I0815148

ABRAHAM LINCOLN
— AND THE —
HEROIC LEGEND

CONFLICTING WORLDS

New Dimensions of the American Civil War

T. Michael Parrish, Series Editor

Abraham Lincoln in 1860. Photograph by Alexander Hesler, June 3, 1860, Herbert George Studio, Springfield, Illinois. Alfred Whital Stern Collection of Lincolniana, Rare Book and Special Collections Division, Library of Congress.

ABRAHAM LINCOLN
— AND THE —
HEROIC LEGEND

RECONSIDERING LINCOLN AS COMMANDER IN CHIEF

KENNETH W. NOE

LOUISIANA STATE UNIVERSITY PRESS
BATON ROUGE

PUBLISHED WITH THE ASSISTANCE OF THE V. RAY CARDOZIER FUND

Published by Louisiana State University Press
lsupress.org

Manufactured in the United States of America
First printing

Designer: Barbara Neely Bourgoyne
Typeface: MillerText
Printer and binder: Sheridan Books, Inc.

Maps created by Mary Lee Eggart.

Jacket illustration: Detail of *Our Patriots of the War, Abraham Lincoln,* ca. 1863. Prints and Photographs Division, Library of Congress.

Portions of chapters 1 and 2 first appeared as "The Military Education of Abraham Lincoln," *Civil War Monitor* 15, no. 3 (Fall 2025), 26–37, 68.

Cataloging-in-Publication Data are available from the Library of Congress.

ISBN 978-0-8071-8521-6 (cloth: alk. paper) —
ISBN 978-0-8071-8596-4 (pdf) — ISBN 978-0-8071-8595-7 (epub)

For Nancy

CONTENTS

ILLUSTRATIONS

FIGURES

MAPS

PREFACE

I AM A LINCOLN BUFF. Even as a child, coloring mimeographed sheets of Lincoln illustrations in elementary school every February, I admired the sixteenth president. As a new graduate student at the University of Illinois, I walked every day past Lorado Taft's statue *Lincoln the Lawyer* in Urbana's Carle Park and sometimes before exams rubbed the allegedly lucky nose of Hermon Atkins MacNeil's bust of the president in the east foyer of Lincoln Hall. The first classical music I ever bought was Aaron Copland's magnificent and sentimental "Lincoln Portrait." I wore a Lincoln campaign button on election days. A poster of Lincoln filled my office-door window at Auburn University, in the heart of the proverbial Heart of Dixie. None of my Civil War classes was complete without a day leading my students to consider the Gettysburg Address for its deeper meanings. Copying my dissertation director, I ended my Appomattox lecture by saying simply, "That night, Mr. Lincoln decided to go to the theater"; the next class I tried not to tear up as I recited portions of Walt Whitman's "When Lilacs Last in the Dooryard Bloom'd." I have read scores of Lincoln biographies and specialized books and essays about everything from his upbringing to his melancholy, to his diet, and even to his dog Fido. Twice I taught Sunday School classes built around Allen Guelzo's book *Abraham Lincoln: Redeemer President.* I have watched innumerable films and television programs about Lincoln. My then-pregnant wife and I camped in the rain at New Salem, and since then I have dragged my family to more Lincoln sites than I want to admit, from the famous to an obscure marker in a cornfield on the boundary of Champaign and Piatt Counties, Illinois. As I write these words, a life-sized cardboard cutout of

Lincoln looks over my shoulder and lilacs bloom in my own dooryard. I own a T-shirt that reads "I Miss Abe." My Lincoln bona fides should be secure.

Yet as the years passed, I began to wonder if Lincoln was always the perfect hero in the black suit and stovepipe hat I once colored with crayons. As a doctoral student of Robert W. Johannsen, Stephen A. Douglas's great biographer, perhaps some latent skepticism toward Lincoln already had entered my intellectual DNA. Then late in 2013, Professor John Ferling and the friends of the library group at the University of West Georgia invited me to present a program about Lincoln. At the time, they were hosting the Gilder Lehrman Institute of American History's traveling exhibit *Abraham Lincoln: A Man of His Times, A Man for All Times.* Having spent my first decade of teaching on that campus, I accepted enthusiastically but with qualms as well. Despite my lifelong interest in Lincoln, I had never pursued the president as a serious research subject. What could I talk about? I finally found a tentative path forward through Lincoln the commander in chief. I had, in fact, written about him before. In my dissertation and first book, I described how a frustrated Lincoln pushed his reluctant army leadership to seize Southwest Virginia and the Virginia and Tennessee Railroad, which connected eastern Virginia to the western Confederacy through the upper Valley of Virginia. In a later narrative of the Battle of Perryville, I discussed Lincoln's relative inattention to events in the western theater as the war swirled in Virginia and Maryland, related his deep dissatisfaction with Federal Maj. Gen. Don Carlos Buell, and described the pressure he placed upon General in Chief Henry Halleck to replace Buell. Lincoln would have had his way had Maj. Gen. George Thomas agreed to take command of the Army of the Ohio on the eve of battle, but Thomas refused. After Perryville, Buell again drew Lincoln's ire for refusing to pursue the Confederates into East Tennessee, a barren place without food and forage according to the general, but also a Unionist enclave that the president yearned to liberate. Buell, I maintained, was right to hesitate.

A week after Lincoln's 205th birthday, I delivered my talk, "Lincoln the War President Revisited." Using the Kentucky Campaign as the basis of the presentation, I still largely depicted Lincoln as the great commander in chief found in T. Harry Williams's classic *Lincoln and His Generals,* but he was also one who could interfere with his generals' plans, play favorites, and fire those with whom he disagreed. Many of the same criticisms that historians had leveled at Jefferson Davis—meddling, developing unrealistic expectations, holding grudges—could be applied to Lincoln as well, I suggested, well aware of the heresy. Lincoln was not perfect. Driving home that night, it struck me that revisiting Lincoln the war president might be a good topic to pursue.

But I did not, at least not at first. By the time of my West Georgia talk, I was engaged in researching *The Howling Storm,* a history of climate, weather, and their influence on the Civil War. Writing that book, however, Lincoln kept coming up; his final listing in the index became second only to "Grant, Ulysses S." in extent. At length I concluded there that Lincoln's inability or unwillingness to consider weather and logistics in his understanding of campaigns and commanders was another flaw in his career as war president—indeed, a crucial one that helped shape his familiar positive or negative assessments of his generals. To my surprise, I came to believe that Maj. Gen. George G. Meade could not have trapped Gen. Robert E. Lee north of the Potomac River after Gettysburg, which Lincoln fervently believed. Looking at the war with climate and weather in the foreground made me understand why Maj. Gen. George McClellan did some of the things he did during the Peninsula Campaign, an even more blasphemous thought. I came to see Lincoln in the same way that historian Mark Fiege described him: a man of his times who believed that modern people could conquer nature through sheer will and ingenuity, just as the young Lincoln himself once found a way to move a loaded flatboat over the shoals of the Sangamon River at New Salem or maneuvered his buggy through flooded rivers while riding the Eighth Judicial Circuit. He now expected his generals, sometimes unrealistically, to accomplish the same thing on a vast scale. In Grant he finally found his general, to paraphrase historian Kenneth P. Williams, in that Grant was willing to push ahead and not look back, however it damaged his army in the process.

The Howling Storm came out at last in 2020, during the lost year of Covid quarantine. All my initial book talks were online. There I noticed a curious phenomenon. As expected, audiences asked questions about the war and weather. But some listeners also wanted to know—sometimes demanded to know—how I could defend McClellan or Meade even partially, or how I could suggest that Lincoln had been less than perfect as a commander in chief. I had discovered a third rail. This phenomenon reached its height during a live talk at Gettysburg in 2023, when a distinguished veteran officer joked that he wished he had attended the U.S. Naval Academy instead of West Point, since the Military Academy made him a fellow alum of George McClellan. The audience loved it. My eyes grew wide.

By then, with typically enthusiastic encouragement from my late friend Peter Carmichael, I already was at work on the present volume. Why, I wondered, were knowledgeable readers of the Civil War so ready to defend Lincoln the war president as flawless or to attack generals such as McClellan or Meade as incompetent, just as I had myself in so many past classrooms. Was it simply that we all had read T. Harry Williams and the many newer works in that tradition? From where did this idea come in the first place? Was it even true? The more I dug into the idea, the more complicated and fascinating the search became. Herein lies the complex tale that follows, about the history and powerful if complicated memory of Lincoln as the nation's greatest commander in chief. I call it the heroic legend.

ACKNOWLEDGMENTS

FIRST AND FOREMOST, this book exists because Peter Carmichael talked me into writing it. My deep gratitude to Pete is only equaled by the heartbreak that he did not live to see it completed. I hope that in some small way it at least serves as a tribute to my friend's too-brief life, his infectious enthusiasm, and his marvelous career.

Once I embarked on the project, numerous librarians and archivists graciously assisted me with my research. I owe great thanks to Laurie Rossi of Brown University; Jeremy Floyd, Dina Kellams, Carrie Schwier, Bradley D. Cook, and Ralph R. Vargas of Indiana University; Tomeka M. Myers at the Library of Congress; and Germain J. Bienvenu of Louisiana State University. I am grateful to those in the Interlibrary Loan Department at Auburn University Libraries who tracked down several obscure publications for me. Staff members at the University of Illinois's Main Library and the History, Philosophy, and Newspaper Library—places where many years ago I researched my dissertation—were uniformly helpful. Thomas Wolfe was right that you can't go home again, but sometimes we can at least check out books at the same counters.

It has been a great pleasure working with LSU Press once again. Series editor Michael Parrish and Editor in Chief Rand Dotson make LSU Press incredibly welcoming to Civil War authors. Kevin Brock once again was a superb and patient copyeditor. Ashley Gilly guided me through the production process. I am also most grateful to the anonymous press reader who not only provided a useful and detailed evaluation of my manuscript but also delivered it in what must be record time. He caught enough sins of omission and commission to keep me from being driven from the history profession.

Any remaining errors, of course, are mine and mine alone. Mary Lee Eggart in the meantime provided excellent maps, and in so doing she put to shame the assumption of T. Harry Williams's book designer in 1951 that surely no one in Baton Rouge could produce good maps.

Writing history sometimes can be as lonely as the stereotype suggests, but often it is a collaborative effort as well. Many friends played a role in bringing this book to fruition, and I am so grateful to all of them. John Ferling's kind speaking invitation first led me to explore Lincoln as commander in chief many years earlier. The late Eric Wittenberg gave me a new avenue to put together some early thoughts on Lincoln as commander in chief to an audience. He is someone else that will never see this book, to my great regret. I have benefited greatly from lunches and conversations with John Hoffmann and Carl Caldwell. John once served as my boss at the Illinois Historical Survey, and he has been my friend ever since. His knowledge of Illinois history especially is both vast and freely shared.

Christopher Ferguson, Matt Hulbert, Jennifer Murray, George Rable, and Frank Wetta read portions of the manuscript and saved me from more embarrassing gaffes than I can count. Stephen Berry discussed with me his views of Commander in Chief Lincoln. Brooks Simpson allowed me to quote a comment from a blog post and then explained to me the origins of his brief but still vital study of Lincoln as commander in chief. Harold Holzer encouraged me with great kindness at an anxious moment. Darin Rock and Dan Svyantek introduced me to the literature of the psychology of leadership under stress, and Darin helped me carry some of my own stressors. Terry Beckenbaugh, Barbara Gannon, and Tim Talbott helped me identify an obscure author. Melissa Blair, Kevin Brock, William H. Brown, Cate Giustino, Chris Kolakowski, Dan Masters, Jennifer Murray, Barton Myers, Mark Sheftall, Darryl Smith, Mark Smith, Joan Waugh, and John Walsh all suggested books when I dared to venture outside 1860s American historiography. Bob Bradley, Bryan Cheeseboro, Jake Clawson, Dan Cone, Barbara Gannon, Andy Hall, Will Haynes, Richard Heisler, Jordan Henderson, Bob Huddleston, Martin Husk, Bob Hutton, Chuck Kays, Ari Kelman, Kelly Kennington, Chris Kolakowski, Kevin Levin, Dan Masters, Jennifer Murray, Dan Modes, Steve Nash, Bruce Nave, Al Nofi, Mike Peters, David Powell, Logan Shaddix, Donald Shaffer, Darryl Smith, Cara Stoddard, Bruce Tap, Lee White, and David Woodbury all helped me clarify my thoughts on what Dave Powell calls the "great stories" of Civil War memory and legend. And some people just helped me deal with life: David Carter, Mark Franklin, Kristi Gresch, and the other five members of the Shawsville 6—Chuck Akers, Randy Butt, Roger Butt, Steve Butt, and Jimmy Lawrence.

I am grateful as always to my family. To my late father, my sister, my brothers, and their families, thank you for your love and your grace. The "three-dollar words" are still here for you dad. That goes as well for Jesse, my amazing son across the sea. Finally, and most importantly, I once again thank Nancy Noe for pretty much everything good in my life—and in sickness and in health these late autumn days. I do not think she anticipated that retirement would mean watching me disappear upstairs to the office most afternoons only to emerge for dinner rubbing my aching eyes and quoting Gideon Welles. Still, she patiently listened to me as I wrestled with Lincoln and his chroniclers. We drove around central Illinois to find Lincoln markers, she read every word of this manuscript before anyone else did, and she made this a better book. I am a better and braver person for her presence in my life. She's the best.

ABRAHAM LINCOLN
— AND THE —
HEROIC LEGEND

INTRODUCTION

THIS BOOK IS an extended essay about an idea, which for reasons explained in depth below I call the *heroic legend.* By that I mean the now-canonical assertion that Abraham Lincoln as commander in chief was a military genius both strategically and tactically, not to mention a naturally intuitive and self-taught military thinker so modern in his views that he became a superior commander to his generals. In this introduction I define "heroic legend" in greater detail, offer suggestions as to why it deserves revisiting, explain why I call it a legend, and set the stage for relating its complicated history in the chapters that follow.

At the outset one might well wonder with fairness why anyone needs another book about Abraham Lincoln. There are a lot of them already, after all. During the presidential campaign of 1860, publishers churned out the first baker's dozen of hastily written book-length biographies about Lincoln, still a relatively unknown candidate from Illinois. The first to appear, only two weeks after he secured the Republican nomination and known as "the Wigwam Edition," misspelled his given name as "Abram." Since that unfortunate beginning, an estimated 16,000 more books on Lincoln have appeared, leaving him second in biographic popularity only to Jesus Christ.[1] A few years ago, book critic and novelist Lev Grossman wondered why there were so many. He asked if "the volume of it suggests something more" than simple scholarly interest in a pivotal president, then determined that it represented "an obsession, an addiction, a Lincoln compulsion." Alluding to the president's assassination on Good Friday, 1865, Grossman concluded that Lincoln had become the Christ figure in an American secular religion. "At the time," he observed, "Lincoln's death was fused with Jesus' in the popular imagination—people needed Lincoln to be more than human in order to give meaning to the slaughter over which he presided. We still seem to need that, even while we know it's not true. Maybe it's that gap, between Lincoln's mortal and immortal natures, that we're trying to fill with all these words." True or not, "all these words" about Lincoln keep coming. Many of them touch directly on that liminal space Grossman delineated between Old Abe's earthy humanity and a sanctified aura, dating back to the first biographies published after his assassination.[2]

Writing three decades ago about the flood of Lincolniana that began after the president's death and swept on into the twentieth century, historian Merrill Peterson identified five interconnected core themes. Lincoln became in the American mind the "Savior of the Union," a powerful symbol of vibrant and triumphant American nationalism and victory who came to rival George Washington in primacy. Around the globe, other people looked to him as "the First American," an exemplar of the nation and of the promise of "government of the people, by the people, and for the people." To others still he was the "Great Emancipator" who broke the chains of slavery for millions. Born in a log cabin on the frontier, Tom Lincoln's son became the "Man of the People," an infinitely human hero who demonstrated the inherent worth of the common man and the triumph of democracy. Other authors celebrated a related "Self-Made Man" who rose from poverty to the White House and became a role model for the masses.[3]

There were naysayers all along, of course. Many of Lincoln's wartime opponents and their children's generation clung to the Confederacy or else their northern conservative opposition to his administration and the war. They obsessively recycled wartime rhetoric about his alleged atheism, crude vulgarity, illegitimacy, and bloodthirsty tyranny, not to mention his views on race.[4] Modern "neo-Confederate" and libertarian authors writing in that tradition, paleoconservatives and libertarians alike, sometimes depict Lincoln in much the same way but more often now play down his personal failings to describe him instead as a hypocritical racist and a flaming liberal/progressive/Marxist/communist. Their Lincoln is a despot and war criminal who allegedly destroyed the constitutional republic of the Founding Fathers and erected the foundations of the welfare state and centralized government. Yet in the end, their often internet-borne critiques are nothing more than the warped carnival-mirror reflections of Peterson's five archetypes.[5]

For most other Americans, however, from extreme left to hard right politically, "getting right with Lincoln" remains as important as it was when historian David Herbert Donald coined that phrase during the Cold War. Two recent presidents possessing vastly different ideologies, Barack Obama and Donald Trump, sometimes compared themselves to Old Abe. Rhetorician David Zarefsky is also correct that many people today also care more about Lincoln getting right with them and their causes.[6] They have enlisted Lincoln in a dizzying array of issues and ideologies across the political spectrum and around the globe. Even today he can be found in many places at once: the man of the people on the humble penny, the towering but somehow approachable savior of the Union, the emancipator sitting like a marble Zeus in the Lincoln Memorial, the axe-wielding vampire slayer of arch fiction, the comic television actor in a stovepipe hat hawking sheets on Presidents' Day, and ultimately the icon to whom politicians worldwide pay lip-service when they ask "What would Lincoln do?" Building upon the work of Peterson, sociologist Barry Schwartz explained this in part by suggesting that collective memories of Lincoln by the time of World War I had become "part of the soul of American society," sometimes serving as a "lamp" or model, while at other times as a "mirror" to what Americans wanted to see in themselves.[7]

Historians still work within and around Peterson's parameters, but as a group they have been more willing than the public to question conventional wisdom, dispute each other's conclusions, challenge the archetypes, and question Lincoln's "immortal nature." Indeed, nearly every aspect of his life and work engenders spirited debate. Take, for example, the "Great Emancipator." Did Lincoln really "free the slaves," or did they liberate themselves in small, local rebellions that forced a reluctant president to react when the army asked what do with all those people coming into their lines? Was he a racist typical of his times, a white supremacist, or a leader with a progressive racial vision? Was his primary goal simply to save the Union, or from the first did he really want to extinguish slavery? Was he a conservative, a moderate, or a radical? Why did the Great Emancipator spend so much time discussing compensation to slaveowners and voluntary colonization of freed people beyond U.S. shores? Was he sincere when he talked about colonization or just skillfully bringing Americans along toward Black freedom? Was the Emancipation Proclamation ultimately about filling the ranks, as the document itself suggests, or did it derive from justice and morality, as his Second

Inaugural later implied? Disputed answers to these questions abound, but any consensus has remained elusive.[8]

The same can be said today of the "Man of the People" and the "Self-Made Man." Lincoln had not been in his grave for long before authors began to argue about how best to depict him. Writing in 1947, biographer Benjamin Thomas looked back to the previous century to denote two schools of thought that had developed since 1865: one that "would depict him as a national hero with all the attributes a national hero was supposed to have" and the other as a good but flawed man "as he was." When he wrote those words after World War II, Thomas was confident that the latter school had won the field.[9] So-called scientific historians of his time—led by James G. Randall at the University of Illinois, academia's first true Lincoln scholar—had set aside the "common man" topics that had been rife in popular discussions of Lincoln up through the Great Depression, as best epitomized in the often-sentimental work of the poet and biographer Carl Sandburg and the plays and films his work subsequently spawned. The poet made much of Lincoln's alleged relationship with the doomed Ann Rutledge of New Salem, for example, while Randall consigned his eye-rolling disbelief to an appendix in the second volume of his own biography of Lincoln, tacked on after a discussion of the Gettysburg Address. Such works as Sandburg's, Randall and others claimed, were amateurish, tended toward mawkishness, and in the end were unreliable folklore. What was needed was hardnosed academic scholarship about *President* Lincoln. His fellow professors and graduate students took up the challenge. Randall's academic leadership, the opening of the Lincoln Papers at the Library of Congress after World War II, the publication of Lincoln's collected works and other primary sources, and advances in archives all together spurred scholarly interest in his public life at the expense of "Lincoln Lore."[10]

Yet as the twentieth century advanced toward its conclusion, a sincere desire to understand Lincoln better unleashed a plethora of new searches for the key to the elusive inner man. Shifting opinions of sources were critical too. Law partner William Herndon's early oral histories of Lincoln's life before Washington, dismissed by Randall as unreliable hearsay, found new appreciation.[11] As with emancipation, this renewed scholarship abounded in remarkably diverse questions, interpretations, and debate about the "Man of the People" that stretched discussions to their limit. What was Lincoln's relationship with his father, or for that matter the Founding Fathers? Did he love his mother, or was he ashamed of her? Was he well adjusted, melancholic, clinically depressed, or physically ill? Did he have nervous breakdowns and attempt suicide? Did he have a midlife crisis? Was he a passive personality borne from point to point by larger currents, or was he instead an aggressive pathfinder? Was he a good friend or an aloof loner? Was he voraciously heterosexual, essentially gay, or bisexual? Did he love Mary Todd or marry her out of a growing sense of duty while still pining for either Ann Rutledge or Joshua Speed? Was he happily married or a scolded and physically abused cuckold? Or was Mary the victim, married to a distant husband who absented himself from her side at every opportunity? Was he an atheist, a fatalist, a secular moralist, a Christian, or the wounded son of a harsh Calvinist, expecting God's damnation? As for the "Self-Made Man," was Lincoln truly sui generis—born to greatness—or did he rise within the context of family, friends, associates, communities, a frontier culture, period politics, and wider Western civilization? If the latter, who were his mentors? How did his careers as a storekeeper, surveyor, lawyer, writer, and Whig partisan contribute to his climb up the ladder? One cannot help but wonders if Randall would be more appalled or vindicated knowing that he had been right in 1934 when declaring that "the Lincoln Theme" was not "exhausted."[12]

Yet "all these words" and 16,000 books to the contrary, critical voids still exist in Lincoln scholarship. During the bicentennial of his birth, for example, historian Catherine Clinton pointed out how the international dimension of Lincoln as "First American" remained relatively unexamined. Nor, she continued, had scholars done enough with those people around him who had not been white men. The "Savior of the Union" fared better, but specialists still saw a need for exploration of issues such as the nature and day-to-day operations of Lincoln's parties and opponents as well as the activities of lesser-known players in his political circles.[13] Despite recent efforts to the contrary, historians also had neglected Lincoln's policies in the American West. Holding on the to the West and its natural resources, blocking Confederate expansion and slavery, supporting free-labor settlement through legislation such as the Homestead Act and a transcontinental railroad, forcing native peoples off millions of acres of usable land, building new states, and securing western votes were all secondary or tertiary agenda items in the Lincoln White House. A group of prominent Republicans, including Secretary of the Interior John Usher and White House secretary John Nicolay, used their ties to Lincoln to defraud the Lenape (Delaware) of over 200,000 acres of tribal land in Kansas. Minnesota's Dakota War of 1862 led to both the largest single-day execution and largest mass commutation of the death sentence in American history, with Lincoln staying 266 death sentences but still allowing thirty-eight other Dakota men to hang. The commander in chief's army committed ethnic cleansing and genocide in the West at the Bear River Massacre of the Newe (Shoshone) in modern Idaho, the forced removal of the Diné (Navajos) and Mescalero Apache to the hellish Bosque Redondo reservation, and the Sand Creek Massacre in Colorado—none of which Lincoln ever mentioned in public despite sporadic public outcry within Congress and even in the regular army.

Yet most pioneering scholars, who otherwise are doing yeomen's work integrating Civil War and American West history into a broader consideration of the mid-nineteenth century's expansive nationalism, do little with the president himself. With a few exceptions, Lincoln appears infrequently in their pages, a harried executive concerned with appointments and party building, pushing western railroad construction, acting condescendingly in his dealing with occasional indigenous delegations, and otherwise too distracted by the conventional war to rein in a corrupt Bureau of Indian Affairs run by a crony from Illinois. Lincoln did occasionally acknowledge inequities in the reservation system, but he did little to correct them or change his own views. Some scholars believe that he would have done more in a second term. Yet in the end, the Great Emancipator and the commander in chief who held his tongue about Sand Creek almost end up seeming to be two different historical people with the same name.[14] Historian Michael S. Green, one of the few scholars to focus on Lincoln and his western policies in depth, has warned, "any examination of Lincoln and Native Americans reveals much that should disturb his fans. . . . [W]hile Lincoln advanced considerably in his thinking about African Americans, Native Americans were another matter."[15]

It is Lincoln the commander in chief who begs most for scholarly reevaluation. The Savior of the Union preserved the nation through war. To be sure, Lincoln biographers and other Civil War scholars hardly have ignored his activities as commander in chief, although the niche of the literature that focuses particularly on that role is surprisingly small given the total extent of Lincoln historiography.[16] The real issue, rather, is that with a scant few dissenters to the contrary, Lincoln-as-commander-in-chief scholarship past and present lacks the spirited debates that now mark all the other aspects of his life, even within works that challenge boldly those other norms. Since the Cold War, with only a handful of exceptions, it has fallen into two remarkably similar categories: either Lincoln's innate perfection or his developing march to it, as symbolized respectively by unrelated scholars Kenneth P. Williams and T. Harry Williams.[17] Otherwise, as historian Glenn LaFantasie maintained, there has been a "glaring blind spot" to Lincoln's "inconsistencies and contradictions" beneath the surface image of his mastery of war.[18] Conference panelists adjourn to the hotel bar and argue vehemently until closing time about colonization, Lincoln's marriage, or his racial views, but most Civil War historians and enthusiasts still agree with the two historians named Williams: Lincoln became the nation's best commander in chief thanks to a better military mind than his generals. To suggest otherwise, according to dissenter Elizabeth Pryor Brown anyway, is "taboo."[19]

On this single topic—arguably the most important of all of Lincoln's presidential roles given his wartime presidency—we return again and again to the heroic legend. Consider a recent popular iteration of the standard recitation. In February 2022 the *History* television network premiered a three-part, seven-and-a-half-hour miniseries entitled *Abraham Lincoln.* Its pedigree was sterling. The executive producer was Pulitzer Prize–winning biographer Doris Kearns Goodwin, whose best-selling book *Team of Rivals* served as the basis for Steven Spielberg's award-winning film *Lincoln* a decade earlier. There was much to commend in it, including well-acted recreations and a refreshingly diverse group of expert commentators that included noted historians. President Obama and Gen. Stanley McChrystal, two men whom journalists sometimes had depicted as the modern incarnations of Lincoln and Maj. Gen. George B. McClellan, also participated. The creators paid serious attention to slavery and abolition, wrestled with the reality of race in Lincoln's mind, and identified slavery as the unquestioned cause of the war.[20]

Some viewers were nonetheless disappointed. Historian Kevin Levin, for example, found the program "entertaining and informative" but added, "I didn't expect anything new and in the end the documentary failed to deliver anything new."[21] That was especially true when it came to Lincoln's role as commander in chief. Unlike much of the rest of the narrative, the story *Abraham Lincoln* told about the commander in chief was reassuringly conventional, the heroic legend spun yet again. As always, it began on the frontier. Born in that famous log cabin, young Abe Lincoln rose from poverty and his father's neglect thanks to his remarkable intelligence, diligence, and inherent honesty. He served as a militia captain during the Black Hawk War of 1832. Young Lincoln saw no fighting but learned pivotal lessons about war, leadership, and the soldier experience. He then faced numerous challenges and painful defeats in civilian life as he emerged as an enemy of slavery, something he had hated since his youth. Becoming a force in state politics, he served in Congress, won the hand of politically astute Mary Todd, and debated Stephen A. Douglas. As he matured, Lincoln set aside his edgy sarcasm and became a statesman. He lost a Senate seat to Douglas in 1858, but his ringing opposition to slavery's expansion spread his fame nationally. He then secured the Republican presidential nomination and won in 1860.

Southern secession followed. Lincoln arrived in Washington to learn that Fort Sumter in South Carolina was running out of food and soon would have to surrender without resupply. Spurning timid counsel, he took the reins. When he sought to resupply the garrison, the Confederates fired the first shot and started a war that would put the American nation and democracy worldwide to the test. Lincoln responded with firmness. He instituted a blockade of the southern coast and asserted his full constitutional war powers as commander in chief as no previous president had done. Desperate not to lose the remaining slave states, he soft-pedaled emancipation at first and focused on preserving the Union. He hoped that a quick victory would bring peace, but after the defeat at First Bull Run in July 1861, he accepted the reality of a long war and built a massive army. Lincoln also developed a personal connection with the troops and began to master war through voracious reading and informal tutoring with trusted officers. Armed with natural sagacity, the president became a better tactician and strategist than his generals, not to mention West Point graduate Jefferson Davis. He embraced new weapons in defiance of stodgy officers and led his own victorious campaign at Norfolk, Virginia. All the time, he worked to end slavery through the Emancipation Proclamation.

Lincoln faced dogged opposition in response. The worst of his foes were not the Confederates, but timid and insubordinate Maj. Gen. George B. McClellan, portrayed in *Abraham Lincoln* with the melodramatic sneer of a silent-movie villain. The general repeatedly refused to heed the president's sound but unorthodox advice and at length failed. Lincoln fired McClellan after Antietam, but the initial successors were no better—all of them failed to grasp Lincoln's military genius. Maj. Gen. George G. Meade let the Confederates escape certain destruction again after the pivotal Battle of Gettysburg in

July 1863, but at least the war somehow had turned a corner. A few months later, Lincoln enunciated bedrock American principles in a classic speech on that field. He finally found a likeminded general in the western theater. Lincoln supported Ulysses S. Grant when others wanted him fired for alleged drunkenness because, unlike McClellan, Grant won battles and followed orders without complaint. The president brought his fellow westerner east in 1864 and let him fight the war fiercely and without interference. Grant, like Lincoln, saw the need for multiple, simultaneous attacks across the Confederacy. Many men died, but despite the political costs, Lincoln stuck with Grant and rejected calls to abandon emancipation. He achieved reelection with the votes of loyal soldiers who loved him for his kindness to them, even to their prisoners in gray, having saved many from executions and prison. Grant won the war and crafted a generous peace at Appomattox. Lincoln's assassination prevented him from reuniting the nation fully, but the country's greatest president—and first modern commander in chief—had saved the Union, freed the slaves, and preserved democracy for the world.[22]

This is the heroic legend of how Lincoln as commander in chief won the Civil War, retold once again for new audiences.

The heroic legend as it appears in such venues is so pervasive, so powerful, and indeed sometimes so akin to a gospel reading recited before a sermon that one must reexamine it before even beginning to consider the reality of Lincoln as a commander in chief. Anyone attempting that sort of deconstruction, however, soon will discover that parts of the structure are suspect immediately upon closer inspection. Much of the heroic legend is true enough, yet oversimplification, hyperbole, bias, and the heavy weight of previous storytelling also exist in abundance. It ignores contradictory evidence at times, and it sometimes provides questionable conclusions.

Lincoln's Black Hawk War experience, for example, was not all that successful. His men, encouraged and led by his carousing New Salem pals, did elect him captain. Unfortunately, the young man proved so unable to discipline them that his own commander ordered him to carry a wooden sword for two days, punished him again for accidentally firing his weapon in camp, and later sent the troublesome bunch home early. Lincoln reenlisted twice more as a private—he needed the money—but only served a few weeks without ever seeing any fighting. No doubt he learned hard lessons about leadership and the plight of poorly supplied soldiers—not to mention a healthy admiration for those same volunteers—but even his most favorable modern biographers admit that what most came out of the experience were contacts with influential men who aided his subsequent climb up the political ladder. Lincoln acknowledged as much in public and joked about his service in Congress to score political points, yet he still considered himself a veteran.[23]

As for the Civil War, the heroic legend again is often oversimplified and unbalanced. Like too much Civil War historiography, it rotates on an axis running from Richmond and Petersburg, through Washington, to the alleged turning point at Gettysburg. The western theater mainly exists to supply Grant and an unvexed Mississippi River flowing to the sea. Western battles not featuring Grant—Perryville, Stones River, Chickamauga—receive relatively little notice in the legend. The war west of the Mississippi hardly exists at all; there is no room for the Battle of Mansfield, much less Sand Creek. The naval war surfaces with the blockade and the *Monitor* fighting the "*Merrimack*"—actually the *Virginia*—only to disappear beneath the rhetorical waves. The heroic legend privileges the land war in the eastern theater.

Even then, complications abound. In 1890 Lincoln's former personal secretaries, John Nicolay and John Hay, described Lincoln's intensive study of military history beginning in the closing months of 1861 in their mammoth ten-volume biography of the president they adored. "He gave himself, night and day, to the study of the military situation," they wrote. "He read a large number of strategical works. He pored over the reports from the various departments and districts of the field of war. He held long conferences with eminent generals and admirals, and astonished them by the extent of his special knowledge and the keen intelligence of his questions."[24] Yet as discussed more fully in chapter 1, Lincoln's much-related mastery of volumes on military strategy, a staple of most books about Lincoln, runs counter to everything else we know about him and his reading habits.

As for his generals, "it is easy now," historian George Rable has observed, "for Americans to forget how many people lacked confidence in Lincoln's decisions as commander-in-chief and therefore fail to realize how high McClellan stood in the estimation of many contemporaries."[25] There was no agreement about Lincoln's military genius—far from it. Heavy rain really did slow down McClellan on the Peninsula in 1862, and similar conditions made Meade's capture of Lee after Gettysburg much less of the sure thing that it seemed to an impatient White House. Both generals were difficult and touchy men, but one cannot automatically dismiss them as fools at their craft.[26] Or take the matter of Lincoln's loyalty to Grant and his promise in 1864 to stay out of the general's way. As Grant biographer Brooks Simpson has countered—and as this volume backs in a later chapter—Lincoln's support of Grant was far more conditional and complex than the heroic legend would have us believe.[27]

Nor would some of Lincoln's generals and others agree with many biographers that as the man grew older, he lost what historian Robert Bray has called his "power to hurt," Lincoln's tendency to wield sarcasm and abusive tongue lashings that delighted his political supporters on the stump. His sarcasm had once nearly resulted in a duel with fellow Illinois politician James Shields—who later became one of his generals. As later chapters demonstrate, an impatient and exhausted President Lincoln remained quite capable of cruel invective and even "something close to malice," in historian Allen Guelzo's words, toward some of his generals and cabinet members, sometimes to the face of the recipient but all too often behind their backs.[28]

Nicolay and Hay's much-quoted description of Lincoln's study habits additionally points to a more fundamental problem with the heroic legend. "He held long conferences with eminent generals and admirals," they wrote, "and astonished them by the extent of his special knowledge and the keen intelligence of his questions." The wording here is crucial. Their passage is a direct allusion—one obvious to nineteenth-century Americans if not modern readers—to Saint Luke's description of twelve-year-old Jesus in the Temple, as described in the King James Version of the gospels that dominated the era. "And it came to pass," Luke wrote, "that after three days they found him in the temple, sitting in the midst of the doctors, both hearing them, and asking them questions. And all that heard him were astonished at his understanding and answers." Lincoln became more than a commander in chief reading books in the Nicolay and Hay passage. As he had been to his pious previous biographers, Lincoln was another savior who "astonished" those around him with his remarkable knowledge, the literal "Savior" of the Union, touched with divine genius and thus the hero of a powerful legend.[29]

Here I used the word *legend* deliberately. Definitions of the words *myth* and *legend* vary from scholar to scholar to be sure, even among those who study them professionally. Neither at least refers to fiction. The Civil War was not a fairy tale, parable, or tongue-in-cheek send-up. No one begins a Civil War story with "once upon a time," which folklorist Alan Dundes cited as a dead giveaway that a story is a fictional folktale.[30] It happened. When it comes to more exact definitions, many scholars follow the lead of anthropologist William Bascom, who identified *folktales* as "fiction. . . . almost timeless and placeless." Here one finds the "once upon a time" fairy tales that often end with "and they all lived happily ever after." *Myths,* in contrast, are narratives from a far-distant past that a given society once regarded as true. They are "usually sacred, and they are often associated with theology and ritual." They deal with matters such as "the origin of the world, of mankind, [and] of death," often through tales of supernatural gods. Finally, *legends* "are regarded as true by the narrator and his audience, but they are set in a period considered less remote, and the world was much as it is today." They are usually secular, revolve around mortals, and often are regarded as historic. Lincoln lived relatively recently, hence stories about him properly are *legends,* not myths.[31]

As the classicist G. S. Kirk warned, however, the dividing line is not always clear. The *Iliad,* for example, contains elements of both mythology (meddling gods) and legend (a real war). "A more or less realistic account of a historical action is not a myth," he wrote, "although it may eventually take on mythical characteristics."[32] So-called gods and generals fought the Civil War too, according to one influential novel.[33] Many historians likewise use the word *myth* when describing what Bascom would call a legend. According to historian David Blight, for example, reality, nostalgia, and wishful thinking combined into an "abiding myth" of the Civil War after it ended.[34] Starting with the veterans themselves, generations of Americans told and retold stories so many times—minimizing or ignoring others—that they turned a bloody war into a structured epic tale that brought them and their sacrifices meaning. The war became an "American Iliad," complete with familiar allusions and must-tell episodes as familiar today as Homer's "rosy-fingered Dawn" and "wine-dark sea."[35] Such oft-repeated mantras often are "simplistic, golden-rule impressions," as historian Thomas Rowland asserted.[36] U. S. Grant worried about the process and its perils as early as 1885, when he commented regarding one popular tale that "wars produce many stories of fiction, some of which are told until they are believed to be true. The war of the rebellion was no exception to this rule."[37]

Little has changed since Grant's warning. We like our comfortable, familiar stories. "The American Civil War suffers from a particular form of mythmaking," historian David Powell has observed. "There grew up a tradition of 'great stories.' Some of these were driven by reconciliation mythology, but most were simply overgrown dining-out tales. . . . [W]hole generations of historians from the 1930s to the 1960s repeated these stories, because they make for great reads—and in some cases, added to them. Not all, of course, and much of the best historical work is now about correcting the tall tales, but they persist."[38]

Anyone familiar with the Civil War has encountered those persistent "great stories" and allusions many times. Just as Achilles was always "swift-footed" and Odysseus always "cunning," Robert E. Lee (never just "Robert Lee" or "R. E. Lee") hated slavery and secession but chose Virginia and became the most brilliant general of the war. Thomas J. Jackson stood like a stone wall and sucked lemons—if only he had been at Gettysburg. McClellan was cowardly, petulant, laughably messianic, and rude to Lincoln. Confederate troops were always ragged, outnumbered, badly fed, and born to the saddle; few of them owned slaves. Any Johnny Reb could whip ten Billy Yanks—mostly immigrants right off the boat—until the Yanks whipped him after all. The rifle musket and Minié ball made Napoleonic tactics obsolete, but the generals were too foolish to grasp the first modern war. Meade, the "Goggle Eyed Snapping Turtle," prolonged the war by letting Lee escape from Gettysburg, yet it was the turning point in the war. Everyone hated Gen. Braxton Bragg, Gen. John Bell Hood was a drug addict, and Lt. Gen. Nathan Bedford Forrest was a genius. On the other (never "United States") side, Grant was a drunken butcher, Maj. Gen. William Tecumseh Sherman burned everything in his path except when fellow Masons or numerous former sweethearts stopped him, and the war in the West never mattered. In the end, a tragic "brother's war" led to national reconciliation when Grant and Lee shook hands at Appomattox Court House.[39]

Much of this is at best exaggerated or simply not true. Yet despite the best efforts of historians to offer nuance if not correction, such legends not just survive but prosper in popular culture. Indeed, they summon enthusiastic defenders when challenged. Many listeners hold these stories and tropes so dear that they demand to hear the same stories over and over, with detail down to the regimental and brigade level, just as banqueting Greeks wanted to hear passages of favorite tales recited from Homer. The very existence of a canon testifies to what David Blight called the "symbolic power" of what David Powell called "great stories."

Canonization is an ongoing process as well. While most of the "great stories" go back to the nineteenth century, others display a more recent vintage. A potent example was the admission of Col. Joshua Lawrence Chamberlain into the pantheon of Civil War heroes after the 1974 publication of Michael Shaara's Pulitzer Prize–winning novel *The Killer Angels,* later the basis for the 1993 film *Gettysburg.* Before *The Killer Angels,* the professor from Maine was a minor figure in the standard Gettysburg narrative. Maj. Gen. Gouverneur K. Warren's statue stands atop Little Round Top, not Chamberlain's. After the book and movie, however, so many visitors wanted to see where his 20th Maine launched its bayonet charge down Little Round Top that the National Park Service installed a sign pointing them toward the regiment's monument, fenced in the path to the monument to protect the hillside, created a wayside exhibit, added a parking lot, and eventually acquired more property. All that was lacking was a marker for Buster Kilrain, a fictional character that park visitors sometimes seek out. The flood of visitors brought site damage with them. In the summer of 2022, the Park Service closed Little Round Top for two years to rehabilitate "overwhelmed parking areas, poor accessibility and related safety hazards, significant erosion, and degraded vegetation" caused by visitors eager to see where Chamberlain and Kilrain fought. Such is the power of legend.[40]

Many of the "great stories" are benign. Chamberlain's growing centrality to popular culture only annoys Gettysburg fundamentalists. But other stories are less so. Historians Joseph Harsh and later Thomas Rowland delineated a "Unionist interpretation" of the war that they believed emerged in the 1890s out of Nicolay and Hay's ten volumes; I argue in this book's later chapters that it had earlier and later antecedents. Support for the Union, a near-idolization of Lincoln and Grant as the harbingers of modern warfare, and enthusiastic lambasting of the arch-villain McClellan were its main tenets. So strong was this "modernist" interpretation, Harsh maintained, that it made any reasoned analysis of McClellan impossible. His name—Harsh would say his "caricature"—remains a modern synonym for military imbecility.[41]

Historian Wesley Moody and contributors to his book, meanwhile, identified seven less benign "myths" about the Civil War that not only prosper in modern America but also in some cases shape current politics and society.

They are the internet-driven fantasy that thousands of so-called Black Confederates fought willingly in gray for constitutional issues in a multiracial Confederacy, the durable notion that all Confederates fought for states' rights and not slavery, the continuing partisan finger-pointing over the horrors of Civil War prisons, the assertion that guerrilla insurgency was unimportant, the old saw that a soused Grant was a clumsy butcher, the dubious claim that Sherman invented total war in Georgia, and finally the ongoing argument that Lincoln was a hypocritical racist. In a similar vein, historians Elizabeth Varon and Michael Vorenberg each asserted that the benign "myth" of the war ending with a gentlemanly handshake, reconciliation, and reunion at Appomattox on April 9, 1865, is both incorrect factually and deleterious in its later effects on American society. The Appomattox legend distorted the reality of the war, papered over the continuing violence of Reconstruction, ignored tensions along the Rio Grande, recast ongoing wars in the West, and contributed to the survival of American racism and southern defiance through equating the blue and the gray. Vorenberg added the ongoing search for similar exactitude negatively shaped American exits from other wars, such as in Vietnam, Afghanistan, and Iraq.[42]

The rhetorical assault on Lincoln arose in turn from the most prevalent and familiar surviving "great story" of all, the Myth of the "Lost Cause." Taking its name from Richmond editor Edward Pollard's 1867 book, the Lost Cause Myth first developed after the war as a balm to defeated white southerners. Historian Alan Nolan listed its main beliefs: abolitionists stirred up a needless war, Confederates legally seceded and fought for constitutional issues instead of slavery, Lincoln was a vicious tyrant who cared little about the enslaved, well-treated slaves were content and loyal, Confederate armies consisted of superior Christian generals and braver men who only succumbed to what Lee at Appomattox called "overwhelming numbers and resources," Lt. Gen. James Longstreet's Judas-like betrayal of Lee cost the Confederacy its independence at Gettysburg, and on the southern home front everyone united in support of the Confederacy. Ultimately, the Confederates were the good guys.

The Lost Cause did not spring from a vacuum. Like any good story, it drew richly from older narratives, myths, and legends. Historian Charles Reagan Wilson argued that the Lost Cause's originators borrowed chiefly from American Christianity, as intellectual leaders within the church essentially superimposed the Confederacy upon the Bible. Confederates were God's most recent chosen people, its proponents declared. Slavery was biblical and ordained by God. Lincoln and the Union were akin to the sinful heathens who subdued the Israelites. Heroes and martyrs such as Lee and Jackson had been holy warriors. Given these familiar tenets, churches and lay organizations proselytized with zeal. Southern holy days developed. The Confederate battle flag became the "Southern Cross," the faithful collected relics, and monuments went up with prayers and solemn ceremony. Rituals developed to honor the living and bury the dead. True believers wrote catechisms for children and taught them the Lost Cause just as churches prepared the young for their first communion.[43]

Other scholars, however, have countered that Christianity alone did not provide the models for the Lost Cause. Alan Nolan called it "an American legend, an American version of great sagas like *Beowulf* and the *Song of Roland*." When it was useful, he argued, the creators of the Myth of the Lost Cause drew eclectically from other sources than the Bible: King Arthur tales, the popular works of Sir Walter Scott, the hagiography of the American Revolution, and—especially when it came to Confederate heroes—the mythology of Ancient Greece and Rome. Lee, Jackson, and the common Johnny Reb had as much in common with Galahad, Ivanhoe, and Achilles as with Joshua and Sampson, while Lincoln emerged as a modern King John or George III.[44]

On this final point, Wilson specifically cited the popular and influential work of Joseph Campbell and his concept of "the hero's journey," as first depicted in his monumental, award-winning study *The Hero with a Thousand Faces,* first published in 1949 in the depths of the post–World War II Cold War.[45] Campbell deserves additional attention at this juncture if we are to understand the most modern popular iteration of the heroic legend. He was a twentieth-century literature professor who by "following his bliss"—a phrase he coined—grew increasingly interested in folklore and world mythology.[46] Borrowing from Sigmund Freud and especially Carl Jung's concept of a "collective unconscious," Campbell postulated the existence of a "monomyth," a deep, universal expression of the human psyche that crossed time and distance to emerge again and again in the world as mythology. Essentially, every world culture's central myth was a localized variation of the same "universal adventure." This he called the hero's journey, "one, shape-shifting yet marvelously constant story." In turn it consists of three distinct legs: "separation or departure" from the familiar world, "trial and victories of initiation," and finally "the return and reintegration with society."[47] Campbell summarized the hero's journey in his own distinctive prose:

> The mythological hero, setting forth from his common-day hut or castle, is lured, carried away, or else voluntarily proceeds, to the threshold of adventure. There he encounters a shadow presence that guards the passage. The hero may defeat or conciliate this power and go alive into the kingdom of the dark (brother-battle, dragon-battle; offering, charm), or be slain by the opponent and descend in death (dismemberment, crucifixion). Beyond the threshold, then, the hero journeys through a world of unfamiliar yet strangely intimate forces, some of which severely threaten him (tests), some of which give magical aid (helpers). When he arrives at the nadir of the mythological round, he undergoes a supreme ordeal and gains his reward. The triumph may be represented as the hero's sexual union with the goddess-mother of the world (sacred marriage), his recognition by the father-creator (father atonement), his own divination (apotheosis), or again—if the powers have remained unfriendly to him—his theft of the boon he came to gain (bride-theft, fire-theft); intrinsically it is an expansion of consciousness and therewith of being (illumination, transfiguration, freedom). The final work is that of the return. If the powers have blessed the hero, he now sets forth under their protection (emissary); if not, he flees and is pursued (transformation flight, obstacle flight). At the return threshold the transcendental powers must remain behind; the hero re-emerges from the kingdom of dread (return, resurrection). The boon that he brings restores the world (elixir).[48]

The Hero with a Thousand Faces, the author's subsequent books, and his many speaking appearances made Campbell himself an integral part of Western popular culture. A PBS series about him that first aired in 1988 remains one of the most watched programs in television history and continues to be rerun. Assisting with that program was Campbell devotee and filmmaker George Lucas. Millions of moviegoers unknowingly imbibed the monomyth through Lucas's popular *Star Wars* movies; Lucas rewrote the initial draft of the first *Star Wars* film after reading *The Hero with a Thousand Faces* to bring the adventures of fictional Luke Skywalker more in line with Campbell's hero's journey and deliberately craft a modern myth for new generations. Hollywood screenwriter and studio executive Christopher Vogler's subsequent summaries of Campbell's hero's journey guided the development of many additional films, especially at Disney studios, which not only acquired the *Star Wars* empire but also produced other successful, Campbell-inspired films such as *Aladdin* (1992) and *The Lion King* (1994). Anyone searching the internet for Joseph Campbell will find analyses, explanations, homages, quotations, self-help sites, and teaching guides. Modern Western popular culture is steeped in Campbell's hero's journey much more than many people realize.[49]

But not everyone was impressed. Campbell was controversial from the first. Some early reviewers of *The Hero with a Thousand Faces* admitted to "incomprehension." A *New York Times* reviewer praised its ambition but lamented "the mystical and pseudo-philosophic fog of Jung."[50] Within the academy, professional folklorists and other scholars have remained skeptical. They have criticized Campbell's methodology as amateurish, biased toward European sources, and prejudiced against Judeo-Christian traditions. Others have questioned the rigor of his research, rejected the existence of timeless truths and universal archetypes, and lamented his conflation of folklore, myth, and legend. They complained that he ignored stories and regions that contradicted his argument, cherry-picked from the rest, and divorced his sources from context. Many have found his Jungian mysticism worrisome. Alan Dundes admitted that at least Campbell got people interested in myths—including many a new graduate student—but in the end concluded that he was no more than a clumsy dilletante.[51]

And there were other problems still. Feminists noted that Campbell's hero was almost always male despite the existence of many heroine-centered myths he ignored. He left little space for women except as nurturing mothers, damsels in distress, or plucky sidekicks.[52] Sarah E. Bond and Joel Christensen complained that "one of the most troubling things about Campbell's Monomyth is its omission of the truth of Greek heroic myth: heroes hurt people. . . . The hero with a thousand faces turns out to have a depressingly constant appearance. He projects a toxically masculine, heteronormative point of view that often marginalizes other voices and bodies."[53] Charges and counterarguments swirled after his death that, at least privately, Campbell was antimodern, anti-Christian, anti-Semitic, elitist, racist, and sexist. Novelist David Brin has censured both Campbell and George Lucas for fostering an antidemocratic world far, far away in which elites deserve to rule without plebian interference. Theologian Robert Jewett and philosopher John Shelton Lawrence have depicted the Campbell-Lucas *Star Wars* universe as unintentionally fascist.[54]

Jewett and Lawrence offered yet another critique still: Campbell's hero had become irrelevant. They described, starting in colonial New England but picking up steam with the creation of the cowboy hero in the late nineteenth century, a new "American Monomyth" that had displaced the one Campbell described. In that homegrown hero's journey, "a community in a harmonious paradise is threatened by evil; normal institutions fail to contend with this threat: a selfless superhero emerges to renounce temptations and carry out the redemptive task; aided by fate, his decisive victory restores the community to its paradisial condition: the superhero then recedes into obscurity." Novelist Owen Wister's Virginian, Buffalo Bill Cody, the Klansmen of *Birth of a Nation* (1915), the Lone Ranger, Superman, Capt. James T. Kirk of the starship *Enterprise,* and the vigilante of the *Death Wish* movies are among its manifestations. All of them are outsiders who offer violent redemption to a "monomythic Eden" before riding or flying off into the sunset. Jewett and Lawrence damned this new "escapist fantasy" as "pathological." Instead of turning to science or flawed leaders in an imperfect democracy to deal with difficult trials, too many citizens now waited for "messianic" political superheroes to save them through law-breaking and violence. "It is as if Joseph Campbell's' 'hero' has become an anonymous killer in search of an enemy 'with a thousand faces,'" they lament.[55]

But what does this have to do with Abraham Lincoln? Quite a bit, according to Lincoln biographer Benjamin Thomas, who almost a century ago described the "hero-myth" of Lincoln's life and death that emerged remarkably soon after the assassination. Before Horatio Alger began to put to paper his "rags-to-riches" tales of plucky youths, authors routinely described Lincoln as a providential and prototypical "model youth" and hero who rose to greatness, the Self-Made Man.[56] Another significant Lincoln scholar, David Donald, viewed "the Lincoln Legend" as much as part of Western folklore as "a Paul Bunyan, a Mike Fink, [or] a Davy Crockett." Authors who sought out a "real" Lincoln, he added, were just as likely as hero worshipers to view their subject through the lenses of legend.[57] On the cusp of the president's birth centennial, historian Clinton Rossiter, too, deemed Lincoln "the supreme myth, the richest symbol in the American experience." Lincoln was America.[58] As later chapters relate, some of Lincoln's contemporaries deliberately depicted him as a Christian hero, while Carl Sandburg sought to recreate the Lincoln legend for Americans in the depths of depression and war. More recently, historian Mark Grimsley has analyzed the "myth" of the Lincoln-

McClellan relationship through the lenses of Campbell, Lucas, and Jungian scholars. Lincoln's life story always has been shrouded in legend.[59]

Indeed, Jewett and Lawrence themselves depicted Lincoln as the proto-superhero who helped create the American Monomyth in the first place. The evil of slavery threatened an Edenic United States in their telling. When the government failed to deal with divisions over slavery and the nation careened toward collapse, Lincoln the outsider and hero emerged from the obscurity of the prairie to save it. Renouncing temptations and aided by fate, he fought enemies, vicariously killed quite a few of them, and redeemed the nation through four years of carnage before falling at Ford's Theatre. Stressing that the real Lincoln was a much more complex and moral man, they add that, unfortunately, he also helped establish the cultural trope of the "legitimate law breaker," a man above the law who violated the Constitution repeatedly to rescue it from worse. According to them, Lincoln "acted as teacher for the nation, repeatedly justifying the extraordinary actions he had taken as well as clarifying how best to preserve the republic. . . . [He] deliberately circumvented laws to serve a higher purpose. We see variations of these traits in every monomythic hero." In the depths of the Great Depression, just as Superman took off in Metropolis, Sandburg was in his ascendance, and another world war loomed, John Ford's film *Young Mr. Lincoln* (1939) cemented Lincoln's Sandburg-like image as a superhero long before he picked up his fictional axe to kill proslavery vampires. Ford's Lincoln is folksy and shy, the best of the common folk, but he defies a lynch mob and uses courtroom tricks to save an innocent man. At the end he walks alone into a storm representing the future, "a superman whose physical threats and actual psychological violence restore moral balance."[60]

One need not accept Jewett and Lawrence's specific ideas of the American Monomyth any more than Campbell's flawed hero's journey. The point here is to see how others have borrowed from the structures of myth and legend to understand and tell Lincoln's story as a warrior legend. Campbell's original hero's journey, however challenged by the experts, permeates storytelling in modern popular culture more than ever. Consider again the story told in the documentary *Abraham Lincoln,* or perhaps that told with Disney-inspired sets that depict Lincoln's life in two "journeys"—tours—at the Abraham Lincoln Library and Museum in Springfield, Illinois.[61] The unlikely hero from the frontier sets forth from his father's hut to the threshold of adventure. Gatekeepers confront him as he wrestles foes into friends, fights in a brief war, reads the law, and enters politics. He moves deeper and deeper into a strange new world, enduring many legendary trials and defeating many foes. He also finds allies. When he reaches the "nadir" of civil war in Washington, Lincoln undergoes his supreme ordeal. He encounters not only helpers (U. S. Grant, William Henry Seward, Frederick Douglass) but also new enemies (Confederates, slaveowners, Copperheads, Meade at the Potomac, and especially McClellan). Lincoln ends slavery, triumphs over the South, becomes one with the Founding Fathers, and is harried to his doom by those who wish to harm him. Yet he brings three boons that "restore the world"—emancipation, a reunited nation, and a successful democracy—before he dies and is resurrected as the very Savior of the Union that Lev Grossman described. His life was a hero's journey.

None of that is necessarily false. Much of it is true. What matters here is the *structure,* the way the story is conceived and told as the journey of a warrior-hero. The documentary *Abraham Lincoln* as well as the Lincoln Museum depict a hero's journey just as surely as *Star Wars* does. But what then of the real commander in chief and the real war? To understand Lincoln better, we first must hack our way through the historic legend that has grown up since 1861 and clear the ground for a proper reevaluation of a real human being who commanded the armies of the United States at its most perilous hour. But to do even that, we must come to understand the complicated story of how and why storytellers constructed the heroic legend in the first place as well as how and why it evolved over time until reaching its ascendance in the 1950s.

As it turns out, that is a tale in itself, one with twists and turns worthy of the mythical hero Theseus in the Minotaur's labyrinth. And it begins with Abraham Lincoln himself, the progenitor of his own legend. Part 1 of this volume, entitled "War," maintains that before anyone else concluded that he was smarter than his generals, Lincoln came to believe it himself, doing so remarkably early in his presidency. Because every blade needs a whetstone and every legendary hero needs a foe to overcome, Maj. Gen. George McClellan emerged in Lincoln's mind and the American psyche as his chief adversary. To this day, the Lincoln-McClellan relationship remains at the heart of any evaluation of Lincoln as commander in chief, and it is central to the heroic legend. As historian George Rable wrote, it "at times dominated the course of the conflict" in the war's first years.[62] McClellan "is so central to the story," historian Joseph Harsh wrote, "that any interpretation of the war must be made to fit him in order to be plausible." Unfortunately for Little Mac, that meant riding a "see-saw" with Lincoln that rarely teeters. "It is assumed," Harsh observed, "that one was right and the other wrong. . . . When one is up, the other has got to be down."[63] Or as Mark Grimsley has put it, someone had to take "the *blame* for the relationship's failure. The tendency to think in terms of blame is . . . the single strongest feature of the conventional telling of the relationship." McClellan's misfortune was "a stormy relationship with the most beloved president in American history."[64] Lincoln and McClellan take up much of the first two chapters here, both to explain how Lincoln came to view himself as the wiser warrior and to offer a tentative counternarrative to much of the heroic legend.

As the war proceeded, a few members of Lincoln's inner circle began to echo his thoughts on his military prowess, notably loyal secretaries and future biographers John Nicolay and John Hay. That occurred simultaneously with the failure of McClellan's immediate replacements in Virginia and the rise of U. S. Grant to high command and victory, as depicted and analyzed in chapters 3 and 4. Kenneth Williams's now-familiar "Lincoln Finds a General" trope, culminating in Grant's arrival and eventual triumph, helped solidify the historic legend as canon in the 1950s. Grant was Williams's anti-McClellan. There is much truth in that too. Yet Lincoln was not always the patient and all-knowing commander in chief that Williams depicted, his other generals were not always the failures Williams gleefully denigrated, and the Grant-Lincoln relationship was never immune to presidential intervention. Self-confidently and impatiently, Lincoln continued to exert his views on the proper conduct of the war at every level, still an active if sometimes imperfect commander in chief. It was Lincoln after all, not Grant, who demanded the "hard, tough fighting" of the Overland and Petersburg Campaigns, when Grant's first instinct was to emulate McClellan and swing into the Confederate rear.[65]

Part 2, *Memory,* begins with Lincoln's assassination and, over four chapters, narrates how the heroic legend spread beyond the Lincoln White House, struggled against competing interpretations, and after years of debate and neglect finally became canonical in the Cold War of the 1950s. To be sure, the heroic legend debuted in print only months after Lincoln's death, but it arrived so cloaked in religious piety that for decades it did not withstand the counternarratives offered by secular contemporaries such as William Herndon, writers who concerned themselves with an earthy prairie lawyer rather than a divinely inspired president. As other biographers and historians vied for sales and respect, as discussed in chapter 5, Nicolay and Hay became the torchbearers of the heroic legend as well as much else that we know about Lincoln. They reoriented Lincoln biography forever. Yet when it came specifically to Lincoln's military genius, they made surprisingly few converts among their contemporaries. Into the next generations, Nicolay and Hay's heroic legend remained the exception to a historiography that could celebrate Lincoln within all of Merrill Peterson's tropes without depicting him as a self-taught military genius. Chapter 6 explains how minimizing, ignoring, or denying the legend outright remained the rule in the United States right up to the beginning of World War II, with the prominent exception of the ubiquitous McClellan-as-villain trope. If anything, the heroic legend was in decline through the 1930s thanks to its emphatic rejection by the dominant Civil War historians of that era.

The revival of the heroic legend was international, as explained in chapter 7. In Great Britain as elsewhere, army leadership also emphatically rejected the heroic legend from its beginnings. Prominent intellectuals in uniform, who also were sympathetic to the Confederacy, depicted Lincoln as a clumsy meddler who paled in comparison to the great Confederate heroes. They taught young officers to emulate Stonewall Jackson and Robert E. Lee, not Lincoln and his generals. The carnage of World War I's Western Front, however, with its modern barbed wire and trenches, convinced a few of those young officers that they had heard the wrong lessons at Sandhurst and at the Staff College. In the 1920s and early 1930s, those embittered men enunciated a new vision of Lincoln's military genius that resembled Nicolay and Hay's. Given the authoritarian drift of the era, they also imagined and celebrated Lincoln as a benign dictator whose centralized model offered hope of winning the next war. After the Second World War came and went, as chapter 8 demonstrates, Americans Kenneth P. Williams—yet another veteran of the Western Front—and T. Harry Williams joined others in rejecting previous interpretations. They drew deeply upon the British soldier-historians, whose ideas seemingly had been vindicated by victory in 1945, and revived the heroic legend for a Cold War America finally ready to accept it. Their arguments, based on lessons and language taken from the world wars, were so timely and so powerful that they seized the field. As I argue in the conclusion, they have never really relinquished it.

The heroic legend that we know, then, is complicated. Gestated in the Lincoln White House, preserved by a few of the president's early admirers despite significant opposition from a majority of contemporary authors, all but reborn in early twentieth-century Britain in the muddy and bloody shadow of the Western Front as part of local British agendas, and canonized after World War II in the Cold War United States and its Civil War centennial, the heroic legend somehow is the last element of Lincoln historiography to defy reconsideration. As I suggest in a brief afterword, it deserves reassessment—and not just for historical reasons. Since the Cold War, modern presidents beginning with Harry Truman have referred to the Lincoln presidency as a foundation to expand their powers, creating what historian Arthur M. Schlesinger Jr. famously called an "imperial presidency" that defied Lincoln's adamant assertion that he did not want to create precedents. As presidential power continues to augment in the twenty-first century, Abraham Lincoln's foundational heroic legend deserves more attention than ever.[66]

PART I

WAR

ABRAHAM LINCOLN AND THE HEROIC LEGEND

1

THE WAR POWER

Lincoln and the Genesis of the Heroic Legend, January 1861–January 1862

On December 1, 1862, as the announcement of the Emancipation Proclamation drew near and armies gathered near Fredericksburg, Virginia; Nashville, Tennessee; and Vicksburg, Mississippi, President Abraham Lincoln sent his annual message to Congress. Its conclusion concerned his ultimately failed proposal that Congress amend the Constitution to end slavery in the United States over the course of thirty-seven years, with compensation to slaveholders and voluntary colonization for African Americans who chose to emigrate. If the reason for his soaring rhetoric surprises modern readers, the words still ring. "The dogmas of the quiet past," he wrote, "are inadequate to the stormy present. The occasion is piled high with difficulty, and we must rise—with the occasion. As our case is new, so we must think anew, and act anew. We must disenthrall ourselves, and then we shall save our country."[1]

Lincoln practiced what he preached. Starting at the end of 1860, he greeted the "stormy present" by thinking anew and acting anew to save his country. Nowhere was his willingness to challenge conventional wisdom more evident than as commander in chief. Coming to office with scant background in military affairs but possessing remarkable self-confidence, he seized the reins of the war like no president before him. "Lincoln," historian Harold Holzer later observed, "seldom lacked for self-assurance, even in solitude."[2] He would go on to oversee the war virtually by himself, concluding, in historian Russell Weigley's words, "that the office of Commander in Chief vested him during war with all the powers pertaining to sovereignty under the internationally accepted rules of war—and under a loose construction of the international rules at that. . . . [A]s Commander in Chief and thus the embodiment of the sovereignty of the United States he held war powers exceeding those of Congress."[3]

Lincoln never spelled out a consistent theory of what he called his "war powers" or explained why he charted such a remarkable course away from precedent. Perhaps he could not. Historian Brian Dirck has found no "Lincoln Doctrine," only "broad tendencies and a rather loose set of principles and strategies" in Lincoln's administration of the war that were reactive and sometimes inconsistent.[4] "My policy is to have no policy," Lincoln often said.[5] But from the first, he did believe firmly that his office was invested with American sovereignty, that his powers were broad in the national emergency, and that in such an unprecedented crisis, he might have to violate specific sections of the Constitution from time to time to save the nation that rested upon it. Such a novel theory of a president's broad constitutional authority was all but nonexistent in 1861. By himself, Lincoln invented the modern commander in chief.[6]

Commander in Chief Lincoln wielded two kinds of "war powers," Dirck continued. "First-order presidential warmaking" involved tasks previous chief executives carried out without much controversy, such as appointing officers, strategizing, and providing logistical support. "Second-order warmaking powers," in contrast, "blurred the lines" in unprecedented ways between the previously accepted duties of a wartime commander in chief and a peacetime president, as with emancipation. Ironically, it was in the more traditional role that Lincoln moved with hesitation and deference, especially at first.[7] But his self-confidence grew apace. He soon came to trust his own instincts more than his generals. While he remained loathe to issue direct orders to them for most of the war, they knew what he wanted. "To a greater degree than other war presidents," historian Mark Grimsley wrote, Lincoln "involved himself in military operations: the actual nuts and bolts of maneuvering troops through time and space and influencing the conduct of battles."[8]

Part of that gelling self-reliance grew from impatience. He wanted to end the war as soon as possible. Historians who study Lincoln as commander in chief cite that impatience again and again as a defining characteristic. Most see it as positive, a necessary spur to victory.[9] Historian Elizabeth Brown Pryor was among the few to differ, observing that because of his restiveness, Lincoln sometimes "blundered through military labyrinths with all the agility of an angered buffalo, while thousands of people died."[10] The president had little interest in the military "dogmas of the quiet past" either, not when they rubbed against his common sense, public opinion, or political reality. At times he could be an indecisive and passive-aggressive boss, at others an intrusive meddler. His impatience with his generals, his eagerness to draw up and advocate for his own campaign plans, and even his frequent snippiness usually came couched in concerns that "the people" would not tolerate inaction. Generals roundly decried the notion that they needed to satisfy the public's thirst for victory. They complained that campaigning in the real world was far different than locating on a map the shortest line between points A and B—which the analytical and Euclidian Lincoln, an enthusiastically self-taught geometer and surveyor, tended to do.[11] While the brass saw Lincoln as an amateurish meddler, however, others then and now have defended him as realistic in his approach and prescient in understanding that a military struggle between two erstwhile republican governments invariably relied on popular support.[12] To Lincoln the politician, the war always was "essentially a People's contest."[13] Government and strategy had to be responsive to public opinion.[14]

Lincoln's health played a role as well, one that deserves more reevaluation. Observers frequently described Lincoln as tired, worn-out, stooped, sickly, angry, and depressed, from Fort Sumter to the very end. Leadership is stressful at the best of times, but Lincoln sat as president during a national nadir, making decisions at crucial moments that affected millions of lives. As psychologists of leadership have come to know, the pressure of time, incomplete or ambiguous information, the lack of a clear course, and the fear of dire personal and national consequences can overwhelm the most stable leaders. Some statesmen rise to the occasion and even thrive. Others falter. Lincoln persevered to a successful end that saw his goals accomplished. Yet as familiar comparisons of his 1860 and 1865 photographs make clear, the stress also took a mighty toll. He was not a superman, but rather a troubled individual who had experienced depression and even despair at low moments throughout his life. In Washington, Mary Lincoln and many others worried about his health and occasionally his mental stability. Often, he could not sleep, ate but little, and increasingly struck observers as a prematurely old man who seemed to be sleepwalking. Modern neuroscience and psychology again remind us how stress takes a toll on body and mind. Chronic sleep deprivation undermines decision making and heightens anxiety. Negative events begin to shape decision making as well. Exhausted people cannot process new information as completely as before. Problem solving suffers, leading to a stubborn reliance on what worked (or did not work) before. Emotions come to the fore. Grievances expand.[15]

Lincoln kept going. He possessed many of the characteristics that political scientist Robert S. Robins and psychologist Robert M. Dorn identified as crucial to successful leadership in stressful moments. He had a firm world view, a deep commitment to a cause, a willingness to face challenges, no shortage of ambition, and the ability to absorb criticism. His fabled humor and storytelling gave him a powerful tool for relaxation, as did riding horseback and his love of theater. He lacked other coping abilities, however. Healthy leaders believe that they can shape events, for example. Lincoln, sometimes at least, said that he did not.[16] Historian David Donald controversially argued for "the essential passivity of his nature" and his "reluctance to take the initiative."[17] Certainly, when he assigned responsibility for war or peace to the Confederacy in his First Inaugural Speech, told opponents of emancipation in April 1864 that "events have controlled me," or described himself as a tool of God's will, Lincoln confessed—or at least pretended to avow—a perceived powerlessness. He increasingly grew averse to criticism as well. Leaders need to know they have support; Lincoln often did not. The death of his favorite son in the White House and his wife's deep mourning, overspending, and increased instability made his home no refuge.[18] One can only speculate in the end how exhaustion and its corollaries affected his decision making as commander in chief; we cannot take Lincoln to a physician or psychologist for evaluation. But at the same time, we should not pretend that he was a Nietzschean Übermensch when his 1865 portrait and so many observers tell us otherwise.

These six factors—his loose ideas about extensive executive war powers, a healthy self-confidence, his deep impatience, a philosophical gravitation toward Euclidian simplicity, the constant need to retain public support, and sheer physical and mental exhaustion—combined to shape much of what Lincoln did as commander in chief. They also are the guideposts to much that follows, leading us to Lincoln's conclusion that he knew better than his own generals when it came to making war.[19]

In April 1861 Abraham Lincoln seemed most unlikely to win renown as an intuitive military genius. Aside from his brief militia service, he came to the

White House with no military expertise and an antiwar reputation earned through opposition to the conflict with Mexico. Democrats such as Stephen A. Douglas still blasted his antiwar speeches from the 1840s. In truth, Lincoln did not oppose war itself, only Democrat James K. Polk's against Mexico. He looked back with pride to American wars he deemed just, especially the Revolution. Like most Whigs, he voted to fund the war in Mexico despite his opposition, supported Latin American wars of independence, and stumped for Whig and Republican politician-generals such as Winfield Scott. But there were inconsistencies too. As historian Cecily Zander has maintained, Republicans including Lincoln distrusted West Point and the regular army's officer corps, viewing them as tools of the Democratic Party and a wider southern slavocracy that allegedly controlled the federal government. He voted against funding West Point while in Congress, ridiculed military pomp, and stressed his questionable Quaker roots in 1860. Never calling himself Captain Lincoln, he joked about his time in the militia. But mostly, he ignored military affairs. Lincoln's real concerns were economic and domestic.[20]

South Carolina's secession on December 20, 1860—Lincoln previously had assumed it was simply bluff—changed all that. A tough new consistency emerged overnight. Only one day later, the president-elect wrote confidentially to fellow Republicans supporting the use of force if necessary to prevent secession. Privately he sent word to Scott, the aged and rotund commanding general of the U.S. Army, to prepare to "either *hold,* or *retake,* the forts" in Charleston "as the case may require, at, and after the inauguration."[21] He told others the same thing. At the same time, Lincoln refused to countenance compromises that would surrender government property, provide more space to slavery, or leave the nation divided. He worried with good reason that Congress might forge ahead to a deal without him. He would accept a just war, although he still expected that time, delicacy, and resurgent southern Unionism first would heal the nation's wounds. Meanwhile, as President James Buchanan floundered, six more states followed South Carolina before Lincoln's inauguration on March 4, 1861. Corresponding with Scott, the president-elect developed his own embryonic strategic views that centered on holding U.S. properties in the seceding states and retaking those already lost. Historians Michael Burlingame and Harold Holzer each note that fellow Republicans and cheering crowds on the way to Washington further encouraged his growing militancy.[22] When Lincoln put all those ideas in his draft inaugural speech, however, both incoming Secretary of State William Henry Seward and old friend Orville Browning urged him not to mention retaking the forts. Ultimately, Lincoln only pledged to "hold, occupy, and possess" federal property. Prompted by Seward, he also assured secessionists that "in *your* hands, my dissatisfied fellow countrymen, and not in *mine,* is the momentous issue of civil war. The government will not assail *you.* You can have no conflict without being yourselves the aggressors."[23]

Still underestimating the depth and breadth of secessionism in the slave states, Lincoln continued to assume that he had time to reach a peaceful end to the crisis. One day after he took his oath, he found out differently. After Christmas, Col. Robert Anderson had moved his garrison at Charleston, South Carolina, from vulnerable posts ashore to Fort Sumter in the harbor. In January 1861 Buchanan's attempt to resupply the fort failed when shore batteries drove off the relief ship. Two months later the garrison was running out of food. According to Anderson, it also would require 20,000 U.S. troops to seize the hostile forts and batteries ringing the harbor. The U.S. Army had but 16,000 men in all, most stationed out west. Scott also doubted that ships could stand up to land batteries—a notion the navy hotly disputed—and believed that it would take months to prepare such an expedition anyway. Scott advised evacuation. It was a momentous decision for a president and a cabinet without practical military experience. Except for Postmaster General Montgomery Blair, the cabinet agreed with the expert officer. At the same time, they rejected an aggressive plan from former naval officer Gustavus Fox, Blair's brother-in-law, to run the batteries and resupply the fort, an idea Buchanan already had dismissed. Seward was especially adamant that Lincoln not set off a war or drive away more states by attempting to relieve Fort Sumter. Others feared the political effects of a defeat.[24]

Lincoln intuitively liked Fox's idea, however, and on his second day in office, the president refused to give in to Scott despite the general's monumental national stature and military expertise. He was the boss now. With his inaugural pledges boxing him in, Lincoln also feared that Republicans would abandon him if he wavered. Nor did he quite trust Anderson, a southerner. Prone to deliberate decision making, the new president just was not sure what else to do. Hoping to buy time, he sent three men, including Fox, to Charleston to gauge opinion and interview Anderson. Their reports were dim: Unionism was dead in the city, and it was true that the colonel's garrison could last only to mid-April. The news depressed Scott so much that he advised evacuating both Fort Sumter *and* Fort Pickens near Pensacola, Florida, the only other significant U.S. post left in the self-proclaimed Confederacy. With growing cabinet support except for Seward—and a nudge from Blair's politically powerful father—Lincoln again rejected Scott's conservative counsel. He would honor his promises.[25]

Risking war and standing up to "the Seward and Scott policy," as a jealous Secretary of the Navy Gideon Welles derisively called it after the war, was not easy for a new president lacking a military background or executive experience, especially at such a traumatic moment.[26] One symptom of that inexperience and desperation—also one that testified to his complete lack of military acumen at the beginning of his administration—was Lincoln's initially enthusiastic support of a bizarre plan hatched by a young favorite to nationalize the rallying state militias. Only twenty-three years old in March 1861, Elmer Ellsworth was an itinerant clerk and indifferent law student originally from upstate New York whose real passion in life was military pomp. Apparently unable to enter West Point and unwilling to join the regular army, Ellsworth moved west, joined several militia units, and became known as a skillful if priggish drillmaster. Discovering the French Army's colorful Algerian Zouaves, with their quick drill and fanciful turbaned uniforms, he taught himself French and mastered their manual. In 1860 his Chicago-based U.S. Zouave Cadets toured the North and created a Zouave craze, with mock battles and performances that included somersaults, handstands, and the intricate movements of modern marching bands. Among his fans were Lincoln and his son Tad, who saw the Zouave Cadets perform in Springfield. Suddenly a national celebrity, Ellsworth moved to Springfield at Lincoln's invitation and became Lincoln's last law clerk in hopes of pleasing his future father-in-law with a real job. All the Lincolns came to adore Ellsworth. He became active in the presidential campaign, gave numerous speeches, and managed crowd control on the trip to Washington.[27]

When Lincoln unsuccessfully proposed making the untried Ellsworth the chief clerk in the War Department, the young man countered with an even more ambitious plan of his own based on an idea he and Lincoln first had broached in Illinois (only to see it fail in the state legislature). He convinced the president to create a new federal bureau of militias, with Ellsworth at the top as adjutant and inspector general. The new bureau in theory would coordinate organizing and equipping state militia units while providing standard drill and moral parameters—Ellsworth essentially would become the nation's drillmaster. Lincoln beamed that his untried young protégé possessed "a real genius for war!" The plan went nowhere after new Attorney General Edward Bates warned the president that the whole scheme was unconstitutional: Only Congress could create a new executive department, while the states controlled their own militias. Moreover, General Scott already had appointed an officer to oversee the militia units entering Washington. The regular army wanted no part of the pretend soldier either. When the press turned on the young celebrity and depicted him as an ambitious fraud, Ellsworth backed off, resigned his new commission, and went to New York City to recruit a Zouave regiment from the city's rough-and-tumble firemen. Lincoln continued to support him despite the regiment's increasingly notorious hell-raising once it arrived in Washington. The bureau of militias proposal continued to loom until late May, when Ellsworth died just across the Potomac River in Virginia while tearing down a secession flag hoisted by its shotgun-wielding hotel owner. Lincoln wept repeatedly at the loss of his youthful friend, the first officer to die in the war.[28]

The odd Ellsworth gambit was only one example of Lincoln's shaky beginnings as commander in chief. Lacking executive experience, he did not know how to prioritize, delegate, or administer systematically. Exhausted and careworn since the election by both the gathering war clouds and the incessant crowds of fellow Republicans seeking patronage positions, Lincoln could not sleep, endured painful headaches, and fainted at least once. In Springfield he had imagined himself in the Garden of Gethsemane. Now he compared the White House to hell. Over the next days, anxiety, inexperience, and confusion bedeviled him. Seward stalked him as well, still aggrieved that he was not president and this unknown rube from the frontier was. As if he were chief executive, the secretary engaged in covert talks to prevent Virginia's secession, offering to evacuate Fort Sumter in exchange and secretly pledging that Lincoln would not use force. Any threatening move would look like coercion and wreck everything. Working closely with three highly ambitious junior officers—Lt. Col. Erasmus Keyes, Capt. Montgomery Meigs, and Cmdr. David Dixon Porter—Seward concocted an odd diversion of reinforcing Fort Pickens. Lincoln approved. Convinced of disloyalty in the Navy and War Departments, Seward and Porter then remarkably convinced the president not to tell anyone about it, not even Scott, Welles, or Secretary of War Simon Cameron. The two operations proceeded in parallel until Lincoln blundered, assigning to both expeditions the most powerful warship available, the sixteen-gun steamer USS *Powhatan.* He later confessed that he signed the orders Seward gave him without reading them, an indication of his already stress-compromised decision making. Some historians agree with Welles that Seward's real aim was to kill the Sumter expedition. Lincoln apologized, but the damage was done. That ship had sailed—to Florida.[29]

Still, Seward would not give in. On April 1 he suggested picking a fight with France and Spain in hopes of reuniting the nation through a common foe while he jockeyed to become a sort of prime minister. Lincoln quickly rejected Seward's power grab just as he had Scott's advice; he was the president and commander in chief. Five days later he dispatched the Fort Sumter expedition. At Seward's suggestion, however, he informed South Carolina of its intentions. Lincoln hoped that the Confederates would let the relief party land, but unlike some in his inner circle, he pessimistically expected resistance. He felt no guilt; he would have fulfilled his pledges. The now-alerted Confederate shore batteries opened fire on Fort Sumter before dawn on April 12. Anderson surrendered thirty-four hours later. Farther south, U.S. Marines easily secured Fort Pickens before Seward's effort at diversion came to nothing.[30]

Historians have differed among themselves for years when evaluating Lincoln's performance during the Sumter crisis. Many insist that he was responsible for the war by cleverly maneuvering Confederate President Jefferson Davis into firing the first shots and unifying the North, an argument that among other things absolves Davis from ordering the actual attack. Others depict a man of peace who would countenance war only if all else failed. Others still see Lincoln inadvertently starting the war through indecision and bumbling. The debate continues in part due his own defensive retrospective insistence that he made no mistakes at all.[31] His friend Orville Browning wrote weeks later that Lincoln told him: "The plan succeeded. They attacked Sumter—it fell, and thus, did more service than it otherwise could."[32] Loyal presidential secretaries John Hay and John Nicolay later echoed that observation, writing that "whether the expedition would fail or succeed was a question of minor importance. He was not playing a game of military strategy. . . . He was looking through Sumter to the loyal States; beyond the insulted flag to the avenging nation."[33]

This was retrospective public relations, although in time many accepted it as proof of Lincoln's sagacity. In truth, his actual response from the inauguration to the attack on Fort Sumter reveals no concise "plan" at all beyond keeping his vows to the voters to resist secession and his willingness since January to accept a military solution and a limited war if necessary. Hardly a benign Machiavelli seeking to galvanize the North, the exhausted neophyte president zigzagged hesitantly, rejected professional advice, largely ignored his cabinet except for the manipulative Seward, cooperated secretly with Seward's Fort Pickens gambit, saddled two naval expeditions with his confusion, and finally alerted suspicious Confederates of the administration's plans.[34] Lincoln could have been more "energetic and decisive," Welles later complained, but he instead had been hesitant as the nation divided. Worse, the president ceded "extraordinary powers and authority" to Seward and a small circle of junior officers. That "would have alarmed the country and weakened the public confidence in the administrative capacity of the Executive had the facts been known. . . . It betrayed weakness in the executive head."[35] Lincoln did not stir up hostilities on purpose, he did not shoot first, and the firing on Fort Sumter did unite the North for a time. Yet the new president also committed enough unforced errors throughout the crisis that the beginnings of his tenure as a wartime commander in chief were ominous.[36]

What followed Fort Sumter, according to historian Eric Foner, was "among the boldest unilateral exercises of executive authority in American history."[37] Those actions must be understood first within the immediate context of fear that had Washingtonians and especially Republicans terrified of potential invaders across the Potomac and alleged traitors—some real—embedded within. Defectors from the army officer corps created general paranoia and heightened Lincoln's preexisting disdain for the fuss and feathers of the old army. The resignations of Robert E. Lee—whom Lincoln just had promoted to colonel in a bid for his fidelity—and fawning Lt. Col. John Bankhead Magruder particularly infuriated him. Many of the officers who did remain loyal nonetheless looked down on the president as a shabby yokel who could not even salute properly. They also despised Cameron, known in military circles as a crooked politician whose supporters had used the army to line their pockets. Few precedents existed to guide Lincoln either. Washington had suppressed the Whiskey Rebellion in 1791, while Andrew Jackson and Zachary Taylor both had threatened to use the military to preserve the Union. Yet the Whig-Republican traditions that Lincoln had championed subordinated the Executive Branch to Congress, in part in reaction to Jackson's saber rattling.[38]

Adamant that no right to secede existed and an insurrection was in process, worried that his capital might fall, and concerned that the nation and indeed worldwide democracy might collapse, Lincoln defined his wartime role as commander in chief in a most nondeferential, non-Whig, and thoroughly Jacksonian way. The results were mixed. After Fort Sumter, he called Congress back to Washington for a special session, but only in July, once seven states had concluded their congressional elections—and because Seward convinced him that Congress might seek a weak compromise, something that had concerned Lincoln all spring. Using existing law, he called for 75,000 three-month state militiamen—an arbitrary number gestated in a cabinet meeting—to both defend the capital and retake lost U.S. property. Greeted enthusiastically in the free states, the call alarmed the border slave states so much that the Virginia Secession Convention voted to secede, with three more slave states to follow, to extend the Confederacy to the outskirts of Washington. On April 19, again following Seward's lead, Lincoln proclaimed a naval blockade of the Confederate coast. Welles warned that the proclamation, as opposed to simply closing the ports, would strain international laws and could lead European powers to grant the Confederacy belligerent status and aid. He was right, and that self-inflected wound festered the next four years despite the blockade's eventual centrality to victory. Alarmed by secessionist guerrillas in Maryland, Lincoln became the first president to suspend the writ of habeas corpus (between Washington and Philadelphia), took control of railroads in the state, and allowed Federal troops to place artillery on the heights overlooking Baltimore. Even Republicans were shocked when troops arrested Baltimore's mayor, city council, police commissioner, and others.[39]

With at least the capital safe for the moment, Lincoln dug in for a longer war. In early May he asked for an additional 42,034 volunteers and 18,000 sailors to serve for three years. To the dismay of many congressional Republicans who continued to distrust the professionals, he also enlarged the regular army with ten new regiments. To arm and equip them all, the administration routinely bypassed executive agencies and bureaucrats it feared to be disloyal. It contracted directly with private manufacturers and European armories, inadvertently driving up prices in a bidding war with states and leaving a trail of mismanagement. Borrowed money came from the Treasury without congressional approval. As the army expanded, Lincoln—much like Polk—appointed generals with little or no military experience to shore up political support. He widened suspension of habeas corpus, ordered marshals to seize telegrams, and restricted the mails.[40]

All of this seemed shocking in 1861, even to Lincoln himself. He admitted and defended his extraordinary actions in his July 4 message to the reassembled Congress as vital to save the republic and all republics from disgruntled minorities who would "practically put an end to free government upon the earth. . . . [N]o choice was left but to call out the war power of the Government; and so to resist force, employed for its destruction, by force, for its preservation." The president knew that he was on shaky constitutional ground. But it was not a course he had taken lightly, he promised, asserting that "it was with the deepest regret that the Executive found the duty of employing the war-power, in defense of the government, forced upon him. He could but perform this duty, or surrender the existence of the government." Secession was unconstitutional, while his constitutional sins had been venial. "These measures," he wrote, "whether strictly legal or not, were ventured upon, under what appeared to be a popular demand, and a public necessity; trusting, then, as now, that Congress would readily ratify them. It is believed that nothing has been done beyond the constitutional competency of Congress." In the end, Congress retroactively agreed, passed the necessary legislation, and authorized an army of a half-million men to be enlisted for three years.[41] As historian Paul A. C. Koistinen noted, congressional Republicans at that crucial moment feared "a lack of leadership . . . much more than acts that bordered on the dictatorial."[42]

In late April, as the first units arrived to defend Washington, Lincoln militarily was still thinking simply about holding vulnerable positions—Washington and Fort Monroe on Virginia's Peninsula—and then sending Federal troops "down to Charleston . . . [to] pay her the little debt we are owing her."[43] He envisioned a limited East Coast war, with the blockade doing the rest. Others saw a larger canvas. On April 27 George B. McClellan sent Scott an unsolicited plan to win the war. Once an army wunderkind and most recently a railroad president who supported Stephen A. Douglas in his 1858 Senate race against Lincoln, McClellan had commanded Ohio's militia for exactly four days when he wrote the general in chief. Never lacking in ambition or ego—not to mention an insecure tendency to try to impress his wife with blustering letters that ill-served him with later scholars—McClellan consistently from the first imagined the necessity of a bigger war. His plan depended upon massive armies moving along roads and rivers, decisive campaigns, and gentle treatment of white southerners to hasten reunion. Like all the star West Point students and Mexican-American War veterans of his era, he distrusted volunteers and was wary of costly frontal assaults. In his initial scheme, one army (presumably under his command) would cross the Ohio River into western Virginia, fight its way to Richmond, move on to Charleston, and then march clockwise around the enemy coast. A complimentary movement would drive south to the Confederate capital at Montgomery, Alabama. Scott passed this plan to Lincoln, but with reservations. Even more convinced than McClellan that many white southerners still supported the Union, the elder general was loath to send armies across its territory, spilling blood and creating hatred. Better to build up the army, he thought, isolate the Confederacy with the blockade, and launch a campaign down the Mississippi River to cut it in two. In time, the constricted and isolated Confederacy would implode.[44]

Scott's ideas eventually became a basis for western operations especially, but in June 1861 Lincoln did not believe that he had that kind of time. The general's lampooned "Anaconda Plan," once leaked and publicized, met with popular derision. Editors, governors, cabinet members (especially Blair and his powerful clan), and many average Americans demanded a quick victory. When the Confederates moved their capital to newly seceded Virginia, powerful New York newspaper editor Horace Greeley's front page bellowed "Forward to Richmond!" It was more than jingoism; the Senate debated endorsing Greeley's demand that the army take Richmond before the Confederate Congress sat on July 20. And Lincoln faced other pressures. The enlistments of three-month volunteers would soon expire, European involvement was possible, and the government was running on borrowed money. Then, too, there was the beloved Ellsworth's death across the Potomac, which according to biographer David Donald pushed Lincoln to a more aggressive stance. The president's thinking thus evolved quickly toward forgoing the "trip to Charleston" and launching a quick strike in Virginia to end the war then and there. On July 29 the cabinet met, joined by Scott, Meigs, Brig. Gen. Irvin McDowell (another favorite of Scott's), and Secretary of the Treasury Salmon P. Chase. McDowell commanded the Federal army of 35,000 men coalescing around Washington. Lincoln finally rejected Scott's Anaconda and endorsed McDowell's

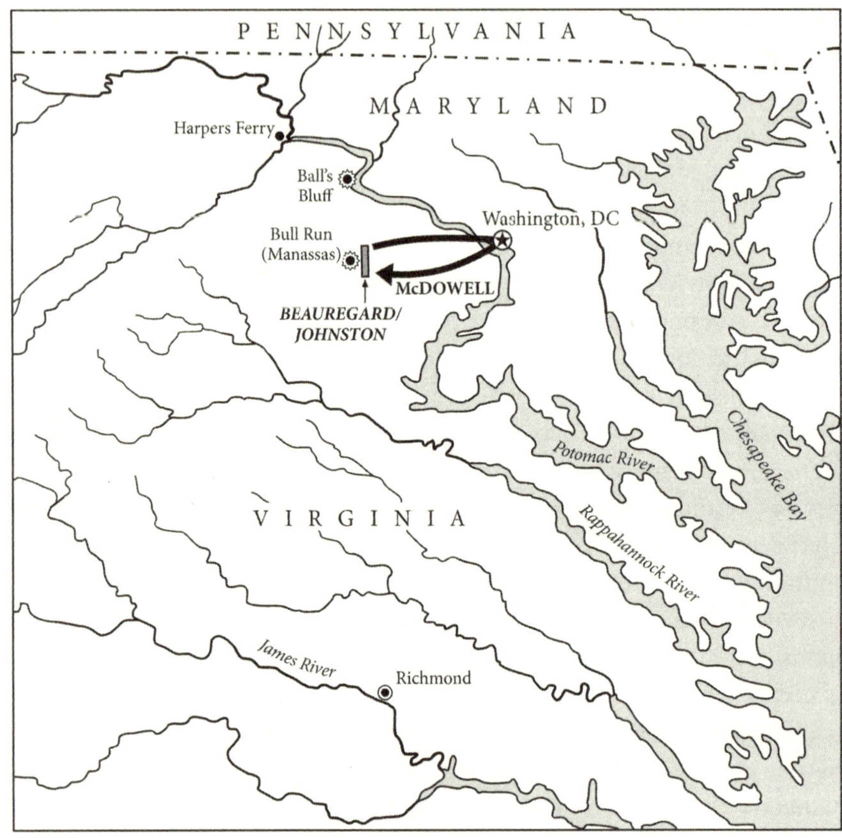

Virginia Theater, 1861.

proposal to march against the Confederate forces at Manassas Junction, thirty miles southwest of Washington. Defeating the enemy, the army would go "on to Richmond" and somehow end the war. McDowell begged for time to better prepare his troops, but with support from Meigs, Lincoln declined, commenting that the enemy was also "green."[45] In historian T. Harry Williams's words, the tyro president alone had "initiated and planned" the war's first major campaign and "forced" it upon his generals. It was his "first important exercise of his power as commander in chief."[46]

It almost worked. McDowell commanded the largest field army in American history to that point. A smaller force of about 22,000 Confederates under Brig. Gen. P. G. T. Beauregard waited at Manassas. In the Shenandoah Valley,

Brig. Gen. Joseph E. Johnston's 11,000 Confederates opposed Maj. Gen. Robert Patterson's 15,000 Federals. Patterson's job was to pin down Johnston. He failed. McDowell's "green" recruits, meanwhile, dawdled in the summer heat and, despite constant pressure from Lincoln, approached the enemy ten days behind schedule. On the morning of July 21, McDowell attacked and drove the Confederates' left flank back steadily until Johnston's recently arrived reinforcements stopped the exhausted Federals. As confusing reports came in during the morning, Lincoln consulted a napping Scott, who told him not to worry and rolled over. That afternoon a Confederate counterattack sent McDowell's men and a crowd of civilian sightseers reeling back to Washington. Lincoln stayed up all night conversing with some of them and reading telegrams.[47] He feared viscerally for the safety of the capital and acted broadly to prevent its occupation and the political nightmare that assuredly would follow. As Nicolay and Hay recalled, "all available troops were hurried forward to McDowell's support; Baltimore was put on the alert; telegrams were sent to the recruiting stations of the nearest Northern States to lose no time in sending all their organized regiments to Washington; McClellan was ordered to 'come down to the Shenandoah Valley with such troops as can be spared from Western Virginia.'"[48]

Defeat mortified Lincoln, but as with Fort Sumter, he took no responsibility for it. When Scott postured and pretended to blame himself for not talking Lincoln out of the attack, the president angrily denied that he had forced Scott to do anything. Ignoring the old general, on July 23 he compiled a nine-point memorandum on "Military Policy." Some of it was familiar, such as the blockade and holding Fort Monroe and Baltimore. But Lincoln also called for reinforcing both the Shenandoah and McClellan and for reorganizing the army around the new volunteers. He looked west for the first time too, asking Maj. Gen. John C. Frémont—former explorer and 1856 Republican presidential candidate—to build an army in Missouri. Three days later Lincoln approved a call for 500,000 more men. On July 27 he added two additional items: control of Manassas and its railroads to Washington and Harpers Ferry, Virginia, and "a joint movement" of two armies from Cairo, Illinois, down the Mississippi River to Memphis and from Cincinnati into East Tennessee, where Unionists had won his admiration. Both Scott's and McClellan's influence were evident in Lincoln's newly expanded martial thoughts, but the resolve to accomplish them was his alone.[49] "Lincoln never swerved from his memorandum of July 27, 1861," historian and soldier Francis V. Green wrote nearly a half century later. Lincoln concluded that he just needed to find generals who would implement his ideas and fight a successful, war-winning battle, preferably sooner than later.[50]

A month after Bull Run, Lincoln brought McClellan to Washington to rebuild the beaten army. Coming off victories in western Virginia, "Little Mac" was "the unquestioned hero of the hour," according to Hay and Nicolay. As George Rable has noted, Lincoln and McClellan already knew each other. McClellan may have supported Douglas in 1858 and 1860, but as president of the Illinois Central Railroad, he had hired Lincoln the lawyer over forty times. Regardless, even the most ardent critic agrees that McClellan, once in Washington, proceeded to excel in rebuilding the Federal army. He integrated new units, equipped and trained them, discarded bad officers, spearheaded the construction of Washington's fortifications, and revived morale. He seemed to be everywhere to such a degree that the long hours undermined his health.[51]

McClellan also thought a lot about victory. His "personality and actions have inspired hatred and adoration—mostly the former," historian Donald Stoker wrote, but "something critical has received short shrift: McClellan the strategist."[52] In a new proposal that Lincoln solicited directly—ignoring Scott and the chain of command in what would become a common and corrosive feature of the Lincoln presidency—McClellan again envisioned massed armies launching coordinated Federal thrusts meant to smother the Confederacy in the crib. But this time the main effort would be Virginia, where the general now found himself. He would lead an army of 273,000 men (including all the U.S. Army regulars) out of Washington and, as he had proposed earlier, march it clockwise along the Confederate coast to New Orleans with naval cooperation. Smaller armies would operate on the Mississippi, in East Tennessee, and in the Southwest. Overwhelming victory coupled with paternal concern for white southerners' lives and property (including the enslaved) would reunite the nation. When this plan went nowhere due to the cost, manpower, and time required, the general sent a new proposal at the president's request that still involved a huge army in Virginia.[53] Scholars usually chide McClellan, but his ideas "as always, had merit," according to Stoker. Little Mac, as he came to be known, saw the need for "unity of command and planning, coordinating various armies, vigorous action, [and] viewing the various fields of conflict as parts of a contiguous whole. . . . He was also correct to think of targeting the Confederate army; Lincoln would come to the same conclusion."[54]

Nor was McClellan alone in drawing up questionable campaign plans that autumn. Seemingly everyone was doing it.[55] That included Lincoln himself.[56] British war correspondent William Howard Russell first met Lincoln at McClellan's headquarters in October, "a tall man with a navvy's cap, and an ill-made shooting suit, from the pockets of which protruded papers and bundles." Lincoln asked to see "George," only to be told that McClellan was resting. "This poor president" was a man to be "pitied . . . trying with all his might to understand strategy, naval warfare, big guns, the movements of troops, military maps, reconnaissances, occupations, interior and exterior lines, and all the technical details of the art of slaying." Lincoln, Russell continued, "runs from one house to another, armed with plans, papers, reports, recommendations, sometimes good humoured, never angry, occasionally dejected and always a little fussy."[57]

Often lost in historians' fascination with the Lincoln-McClellan relationship that autumn, Lincoln's developing military ideas merit more attention. He already was fixated with liberating largely Unionist East Tennessee by then, largely for political and emotional reasons, although he made a good military case for cutting the rail line that connected Virginia to Georgia. Around October 1, after the Confederates violated Kentucky's tenuous neutrality—an odd situation that Lincoln had tolerated in hopes of a revival of Unionism while quietly arming antisecession elements—he wrote a detailed memorandum for securing East Tennessee. Typically, he wrote it "not in the form of an express order," according to Nicolay and Hay, but "nevertheless intended as a substantial direction of military affairs." It would occur in conjunction with a naval campaign against Port Royal, South Carolina, designed by Flag Officer Samuel F. Du Pont and the Welles-appointed Blockade Board to acquire a safe harbor on the Atlantic Coast. Lincoln even suggested specific troop movements and supply lines in his "almost express order." The War Department and Brig. Gen. William Tecumseh Sherman, commanding in Kentucky, were "in no mood for the enterprise" and ignored orders couched as advice.[58] Sherman had met Lincoln and judged him to be a well-meaning man in over his head. Nor had the general appreciated being told to take command in Kentucky after Lincoln promised not to do that. Historians still disagree on the East Tennessee plan's viability. James Lee McDonough maintained that it would have cut Confederate communications and hampered troop movements and logistics, while a friendly population would have eased supply concerns. Others support Sherman's skepticism, noting the logistical difficulties involved in supplying troops operating in mountains with bad roads, little available forage, no useful railroad, and winter approaching.[59]

Undaunted, later in October Lincoln suggested an additional western "plan of campaign" in Missouri as well, calling for an end to the pursuit of Confederates under Maj. Gen. Sterling Price into Arkansas so that additional men could be sent elsewhere. Price's renewed activity scotched that.[60] Lincoln strained logistical realities even more in December. Horrified at the executions of East Tennessee partisans who had burned railroad bridges in anticipation of a rumored Federal incursion that the president funded—Sherman had blocked it—he unsuccessfully asked Congress to pay for a mountain railroad from the Kentucky Bluegrass to Knoxville. It would only take six or eight months to build, he claimed, a remarkably rosy timetable the War Department promptly dismissed.[61]

In addition to setting strategic goals, Lincoln by October 1861 had developed operational plans with tactical elements as well. Like McClellan's, they embodied cooperation on separate fronts and questionable logistics. He refused to order their execution, but he fumed when nothing happened. A pattern was emerging.

On November 1 Lincoln made McClellan general in chief of the U.S. Army. Little Mac, who often distrusted authority figures, had scapegoated Scott for the stalemate in Virginia, questioned the old man's loyalty (Scott was a Virginian by birth), raised unnecessary alarms, gone behind Scott's back to Lincoln (who permitted such behavior), and promised action. Yet once in power, McClellan seemingly did nothing but drill and parade. He especially ignored Lincoln's ongoing desires for a quick strike against the enemy at Manassas, something the president had wanted for months if only to get the press and congressional critics off his back.[62]

McClellan wanted to prepare the army carefully for "the next great battle," he wrote his chief quartermaster.[63] None of this should have been surprising. George Rable has observed that "caution, careful planning, an obsession with detail, and hesitation at the moment of crisis" already had been hallmarks of the general's victories in western Virginia. Rable added that by November, however, "there was something schizophrenic about the seemingly frantic activity and continuous delays."[64] At first condescending and then fed up with Lincoln's unexpected visits, pressure, unpolished personality, jokes, and operational plans—Little Mac thought this an amateurish hobby—the prim and proper McClellan began avoiding the president. The disastrous little battle at Ball's Bluff along the Potomac on October 19 increased both McClellan's hesitation to hit the enemy directly and Lincoln's need for positive action. Worse, Col. Edward D. Baker, Lincoln's old friend and the namesake of the president's dead son Eddie, died at Ball's Bluff. The president's inner circle, especially John Hay, came to reciprocate the general's loathing. Later, according to Hay—but no other source, historian Thomas Rowland has pointed out—an exhausted and possibly tipsy McClellan openly snubbed Lincoln at his home on November 13.[65]

Lincoln and McClellan at least agreed that the main effort had to come in Virginia—but where? The president's latest iteration of his operational ideas, December's Occoquan Plan, proposed sending half the army against nearby Centreville while two smaller forces moved up the Occoquan River into the Confederate rear. Historian Ethan Rafuse noted that it reflected McClellan's earlier ideas, but by then the general thought the enemy was both too strong there and too prepared. He instead began conceptualizing a massive turning movement down the coast rather than the frontal assault at Manassas that Lincoln expected. He would insert his army somewhere between Manassas and Richmond, the latter would fall, and the war would end. But he said nothing of this to the desperately curious president other than alluding to a campaign in the East while Sherman's replacement, Maj. Gen. Don Carlos Buell, led his army into East Tennessee. Lincoln liked that. But no troops marched.[66]

Then it got worse. McClellan went to bed with typhoid fever just before Christmas. "The timing for McClellan's bout with typhoid," George Rable has maintained, "could not have been worse."[67] Radical Republicans on the new congressional Joint Committee on the Conduct of the War, men who already not only hated the Democrat McClellan's conservatism and dawdling but also doubted his loyalty, met with Lincoln on New Year's Eve to demand that the president fire him and bring back McDowell. Melancholy and becoming desperate, Lincoln reacted with a flurry of activity designed to accommodate the Radicals. Privately he began to wonder if victory was inevitable after all. Already he had telegraphed Brig. Gen. Ambrose Burnside, urging him to launch his delayed expedition against the North Carolina coast that McClellan had initiated in September without navy input. Now he wired his western commanders, Buell in Kentucky and Maj. Gen. Henry Wager Halleck—who had replaced Frémont after a bitter struggle with Lincoln over who controlled emancipation in Missouri—asking what McClellan's plans were for them. They had no clue. Halleck was weeks from marching as well, and neither commander was interested in cooperation. Buell had sent troops into eastern Kentucky under Brig. Gen. George Thomas but ordered him to keep out of East Tennessee. Buell openly confessed that he saw no reason to go there other than to please the president. Lincoln was appalled by such honesty, as was even McClellan. The next evening the president and the cabinet received another earful from the joint committee, which still wanted McDowell to replace McClellan. He fired off more telegrams to Buell, Halleck, and Brig. Gen. U. S. Grant at Cairo, Illinois. Only Grant complied, with a limited demonstration up the Tennessee River into Kentucky that Halleck promptly recalled.[68] "Delay is ruining us," Lincoln wrote. "It is indispensable for me to have something definite."[69]

On the very next day, January 8, 1862 (as Library of Congress records confirm), Lincoln checked out Halleck's *Elements of Military Art and Science.* His cramming of treatises in the military art allegedly led to his quick mastery of the literature and turned him into a warmaking genius.[70] This is a cornerstone of the heroic legend, yet in retrospect it is based on only three sources. In 1890, as noted previously, Nicolay and Hay described Lincoln's intensive study of military history beginning at the end of 1861.[71] Their sometime assistant, "third secretary," and future rival William O. Stoddard already had written much the same in his 1885 biography of Lincoln: "In one corner of the room was an upright frame of wood, upon which were many maps, conveniently mounted on spring-rollers. . . . Folios of maps leaned against the walls or hid behind the sofas. Volumes of military history and kindred literature came and went from various libraries and had their days of lying around the room or on the President's table." Lincoln, Stoddard continued, studied them diligently.[72] Five years later in a book that came out roughly the same time as Hay and Nicolay's massive opus, Stoddard again remembered maps festooned with pins and "many books in the Executive business office. . . . They come and they go from this place and that. They litter the tables and they lean against the walls, and they look out from under the sofa, as if they were asking if their turn for consultation had come. Nobody knows when the President finds time for reading, but he does find it, somehow, between times and between days."[73] In between the publication of Stoddard's two books in 1888, journalist Noah Brooks, once a close friend of the Lincolns who would have replaced Nicolay as a secretary after the war, wrote a brief but similar description of Lincoln's study habits in yet another biography.[74]

Generations of scholars, not surprisingly, have accepted these passages as fact—Nicolay, Hay, Stoddard, and Brooks were the prototypical White House insiders after all and augmented their memoirs to the point of guessing what Lincoln must have read based upon his writings and actions. Some find traces of the Swiss theorist Antoine-Henri Jomini, who questionably interpreted Napoleon's wars for later generations. Others detect the mind of Carl von Clausewitz, unpublished in English in 1861 but conceivably filtered through the German-born professor and presidential advisor Francis Lieber.[75]

Yet the notion of Lincoln's intense self-study as described by Nicolay and Hay is problematic upon closer inspection. The images of Lincoln pouring through "a large number of strategical works" flies directly in the face of everything else scholars otherwise know about his study habits. By his own admission, Lincoln was never a wide reader. He habitually read methodically in a few key books. As a child he had little choice. He loved to read, but little was available. As a young adult he probably first learned grammar from a single textbook and borrowed a few other eclectic volumes, such as Thomas Paine's *Common Sense* and *Age of Reason,* from his notoriously freethinking New Salem neighbors. He taught himself surveying from two standard texts and enjoyed geometry so much that eventually he made his way through Euclid. Lincoln taught himself political economy from reading Henry Carey, John Stanley McCullough, John Stuart Mill, and Francis Wayland. His law career began with reading, over the course of three years, a copy of William Blackstone's standard *Commentaries on the Laws of England.* Both David Herbert Donald and Robert Bray, the latter the authority on Lincoln's reading habits, note two or three additional standard how-to-do-it law texts that Lincoln probably perused thanks to John Todd Stuart, his fellow Whig legislator and first law partner. Stuart offered little supervision, however, and Lincoln never became known for his mastery of the law's intricacies. On the circuit, many of the jokes he told in the evening around the fireplaces of taverns derived from *Joe Miller's Jests,* an indecorous eighteenth-century joke book. As for pleasure reading, Lincoln again turned repeatedly to a few favorites, notably the Bible, Shakespeare, and the poetry of Robert Burns and Lord Byron. He voraciously read national newspapers before the war, but wartime criticism and the pressure of time ended that habit; Hay thereafter provided clippings to his boss. Pseudonymous humorists Artemus Ward (Charles Farrar Browne), Orpheus C. Kerr (Robert Henry Newell), and Petroleum V. Nasby (David Ross Locke)—their works laced with broad dialect and anti-Democratic satire—replaced the journalists. Lincoln carried a copy of Ward's *His Book* in his pocket and kept an early edition of Nasby in his desk to read to visitors. Much of his reading, according to Bray, was performative as well. The president liked to read aloud to an audience, even his unwilling cabinet or War Department telegraphers. He even read aloud to himself as well, insisting that it helped him learn.[76]

In other words, Lincoln was never a voracious reader as an adult. He never owned a library, preferring to borrow from Herndon's. "I never read an entire novel in my life," he told artist Francis Carpenter: "I once commenced *Ivanhoe* but never finished it."[77] A few months after the assassination, Herndon likewise recalled Lincoln saying: "I cannot read generally. I never read text books for I have no particular motive to drive and whip me to it. As I am constituted I don't love to read generally, and as I do not love to read I feel no interest in what is thus read. I don't, & can't remember such reading." There was a notable caveat, however, that bears closer consideration. If needing information for a client, he told Herndon, he happily conducted extensive research. "When I have a particular case in hand I have that motive," Lincoln explained, "and feel an interest in the case—feel an interest in ferriting out the questions to the bottom—love to dig up the question by the roots and hold it up and dry it before the fires of the mind."[78] But even then, as historian David Donald admitted, Herndon did the lion's share of library research for citations and precedents.[79]

Still, did Lincoln "dig up" military theory "by the roots" while in the White House, as he once approached surveying, geometry, and case law? Historian Carol Reardon has made a compelling case that the president absolutely boned up on war, as his correspondence "reveals an increasing facility with the language and theoretical concepts of the professional soldier, and he applied his newfound knowledge to make clear to his generals both what he wanted to accomplish and how he expected it to be done." She added, however, that we know almost nothing about what Lincoln read except for a single book.

Citing Bray's extensive examination of Lincoln's reading, she pointed out that the president checked out of the Library of Congress only one book on military science during the entire war. And notably, it was the only volume Stoddard identified by name: Halleck's *Elements of Military Art and Science.*[80]

It was the obvious choice. Published in 1846 and revised in 1859 on the eve of war, Halleck's book already had become the standard American text on the art of war. It grew out of twelve lectures that the then first lieutenant delivered in December 1845. Halleck even then was a rising star, a protégé of West Point's influential professor Dennis Hart Mahan, and a published author. With permission from the army, he had traveled to Europe to study French fortifications. His lectures were so successful that, during the following year, they appeared in print as *Elements,* inspired in part by his friendship with Francis Lieber. Halleck made no pretense of innovation. The text largely is a synthesis of other authors' writings, notably Mahan and Jomini. Yet as biographer John Marszalek has noted, there was originality too. Halleck took a middle ground between Jomini and Mahan and filtered their assertions both through his own experiences as a military engineer and his own personal biases. In this way, lessons supposedly taught by Napoleon and Frederick the Great as simplified by Halleck made their way into print and the minds of officers: concentration at a decisive central point before battle, maintaining a numerical advantage over the enemy on the field, protecting one's communications and bases while harassing the enemy's, striking quickly and decisively, maintaining control of interior lines, and seizing strategic points. Halleck championed professional armies, rejecting any reliance on untrained militias. He covered a gamut of other topics as well, from a defense of war to fortifications, logistics, seacoast defenses, defending the Canadian border, and military organization. The 1859 edition reflected recent experiences in Mexico and in the Crimea, and the publisher pushed out a third edition in 1862 to fill the haversacks of novice officers.[81] The result, according to Marszalek, was that it became "essential reading for military men" and was "an excellent distillation of contemporary military thinking." It also won its author the reputation of being an intellectual in uniform, nicknamed "Old Brains."[82] Halleck's *Elements,* in other words, was the rough equivalent to Blackstone on law or Euclid on geometry, the one work that any would-be American strategist had to master.

What else did Lincoln read in the way of "strategical works"? Nothing for which hard evidence exists. Bray found a circulation record at the Library of

Congress showing that Lincoln later checked out a book called *The Rifle* by "Burk." It appears to be one of several editions of English lawyer Hans Busk's *The Rifle, and How to Use It,* an examination of rifles past and present, with three chapters on how to train volunteers to use them. Bray also found that Lincoln in 1863—over a year after Nicolay and Hay's observations—borrowed a new compendium of American military law, U.S. Senate Clerk John F. Callan's *The Military Laws of the United States.* Neither were "strategical works," however.[83]

Anything beyond that is only speculation. As Reardon further discussed, in June 1862 Lincoln received a free copy of Emil Schalk's *Summary of the Art of War* from the author. Schalk was an obscure German émigré who achieved notoriety at the beginning of the war only to return to obscurity two years later. Whomever he was, he knew the literature, and he briefly attracted a wide audience. Schalk advocated massing forces against an enemy's weakest spot, not his strongest, followed by swift movement to exploit advantage. A commander's two choices, he wrote Lincoln, were to hit multiple points on the enemy periphery or to use his entire force against only a part of enemy—such as in this case, Virginia. Lincoln and Halleck had been doing the former; now Schalk advocated the latter. The war would be over in four months if Lincoln took his advice, he claimed. In a later book, Schalk lambasted McClellan while stressing the destruction of enemy armies over seizing territory, just as Lincoln already advocated. But that does not prove that the president ever read either book or even excerpts and reviews. "Civil War historians frequently praise Abraham Lincoln's foresight for urging Major General Joseph Hooker to make Lee's army—and not Richmond—the objective of his Spring 1863 offensive," Reardon observed, "but clearly the idea already had entered the public domain."[84]

In the end, all we know for sure about Lincoln's supposed crash course in military strategy as described by Nicolay, Hay, and Stoddard is that the president had Halleck's book on hand as he taught himself strategy. He kept it checked out for over two years, until mid-March 1864. Lincoln almost certainly read it—he read something—and more than likely as slowly and carefully as he did Blackstone and Euclid. The other books strewn around his office remain anyone's guess. Bray's authoritative list of "what Lincoln read," based upon Library of Congress circulation records and other sources, suggests that most of the books piled in Lincoln's office as described by Stoddard must have been bound plays and poetry, along with some history, law, and reference books. Lincoln also regularly talked to advisors, papered his office with maps, and consumed raw reports from the field, just as Nicolay, Hay, and Stoddard reported. Beyond question he had started to grasp military ideas by January 1862, when his own strategic plan fully emerged, and he eventually discarded contemporary wisdom and moved beyond it. But there is no conclusive proof that he was a self-taught military genius who read widely on war.[85]

All that was in the future. In the present, what Lincoln heard from Halleck two days after checking out *Elements* on January 10, 1862, must have given him second thoughts. The general defended his inaction and pedantically sought to instruct Lincoln about how badly the president understood the rules of war. Lincoln reacted with exasperation. "It is exceedingly discouraging," he wrote. "As everywhere else, nothing can be done."[86]

Another Halleck-related crisis immediately appeared. Lincoln loved new inventions. He remains the only president to hold a patent, and he maintained an open door for inventors, the conmen as well as the legitimate. He loved to test fire weapons. The previous November saw him take a sudden interest in mortar boats. Also called bomb vessels, these were large rafts—some designed to survive open seas—carrying a single mortar for use against enemy fortifications. Gustavus Fox originated the idea, with support from Frémont, but it was Navy Secretary Welles and Cmdr. David Porter who met with Lincoln to convince him that mortar boats could spearhead the capture of New Orleans. The vessels fascinated the president. With McClellan reluctantly providing land troops, the New Orleans expedition seemed ripe for success until January 10, 1862, when Lincoln learned that Halleck had let construction and mortar forging lapse when he replaced Frémont. Few boats or mortars now existed. Naval Capt. Andrew H. Foote, commanding the Western Gunboat Flotilla, did not want them anyway. Fed up with his generals and captains, Lincoln jumped in as de facto project manager. In time, he would demand daily telegrams about progress on the mortar boats, streamline ammunition supply, approve buying a steamer to house the crews, and tell the War Department to pay those men, largely army transfers.[87]

Later on that same January 10—it was becoming a signal day in the Lincoln presidency—he wandered into Meigs office. Since his emergence in April under Seward's sponsorship, Meigs had risen rapidly from the rank of captain to brigadier general and quartermaster general of the U.S. Army, a leap that left jealous peers grousing. “General, what shall I do?” Lincoln pleaded. “The people are impatient; Chase has no money and tells me he can raise no more; the General of the Army has typhoid fever. The bottom is out of the tub. What shall I do?” Meigs was alarmed; typhoid could put McClellan out of action for weeks. He advised Lincoln to meet with McClellan’s subordinates and decide who could command the army in Little Mac’s absence.[88]

But who might that be? The Radicals still wanted McDowell, but he had lost the first major battle of the war. Lincoln instead began to flirt with a desperate idea. Attorney General Bates had encouraged him at least three times to embrace the role of commander in chief and perhaps even take command of the army himself, although privately he did not think Lincoln was up to it. Bates even raised the issue in a cabinet meeting on January 10. “The Prest. is an excellent man,” he wrote in his diary, “and, in the main wise; but he lacks *will* and *purpose,* and, I greatly fear he, has not *the power to command.*”[89]

The commander in chief was developing military ideas, however, and they could not have come from a book he had just acquired. The day after meeting with Meigs, Lincoln told Orville Browning, recently elevated to the Senate after the death of Stephen A. Douglas, that “he was thinking of taking the field himself, and suggested several plans of operation.” He even sketched out ideas that reflected his growing determination to use superior Federal numbers against the enemy across a broad front, an approach that scholars later termed “concentration in time.” To overcome the Confederates’ ability to use interior lines to move elements of their smaller military to single pressure points, Federal forces needed to test several places at once. “One was to threaten all their positions at the same time with superior force,” Browning explained, “and if they weakened one to strengthen another seize and hold the one weakened &c.” He added that Lincoln also envisioned “shelling them out of their intrenchments with guns that would throw very large shell over two miles—the enemy having none of that size. Said [the USS] Pensacola had gone to the Gulf to operate against New Orleans, and the movement from Cairo on Columbus was only a feint to aid Buel at Bowling Green.”[90] Concentration in time, to be sure, was not Lincoln’s invention, as often avowed. Scott’s Anaconda had encompassed the entire Confederacy, for example, while McClellan had advocated coordinated national campaigns since his first week in uniform.[91]

In retrospect, the idea of Lincoln leading the army in January 1862 might seem like little more than a cri de coeur—most recent historians dismiss it as that—but it was not that far-fetched. Biographer Benjamin Thomas took him seriously, noting that Lincoln had as much experience or more as many of the politicians who received general stars from him. Many Republicans already distrusted West Pointers as elitists lacking a moral compass on slavery. Both Phillip Shaw Paludan and Carol Reardon have related how a great many Americans looked for a genius rising from the populace to lead their armies rather than a professional. Still, Lincoln took Meigs's advice and called a meeting with two of McClellan's division commanders, McDowell and Brig. Gen. William B. Franklin. In asking them to go over their superior's head, just as he allowed McClellan to do with Scott, the president augmented a corrosive precedent and contributed to a developing toxic culture within the army's leadership.[92]

Lincoln told the two generals that "if General McClellan did not want to use the army, he would like to '*borrow* it.'"[93] Perhaps he was being more literal than usually assumed. At any rate, the president ordered them to come back the next morning with plans. This second meeting included Meigs as well as Blair, Chase, and Seward. Not invited was Cameron, whose incompetence and insubordination had cost him his job as secretary of war that day. McDowell's proposal looked much like Lincoln's Occoquan Plan—"a remarkable fact," according to Nicolay and Hay—while Franklin's turning movement via Chesapeake Bay reflected McClellan's evolving plans. Lincoln called a final session, asking the generals to consult with Meigs about the cost and time involved in Franklin's proposal. The message was clear: Lincoln preferred his own ideas as faster and cheaper.[94]

The thirteenth of January became yet another pivotal day. Lincoln first outlined his "views" to Buell and Halleck, just as he disclosed them to Browning. Typically, he stressed that they were not orders. Yet here was concentration in time spelled out in almost Euclidian essence. "I state my general idea of this war to be that we have the *greater* numbers," he wrote, "and the enemy has the *greater* facility of concentrating forces upon points of collision; that we must fail, unless we can find some way of making *our* advantage an overmatch for *his;* and that this can only be done by menacing him with superior forces at *different* points, at the *same* time; so that we can safely attack, one, or both, if he makes no change; and if he *weakens* one to *strengthen* the other, forbear to attack the strengthened one, but seize, and hold the weakened one, gaining so much."[95]

That left the war in Virginia. But the scheduled third meeting went off the rails when McClellan showed up. Alerted by his friend War Democrat Edwin M. Stanton, the general had appeared unexpectedly at the White House the previous day and was invited back by Lincoln at the last minute. Still quite sick and angry at what he perceived as backstabbing, he said little in the following meeting except to mutter to Meigs that Lincoln's loose lips would see his plans leaked the next morning in the *New York Herald.* All he would do was affirm that he had a plan and a timetable and that he would make Buell act. That was just enough for Lincoln, who was not yet ready to displace the general. He disregarded Franklin and McDowell's moot endorsement of the Occoquan Plan and adjourned. The next day, urged on by Stanton, McClellan quietly divulged his plans after all—to the *New York Herald.*[96]

In the end, Lincoln did not borrow the army, and he rarely spoke again about leading troops, other than in asides in February and March, and later in a bit of angry daydreaming in July 1863 after Gettysburg. But from mid-January 1862 on, Abraham Lincoln became a more assertive commander in chief with increasingly well-defined strategic and operational ideas, as McClellan would soon come to realize. Using the general like a whetstone, Lincoln would further refine his views on war.[97]

2

THE ARC AND THE CHORD

Lincoln, McClellan, and the Heroic Legend Defined, January–November 1862

AFTER THE "BOTTOM of the tub" days of January 1862, Lincoln kept McClellan in command of Federal forces despite tremendous pressure from the Radical Republicans on the Joint Committee on the Conduct of the War. He hoped to see forward movement from the army in Virginia and Buell's forces in Kentucky. At the same time, he fired corrupt and disrespectful Secretary of War Cameron. Acting on advice from Chase and Seward, Lincoln nominated the Democrat and former attorney general Edwin Stanton to be his new secretary of war on January 13. Abrasive, energetic, and thoroughly conniving—he had both encouraged McClellan's obstinance and convinced Cameron to challenge Lincoln before taking over his job—Stanton became an honest if bullying administrator, although his grasp of military science proved weak. His cozy relationship with McClellan quickly floundered, as Stanton shifted to Lincoln's side. The president, in the meantime, began haunting the War Department's telegraph office, where he read dispatches as they came in and again before bed. When two further weeks of McClellan's inaction passed, a frustrated Lincoln finally flexed his muscles. Consulting no one, on January 27 he issued General War Order No. 1. On Washington's Birthday "a general movement of the Land and Naval forces of the United States against the insurgent forces" would begin in Virginia, Kentucky, from Cairo, and at sea.[1]

Most scholars still agree with historian T. Harry Williams, who observed: "There was a measure of absurdity in ordering an advance on a national holiday four weeks hence without considering what the weather might be then or what the Confederates might do in the interim. But undoubtedly Lincoln did not intend the order to be taken too seriously. . . . His probable purpose was to stir McClellan to some kind of action."[2] Historian Chester Hearn countered that the orders were "intended to protect the administration from accusations of inaction and not to initiate a series of impulsive battles."[3] But in retrospect, it is just as likely that Lincoln meant every word. The order, after all, fully embodied his current ideas as expressed recently to Browning, Buell, and Halleck, even down to specifics. As for not taking the topography, weather, logistics, or the Confederates into account, Lincoln would often fail to do that. Adding to the argument that the president was in earnest is that four days later he issued Special Orders No. 1, specifically ordering McClellan to move against Manassas while alluding once again to his own Occoquan Plan.[4]

McClellan certainly took Lincoln's orders seriously but thought them both unwise and dangerous given the winter's deep mud. He finally revealed his plans to Stanton, who for unknown reasons did not pass them on to the president.[5] When Lincoln finally learned what McClellan wanted to do, he would not budge at first. "You and I have distinct, and different plans for a movement of the Army of the Potomac," he wrote, "yours to be down the Chesapeake, up the Rappahannock to Urbanna, and across land to the terminus of the Railroad on the York River—, mine to move directly to a point on the Railroad South West of Manassas." He posed five leading questions: "Does not your plan involve a greatly larger expenditure of *time,* and *money* than mine? Wherein is a victory *more certain* by your plan than mine? Wherein is a victory *more valuable* by your plan than mine? In fact, would it not be *less* valuable, in this, that it would break no great line of the enemie's communications, while mine would? In case of disaster, would not a safe retreat be more difficult by your plan than by mine?"[6] McClellan responded at length. Attacking the enemy at Manassas would only push the Confederates closer to their base and make them harder to defeat, he wrote. His own campaign, however, would end the war.[7]

Lincoln ceded the field momentarily—he still claimed to feel inferiority when it came to generals—but he never really abandoned his own operational vision, strategic priorities, or doubts. The president still thought his plan was better and that McClellan was making a mistake in going so far afield. In particular, he worried about leaving Washington vulnerable while Confederate artillery batteries still menaced the Potomac. A series of events over the next few weeks gave Lincoln additional second thoughts. Away from Virginia, Federal forces won a string of significant battles: Thomas at Mill Springs, Kentucky, on January 19; Burnside on the North Carolina coast on February 18; Grant and Captain Foote at Forts Henry and Donelson, Tennessee, between February 6 and 16: and Col. Edward Canby in the New Mexico Territory on February 21. Nashville fell on February 25, opening the way to Alabama and Mississippi. Grant shone especially, but they all made McClellan look stagnant in comparison. The death of his son Willie on February 20, meanwhile, left the president despondent and distracted. February 22 came and went with McClellan in camp and Lincoln in mourning.[8]

Lincoln tarried until February 27 before authorizing the accumulation of ships for moving McClellan's army down the Chesapeake coast. The next day McClellan's planned move against Winchester, Virginia, designed to safeguard the capital, failed miserably, with the canal boats specially built to enable the construction of a permanent bridge across the Potomac arriving six inches too wide to fit through the Chesapeake and Ohio Canal.[9] Wags joked that the operation had "died of lockjaw."[10] According to Nicolay, Lincoln hit the roof, complaining that McClellan "doesn't intend to do anything." He shouted at McClellan's chief of staff (and father-in-law) during a "long and sharp talk" that also revealed innocence about what generals did with their time. Lincoln the frontier surveyor asked: "Why in the —nation, Gen. Marcy . . . couldn't the Gen. have known whether a boat would go through that lock, before spending a million dollars getting them there? I am no engineer: but it seems to me that if I wished to know whether a boat would go through a hole, or a lock, common sense would teach me to go and measure it." He added more plaintively: "Everything seems to fail. The general impression is daily gaining ground that the Gen. does not intend to do anything. By a failure like this we lose all the prestige we gained by the capture of Ft Donelson. I am grievously disappointed—grievously disappointed and almost in despair."[11]

Many agreed. This latest failure and loss of popular "prestige," coupled with McClellan's Democratic politics and the party's rabid support of him, stirred up a new fuss. On March 3 members of the joint committee again demanded that Lincoln replace him, preferably with McDowell or Frémont. Lincoln actually did consider firing McClellan this time. Stanton sounded out retired Col. Ethan Allen Hitchcock as a possible replacement. He declined but agreed to direct an informal advisory group, called the War Board, that Stanton assembled to help him grasp military affairs, which he then usually ignored.[12]

On March 6 Lincoln objected to McClellan starting his grand turning movement from Annapolis. In Nicolay and Hay's words, it would look bad. They later wrote: "Taking the whole army first to Annapolis, to be embarked in transports, would appear to the extremely sensitive and impatient public opinion very much like a retreat from Washington. . . . Could not, he asked, 50,000 or even 10,000 men be moved in transports directly down the Potomac? This would be a self-evident forward movement, which the public would comprehend without explanation." When the army objected due to the enemy guns on the Potomac, Lincoln and Welles sent for the new ironclad *Monitor,* which had steamed south to confront the Confederate ironclad *Virginia* at the mouth of the James River.[13]

At Manassas a wary Confederate Gen. Joseph E. Johnston misinterpreted McClellan's limited movements as the beginning of a plan much like what Lincoln wanted—an overland move to Centreville—and began withdrawing on March 7. White House insiders regarded the retreat as proof of both the president's wisdom and McClellan's ineptitude in not stirring earlier. A surprised McClellan followed Johnston for a few days, claiming that it at least was good marching practice for the men. Their discovery of the weaknesses in the abandoned Confederate line, including "artillery pieces" that were in fact logs painted black, deeply embarrassed McClellan and his supporters. Meanwhile, the next day off Fort Monroe, the *Virginia* sortied out against the Federal blockade, inflicting heavy damage on the squadron. The ironclad terrified Lincoln and Stanton well beyond its actual capabilities. They imagined Washington burned, an administration in flight, the blockade wrecked, McClellan's transports sunk, shipping into Boston and New York City menaced, and foreign intervention. After the war, a still-disgusted Welles wrote that he barely prevented a frightened Lincoln from shutting down the Potomac with canal boats loaded with stone to keep the *Virginia* at bay.[14]

Lincoln had ignored McClellan for days, but now in this crisis, he called him in and revived all his previous objections to the coastal campaign. He also warned the general that some congressmen thought him a traitor for his lack of activity, apparently not adding that Stanton was making similar wild allegations. An ugly scene followed. Little Mac finally suggested that he submit his plans to his division commanders for approval. Lincoln approved. They voted 8–4 in the general's favor despite overt pressure from Stanton to do otherwise; the four dissenters essentially endorsed the Occoquan Plan.[15] Lincoln once again agreed to go along with McClellan, but again he did so only begrudgingly. In part, he may have admitted that he was dodging responsibility if things went badly. "We can do nothing else than accept their plan and discard all others," he reportedly told Stanton. "We can't reject it and adopt another without assuming all the responsibility in the case of the failure of the one we adopt."[16]

Yet three new presidential orders simultaneously tightened his control of McClellan, his army, and his campaign while simultaneously revealing Lincoln's growing distrust of the general. General War Order No. 2, written that same frightening day, divided McClellan's army into four corps over Little Mac's objections. The four new corps commanders were the senior generals in the army, but it was hard to ignore the fact that they also all were McClellan skeptics. Three of them had voted against what would become the Peninsula Campaign, and the fourth was Seward favorite Erasmus Keyes, who had expressed doubts. The others, Stanton groused to Hay, were "afraid to fight."[17]

General War Order No. 2 further elevated two of the president's political generals, creating a new corps in the Shenandoah for Maj. Gen. Nathaniel Banks, a former Speaker of the House whom Lincoln admired, and naming McClellan foe Brig. Gen. James S. Wadsworth of New York the military governor of Washington, DC. Simultaneously, General War Order No. 3 ordered McClellan to leave behind enough men to safeguard the capital, with both him *and* his new corps commanders responsible for determining the proper number. Lincoln did not trust McClellan to do it alone. The directive also prohibited him from dispatching more than two corps elsewhere until he had safeguarded the Potomac and unrealistically demanded that he get moving within the next ten days. *Monitor*'s celebrated ability to bottle up the *Virginia* the following day somewhat relieved the panic in the White House, but it did not allay Lincoln's concerns, especially after the press kept laughing at just how weak the Manassas defenses really were. War Order No. 3 on March 11 thus consolidated the western commands that McClellan had created under Halleck (who took the credit for Grant's victories), created a department in western Virginia for Frémont as a sop to Radicals, and—most significantly—removed McClellan as general in chief but did not name a replacement. Lincoln leaked word to McClellan that this last was temporary, but he would not say so directly to him or in public. For the time being, all department commanders instead would report to Stanton, and Lincoln would do the job of a general in chief himself. In part, the president wanted to avoid trouble with the joint committee over not appointing one of their favorites to the top command.[18] But this arrangement also reveals Lincoln's impatient self-confidence. Instead of taking command of the Army of the Potomac, as he had considered doing two months earlier, the commander in chief with a month of field experience in soldiering made himself the de facto general in chief of all the Federal armies.

Confederate retreat, the menace of the *Virginia* on the James River, and the navy's frustrating refusal to cooperate forced McClellan to alter his plans on the fly. Haste bred sloppiness. Lacking good maps, he nonetheless decided to shift his landing to Fort Monroe and approach Richmond on the Virginia Peninsula, created by the York and James Rivers. McClellan expected to fight at Yorktown but assumed (without making sure) that the navy would help. Once he secured West Point on the York River as a new supply base, he could take Richmond.[19] On March 13 Lincoln signed off on the plan, with the usual caveats. McClellan had to leave enough men to hold Manassas and leave "Washington entirely secure."[20] Even generally favorable historians have criticized Lincoln for his conditions, with T. Harry Williams writing: "If he objected to McClellan's plan, he should have required the General to make another or he should have removed him. . . . If ever a general taking the field needed the complete trust of his superiors, McClellan did, and if ever a general lacked it, he did."[21]

As historian Thomas Rowland aptly wrote, defending the capital "hovered like the legendary albatross" above McClellan and of each of his successors.[22] The general and his corps commanders had agreed to leave 40,000 men behind to assuage Lincoln's fears of losing Washington. Those troops soon became another bone of contention. The general thought this a waste of manpower he could use better against Richmond. There were enough troops already in the Shenandoah Valley to blunt Jackson's small army there, McClellan believed, and his own offensive otherwise would protect the capital by forcing the enemy to concentrate nearer to Richmond. In a hurry to leave and apparently none too concerned for accuracy—perhaps acting deceptively as

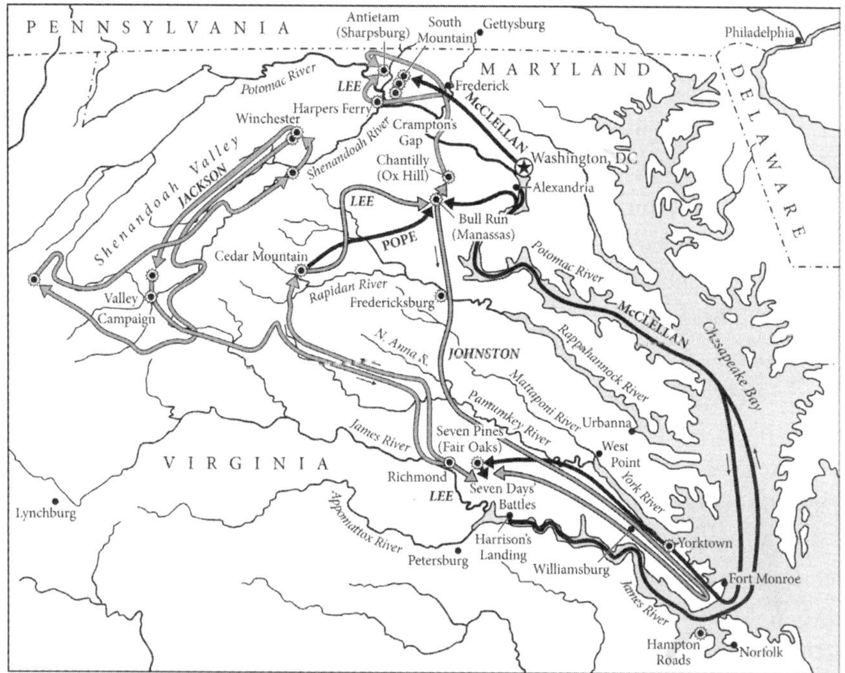

Virginia Theater, 1862.

well—McClellan reported that he had left 73,000 men to defend the capital. His addition was sloppy at best. The general counted some men twice, included nonexistent units, and added an absent division. Stanton's War Board approved the dispositions at first, but opposition soon reared up. Hitchcock, Wadsworth, and Adjutant General of the Army Bvt. Maj. Gen. Lorenzo Thomas all understood War Order No. 3 to mean men specifically left in and near the city. Wadsworth had never trusted McClellan or his numbers. Now they told Lincoln that there were only 19,000 men actually in the capital—many of them recruits—and that McClellan planned to send 7,000 of them elsewhere. Wadsworth wanted 30,000 men for the city works alone.[23]

Stanton panicked again. Fully believing wild rumors spreading among Republicans that McClellan was secretly a secessionist and "under the influence of Jeff Davis," he demanded that the president fire the general, bizarrely pointing to the eminently obscure western brigade commander Col. Napoleon Bonaparte Buford as a possible replacement. Again, Lincoln refused. He told Browning that he still trusted McClellan, saying "that Genl Scott, and all the leading military men around him, had always assured him that McClelland possessed a very high order of military talent, and that he did not think they could all be mistaken." Yet the president confessed that "he was not fully satisfied with his conduct of the war—that [McClellan] was not sufficiently energetic and aggressive in his measures—that he had studied McClelland and taken his measure as well as he could—that he thought he had the capacity to make arrangements properly for a great conflict, but as the hour for action approached he became nervous and oppressed with the responsibility and hesitated to meet the crisis."[24]

In lieu of firing the "nervous" general, Lincoln ordered Stanton to hold one of the two divisions yet to depart and place it near Manassas to guard the capital. For political reasons alone, Washington had to be safe. Yet McClellan already was in a fix on the Peninsula when he got the news that McDowell's corps was not coming full strength to bring up the rear. Frequent rain had turned soft, sandy roads into red goo. His maps were inaccurate. The extent of Yorktown's defenses shocked him and his corps commanders, although they were not as impregnable as they looked. The navy refused to help. Now Lincoln's intervention cost a commander who based his plans on overwhelming numbers more than 40,000 troops, a third of his planned army. McClellan badgered Washington for them, erroneously reporting that most of the enemy had gathered to outnumber him at Yorktown. He needed the Fort Monroe garrison, he said, along with siege guns, the navy, and especially McDowell.[25]

Lincoln was unsympathetic. He had concluded that McClellan already had enough men to fight. Indeed, confidence was high enough in Washington when it came to overall manpower that Stanton shut down recruiting stations across the nation on April 3. Possibly he wanted to not only rationalize a system partially developed by McClellan to minimize state interference but also to save money as well, yet certainly he acted in response to ongoing Federal success in the West and expectations of a final victory soon in the offing. Almost immediately, the secretary received a rude awakening. Three days after Stanton's order, the Battle of Shiloh began in Tennessee. That two-day bloodbath of historic American horror cost the Federal army over 13,000 casualties, the Confederates almost as many, and made Stanton's decision to halt recruiting look irresponsible once officials in Washington began to learn of the battle on April 9.[26]

The day before that shocking news arrived from Tennessee, however,

Lincoln wrote McClellan erroneously: "You now have over one hundred thousand troops. . . . I think you had better break the enemies' line from York-town to Warwick River, at once."[27] Lincoln was close to the truth; Little Mac outnumbered the Confederates four-to-one. But to be fair, his numbers were guesswork, too. Unmoved, McClellan wrote his wife, "I was much tempted to reply that he had better come here & do it himself."[28] Privately, Lincoln admitted to Browning again that "he was becoming impatient and dissatisfied with McClellan's sluggishness of action, and read me a letter he had written him in reply to his demand for more troops, in which he talked to him in exceeding plain terms about his delays and urged upon him the indispensable necessity of his striking a blow if he expected to maintain his character before the Country."[29]

While some historians have defended Lincoln's April 8 letter as kind and paternal per Nicolay and Hay's original interpretation, in reality it reeks of frustration, a sour mood born of a sudden illness, and Lincoln's "power to hurt."[30] McClellan had left "less than twenty thousand unorganized men, without a single field battery" to defend the capital. That would have "presented . . . a great temptation to the enemy to turn back from the Rappahannock, and sack Washington"—it had not. Stop complaining, the president demanded, "strike a blow." McClellan was responsible for his problems because he had dismissed the Occoquan Plan. "I always insisted," the president wrote in an I-told-you-so manner, "that going down the Bay in search of a field, instead of fighting at or near Mannassas, was only shifting, and not surmounting, a difficulty—that we would find the same enemy, and the same, or equal, intrenchments, at either place." And he then rubbed more salt into the Manassas wound: "The country will not fail to note—is now noting—that the present hesitation to move upon an intrenched enemy, is but the story of Manassas repeated. . . . [Y]ou must act."[31]

But McClellan did not act, not as Lincoln wanted anyway, and the president still refused to order him to move, again couching his desires as advice. The army settled down at Yorktown to a siege that lasted a month. Lincoln partially gave in, sent one of McDowell's divisions to the Peninsula despite Stanton's fierce opposition, and after complaining about McClellan's "indefinite procrastination," shipped him more big guns. When the Confederates abandoned Yorktown on May 3, McClellan hesitated to advance, still complaining that he needed all of McDowell's corps and that Washington officials had abandoned him.[32] In a sense they had. His demands for men, according to Nicolay and Hay, led Stanton to say that "if he had a million men, he would swear the enemy had two millions, and then he would sit down in the mud and yell for three."[33]

After the fall of Yorktown and a bloody pursuing fight at rainy Williamsburg, a frustrated Lincoln impatiently went to the front with Chase and Stanton. According to Nicolay and Hay, the president wanted to "ascertain by personal observation whether some further vigilance and vigor might not be infused into the operations of the army and navy at that point."[34] McClellan foolishly told him was too busy to meet. That was a major mistake. Lincoln expressed confusion to others as to why the army had not taken Norfolk, the *Virginia*'s base. McClellan had assumed that the enemy would abandon Norfolk in retreat, but he never bothered to explain that to the president. Lincoln, having once flirted with leading the army, suddenly decided to seize Norfolk himself. Securing men from Fort Monroe, the president and his cabinet officers went upriver to find a place for an amphibious landing, wading ashore under fire. The next night over 5,000 Federal troops landed before McClellan could stop them and marched into Norfolk. They found the Confederates gone; McClellan had been right. To him, the president's Norfolk operation was a sad stunt that offered more proof of his ignorance. But for Lincoln—and many scholars since—the lark proved his tactical sagacity. The destruction of the *Virginia* the next night, blown up to avoid capture, added credence to that assertion.[35]

McClellan offered no congratulations to the president for his little campaign but instead continued to complain. Blaming Lincoln's "very bad" new corps arrangement for "very nearly . . . a most disastrous defeat" at rainy Williamsburg, he asked for permission to either scrap it or fire certain corps commanders. He mentioned no names, but he believed that both Brig. Gen. Samuel P. Heintzelman and Brig. Gen. Edwin V. "Bull" Sumner had performed poorly. Both had supported Lincoln in voting against the campaign, however, and Sumner had been part of Lincoln's entourage in February 1861 until his bellicosity left him ditched in Baltimore. Lincoln gave in, but not before firing back that none of it was his fault. He had "ordered the Army Corps organization not only on the unanimous opinion of the twelve Generals whom you had selected and assigned as Generals of Division, but also on the unanimous opinion of every *military man* I could get an opinion from, and every modern military book, yourself only excepted. Of course, I did not, on my own judgment, pretend to understand the subject." But he understood politics. Lincoln went on that it was "indispensable for you to know how your struggle against it is received in quarters which we cannot entirely disregard. It is looked upon as merely an effort to pamper one or two pets, and to persecute and degrade their supposed rivals. I have had no word from Sumner, Heintzelman, or Keyes . . . but I am constantly told that you consult and communicate with nobody but General Fitz John Porter, and perhaps General Franklin."[36] Michael Burlingame has suggested that the president might have fired the general then and there except that the Senate had just praised McClellan. Later in May the general created two new provisional corps, although that diminished the military power of all of his corps individually, and assigned them to his alleged "pets," Franklin and Porter. The Fifth and Sixth Corps thus would become the nexus of pro-McClellan sentiment within the Army of the Potomac.[37]

Lincoln nonetheless had returned to Washington enthused. Good news from the West—the capture of New Orleans on May 1, accomplished without the still uncompleted mortar boats—helped. Yet McClellan remained his chief vexation. The president asked how the enemy could move through red Peninsula mud faster than Federals, not considering that thousands of rebel feet, hooves, and wheels made the mud infinitely worse for pursuing troops. Still, he rounded up reinforcements and even agreed to release McDowell—but only with conditions. Lincoln told McDowell to obey McClellan's orders only if Washington remained protected, an unorthodox proviso that even bothered the usually loyal Meigs, who otherwise strenuously opposed the Peninsula Campaign. Lincoln also disregarded McClellan's request that McDowell's men come quickly by ship. They instead would march overland, staying between Washington and Confederate forces at Richmond. McClellan would have to extend his right to meet them, fatally pulling his right flank north across the flooded Chickahominy River.[38]

Then Stonewall Jackson struck. He already had defeated Frémont on the western rim of the Shenandoah Valley on May 8. After pausing, he moved north, routed Lincoln favorite Banks on May 25, and drove the Federals out of the Valley and into Maryland. Once again the specter of Bull Run and a burning Washington loomed. Historians have differed as to whether Lincoln panicked, saw an opportunity to destroy Jackson's army, or both. In any event, he suspended McDowell's move south and ordered him to send two divisions west into the Valley instead. In effect, as Mark Grimsley observed, Lincoln diverted 40,000 men from the Peninsula Campaign to capture 17,000 Confederates in the Valley. He also advised McClellan out of the blue to either "attack Richmond or give up the job and come to the defence of Washington," later asking in a coded message, "Can you get close enough [to Richmond] to throw shells into the city?" An angry McClellan quipped that the president was frightened and correctly deduced Jackson's intentions to weaken his strength. He neither moved nor shelled Richmond civilians as Lincoln suggested, which would have been the war's first bombardment of a major populated city. With McClellan refusing to attack or bring the army back to Washington, and with Norfolk fresh in mind, Lincoln as de facto general in chief then acted tactically, dictating detailed troop movements in the Valley from the War Department telegraph office. His plans, drawn up with Stanton, looked geometrically feasible on paper. They sent Frémont from the west and McDowell's divisions from the east into the Valley. Both pincers would block Jackson's retreat south while Banks pressed from the north. Lincoln would coordinate from Washington. Unfortunately, he again struggled to grasp the friction of war, especially the reality of miry roads that looked fine on dry maps. Jackson had a macadamized pike; the Federals had ruts and mud. But to Lincoln, who had appointed the political generals Banks and Frémont in the first place, had never led troops, had lost track of Jackson, and worried little about logistics and transportation, the shape of the road was no concern. It was "for you a question of legs," he told McDowell. "Put in all the speed you can." When Jackson avoided the Federal trap on June 2, won two more battles, and escaped, the president (and many later scholars) blamed Frémont for not taking the slow and sloppy road Lincoln preferred on his map.[39]

By then, McClellan—now sick with malaria—had fought a defensive battle at Seven Pines (or Fair Oaks) east of Richmond on May 31 and June 1. It was a confused affair shaped by the flooded Chickahominy River that unequally divided his army due to the White House's determination to send McDowell overland. After the Confederate commander, Gen. Joe Johnston, went down wounded, Davis appointed his advisor, Gen. Robert E. Lee, to replace him. Lee fell back to Richmond's edge and began entrenching. Ill, exhausted, and shaken by the battle's carnage, McClellan approached the city gingerly despite Lincoln's renewed demands for decisive action. Incorrectly convinced as always that he was outnumbered, the general again asked for more men.

Lincoln, at least happy that McClellan had not retreated, obliged by sending a division from McDowell, garrison troops from Washington and elsewhere, and men freed up from Fort Monroe.[40]

Still, nothing happened. On June 23 a frustrated Lincoln made another spur-of-the-moment decision to slip out of the capital secretly and take an overnight train to West Point, seeking advice from retired Winfield Scott. Word got out; rumors flew. No verifiable record of their meeting exists, but based on a document Scott wrote, he defended McClellan to the hilt, advising Lincoln that Washington was secure, the war would be won or lost at Richmond, and the president had placed McDowell too far north to help McClellan. They also may have discussed Lincoln's newest notions: appointing Halleck as general in chief—both Scott and Dennis Hart Mahan supported that—and combining the troops that just had fought Jackson into a new Army of Virginia under Maj. Gen. John Pope. A distant relation through Mary Lincoln and a friend who had accompanied Lincoln to Washington, Pope had achieved victory at Island No. 10 in the Mississippi River in early April. His successful implementation of Lincoln's prized mortar boats at Island No. 10 had thrilled the president. An antislavery Republican and aggressive general, Pope also was a darling of the Radicals and Stanton's latest choice to supersede McClellan.[41]

While Pope's primary mission would be protecting Washington, Lincoln had an older operational idea brewing in mind when he summoned him from the West on June 19. He had never ceased believing that the best way to Richmond was overland south from Washington, telling Browning that "his opinion always had been that the great fight should have been at Manasses—that he had urged it upon McClellan that if the enemy left Manasses he would entrench at York Town, and we would have the same difficulties to encounter there. . . . [S]ubsequent events had satisfied him he was right." Perhaps in some manner Pope and his new army could do that.[42]

On the Peninsula an ill McClellan promised action, then halted to ask again for more men when he learned that Jackson's army had arrived, supposedly with P. G. T. Beauregard and some of his western army as well. He concluded that the Army of the Potomac now was outnumbered more than two-to-one. McClellan in fact still had a numerical advantage, while Beauregard remained in Mississippi. He nonetheless wrote dramatically about his fears. The general blamed Lincoln and especially Stanton for the "disaster" he expected to come, writing, "I am in no way responsible for it, as I have not failed to represent repeatedly the necessity of reinforcements." His frantic tone very much suggests a leader collapsing under pressure. Lincoln again denied any responsibility and revealed his own frustrations. The allegation of lack of support "pains me very much," Lincoln replied on June 26. "I give you all I can, and act on the presumption that you will do the best you can with what you have."[43] Lincoln, according to Nicolay and Hay's glowing account two decades later, was "already convinced of the substantial failure of McClellan's campaign." They attributed that conclusion to his superior military mind. "It is safe to say," they later wrote, "that no general in the army studied his maps and scanned his telegrams with half the industry—and, it may be added, with half the intelligence—which Mr. Lincoln gave to his." It was for that reason, they maintained, that Lincoln created the Army of Virginia under Pope that very day: to bring about victory after all from Washington south.[44]

That same day Lee struck McClellan's right, where the flooded Chickahominy isolated Porter's corps as it awaited McDowell. His corps was not in position where McClellan had wanted him thanks to Lincoln's intervention. The last thing Lee had wanted was to fight "a battle of posts," he had told Davis earlier. "He [McClellan] will take position from position, under cover of his heavy guns, & we cannot get at him without storming his works. . . . I am preparing a line that I can hold with part of our forces in front, while the rest I will endeavor to make a diversion to bring McClellan out."[45]

For the next week, Lee hammered the Federals from north to south toward the James River. McClellan floundered, ignored his corps commanders' reasonable pleas for a counteroffensive, and spent much of the last two days cruising on a gunboat in the James. Events had shattered him.[46] In a dispatch on July 28, he took no responsibility for the retreat, complaining that Stanton and Lincoln's refusal to send more men had doomed them all. "Had I 20,000 or even 10,000 fresh troops to use to-morrow I could take Richmond," he wrote, "but I have not a man in reserve, and shall be glad to cover my retreat and save the material and *personnel* of the army. . . . I have seen too many dead and wounded comrades to feel otherwise than that the Government has not sustained this army. If you do not do so now the game is lost. . . . If I save this army now, I tell you plainly that I owe no thanks to you or to any other persons in Washington. You have done your best to sacrifice this army." Contrary to the accepted story that someone in the telegraph office deleted the last accusation before Lincoln saw the telegram, historian William Marvel has made a convincing case that both Lincoln and Stanton must have read it.[47] Lincoln certainly reacted as if he had. "Save your Army at all events," the president replied at first. "Will send re-inforcements as fast as we can." Then he once again defended himself and his operational decisions: "I feel any misfortune to you and your Army quite as keenly as you feel it yourself. If you have a drawn battle, or a repulse, it is the price we pay for the enemy not being in Washington." Lincoln added that Pope, now acting as his advisor, urged McClellan to fall back on the York instead of the James.[48]

That was only part of the story of Pope's ascendancy. Lincoln did not mention the general's attacks on McClellan in a cheering House of Representatives or while meeting with the Joint Committee on the Conduct of the War. But McClellan knew enough. He viewed Pope's appointment as a personal insult, as did other officers with more seniority. Little Mac ignored the advice and retreated down the river to Harrison's Landing, thirty-five miles from Richmond, where naval guns could protect the army. Lincoln at first was willing to let him sit there. Sending McClellan more men from Washington or from the West, he believed, would result either in the loss of the capital or in giving back territory gained in Tennessee, Missouri, and Kentucky. Better to focus on the Mississippi and East Tennessee for now and then add 100,000 (later 150,000 and finally 300,000) new recruits.[49] "It is impossible to re-inforce you for your present emergency," Lincoln wrote on July 1. "If we had a million of men we could not get them to you in time. . . . If you are not strong enough to face the enemy you must find a place of security, and wait, rest, and repair. . . . [S]ave the Army at all event even if you fall back to Fortress-Monroe. We still have strength enough in the country, and will bring it out."[50]

But Lincoln soon changed his mind. Public morale sank after McClellan's retreat to his "place of security," while the price of gold rose. Many in the press and public acted as if McClellan's failure to take Richmond negated all the western victories combined, which rankled the president. Others again accused the general of cowardice and wanted him relieved. Republicans in general demanded a harsher war and stronger measures against slavery, the institution that propped up the Confederacy. They reveled in Pope's first orders in command of the Army of Virginia, which among other things verbally backhanded McClellan's hesitancy and his men's alleged cowardice while announcing hard new measures against secessionist civilians and drumhead executions of suspected guerrillas. Pope got the subsequent blame, but Lincoln and Stanton at least preapproved those orders, marking their final shift from the "conciliatory" or "soft war" position that McClellan championed to a more "pragmatic" phase without much concern for white southern sensibilities. An undercurrent of panic ran through the capital as well. Stanton worried that McClellan would surrender to Lee, who would then move against Washington. An anxious Meigs woke up Lincoln one morning to tell him to bring the army back and save the capital. Lincoln refused and went back to bed, but he was struck by Meigs's fear. Was it as bad at the front? A week later, still worried, the president went to Harrison's Landing to see for himself. He concluded that the army was not nearly as battered as he feared and was delighted that some corps commanders still spoiled for a fight. McClellan, who distrusted the president's private meetings with his subordinates—another breach of standard protocol—found Lincoln's manner otherwise to be odd.[51] He had no interest in hearing about the battles, McClellan wrote, only asking how strong the army was, where the enemy was, and could it safely withdraw. Wary of a "paltry trick," McClellan thought Lincoln "a man about to do something of which he was much ashamed."[52]

But McClellan did something strange as well. As Lincoln left, the general handed him a letter. Admitting that his army's situation was "critical," McClellan wanted to discuss instead his "general views concerning the existing state of the rebellion; although they do not strictly relate to the situation of this Army or strictly come within the scope of my official duties." He again stressed the need for kid gloves in dealing with white southerners, and for conducting the war "upon the highest principles known to Christian Civilization. It should not be a War looking to the subjugation of the people of any state, in any event. It should not be, at all, a War upon population; but against armed forces and political organizations. Neither confiscation of property, political executions of persons, territorial organization of states or forcible abolition of slavery should be contemplated for a moment." Like many a conservative Democrat, McClellan long had opposed dragging emancipation into the war. He did not oppose the new Second Confiscation Bill per se, he declared—ironically, no Federal army had liberated more enslaved people than his Army of the Potomac—but he feared "radical views" that might undermine the military and make national reunion less likely. Finally, he championed "concentrations of military power" instead of dispersing troops "in expeditions, posts of occupation and numerous Armies"—clearly a direct jab at Lincoln's recent decisions—and the returned to the need for a real "Commander [that is, General] in Chief of the Army; one who possesses your confidence, understands your views and who is competent to execute your orders by directing the military forces of the Nation to the accomplishment of the objects by you proposed." He added, "I do not ask that place for myself."[53]

Historians have debated the "Harrison's Landing Letter" ever since. Many McClellan critics find it presumptuous and further evidence of the general's arrogance. Others believe it was well meaning at heart, a statement of views that McClellan imagined Lincoln would support. In fact, there was little at all new in it, aside from apprehension that men like Pope suddenly were taking the war in the wrong direction with support from the president.[54] It encompassed all that McClellan had been saying for a year. But it was just too late now. The letter was, historian Mark Grimsley observed, "perhaps the most powerful expression of the conciliatory policy crafted during the war," written just at the moment that policy was collapsing.[55]

It fell on deaf ears. Lincoln and other Republicans had given up on "soft war." The president signed a watered-down version of the Second Confiscation Act in mid-July after his initial veto, and he supported congressional action to bar the return of the liberated enslaved to slaveowners. A longtime supporter of voluntary colonization efforts for African Americans, he especially championed a project at Chiriqui on the modern Panamanian coast that the Blairs and his in-law Ninian Edwards backed. Their agents promised a cheap supply of coal for the U.S. Navy and naval bases as well as land for willing freed people who wanted to leave a racist United States that Lincoln believed might never grant them equality. At the same time, he opened internal discussions regarding his "last trump card"—a presidential emancipation proclamation. Drawing from a variety of historic and legal precedents, Lincoln believed that he had the "second order" wartime power as commander in chief to emancipate the enslaved in areas where their involuntary labor supported the rebellion, all without approval from Congress or the states. It was a way to win the conflict as well as a logical extension of Republican beliefs. Only the sad shape of the war in the field and his fears of the public's potentially negative reaction held him back. Seward convinced Lincoln to wait until a military victory somewhere, lest Europe see the move as a sign of weakness. In the meantime, the president widened the suspension of habeas corpus to the entire nation in September. Echoing Pope, he had Stanton issue orders allowing other commanders to seize or destroy enemy personal property and to execute guerrillas. With renewed enlistments tanking, he called out 300,000 militiamen for nine months' service, permitted conscription in states not meeting quotas, and supported legislation that allowed African Americans to enlist as laborers. He also backed up Stanton's questionable policies of banning eligible men from leaving the country while prosecuting draft evaders in military courts.[56]

Under pressure from Republican leaders, Lincoln also moved beyond McClellan and more toward aggressive Republican generals like Pope. He signaled the change in July when he promoted Russian-born Col. John Basil Turchin to the rank of brigadier general after Buell successfully court-martialed the popular officer and tried to drive him from the army for encouraging his men to sack Athens, Alabama, two months earlier. His weariness and depression aside—"Browning I must die sometime," he moaned to his friend—Lincoln forged on. The army in the East was in good shape, he said. Lincoln defended Stanton against McClellan's charges that the secretary was responsible for defeat. Now convinced that the general would never go on the offensive despite his new talk of an advance up the James to the railroad junction at Petersburg, Lincoln acted.[57] But with elections still approaching in most states, he would not fire McClellan outright and risk political losses. Instead, on July 11, having consulted no one except Pope, he ordered Halleck to come east as the new general in chief, explaining disingenuously that it was McClellan's idea when it was not. In truth, Lincoln and some in the cabinet almost certainly wanted someone who would fire McClellan as Army of the Potomac commander and take the heat for it. Historians wonder if Halleck's appointment also reflected Lincoln's need for a strategist, a bureaucrat, a general who opposed conciliation, or an advisor other than Stanton.[58] But as historian David Donald put it, the choice if nothing else absolutely "signaled a repudiation of McClellan, and of McClellan's view of the war."[59]

Yet McClellan survived. When Halleck arrived, Lincoln sent him to Harrison's Landing with permission to dump the army commander if he wished, adding with a thumb on the scales that in his opinion McClellan would never fight. Browning reported that Lincoln expected Halleck to fire McClellan and assume command. That did not happen. Halleck was disappointed with what he found to be sure. McClellan wanted 30,000–50,000 reinforcements to start a campaign against Petersburg, the vital railroad junction south of Richmond, or else move more broadly up the James. In yet another breach of the chain of command that the president tolerated, corps commander Heintzelman sent a letter by his wife to Lincoln to ask for more men. Yet Halleck would not take the onus of firing a man he admired, even after Lincoln and Stanton had him sound out Burnside about the job. Nor did he believe in second-guessing field commanders. When McClellan still refused to advance, however, Halleck finally ordered him to ship his sick and wounded to Washington, then bring the army back, too—Chase, Stanton, and Generals Franklin and Keyes had advocated this for weeks. The Peninsula Campaign was over. The withdrawal that Lincoln broached at Harrison's Landing now became a reality. Slowly—too slowly Lincoln and others complained—the Army of the Potomac retraced its steps. It abandoned hard-won positions that it would not hold again for two years, then during an actual drive on Petersburg and after sustaining roughly 122,000 additional battle casualties—a full field army of dead, missing, and maimed Federal soldiers.[60]

Withdrawal cemented Lincoln's Virginia overland preferences for good, but for now it was a godsend to Lee. With McClellan not stirring, he dispatched Jackson north to check Pope. Jackson's furious attack on Banks at Cedar Mountain on August 9 created enough consternation in Washington that the White House hurried up McClellan. Little Mac replied—with a dig at Meigs—that he did not have enough ships to move quickly. With McClellan now clearly leaving the Peninsula, Lee left a token force at Richmond and took off with the rest northward, welcoming the chance to fight a divided enemy in open country instead of being hemmed in before his capital. Pope fell back toward Manassas, where Jackson attacked him on August 28. For the next two days, Pope hammered Jackson's divisions, so intent on breaking his line that he did not see Lee arriving with massive reinforcements. Disaster followed. Lee smashed Pope's new army and drove it from the field in another Bull Run panic. There was chaos in the rear, too. McClellan had arrived in Washington on August 24, but with the situation and command situation both murky—Halleck did not know where Pope was—he did little. Fitz John Porter's bitter comments and a refusal to obey an ill-timed order from Pope led the administration to suspect that McClellan wanted the Army of Virginia to lose. He did not, but Little Mac and his staff certainly expected a defeat from a man they loathed. Worse, stress and indecision overwhelmed the new general in chief. Halleck, too, had little faith in Pope, while Lincoln had opened a second front, determined to dump Buell and his soft-war policies after he failed to take East Tennessee from the west. Instead, Buell had retreated from northern Alabama in the face of a Confederate strike north through Tennessee into Kentucky. Halleck broke down. Reluctant to race to Pope's battlefield—no one in Washington knew where it was anyway—McClellan went over Halleck's head and told Lincoln on August 29 that the administration had two choices: either concentrate the two armies or use the Army of the Potomac to save Washington and let Pope "get out of his scrape" on his own. He advised the latter. McClellan was in no mood to help Pope, Halleck could not compel him, and Lincoln would not order it.[61]

Unable to sleep, exhausted, and cranky, Lincoln anxiously haunted the telegraph office for the next week, often staying all night. He expressed dismay at the Second Bull Run defeat and Halleck's poor showing thus far, but it was McClellan who infuriated him. He told Hay that "it really seemed to him that McC wanted Pope defeated," while his advice to destroy a bridge over the Potomac displayed "dreadful ~~cowardice~~ panic." Hay continued: "The President seemed to think him a little crazy. Envy jealousy and spite are probably a better explanation of his present conduct." Once again, whatever the cause, enemy forces threatened Washington. "Well, John," Lincoln told Hay, "we are whipped again, I am afraid." He once again took no responsibility; it was his generals' fault. The president looked for an opportunity to rebound aggressively. "We must hurt this enemy before it gets away," he said frequently.[62]

Finger pointing took over. Pope and McClellan censured each other. Lincoln and the cabinet (minus Seward, who conveniently had left town) blamed McClellan while excusing Pope, except for Blair, who castigated them both. Stanton and Chase started an effort to court-martial McClellan; Chase said he wanted him shot. Welles refused to join them but only because he worried that the effort might blow up into a wider condemnation of Lincoln. No one was happy with Halleck, who was close to a breakdown, probably swallowing opium, and perhaps drinking too much wine as well to ease a flare-up of hemorrhoids. Still, the cabinet raged when Lincoln—who allegedly had not slept for a week—announced summarily on September 2 that he was putting McClellan in charge of defending Washington after Burnside had turned him down a second time. Lincoln admitted deep misgivings, but he said that McClellan was the only man who could restore the army's morale, and he at least fought well on the defensive. "We must use the tools we have," the president said. Besides, he pleaded, this was only a temporary appointment. Unconfirmed gossip that the army might try to overthrow him and put McClellan in his place also mandated restoring him for the moment, he believed. Still, Lincoln groaned that he had thought about hanging himself, and he frankly lied to Welles that Halleck made him restore Little Mac. The president also publicly scapegoated Pope—his private belief was that Second Bull Run was all McClellan's fault—and sent him far away to Minnesota, where the Dakota (Sioux) were in rebellion. Lincoln hesitated to fire McDowell for his role in the debacle, but the same day he sent word to him by Chase that he himself should request a court of inquiry, despite the absence of any existing formal complaints. That effectively took McDowell out of the command picture for good. To replace him as corps commander, McClellan asked for Maj. Gen. Joseph Hooker, unaware of that general's plots against him. Finally, and without making it official, Lincoln reasserted his role as de facto general in chief during Halleck's collapse. Official Washington was in chaos.[63]

But Lee had no designs on Washington. Instead, he veered westward into Maryland, hoping to feed his army while influencing the northern electorate and potential allies in Europe with a smashing victory. McClellan's Federals followed on September 6. Later historians disparaged Little Mac's pace, but it surprised Lee, who had counted on three or four unmolested weeks. He had divided his Army of Northern Virginia and was shocked when McClellan assaulted its rear guard at the South Mountain passes on September 14. Along the way, a sickly Lincoln peppered McClellan's headquarters with requests for updates and advice. The general responded with his usual pleas for reinforcements. Lee began to reassemble his army near Sharpsburg, Maryland, west and north of the Potomac. On September 17 McClellan attacked the Confederates all along Antietam Creek but failed to destroy them. Lee retreated to Virginia, his campaign ruined. Instead of following, McClellan claimed victory and stopped to refit his battered army. Lincoln thought that he was watching the end of the war slip away, so he pushed McClellan to give chase and destroy Lee. The general's critics, including Meigs, stirred the pot, charging that he deliberately let Lee escape in anticipation of a rumored military coup to put McClellan and the Democrats in power. For his part, McClellan smarted that he did not receive the praise—and reappointment to general in chief—that he thought he deserved. He wanted Halleck and Stanton fired, and he opposed the Preliminary Emancipation Proclamation of September 22. Ironically, the proclamation was a direct result of his actions, as Lincoln privately had sworn that he would issue the order if McClellan drove the enemy from Maryland. It still encompassed compensation of enslavers and colonization for the formerly enslaved while giving the Confederates until January 1, 1863, to lay down their arms and keep their slaves.

Finally, like most Democrats, McClellan damned Lincoln's latest suspension of habeas corpus. Two days after releasing the preliminary proclamation, in an attempt to quell violent protests against recruiting and the state militia drafts, the administration remanded alleged traitors to military tribunals and martial law. McClellan came close to resignation over this issue before friends such as Burnside and Porter talked him out of it.[64]

Lincoln arrived on the battlefield on October 1, still hoping to get the Army of the Potomac moving and almost certainly to reassure himself of both McClellan's fidelity and the troops' loyalty. Historian Scott Hartwig has suggested that Lincoln was disingenuous in his meetings with McClellan and his generals. The president repeatedly urged a pursuit and gently warned McClellan of being too cautious, but always while applying liberal doses of humor and disarming praise. When Lincoln left four days later, McClellan and his generals genuinely believed that they had won his support for army reorganization and resupply after the brutal battle. To be sure, it continued to surprise McClellan that again Lincoln had no interest in hearing about the fighting except for Hooker's role and that the president reviewed the troops listlessly. He had misread the man completely. The rank and file's positive reaction had convinced Lincoln that he need not fear their wrath if he replaced Little Mac and his inner circle.[65] Behind McClellan's back, an annoyed Lincoln openly accused him of cowardice. According to Nicolay and Hay, he asked his travelling companion, Illinois Secretary of State Ozias Hatch, "'Do you know what this is?'" Taken aback, Hatch replied, "'It is the Army of the Potomac.' 'So it is called,' Lincoln continued, 'but that is a mistake; it is only McClellan's bodyguard.'"[66]

Once back in Washington, Lincoln had Halleck order McClellan to go after Lee. When a shocked McClellan replied with more requests, excuses, and fears that Lee might double-back and return north, Lincoln grew testy. His mood worsened even more when Maj. Gen. Jeb Stuart's cavalry rode completely around the Army of the Potomac on October 10–12.[67] On the thirteenth Lincoln wrote McClellan a letter that historian Mark Neely correctly characterized as dripping with "withering scorn." It also was his last attempt to get the general moving. Yet it displayed Lincoln's evolved operational thinking as well, as he cited "the standard maxims of war." Referring again to McClellan's "over-cautiousness," the president first accused him and his men of being "unmanly"—a major insult in the era, as Neely pointed out. Lee's rebels got along well without the quantity of provisions the Potomac army received, he argued, pointing to Lee's twice-as-long supply line while in Maryland. Nor was McClellan equal to Lee as a general, he snapped. "Change positions with the enemy," Lincoln observed, "and think you not he would break your communication with Richmond within the next twentyfour hours."[68] He then applied his knowledge of Euclid and his maps:

> Exclusive of the water-line, you are now nearer Richmond than the enemy is by the route that you *can* and he *must* take. Why can you not reach there before him, unless you admit that he is more than your equal on a march? His route is the arc of a circle, while yours is the chord. The roads are as good on yours as on his. You know I desired, but did not order, you to cross the Potomac below, instead of above the Shenandoah and Blue Ridge. My idea was that this would at once menace the enemy's communications, which I would seize if he would permit.

Nor could he resist a final dig. "At least, try to beat him to Richmond on the inside track," he wrote. "I say 'try'; if we never try, we shall never succeed. . . . In coming to us he tenders us an advantage which we should not waive. We should not so operate as to merely drive him away. As we must beat him somewhere or fail finally, we can do it, if at all, easier near to us than far away. . . . If we cannot beat the enemy where he now is, we never can, he again being within the entrenchments of Richmond." The president concluded, "This letter is in no sense an order," although Nicolay and Hay indicated that the general would have been wise to treat it as such.[69]

Hartwig judged Lincoln's advice "as good and sound as an example of strategic advice as any general received during the Civil War."[70] Yet McClellan resisted, now citing his need for fresh horses. Lincoln shot back with what Neely termed "one of the few ill-tempered and mean-spirited letters of his life."[71] "I have just read your despatch about sore tongued and fatiegued horses," the president wrote. "Will you pardon me for asking what the horses of your army have done since the battle of Antietam that fatigue anything?" The general's attempts to explain went nowhere.[72] Disgusted with Lincoln, McClellan agreed to cross the Potomac on October 22, then waited four additional days. By then, Lee was across the Blue Ridge Mountains. For an exhausted Lincoln, that was the last straw. He already had fired Buell on October 30 for his failure to pursue the Confederates into barren East Tennessee after defeating Gen. Braxton Bragg's Army of Tennessee at Perryville,

Kentucky. Discarding his brief musings about making McClellan general in chief again while stripping him of a field-army command—something Little Mac might have accepted—Lincoln decided to cut the cord entirely. On a snowy November 7, with the elections over and the rallying Democrats no longer able to make it a campaign issue, he fired McClellan, too, finally ordering Ambrose Burnside to take command, like it or not. The men would follow Burnside, the president had concluded during his recent visit to the Army of the Potomac. Lincoln had accepted the general notion that McClellan was, if not a traitor, at least weak. He then worried that McClellan might refuse to step aside and even launch a coup. Little Mac did not, although some in his circle broached the idea.[73]

Lincoln ultimately explained to Hay that McClellan "was playing false—that he did not want to hurt the enemy." But worse still was rejecting Lincoln's military advice. "I saw how he could intercept the enemy on the way to Richmond," the president continued. "I determined to make that the test. If he let them get away I would remove him. He did so & I relieved him."[74] Only the following spring did Lincoln suggest to Noah Brooks that political ramifications played a larger role. "I kept McClellan in command after I had expected that he would win victories," Brooks remembered him saying, "simply because I knew that his dismissal would provoke popular indignation and shake the faith of the people in the final success of the war."[75]

Early in November 1862, Chicago relief worker and journalist Mary Livermore arrived in Washington. "It was a gloomy time all over the country," she remembered, "and the fruitless undertakings and timid, dawdling policy of General McClellan had perplexed and discouraged all loyalists, and strengthened and made bold all traitors." When Lincoln invited her and her associates to the White House, they readily accepted. What she saw, she remembered later in life, gave her a shock. Lincoln's "introverted look and his half-staggering gait" reminded her of "a man walking in sleep. He seemed literally bending under the weight of his burdens. A deeper gloom rested on his face than on that of any person I had ever seen." His mood matched his mien. When someone asked for "a word of encouragement," Lincoln refused. "The military situation is far from bright," he replied, according to Livermore, "and the country knows it as well as I do." Instead, he let off steam:

> The fact is . . . the people haven't yet made up their minds that we are at war with the South. They haven't buckled down to the determination to fight this war through; for they have got the idea into their heads that we are going to get out of this fix, somehow, by strategy! That's the word—*strategy!* General McClellan thinks he is going to whip the rebels by strategy; and the army has got the same notion. They have no idea that the war is to be carried on and put through by hard, tough fighting, that will hurt somebody; and no headway is going to be made while this delusion lasts.

The president then complained bitterly about the soldiers he allegedly loved, according to the heroic legend, as he had since Second Bull Run. He told Livermore, "there are whole regiments that have two thirds of their men absent—a great many by desertion, and a great many on leave granted by company officers, which is almost as bad. General McClellan is all the time calling for more troops, more troops; and they are sent to him; but the deserters and furloughed men outnumber the recruits. To fill up the army is like undertaking to shovel fleas."[76]

Some scholars have questioned the veracity of Livermore's account, written with direct quotations over two decades after the end of the war, but Lincoln's comments about "strategy" ring true enough, while others have noted his other comparisons of absent soldiers to fleas. For Halleck, Lincoln, and Halleck's other nineteenth-century readers, "strategy" at its most basic included campaigning and theaterwide activities that today are separated out by modern militaries as "operations." Strategy was, Halleck wrote in *Elements of Military Art and Sciences,* "the art of directing masses on decisive points," involving almost everything "beyond the range of each other's cannon. . . . [It] regards the theatre of war, rather than the field of battle. It selects the important points in this theatre, and the lines of communication by which they may be reached; it forms the plan and arranges the general operations of a campaign." Individual campaigns thus were expressions of strategy, as he understood the word.[77]

But Lincoln meant more than that in his comment to Livermore. What did strategy entail specifically in 1862? As historians Herman Hattaway and Archer Jones observed, West Pointers who wanted to move beyond the tactical lessons they gained at the academy had to read military history and theory and absorb lessons gained in Mexico. The greatest operational model to emerge from that war for most was the preferability of turning movements over bloody frontal assaults—the arc instead of the chord. Frontal assaults traditionally meant heavy casualties. Skillfully planned maneuvers around an enemy's flank and into his rear instead could minimize or eliminate battles and lessen casualties. That was the "strategy" McClellan had followed to the Peninsula and that led to his ouster.[78] As for the modern conception of strategy, as Carol Reardon has observed, the army "had no officially adopted doctrine" and only a brief definition that went little beyond the idea of coordinated campaigns.[79]

At the end of the McClellan era, Lincoln and his fellow Republicans had rejected both the general and the wider military's "delusion" of turning movements and strategy as demonstrated most notably on the Peninsula. He trusted his own martial ideas more than ever precisely because McClellan had failed again and again while ignoring them. What Lincoln demanded now was something more primal, the direct chord of "hard, tough fighting, that will hurt somebody" but end the terrible war sooner rather than later. Conciliation, soft war as exemplified by Buell and McClellan, and clever maneuvers had failed. The commander in chief's agenda now was clear: replenish the army, protect Washington from a politically catastrophic occupation, find an anti-McClellan who could win a war-decisive battle north of Richmond by driving straight at the enemy, utilize similar tactics and concentration in time in the West, and stop worrying about secessionists' feelings. But as he would learn in 1863, finding generals who would ignore "strategy" and do what he wished was easier said than done.[80]

3

I COULD HAVE WHIPPED THEM MYSELF

Lincoln, His Generals, and the Heroic Legend, November 1862–November 1863

When Lincoln fired Don Carlos Buell and George McClellan in the autumn of 1862, he acted within the constraints of a specific political environment. For all the complaints past and present about Lincoln becoming a dictator, free elections continued in the nation. There was no single election day as today, however. Two states already had cast ballots in 1862 (Oregon on June 2 and Maine on September 8), while eight others would not hold congressional elections until 1863. The rest hewed to three dates that fall: October 14, November 1, and November 4. On them rested control of the House of Representatives, several state legislatures, and six governorships. Aware of his growing unpopularity and developing conservative opposition to emancipation, Lincoln could say little in public to help Republicans. Voters in Indiana, Iowa, Ohio, and Pennsylvania went to the polls in October, just after Confederate armies had escaped from Antietam and Perryville. The Democrats added House seats, but at least Lincoln no longer had to fret about midwestern Buell supporters. Ten days later—the same anxious day he scolded McClellan about tired horses—Lincoln replaced Buell with another Ohioan, Maj. Gen. William S. Rosecrans. Halleck told Buell bluntly that his refusal to enter East Tennessee had been a political disaster for the president as well as a military setback. November brought more political defeats. New Jersey and New York elected Democratic governors. Republicans held on to

Congress and most legislatures, but the Democrats added thirty-four House seats as well as control of the statehouses in Indiana, New Jersey, and Illinois. Republicans even lost Lincoln's home district in Illinois.[1]

The results mortified Lincoln, but they did nothing to curtail his continuing shift toward a harsher war. He blamed his party's losses on the battlefield stalemate that his soft-war generals had left him, not his own policies or the lengthening casualty lists. He thus did little to conciliate Democrats. Indeed, the day after the November 4 elections, Lincoln had Halleck fire Democratic favorites Fitz John Porter and McClellan. Stanton then had the army court-martial Porter for disobeying orders at Second Bull Run. The prosecution, in one real sense a political trial of McClellan in absentia, marked the apogee if not the end of the administration's fears of a military coup. Late in January 1863, a court handpicked by Stanton found Porter guilty and dismissed him from the U.S. Army. Determined to clear his name from similar allegations, Buell requested a court of inquiry that dragged on into May 1863. It eventually ruled that he had been incompetent but not disloyal. The moral was obvious. Lincoln's generals not only needed to win victories, but they also had to do so in the direct manner that the president wanted; as he told Mary Livermore, "hard, tough fighting, that will hurt somebody." Lincoln had taken charge to shape the fighting and bring an end to the war. And so the command carousel turned, with generals rising and falling like toy horses as it spun in a flat circle.[2]

In Virginia Maj. Gen. Ambrose Burnside was the first new man on the generals' merry-go-round. Lincoln liked him. He was loyal, aggressive, and had fought well independently in North Carolina. His well-known friendship with McClellan, however weakened in private by recent events, and his great popularity within his own corps both made him less objectionable to the Army of the Potomac. His relative aloofness from army and partisan politics made Burnside acceptable as well to a wide range of Washington politicos. The problem was that he already had turned down Lincoln and the job twice before, most recently when Lee entered Maryland. Burnside simply did not believe that he was up to it.[3] Senator Orville Browning reported that the general told Lincoln that "the responsibility was too great—the consequences of defeat too momentous—he was willing to command a Corps under McClellan, but he was not willing to take the chief command of the army."[4] Yet despite that red flag, Lincoln wanted him anyway. After axing McClellan, he presented the reluctant general with a Hobson's choice—take the job or see it go to Maj. Gen. Joseph Hooker, whom Burnside despised as much as Hooker disliked him in return. With apologies to McClellan and a gnawing sense of inadequacy that never dissipated, Burnside gave in.[5]

Lincoln made it clear to the new army commander that he had to win battles soon for political reasons—to stem the rising Democratic tide and placate the Radicals—as well as military ones. Rosecrans in Tennessee and Maj. Gen. Ulysses Grant in Mississippi were preparing to strike; utilizing concentration in time could end the war. Burnside was eager to please, but disagreements emerged. Lincoln wanted him to go right at Lee up the south bank of the Rappahannock River. Here was Lincoln's direct operational thinking at its bluntest. Historian William Marvel, one of Lincoln's sharpest modern critics, nonetheless found the president's ideas about this "entirely sensible." Burnside and Halleck pushed back, however, pointing out that the Army of the Potomac would have to rely on a deteriorating, single-track railroad for supplies if it took that route. Burnside instead wanted to continue what McClellan had started, a flanking march toward Fredericksburg along the north bank. To Lincoln, such relative finesse smacked of more "strategy." He hesitated, gave in, and then insisted on celerity. Instead, the operation slammed to a stop opposite Fredericksburg when the pontoon bridges Burnside needed to cross the river arrived late, probably thanks to Halleck's inattention. Lee arrived, arrayed his men along the heights on the south bank, and waited.[6]

Stooped, sickly looking, and weary according to observers, Lincoln sensed a disaster looming. Even if Burnside crossed the river and won a battle, he realized, Lee would just retreat toward Richmond and pick a new place to fight, just as McClellan had warned. The president thus suggested a new alternative that much resembled his own Occoquan Plan. It involved placing 25,000 Federals, supported by gunboats, in Lee's rear. Halleck and Burnside objected again, claiming that it would take too much time to assemble such an effort. Stymied, Lincoln then radically changed his imperative, telling Burnside that he did not need to attack at all. Instead, on December 13, the general initiated a debacle. The Army of the Potomac's repeated assaults against high ground and rough terrain just outside Fredericksburg cost it almost 13,000 casualties, more than double what Lee absorbed. Shocked by eyewitnesses who brought him close to physical collapse, Lincoln told Halleck to order a retreat. Old Brains even refused to do that, saying to Lincoln that he could tell Burnside that himself.[7]

Once Lincoln steadied himself, he appreciated Burnside for at least taking the blame rather than shifting it to Washington, as McClellan had done.[8] Still, his despair lingered. "'If there is a worse place than hell,' he remarked, 'I am in it.'" To the governor of Pennsylvania, he asked, "What has God put me in this place for?"[9] On December 18, referring to the battle as well as the attempts by fed-up Radicals to purge Secretary of State Seward from the cabinet and take control of his administration, a depressed Lincoln told Browning: "[W]e are now on the brink of destruction. It appears to me the Almighty is against us, and I can hardly see a ray of hope."[10]

What historian Orville Vernon Burton later called "the tragedy of Fredericksburg" was that Lincoln learned "the wrong lessons" from the battle. All he needed, the president concluded, was better leadership and more attacks.[11] William O. Stoddard remembered Lincoln expressing this notion with cold precision:

> [I]f the same battle was to be fought over again, every day, through a week of days, with the same relative results, the army under Lee would be wiped out to its last man, the Army of the Potomac would still be a mighty host, the war would be over, the Confederacy gone, and peace would be won at a smaller cost of life than it will be if the week of lost battles must be dragged out through yet another year of camps and marches, and of deaths in hospitals rather than in the field. No general yet can be found to face the arithmetic, but the end of the war will be at hand when he shall be discovered.[12]

"The message was kill and destroy," historian Gabor Boritt later wrote of this bloody formula. "What had happened to the little boy who shot the turkey in the Indiana wilderness and whose heart had ached so?"[13] But Lincoln's "arithmetic" was wrong. To be fair, he did not have the exact butcher's bill in front of him, but nonetheless his addition was most faulty. Using now-accepted numbers, a week of Fredericksburgs would have produced 87,571 Federal casualties compared to 37,163 for the Confederates. Lee would have emerged with the larger if battered army, while the Army of the Potomac essentially would have been ruined and the road to Washington left wide open.[14] Even one day of such battle, however, had left Washington despondent. "Most uncheerful were the so-called holidays of that season," correspondent Noah Brooks wrote. "The city was filled with wounded and dying men; and multitudes of people from the North, seeking lost, missing, or wounded relatives, crowded the hotels."[15]

Eager to redeem himself and reward the president's trust, Burnside decided to cross the Rappahannock south of Fredericksburg and try it again. McClellanites in the Army of the Potomac had never regarded Burnside as worthy of his position and had opposed the assault at Fredericksburg. They now deemed this new proposed operation to be as doomed as the previous one. Recognizing Lincoln's continuing willingness to ignore the chain of command and undermine his commanders, "grand division" commander Maj. Gen. William B. Franklin and corps commander Maj. Gen. William F. "Baldy" Smith wrote directly to the president that the army should return to the Peninsula rather than fight again on the Rappahannock. Lincoln replied, without alerting Burnside, that he would share their thoughts with Halleck. Two other malcontents, Brigadier Generals John Cochrane and John Newton of Smith's corps, went straight to the White House in person to complain that Burnside was incompetent and soldier morale was terrible. Lincoln once again ignored protocol by not only hearing them out but also, thoroughly rattled by what they reported, then ordering Burnside to halt. Two days later, on January 1, 1863, Lincoln and Burnside met. The general wanted presidential support, but he was willing to resign. Lincoln demurred but also refused to identify his army critics. The toxicity in the Army of the Potomac's higher ranks, a culture that Lincoln and McClellan both had fostered and tolerated since the beginning of the war, stewed.[16]

Later that same remarkable day, Lincoln signed the Emancipation Proclamation. Like the preliminary version, he framed it as a "second order" war measure, designed to weaken the Confederate military by liberating their unwilling labor force. The Constitution and continuing support of slavery in the border states constrained him, and it only applied to areas under Confederate control on that date. Unlike the September document, however, the final version said nothing about compensation or voluntary expatriation. Colonization schemes would continue to play out privately well into 1864 to be sure, while as late as February 1865, Lincoln again proposed compensating slaveholders. He imagined colonies of freed people as prejudice-free asylums. He had backed away from the Chiriqui scheme by then due to local turmoil, but just one day before he signed the final proclamation, he approved resettling freed people on an island off Haiti. Until February 1864 and that experiment's catastrophic failure, Lincoln supported it, but he was done stumping for colonization in public after January 1863. Nor did he express any sympathy for slaveholders, loyal or otherwise, as historian Eric Foner has noted. The proclamation finally authorized something as well that Lincoln had resisted: recruiting African American soldiers. Men had been enlisting in small numbers for months, but tens of thousands of Black soldiers now would join the ranks at a time when white enlistment had declined precipitously.[17]

Contrary to conventional wisdom, the proclamation freed thousands of people on January 1 in some occupied areas, and it would keep doing so as the months passed. Its real power, however, depended on the ability of Federal armies to win battles and advance. As Foner put it, "freedom would follow the American flag."[18] Lincoln's meeting with Burnside and his signing of the Emancipation Proclamation on New Year's Day thus were linked inexorably. Yet immersed in saving Seward from a Radical coup and the blowback to emancipation, Lincoln tried to pass the buck to Halleck and let him decide if Burnside should attack again. "If in such a difficulty as this you do not help, you fail me precisely in the point for which I sought your assistance," he pleaded. "[G]o with him to the ground, examine it as far as practicable, confer with the officers, getting their judgment, and ascertaining their temper, in a word, gather all the elements for forming a judgment of your own; and then tell Gen. Burnside that you do approve, or that you do not approve his plan. Your military skill is useless to me, if you will not do this." Insulted, Halleck again refused a presidential request and instead tried to quit. Burnside in the meantime submitted his resignation from the army on January 7.[19]

"Lincoln was facing opposition and veritable rebellion in the leadership of the army," historian John Marszalek wrote. The president backed down, refused to accept Burnside's resignation, and finally approved his new operation on January 8—three days after Halleck did—but again advised caution.[20] But his support for Burnside was wavering. "I do not yet see how I could profit by changing the command of the [Army of the Potomac]," Lincoln bluntly wrote the commanding general with what was hardly a ringing endorsement.[21] By then, the plan had leaked. Scrambling for an alternative, Burnside clutched at Meigs's idea to cross the fords north of town. On January 17 the army finally left its camps. Lincoln unknowingly had held them up too long. Temperatures plummeted, then a low-pressure system moving up from the Gulf of Mexico brought torrential rain. The flanking movement became stuck in the mud, a "Mud March." The anti-Burnside chorus howled;

many wanted McClellan back. The commanding general told Lincoln that either his detractors had to go or he would. Lincoln gave up and accepted Burnside's resignation.[22]

Lincoln, his cabinet, and Halleck discussed possible replacements, including Rosecrans. The president, however, was wary of bringing another successful western general to Virginia after Pope's failure. Consulting no one in the end, Lincoln chose Hooker to replace Burnside. He liked Hooker, too. He was aggressive and the senior corps commander aside from McClellan's "pet" Franklin and the aging Sumner. Flexible politically, Hooker was a former War Democrat who had become popular with the joint committee's leadership, other Radicals, and the wider populace. He also had been working busily behind the scenes for months to gain command. Not everyone was pleased. Franklin and Sumner refused to serve under him and went home to await orders. Halleck had hated Hooker for years and preferred Maj. Gen. George G. Meade, which may have helped Hooker, too, given Lincoln's frustrations with his general in chief. Indeed, in yet another presidential violation of the chain of command, he gave Hooker permission to bypass Halleck entirely and work directly with the White House. Lincoln was gambling, but he hoped that he could deal personally with Hooker's intrigues, questionable moral compass, well-known dissipation, unpopularity among his peers, and recent complaint that "the Army and the Government needed a Dictator," which Lincoln addressed: "Of course, it was not *for* this, but in spite of it, that I have given you the command. Only those generals who gain successes, can set up dictators. What I now ask of you is military success, and I will risk the dictatorship. . . . [G]o forward and give us victories."[23]

The "Mud March" in retrospect was an apt symbol of the mess that Lincoln's aggressiveness, impatience, hesitations, and interventions had helped stir up. Indeed, from the Atlantic Coast to the Great Plains, the war was stuck in a metaphorical mud. Frustrations and disappointments piled up everywhere like the dead army horses and mules rotting along the Rappahannock.

Lincoln's decision to send Pope to Minnesota, for example, backfired. In mid-August 1862, famine, ongoing treaty violations, and the callous response of Lincoln's political appointees led a faction of starving Dakota (Sioux) in the state to rebel. John Nicolay, who already was in St. Paul negotiating a land grab with the Chippewa (Ojibwe), shrilly called for a "war of extermination"

The Far West, 1862–1864.

against all the local nations. After assuming command on September 16, Pope did much the same, boasting that he would "exterminate" the Dakota and their allies like "maniacs or wild beasts." When the uprising petered out soon thereafter, a military commission in Minnesota sentenced 303 men to die. Lincoln intended not to interfere at all until Judge Advocate General Joseph Holt told him that he could not delegate the pardon power. After writing his annual message, Lincoln diligently combed through the trial proceedings. He approved thirty-nine death sentences—later reduced by one—but granted clemency to the rest of the condemned. One day after Christmas, as Lincoln dealt with Burnside, fought to save Seward, and prepared to issue the Emancipation Proclamation, thirty-eight men hanged in the largest mass execution in American history. Lincoln had said that he would not sacrifice lives for votes, but when white Minnesotans objected loudly to his commutations, he agreed not only to compensate victims but also to drive from the state all the Dakota and the peaceful Ho-Chunk (Winnebagos) as well.[24]

Rosecrans in Tennessee came up short as well. Instead of moving promptly into East Tennessee as the president wanted, the general completed his predecessor's planned movement to Nashville. He then spent two months getting ready to fight, despite pleas and threats from Washington. Rosecrans's inactivity allowed General Bragg to shift 10,000 men from his army to Vicksburg, exactly what concentration in time was meant to prevent. Rosecrans finally marched out of Nashville after Christmas 1862. Along cold and wet Stones River near Murfreesboro, his men turned a near-collapse into victory just after the start of the new year. But Lincoln's joy soon gave way to consternation. Rosecrans sat in Murfreesboro for the next five months, methodically amassing supplies and men for a march into southern East Tennessee despite bad weather and rampant disease. Distrustful of Stanton and Halleck, he also nagged Lincoln for a revised date of commission that would allow him to outrank Grant, under whom he had served unhappily in Mississippi. Commander in Chief Lincoln, who never comprehended why rank mattered so much to military men, refused. Moreover, frustrated with generals' refusal to march as the enemy did without long supply trains, Lincoln and Halleck were moving in quite a different theoretical direction that emphasized mobility and minimal baggage.[25] To a reassigned General Banks, who wanted a thousand wagons in Louisiana, Lincoln wrote, "this expanding, and piling up of *impedimenta*, has been, so far, almost our ruin, and will be our final ruin if it is not abandoned."[26] Banks relented, but Rosecrans dug in. Lincoln pushed him to act in the Tennessee Valley in other ways, urging cavalry "counter-raids" to secure supplies, emancipate the enslaved, and prevent Confederates from concentrating at Vicksburg. It was to no avail. Rosecrans cached "impedimenta" as Lincoln fumed.[27]

The third major element of Lincoln's hoped-for concentration in time that winter involved the Mississippi River. After David Farragut's capture of New Orleans in May 1862, Federal forces controlled the river south to Memphis and north to Port Hudson, Louisiana, and Vicksburg, Mississippi. At the last city, however, the Confederates had constructed a veritable "Gibraltar of the West" on the bluffs overlooking the river. Lincoln was anxious to get the entire Mississippi back under Federal control and reopen it to midwestern commerce. After two abortive waterborne campaigns, Farragut ran the

Vicksburg batteries and met Federal gunboats coming south in July. Without control of Vicksburg and Port Hudson, however, the meeting largely was symbolic. The river remained blocked.[28]

Lincoln's impatience grew. As Rear Admiral David Porter later observed, no one wanted control of Vicksburg more than the president, both for an open Mississippi River and the logistical necessities that Lincoln was now grasping. "See . . . what a lot of land these fellows hold, of which Vicksburg is the key," the president told him, referring to his maps. "Here is Red River, which will supply the Confederates with cattle and corn to feed their armies. There are the Arkansas and White Rivers, which can supply cattle and hogs by the thousand. From Vicksburg these supplies can be distributed by rail all over the Confederacy. Then there is that great depot of supplies on the Yazoo. Let us get Vicksburg and all that country is ours. The war can never be brought to a close until that key is in our pocket."[29]

But that key was currently out of reach. In July Lincoln asked Maj. Gen. Ormsby M. Mitchel, commanding a division under Buell, if he could take Vicksburg. Manpower from the Mississippi Valley's friendly Black majority could augment his numbers, Lincoln thought—his first real expression of willingness to enlist African Americans. Mitchel was willing if white Federal troops in Arkansas supported him too, but Halleck refused to approve. Old Brains had his own plan for a joint army-navy campaign, but nothing came of it. That left it to Grant and Rosecrans in northern Mississippi. They won victories there that autumn, but the river remained blocked.[30]

When Rosecrans went to Tennessee, Grant assumed command of the region and began preparing his own campaign against Vicksburg. But then Lincoln impatiently jumped in with both feet and muddied the waters. All the way back to the Sumter crisis, as Elizabeth Brown Pryor maintained, the president had planted "the seeds of chronic disobedience. . . . If the commander in chief was ignoring hierarchy, established procedure, and customary courtesy, and rewarding unregulated behavior, the path was cleared for irregular actions at every level."[31] Pryor was right; such behavior repeatedly had plagued Scott, McClellan, and Burnside. Now it confronted Grant. Anxiously eager for progress, Lincoln began to listen to other men with big plans for the West. In October Porter became the new commander of the Mississippi Squadron (as he rechristened the Western Gunboat Flotilla) after he convinced Lincoln that he could take Vicksburg, unlike his foster brother Farragut.[32] Maj. Gen. John A. McClernand, meanwhile, a former Illinois

Democratic congressman and old acquaintance who had fought under Grant, captured the president's attention. In 1861 Congressman McClernand had made manifest his distrust of professional army officers before joining the ranks himself. After the first-round of 1862 elections, he obtained a leave and traveled east. McClernand dazzled Chase, visited Antietam with Lincoln, and persuaded the president to let him recruit a new army and take the city. Here was a fighting War Democrat who could bring midwestern men and support to the administration. Expecting that Halleck and Grant would object, Lincoln then decided to keep them in the dark while developing his own operational plan for a pincer movement to take Vicksburg. Banks—somehow still a favorite despite his failures in Virginia—had replaced Maj. Gen. Benjamin Butler in New Orleans. In Lincoln's developing scheme, Banks would march north from New Orleans while McClernand brought his new army south with support from Porter's naval squadron.[33]

"Why Lincoln passed over Grant and selected two incompetents to accomplish one of the most important objectives of Union strategy," T. Harry Williams later wondered, "is hard to explain." Perhaps it was simple frustration, he suggested, but raw politics seemed just as likely a reason. Banks shored up Lincoln's party in New England, while a War Democrat like McClernand could help reclaim the Midwest after the disappointing recent elections. "More probably," Williams continued, "the autumn of 1862 was a period when Lincoln's powers of human evaluation were not as sharp as usual."[34] Porter said as much when he remembered Lincoln asserting bizarrely that McClernand the Illinois politician was "a natural-born general" who deserved the credit for winning at Shiloh, not Grant, and was a better general than either Grant or Sherman.[35] Historian Brooks Simpson noted that the rise of McClernand made it evident that at that time Lincoln's vaunted "faith in Grant was conditional and qualified."[36]

Whatever the reasons, Lincoln had created chaos on the Mississippi. No one in Washington could explain how McClernand and Grant were supposed to cooperate. Halleck had so little faith in political generals or raw troops that he ignored Lincoln and gave his recent rival Grant permission to assert his authority over McClernand. In December Grant hastily threw together his own operation to take Vicksburg before McClernand could. While he moved half of his army overland, the balance under Sherman took riverboats to a point north of the city. Old Brains and a wavering Lincoln refused to stop Grant, but Confederate cavalry did, destroying his supply base on De-

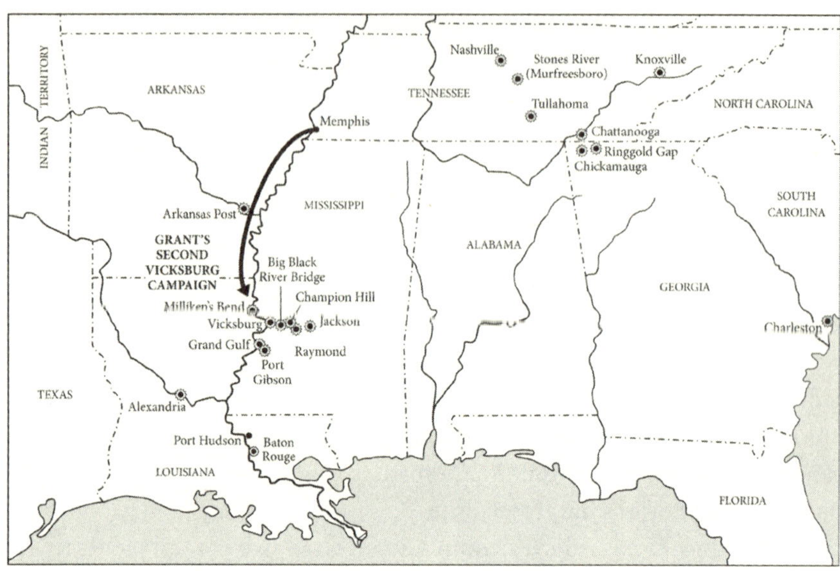

Western Theater, 1862–1863.

cember 20. Not knowing that Grant consequently had retreated, Sherman landed six days later. Stuck on a soggy floodplain below well-defended bluffs, he thrashed about in the mud until January 2, 1863, before withdrawing. McClernand once arrived promptly asserted command over Sherman and headed up the Arkansas River to reduce the bastion at Arkansas Post. Furious, Grant recalled them both and reduced the Illinoisan to corps command.[37] McClernand howled that Grant and Halleck had violated his deal with the White House. Lincoln tried to soothe him, but citing "too many *family* controversies . . . already on my hands," he refused to endorse "open war with Gen. Halleck." He continued, "Allow me to beg, that for your sake, for my sake, & the country's sake, you give your whole attention to the better work." Lincoln had made, then abandoned, Major General McClernand.[38]

Vicksburg remained unconquered in early 1863. Unwilling to retreat, in part due to the potential political fallout, Grant moved his army to the rainy, flooded banks north of the city and began to contemplate a spring offensive. He would march his army down the west bank of the Mississippi, recross, and take Vicksburg from the east. In part, as Brooks Simpson maintained, Grant designed his plans to placate Lincoln, who still wanted Banks involved. In the meantime, Grant put his men to work digging canals that might create a usable bypass for river traffic but would at least keep the troops busy. At first Lincoln supported these engineering efforts. He knew from his youth that the Mississippi could change channels. As historians Lisa M. Brady and Mark Fiege have each noted, Lincoln and Grant shared a "Whiggish" mentality that saw modern man as a hero conquering nature. But as spring drew near and men's flesh grew weak, Lincoln grew disenchanted. The digging accomplished nothing practical. Reports of rampant sickness and bad morale alarmed the folks back home. Then there were new rumors of Grant's drinking. A worried Lincoln dispatched investigators to find out if they were true, and he allegedly told U.S. Army Adj. Gen. Lorenzo Thomas to fire Grant if necessary.[39] "Grant's attempt to take Vicksburg looks to me very much like a total failure," Nicolay opined.[40] Grant held on, but as Simpson observed, Lincoln was never as fully supportive of him at this stage of the war as the heroic legend would have us believe.[41]

The spring of 1863 brought what biographer David Donald called Lincoln's "great spring assault on the Confederacy."[42] The president had high hopes, but the first great effort only brought more disappointment. As with the army, naval favorites had gained the president's ear. Chief among them was Cmdr. John A. Dahlgren, who took command of the Washington Navy Yard in 1861 at Lincoln's insistence and later became head of the Bureau of Ordnance. Dahlgren was best known for designing the advanced naval guns bearing his name. His technological gifts appealed to Lincoln the inventor. While he quickly became a White House confidant, Dahlgren found less appreciation elsewhere. Promotions went to victorious sea captains in the old navy, not to bureaucrats and engineers. After David Porter's promotion and reassignment, Dahlgren lobbied Lincoln directly for higher rank. The president was supportive, but Welles resisted.[43] The navy secretary thought that Dahlgren lacked the necessary skills, was "intensely ambitious, and . . . too selfish." He also dreaded the blowback from other officers, disliked Dahlgren and Lincoln's dealings with "sharpers and adventurers" with weapons to sell, and deplored "the army practice" of presidential favoritism.[44]

Blunted but undaunted, Dahlgren set his sights on gaining command of the anticipated assault on Charleston as the surest route to higher rank. Lincoln had longed to punish the South Carolina city since April 1861. While its capture would have little strategic value, symbolically it would be a triumph—and a sure path to promotion for the man who accomplished it. Unfortunately for Dahlgren, Flag Officer Samuel F. Du Pont stood in his way. Du Pont did not care much for Lincoln or his cabinet, and he refused to step aside for a man he disdained as a slick courtier but poor sailor. He kept his command but clashed constantly with Welles and Assistant Navy Secretary Fox. They were convinced that Du Pont could compel the city to surrender without the army by utilizing the new armored monitors to race past the fort and pound the city into submission. Lincoln liked this direct approach using new technologies—there was no "strategy" involved. Du Pont, however, believed that army involvement and a siege were inevitable. He quietly doubted the monitors' capabilities but said nothing and did nothing. Welles condemned his "shirking," while Du Pont's delays and calls for more ships led Lincoln to compare him to McClellan, an analogy that was fast becoming a regular presidential insult.[45] "Abe is restless about Charleston," Dahlgren wrote on February 14. Two days later the president ordered Dahlgren's promotion to rear admiral. The message to Du Pont was clear.[46]

Welles finally told Du Pont to either attack or send his ships west for service against Vicksburg. He gave in. Seven monitors and two larger ironclads entered Charleston harbor on April 7, only to be repulsed after forty minutes. Capt. John Rodgers angrily told a visiting John Hay that the results proved that "the country" had been wrong to believe in "the invincibility of the Ironclads." For his part, Du Pont complained that they were defective. In Washington, however, Lincoln and his circle defended the wonder ships and blamed the commander, expressing incredulity that Du Pont had given up after an hour; it was pure "timidity," Hay complained in his journal. An angry war of words followed until Dahlgren replaced Du Pont in July. His joint operation with the army to capture Morris Island and reduce Fort Sumter from there—the very siege that Lincoln and Fox had opposed while it was Du Pont's idea—followed. The president grew deeply interested in the operation and even presented tactical plans to Halleck, who dismissed them, as usual, as the work of an amateur. The Confederates finally abandoned the island on September 6–7, but Dahlgren's botched attempt to storm Fort Sumter two nights later failed miserably. So did his body. Constantly seasick, the admiral collapsed physically. Army sources whispered that he had lost his mind, too.[47] "Dahlgren has been in wretched health," a source told Hay, "dyspeptic, distraight, and overworked. His brain seems to be a little affected. He seems to have lost continuity of thought. . . . The business of the fleet is in chaos."[48]

Dahlgren managed to continue his friendly correspondence with Lincoln, however, and so kept his command. He maintained the blockade and would support Sherman after the March to the Sea in late 1864. But Dahlgren never again tried to take Charleston, which remained in Confederate hands until February 1865.[49]

By the time of Dahlgren's last, failed attempt to capture Fort Sumter in September 1863, the wider war had evolved dramatically. Lincoln had faced other severe challenges during that time. Most remained enmeshed in "first order" issues of commanders and campaigns, but some involved "second order" war-making powers. Politics loomed like a shadow over all of them. Fueled by the ongoing carnage, emancipation, and restrictions of civil liberties, Peace Democrats gained ground. Openly racist, ready to declare an armistice, and perhaps willing to give up on a united nation, "Copperheads" threatened an administration they called tyrannical and murderous. When Congress instituted a draft in March 1863—almost a year after the Confederates did the same thing—Copperheads denounced Lincoln for making white men die for Black freedom. Class was another factor. The draft law provided ways to avoid service that favored men with money. The reaction, especially in the Midwest and in northeastern cities, was swift. Republicans who recently dreaded a military coup now feared popular disorder and clandestine cabals. While they exaggerated the threat, mass demonstrations, draft resistance, intimidation, and the murders of recruiters and draft officials were real. Lincoln and his supporters saw no loyalty in such violent opposition. Aided by citizens informing on their neighbors, officials jailed suspects, shut down newspapers, and tried to mute the opposition.[50]

In such a stormy and divisive climate, Lincoln needed victories more than ever. Du Pont, Grant, and Rosecrans had been no help, however. The same was true of Hooker. In Virginia Lincoln initially hoped for a quick resumption of campaigning. Mother Nature had other plans. Well into April, the weather was cold and unusually wet, with rain or snow more than half the winter. Deep red-clay mud alternated with frozen soil, while frozen or flooded rivers and roads impeded supply. Any offensive was impossible until the roads dried out. All Hooker could do was rebuild.[51]

On April 4 Lincoln went to the soggy front for a week. He reviewed troops, met generals (including Meade), and visited the wounded. Peering through a telescope at Fredericksburg, he saw the destruction of the war as never before. His real purpose, however, was to spur Hooker. The president stressed that wrecking Lee's army in open battle, not taking Richmond, was the general's objective. He wanted no more McClellan-like flanking or strategy, he said, but then promptly confused Hooker by warning against the costly frontal assaults that ruined Burnside. In an added dig at both Burnside and McClellan, Lincoln also told him to engage his entire Army of the Potomac and not worry about holding a reserve force. Hooker was eager to comply if he could; he told Brooks that he now regarded Lincoln as a father. He developed a detailed plan, reflecting the president's priorities, that involved crossing the Rappahannock River upstream while cavalry rode into Lee's rear. Lincoln liked it, as it resembled his own Occoquan Plan's dual movements, but heavy rain starting on April 15 ruined the operation. The failure frustrated Lincoln so much that he opened his door briefly to another fraud who claimed the ability to predict the weather. He then returned to Hooker's headquarters on April 19. The general had a new plan based upon correct intelligence that Lee had sent part of his army off to the south to forage. Hooker wanted to cross upriver while those units were gone, tying down Lee with a diversionary assault at Fredericksburg. He would crush Lee between his pincers or else drive him south. As historian Donald Stoker observed, it looked much like the plan Meigs had suggested to Burnside before the Mud March. Lincoln approved.[52]

More rain delayed Hooker until April 30. News trickled in slowly to Washington after that, but by May 6, reports confirmed that Lee had won a pitched battle at Chancellorsville. It was another Federal disaster. "Lost, lost, all is lost!" Stanton exclaimed to Welles.[53] Lincoln was so distraught that the secretary of war worried that he was suicidal.[54] "The appearance of the President," journalist and friend Noah Brooks wrote, "was piteous. Never, as long as I knew him, did he seem to be so broken, so dispirited, and so ghost-like. Clasping his hands behind his back, he walked up and down the room, saying, 'My God! my God! What will the country say! What will the country say!' He seemed incapable of uttering any other words than these, and after a little time he hurriedly left the room."[55]

Lincoln pulled himself together, left for the front, and he tried to get Hooker to counterattack. The men seemed willing, the president thought. He promptly undermined Hooker and the chain of command by again meeting with subordinates who complained that Hooker had thrown away a victory. They wanted Lincoln to fire him, as did Halleck. The president himself blamed Hooker for ignoring his advice and not using his reserves. "An early movement," he wrote the general, "would also help to supersede the bad moral effect of the recent one, which is sure to be considerably injurious. Have you already in your mind a plan wholly, or partially formed? If you have, prosecute it without interference from me. If you have not, please inform me, so that I, incompetent as I may be, can try [to] assist in the formation of some plan for the Army." Hooker did neither. Another week passed. Lincoln called him to Washington. It was too late now to counterattack, he said, so the general should just harass the enemy and rebuild his army. As with Burnside, Lincoln also informed Hooker that he had lost the confidence of his subordinates and many politicians but once again refused to name names, thus protecting the officers' subversion.[56] Supportive face to face, Lincoln sounded a harsher note behind Hooker's back. Referring to the concussion Hooker suffered during the battle, Secretary Welles wrote, "the President says if Hooker had been killed by the shot which knocked over the pillar that stunned him, we should have been successful."[57]

"The weeks after the battle of Chancellorsville," biographer David Donald wrote, "were among the most depressing of Lincoln's presidency."[58] The press jabbed at both Mary Lincoln's controversial interest in spiritualism and the president's apparent lack of strategic acumen by jesting that he had held a séance to seek military advice from George Washington, the Marquis de Lafayette, Benjamin Franklin, and Napoleon. As historian David Reynolds observed, "Lincoln joked that these great souls seemed just as confused about how to conduct the war as his cabinet was."[59]

More ominously, the Democratic-led peace movement kept growing. In May Burnside, who was building a new army in the Midwest, clumsily sanctioned the arrest and imprisonment of alleged Confederate sympathizers broadly defined, ultimately including a congressman, Copperhead Democratic leader Clement Vallandigham of Ohio, for an antiwar speech. As with Pope, Lincoln's attempt to ease out a defeated commanding general had backfired. Burnside's gaffe gave the growing opposition a martyr and symbol—Vallandigham's plan all along. Lincoln commuted the sentence and banished the politician to the Confederacy but still refused to admit any overreach.[60]

Responding in writing on June 12 to a protest meeting days after Burnside shut down the Democratic *Chicago Times,* Lincoln for the first time defended in public his civil-liberties record as constitutional in hopes of bringing a majority of voters along with him. He partially threw Burnside under the omnibus, admitting, "I do not know whether I would have ordered the arrest of Mr. Vallandigham." But he justified himself. Free speech was not at stake, the president argued with some legerdemain, but the army was. "Long experience has shown that armies cannot be maintained unless desertion shall be punished by the severe penalty of death," he wrote. "Must I shoot a simple-minded soldier boy who deserts, while I must not touch a hair of a wiley agitator who induces him to desert? This is none the less injurious when effected by getting a father, or brother, or friend into a public meeting, and there working upon his feelings, till he is persuaded to write the soldier boy, that he is fighting in a bad cause, for a wicked administration of a contemptible government." Such an assessment left little room for dissent. Even "the man who stands by and says nothing when the peril of his government is discussed," Lincoln contended, "can not be misunderstood. If not hindered, he is sure to help the enemy; much more if he talks ambiguously—talks for his country with 'buts,' and 'ifs' and 'ands.'" Patriots supported the government wholeheartedly, Lincoln concluded. It seems everyone else carried the stench of treason.[61]

By then, Lincoln needed all the support he could get. Promising military advances did little to end the stalemate in the West. Concentration in time failed again. Rosecrans ignored entreaties to get moving until late June. When he did, his brilliantly planned and relatively bloodless Tullahoma Campaign drove the Confederates back into Chattanooga. He stopped short of taking that city, however, much less liberating East Tennessee. Instead, Rosecrans began amassing supplies once again before entering the mountains. Unconcerned with the realities of logistics or mountain topography, Lincoln smarted at what he saw simply as more strategy without headline-grabbing battles that would destroy an enemy army. He worried that the Confederates would send more men to Vicksburg and denigrated Rosecrans's real triumph in occupying the rest of Middle Tennessee without spilling much blood. All that mattered was that Bragg's Army of Tennessee survived.[62]

The president also put on hold his hopes regarding Grant. At the end of March, the general sent his Army of the Tennessee down the west bank of the Mississippi River, just as Lincoln had hoped. As it slithered south in deep mud, Admiral Porter ran his fleet past the guns of Vicksburg, which delighted Lincoln. On April 30—the same morning that Hooker began his Virginia campaign—Porter began shuttling Grant's army to the east bank. Ignoring Lincoln's wishes that he cooperate with Banks, Grant instead fought his way northeast to the Mississippi state capital at Jackson. In hindsight, that turned out to be the correct decision. With a relief force under General Joe Johnston blocked, Grant then turned west. In successive battles he drove the Confederates back into Vicksburg. His attempts on May 19 and May 22 to break through fieldworks surrounding the city, however, ended in failure. The general thereafter settled down to another siege that Lincoln did not want. According to rumors, Grant turned back to the bottle too. Chase demanded his dismissal, perhaps with Rosecrans as his replacement.[63] Lincoln wanted no part of that. The White House argued that Grant was "making some headway," in Nicolay's words.[64] "If I knew what brand of whisky he drinks," Lincoln joked, "I would send a barrel or so to some other generals."[65]

It is doubtful that Lincoln was thinking of Hooker with his whiskey quip, considering similar rumors of overindulgence there. Affairs in Virginia soon occupied more of his attention than did Grant or Rosecrans anyway. Hooker held on to his powerful constituency of Radicals, led by Chase. As with Burnside after Fredericksburg, however, an increasing number of his unhappy generals wanted Hooker ousted, some since the aftermath of Chancellorsville, to be replaced by George Meade. Maj. Gen. Henry Slocum went straight to Washington to persuade Lincoln. The president did not give in at first—he still liked Hooker personally—but he again warned the army commander that he was losing his subordinates' confidence. Lincoln then undermined the general's support by stoking the fire, quietly sounding out possible replacement Maj. Gen. John Reynolds, who visited the White House both to complain about Hooker and to avoid superseding him.[66]

In Richmond, Grant's slow strangulation of Vicksburg worried Mississippian Jefferson Davis enough that the Confederate president wanted to detach part of Lee's army and send it west. Lee countered that the best way to save Vicksburg was to allow him to invade the North a second time. A successful operation might pull Grant away from the stronghold or even force Lincoln to flee Washington. Davis gave in on May 26, and the Army of Northern Virginia soon began moving.[67] Hooker was confused at first, but by June 5, he grasped Lee's intentions. His response was to ask for permission to cross the Rappahannock, "pitch into his rear" at Fredericksburg, and force Lee to retreat. Donald Stoker correctly noted that this message reveals much about Hooker's lost self-confidence since Chancellorsville—the general would not act without Lincoln's blessing. The president said no. He recoiled from fighting at Fredericksburg again, feared a trap, and as usual refused to uncover Washington. Hooker's proposal also smacked of McClellan.[68] Lincoln revealed his full thoughts to the general in a dispatch:

> [I]n case you find Lee coming to the North of the Rappahannock, I would by no means cross to the South of it. If he should leave a rear force at Fredericksburg, tempting you to fall upon it, it would fight in intrenchments, and have you at disadvantage, and so, man for man, worst you at that point, while his main force would in some way be getting an advantage of you Northward. In one word, I would not take any risk of being entangled upon the river, like an ox jumped half over a fence, and liable to be torn by dogs, front and rear, without a fair chance to gore one way or kick the other. If Lee would come to my side of the river, I would keep on the same side & fight him, or act on the defence, according as might be my estimate of his strength relatively to my own.[69]

Hooker did none of those things. Instead, five days later he proposed "a rapid advance" against Richmond, somehow deluded that only 1,500 men defended it. There were enough troops to the north to deal with Lee's advance in the meantime, he stressed. Lincoln again said no, questioned Hooker's courage, and referred to his own mastery of geometry:

> If left to me, I would not go South of the Rappahannock, upon Lee's moving North of it. . . . If you had Richmond invested to-day, you would not be able to take it in twenty days; meanwhile, your communications, and with them, your army would be ruined. I think *Lee's* Army, and not *Richmond,* is your true objective point. If he comes towards the Upper Potomac, follow on his flank, and on the inside track, shortening your lines, whilst he lengthens his. Fight him when oppertunity offers. If he stays where he is, fret him, and fret him.[70]

Most scholars defend Lincoln on this point, but not all. Donald Stoker and Brooks Simpson each have argued that Lincoln never grasped that Hooker's intention was to draw Lee back south. It might have worked. But all Lincoln saw was another McClellan, so obsessed with taking Richmond that he risked

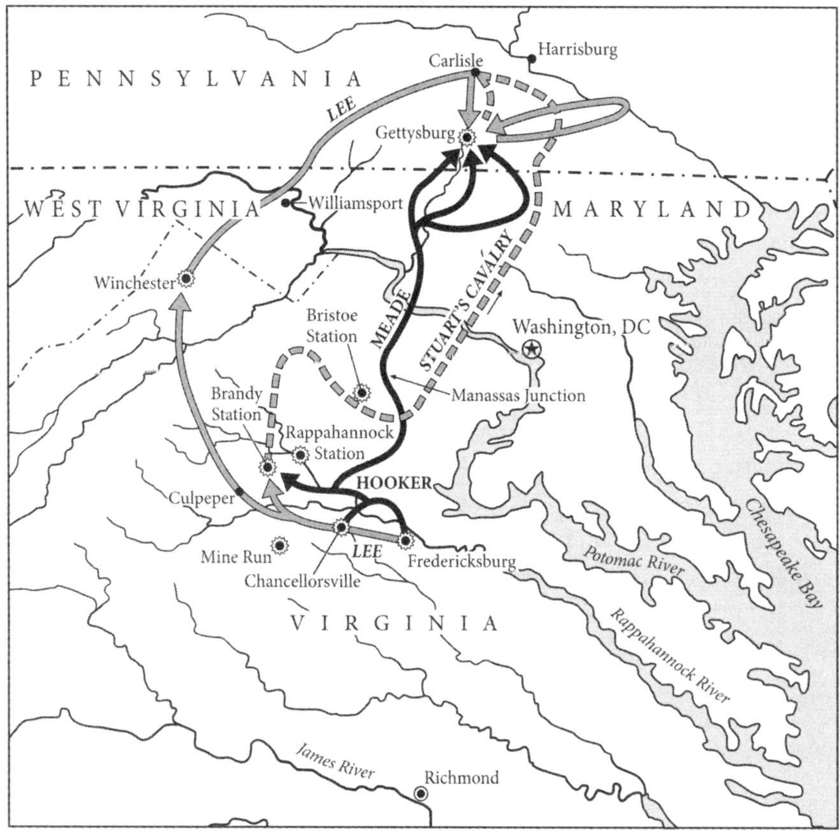

Virginia Theater, 1863.

Washington.[71] The president's tense displeasure worsened over the next few days. When Welles asked why Hooker did not hit Lee in the flank or rear, Lincoln replied, "our folks appeared to know but little how things are, and showed no evidence that they avail themselves of any advantage."[72]

The president said much the same to Hooker himself. "If the head of Lee's army is at Martinsburg and the tail of it on the plank road between Fredericksburg and Chancellorsville," he wrote the general, "the animal must be very slim somewhere. Could you not break him?" Hooker waited another day—and until he received orders—to reluctantly follow.[73] Lee then called up his rear corps from Fredericksburg, convinced that Richmond finally was safe. Once again, as in the Valley Campaign and later after the Seven Days' Battles, Lincoln's intervention was a gift that provided Lee more freedom to move. But the president was not wrong entirely. "The animal" was quite elongated, with cavalry in Pennsylvania, infantry crossing the Potomac, and one corps barely out of Fredericksburg. There indeed was an opening for a counterstrike, but Hooker's aggressiveness was too beaten down to take advantage of it.[74]

Careful to keep between Lee and the capital as Lincoln wanted, Hooker headed north, but the muddled command situation bedeviled his response. Pressure increased on Lincoln to fire Halleck, who seemed constantly dazed and, according to rumor, continued to abuse alcohol and opium.[75] "Halleck sits, and smokes, and swears, and scratches his arm, and [s]hakes it," Welles grumbled, "but exhibits no military capacity or intelligence. Is obfuscated, muddy, uncertain, stupid as to what is doing or to be done."[76] Hooker complained that Halleck had no confidence in him. Until Lincoln fixed that, he warned, "we may look in vain for success." Lincoln defended Halleck, adding that the general in chief's only problem was jealousy: they had kept him out of the loop. Looking back to Antietam and perhaps as well his firing of McClellan, the president stressed to Hooker that Lee's movement provided an opening to reset history, as it "gives you back the chance that I thought McClellan lost last fall. Quite possibly I was wrong then and now; but, in the great responsibility resting upon me, I cannot be entirely silent." A few hours later, "to remove all misunderstanding," Lincoln placed Hooker under Halleck's command, exactly what Hooker had feared.[77]

Halleck's refusal to give Hooker control of the Harpers Ferry garrison was the last straw.[78] Always jealous of his peers, Welles thought it was a base ruse to get rid of the general and that Halleck, Stanton, and Seward were duping Lincoln into doing their bidding. "The President has been drawn into the measure," he complained, "as he was into withholding McDowell from McClellan, by being made to believe it was necessary for the security of Washington" to hold Harpers Ferry.[79] If so, it worked. On June 27 Hooker asked to be relieved from command. In a cabinet meeting, Lincoln defended himself. Hooker had committed the cardinal sin. According to Welles, "the President said he had, for several days as the conflict was imminent, observed in Hooker the same failings that were witnessed in McClellan after the battle of Antietam. A want of alacrity to obey, and a greedy call for more troops which could not, and ought not to be taken from other points." The name "McClellan" was now a pejorative.[80] Lincoln's "power to hurt" came into play, too. When Hooker asked Noah Brooks what the president said about him, Brooks replied: "Lincoln had told me that he regarded Hooker very much as a father might regard a son who was lame, or who had some other incurable physical infirmity. His love for his son would be even intensified by the reflection that the lad could never be a strong and successful man. The tears stood in Hooker's eyes, as he heard this curious characterization of himself" as a "cripple."[81]

With Lee in Pennsylvania, the choice of a replacement for command of the Army of the Potomac was critical. In the end it came down to availability. Maj. Gen. Darius Couch and Reynolds had refused the job already. Maj. Gen. Winfield Scott Hancock was unwilling as well. That left Meade, who at least had the support of many peers. While no friend of Hooker, he largely had stayed out of the army's infighting. Consulting Stanton but not Halleck, who had recommended him months earlier, Lincoln ordered Meade to assume command, leaving the general no choice but to accept a position he did not desire. Halleck promptly gave Meade access to the Harpers Ferry garrison, which added credence to Welles's suspicions. Controversy continues over whether the new commander wanted to fight aggressively or on the defense, but any plans went awry when his cavalry encountered Confederates near Gettysburg on July 1. Lee attacked Meade through July 3 in the bloodiest battle of the war before retreating on the Fourth of July. The Army of the Potomac finally had defeated the Army of Northern Virginia. Other than the massive amounts of supplies gleaned from Pennsylvania farmers and burghers, Lee had failed. On that same July 4, the Confederates surrendered Vicksburg to Grant after forty-seven days of a textbook siege.[82]

Despite Mary Lincoln's serious injury from a carriage accident on July 2, the president had camped in the telegraph office awaiting war news. According to newly wounded White House insider Maj. Gen. Daniel Sickles—admittedly never the most reliable of witnesses—Lincoln prayed earnestly, convinced that the cause could not take another defeat. The twin victories elated him. The end of the war finally seemed close.[83] On July 5, just before news of Vicksburg arrived, Lincoln praised Grant as the anti-McClellan. "He doesn't worry and bother me," he told one officer. "He isn't shrieking for reinforcements all the time. He takes what troops we can safely give him . . . and does the best he can with what he has got, and doesn't grumble and scold all the while." The president added, "if Grant only does this thing down there—I don't care much how, so he does it *right*—why, Grant is my man and I am his the rest of this war!"[84]

On July 13 he wrote Grant an apology that also displayed his operational thinking.[85] "I never had any faith," he admitted, "except a general hope that you knew better than I, that the Yazoo Pass expedition, and the like, could succeed. When you got below, and took Port-Gibson, Grand Gulf, and vicinity, I thought you should go down the river and join Gen. Banks; and when you turned Northward East of the Big Black, I feared it was a mistake. I now wish to make the personal acknowledgment that you were right, and I was wrong."[86]

Meade, however, never became Lincoln's man. The trouble began on that otherwise glorious July 4 in the War Department telegraph office when Lincoln learned that Meade was not in hot pursuit. Then he saw the commander's congratulatory order to his men. "Our task is not finished," Meade wrote. The war would require "greater efforts to drive from our soil every vestige of the presence of the invader."[87] An observer recalled that when Lincoln read that sentence, "an expression of disappointment settled upon his face, his hands dropped upon his knees, and in tones of anguish he exclaimed, '*Drive the invaders from our soil! My God! Is that all?*'"[88] To an increasingly like-minded Hay, who was coming to think of Lincoln as a military genius, the president sighed, "this is a dreadful reminiscence of McClellan."[89]

Two days later the congratulatory orders still steamed Lincoln. He wrote Halleck: "I left the telegraph office a good deal dissatisfied. You know I did not like the phrase . . . 'Drive the invaders from our soil.'" Worse, Lincoln incorrectly believed that Meade was not in pursuit. Another chance to end the war quickly was vanishing. His distrust of the army's fidelity erupted yet again as he seemingly forgot that on June 28 he had ordered Meade to stay between Lee and the capital, directions that he had never altered. "These things all appear to me to be connected with a purpose to cover Baltimore and Washington," he complained anxiously to Halleck, "and to get the enemy across the river again without a further collision, and they do not appear connected with a purpose to prevent his crossing and to destroy him."[90]

"It was as unfair an assessment as Lincoln ever made," historian Russell Weigley observed. "Lincoln and the war department [sometimes] underestimated the shattering impact of a major battle and expected too much renewed action too soon."[91] The Army of the Potomac had suffered over 23,000 casualties at Gettysburg, over four times as many losses as Grant absorbed during the entire Vicksburg Campaign from March through July. Such a battering required restructuring. The men needed food and shoes. Confusion abounded as to whether Lee was in retreat or simply pulling back to better ground. There was also the weather. Hard rain fell on the fourth and persisted with little interruption for the next ten days; it amounted to 3.24 inches, roughly what fell in an average month. The deluge not only raised the Potomac high enough to block Lee's retreat but also turned roads into mires. Once he began pursuit, Meade tried to compensate by moving south along macadamized pikes, but it was still slow going.[92]

But as he paced in the telegraph office, agitated and sleep deprived, Lincoln saw only another opportunity to end the war slipping away due to a general's McClellan-like lack of will. He urged Meade to strike and destroy Lee's army. On July 7 he had Halleck inform the commander that Vicksburg had fallen. "Now, if General Meade can complete his work, so gloriously begun so far, by the literal or substantial destruction of Lee's army," Lincoln added, "the rebellion will be over." Meade tried to point out his difficulties, but his clumsy word choice made matters worse. "I wish in advance," he wrote, "to moderate the expectations of those who, in ignorance of the difficulties to be encountered, may expect too much."[93]

Unwilling to accept logistical reality and convinced that the decisive moment of the war was slipping away, Lincoln heard none of it. As historian William Marvel has noted, Lincoln never seemed to have contemplated what would have happened had Meade attacked and failed. He still sounded too much like McClellan, just as Hooker had. Halleck wrote Meade, "the President is urgent and anxious that your army should move against him [Lee] by forced marches." Lincoln sent Vice President Hannibal Hamlin to Maryland to goad Meade. The army caught up with Lee on July 12, but wary subordinates and entrenchments that looked more daunting than those faced at Fredericksburg gave the commander pause. By the time he was ready to attack on July 14, Lee had escaped. "I need hardly say to you that the escape of Lee's army without another battle has created great dissatisfaction in the mind of the president," Halleck advised, "and it will require an active and energetic pursuit on your part to remove the impression that it has not been sufficiently active heretofore." Meade responded, "the censure of the President . . . is, in my judgment, so undeserved that I feel compelled most respectfully to ask to be immediately relieved from the command of this army." Halleck refused.[94]

Lincoln's mood soured even more in mid-July. An ugly antigovernment and openly racist draft riot in New York City July 13–16 seemed to bode ill, although in retrospect it embarrassed the Copperheads more. Lincoln was "depressed" and "deeply grieved" on the fourteenth, according to Hay. "'We had them within our grasp' he said. 'We only had to stretch forth our hands & they were ours. And nothing I could say or do could make the army move.'"[95] Hay added that son Robert Todd Lincoln remarked, "the ~~Tycoon~~ President is grieved silently but deeply about the escape of Lee. He said 'If I had gone up there I could have whipped them myself.' I know he had the idea." The younger Lincoln said it was the only time he ever saw his father tear up.[96] But the president was suspicious too. "There is bad faith somewhere," Lincoln told Welles "Mead has been pressed and urged but only one of his generals was for an immediate attack—was ready to pounce on Lee—the rest held back—What does it mean, Mr. Welles?—Great God what does it mean?"[97]

Frustrated beyond measure, Lincoln wrote Meade a long and accusatory letter. "I am very—*very*—grateful to you for the magnificent success you gave the cause of the country at Gettysburg," he began, "and I am sorry now to be the author of the slightest pain to you. But I was in such deep distress myself that I could not restrain some expression of it. I had been oppressed nearly ever since the battles at Gettysburg, by what appeared to be evidences that [you and others] . . . were not seeking a collision with the enemy, but were trying to get him across the river without another battle." As always, Lincoln refused to identify a commanding general's accusers, but he flailed at Meade for letting Lee's army escape. He had more than enough men, Lincoln complained, it would have been easy, but the general "stood and let the flood run down, bridges be built, and the enemy move away at his leisure, without attacking him." His conclusion especially stung.

> I do not believe you appreciate the magnitude of the misfortune involved in Lee's escape. He was within your easy grasp, and to have closed upon him would, in connection with our other late successes, have ended the war. As it is, the war will be prolonged indefinitely. If you could not safely attack Lee last monday, how can you possibly do so South of the river, when you can take with you very few more than two thirds of the force you then had in hand? . . . Your golden opportunity is gone, and I am distressed immeasureably because of it.[98]

Not since Antietam had Lincoln penned anything so angry. In the end, he thought better of it and never sent the letter, although he kept it in his files. There is little doubt that it expressed his views, however, as Meade sensed.[99]

Days later, according to Nicolay and Hay, Lincoln groaned, "We had gone through all the labor of tilling and planting an enormous crop, and when it was ripe we did not harvest it." While his anger had eased enough to appreciate what Meade had accomplished, his conviction that the general had failed to end the war lingered like a cancer.[100] On July 17, according to Welles, he reluctantly told the cabinet that he would keep Meade in command. "He has committed . . . a terrible mistake," Lincoln said, "but we will try him farther." It was no endorsement, and the cabinet withheld theirs. Ten days later, as the armies sat quietly and more unhappy generals wrote directly to Lincoln, the president told Welles: "I have no faith that Mead will attack Lee—nothing looks like it to me. I believe he can never have another as good opportunity as that which he trifled away. . . . No I dont believe he is going to fight."[101]

The relationship between Lincoln and Meade never recovered. Both distrusted the other. Lincoln was unfair in repeatedly insisting that Meade was moribund, but Virginia was relatively quiet in the weeks after Gettysburg. The two battered armies spent a stifling August and September arrayed on opposite sides of the Rappahannock and Rapidan Rivers, shielding their capitals, occasionally probing, but otherwise content to wait and rest. The president grew increasingly impatient, once again drawing up his own tactical plans while still insisting that wrecking Lee's army in the open—and not taking Richmond—was the proper goal. He also tried to convince Meade to make a place in the army for Hooker, whom he strangely thought might provide some backbone.[102] Then on September 19—the same day that the Battle of Chickamauga began in the West—Lincoln wrote Halleck regarding Meade's request for more troops. To him, both the hard arithmetic and his distrust of the man demanded a negative response:

> General Meade estimates the enemy's infantry in front of him at not less than 40,000. Suppose we add 50 per cent. to this for cavalry, artillery, and extra-duty men, stretching as far as Richmond, making the whole force of the enemy 60,000. General Meade, as shown by the returns, has with him, and between him and Washington, of the same classes of well men, over 90,000. Neither can bring the whole of his men into a battle, but each can bring as large a percentage in as the other. For a battle, then, General Meade has three men to General Lee's two. Yet, it having been determined that choosing ground and standing on the defensive gives so great advantage that the three cannot safely attack the two, the three are

> left simply standing on the defensive also. If the enemy's 60,000 are sufficient to keep our 90,000 away from Richmond, why, by the same rule, may not 40,000 of ours keep their 60,000 away from Washington, leaving us 50,000 to put to some other use? Having practically come to the mere defensive, it seems to be no economy at all to employ twice as many men for that object as are needed. . . . I can perceive no fault in this statement, unless we admit we are not the equal of the enemy, man for man.[103]

Lincoln went on to disparage Meade by again comparing him to Little Mac, a trope that fast had become his worst insult:

> To attempt to fight the enemy slowly back into his entrenchments at Richmond, and then to capture him, is an idea I have been trying to repudiate for quite a year. My judgment is so clear against it that I would scarcely allow the attempt to be made if the general in command should desire to make it. My last attempt upon Richmond was to get McClellan, when he was nearer there than the enemy was, to run in ahead of him. Since then I have constantly desired the Army of the Potomac to make Lee's army, and not Richmond, its objective point. If our army cannot fall upon the enemy and hurt him where he is, it is plain to me it can gain nothing by attempting to follow him over a succession of intrenched lines into a fortified city.[104]

Lee settled the matter. On October 8 he crossed the Rappahannock and forced Meade to retreat until a bloody rebuke at Bristoe Station on October 14. Lincoln demanded a counterattack, assuring Halleck that "the honor will be his if he succeeds, and the blame may be mine if he fails." Ready to resign, Meade waited until November 7 before recovering the lost ground. On November 26 he advanced again. Meade had wanted to swing east to Fredericksburg, but while Lincoln still demanded an attack, the president did not want it there. Lee then fell back to formidable entrenchments along chilly Mine Run. Meade almost attacked them, but he called off the impending assault. His discretion almost certainly prevented a repulse, but miles away the White House did not agree.[105] "For Lincoln," Brooks Simpson observed, "Mine Run proved the last straw. He now believed that Meade was incapable of conducting offensive operations. Meade might not lose the war, but he would not win it."[106]

As the winter of 1863–64 passed, Lincoln grew more convinced than ever that he understood how to win the war better than his failed generals. Lee's apparent escape from Gettysburg had taught him that he "could have whipped them myself." Only Meade and his generals in the Army of the Potomac stood in the way of quick pursuits, heavy counterattacks, and victory. As he had done with Pope during the McClellan era, Lincoln once again began to look westward for a new solution to the ongoing stalemate in Virginia: his man Grant.

4

MARTYR VICTORIOUS

Lincoln, Grant, and the Heroic Legend, September 1863–April 1865

WHILE THE WAR REACHED another stalemate in Virginia in the autumn of 1863, Lincoln's cause eventually found greater success in the West. No one could have predicted that in the late summer, however, as Federal forces and the president endured another major defeat, this time in North Georgia.

After two months of impatient telegrams and threats from Washington, General Rosecrans's Army of the Cumberland had finally marched on Chattanooga in mid-August. All went splendidly at first. General Bragg abandoned the city on September 7 lest his Army of Tennessee be cut off from the rear. The deliberate Rosecrans for once ordered a quick pursuit, but that was difficult to accomplish in the rugged North Georgia mountains. Bragg tried to attack isolated portions of the Federal army, but his own cancerous command problems stymied his efforts until an all-out assault on September 19. Along Chickamauga Creek, Rosecrans held fast the first day, but two divisions of reinforcements dispatched from Lee's army led by Lt. Gen. James Longstreet helped break his line on September 20. Rosecrans and much of his army reeled into Chattanooga, protected by a stubborn rear guard led by Maj. Gen. George Thomas. Bragg did not have enough men to take the city or completely encircle it, but he cut off the main arteries of supply and hoped to starve out the Federals.[1]

Rosecrans was trapped. The denouement came as no surprise to Lincoln, who again had spent days in the telegraph office. "Well, Rosecrans has been whipped, as I feared," he told Hay. "I have feared it for several days. I believe I feel trouble in the air before it comes."[2] Once again, concentration in space had helped the Confederates, while the Federal forces had failed to act in unison east and west, allowing Longstreet to shift from Virginia to Georgia. Lincoln bitterly blamed Meade for the disaster, telling Secretary of the Navy Welles that he was not "doing any thing, or wanted to do any thing." Defeat at Chickamauga, Lincoln believed, indeed stretched back to McClellan and up to the failure to stop Lee after Gettysburg. "It is . . . the same old story of the Army of the Potomac," he went on. "Imbecility, inefficiency—dont want to do. . . . [I]t is terrible, terrible, this weakness, this indifference of our Potomac generals, with such armies of good and brave men." Why not fire Meade, Welles asked. "'What can I do,' he replied, 'with such generals as we have? Who among them is any better than Mead?'"[3] A month later Lincoln remained annoyed, as he knew exactly what he wanted his generals to do. Warning General in Chief Halleck of reports that Lee had sent a corps from his Army of Northern Virginia to Tennessee while continuing to dismiss Meade's ideas, he asked: "What is to be done? If you have a plan matured, I have nothing to say. If you have not, then I suggest that with all possible expedition the Army of the Potomac get ready to attack Lee; and that, in the meantime, a raid shall, at all hazards, break the Railroad at or near Lynchburg [Virginia]."[4]

Defeat at Chickamauga also was sobering personally. Lincoln bore up well enough until he learned that his favorite brother-in-law, Confederate Gen. Ben Hardin Helm, had died in the battle. The report shook him emotionally. Old friend David Davis wrote: "I never saw Mr. Lincoln more moved. . . . I found him in the greatest grief. 'Davis,' said he, 'I feel as David of old did when he was told of the death of Absalom. "Would to God I had died for three, oh Absalom, my son.my son!"' I saw how grief stricken he was so I closed the door and left him alone."[5] But while Lincoln's mood remained dark over the next several days, he also saw a chance to redeem what was lost at the Potomac River crossings. "If we can hold Chattanooga, and East Tennessee," he wrote Rosecrans, "I think this rebellion must dwindle and die."[6]

Lincoln first turned to General Burnside, whom he had continued to support at arm's length, to send help. Burnside's new army occupied Knoxville at last; with it, much of East Tennessee finally was in Federal hands. Unfortunately, he had gone off in the opposite direction, northeast to Jonesboro, chasing guerrillas. Despite several entreaties, Burnside refused to change course or abandon the hunt. "Damn Jonesboro!" Lincoln shouted.[7]

He penned another caustic letter that he never sent. "Yours of the 23rd. is just received," he wrote, "and it makes me doubt whether I am awake or dreaming. I have been struggling for ten days, first through Gen. Halleck, and then directly, to get you to go to assist Gen. Rosecrans in an extremity, and you have repeatedly declared you would do it, and yet you steadily move the contrary way."[8]

By then, other relief efforts were in motion. Sherman received orders to bring four divisions from Mississippi to the Chattanooga area. Near midnight that same day, September 23, Secretary of War Stanton convened a meeting at the White House that included Treasury Secretary Chase, Halleck, Secretary of State Seward, Stanton, and eventually Col. Daniel McCallum, the superintendent of the U.S. Military Railroad. Stanton proposed stealing a trick from Richmond and sending two corps from Meade's largely idle Army of the Potomac to reinforce Rosecrans. He thought their transit would take five days. Lincoln scoffed. Both his mood and his opinion of that army remained ugly. "I will bet," he said, "that if the order is given tonight, the troops could not be got to Washington in five days." Lincoln gave in, but only after McCallum approved the idea. To lead the effort, Stanton appointed General Hooker, who had been idling in Washington, dining frequently with Hay. Lincoln was wrong and McCallum was almost right: the first troops from Virginia arrived in Chattanooga in eleven days.[9]

In the meantime, the White House abandoned Rosecrans as it had so many other defeated field generals. Reports that he had fled from the field at Chickamauga demanded a change. So did damning reports about his alleged mental breakdown from the War Department's Charles Dana, the Grant loyalist who was with the Army of the Cumberland as Stanton's eyes and ears. Drawing his information from a biased Dana, Lincoln told Hay that Rosecrans was "confused and stunned like a duck hit on the head." Stanton wanted to replace him with George Thomas. Lincoln hesitated until after the October 13 elections in Ohio, where Old Rosy remained popular. He would not take a chance of aiding Vallandigham, who was running for governor from Canadian exile, even if that meant leaving an alleged incompetent and coward at the head of the army in Chattanooga. The Republicans won big in the state. Three days later Lincoln and Stanton combined the western military departments into a single one to be commanded by Grant, the general Lincoln now most trusted. Stanton sent the new department head to Chattanooga, giving him the choice of keeping Rosecrans or replacing him with

Thomas. Grant wanted no part of Rosecrans; Thomas got the job. Lincoln eventually sent Rosecrans to Missouri to replace Maj. Gen. John Schofield, who had caused a ruckus by taking sides in the state's labyrinthine politics.[10]

Using unguarded back roads, Grant arrived in Chattanooga on October 23. Working with Maj. Gen. Baldy Smith, he engineered a supply line that provided food and forage. Once Sherman arrived on November 14, Grant made plans to fight his way out. Bragg, in contrast, weakened his army by sending his new rival Longstreet and his veterans against Knoxville. In the Battles of Chattanooga, fought from November 23 through November 25, Grant defeated Bragg and drove him into North Georgia. Four days later Longstreet's attempt to take Knoxville ended in failure.[11]

Lincoln kept up with events as best he could from his sickbed. Returning from Gettysburg, where he had just delivered his legendary address—in it, among other things, he called for "increased devotion" to the "unfinished" war effort—the president had come down with what doctors diagnosed as varioloid, a mild form of smallpox. The illness, which may well have been full-blown smallpox, did little for his mood. According to Hay, he was "very anxious" about Burnside and "a little despondent" about Grant until word came on November 23 that the latter had attacked. With that, the president "took heart."[12] On December 7, with Knoxville secure and Longstreet in retreat, Lincoln announced the occupation of East Tennessee as a matter of "high national consequence" and called upon citizens to thank "Almighty God, for this great advancement of the national cause." Two days later he sent Grant and his men "more than thanks—my profoundest gratitude."[13]

Aside from a sliver of northern East Tennessee where Longstreet wintered, the president's long hope of liberating the region was fulfilled at last. Yet he was not satisfied. The same day he thanked Grant, he returned to castigating Meade and his army. Meade was no Grant, and the Army of the Potomac did not match up to the western armies. "Now . . . if this Army of the Potomac was good for anything," he complained to Nicolay, "if the officers had anything in them—if the army had any legs, they could move thirty thousand men down . . . and catch Longstreet. Can anybody doubt," he continued, "if Grant were here in command that he would catch him?"[14]

By the winter of 1863–64, "a streak of ruthless determination, not hitherto noticeable, began to appear in Lincoln's character," according to biographer

David Donald. Lincoln "betrayed his sense that the war had gone on too long, with too much loss of blood and treasure, and that it was time to force it to a close." That impatient "determination" revealed itself in various ways. The president authorized executing one Confederate prisoner for every captured African American Federal soldier killed, and he imposed potential sentences of hard labor in retaliation for enslaving Black combatants. Fearing a slippery slope of killing, he never followed through.[15] But in August what historian Mark Neely called Lincoln's "instinct for the jugular" led him to support Brig. Gen. Thomas Ewing's General Orders No. 11 in Missouri, which depopulated four counties along the Kansas border in response to a massive guerrilla attack on Lawrence, Kansas.[16]

In mid-September Lincoln exploded in anger at judges attempting to release conscripts from the army with writs of habeas corpus while ordering the arrests of enrolling officers. He proposed suspending the writ, ignoring the injunctions, and arresting the judges instead. An alarmed cabinet persuaded him to adopt a lesser and more legal remedy. Meanwhile, the president had called for another 300,000 volunteers in October, to be supplemented by a draft if not enough men came forward, and he added a request for 200,000 additional men in February 1864. In March he requested yet another 200,000 soldiers, with deadlines extended to May because of the tepid response. In December 1863, meanwhile, he had issued his Proclamation of Amnesty and Reconstruction, the so-called Ten Percent Plan, which was designed to organize loyal governments quickly in occupied parts of the Confederacy. Lincoln intended to enforce his proclamation in part through military action. In January 1864 he ordered a Federal expedition into Florida to spread word of the reconstruction proclamation, recruit African American soldiers, and seize food and supplies. Confederate troops repulsed it at the Battle of Olustee on February 20 and drove the battered Federal force back to its toehold in Jacksonville. A week later Brig. Gen. Hugh Judson Kilpatrick and Rear Admiral Dahlgren's son Ulric led a cavalry raid toward Richmond, ostensibly aiming to free Federal prisoners, disrupt enemy communications, and announce the proclamation. It ended in defeat and controversy. Confederates claimed that papers found on young Colonel Dahlgren's corpse called for the assassination of President Davis as well as burning the capital city. Lincoln probably was not involved in those specifics, even though he and Stanton had originated the raid, overruled Meade's opposition to it, and directly given Kilpatrick permission to proceed, once again ignoring the chain of command.[17] In Donald's words, the Kilpatrick-Dahlgren Raid nonetheless reflected "the President's determination to take whatever steps were necessary to end the rebellion."[18]

Grant wanted to end the war, too, but he also began to run afoul of White House priorities and Lincoln's strategic vision. Winter weather, mountains, and bad roads around Chattanooga made it impossible to operate there. The alternative plan he offered early in December 1863 instead involved a quick movement of 35,000 men from the Mississippi Valley against Mobile, one of the Confederacy's last open ports. Once Mobile was invested or taken, Grant could turn on Alabama and perhaps Georgia. The Army of the Potomac—to be commanded by Sherman or Baldy Smith instead of Meade, Grant suggested—could shift troops west and take care of Longstreet before he could reunite with Lee. The general sent Dana to Washington to make his case. Two weeks later Lincoln, Stanton, and Halleck said no. They worried that Longstreet remained a threat to East Tennessee, while they believed that North Georgia and West Tennessee also had to be secured before initiating any Mobile campaign. They also wanted to send General Banks from New Orleans up the Red River and into Texas, perhaps reinforced by Grant. Such an expedition would do nothing to end the war, but it would secure cotton for New England mills before the 1864 elections, rattle sabers against France's recent military and imperial expansion into Mexico, and help create a loyal Louisiana government through the provisions of the Proclamation of Amnesty and Reconstruction.[19]

Grant regrouped and in mid-January 1864 suggested a second, less ambitious plan for western operations. He would divide the army group then under him in Chattanooga, with part of it driving on Atlanta and the rest moving on Montgomery. Lincoln and Halleck vetoed that idea, too, still worried about East Tennessee. Now won, that region could not be lost again. Grant in the end sent Sherman back to Vicksburg to mop up resistance in Mississippi east of the river while keeping him away from Banks. Sherman's resulting Meridian Campaign of February–March 1864 became a dry run for what he would do months later in Georgia. Yet Halleck had found that he enjoyed discussing strategy with Grant, unlike with Meade, and he now solicited his ideas about Virginia. Grant, still only commanding in the West, now sent the general in chief a third operational plan. He recommended landing a 60,000-man expeditionary force at Suffolk, Virginia, and swinging it into North Carolina toward Raleigh, cutting Lee's communications as it went, compelling him to abandon Richmond and perhaps all of Virginia to save his army. It was McClellan's last Peninsula plan, only greatly enlarged geographically. Agreeing with Lincoln that the Army of Northern Virginia was the true objective, Halleck rejected the proposal as already discarded and contrary to the example of Napoleon. To assemble such a force, he explained, would weaken the Army of the Potomac and endanger Washington. Lincoln would never allow it.[20]

"Neither Lincoln nor Stanton nor Halleck seemed to comprehend the merits of Grant's proposals," historian Joseph Glatthaar later maintained. "Both the North Carolina and Mobile plans were so contrary to the traditional notions of warfare that had emerged from the Napoleonic era, so rooted in actual experience in the Mississippi River Valley, that the leadership in Washington had no basis from which to evaluate their strengths and weaknesses. . . . To expect Lincoln to grasp this bold approach to the war without extensive explanations of its merits . . . was asking too much of the man."[21] Grant's Virginia plans instead violated Lincoln's essential strategic maxims: defend Washington, confront and crush Lee in the open with more men, and avoid strategy. "One looks in vain for the unimaginative slugger and butcher" of legend, Brooks Simpson observed of Grant's rejected proposals. The general here advocated "a war of maneuver." It was Lincoln who come spring would demand "bloody attrition."[22]

Halleck treaded lightly in his responses to Grant, however, because he saw the proverbial writing on the wall: Grant was about to become his boss. In December 1863 Illinois Senator Elihu B. Washburne had announced that he would introduce a bill reviving the rank of lieutenant general. It would trample on the president's right to appoint generals, but he hoped that it would dissuade those who wanted to nominate Grant for the presidency while also dehorning Halleck. Lincoln, eager for reelection in 1864 despite his many woes, refused to support the bill until he received Grant's pledge that he had no presidential ambitions. Once assured that Grant was no rival, he not only gave his imprimatur but let it be known that he would appoint Grant to be the new general in chief. Grant arrived in Washington on March 8, 1864, and met Lincoln the night before his commissioning. Formalities out of the way, Grant traveled to meet Meade. Much to Meade's surprise, as Grant had brought Baldy Smith along with him, the new general in chief decided to leave him in command. Grant eventually decided that he would ride with the Army of the Potomac too, avoiding Washington and its political atmosphere.

Unlike McClellan, whom he had distrusted, Lincoln allowed this general in chief to command from the field. Halleck happily became U.S. Army chief of staff in Washington, acting as Grant and Lincoln's go-between, while the western command went to Sherman.[23]

"The long search was over," historian Kenneth Williams wrote at the end of volume two of *Lincoln Finds a General.* Quoting William O. Stoddard, he went on, "within a few weeks, Lincoln would remark, 'Grant is the first General I have had.'"[24] The actual situation was much more complicated.

Stoddard's full passage amplified Lincoln's often-expressed views on his role of commander in chief. After the president's exclamation, Stoddard continued:

> That is a curious remark for him to make, when you know how high has been his opinion of Mc-Clellan, and Burnside, and Hooker, and Meade. "How do you mean, Mr. Lincoln?" "Well, I'll tell you what I mean. You know how it's been with all the rest. As soon as I put a man in command of the army, he'd come to me with a plan of campaign and about as much as say, 'Now, I don't believe I can do it, but if you say so I'll try it on'; and so put the responsibility of success or failure on me. They all wanted me to be the general. Now it isn't so with Grant. He hasn't told me what his plans are. I don't know, and I don't want to know. I'm glad to find a man who can go ahead without me."[25]

Grant remembered similar sentiments expressed. As usual with his top generals, Lincoln initially pleaded a lack of military knowledge and unwillingness to intrude. "In my first interview with Mr. Lincoln alone," Grant wrote in his memoirs, "he stated to me that he had never professed to be a military man or to know how campaigns should be conducted, and never wanted to interfere in them." Only the public and "procrastination on the part of commanders" had induced him to do so. "All he wanted or had ever wanted," the president assured him, "was some one who would take the responsibility and act, and call on him for all the assistance needed, pledging himself to use all the power of the government in rendering such assistance"[26]

The rub was that immediately—and tellingly—Lincoln completely contradicted himself. Truly unaware of Grant's plans—insisting that he did not want to know them—Lincoln whipped out "a plan of campaign of his own which he wanted me to hear and then do as I pleased about. He brought out a map of Virginia on which he had evidently marked every position occupied by the Federal and Confederate armies up to that time." It essentially was the old plan that he had presented to Burnside before Fredericksburg, which itself was a mere variation of the Occoquan Plan of late 1861. Lincoln's pride in his ideas and dogged tenacity in proposing them again and again to his generals are striking. In a way, he did "want to be the general." But Grant was not interested in it any more than McClellan or Burnside had been. He, too, found the plan flawed. "I listened respectfully," he continued, "but did not suggest that the same streams would protect Lee's flanks while he was shutting us up." Grant said nothing to Lincoln about his own plans either because both Stanton and Halleck had warned him that the president was a security risk who "was so kind-hearted, so averse to refusing anything asked of him, that some friend would be sure to get from him all he knew"—McClellan once had said the same thing.[27]

As several commentators later noted, both Stoddard's recollections and Grant's memoirs—the latter written as the general was dying—sometimes seem unreliable. If Lincoln did indeed give Grant "carte blanche," to quote Michael Burlingame, he surely withdrew it as soon as the general presented his fourth operational plan. This one was more realistic in that it was thoroughly Lincolnian, unlike the previous efforts. Grant had learned the essential lesson. Now, while Meade went overland at Lee, shielding Washington, Federal forces in the Shenandoah Valley currently commanded by Maj. Gen. Franz Sigel and on the Peninsula by Maj. Gen. Benjamin Butler would harass Lee's supply lines, flanks, and rear. At the same time Sherman would move against the Confederates in Georgia, now commanded by Gen. Joe Johnston. Banks would take Shreveport and then turn around to move on Mobile. Concentration in time would overwhelm the enemy.[28] Lincoln expressed delight with most of it. The plan was what he had wanted all along, he told Hay, as it "powerfully reminded" him of his own "old suggestion so constantly made and constantly neglected, to Buell & Halleck et al. to move at once upon the enemy's whole line so as to bring into action our advantage our great superiority in numbers." He greeted with "especial pleasure" Grant's determination to "make all the line useful—those not fighting could help the fighting." Lincoln reiterated that "those not skinning can hold a leg."[29]

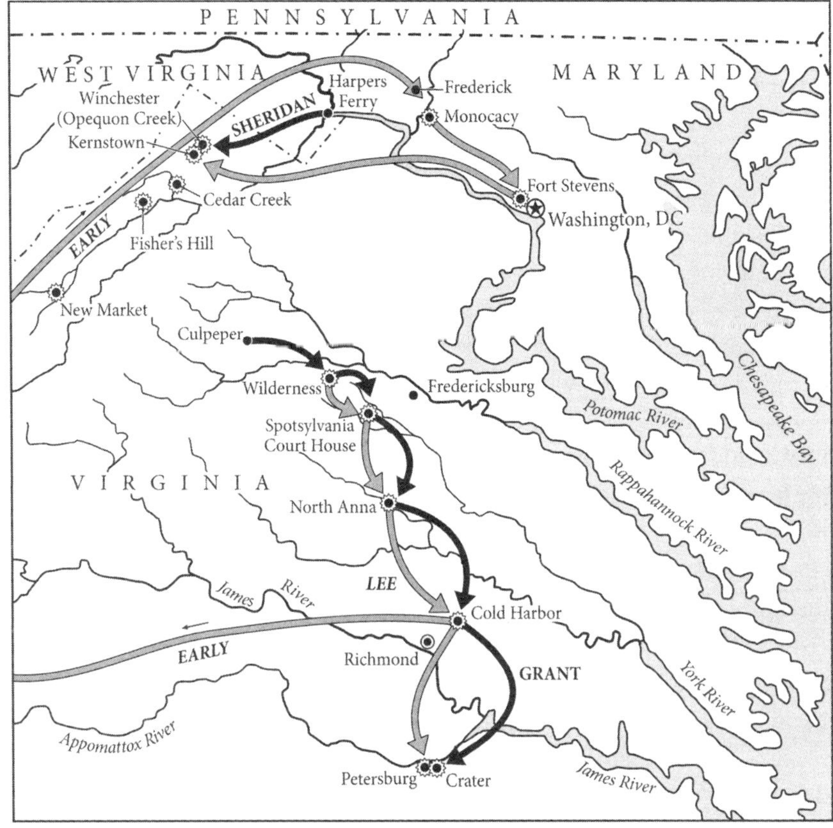

Overland and Valley Campaigns, 1864.

Yet the president forced concessions from Grant, too, reshaping his planned operations in many ways. He balked at removing the inept Banks and Sigel from command, as Grant wanted, for they still commanded powerful political constituencies. He asked the general in chief to give positions to others with political connections while continuing to doubt the loyalty of some officers in the Army of the Potomac who had survived reassignment elsewhere. The congressional Joint Committee on the Conduct of the War encouraged Lincoln's thinking in this regard. More fundamentally, he redirected Banks away from Mobile and toward Texas after taking Shreveport. Rosecrans retained his new command in Missouri despite Grant's concerns. Lincoln further expected daily updates from the field. "Grant would not be left alone," Brooks Simpson observed. "Washington in general and Lincoln in particular would always be looking over his shoulder," just as it had every other Potomac general. He had to "win early enough and often enough to meet the demands of the election year calendar." But the general took his measure of the president as well. As Simpson added, Grant was wary of how Lincoln had treated McClellan and Meade, and he made sure to nurture his relationship with the president. Lincoln clearly required careful handling, which included refraining from any criticism. He sent an unctuous letter to him on the eve of battle. At the same time, Grant finally stopped subordinates from running to the White House's open door with their complaints. With permission from his civilian superiors, he consolidated the cavalry in the East under protegee Maj. Gen. Philip Sheridan, and he persuaded Lincoln to overrule Stanton and release garrisons in the rear (including Washington) for frontline service. The general who once pleased Lincoln by never asking for reinforcements now did just that—and received them.[30]

As impatient to act as Lincoln, Grant wanted to get started in late April, but spring Virginia weather delayed him until May 4, when Meade's army crossed the Rapidan River northwest of Chancellorsville. Three days later Sherman attacked Johnston's entrenchments in North Georgia on Rocky Face Ridge. Over the next six weeks, the Army of the Potomac battered Lee, pushing him south to positions east of Richmond that McClellan had abandoned two years earlier. Allowing Meade to direct his army at first, a frustrated Grant increasingly took de facto control of operations. The Overland Campaign ultimately reflected what Lincoln had wanted for years. The fighting was relentless, almost daily, and bloody. Lee was a wilier opponent than Grant expected, however, refusing to let him maneuver the Confederates into the open for a death blow. A war of attrition followed, by Lee's choice as much as Lincoln's. By mid-June, Grant had suffered 65,000 casualties, culminating with a bloodbath at Cold Harbor on June 3. As James McPherson noted, this amounted to roughly half of the casualties that the Army of the Potomac had taken in the entire war to that time. Little went as planned either elsewhere in Virginia, as both Butler and Sigel fought just as poorly as Grant feared. Banks floundered as well in northern Louisiana and never reached Texas. In Georgia Sherman made progress, but even he had to lay siege to Atlanta in late July after a series of equally murderous contests.[31]

For Lincoln, a reelection campaign that opened with such hope was fast becoming another military and political disaster. Despite War Department censorship, casualty numbers got out. Critics including Mary Lincoln assailed Grant as a "butcher . . . not fit to be at the head of the army." Gold prices soared, the Copperheads rebounded, and at the opposite end of the political spectrum some Radicals moved to dump Lincoln at the upcoming Republican national convention. Their attempt failed thanks to a combination of loyalty and the president's skillful use of patronage, but volunteering for the military cratered so badly that in July Lincoln called for another half-million men, despite warnings that it would wreck his reelection hopes. Once again unable to sleep for days at a time, he was bent and exhausted during the day and given to occasional anguished outbursts and near-constant anxiety. The sights of wounded men streaming into Washington each day especially sickened and stunned him.[32] When he met former Illinois Congressman and old friend Isaac Arnold on the road at the end of a long line of ambulances, Lincoln exclaimed: "Look yonder at those poor fellows. I cannot bear it. This suffering, this loss of life, is dreadful."[33]

Lincoln had brooded privately on his part in the national slaughter since Second Bull Run and Antietam, but now in 1864 he increasingly began looking to the Bible for solace. Perhaps he was merely a tool in God's great purpose, he hoped, and not the architect of such death. The Confederates had started the war, after all, not him. Yet he continued to ache at what his warmaking vision had helped bring about as the capital's hospitals filled up. "Doesn't it seem strange to you that I should be here?" he asked another congressman. "Doesn't it strike you as queer that I, who couldn't cut the head off of a chicken, and who was sick at the sight of blood, should be cast into the middle of a great war, with blood flowing all about me?"[34]

Nonetheless, Lincoln stuck with Grant, the blood, and the "hard, tough fighting" he had wanted. Grant did not retreat after his first encounter with Lee. He kept moving, pushing, and attacking. Grant's declaration on May 11 that he was prepared to "fight it out on this line if it takes all summer" thrilled Lincoln, even after the general abandoned that line and flanked to the south. After securing renomination from the so-called National Union Party—it comprised the vast majority of Republicans and some War Democrats—Lincoln called for yet another half-million recruits. On May 20 he visited Grant to offer his personal support. As the fighting dragged on to Cold Harbor, he unironically tried to minimize others' impatience.[35] Lincoln asked Noah Brooks to report "that we are to-day farther ahead than I thought, one year and a half ago, that we should be; and yet there are plenty of people who believe that the war is about to be substantially closed. As God is my judge, I shall be satisfied if we are over with the fight in Virginia within a year."[36]

Stymied east of Richmond, Grant took the Army of the Potomac across the James River to strike at Petersburg and its vital railroad junction, seeking to cut off Lee's communications to the south. Not only was it a reversion to his original operational ideas of the previous winter, as David Donald noted, but it also resembled very much what McClellan had proposed after the Seven Days. In addition, it actually left Lee between the army and Washington, which previously had been anathema to Lincoln. Halleck fumed, but the president said nothing, trusting Grant for the moment. The initial movement, starting on June 14, surprised Lee, but stubborn Confederate resistance plus extreme heat and worn-out attackers checked attempts to take Petersburg.[37] When Lincoln visited Grant again on June 21, staff officer Horace Porter described the president in his black suit as looking like a "boss undertaker."[38] Grant looked for a new way to break Lee's lines, conscious that any long lull might allow his opponent to shift men to Georgia. The attempt to explode a passage through Confederate fortifications on July 30, however, ended in a crater full of death and unmitigated disaster for the Federals.[39]

Just as bad were events in the Shenandoah Valley. In mid-June Lee had sent Lt. Gen. Jubal Early and 14,000 men there. Defeated at Lynchburg, Maj. Gen. David Hunter (who had replaced Sigel) retreated into West Virginia rather than back down the Valley, leaving the road north wide open. Early quickly took advantage, crossed the Potomac on July 6, and defeated a small but dogged force at the Monocacy River in Maryland on July 9. Delayed by this Federal resistance and the blistering heat, Early headed straight for a Washington largely stripped of troops sent to Grant. In the middle of a bitter fight with Radicals over Reconstruction, not to mention the Peace Democrats' resurgence and a widening war weariness, Lincoln reacted predictably. With the main army now south of the James, Grant had left both him and Washington exposed and vulnerable. Lincoln foresaw absolute political disaster if Early entered the capital or Baltimore. He also stressed the opportunity presented to destroy a detached part of Lee's army north of the Potomac. Yet the president clearly was unhappy with his general in chief for letting this happen in the first place. When Grant assured Halleck that there still were enough men there to protect the capital, just as McClellan once had said, Lincoln replied bitterly and incorrectly that there were only "hundred-day men, and invalids" beyond the 8,000 unreliable men at Harpers Ferry. He first suggested and then ordered Grant to bring most of the Army of the Potomac north. Grant instead dispatched one corps and part of another to meet the president's wishes, but he drew the line at abandoning Petersburg entirely. The new men arrived in Washington just in time to help ward off Early's assaults on hot and dusty July 11 and July 12, as the exhilarated president from the city's defenses watched his first battle under fire. The Confederates escaped when ineffective local military leadership failed to pursue them, and Lincoln refused to order the chase. Early had not taken Washington, but he fueled a crisis of will in the North that saw many longing for peace. Lincoln's reelection now seemed more unlikely than ever. Stanton and Halleck blamed Grant for this. When Early began terrorizing Maryland and Pennsylvania towns, they pressured him to respond. The general in chief proposed combining the troops around Washington but argued with Lincoln about who would command. Rejecting Grant's fascinating recommendations of McClellan (who remained on the sidelines but was on track to be the Democratic presidential nominee), Franklin, or Meade, they reluctantly agreed on Sheridan, then commander of the Army of the Potomac's Cavalry Corps.[40] Grant told Sheridan to "give the enemy no rest," follow Early "to the death," destroy crops and the railroad in the Shenandoah, "carry off stock of all descriptions, and Negroes so as to prevent further planting," and turn the Valley into "a barren waste."[41]

Lincoln had embraced hard war by 1864 and had no qualms about his generals' gravitation toward scorched earth, but he did worry that Halleck would continue to muck up things. "He had before this remarked," Nicolay and Hay remembered, "with pain and disappointment, a tendency in General Halleck to shrink from the exercise of authority in emergencies, and to throw upon himself or Grant the burden of all important decisions. He saw . . . that if he did not interfere the campaign would be lost by hesitation and delay. In violation, therefore, of all official etiquette, and, as some critics think, of propriety," Lincoln telegraphed Grant on August 3.[42]

> I have seen your dispatch in which you say "I want Sheridan put in command of all the troops in the field, with instructions to put himself South of the enemy, and follow him to the death. Wherever the enemy goes, let our troops go also." This, I think, is exactly right, as to how our forces

> should move. But please look over the despatches you may have receved from here, even since you made that order, and discover, if you can, that there is any idea in the head of any one here, of "putting our army *South* of the enemy" or of following "him to the *death*" in any direction. I repeat to you it will neither be done nor attempted unless you watch it every day, and hour, and force it.[43]

At Petersburg Grant settled down to a long siege. Lincoln knew the risks, but he stuck with him despite opposition from Halleck and the cabinet. Grant was his man, and he had little choice otherwise. "I have seen your dispatch expressing your unwillingness to break your hold where you are," he wrote succinctly on August 17. "Neither am I willing. Hold on with a bull-dog grip, and chew & choke, as much as possible."[44] Nicolay found the president "patient, plucky and confident."[45] Other evidence, however, points to his fading hopes of reelection. Lincoln played along with Horace Greeley's plan to broach peace talks with Richmond, only to be embarrassed when Confederates released a letter he had written that seemed intended to make negotiations impossible. He enlisted Frederick Douglass in a scheme to spread the Emancipation Proclamation behind Confederate lines and free as many of the enslaved as he could before McClellan's March 1865 inauguration.[46] In the secret "Blind Memorandum" of August 23, a weary Lincoln wrote: "This morning, as for some days past, it seems exceedingly probable that this Administration will not be re-elected. Then it will be my duty to so co-operate with the President elect as to save the Union between the election and the inauguration; as he will have secured his election on such ground that he can not possibly save it afterwards."[47]

Lincoln could not know when he wrote those dire words that his fortunes were about to rise from the pit. On that same August 23, a joint operation under Admiral Farragut secured full control of Mobile Bay after nearly three weeks of fighting. While Confederates still held the city, its value as a port ended. McClellan secured the Democratic presidential nomination on August 31, just as a fourth battle for control of Atlanta was erupting near Jonesboro. Defeated yet again, the Confederates fled. Sherman occupied the city on September 2. Union morale rebounded while mass celebrations broke out across the North.[48] McClellan now hesitated to respond to the convention. Lincoln, "with a characteristic twinkle of the eye," joked to Dana and another visitor, "Oh! . . . '*he is intrenching*.'"[49]

Six days later, with Atlanta still in mind, McClellan formally accepted his nomination while disavowing the suddenly embarrassing planks of his party's platform inserted by Copperheads. Refusing to describe the war as a failure—a potential disaster for gaining soldiers' votes—or to countenance an immediate and unconditional armistice, Little Mac demanded the restoration of the Union as his price. Confusion and a divided party followed.[50] Nicolay noted with glee how War Democrats despised the "surrender platform." He added a few days later, "the political situation has not been as hopeful for six months past as it is just now. There is a perfect revolution in feeling."[51] Lincoln, meanwhile, had Grant lean on Sheridan to negate the threat posed by Confederates in the Shenandoah Valley. Sheridan defeated Early at Winchester on September 19, at Fisher's Hill three days later, and then again in spectacular fashion at Cedar Creek a month later. Most of the Valley was tamed at last.[52]

Thrilling battlefield victories and Democratic missteps altered the national mood. Lincoln began to think that he could win a close election. But the administration left little to chance. It saw a potential well of support in uniform. After the 1862 elections, nineteen states enacted laws permitting absentee voting in some form. Six others, however, still required that voters appear in person at their local polls. To save the nation from McClellan and the Copperheads, Lincoln wanted the soldier vote. The administration could be heavy-handed to get it. It pressured generals, including Grant and a wary Sherman, to grant leaves of absence and furlough probable Republicans from their active fronts so that they could go home to cast ballots. Lincoln asked Welles to allow a delegation from New York to collect votes from the Mississippi Squadron. Stanton drove a few dozen Democrats from the army and the War Department while interrupting the flow of pro-McClellan literature into camps. In the field Republicans openly electioneered for Lincoln and sometimes intimidated Democrats into silence. A few Democrats stood court-martial. In the end, 78 percent of men in uniform—at least those from the states that counted them separately—voted for Lincoln's Union Party. Most voted their conscience for Lincoln and the Union, and many eagerly supported emancipation after their exposure to the ugly realities of slavery. Ongoing Republican-Union coercion of Democrats inflated the tally as well, although historians disagree on whether such tactics were widespread or statistically significant. Lincoln won reelection on a generally rainy November 14 with 212 electoral votes to McClellan's 21, receiving about 55 percent of the total vote. The soldier vote did not sway the election, but it did give Lincoln razor-thin margins in Connecticut and New York.[53]

As Brooks Simpson observed, the 1864 elections freed Grant from worrying about politics or, to an extent, Lincoln. The ramifications soon became apparent. He began to challenge the president openly and with increasing success. In October Sherman requested permission to let Gen. John Bell Hood's Army of Tennessee, moving northward toward Tennessee, escape without a fight. Once reinforced, he argued, Federal forces in that state had enough men to deal with Hood. Instead, he wanted to cut across Georgia to the sea, breaking the state's will to keep fighting and sending a message to the rest of the Confederacy and the world. Sherman's plan violated two of Lincoln's main precepts: finding the enemy army to destroy it and protecting East Tennessee. The president further worried that Sherman would get into deep trouble. Grant was not convinced either, but he trusted the general enough to persuade the president to approve the plan after the October ballots went in his favor. Sherman left Atlanta a week after the election and seemingly disappeared. Lincoln remained disquieted about his army's progress until Sherman reemerged and occupied Savannah a month later.[54]

Lincoln expressed no more reservations about Sherman's tactics on the March to the Sea than he did about Grant or Sheridan's burnings in the Valley. "When you were about leaving Atlanta for the Atlantic coast," a chastened Lincoln replied, "I was *anxious,* if not fearful; but feeling that you were the better judge, and remembering that 'nothing risked, nothing gained,' I did not interfere. Now, the undertaking being a success, the honor is all yours, for I believe none of us went farther than to acquiesce. . . . But what next? I suppose it will be safer if I leave General Grant and yourself to decide."[55] Swayed by Sherman's rosy estimate of the time required and unfettered by the president, Grant let him march toward Petersburg through the miry Carolinas rather than ship his army to Virginia by sea, which in the end prevented their junction before the war ended.[56]

In his telegram to Sherman, Lincoln referred to another triumph, this one in Tennessee. There, General Thomas had smashed Hood at Nashville a few days earlier. Together, Thomas and Sherman had made "a great success" in the West.[57] The events leading to that Tennessee triumph, however, were fraught with tension. On November 30 Hood attacked part of the Federal forces defending the state at Franklin, south of Nashville. Despite massive casualties, the Confederate commander quixotically marched on toward the state capital. As James McPherson has pointed out, Lincoln saw Hood's invasion as a raid eerily similar to Early's. He pressed Grant to make Thomas leave his works and fight. Stanton, too, decried Thomas's alleged McClellan-like tendencies to wait and make excuses. Grant shocked them both, however, when he moved to fire Thomas, whom he had disliked since Chattanooga. Lincoln wanted no part of that; he appreciated Thomas as a soldier and as a southern Unionist. He did his best to dissuade the general in chief, and failed. Grant sent Maj. Gen. John Logan to relieve Thomas if he had not attacked by his arrival. Thomas saved himself at the last minute with a decisive victory amid cold and ice in December.[58] Relating a tall tale about a man from Illinois named Slocum and his once-fierce dog, Lincoln told Noah Brooks: "Hood's army was a good army. We have been very much afraid of it. But, as an army, I reckon its usefulness is gone."[59]

Lincoln and Grant butted heads yet again about Ben Butler. Fort Fisher, near Wilmington, North Carolina, protected the Confederacy's last connection to the outside world. Both Welles and Grant wanted it taken. Grant put together a joint army-navy expedition involving Admiral Porter. Lincoln had wanted Maj. Gen. Quincy Gillmore to lead the army component, but he agreed to let Grant choose Maj. Gen. Godfrey Weitzel instead. Then Butler pulled rank and demanded to command himself. He also proposed the odd idea of loading a ship with explosives and setting it off near the fort to breach its walls. Grant through the idea and Butler both ridiculous, but Lincoln and Porter loved it. Grant was proved right; exploding the ship accomplished nothing. Butler landed his troops afterward on Christmas morning only to give up early and retire. That was enough for Grant, who finally was able to convince Lincoln to let him fire the politically imposing Butler. Only Welles prevented Grant from getting rid of Porter too. Two weeks later a second assault succeeded, and Fort Fisher fell.[60]

While Sherman had marched, Thomas had fought, and Butler had wavered, Grant pursued the Richmond-Petersburg siege. After the Battle of the Crater on July 30, he began extending his entrenchments first to the south and then west. Grant and Meade's soldiers fought nine named battles and countless skirmishes as they sought to cut the three major railroads and additional byways that ran into Petersburg, all the while keeping pressure on Richmond. Lee's increasingly thin army had to match every move. A harsh winter called a halt to major fighting. Grant waited for spring's dry roads and Sheridan's return from the Valley. In mid-December 1864 Lincoln issued yet another call for volunteers, 300,000 more this time. Then in mid-February 1865 Grant resumed operations.[61]

On March 24 Lincoln and his entourage arrived at Grant's massive supply base at City Point at the general's invitation. Grant thought the trip away from Washington might do the president's health good. Already thin, Lincoln had lost more weight that winter to the point of looking cadaverous. He ate less than ever and struck observers as nervous, worn down, and prematurely aged, with deep wrinkles and graying hair. His second inauguration had wearied him, as was apparent in his soaring jeremiad of an address and especially his assertion that the war's end was in God's hands, not his, and could well go on indefinitely. At least as burdensome was a public scandal involving two well-connected naval contractors. Lincoln took to his bed in mid-March after the inaugural and chaired cabinet meetings in his bedroom. The trip south cheered him, however, despite a fatiguing fever he developed en route. Lincoln arrived at City Point with his maps, eager to make sense of his generals' dispatches. Then the next day, before a planned presidential review of the troops could begin, Lee struck Fort Stedman in the Federal line, preparatory to a breakout and escape. The Federals regained the position and closed up their lines after vicious fighting that left over 5,000 casualties.[62]

Grant would not allow the president to watch the fighting, but the next day he took him to the battlefield, first by train and then on horseback. Traveling with Lincoln, naval Capt. John S. Barnes recalled "great numbers of dead . . . with burial parties at their dreadful work. Many Confederate wounded were still lying on the ground. . . . We passed by two thousand rebel prisoners of war, herded together, who had been captured within our lines only a few hours before. Mr. Lincoln remarked upon their sad and unhappy condition." The president previously had seen battlefields days and weeks after the fighting, notably at Antietam and Fredericksburg, but had observed nothing so immediate and so gruesome as Fort Stedman. He was "quiet and observant," Barnes remembered, "making few comments, and listened to explanations in a cool, collected manner, betraying no excitement, but his whole face showing sympathetic feeling for the suffering about him." The train back was packed with the wounded. "Mr. Lincoln looked worn

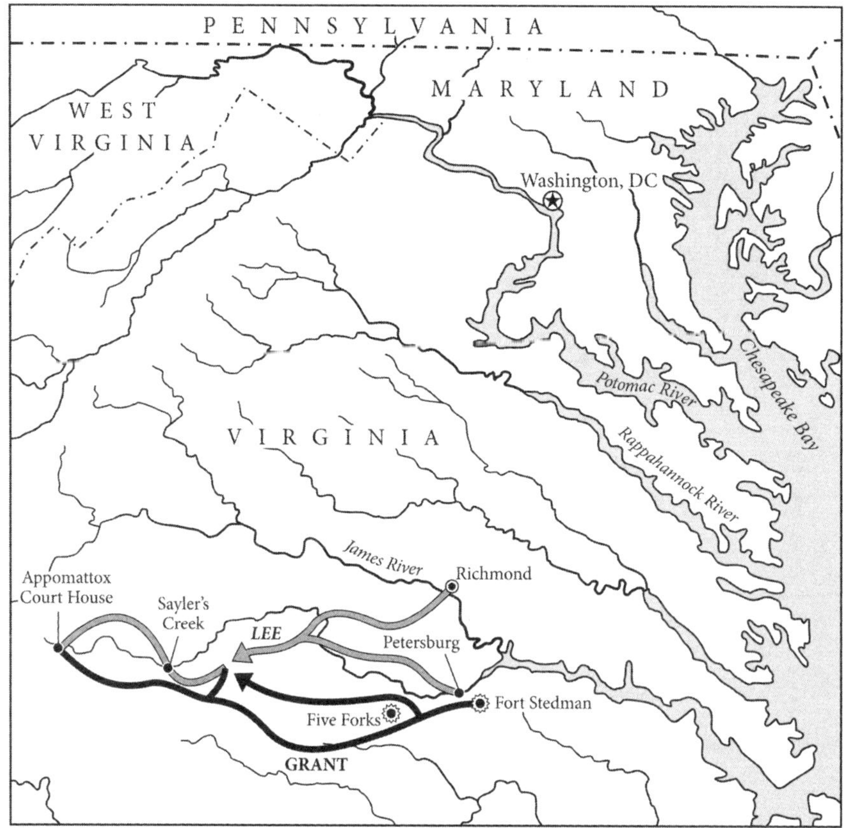

Appomattox Campaign, 1865.

and haggard." Barnes continued. "He remarked that he had seen enough of the horrors of war, that he hoped this was the beginning of the end, and that there would be no more bloodshed or ruin of homes." The captain also recalled a dying "little red-headed boy" in Confederate uniform wailing for his mother. "Mr. Lincoln's eyes filled with tears and his voice was choked with emotion, and he repeated the well-known expression about 'robbing the cradle and the grave.' . . . Mr. Lincoln, overcome by the excitement and events of the day, desired to rest . . . and, declining the invitation to take supper at General Grant's headquarters, saw no one again that evening."[63]

The horribly tragic sights of Fort Stedman shook Lincoln. At no point in the war had he seen so much fresh gore and pain. Now he seemed more desperate than ever for the end of the war, to be followed by a generous peace that nonetheless had to include abolition and the restoration of the nation. Observers continued to describe him as worn out, alternately upbeat and downcast. But his confidence in himself as a tactician had not waned. Admiral Porter recalled Lincoln often pulling a well-marked map from his pocket to indicate what he would do were he in command. When Sherman arrived, he met Lincoln, Grant, and Porter. Afraid that the Confederates might slip their grasp yet again, as he had seen so many times before, Lincoln now wanted to know his generals' plans for achieving that final victory. He recoiled from more killing, more Fort Stedmans. Grant was reticent, still unwilling to divulge his plans to the president, but more fighting lay in the offing, he said.[64] "Mr. Lincoln exclaimed, more than once," Sherman later remembered, "that there had been enough blood shed, and asked us if another battle could be avoided."[65]

On March 29 Grant opened his final campaign. Maj. Gen. Horatio Wright's corps finally broke through the Confederate lines on April 2. Lee had no choice but to flee to the west. "Thank God . . . that I have lived to see this!" Lincoln exclaimed. "It seems to me that I have been dreaming a horrid dream for four years, and now the nightmare is gone."[66] With part of the Army of the Potomac pressing Lee and the rest sweeping ahead, the end seemed near. On April 4 Lincoln arrived in Richmond, where he met Grant and Porter. The president was thankful, as were the many formerly enslaved who gathered joyously to see him. Back at City Point, Lincoln sent a steady stream of blow-by-blow telegrams to Washington, while unusually obsessing about three hungry and motherless kittens he discovered in the telegraph hut.[67] He telegraphed Grant on April 8: "Gen. Sheridan says 'If the thing is pressed I think that Lee will surrender.' Let the *thing* be pressed."[68]

Grant's forces corralled Lee at Appomattox Court House on April 8. The next morning, Palm Sunday, Lincoln returned to Washington as Lee surrendered. Lincoln was overjoyed when he heard the news. He disclaimed any part in the final triumph and joked at how Grant had again rejected his military advice. On April 14, the fourth anniversary of the firing on Fort Sumter, reunion was the main topic at a cabinet meeting. Lincoln again advocated an easy peace, praising Lee and his men. He also wondered if there was news from North Carolina, where Sherman remained in the field. The war was not over, yet Lincoln did not worry.[69] According to Secretary Welles, he told the cabinet that he had a dream the previous night, calling it "the usual dream which he had preceding nearly every great and important event of the War.

. . . He seemed to be in some singular, indescribable vessel," Welles continued, "and that he was moving with great rapidity towards an indefinite shore; that he had this dream preceding Sumter, Bull Run, Antietam, Gettysburg, Stone River, Vicksburg, Wilmington, etc." Grant, who was at the meeting, predictably downplayed his rival Rosecrans's triumph at Stones River. Lincoln ignored him. "'I had,' he remarked, 'this strange dream again last night, and we shall, judging from the past, have great news very soon. I think it must be from Sherman.'"[70]

Lincoln was happy at last. The end was close. He had endured. Although it was Good Friday, a day for churches and mourning, he decided to celebrate that drizzly night by attending a play at Ford's Theatre.

That wet night, Lincoln's hero journey moved on into the darkness, toward an "indefinite shore" of martyrdom and legend.[71] Now he belonged to the ages. His assassination on Good Friday, not a week after Lee's surrender, brought forth unprecedented tidal waves of shock and sorrow. Men and women, soldiers and civilians, wept for Father Abraham, searched for God's purpose in his death, and demanded the heads of those responsible. Churches shuddered with organs and lamentations on the day that became known as Black Easter. Schools and businesses shut their doors. Black drapery shrouded private and public buildings. Civilians donned their black clothing and mourning garb as well, collected relics, and committed to memory exactly where they were when they first heard the terrible news. In Washington 25,000 mourners viewed the president's remains. His funeral train back to Illinois, punctuated by additional solemnities across the northern states, prolonged the grief while spreading participation geographically, racially, and socioeconomically. An estimated one million mourners across the North bade Lincoln farewell before internment in Springfield. The dominant national mood rushed toward what Merrill Peterson termed Lincoln's "apotheosis." As these eulogies and rituals spread across the nation, sociologist Barry Schwartz observed, Lincoln became in memory a perfect man almost overnight. As John Sartain's popular print *Abraham Lincoln, the Martyr, Victorious* made clear visually, the president who never joined a church now surely resided in heaven with George Washington and the angels.[72]

Martyrs, as historian Wallace Hettle pointed out, always need "one or several mythmakers to recount the saga," for "martyrdom is a fundamentally literary act" that "reveals as much about the author as it does about the subject." The prominent Confederate Presbyterian theologian Robert Dabney, Hettle continued, recently had drawn upon John Bunyan's *Pilgrims Progress* (1678) and John Foxe's *Actes and Monuments* (1563) (later known as *Foxe's Book of Martyrs*) to pioneer the American notion that death in a Civil War uniform by itself counted as martyrdom.[73] Ironically given the author, that idea resounded doubly for Lincoln. His near-deification began in April 1865 and continued for decades, with portraits and monuments, the mass production of keepsakes and melodramatic folklore—what historian Harold Holzer called "a thriving industry of Lincoln reminiscence"—and hagiographic books and biographies featuring a larger-than-life and often devoutly Christian hero.[74]

Historian Benjamin Thomas later categorized the authors of such adoration as "idealists." Others, termed "realists," soon began to depict a Lincoln who was much more human and imperfect, usually with a focus on the pre-presidential years. Barry Schwartz referred to the same approaches respectively when depicting "the epic hero," as ultimately symbolized by the Lincoln Memorial, and the "the egalitarian hero," celebrated at the simple log cabin at the Lincoln birthplace. As a matter of course, Lincoln's actions as commander in chief more often drew the attention of the idealists, but their treatments were far from uniform. Indeed, most of them among Lincoln's contemporaries, soldiers and civilians alike, would reject much, if not all, of the heroic legend of Lincoln as commander in chief. As with Grant, the president had not convinced them of the military prowess that he sometimes played down in conversation yet clearly had seen in himself, at least if his actions and more private asides offer any guide. Convincing others beyond his inner circle now would require decades and the toil of devoted acolytes after the rifles fell silent and the man slipped into memory.[75]

President Lincoln in 1865. Photograph by Alexander Gardner, February 5, 1865, Philip & Solomons, Washington, DC. Prints and Photographs Division, Library of Congress.

President Lincoln and Maj. Gen. George B. McClellan at Antietam, 1862. Photograph by Alexander Gardner, October 3, 1862. Civil War Photographs, 1861–1865, Prints and Photographs Division, Library of Congress.

Allan Pinkerton, President Lincoln, and Maj. Gen. John A. McClernand at Antietam, 1862. Photograph by Alexander Gardner, October 3, 1862. Civil War Photographs, 1861–1865, Prints and Photographs Division, Library of Congress.

Abraham Lincoln, the Martyr, Victorious, 1866.
Engraving by John Sartain and W. H. Hermans. Alfred Whital Stern Collection of Lincolniana, Rare Book and Special Collections Division, Library of Congress.

John Nicolay, Abraham Lincoln, and John Hay, 1863.
Photograph by Alexander Gardner, November 8, 1863, Washington, DC.
Prints and Photographs Division, Library of Congress.

James G. Randall in his study, ca. 1935. Image 0003176, University of Illinois Archives, Urbana.

Sir Frederick Barton Maurice, ca. 1917. Photograph by Walter Stoneman. NPG x43776, © National Portrait Gallery, London.

Kenneth P. Williams, ca. 1917. Image P0052578, Indiana University Office of University Archives and Records Management, Bloomington.

T. Harry Williams on the cover of *Saturday Review,* February 23, 1952. Author's collection.

PART 2

MEMORY

HISTORIANS AND THE HEROIC LEGEND

5

LINCOLN MEN

Lincoln's Generation and the Heroic Legend at Bay, 1865–1911

WITH LINCOLN'S tragic death in April 1865, elements of the heroic legend began flowing from the White House into the general conversation about the assassinated president. But like the seeds sown in the biblical parable, those seeds of memory sometimes fell on stony ground and quickly withered, onto good ground and took root, or among thorns that choked them out. During the lives of Lincoln's contemporaries, all three scenarios were present. By the beginning of the twentieth century, however, despite the strenuous efforts of former White House secretaries John Hay and John Nicolay, thorns and stones largely surrounded their literary field.[1]

As early as the winter of 1863, historian Glenn LaFantasie has pointed out, the poet Walt Whitman had sketched out in a private letter the rough outlines of the heroic legend. It took the tragic events at Ford's Theatre, however, to bring them into public discussion. Henry J. Raymond, the staunch Republican Party leader who founded and edited the *New York Times,* rushed out the first of the post-assassination Lincoln biographies not long afterward. It set a pattern for the idealist Lincoln scholars to follow. Although an angry Lincoln had denied him a patronage job due to the *Times*'s criticism, Raymond greatly admired the president. Working quickly, he bookended his previously authorized 1864 campaign biography with fifty new pages of prewar biography, added chapters on the end of the war and the assassination, and provided a eulogy. Military affairs figured into both of Raymond's narratives, but Lincoln as commander in chief only appeared in the president's own words through a plethora of inserted letters, speeches, and proclamations, and in the author's discussion of Lincoln's impatience with McClellan. Raymond had chaired the National Union Party Executive Committee in 1864 and written the party platform, but he said little otherwise about presidential candidate McClellan, saving his real venom for rival editor and former employer Horace Greeley.[2]

The result was dry. Raymond's biography only came to life in an appendix, a previously published reminiscence by the artist Francis Bicknell Carpenter. In 1864 Carpenter spent six months in the White House working on his celebrated painting *First Reading of the Emancipation Proclamation of President Lincoln.* The artist soon published his own book, the first of the many White House–insider accounts to follow. Like Raymond, Carpenter stressed Lincoln's kindness and Christian compassion but not his generalship. His book was not the first personal reminiscence of Lincoln—at least one predated the assassination—but it heralded what Merrill Peterson called a "flood" of memoirs that lasted into the centennial of Lincoln's birth.[3]

Lincoln scholars usually dismiss Raymond's volume and the other early biographies that followed as little more than forgettable paeans, pseudoreligious tracts, and sources for anecdotes. Two of the early idealist treatments require more consideration and reevaluation, however, as they pointed toward the heroic legend to follow. The deeply devout novelist and editor Josiah Gilbert Holland wrote one of them. The founder of what later became *Century* magazine, he wrote in 1866 what later critics regarded as the best of the unctuous first lot of idealist biographies. Unlike Raymond, Holland did not rush out his narrative. Based in part on interviews he conducted in Springfield that included Lincoln's junior law partner, William Herndon, his massive *Life of Abraham Lincoln* took time but nonetheless sold well at publication. Lincoln in Holland's eyes was "the incarnation of power and goodness" to the freed people and died a martyr in a holy cause. With occasional Lincoln expressions of piety he created from whole cloth, Holland asserted that the unbaptized president's "was eminently a Christian administration . . . the finest exhibition of a Christian democracy the world has ever seen. . . . Mr. Lincoln will always be remembered as eminently a Christian President."[4] Holland's Lincoln, sociologist Barry Schwartz observed, was a biblical prophet.[5]

What scholars later neglected to note while wading through Holland's effusive hagiography was that he also made the earliest postwar case for Lincoln as a perfect commander in chief, at least when it came to Brian Dirck's later category of second-order warmaking. Military perfection was part and parcel of Holland's argument that Lincoln was God's chosen leader. He was not just a wise Solomon but a modern Joshua or Gideon. Lincoln put the nation on a war footing in 1861, moved prayerfully toward emancipation as "the will of God," overcame "pestilent" Copperheads and difficult generals, won the hearts of the army and the people, and preserved the nation. To make his case, Holland glossed over defeats, defended Lincoln's early reluctance to confront slavery, and explained that the president broached colonization schemes because "he loved the negro too well" to have them suffer prejudice in America. Meanwhile, his harsh treatment of McClellan, that power-hungry stumbling block to Providence's intentions, helped lay another foundation. "The difficulty was that he was great mainly in his infirmities," he wrote of McClellan. "He was not a great man, nor a great general. He was a good organizer of military force, and a good engineer; he was a good theorizer, and wrote good English; he had that quality of personal magnetism which drew the hearts of his soldiers to him; but he was not a man of action, of expedients, of quick judgment, of dash and daring, of great, heroic deeds. He was never ready."[6]

Isaac Arnold's early idealist effort also dealt significantly with Lincoln as commander in chief. A former Republican congressman from Chicago, Arnold was one of the president's closer friends and advisors going back to Illinois and before the war. Yet his *The History of Abraham Lincoln and the Overthrow of Slavery* was more of a general biography like Raymond's, cranked out quickly from secondary sources and additional correspondence with Herndon. It was as pious as Holland's treatment, too; at one juncture Arnold compared the Second Inaugural Address to the Sermon on the Mount. He also agreed with Holland that Lincoln's exercise of the war powers and curtailment of civil liberties were constitutional. He was even tougher on McClellan than Holland, describing the general as slow, timid, ungrateful, and the "most conspicuous failure of the war. . . . I have dwelt upon his campaigns, and lingered over the correspondence between him and the President," Arnold explained, "because in 1864 he was the opposing candidate for the presidency to Mr. Lincoln, and because I wished to exhibit truthfully, clearly and fully, the patience, the faithfulness and generosity with which he was supported by Mr. Lincoln." McClellan's greatest sin was that he was a Democrat.[7]

Arnold's Lincoln was also a successful commander in chief. And unlike Holland, he sometimes praised the president's first-order warmaking as well. Arnold's Lincoln was a born general. Discussing the Peninsula Campaign, for example, he wrote, "the dispatches of President Lincoln to the various military commanders exhibit great sagacity and natural military skill and judgment." Arnold made spurious claims that Lincoln planned Grant's Vicksburg Campaign, mentored the general, and helped draft the war's conclusion. Among Lincoln's many lasting accomplishments, "he was the Commander-in-Chief . . . of the largest army and navy in the world; and this army and navy was created during his administration, and its officers were sought out and appointed by him."[8]

By 1867, still in mourning, Holland and Arnold had sketched out an early, idealistic, and pious outline of Lincoln as the perfect commander in chief inspired by the Almighty. They also set a precedent of expressing their ideas through general histories of the war with Lincoln at the center. It was a false spring of the heroic legend, however. Their seeds sprouted in stony ground. By then, William Herndon had hijacked Lincoln biography.

There were always critics. For vastly different reasons, some former Copperheads, a few extreme Radicals wary of Lincoln's plans for an easy peace, and many southern whites all welcomed the news of Lincoln's death. Most of them laid low at first, unsure of what was next to come and often intimidated by rage-filled boys in blue.[9] In time, however, southern hatred of Lincoln became central to the myth of the Lost Cause. White women gathered in cemeteries to mourn and memorialize their dead by tending soldiers' graves and erecting markers. The end of Reconstruction opened the way to male participation in such remembrances. Ex-soldiers defended themselves in a "battle of the books." As men elbowed their way into memorialization, wrapped in the battle flag, they shaped the post-Reconstruction South around white supremacy and the alleged horrors of Reconstruction. Sometimes they openly linked white supremacy to their Confederate statuary. Some of them lied deliberately for personal or political gain. Gatekeepers appeared, such as former Lt. Gen. Jubal Early and his Southern Historical Society and in the next generation Mildred Rutherford and the United Daughters of the Confederacy. They crafted a canon of their own, determining what could be taught in schools while suppressing African American countermemories. Their collective negative portrait of Lincoln as a villainous tyrant, warmonger, and crude atheist who dispatched Sherman's torch-wielding vandals through Georgia became a crucial part of this Lost Cause.[10]

Indeed by the 1880s, the Lost Cause already had reached the point that many northerners such as Frederick Douglass saw it as an ideological threat to what Lincoln had accomplished. They worried as much about the related "reconciliationist vision" growing among their largely white northern neighbors, one that favored letting bygones be bygones while papering over the causes of the war, ignoring the freed people, getting on with business, and letting the South claim a moral victory. The Lost Cause "locked arms with reconciliationists" and agreed upon what historian David Blight called "a segregated memory of the Civil War on southern terms" that sometimes even included slighting and denigrating Lincoln.[11] Not every northerner favored sectional reconciliation. Historians Gary Gallagher, Barbara Gannon, and Caroline Janney, among others, have described many objections to reconciliationism, especially among Federal veterans who clung to what Gannon called "the Won Cause." African Americans themselves endorsed an "emancipationist vision" that put their freedom at the war's core. But there still were more than enough people who were ready to move on.[12]

One powerful reconciliationist directly took on the Holland-Arnold thesis that Lincoln was a masterful commander in chief who won the war. Lincoln's former minister to Great Britain, Charles Francis Adams, was the son and grandson of presidents. Many Americans credited him for keeping Europe out of the Civil War. Disillusioned by corruption in the Grant administration, however, in 1872 he joined the Liberal Republican splinter movement and supported the Democratic reconciliationist Greeley for president. A year later, in a eulogy for William Henry Seward, Adams proclaimed that Seward had saved the Union, not Lincoln. The president had been "a pure, brave, honest man, faithful to his arduous task," Adams admitted, but he was sadly out of his depth. "In the history of our Government down to this hour," he orated, "no experiment so rash has ever been made as that of elevating to the head of affairs a man with so little previous preparation for his task as Mr. Lincoln." Thankfully, Lincoln recognized that Seward was "a superior in native intellectual power, in extent of acquirement, in breadth of philosophical experience, and in the force of moral discipline." Seward in turn patriotically chose "self-abnegation. . . . in exchange for a more solid power to direct affairs for the benefit of the nation, through the name of another, who should yet appear in all later time to reap the honors due chiefly to his labors." Lincoln, in sum, was Seward's willing puppet, and thank goodness for it. Adams dismissed him as commander in chief altogether: "I am not going to touch upon the incidents of the great war. It is enough to say that Gettysburg and Vicksburg turned the tide; and the Administration had nothing more to fear from popular distrust."[13]

Worse still were those voices who challenged the apotheosis of Lincoln back home. Many of the president's old Whig friends in Illinois had soured on him due to his wartime policies, his unpopular widow, and especially what many deemed his stingy distribution of patronage. Some eventually became Liberal Republicans and Democrats just as Adams had. Ultimately, the most notorious apostate was Lincoln's "surrogate son," the eccentric bookworm and soapbox philosopher William Herndon. The prodigal son of a Southern Democrat, Herndon found in "Mr. Lincoln" his north star. Lincoln returned the friendship of "Billy," but he never regarded him as an equal. Especially wary of Herndon's hard drinking, the president-elect left him in Springfield in 1861. After the assassination, Herndon grew obsessed with collecting primary-source material for a biography. Holland and Arnold encouraged him. No one allegedly knew Lincoln better than he did. But Herndon envisioned something quite different than his correspondents, an honest warts-and-all biography that would explain a great man he also increasingly regarded as ambitious, calculating, prone to depression, and often cold—hardly the perfect Saint Abraham emerging in popular culture. Herndon read widely, sought documents, and conducted over 250 interviews with people who claimed to have known the president. Mary Lincoln even granted him an audience, despite their long mutual loathing. Lincoln's eldest son Robert, however, drew the line at allowing him access to his father's voluminous White House correspondence, over 18,000 items that executor David Davis had scooped up with help from Hay and Nicolay after Lincoln's death and locked up in an Illinois bank.[14]

Herndon was undaunted. Out of his interviews came material that would power both Lincoln folklore and modern scholarship to this day, not to mention immediately shifting the Lincoln debate from the war years to the period before 1860. Excited to reveal what he had found, Herndon launched a series of lectures in Springfield in December 1865. The first two received applause, including from Arnold. Carpenter liked the first speech so much that three years later he reprinted it in its entirety—initially without Herndon's permission—

in his new and chatty insider's account of the Lincoln White House. All went well until a fourth presentation in November 1866, when Herndon publicized his findings on New Salem's doomed Ann Rutledge and asserted that she—not Mary Todd—had been the love of Lincoln's life, her death being the key to his melancholy. The blowback was immediate. Widowed Mary Lincoln was outraged. Robert Lincoln, unwilling to see his family's laundry aired in public, tried to silence Herndon. Holland joined him in the fray, while Arnold blanched that such unseemly gossip might push the late president from his pedestal. Carpenter faced pressure to expunge the first speech from a retitled edition of his memoir. Others deemed Herndon's assertions to be indecent. According to the Lincolns' pastor, Herndon was worse than John Wilkes Booth. The *New York Herald* compared him to Judas.[15]

Shunned, cursed with writer's block, and short of cash, Herndon eventually sold copies of his research to another questionable member of Lincoln's circle, Falstaffian attorney and wartime bodyguard Ward Hill Lamon. Lamon's biography—it only ran through the first inauguration—appeared in 1872, fueled by Herndon's papers and oddly ghostwritten by a fiercely partisan Democrat named Chauncey Black. His father having served in Buchanan's cabinet, Black gloried in describing Lincoln's atheism, alleged illegitimacy, incapacity for friendship, bad marriage, and taste for bawdy stories. Although the book contained anecdotes that later became central to Lincoln lore, Black's caustic tone pleased no one except Lincoln haters. Here was proof, they crowed, that Lincoln was little more than poor white trash, a bastard, an atheist, and a smutty fool married to a shrew. Everyone else found the book shocking. Holland called it a national tragedy. Arnold and Orville Browning wrung their hands. Mary Lincoln's former pastor took to the lecture circuit to refute it. Hay, Nicolay, and the surviving Lincolns were incensed. They all blamed Herndon, who retreated into his bottle.[16]

Herndon, Lamon, and Black's "realist" approach nonetheless turned Lincoln biography away from the White House and back toward the prairie.[17] John Hay and John Nicolay eventually would respond for the idealists, but that took years to bear fruit. To be sure, both had mused about writing about the president since before Appomattox. Hay kept a diary, while Nicolay had kept documents, his letters to his future wife, and his notes. Much delayed their progress, however. Their ties to Lincoln brought major dividends. Both sailed to France after the war as diplomats. Nicolay returned after four years to run an Illinois newspaper, then in 1872 became marshal of the Supreme Court, a sinecure that he retained fifteen years. Hay was more directionless. He crisscrossed the Atlantic, accepting and resigning from both government and private positions. He worked for Greeley at the *New York Tribune,* becoming the first reporter to interview James O'Leary after his wife's cow allegedly burned down much of Chicago. He penned anti-Grant editorials for the Liberal Republicans when his employer Greeley headed the Democratic-Liberal Republican fusion ticket for president, published a travel book, and wrote poetry in Illinois dialect that won him praise from Mark Twain. Hay then married the daughter of an Ohio millionaire in 1874, assumed a modicum of duties for a hefty salary, and made friends among the American elite; Henry Adams, son of Charles Francis Adams, became the closest of them.[18]

Yet by the end of 1872, the growing anti-Lincoln chorus, the deaths of Salmon Chase and William Henry Seward, and the practical matter that both Nicolay and Hay had time to spare called them back to the projected biography. Hay, who according to a biographer never stopped mourning Lincoln, bristled at the "contemptible assertions and insinuations of Chas. Francis Adams in his eulogy" despite his brotherly bond with Adams's son. Lamon's biography positively reeked.[19] Outraged by it, some Lincoln supporters urged Nicolay and Hay to redress the wrong. Hay's uncle, Milton Hay, once Lincoln's law student, wrote Nicolay on Christmas Eve, 1872, that he was "glad to hear that you will resume your work on Lincoln. Lamon's abortive work, has in my opinion increased the necessity for something more satisfactory to the public." Lincoln "was the greatest figure in that revolutionary period that began with the defeat of the Missouri compromise," he continued. Upright people would not "bring into their family libraries, a Book which shall either depreciate Lincoln, or clothe him with heterodox religious views. They want a model for all the good little boys to follow, and Billy Herndon's model won't do."[20]

Writing such a book meant access to the Lincoln papers, however, and it took two years and the Lamon book to persuade Robert Lincoln to make them available. Massaging the president's son took regular effort and patience. Nicolay, for example, urged the younger Lincoln not to respond to Charles Francis Adams directly or release any documents to Seward's old rival Gideon Welles, who was writing a fierce rejoinder. Lincoln especially wanted to give Welles the memorandum of April 1, 1861, that demonstrated how Seward wanted to provoke a foreign war while wresting control of the administration. Nicolay objected vehemently. "Having chosen me as your father's biographer," he plead, "you must not cripple me at the very outset by giving my trump card to another player."[21] He further cautioned him to provide everything, including papers Lincoln's son kept in his office to show off or give away as souvenirs. Nicolay was "especially anxious—and I press this point particularly—that not a scrap of paper of any kind be destroyed" before he could get to Illinois, as "the only good rule," he concluded, "is to *save everything*."[22] Robert Lincoln finally relented. His father's papers arrived in Washington in July 1874, the boxes "still unopened and iron-bound."[23] No one else would see them again until after World War II.[24]

Yet another fifteen years passed before Nicolay and Hay completed the ten fat volumes of *Abraham Lincoln: A History*. They acquired a library of research material, divided the effort, put pen to paper, and edited each other. Unwilling to write a mere memoir or trust others' memories, they corresponded with participants in search of specifics but soon abandoned interviews entirely, a decision that in itself was a rebuttal to Herndon. The truth was in documents, yet their rooms full of paper became as much a curse as a blessing. Meanwhile, they fended off interlopers such as Arnold, who wanted their help to expand his book and to publish Lincoln's papers before they could.[25]

Nicolay and his wife Therena—the still unsung but vital third collaborator—diligently carried the heavier load until her death late in 1885. Hay, in contrast, worked on the book in fits and starts, given his frequent relocations, service as assistant secretary of state under President Rutherford Hayes, long vacations, extramarital infatuations, and illnesses that always cropped up when writing. Promising Nicolay that he would bear down at last, he promptly took several months off in 1882 to write an anonymous novel entitled *The Bread-Winners*, intending to vigorously defend industrialists like his father-in-law and himself against organized labor. And even Nicolay wandered off task. Tempted by an offer of $600, he devoted the second half of 1880 to slashing out *The Outbreak of the Rebellion* for a new twelve-volume history of the war published by Charles Scribner's Sons. A full-throated attack on Lost Causers and reconciliationists, it trumpeted what was stewing in Nicolay's library. Secession was treason. The word "conspiracy" and its variations appeared seventy-six times. President Lincoln had wanted peace but reacted to Fort Sumter constitutionally. First Bull Run's hard lessons led to victory in 1865.[26]

Both Hay and Nicolay judged *Outbreak of the Rebellion* to be fair, as did self-interested characters such as Gustavus Fox. "I had lost all faith in history till I received your book," former Maj. Gen. David Hunter wrote to Nicolay.[27] But not everyone was pleased. William Tecumseh Sherman adamantly refused to believe that Brig. Gen. Nathaniel Lyon dressed as a woman while reconnoitering secessionists in Missouri.[28] More predictably, the Lost Causers erupted. One English reviewer, quite possibly the pro-Confederate ex-parliamentarian A. J. B. Beresford Hope, complained that Nicolay wrote "in the language of a man who has learnt nothing and forgotten nothing, repeating all the nonsense about treason and conspiracy which at the outset of the conflict was in vogue among fanatical Federalists. . . . His misrepresentations of facts are as monstrous as his misuse of words."[29]

Even Hay admonished Nicolay after the negative reviews for *Outbreak of the Rebellion* that they had to avoid writing "a stump speech" dripping with what he called "the present tone of blubbering sentiment." Yet they never gave up their self-image as "Lincoln men."[30] That was impossible anyway, with Robert Lincoln hovering over their shoulders. The heir, according to historian David C. Mearns, "had given them monopoly in return for faithful and exacting service."[31] Nicolay repeatedly assured Lincoln of their fidelity; his father was their "ideal and hero." Nor were they now the "mere boys" the younger Lincoln had known in Washington.[32] Yet they submitted every word they wrote to him for editing, which became heavy-handed regarding the family. Robert Lincoln defended his grandfather more than his father ever did in life while also demanding a more positive depiction of the frontier. Hay and Nicolay soon began self-editing; anything that might trouble Lincoln had to go first. He also continued to ask for papers to defend his father, notably in 1878 when Nicolay strained to keep the younger Lincoln from debating George Meade's refusal to attack after Gettysburg.[33]

The years passed. Both men ruined their eyes in this task. Hay's frequent headaches and other ailments—his biographer suggests they were also psychosomatic reactions to a lucrative but loveless marriage—finally forced him to dictate his chapters. The more the two wrote, the longer the manuscript became. Nicolay, Hay complained privately, could not rein himself in. He even wondered if he would live to see the massive work finished. Yet with a Democrat in the White House for the first time since the Civil War and no hopes for a political appointment, Hay returned to the biography with seriousness in 1885. He moved back to Washington in part to finalize the manuscript with his widowed old friend and colleague.[34]

Rivals spurred on Nicolay and Hay. The twenty-fifth anniversary of Lincoln's election and the twentieth anniversary of his assassination were watersheds that brought forth three significant insider biographies. Arnold's long-expected book, accomplished in the end without the help from Hay and Nicolay he wanted, appeared to strong reviews. It added little that was new in information or interpretation to his older work, however. If anything, Arnold downplayed his earlier arguments about Lincoln as commander in chief.[35]

In stark contrast, William O. Stoddard's biography offered a bold depiction of a powerful strategic mind. Like Nicolay, Stoddard had edited an Illinois newspaper before the war and supported Lincoln's election, which gained him entry into the White House. Until mid-1864, when he departed for a position as a U.S. marshal in Arkansas, Stoddard was Hay and Nicolay's assistant and third secretary. He was in fact the often-shunned odd man out whose duties included handling extra paperwork, opening and sometimes shredding the mail, and dealing with Mary Lincoln. Mrs. Lincoln liked him, but Nicolay and Hay quietly disdained Stoddard as unreliable and too interested in trying to get rich on the stock market. After the war, he returned to journalism and became a prolific author of boys' books.[36]

In his *Abraham Lincoln,* Stoddard admitted his debt to Herndon and Lamon regarding his early chapters and announced that would "not even enter the field" that "his former office-associates, Messrs. John G. Nicolay and John Hay have preempted, . . . an exhaustive historical record of the 'life and times' of Mr. Lincoln" that was in preparation. Such praise did not mollify Hay and Nicolay, who expressed annoyance that the upstart former underling dared to compete with them openly and muddy the market for Lincoln books. Stoddard omitted details about battles and campaigns but otherwise followed the Arnold-Raymond model of Lincoln-centric war histories. Like them, he also depicted Lincoln as a near-perfect commander in chief and—with a word he used twenty times—a benevolent "dictator," in the positive sense of the Roman Republic, chosen by Providence and the people to save the nation before stepping aside. "It was needful for him to assume dictatorial authority," Stoddard argued at one juncture, "and the people tacitly expected of him that he should do so." Before Hay and Nicolay, it was he who first crafted the image of Lincoln the military student. The president created "the vast machinery of the new government"; studied maps and military science until "he knew every river, mountain-range, creek, hill, valley, on the broad areas through which the tides of the war were to ebb and flow"; embraced new technologies (often allegedly with Stoddard at his side); and knew more about war than his generals, especially McClellan. He built the Federal army and staffed the Army of the Potomac. The western armies counted for little in Stoddard's telling—McClellan appears twice as often as Grant—and he mentioned Vicksburg only three times.[37]

But there was a caveat. Lincoln may have been a supreme commander and visionary, but he was never an operational commander or a tactician, according to Stoddard. He pushed his generals to act decisively but always followed protocol and never mandated specific troop movements. "It has been said and printed that he 'disclaimed all military ability,'" Stoddard explained, "and it is true that he often spoke very modestly of his pretensions; but the necessity was upon him, and he continually and distinctly and from the beginning exercised the important functions of a military umpire. His decision was final in the plans and in their modifications as campaigns progressed." That was notably the case with Ambrose Burnside. "That [Lincoln] had earnestly insisted upon active operations was true. He had done that daily, from the outset; but he had not undertaken to direct details; and the inexcusable blunders of the Fredericksburg fight were committed without his knowledge."[38]

Another White House insider who began publishing Lincolniana, Noah Brooks, was yet another old rival of Hay and Nicolay. Few other men had been closer to the president during the war or spoken with him more often. Yet another small-town Illinois newspaper editor who gravitated toward Lincoln, Brooks moved first to Kansas and then to California but came back east as a war correspondent in November 1862 after his wife's death. He grew close to the Lincolns while filing 258 columns filled with admiration of the president. Like Stoddard, Brooks proved adept at cultivating and defending Mary Lincoln. She responded by urging her husband to replace Nicolay with Brooks, which he would have done had he lived. Hay and Nicolay despised Brooks as much as they did "Her Satanic Majesty," and their animus was warmly mutual.[39]

Two decades after the war, Brooks was a celebrated American newspaper editor and author of popular-magazine articles and—like Stoddard—boys' books. In 1888 he published a Lincoln biography for young people that found an appreciative adult audience that included Robert Lincoln. Acknowledging his research debt to Herndon and Lamon as well as to Arnold, Holland, Hay, and Nicolay, Brooks like Stoddard strove to establish his credentials as a close friend of Lincoln. Yet again he included few passages that suggest firsthand observation beyond discussions of the Lincolns in the White House. Like previous idealists, Brooks's biography was more of a general history of the era with the president as the central figure. His Lincoln was as pious as Holland's, a man of sorrows who was also invariably kind, gentle, generous, and anxious. As commander in chief—about half of the book covers the war years—Lincoln made the initial decision to meet force with force, outlined an overall strategy, and "strained his authority to the utmost to collect a force for the defence of the capital and to serve as a framework on which should be organized a large and aggressive fighting army." In contrast to Stoddard, however, Brooks described Lincoln as "a Western man" who from the first saw the importance of opening the Mississippi River, leading to Grant's later successes. He, too, picked up on the idea of the president as a self-educated military genius. "Lincoln," Brooks wrote, "with that insatiate desire to know all that man could know by hard study, read all the books on war and strategy that he could find, and speedily mastered all that these could teach him. Far into the night, when the ceaseless importunities of those who desired audience with him would allow him an hour or two of seclusion, he pored over books and maps, plans of battles and sieges, slowly absorbing the details of military science, as he had, in earlier years in the backwoods, grasped the parts of the various knowledge that he had made his own."[40]

Yet Lincoln did little with that great knowledge, if Brooks was to be believed. Aside from sometimes pushing McClellan to act, campaigns and battles happened with little direction from a passive president. The great tactician and general was nowhere to be found in Brooks's *Abraham Lincoln*. The narrative rang especially false to Hay, who caustically complained to Nicolay that an editor "wants a lot of the Noah Brooks rubbish, which of course we could invent by the ream just as Noah does. It is very readable, I suppose."[41]

Hesitant for years to contract their book too early, the "fair sale even of Stoddard's book" helped convince Hay and Nicolay at last to agree in 1885 to publish with *Century* magazine. The competition was becoming too fierce to wait any longer.[42] It was a curious choice on the surface. Founded by Josiah Holland, who died soon after, the journal passed to editor Richard Gilder, a Civil War veteran and Progressive New York urban reformer. He promptly rebaptized it in reconciliationism. The *Century* became home to the Old South plantation nostalgia of writers such as Thomas Nelson Page. It published works from northern luminaries as well, including the serialized version of Hay's *The Bread-Winners* in 1883, yet reconciliation remained the great theme. In 1884 the "Century War Series" began under the guidance of associate editors and fellow reconciliationists Richard Underwood Johnson and Clarence Buel. For the next four years, the luminaries of the war, including James Longstreet, Joe Johnston, McClellan, Grant, and Sherman, refought campaigns in return for handsome reimbursement. The editors studiously avoided anything divisive enough sectionally to dampen sales. Both sides had boasted heroic Americans, the *Century* suggested. The public loved it, and subscriptions nearly doubled. Published as *Battles and Leaders of the Civil War,* the essays became a successful (and still much-cited) four-volume book. The *Century* thus took control of Civil War memory while defanging, shaping, and commodifying it. Memory now had a price tag.[43]

Hay and Nicolay's biography had one, too. The diehard Unionists went with the arch-reconciliationist *Century* for the money. The publisher and editor wooed them with an open checkbook, offering the mammoth sum of $50,000—roughly $1.5 million today—for the serial rights plus book royalties. "We want your Life of Lincoln—we must have it," *Century* publisher Roswell Smith wrote Hay. "If you say so, I shall give you all the profits. We will take it & work it for nothing in order to start a subscription Book Business as we have in mind. . . . It is probably the most important literary venture of the time—or of the past twenty-five years."[44] Hay and Nicolay resisted for months, leery of serialization and an ambitious proposed timetable for completion. Finally, after months of negotiations and Gilder's week-long intrusion into Nicolay's New Hampshire vacation, the authors agreed to a book contract unmatched in American letters.[45]

The arrangement, however lucrative, was strained. *Century* wanted to delay publication until the completion of *Battles and Leaders,* which meant at least two years of serialization in the magazine. The authors, meanwhile, chafed against Gilder's reconciliationism, which fully revealed itself in his alarm over Nicolay's quip that Lee should have been shot for treason. Such "violent" language, the publisher warned, would hurt sales. Tempering their views only somewhat, Nicolay and Hay refused to depict any secessionist in even a dim heroic light. As in *Outbreak of the Rebellion,* secession was a traitorous conspiracy to them, slavery was the evil cause of a war, and African Americans helped win it. Hay happily waved the bloody shirt in public addresses. Their Unionism, hatred of men such as Lee, and readiness to defend Lincoln created repeated editorial conflicts.[46]

Their lack of military experience did not help matters. The associate editors, who had spent years reworking the memories of soldiers, found Nicolay and Hay's military history "somewhat inadequate" and devoid of new research—the authors had not read the Century War Series articles. Gilder suggested that they "cut all you can" or else let the *Century* do it.[47] More than once, Nicolay pushed back. He argued in mid-1887, for example, that his narrative of Fort Sumter was correct, and at any rate, "there is no such thing as reconciling the accounts. We gave that up a long time ago. . . . Life is too short, and the editors of the Century would lose their summer vacation"—just as he had.[48] Hay, who had written most of the battle narratives, hated the criticism even more. He would rewrite nothing, he said, and Gilder could do what he wanted. Hay then complained about how much the editors cut.[49]

The *Century* editors were not alone in carping. In November 1886 they began publishing excerpts. By February 1890, when serialization ended, over a third of the massive work had appeared in its pages. The response was positive overall, and the staff rejoiced at their sales. There was automatic opposition, however. Confederate apologists not surprisingly hated it. Other readers complained about long digressions, asserting that there was too much history and too little Lincoln. *Life* magazine humorously suggested a game in which the winner would be the first to locate five mentions of Lincoln himself in a single issue of the *Century,* with mere allusions allowed. More seriously, some men whose names appeared in print howled. When Nicolay furnished Herndon with advance copies, the latter privately charged that the authors had suppressed the truth.[50]

The editors did not know about Herndon's grousing, but they did fret about the authors' spread-eagle pro-Lincoln bias, and they wanted it toned down. Readers kept complaining. Proud of the *Century*'s illustrations, the art director struggled to get southerners to volunteer portraits. Gilder worried about harsh depictions of prominent northerners, too, such as the Blair family and John C. Frémont. He warned the authors that prominent sculptor Augustus Saint-Gaudens had complained about their "calling names, pitching in, etc.," exclaiming, "How damn partisan it's getting!"[51]

As the last *Century* installment was about to run, Gilder again raised the specter of the authors' open "partisanship." Nicolay finally blew up. Like his mentor Lincoln, he dashed out a long and impassioned letter he never sent in full. "We stand in no awe" to such charges, he wrote. "We deny it is partisanship to use the multiplication tables, reverence the Decalogue, or obey the Constitution of the United States." Secessionists were traitors—Lee included—and no one could defend them honestly. Trying to do so set a bad precedent for future generations. "The identical old tests of loyalty and of honor, manhood, truth, and faith," he continued, "are omnipresent in every form of government; when they are abandoned nothing remains but anarchy."[52]

After months of exhausting proofreading and indexing, *Century* finally published the full book at the end of 1890. It ran to 1.2 million words across 4,700 pages in ten volumes, including the military history that the editors had struck from the magazine. Anticipation was great, but reactions were mixed. Some reviewers lauded it as one of the great works of American history and national literature. Others complained about its bulk, digressions, and long quotations. As historian Michael Burlingame later noted, Lincoln at one juncture disappears from the narrative for 395 pages. At $50—between $1,500 and $2,000 today—it was exorbitantly costly as well. Merrill Peterson estimated that fifty times as many people read the *Century* excerpts than the book itself. Then as now, some readers also wanted to argue to the death about Civil War minutiae. Soon-to-be rival Lincoln biographer Alexander K. McClure, a former Republican congressman, nationally known newspaper editor, and leading reconciliationist, inaugurated a long and notable brouhaha when he disputed Hay and Nicolay's narrative and Lincoln's honesty regarding the replacement of Hannibal Hamlin as vice president. Former Maj. Gen. Carl Schurz, another Liberal Republican, liked the book but lamented the negative depiction of Chase. Historian Frederic Bancroft, a pioneer of the new academic history that was developing in the United States on German models, disliked the book's ponderous style, the denigration of all Confederates as treasonous, and the depictions of Lincoln's peers as lesser men.[53] "The whole thing is growing very ridiculous," Hay wrote Nicolay. "Every old dead-beat politician in the country is coming forward to protest that he was the depositary of Lincoln's inner most secrets and the engineer of his campaign. And every one of them, who we have not mentioned, is thirsting for our gore."[54]

In retrospect, the reviewers were right all the way around. *Abraham Lincoln* was a stunning achievement. Many of the vignettes that historians still recite when discussing Lincoln first came from its pages. As Joshua Zeitz noted, Seward's willingness to start a foreign war to save the Union, Lincoln's plaintive worries before the first troops arrived in Washington, McClellan's boast that he could "do it all," Lincoln's reaction to Hooker's talk of dictatorship, and Lincoln's pessimism before the 1864 election all came from Nicolay and Hay.[55]

Yet through omission and commission, *Abraham Lincoln* also became an exercise in legend building. Nicolay and Hay papered over embarrassing moments and even corrected Lincoln's misspellings. Lincoln in the book was a flawless hero. Again paraphrasing biblical descriptions of Christ, the authors depicted Lincoln as "incomparably the greatest man of his time. . . . The blessings of an enfranchised race would forever hail him as their liberator." The authors continued, "the nation would acknowledge him as the mighty counselor whose patient courage and wisdom saved the life of the republic in its darkest hour; and illuminating his proud eminence as orator, statesman, and ruler, there would forever shine around his memory the halo of that tender humanity and Christian charity in which he walked among his fellow-countrymen as their familiar companion and friend." Here was a Christ-like Lincoln, a "mighty counselor" complete with "halo," a treatment almost worthy of Holland.[56]

Such exultation naturally extended to their rendering of Lincoln as the perfect commander in chief, which went well beyond anything Arnold, Holland, or even Stoddard attempted. Both Nicolay and Hay had fully imbibed the president's views of his own abilities and actions. He did nothing wrong as a war leader. Acknowledging only inexperience and brief confusion in the *Powhatan* affair—that was due to Seward—they described Lincoln's handling of Fort Sumter as masterfully flexible, constitutional, and unifying. He correctly rejected Scott's Anaconda and launched the First Manassas Campaign. As the president had asserted himself, he was blameless for the resulting defeat. With "calm and resolute patience," he took a firm hand from a well-meaning but hesitant Winfield Scott. "From this time onward to the end of the war," Hay and Nicolay wrote, "his touch was daily and hourly amidst the vast machinery of command and coördination in Cabinet, Congress, army, navy, and the hosts of national politics." As early as December 1861, the "wise and sagacious" president realized that the road to a quick victory required "a direct attack" at Manassas. The campaign against Stonewall Jackson in the Shenandoah Valley failed only because Lincoln's generals ignored his orders, "all admirable in clearness, intelligence, and temper, always directing the right thing to be done and the best way of doing it." The same was true on the Peninsula. "No general in the army," they wrote, "studied his maps and scanned his telegrams with half the industry—and it may be added, with half the intelligence—which Mr. Lincoln gave to his."[57] As for the pedantic Henry Halleck, Lincoln more deserved to be called "Old Brains." Halleck "had emphasized the danger of moving on 'exterior lines' and insisted that it was merely repeating the error committed at Bull Run," they wrote, "and would as inevitably lead to disaster. Lincoln . . . showed that the defeat at Bull Run did not result from movement on exterior lines, but from failure to use exterior lines with judgment and concert."[58]

As Nicolay and Hay gave the world an idealized Lincoln, they happily undermined the reputations of others. Hay particularly disliked Chase and Frémont, both of whom had schemed to replace Lincoln in 1864. Both were disloyal, he thought, but at least Chase's daughter let them use his diary. There was little redeeming about Frémont, however, whom he and Nicolay depicted as a weak man blinded by flatterers and an assertive wife, crippled by his ambitions, and weighted down with his "unfitness" to command. They only tempered their criticism of Brig. Gen. James Shields, the man who once in Illinois had challenged Lincoln to a duel, to placate the publisher. Don Carlos Buell was stubbornly unwilling to attempt to liberate East Tennessee or to do much else.[59] Halleck learned how to fight a real war from the president, but he "was not fitted by character or temperament for the assumption of such weighty responsibilities as the military situation required." As Lincoln said, his second general in chief "shrunk from responsibility whenever it was possible."[60] The Burnside "experiment" with the Army of the Potomac failed because that general rejected the president's smarter tactical ideas. The same was true with the timid Flag Officer Samuel Du Pont, the confused and increasingly "sullen" Hooker, and the insubordinate Rosecrans. Meade's refusal to honor Lincoln's wishes and attack Lee at the Potomac following Gettysburg led to disaster, while his subsequent inability to accomplish the president's aims did little to redeem him. Each of them could have ended the war faster had he only obeyed the wise commander in chief's wishes.[61]

Even Grant came up short in their telling. He had died of throat cancer in July 1885 just as he completed his two-volume *Personal Memoirs*. Grant wrote for money, too, hoping to recoup his heirs' future after being swindled out of a fortune. He initially looked to the *Century*, having already written for the War Series, but Mark Twain convinced him correctly that Gilder had low-balled him with his offer. Instead, Twain and his brother-in-law Charles Webster's new company published the memoir and sold it door to door, confident of profits despite generous royalties. In the wake of Grant's death, it became a bestseller. In *Personal Memoirs* Grant wrote with what David Blight called "stoic detachment" about his life and the war. His message was thoroughly Unionist: Secession was treason. Slaveholders duped the Confederate rank and file into war. Lee was not the genius of Lost Cause rhetoric.[62] The southern cause "was one of the worst for which a people ever fought."[63]

As for Lincoln, Grant was ambivalent. Admitting that he had been a Democrat before the war, Grant came to like and admire Lincoln personally. He did not forget how he believed that the president had stuck with him during the long Vicksburg winter and again in Virginia. Grant trusted that his "goodness of heart" would have brought about a better peace and mourned his loss deeply. Yet however great Lincoln was as a person, friend, and political leader, he was no general, as his flawed military plans made clear. The McClernand appointment was a mistake: "I doubted McClernand's fitness." Lincoln pushed the canal digging at Vicksburg simply because as a youth he had seen the Mississippi shift channels. Grant withheld his plans from him just as McClellan had and for the same reason: Lincoln would have divulged them. The president did not understand the move across the James River. His comment that "if a man can't skin he must hold a leg while somebody else does" was not an assertion, according to Grant, but a revelation. Lincoln misunderstood Grant's intentions regarding Jubal Early's Valley operations. The president's naïve tactical ideas would have resulted in disaster.[64]

Hay and Nicolay had to tread carefully in disputing a national hero, but disagree they did. Minimizing the McClernand embarrassment, they focused on Lincoln's support for Grant. The general in chief's brilliance was in doing what the president wanted in Virginia. He made mistakes in not safeguarding Washington as much as Lincoln knew was necessary and in the soft terms he gave to Lee. There was no confusion or lack of military acumen in the

White House, they asserted. On the road to victory, the strategy and vision were Lincoln's.[65]

But it was George B. McClellan who was at the dead center of their crosshairs. Indeed, one cannot fully understand their *Abraham Lincoln* and its depiction of the president as a brilliant commander in chief without imagining it in the context of Lincoln's growing wartime dislike of his first general in chief and a subsequent decade-and-a half of vigorous reaction to dissenting voices still defending McClellan.

Prince Phillipe, the comte de Paris, was the most prominent McClellan advocate of the era. A pretender to the French throne, he served as an aide to the general from the fall of 1861 through July 1862. Twelve years later the comte began publishing in French a seven-volume general history of the American Civil War. The first two volumes appeared in English in 1875 and 1876, followed by two more in 1888. In them he depicted McClellan as a genius and martyr. The general was not faultless: He inflated enemy numbers, kept a politicized staff, and exhibited "habitual circumspection." But those sins paled in comparison to Lincoln's, the comte asserted. The president was a clumsy amateur who made major blunders such as the blockade, operations in the Valley, holding McDowell to cover Washington, and otherwise hamstringing McClellan. Worse, he caved to Little Mac's Republican critics. "Honest Abraham" was a dishonest coward who "had not the courage" to tell McClellan about his demotion until he was out of Washington, the comte concluded, and he lied to the general again before the army left Alexandria.[66] The comte's serious allegations made Hay physically sick when he read them, even as he begrudgingly admired the technical quality of the work.[67]

Others weighed in as well. Harvard-educated attorney John Codman Ropes missed Civil War service due to a twisted spine, but he emerged afterward as the most prominent American outside the U.S. Army writing military history. Charles Scribner's Sons recruited him to write the fourth volume of their Civil War series. *The Army Under Pope,* published in 1881 along with Nicolay's contribution to the series, hardly was an attack on Lincoln. Ropes chided the president and his cabinet for muddling the military effort in Virginia in the summer of 1862 and for not firing McClellan after the Harrison's Landing Letter, but he sympathized with Lincoln. McClellan was difficult.

But he also absolved McClellan and Porter from any blame for the defeat at Second Manassas. Halleck's "infirmity of purpose and want of explicit directions" were responsible for that disaster, Ropes argued, not to mention Pope's miscues. Ropes's defense of Porter was so powerful that it seems to have played a role in the former general's s final exoneration by President Grover Cleveland and Congress five years later. Lincoln and Stanton, many now agreed, had ruined an innocent patriot.[68]

While the French noble and the Boston attorney were bad enough, it was McClellan's own attempts to defend himself, in his *Century* essays and then his memoir, that sealed his fate with Nicolay and Hay. *McClellan's Own Story* came out late in 1886, over a year after the general's fatal heart attack. Rough and incomplete—the first draft burned in a fire, and McClellan was only up to May 1862 as he rewrote it when he died—ham-fisted editor and Democratic wire-puller W. C. Prime clumsily padded it with letters from McClellan to his wife, lengthy passages from the general's overwrought 1864 report, articles from *Battles and Leaders*, and his own fawning opinions. None of it did the general's reputation any favors. Repeating the comte de Paris's charges with spleen, McClellan defended himself as the target of a conspiracy of abolitionists, Radicals, and disloyal officers led by backstabbing Edwin M. Stanton. They all had crippled his outnumbered army. Prime edited out the ugliest passages about Lincoln, but in what remained the president still came off as no better than a well-meaning puppet. Swayed by the "conspiracy" and handicapped by ignorance, Lincoln had been a hapless commander in chief.[69]

The reaction to *McClellan's Own Story* was brutally negative. In 1885 Republican Congressman William D. Kelley of Pennsylvania—a party founder, wartime ally of Lincoln, and fierce critic of McClellan—wrote an entire book disputing McClellan's *Century* essays as having "no historic value." Playing up his own inside information as well as drawing on Arnold, Kelley also looked to the initial volumes of the War Department's massive *War of the Rebellion* project, which began publication in 1881 and would become complete in 1901. Historian Yael Sternhell argued that the initial audience for the *Official Records* consisted of veterans and other contemporaries seeking to refight old battles. Kelley certainly fit the bill. In his book he dismissed Little Mac as slow, insubordinate, probably treasonous, and intent on supplanting the "great-hearted, patient, long-suffering President" as commander in chief. The general only succeeded, Kelley continued, in "illustrating the confusion into which the author's morbid imagination led him when in pursuit of an evil genius upon whom to devolve the consequences of his failures."[70]

Kelley was rabidly partisan, but even Ropes panned McClellan's book, observing that it demonstrated that the general had lived in a fantasy world. He had become a stubborn and bitter man, his mind "warped. . . . his egotism is simply colossal—there is no other word for it."[71] Donn Piatt agreed. Described by a biographer as a "gadfly," Piatt had been a lawyer, journalist, diplomat in the Franklin Pierce administration, regimental colonel of infantry, chief of staff to Maj. Gen. Robert C. Schenck, a Republican legislator, and humor editor for the *Galaxy* magazine. Before the 1860 election, he and Schenck stumped for Lincoln and met with him in Springfield. But Piatt's loyalty only went so far. Lamon's publishers deemed Piatt's diary entries about the president-elect's casual naïveté so incendiary that they made Lamon and Black omit them. During the war, Piatt's brief attempts to help abolitionist James G. Birney build an African American regiment in Maryland, which threatened to cost Lincoln the support of Unionist slaveholders, drew the president's fury to the degree that he blackballed him from promotion and threatened to drum him out of the army.[72]

Yet even Piatt had no use for McClellan's autobiography. "One rises from a reading of 'McClellan's Own Story' with a feeling of depression," he wrote.

> It is of sorrow for the author. It were better for his memory had he left his story all untold. . . . We are awakened to the fact that he was a weak man, cautious almost to cowardice. . . . His one plea, put forward at the beginning, and dwelt upon to the last, is based upon the monstrous assertion that Lincoln was an imbecile, controlled by Stanton, Chase, and Seward, and that these three, especially Stanton, hated him so intensely that they were all the time interfering to defeat his army, in order that they might destroy him. . . . [E]liminate this from the book, and nothing remains.[73]

McClellan and his many remaining defenders made Hay furious, while he ignored critics such as Piatt. "We are all alone in condemning" McClellan, he complained, with some hyperbole and a great deal of partisanship, to Nicolay in August 1885. "A big majority of the American people believe him innocent," Hay went on, "all the Democrats, all the Mugwumps, which means nearly all the literary folks, all the Southerners, & half the Republicans of the north."

According to his biographer, Hay sought revenge. "I have toiled and labored through ten chapters over him (McC)," he continued. "I think I have left the impression of his mutinous imbecility, and I have done it in a perfectly courteous manner. . . . It is of the utmost moment that we should *seem* fair to him, while we are destroying him."[74]

Over three volumes, Nicolay and Hay purposely did their best to destroy McClellan's reputation once and for all. They opined that the flattery and deference he received in Washington eroded his "temper and character." Citing his "pathetic" memoirs, the two argued that the "young and ambitious" general developed a massive ego and "a fatal degeneration of mind" that led to a "strange and permanent hallucination" that he was always outnumbered. He snubbed and insulted the president and Congress while resisting attempts to get him moving. Pompous and deluded, the general refused to recognize Lincoln's military genius and scorned his advice to attack straight at Manassas, a decision "absolutely without excuse. . . . [E]verything now indicates that if McClellan had chosen to obey" General Order No. 1, "one of the cheapest victories ever gained by a fortunate general awaited him. . . . He would have won the battle that was to end the war. . . . [T]he President was right and McClellan was wrong." Instead, he concocted the poorly planned Peninsula Campaign and then made the situation worse by leaving too few troops to defend Washington. McClellan also scorned the president's brilliant ideas in the Valley. On the Peninsula he was "absolutely without initiative" and a general "who answered every suggestion of advice with demands for reinforcement; who met entreaties and reproaches with unending arguments to show the superiority of the enemy and insufficiency of his own resources." In the Seven Days' Battles, his cowardice emerged fully. "The evident panic and mental perturbation which pierced through" his dispatches' "incoherence," they wrote, "filled the President with such dismay that its mutinous insolence was entirely overlooked." McClellan then undermined Pope and refused to pursue Lee after Antietam. "The general's inexplicable slowness . . . at last excited the President's distrust. He began to think . . . that McClellan had no real desire to beat the enemy."[75]

Egotistical, timid, insubordinate, whining, conceivably mad, and just as possibly traitorous—here finally was the fully formed McClellan of the heroic legend, crafted deliberately by two partisans who had loathed him for decades and who set out deliberately to ruin what was left of his reputation after the general's ill-fated memoirs appeared. It was, perhaps, their greatest triumph.

In the end, Hay and Nicolay had written, in the words of historian Joshua Zeitz, "the authorized biography of a slain leader and the unofficial Northern, Republican Party interpretation of the Civil War," which was also "a master narrative whose influence would ebb and flow over the years but that continues to command serious scrutiny and engagement." They "left behind a thesis that remains embedded in historical consciousness to this day." Filmmaker Ken Burns laid "the myth of Lincoln" at Hay and Nicolay's feet.[76] Their book was so massive and so seemingly authoritative that it came to function much like a sun, drawing literary planets and asteroids into a solar system. Other works of Lincoln historiography could not compete and instead began to revolve around it and its idealist depiction of the president.

Yet despite its centrality, most authors writing before World War I disagreed with some of the conclusions in Nicolay and Hay's biography. The *Century* essays, for example, encouraged Herndon that there still was an audience for Lincoln books. So, in 1889 he and young admirer Jesse W. Weik published in three volumes *Herndon's Lincoln: The True Story of a Great Life*. Herndon supplied the material, wrote drafts, and edited the chapters that Weik whipped into shape or wrote from scratch. The polarized public reaction that followed exceeded that to Lamon's book. Hay hated it. Robert Lincoln allegedly bought up every copy in London, where he was serving diplomatically, and then convinced Charles Scribner's Sons to back out of issuing a revised edition when the original publisher went under. Herndon's focus remained the antebellum Lincoln, but the book did include two chapters on the presidency, built upon the writings of Hay and attorney Henry Clay Whitney, among others. An old friend to both Herndon and Lincoln, Whitney unfortunately was far from trustworthy. Later, in 1896, he published a forgery of Lincoln's legendary "Lost Speech" of May 1856 that was so obviously off the mark that Nicolay had him barred from the *Century*. Not surprisingly, Whitney's account of a White House visit in 1861, which is about all Herndon and Weik offered about Lincoln as commander in chief, is suspect. While he correctly outlined Lincoln's basic views, Whitney oddly claimed that Lincoln opposed fighting at Manassas until Scott launched a feint against Richmond. When a revised edition came out in 1892 after Herndon's death, Weik toned down the accounts of Lincoln's parentage and freethinking, but he changed little about the war.[77]

One might well view Herndon and Weik's "realist" efforts as comparable to a comet passing through Hay and Nicolay's solar system. The same was true of Donn Piatt. In a series of articles afterward published in book form in 1887, Piatt iconoclastically defended George Thomas and his old friend Stanton, denigrated Grant and Sherman, and admitted his mixed feelings about the president. Never mentioning Hay or Nicolay by name, he nonetheless scorned the growing "hero worship" and "fanaticism" of Lincoln's defenders. "To have such hero-worship healthy," Piatt opined, "it must be true. The false heroes, like false gods, degrade their worshippers. . . . We see it illustrated in the men and matters made prominent by the late war. Hence to question the greatness of Lincoln is to excite pity or contempt, to doubt that of Grant is to run the chance of being knocked down. The true believers walk backward and cover their dead with the mantle of concealment, and in so doing it matters nothing to them that other dead are trampled on."[78]

Piatt described the real Lincoln as "a man of coarse, tough fibre through which ran a vein of humor; and who, while good-natured in manner, was not remarkable for kindness of heart." Ambitious and cold in the Herndon mode, he had climbed the ladder of success, leaving "wrecks" of men who stood in his way. Not surprisingly, Piatt went on, Lincoln felt little remorse for casualties despite all the hagiographic stories of his piety, kindheartedness, and emotions. He was the "man who said to General Schenck and me," the author revealed, "in the darkest period of that dreadful war, that he 'ate his rations and slept well,' and his looks sustained his assertion." His kindness toward the rank and file and hesitance to permit executions, Piatt believed, were politically calculated. Admitting Lincoln's sense of "fair play," he added: "Our war President was not lost in his high admiration of brigadiers and major-generals, and had a positive dislike for their methods and the despotism on which an army is based. He knew that he was dependent on volunteers for soldiers." Lincoln had a strong bias against "a West Point Democrat" and especially Thomas—Piatt thought him the best general of the war—because he was a Virginian. He also was a commander in chief who admitted to Piatt that he had "been so busy with this war I have never read the [Army] Regulations." Lincoln's calm and self-confidence helped win the war, Piatt added, but the much-denigrated Stanton, not Lincoln, had been its military "master-mind."[79]

Herndon and Piatt were exceptions. Most of the other new offerings during this period were akin to orbital planets. Yet the idealist insiders also failed to fully endorse the Nicolay and Hay thesis of Lincoln as masterful commander in chief, even when they accepted the rest of the narrative. Like Piatt, most now also eschewed straight biography in lieu of shorter "I was there" memoirs that began to supplement Nicolay and Hay rather than compete head on. Lincoln-related memoirs of every description began to swamp the market.[80]

The eccentric veteran Osborn Oldroyd was one of the first of these authors. Probably the first Lincolniana collector, he went so far as to rent Lincoln's house in Springfield from Robert Lincoln and turn it into a museum. He also set the literary stage in 1882 with *The Lincoln Memorial.* A hefty olio of presidential documents, it also contained randomly interspersed autographs, brief bromides, poems, and occasional long reminiscences from 200 prominent and lesser-known Americans, including twenty-three former high-ranking officers. Arnold and Herndon provided biographical sketches. The contributors said much about Lincoln's compassion, patriotism, divine mission, and martyrdom. In contrast, they added next to nothing about the commander in chief other than a few brief anecdotes about his criteria for commissioning generals ("fitness" and political considerations), his eagerness to end the war, his maps, and especially his kindness toward prisoners and condemned soldiers, a theme that later became so ubiquitous that it came to be known as the "gentle legend."[81]

Allen Thorndike Rice, who owned and edited the *North American Review,* produced a similar volume in 1886 just after the appearance of Nicolay and Hay's first *Century* essays. He collected recollections of thirty-three men, including Piatt and Kelley as well as some of Oldroyd's contributors, in his *Reminiscences of Abraham Lincoln.* Most of them, including Frederick Douglass, never served in uniform, which skewed the volume toward the personal and political. Despite Rice's intention to gather "a mass of trustworthy evidence" to counter the myths gathering around Lincoln, the volume largely reflected conventional wisdom (and Oldroyd's book) when it came to the president's "masterly common sense," humor, pathos, and patriotism. The editor and some contributors also countered Charles Francis Adams and others who depicted Lincoln as dominated by Seward or Stanton.[82]

Rice's contributors, like Oldroyd's, wrote little about Lincoln as commander in chief. Nowhere in *Reminiscences* did the masterful military genius depicted by Nicolay and Hay appear. Instead, the memorialists again focused largely on the gentle legend and the president's weary disappointment in his generals. Some did provide additional anecdotes. Abandoned passages from Grant's *Personal Memoirs,* submitted by son Fred Grant, reflected Lincoln's dissatisfaction with generals who constantly asked for more men. New York Congressman and later Governor Reuben E. Fenton recalled Lincoln's defense of McClellan early in 1862. Kelley explained why Lincoln preferred Burnside to Hooker when he fired McClellan, while Massachusetts Congressman George Boutwell asserted that the president replaced Hooker with Meade in part to forestall recalling Little Mac. Former Provost Marshal General James B. Fry remembered that Lincoln promoted Alexander Schimmelfennig to the rank of brigadier general over more qualified men because he liked his name and thought that it would attract more German-speaking recruits. Ben Butler claimed that he convinced the president to appoint more Democrats as generals and praised Lincoln's courage when in range of enemy guns. None of these memories suggested a towering commander in chief.[83]

Then in 1890 William Stoddard returned to the Lincoln field with *Inside the White House in War Times,* an odd, rambling, second-person, present-tense autobiography as full of dialogue as his fiction. He again portrayed himself as a peer to Hay and Nicolay. As in his earlier biography, Stoddard depicted the commander in chief as the strategic guiding hand of the Federal war effort, immersed in his maps and insistent that his generals fight it his way, yet unwilling to get involved in tactical and operational planning. Lincoln again acted as an umpire.[84]

There were other memoirists. Former Treasury Department official Lucius Chittenden published yet another reminiscence of Lincoln. Referring those interested in a full biography to Hay and Nicolay or alternatively Arnold's shorter work, Chittenden produced a digressive account that depicted Lincoln as a near-perfect president, pious Christian, and patriot. He said little about commander in chief Lincoln, however, except to note his "common-sense," his readiness to try new technologies, and his courage at Fort Stevens.[85] Adolphe Pineton, the marquis de Chambrun, supplied another brief reminiscence, having observed the end of the war for France. In 1893 he remembered Lincoln at City Point and in the field with Grant as a sort of tourist, following his generals' reports with his maps, visiting the wounded, and assessing the debris of war without directing anything. Only once did the president leave their traveling party, "he told us, to draw up instructions for the Lieutenant-General."[86]

That same year combative Alexander McClure finally published his long-awaited reminiscences, both "to correct some popular errors as to Lincoln's character and actions" and to challenge anyone who claimed to have been the president's confidants, when in fact he had none. McClure praised Lincoln to a degree—he had saved the Union, after all—but nonetheless found him to be far from perfect. Honest, able, and practical he might have been, McClure maintained, Lincoln also was overly political and too receptive to Stanton's toxicity. He also heretically endorsed Charles Francis Adams's views of Lincoln and Seward, exonerated McClellan's generalship if not his paranoia, and defended Buell, Meade, Porter, Thomas, and Maj. Gen. Gouverneur Warren, all of whom had received unfair treatment from Lincoln or Grant. McClure admitted that the president was right to bring back McClellan before Antietam, to stand by Grant after Shiloh—McClure confessed that he had demanded Grant's dismissal at the time—and to elevate Grant in 1864. It was to McClure that Lincoln famously said about Grant, "*I can't spare this man; he fights.*" Yet this account hardly was a ringing endorsement. McClure also refused to bury the hatchet with Hay and Nicolay. He cited Herndon's biography and again challenged Nicolay on Hamlin with a full chapter and a twenty-four-page appendix. The administration had bungled the dismissal of Cameron, too, he added.[87]

McClure's public doubts about Lincoln confiding in anyone did little to deter others who wanted to be seen as close to the president. In 1894 Noah Brooks's publisher issued a new edition of his earlier biography, retitled and issued explicitly for adults, while the *Century* serialized portions of Brooks's entirely new book. *Washington in Lincoln's Time.* It appeared the following year to strong reviews and steady sales. Based on his wartime writings, Brooks depicted Lincoln as a weary hero, almost overwhelmed but always expressing kinship with the common soldier. He also was a close friend, Brooks asserted, who shared secrets with him. The president took him along to meet Hooker in April 1863, then sent Brooks to observe the Gettysburg Campaign for him.[88]

Yet Lincoln still was not the brilliant president-general portrayed in Nicolay and Hay, but rather more like the passive observer of Stoddard and marquis de Chambrun. Lincoln had "common-sense. . . . It is not true that President Lincoln was ruled completely by General Halleck, as so many ill-informed people used to say," Brooks observed. "Lincoln liked to 'talk strategy' with Halleck, but was never very much under the general's influence even in military matters. He had opinions of his own, and was often impatient with Halleck's slowness and extreme caution." Yet Lincoln always demurred. Brooks, for example, remembered the president's ideas for taking Charleston. Assistant Navy Secretary Fox at the time thought them worthwhile, but Halleck deemed them impossible. Lincoln let it go. Describing Early's raid in June 1864, Brooks noted, "if Lincoln was the meddlesome marplot in military affairs which some have represented him to be, he would have peremptorily ordered a sortie of the Union forces, then numerously massed inside the defenses of Washington; but although he was 'agonized' (as he said) over the evident failure of all attempts at pursuit, he kept his hands off."[89]

New memoirs continued to appear well into the new century, increasingly with de rigueur references to Nicolay and Hay. Most were not truly insider accounts, but rather writings of men who had known Lincoln at arm's length. In 1907, for example, David Homer Bates, former War Department telegrapher and cypher clerk, remembered a commander in chief who used the telegraph to follow troop movements and drive his field commanders in real time, as he did during the Valley Campaign of 1862 and again during the pursuit of Lee from Gettysburg. Lincoln might stay in that office all night. He usually did not try to direct the war by telegraph, Bates added, but simply kept up with events. At other times Lincoln simply used the office to hide out, tell stories, recite poetry, and read aloud from his favorite humorists.[90]

Seven years later former Maj. Gen. Grenville Dodge remembered Lincoln's strengths in civil affairs and his "keen vision, of almost prophetic ken," but in military matters only mentioned Lincoln's support of Grant.[91] William E. Doster supplied yet another memoir. The provost marshal of Washington for a year, his claim to fame was acting as counsel for two of John Wilkes Booth's coconspirators. Doster described Lincoln as honest, gifted, and the son of a "shiftless" race presiding over "a costly and humiliating" war, its "main fruits . . . heaps of coffins sent home by express containing the bodies of lads who had died of camp fever, without having heard a shot fired, or having been near the enemy." He thought that Lincoln showed admirable patience with McClellan and that his political skills, not his military acumen, saved the Union. Doster also slipped in jabs at Hay and Nicolay, insisting that neither were as important as they thought. He even identified Hay as a poet and author while omitting any mention of the biography.[92]

Neither Bates, Dodge, nor Doster could claim to really know much of what happened in the Lincoln White House. As a result, the most important "inside the White House" account of the new century came from a man who by then had been dead for over thirty years. Gideon Welles died early in 1878 but not before wading into controversy. In 1870 he began writing historical essays that lambasted cabinet rival Seward and the New Yorker's longtime sponsor Thurlow Weed while elevating Lincoln's memory and his own role in the administration. Disgusted with the Grant administration, Welles also had become a Liberal Republican. Still, incensed by Charles Francis Adams's "false history. . . . pregnant with error," Welles responded to him with help from Montgomery Blair and Chase, but without the documents he desired from the two biographers Hay and Nicolay. He wrote three magazine articles in 1873 and then a fierce book entitled *Lincoln and Seward* the next year. Bluntly, the former navy secretary compared Adams to Booth while launching a fusillade on Seward's reputation. Lincoln was the better man and wiser statesman, Welles asserted, while his secretary of state was a weak and overrated schemer lacking principles but hungry for power. Seward's "mischievous maladministration" led to the botched Fort Sumter response, the poorly conceived blockade, and diplomatic truckling to the British. In his white-hot zeal to blister Adams and Seward while defending himself, however, Welles grew clumsy. He unintentionally undermined Commander in Chief Lincoln, who after all had agreed to all those things. More positively, Welles highlighted the president's determination to hold Fort Sumter as well as his hard decision to bring back McClellan after Second Bull Run. But Lincoln was not "infallible," as he was too willing to humor Seward while ignoring Welles to the detriment of the country. He was no puppet, Welles concluded, but neither was he as decisive as Hay and Nicolay maintained.[93]

Welles died four years later, but he left additional essays as well as voluminous diaries. Nicolay and Hay used the latter extensively. Then in 1911, having printed about a fourth of their entries in *Atlantic Monthly*, Welles's tycoon son Edgar and granddaughter Alice transcribed, edited, and published the three-volume *Diary of Gideon Welles*. The title was not completely accurate, for Welles kept no diary until August 1862. The former secretary had related events up to that date—including the Fort Sumter crisis, the birth of the blockade, the loss of the Norfolk Navy Yard, Upper South secession, the rise and fall of McClellan, the Battle of Hampton Roads, and Lincoln's decision for emancipation—in a long and often angry chapter "written several years after the events narrated." Worse, he had frequently amended and rewrote what he actually recorded in his diaries as he refought the war in print, apparently preparing to write a Lincoln biography or war history that never came to fruition. Edgar Welles admitted enough trepidation about revealing his father's ardent views that he deleted "a few strong expressions" as well as editing the grammar and spelling. Historian Howard K. Beale—he later would edit his own edition of the Welles diaries—maintained that in incorporating his father's postwar emendations, Edgar Welles had produced an unreliable edition that better reflected the father's postwar bitterness and insecurities than his wartime thoughts and experiences. The former navy secretary certainly pulled no punches when it came to how much he envied and despised Chase, Halleck, Stanton, and especially Seward, his great rival for Lincoln's respect and friendship. He also was damning to the president. Lincoln in the revised narrative was a confused, disorganized, and sometimes weak commander in chief. As the president lacked previous executive experience, Seward and others gulled him constantly. His deference to Seward weakened the response to secession and hastened the war. Chase and the cowardly and corrupt bully Stanton were no better.[94]

The edited wartime diaries, picking up just before Second Bull Run, suggested that Lincoln never improved. He was, Welles observed, a good man: kind, honest, modest, intelligent, and possessing "a sort of intuitive sagacity." He was capable of tough decisions, such as turning to McClellan after Second Bull Run and staying the course with Meade. But he was also a weak commander in chief and a passive observer generally. He lacked the self-esteem and self-confidence, Welles maintained, to stand up to Seward, Stanton, and Halleck. Before Antietam, for example, Welles complained that "there is really very little of a government here at this time. . . . The President has good sense, intelligence, and an excellent heart, but is sadly perplexed and distressed by events." Lincoln "in a great measure has surrendered to military officers prerogatives intrusted to himself." Welles rued his reliance on Halleck, whom he saw as incompetent, insubordinate, and generally useless. "This is the President's error," he complained. "His own convictions and conclusions are infinitely superior to Halleck's,—even in military operations more sensible and more correct always,—but yet he says, 'It being strictly a military question, it is proper I should defer to Halleck.'" Lincoln stuck with other generals he no longer trusted. He played favorites, especially with Dahlgren. Lincoln was naïve when he championed sharpers hoping to profit through colonizing the freed people. He also could be duplicitous and worried too much about the press.[95]

Reviewers picked up on all these themes. Frederick Bancroft damned Welles's "pathetic" and "outrageously unjust" opinions of his peers as well as his "narrow and unphilosophic mind," which led to "literary rabies." Yet he lauded the diaries' immense value overall and accepted in large part Welles's depiction of Lincoln as an honest, "crude," and sometimes lazy man rather than "the over-wrought canvas of Hay and Nicolay. . . . [Lincoln] often hesitated and sometimes vacillated. At one time he would shun responsibilities and allow others wrongly to assume them; then when others were more timid, he feared no responsibility or rank." Lincoln was a great president, Bancroft concluded, but as commander in chief he listened to the wrong people and stumbled through a war.

The heroic legend was at bay.[96]

6

ABRAHAM LINCOLN WALKS AT MIDNIGHT

American Historians and the Heroic Legend in Limbo, 1895–1945

AS THE TWENTIETH CENTURY DAWNED, the Civil War generation and their reminiscences gave way to new historians who had never known Abraham Lincoln. Until World War II, those authors adopted and discarded new approaches to Lincoln, the Civil War, and its interpretation. Talented lay historians and the new doctorate-wielding professionals began to vie with rough elbows for control of the president's story. Yet with a few notable exceptions, when it came to Commander in Chief Lincoln, all of them offered only more of the same. Despite major economic depressions, two international wars, and the advent of a third global conflict, the heroic legend not just remained in limbo in the United States but seemed by 1940 to be withering.

John Codman Ropes served as a transitional figure in the succession from the memoirists to the historians. In 1895 and again in 1898, Ropes piled on new criticism of Lincoln in the first two of four projected volumes on the Civil War up to early 1863. Citing a bevy of now-available sources—*Battles and Leaders,* most of the *War of the Rebellion* volumes, other government documents, Nicolay and Hay's work, and a plethora of memoirs—Ropes praised the president's patriotism, political smarts, and humanity. Yet in the end, he believed Commander in Chief Lincoln's lack of military experience, open partisanship, and poor management harmed the Federal war effort.[1]

The president's initial call for 75,000 volunteers, for example, was "really ludicrous in its minimizing of the facts of the situation," Ropes wrote. Lincoln never "made any real effort to understand" the problems that his western generals faced and simply dismissed the less successful as incompetent. Acknowledging McClellan's "grievous shortcomings" in the East, Ropes blasted General Order No. 1 and scorned Lincoln's "serious defects as an administrator" in General War Order No. 3. No competent commander in chief would have issued such instructions, Ropes asserted. He further damned Lincoln's passive-aggressiveness and criticized the "bad taste" of his "wholly unnecessary, and exceedingly impolitic . . . threat" to McClellan before the general left for the Peninsula.[2] Withholding McDowell might have been "perfectly warranted" by McClellan's refusal to leave enough men to defend Washington, Ropes admitted, but on a strictly military basis, it probably prolonged the war:

> Had President Lincoln refrained from interfering, McDowell . . . could have effected his purpose of uniting his corps of 40,000 men to the Army of the Potomac. . . . That this concentration of 150,000 men in the immediate vicinity of Richmond would have compelled its speedy evacuation, is certainly very probable. It was, at any rate, obviously the true course for the Federal authorities to take. That this course was not taken was due entirely to the action of President Lincoln, who, contrary to the urgent remonstrances of the generals charged with the conduct of operations against Richmond, broke up deliberately one of the most promising combinations for the defeat of the Confederates and the capture of their capital that fortune was ever likely to afford to the Federal cause.[3]

In the end, he asserted, Lincoln should have just fired McClellan instead of agreeing to a campaign that even Ropes found poorly conceived. Instead, the president himself threw away his best chance of winning the war in 1862. There was more. Lincoln made bad choices in choosing McClellan's replacements. Halleck was a disaster as general in chief. Lincoln may have had common sense, as so many memoirists insisted, but if so, he ignored it when he bowed to politicians and sent troops to Frémont, when he and Stanton tried and failed to manage the pursuit of Jackson in the Valley, and once again when he agreed to the creation of new regiments rather than building up existing ones.[4]

One can only imagine what Ropes's criticism of the rest of the war would have looked like had he not died in 1899. It took another fifteen years for Col. William Roscoe Livermore, an engineer and pioneering instructor at the U.S. Army Staff College, to follow up the series with new volumes. He did little with the heroic legend other than to acknowledge Lincoln's overall strategic vision in 1863, reiterate Ropes's negative points about the Peninsula, and defend the president's advice to Hooker during and after Chancellorsville.[5]

Livermore was not the nation's only soldier-historian, however. By the time of Ropes's death, the war with Spain in 1898 and a growing sense of professionalism within the army had created a new climate for military-history studies within the service. Young officers such as Livermore, weary of serving in a force grown top heavy with old generals and older ideas, spearheaded a reformist movement with American military history at its core. Another notable participant was Maj. Gen. Francis V. Greene, who in 1909 offered a spirited if mixed defense of Lincoln as commander in chief. The son of Bvt. Maj. Gen. George Sears Greene, the hero of Culp's Hill at Gettysburg, the younger Greene was a West Pointer who already had written a book about Grant's campaigns for Vicksburg and led a brigade in the Philippines. In *Scribner's Magazine* he praised Lincoln as a hands-on commander in chief with a brilliant strategic and operational mind. The president's decisions at the beginning of the war successfully guided the Federal war effort thereafter, Greene asserted. Lincoln could visualize a battlefield as well as Grant. Unfortunately, Greene continued, the president exhibited "the marks of a great soul, but not of a great general." His Achilles heel was the lack of a hard edge. His "self-effacement," Greene observed, "his diffidence, his doubt whether the country would sustain him, if he peremptorily asserted his opinions against those of his professional military subordinates, left the army with two heads or three heads or no head at all until the really efficient man was found in Grant." Echoing Ropes, he wrote that a truly superb commander in chief would have fired McClellan for insubordination and axed Halleck for incompetence. Lincoln offered too many "suggestions" to his generals and not nearly enough orders. Either Halleck or Lincoln alone should have directed Hooker and Meade in 1863, not both alternatively. No general could deal with such confusion. Lincoln's best decision was to elevate Grant and fade into the background, although Greene added that he was right to demand a strong response to Early's raid in 1864. Yet despite his diffidence, Greene concluded, Lincoln remained a great commander in chief. "Judged in the retrospect of nearly half a century," he wrote, "with his every written word now in print and with all the facts of the period brought out and placed in proper perspective by the endless studies, discussions, and arguments of the intervening years, it becomes clear that . . . in military affairs his was not only the guiding but the controlling hand."[6]

Greene's essay set the stage for the eccentric officer who came to stand at the center of army military history and whose positive assessment of Lincoln would prove to be the most spirited American defense of Commander in Chief Lincoln of the era. Col. Arthur Latham Conger was the son of a distinguished Civil War Federal officer who went on to become a powerful postwar Republican businessman. Disowned after embracing theosophy at Harvard and dropping out of seminary, the younger Conger joined the U.S. Army in 1898. He fought in Cuba as well as in the Philippine Insurrection (1899–1902) and the Boxer Rebellion (1899–1901). In 1902 Lieutenant Conger escaped prosecution for torturing prisoners in the Philippines, while a court-martial found his commanding officer guilty of war crimes. Conger thus suffered no stain on his record. He advanced rapidly thereafter, became a star student at the Army Staff College at Fort Leavenworth, joined the faculty after graduation in 1907, and created a modern, primary-source-based seminar that not only reflected his civilian studies but also became a model for both military and civilian universities. Starting with McClellan on the Peninsula—he despised Little Mac to the degree that he believed the general squashed some of his own reports—Civil War campaigns served as the basis for much of his instruction.[7] "His special talents," as Carol Reardon explained, "made him the army's single most influential advocate of scientific history."[8]

The army dispatched now-Captain Conger to the troubled Mexican border in 1915, but in the following year, he obtained a leave of absence to attend the annual meeting of the State Historical Society of Wisconsin. There he presented "President Lincoln as War Statesman."[9] Directly challenging Lincoln's critics, Conger lamented that the president's "chief" defenders, Nicolay and Hay, "possess no great competence in military affairs and besides, their avowed policy of being 'Lincoln men all through' has perhaps weakened the force of their arguments." They were neither experienced soldiers nor objective observers and thus could not defend Lincoln adequately. No wonder that some historians now echoed wartime Democrats in arguing that the president was a "vacillating imbecile," he complained, while another group then increasing in numbers cast him as a victim of his "combined ignorance and conceit."[10]

Conger set out to stem that tide and buttress the Nicolay and Hay thesis as they could not do themselves by energetically describing Lincoln as a farseeing strategist in the Prussian mold, which dominated American professional military studies before World War I. To him, the president most resembled the militantly expansionist Prussian Prime Minister Otto von Bismarck, who built modern Germany in the 1860s and 1870s through war. Lincoln, too, deliberately chose conflict to unify the North and lose no more states. Defeat at First Bull Run was a necessary shock to the system. He then built a large army and organized it effectively. "Mr. Lincoln knew nothing about military art or of the science of strategy," Conger affirmed, "but he had the advantage of approaching the subject with a trained, logical, and unbiassed mind." The president taught himself tactics and strategy, rejected passé doctrine, and covertly embraced the continent-wide gist of Scott's unpopular Anaconda that found its final fulfilment in Grant. Look to the Germans—at that time winning the Great War from Belgium to the Dardanelles—Conger added, to see its wisdom. To have followed other advisors only would have made for a longer war and produced a bloodbath worse than the Philippines, "with its unavoidable burning and destruction, with its concentration camps and their hardships and consequent wastage of life."[11]

Lincoln's Bismarckian strategy justified his interest in East Tennessee, Conger continued, as well as his reaction to Stonewall Jackson's presence in the Shenandoah Valley. Defeats in Virginia deceived the eye, as the real story was relative Confederate weakness in the West. Lincoln directed a successful coastal war and appointed the best-available men. Tactically, he was far ahead of their time, too. The wisdom of his emphasis on applying numbers to key points could be seen again in the current Great War, Conger asserted, while the Prussian practice of assigning "missions" rather than issuing specific orders reflected Lincoln's suggestions to his generals.[12]

Historian Milo Quaife, who brought the officer to the historical society conference, later termed his thesis "revolutionary" but only after World War I shifted the ground in Conger's direction while raising him to more prominence as a successful staff officer and brigade commander with the American

Expeditionary Forces in France. For the time being, Conger's and Greene's essays were only false starts on a new canon.[13]

Much more influential than Conger or Greene at the time was a new generation of Gilded Age biographers. The sons and daughters of the Civil War generation, however, continued writing more mixed evaluations of Lincoln as warrior. Ida M. Tarbell became the leading and most popular Lincoln chronicler of her time. A child during the war, Tarbell later became famous as a legendary crusading journalist for *McClure's* magazine. Her muckraking exposés notably ended the monopoly that John D. Rockefeller's Standard Oil held on the American petroleum industry; Rockefeller not incidentally had ruined Tarbell's father. But early in 1895, before she went after the oil tycoon, Lincoln buff and magazine owner S. S. McClure sent a reluctant Tarbell out to track down documents and photographs for a series that he hoped would break the hold that the rival *Century* had on Lincoln biography and Civil War history. Nicolay stonewalled her, while Richard Gilder flatly denied her a place in Lincoln studies, calling her a woman out of her proper place in a field of "Lincoln men." Robert Lincoln was only a bit more generous, refusing her access to his father's papers as he did everyone else, but giving her a previously unpublished photograph of his father as a young man that later appeared to acclaim in *McClure's*. Undaunted, Tarbell crisscrossed the country, conducting interviews and visiting libraries and archives while employing others to do the same. She doggedly tracked down 275 Lincoln letters and speeches unknown to Nicolay and Hay while adding 300 new reminiscences to Herndon's tally. In late 1895 and into 1896, her articles on the younger Lincoln brought acclaim and rocketed her magazine's circulation past the *Century* just as McClure had hoped. She promptly retooled them into her first Lincoln book, *The Early Life of Abraham Lincoln*, published later in 1896. More pieces on President Lincoln followed in 1898 and 1899, leading to her two-volume *The Life of Abraham Lincoln* in 1900. Robert Lincoln praised it as at least a worthy supplement to Hay and Nicolay's opus.[14]

Tarbell would return to the Lincolns and their circle again and again over the years, penning nonfiction and fiction that usually focused on the frontier years. As historian Judith Rice observed, Tarbell's depiction of Lincoln thoroughly reflected her Progressive politics. Her Lincoln was not a pious martyr, but rather the best of the common men, a heroic working-class reformer, a manly leader, and the exemplar of the Republican Party before it sold out to big businessmen such as Hay. Benjamin Thomas described Tarbell as "an idealistic realist" in the warts-and-all Herndon tradition who nonetheless challenged some of Herndon's most provocative assertions.[15]

Tarbell's only serious treatment of Lincoln the commander in chief, however, came in the two-volume biography. It offered little that was new while sometimes reflecting her own confusion about the heroic legend. Lincoln did not shy away from war or making major decisions, she wrote initially. He boldly made the call to resupply Fort Sumter, ordered his generals to seize Arlington Heights, and sent them to Manassas to meet the people's demand for action. His post–Bull Run memoranda set the overall tone for the war. Here was the strong commander in chief. But then Tarbell began to contradict herself, asserting that until McClellan fell ill at the end of 1861, Lincoln only exercised "his military authority principally in raising men and commissioning officers; campaigns he had left to the generals." It was only at the bottom of the tub that he "for the first time asserted himself as commander-in-chief." The president commenced the study of war that Nicolay and Hay described, haunted the telegraph office, and issued his war orders. "He evidently had determined to exercise fully his power of commander-in-chief," she wrote, "to force McClellan into battle and to compel him to carry out the orders which he as chief executive gave." Yet he did not use those powers. Aside from emancipation and the appointing and removing of generals, Lincoln in Tarbell's *Life* exercised little of the war power after he fired McClellan. Nowhere in her biography did the brilliant tactician and strategist emerge. Hastily rushing through campaigns, she favored the familiar gentle-legend tropes of Lincoln's common sense and "big heart" for soldiers.[16]

And she could have done otherwise had she desired. Oddly enough, Tarbell had made just such a declaration of Lincoln's military genius in her ghost-written memoir of Charles A. Dana, published after his death but two years before *The Life of Abraham Lincoln.* Dana at one point had argued that Lincoln became "the greatest general we had, greater than Grant or Thomas," after "three or four years of constant practice in the science and art of war[;] . . . [Prussian Helmuth] Von Moltke was not a better general, or an abler planner or expounder of a campaign, than was President Lincoln."[17] Tarbell wrote down these words on Dana's behalf, but his observations did not sway her views.

Depictions of Lincoln as a great president but lesser commander in chief, meanwhile, found their way into the era's textbooks and general histories.

The most popular of all came from James Ford Rhodes, "perhaps the most important Civil War historian of his time," according to James McPherson.[18] Rhodes's seven-volume history of the nation, initially published between 1892 and 1906, was reissued with two additional volumes after World War I. His standalone one-volume *History of the Civil War* (1917), meanwhile, won the second-ever Pulitzer Prize in history. Born in 1848, Rhodes never served in the war, although many young men of his age did. Instead, he went to college, unenthusiastically entered his Copperhead father's Ohio business, and became a wealthy iron-and-steel magnate. Mark Hanna, the wealthy Republican senator and sponsor of President William McKinley, was his brother-in-law. At the age of thirty-seven, Rhodes retired a wealthy man and moved to Boston to write history. His writings won him legions of fans, including Theodore Roosevelt. Rhodes's biographer attributed his popularity to his lucent style, deep research, and the qualities that he shared with his readers: faith in capitalism, middle-class northern values, and racial bias. His racism allowed him to blame the war on slavery, depict emancipation as a political gambit, and condemn Radical Republicans for attempting to elevate African Americans to equality during Reconstruction, all at the same time. He especially opposed African American suffrage. On these final points, at least, even the United Daughters of the Confederacy's chief polemicist approved and cited him. Historian David Blight later pointed to Rhodes's amalgamation of nationalism and reconciliationism as a crucial forerunner to Columbia University historian William A. Dunning's successful denigration of Reconstruction that survived generations.[19]

Relating the Civil War in volumes three through five as well as in the one-volume *History of the Civil War*, Rhodes became the first major modern historian to draw extensively upon the complete 128-volume *War of the Rebellion*. He also cited Nicolay and Hay's edition of Lincoln's papers and other primary sources such as Grant's and McClellan's memoirs, Welles's diary, and the works of many other authors discussed previously. His major source, however, was Nicolay and Hay's biography. Rhodes praised the authors and cited them 273 times in the multivolume history. Indeed, he often parroted them in their descriptions of the slave states' culpability for the war as well and lauded the president's wisdom, responsiveness to the people, "hard-headed" logic, generosity, "common sense," and—using the buzz words of other contemporary historians—"the practical wisdom of the Anglo-Saxon." He further echoed William O. Stoddard in depicting Lincoln as a model dictator. In 1861 "the country attorney of Illinois assumed the power of a dictator" but only because that was what the people wanted, "for never had the power of a dictator fallen into safer and nobler hands." Rhodes later added that Lincoln "was no Caesar or Napoleon and sought no self-aggrandizement." The president's decisions to reinforce Fort Sumter and march on Richmond were responses to popular will, while his civil liberties policies were necessary if sometimes pushed to the limits by others.[20]

Rhodes believed in the heroic legend to a certain extent. He included and passed along Nicolay and Hay's now canonical description of Lincoln's deep reading in "military treatises," and he asserted that strategically Lincoln was wiser than his generals. In his "despatches" to Hooker in 1863, Rhodes wrote that "Lincoln exhibits common-sense. His diligent reading of military books, the acquirement of knowledge from his generals when occasion offered, the study of the field of war, the close observation of the campaigns and battles of his armies had borne fruit, making him now the best of counsellors in the relation of the civil commander-in-chief to his officers of technical training and experience." He was the force behind the Fort Sumter operation and the subsequent drives for Richmond. His War Orders to McClellan may have been written to placate voters, but they also represented "the highest strategy" and as the real need to protect the capital. McClellan could have won the war had he followed the president's wishes, while Hooker should have listened to Lincoln from the first. The president was right to regret Lee's escape from Pennsylvania and blame Meade. Lincoln also recognized the need to control the Mississippi River, and wisely supported Grant.[21]

Nicolay and Hay could agree with all those points. Yet according to Rhodes, Lincoln also made a string of fumbling tactical and operational mistakes that grew out of his lack of military background. He cited McClellan and Ropes when it came to battle. Lincoln's obsession with East Tennessee was "impracticable and romantic." The operation that the president and Stanton designed for the Shenandoah in 1862 was "too complicated to succeed," relied on "imperfect instruments," and took men away from the Peninsula, where they were more needed. Fitz John Porter deserved better treatment. McClellan primarily caused the failure on the Peninsula, but Lincoln and Stanton's inexperience played roles, too. The president should have reinforced McClellan after the Seven Days and fought in front of Richmond rather than elevate an inept Pope in northern Virginia. Nor should he have fired McClellan in October without a better available replacement on hand than an incompetent Burnside; Fredericksburg was Lincoln's fault as much as Old Burn's.[22] "The great man of the Civil War was Lincoln," Rhodes wrote in *History of the Civil War,* but only for his "his love of country and abnegation of self," not for any military genius.[23]

Competing authors weighed in when writing their own grand national histories. Woodrow Wilson was a southerner who claimed that his first memory was the fear surrounding Lincoln's election. He went on to earn a doctorate in political science, became a professor and president of Princeton, and was soon to become a Democratic politician in New Jersey. He rejected the Lost Cause and occasionally professed to be a Lincoln admirer. In 1901, however, in the fourth of a five-volume history of the nation he slashed out in a hurry for a tidy profit, Wilson had next to nothing to say about Lincoln as commander in chief except that he had been wise to offer command of his army to Lee.[24]

In contrast, historian Henry W. Elson of the Ohio State University admired Lincoln and the Union cause so much that in 1910 the United Confederate Veterans and the United Daughters of the Confederacy launched a successful campaign to drive his *History of the United States of America* out of southern classrooms, along with any teachers mad enough to assign it. Citing Herndon, Nicolay and Hay, and Ropes among others, Elson praised Lincoln as "the foremost man of his age," a "great soul, the greatest genius of his generation," the nation's "ablest president," "a Providential instrument," the Great Emancipator, and a better man than Jefferson Davis in every way. Yet in words reminiscent of McClellan and the comte de Paris—whom he cited as well—"Lincoln was greatly handicapped in two ways" as commander in chief: first, "his want of military training, and, it may be added, his commonplace native judgment in military matters; and second, his inability to extricate himself from the all-powerful political influence at the capital." Lincoln overemphasized the defense of Washington, hamstrung McClellan, and erred in the Valley. The blame for the rupture between Little Mac and the president belonged to them both, Elson maintained. Lincoln also listened too much to Halleck while slighting better generals. Lincoln was a great man, but he was no military genius.[25]

Most other authors of that era agreed with Elson's assessment. Greene and Conger aside, that mixed judgment reflected the overall verdict as America's *belle epoque* passed. Merrill Peterson argued that the Lincoln Centennial of 1909—largely observed only in the northern states—brought few new ideas and little important literature about Lincoln other than publication of

Welles's diary. Sociologist Barry Schwartz countered that the birth centennial helped Progressives like Tarbell link themselves to him through a focus on the egalitarian Lincoln. Popular interest gravitated more than ever toward Herndon's common man, with a fascinating obsession with his alleged log-cabin birthplace as a symbol of his character. By order of President Theodore Roosevelt, Lincoln appeared for the first time on the penny, "the commonest of all coins." Among those who heartily approved the change in coinage was the Milwaukee newspaper man and Socialist Party organizer Carl Sandburg. Intellectuals gravitated toward the presidential years, too. None of them had anything much to say about Lincoln the commander in chief, however, except that he was well meaning but flawed.[26]

In 1914, according to the Springfield-born poet Vachel Lindsay at least, a heartbroken Lincoln rose from his tomb. "Near the old court-house pacing up and down," Lindsay wrote in one of his great works, "Abraham Lincoln Walks at Midnight,"

> Or by his homestead, or in shadowed yards,
> He lingers where his children used to play,
> Or through the market, on the well-worn stones,
> He stalks until the dawn-stars burn away.

The First World War would not let him rest. "He thinks of men and kings," it continues,

> Yea, when the sick world cries, how can he sleep?
> Too many peasants fight, they know not why;
> Too many homesteads in black terror weep.
>
> The sins of all the war-lords burn his heart.
> He sees the dreadnaughts scouring every main.
> He carries on his shawl-wrapped shoulders now
> The bitterness, the folly and the pain.[27]

Unlike in Great Britain—discussed at length in the following chapter—World War I came and went in the United States without a significant effect on Lincoln's reputation as commander in chief. This is not to say that interest in Lincoln lagged. On the contrary, as Lindsay's poem suggests, the war and the interwar years increasingly brought about a great deal of discussion about the sixteenth president. Lincoln reemerged as a symbol of democracy and freedom nationally and internationally during the early twentieth century. Lindsay's ghostly Lincoln, after all, could not "rest until a spirit-dawn / Shall come;—the shining hope of Europe free." Even the wartime president, Woodrow Wilson, felt his spectral presence. Wilson was reelected in 1916 after "he kept us out of war." He reversed course the following year while inaugurating a wave of civil-liberties repression that made the Lincoln administration's previous efforts look tame. As for his predecessor, Wilson had spoken at Gettysburg in 1913, on the fiftieth anniversary of the battle, without mentioning Lincoln once. His admiration grew only as he saw their lives draw parallel in the White House, and he gave a stirring reelection speech from Lincoln's birthplace. Government propaganda often depicted the two presidents standing together. Wilson would find likeminded peers in Europe at the war's end.[28]

As Benjamin Thomas observed, the postwar "disillusionments of the war and peace" simultaneously brought about in the interwar United States both a new skepticism regarding "national heroes" and a renewed interest in biographies about those individuals if they were grounded in documents and avoided the obvious hero-worship of previous eras. Lincoln biography suddenly became something of a new cottage industry. Minister William E. Barton, former Senator Albert J. Beveridge, and poet Carl Sandburg emerged as the leading popular Lincoln biographers of this period. Beveridge, however, had reached only 1858 in his thick manuscript before he died in 1927, leaving reconsiderations of Lincoln the commander in chief to the other two.[29]

Born in 1861, Barton later in life described Lincoln as "my contemporary." His earliest memory was of his Illinois family and community mourning the murdered president.[30] A former missionary to Appalachia and successful minister, he had written prolifically about religious topics before turning to Lincoln full-time late in life. Fond of compiling Lincolniana for use in his sermons and in a religious newspaper he edited, Barton amassed a massive Lincoln library. From 1920 until his death a decade later, influenced by Herndon's realism and devoted to ferreting out unknown accounts and documents that his predecessors had missed, he churned out eight books and a stack of popular-magazine articles about the president. The books had such

Herndon-like titles as *The Soul of Abraham Lincoln, The Paternity of Abraham Lincoln, The Lineage of Lincoln* (which incorrectly made Lincoln and Lee distant relatives), *The Women Lincoln Loved* (fourteen in number), and *A Beautiful Blunder,* about Lincoln's letter to the allegedly grieving mother Lydia Parker Bixby. Regularly ignored by academics and criticized by rivals as egotistical, slapdash, and untrustworthy, Barton's works sold well with the reading public and, for a time, made him a leading Lincoln authority.[31]

In 1925 the minister published his rambling masterwork, the two-volume biography *The Life of Abraham Lincoln.* It attracted notoriety largely for his ideas about the alleged illegitimacy of Lincoln's mother, which led to a subsequent war of words with sometimes friend, sometimes rival Ida Tarbell. His limited interest in Lincoln as commander in chief, in contrast, meant that there was little new about that topic in the biography—by design. "This is not a history of the Civil War," Barton warned readers. "Most of its battles will not be mentioned. Many of its leading generals and notable events must go without recognition in these pages." His interest was in Lincoln the man.[32]

Lincoln was not an active commander in chief anyway, according to Barton, although perhaps he could have been. The president "was not without practical wisdom in military matters," Barton observed. "The few suggestions that he made to army officers about plans of the campaign were intelligent suggestions and showed a certain native shrewdness and practical sagacity which had in them the essentials of true military judgment." Much that followed this observation was familiar to readers of Lincoln studies. Barton included an entire chapter on the gentle legend of Lincoln's pardons. Another chapter on Lincoln and McClellan dismissed the general once again as egotistical and contemptuous in his dealings with the kind and supportive president, if possibly right about his need to better train the Army of the Potomac. Lincoln the politician understood that the public required activity, and eventually he lost patience. Rushing through Pope, Burnside, and Hooker in a few pages, Barton provided over two chapters on Gettysburg, including a battle narrative and a longer examination of the Gettysburg Address, which eventually would form a book of its own. A brief explanation of Lincoln's disappointment in Meade's failure to capture Lee segued into a discussion of the "taciturn, bullet-headed soldier from Illinois" who had just taken Vicksburg. Within a few pages in the same chapter, Grant launched his "simple" Overland Campaign. Grant "made no claim to being a great strategist," Barton wrote, but Lincoln "had enough military wisdom to understand and approve."[33]

Nearly a generation younger than Barton, dashing Carl Sandburg cut a much different figure than the prim minister. He already was a successful news reporter, Pulitzer Prize–winning poet, folk singer, children's-book author, and all-round celebrity when he published his two-volume *Abraham Lincoln: The Prairie Years* in 1926. In many ways, his interest in the president came as naturally as his fellow Illinoisan Barton's. Sandburg was a working-class son of Galesburg, the site of the fifth Lincoln-Douglas debate. Galesburg in the 1880s and 1890s was a place where Civil War veterans lived, and people who knew and heard Lincoln still told tales to young Charlie Sandburg. After dropping out of school, he hoboed; worked at an assortment of blue-collar jobs, including traveling sales; soldiered in the Spanish-American War; spent two weeks at West Point before failing the entrance examinations; went back to college in Galesburg, where he excelled at college sports; spent a brief sentence in the Pittsburgh jail; campaigned for the Socialist presidential candidate Eugene Debs; and earned a byline in Milwaukee and Chicago. Sandburg became both a pioneering investigative reporter and one of the nation's first film critics. Steadily, he gained a reputation for both his reportage and his verse. Influenced by Tarbell and likewise convinced that someone needed to return Lincoln to the people and explore his inner life as an avatar of the American soul, Sandburg gravitated toward writing a Lincoln biography as early as 1907. Such a book, he believed, might offer useful lessons to a cynical postwar nation. He used his frequent travel and speaking engagements to compile research materials that filled three rooms, and he began writing what he assumed initially to be another children's book. Sandburg exhausted himself obsessively writing after work into the wee hours, despite his failing eyesight—the same malady that afflicted Hay and Nicolay when they wrote about Lincoln—and he collapsed physically in 1925. The two-volume book that came from his labors grew into an idiosyncratic and sprawling amalgam of history, journalism, folklore, prose poetry, antiquarian digressions, detail, sentiment, subconscious autobiography, and at times even imaginative fiction, as when the sentient moon appears in its pages to watch the young country and Lincoln grow up.[34]

Sandburg admitted after the fact that he had deliberately crafted an American legend for people who needed one, with both Lincoln and the common man as its heroes. In the words of literary critic James Hurt, Lincoln in *The Prairie Years* was a primitive American "nature god" who grew like a stalk of corn from the black midwestern earth. Sandburg also reinforced the prevailing Lincoln "great stories" that had emerged since 1865, added to them, and repackaged it all for a new generation that had just seen one terrible war and increasingly dreaded another. Because of the quirks, or perhaps despite them, the two volumes of *The Prairie Years,* according to Hurt, became "the publishing event of 1926."[35] Hollywood quickly embraced Sandburg's Lincoln and especially his relationships with Ann Rutledge and Mary Todd. The books even attracted the admiration of some academics for the author's skill in bringing Lincoln to life, if not Sandburg's strict adherence to the sources or the facts. Notable among the dissenters was Milo Quaife, who had championed Arthur Conger but now damned Sandburg's lack of professionalism and factual errors. Sandburg and Tarbell's initial public endorsement of fake Lincoln documents in 1928 and 1929—even Barton had rejected them as obvious frauds—did little to help, especially when the fraudsters finally claimed to have transcribed them from the great beyond during seances.[36]

Sandburg's popularity survived, to the degree that he became "the nation's foremost Lincoln spokesman" after Barton's death. That was crucial in a decade marked by economic collapse. Lincoln seemed to matter more than ever to Americans, especially to those left of center politically.[37] Sandburg originally had planned to stop writing with Lincoln still on the prairie, but thirteen years and numerous interruptions later, his four-volume *Abraham Lincoln: The War Years* appeared. It followed some of the same "eccentric and unconventional" approach, minus the poetic flights and nature-god analogies, but with more concern for historical accuracy and hard journalism. That said, Sandburg still never met a Lincoln story he did not like, and he seemed to include them all. The president sometimes even slipped into the background, as at times *The War Years* became a more general history of the Civil War, chock full of quoted documents and prose "portraits" of leading figures. There was a more somber tone as well, as befitted a project written during the Great Depression and completed just as the world went to war again. Sandburg freely admitted that the present shaped his views of the past as his own worldview became Lincoln's. Nonetheless, once published, *The War Years* quickly gained even more acclaim than its predecessor, and it won Sandburg the second of his three Pulitzers. Presidents Franklin D. Roosevelt—often compared to Lincoln—and Harry S. Truman were among its admirers. Taken together in six volumes, according to Hurt, Sandburg's works on Lincoln's life became, "for better or worse, the best-selling, most widely read, and most influential book about Lincoln" in history. Reissued in new editions, published abroad, trimmed down for a children's version of *The Prairie Years,* and eventually updated as a one-volume abridgement of all six volumes in 1954, it provided fodder for playwrights, scriptwriters, and later television producers. "Probably more Americans have learned their Lincoln from Sandburg than from any other source," Hurt observed, yet "it may seem to have aged rather badly: inaccurate factually, grotesquely distended, and lapsing too frequently into a dated and forced 'prose poetry' that charms less now [1999] than seventy years ago."[38]

Like Hurt, historian Robert W. Johannsen and biographer Penelope Niven each has contended that Sandburg wrote inspired and significant epic poetry that was not exactly history.[39] Merrill Peterson observed that *The War Years* "has sometimes seemed the literary counterpart of the Lincoln Memorial." Yet in that otherwise influential monument of words, Sandburg did little more than Barton or their predecessors to further the heroic legend of Lincoln. In a detailed but descriptive narrative typically with relatively little analysis, Lincoln was a great president and a greater man, a remarkable character who could be jocose or melancholy, a man of the people who identified more with privates than generals, and ultimately the best of what the nation had to offer. But he was not a warrior-king or a military genius despite occasional common-sense strategic and operational insights. Indeed, Sandburg was not always complimentary of his hero on that score.[40]

Willing to risk war to save the Union, stop the expansion of slavery, or let the continent devolve into an ongoing series of balkanized wars, Sandburg's Lincoln wanted peace above all. He would have given up Fort Sumter without a fight to keep Virginia, Sandburg contended, or if Montgomery Blair had not demurred. Davis, not Lincoln, started the war. After Fort Sumter, Lincoln began "taking to himself one by one the powers of a dictator" and stretching his constitutional powers, but only because he knew that Congress and the people would support him soon enough. Sandburg did, too, although the former socialist's distaste for political arrests and shutting down newspapers sometimes offered recurring discordant notes. For reasons of "political necessity," Lincoln also pushed McDowell to Bull Run, which should have been a victory. No more favorable to McClellan than most of his predecessors, Sandburg again dismissed that general as a vain and disrespectful snob, "a dazzled, flustered man" wrought by his anxieties and convinced that "war was 'Ugh!' and not 'Ah!'" When McClellan went to his sickbed at the end of

1861, Lincoln began reading military history—Sandburg's passage closely follows Nicolay and Hay's account—and developed his "general principle" of concentrated attacks without ordering it. He issued General War Order No. 1 to remind McClellan who was boss, and he told Orville Browning (one of Sandburg's favorite sources) that he was tempted to take command himself. The president nonetheless allowed McClellan to go to the Peninsula (albeit without McDowell), while Frémont ruined his plans to capture Stonewall Jackson in the Valley. Never again would Lincoln try to direct operations in the field. The affair at Norfolk suggested that he had the stuff to be a good general, but he never tried anything like that again either. When it came to "military affairs," Sandburg observed, Lincoln increasingly strove "to keep peace in the family" and to defer to the West Pointers rather than stir up stubborn opposition. He brought in Halleck, "the living encyclopedia," so that he no longer needed to read about war. The president haunted the telegraph office as an interested observer—or when he needed to flee the public—but only occasionally offered plans that the generals then dismissed.[41]

According to Sandburg, Antietam and Fredericksburg convinced Lincoln that a harder war was required than McClellan would ever provide, as he told Mary Livermore, even if it might last twenty or thirty years and cost untold lives. By 1863, Lincoln had realized another great principle, that victory meant destroying Lee's army instead of seizing Richmond, but he had trouble convincing his generals of this until the emergence of Grant. As a westerner, Lincoln understood the importance of Vicksburg and the Mississippi River more than his generals. Yet blinded by his need to curry support from midwestern War Democrats, he also grossly overvalued John McClernand. Later, the president allowed his thirst to liberate East Tennessee to mask the real logistical problems that Burnside would encounter there and to ask, in Sandburg's blunt paraphrasing, "'How can you be so dumb?'" Lincoln was quick to compare other unsatisfactory generals to McClellan or accuse others unfairly of cowardice. By late 1863, his "warlike mood" extended behind the lines, notably to those who avoided military service or enabled draft evasion. A few Republican editors proclaimed Lincoln's military genius, but Democrats vehemently disagreed. When Grant took command, Lincoln backed away from operations and left that to him and Sherman, neither of whom included the president in their discussions.[42]

Lincoln thus became an enthusiastic but passive observer of military actions. The only exception came after Early's 1864 attack on Washington. That shook him. "For the first time in his life," Sandburg wrote starkly, "Abraham Lincoln saw men in battle action go to their knees and sprawl on the earth with cold lead in their vitals, with holes plowed by metal through their heads." That horror and his disgust at Early's escape led him to force Grant to respond. Otherwise, Lincoln trusted the war to his general in chief, told amusing stories, won reelection, and waited to implement a generous peace. Shaken anew by the ghastly sights of Petersburg at the end of the war, he entirely lost his "warlike mood," worried about the motherless kittens, and implored Grant and Sherman to spill as little blood as possible to end the war. This was the Lincoln who went to Ford's Theatre: gentle, noble, sick of war, and legendary.[43]

Barton's *Life of Abraham Lincoln* and Sandburg's six-volume *Abraham Lincoln* series were "among the last among a dying breed," Robert W. Johannsen later observed. "Lincoln soon became the property of the professors."[44]

Until the 1920s, academic historians beyond those who authored textbooks had been content to leave Lincoln largely to journalists, preachers, and poets.[45] The first to break the ice was the now-forgotten Nathaniel Wright Stephenson. Born two years after Lincoln's death, Stephenson taught college-level English in Iowa and Indiana and had worked as an editor and writer for two Cincinnati newspapers. In 1902 he moved south to the College of Charleston, somehow becoming a professor of history without an appropriate degree or much background otherwise.[46] In the "Cradle of Secession," Stephenson gave up writing novels and his studies of novelist William Thackeray. Toward the end of his two decades in the Deep South, between 1918 and 1926, he published two books about Lincoln and edited a third, a cut-and-pasted *Autobiography of Abraham Lincoln* taken from previously published "Letters, Speeches, and Conversations."[47]

Stephenson promised that his first Lincoln book, *Abraham Lincoln and the Union,* would deal with the "public" man. Most of it, in fact, devolved into a quirky and rambling history of the era in which Lincoln frequently disappeared in its pages. The author blamed the war on ongoing sectionalism between a democratic North and an aristocratic South that represented the Lost Cause at its most benign. He cited especially the final drumbeat of parallel assaults, led by southern fire-eaters and abolitionists in the North, on the one thing still holding the nation together, the Democratic "party of political evasion."[48] Until the unprepared Lincoln's inauguration, Stephenson went on, his silence and "blundering" had hastened the Union's breakup. Skilled "statecraft" followed, however, as a "passionless" and "inflexible" Lincoln seized control of the war effort, managed a difficult cabinet led by the conniving Seward, built an army, announced a war-winning blockade, and dealt with Europe.[49] "The Civil War was in truth Lincoln's war," Stephenson wrote in the shadow of World War I.

> Those modern pacifists who claim him for their own are beside the mark. They will never get over their illusions about Lincoln until they see, as all the world is beginning to see, that his career has universal significance because of its bearing on the universal modern problem of democracy. It will not do ever to forget that he was a man of the people, always playing the hand of the people, in the limited social sense of that word, though playing it with none of the heat usually met with in the statesmen of successful democracy from Cleon to Robespierre, from Andrew Jackson to Lloyd George. His gentleness does not remove Lincoln from that stern category.... He did not scruple to seize power when he thought the cause of the people demanded it.[50]

Like Rhodes's Lincoln earlier and Sandburg's a few years hence, in other words, Stephenson's became a stern but benevolent dictator. He never became a great commander in chief, however, far from it. Dismissing Nicolay and Hay as unreliable on that score, Stephenson ignored any suggestions of Lincoln's martial wisdom, and he specifically criticized the president for his lack of "sensibility" in sticking with McClellan, "a vain man, full of himself, ... [a] tortoise of a general." When defeats followed, all Lincoln knew to do was call for more men and use the North's economic might to acquire more ships and arms. Economics and diplomacy won the Civil War.[51]

In the subtitle to his equally odd follow-up volume *Lincoln,* published the next year, Stephenson promised an explanation of the private man through *An Account of His Personal Life, Especially of Its Springs of Action as Revealed and Deepened by the Ordeal of War.*[52] The clunky amateur psychoanalysis that followed thoroughly reflected what Merrill Peterson called "the latest vogue of psychological interpretation of Lincoln" in the 1920s, which he found correctly to be "provocative but unsophisticated."[53] Stephenson insisted that "there was always a double life" in Lincoln, "the outer quietly companionable," but the studious and "gloomy" inner Lincoln "solitary, mysterious." Before reaching the White House and unification, the two Lincolns "appeared increasingly contradictory, one thing on the surface, another within."[54]

Drawing almost completely on Herndon and Lamon for the prairie years, complete with jabs at "shiftless . . . vagrant" Tom Lincoln and yet another recounting of the Ann Rutledge story, Stephenson moved quickly to bring Lincoln to the national stage. As in his earlier book, he blamed the war on the abolitionists more than the slaveholding elite, arguing that Lincoln understood "the essential rightness in impulse of the bulk of the Southern people" without recognizing the "near horizon" that made them fear the North and follow the slaveocracy. An "inflexible" and equally short-sighted Lincoln, haunted by depression and mysticism, refused to consider a reasonable compromise and thus made war inevitable. From his inauguration until June 1862, the new president stumbled, an odd man riven by doubts and confusion. His "indecision" and inexperience led him to reject General Scott's Fort Sumter advice and to pay too much attention to the cries of "on to Richmond." He only began to emerge as a real statesman after First Bull Run, especially in his give-and-take struggle with a "Cabal" of abolitionists, Radicals, Stanton, third-rate Republican congressmen, and their willing tools in uniform. All of them were "vindictive . . . extremists" who, in Stephenson's telling, were infinitely more dangerous than the Confederates. The goals of the conspiratorial "Vindictives" were emancipation, southern desolation, and postwar revenge. Lincoln opposed them when he could.[55]

The president was no military genius as commander in chief, however. Lincoln foolishly believed that one great battle would end the war. His martial delusions and the Radicals' hatred of the Democrat McClellan, not any superior military vision, pushed him to interfere, challenge, override, and finally fire the general in 1862. In creating Pope's Army of Virginia, Lincoln showed no great martial insight—that general was a woeful choice to command—but that did not matter to Stephenson. With Pope, Lincoln psychologically "broke out of the cocoon of advisement he had spun unintentionally around his will." The two Lincolns finally became one as he battled the Radicals for control of the future.[56]

Newly confident, free of his demons, and whole in psyche at last, Lincoln ignored his advisers and began "gambling in generals." Halleck, Pope, Burnside, and Hooker were all "blunders" that grew out of Lincoln's psychological need for control rather than any military insight. Stephenson forgot to mention Meade at all, but at least the president was right to turn back to McClellan to save Washington. More importantly, Grant emerged as a lucky find in Mississippi. He became the embodied hopes of Lincoln's triumph over the Vindictives (and sometimes the Confederates) once he rejected the president's own flawed operational schemes. Lincoln became a great man in the end, but he was never a military genius.[57]

It would be easy enough to dismiss Stephenson's shallow Lincoln biographies as mere oddities and period pieces had they not announced more significant scholars and works that were remarkably similar in argument. Out of the steaming postwar cauldron of American racism at its worst, a growing and widespread disillusionment with the Great War and its results, and what historian Thomas J. Pressly called the "intersectional commingling" of the new graduate history programs that promoted reconciliation and renewed nationalism came radically new American approaches to the Civil War. Columbia University's Charles Beard and his students, for example, stressed the centrality of broad economic forces in history. The Civil War essentially had been a conflict between agrarianism and industrialization, Beard asserted. "Revisionism" in contrast rejected both Beardian economic history and the heroic explanations of the earlier "Fundamentalists" of the victorious North's wartime generation as well as more recent "Nationalists" such as Rhodes and Wilson. Revisionists denied that slavery was the moral cause of the conflict while turning on its head Seward's assertion that sectional division had hatched an "irrepressible conflict." Beginning with the pioneering Mary Scrugham, a Kentucky suffragist with sympathies for the Confederacy and a Columbia doctoral dissertation directed by William A. Dunning, they countered that the war had been in fact an unnecessary tragedy stirred up by Lincoln and his generation. A "blundering generation" of political leaders, egged on by the extremist voices of neurotic abolitionists in the North and a defensive countermovement of slavery's frightened defenders, stirred up a "needless" and "repressible" war through sheer incompetence and their refusal to compromise. Emancipation was not worth the war's cost to Revisionists little concerned with African Americans, as slavery would have disappeared soon anyway. After the war, so-called northern fanatics sought revenge as the Radicals imposed a harsh and vengeful Reconstruction on the South. In the words of two Revisionists, Reconstruction was a "Tragic Era" and an "Age of Hate." Stephen A. Douglas, James Buchanan, the proponents of compromise in 1860, and Andrew Johnson became the heroes of the era.

Abolitionists, Radical Republicans, and African Americans emerged as villains. Stephenson was no crank, in other words, but a proto-Revisionist.[58]

Revisionists differed somewhat when it came to Lincoln, however. At one end of the spectrum stood one of the two leading lights of the school, University of Chicago Professor Avery O. Craven. Born in Iowa to southern parents and married to a relative of the Georgia populist and lynching advocate Tom Watson, Craven defended antebellum white southerners as victims of a fanatical North. He not only blamed the abolitionists for the war but also scorned Lincoln. In a series of works culminating with *The Coming of the Civil War* in 1942, Craven hammered away at Lincoln as an opportunist who left the nation worse off. Although a conservative in reality, Craven maintained, Lincoln after the Dred Scott decision was willing to join in with other Republicans in stirring up "the false charges of a slave-power conspiracy and arousing the fears of common men against insidious foes" to advance himself and his party. The "House Divided" speech of 1858 was an "extreme partisan appeal to unfounded fears clothed in dignified legal and Scriptural language and softened with homely humor." Republicans nominated Lincoln for the presidency in 1860 because unlike Seward, who "lacked the necessary nerve to carry through measures of southern subjugation," he was the "'proper tool' to do the job" and "plunder slaveholders." Once elected, he did the party's bidding. The "well-meaning but bewildered" president steered a course for war and maneuvered the Confederates into the first shot.[59]

Others provided a more positive appraisal of Lincoln. Leading the way was the other great Revisionist, James G. Randall of the University of Illinois. Randall was the first significant professor ever to become a Lincoln specialist. He was a native Hoosier, born twenty years after Fort Sumter. Lincoln had enamored Randall since his boyhood readings of Ida Tarbell. He earned his doctorate from Chicago in 1911 with a dissertation entitled "The Confiscation of Property during the Civil War." Unable to enlist in 1917 due to his poor health, Randall took a position in the Wilson bureaucracy, then moved to Urbana from a position in Virginia three years later. Avery Craven was a fellow history professor and neighbor until Craven took his new job at the University of Chicago.[60]

In 1926 Randall published his expanded dissertation as *Constitutional Problems under Lincoln.* He prepared the book in the long shadow of the Great War, which occasionally led him to compare Lincoln to Wilson. Constrained by the rule of law and his own honesty, Randall maintained, Lincoln nonetheless had pioneered a wide interpretation of the Constitution and presidential war powers. With the best of intentions, Lincoln believed—and Congress and the courts later agreed retroactively—that as president and commander in chief, he had "large discretionary power" when it came to second-order warmaking. Lincoln defined the war as an insurrection, called out the militia to suppress it, grew the army, spent money on the military and navy without congressional approval, instituted martial law, reluctantly suspended the writ of habeas corpus, had the army arrest the disloyal and seize civilian property, closed newspapers, and carried out other initiatives through presidential proclamation that notably included emancipation. "Probably no president," Randall observed, "not even Wilson, went as far as Abraham Lincoln in the use of proclamations and executive orders." Lincoln "blurred" the lines between civilian and military authority when it came to arrests and military tribunals.[61]

Lincoln never became a despot, however, as "in the actual use of the war powers, great circumspection and lenience were manifested by President Lincoln's administration, and the Government showed a wholesome regard for individual liberty." Most opposition newspapers remained open, Randall observed, the government applied little censorship, freedom of speech remained secure, and no one hanged for treason. No party thugs roamed the streets either. Lincoln even expected to lose the presidency in 1864 in a free election. "Restraint" was the real story. "If Lincoln was a dictator," Randall argued, "it must be admitted that he was a benevolent dictator." Yet he still could not defend the president entirely. Lincoln ignored the rule of law far too many times and overstepped both Congress and the Constitution, Randall noted. "In a democracy it is a serious question," he added, "how far even a benevolent dictatorship should be encouraged." His real concern was that popular future presidents with less moderation and decency might mimic Lincoln's actions to seize dictatorial power. The Civil War precedents "might be dangerous to our democratic institutions" in anyone else's hands.[62]

In the 1930s Randall's interests steadily shifted from the Constitution to Lincoln himself and to the wider war, even as the modern world drifted toward a new cataclysm. With his colleague Theodore Pease, he edited and eventually published the two volumes of Orville Browning's diary that were to be so crucial to Sandburg and other historians ever since. He wrote biographies of both Abraham and Mary Lincoln, among others, for the *Dictionary of American Biography*. Then in 1934 Randall threw down his gauntlet in

Washington at the joint annual meeting of the American Historical Association and its western rival, the Mississippi Valley Historical Association, in a paper entitled "Has the Lincoln Theme Been Exhausted?"[63] Benjamin Thomas called it "a bugle call."[64]

As Randall later confided to fellow Revisionists William B. Hesseltine and Richard N. Current, "as a historian, Sandberg made a very good poet."[65] He proclaimed to his peers that it was time for the academic community to take up Lincoln studies, as the collectors, the amateurs, and the poets—he took particular aim at Barton, Beveridge, Herndon, Tarbell, and Weik—had done a poor job. There was too much silliness about Lincoln's mother's paternity or Ann Rutledge, he believed, and too little hard discussion about the presidency. With a nod to his fellow Revisionists, whom he suggested were nobly bringing scientific detachment to the field, Randall insisted that there remained too much bias. There still was no good biography of Lincoln, he announced, few good studies of Lincoln the politician or president, and no definitive edition of his papers, as Nicolay and Hay had cleaned up the president's spelling and grammar while neglecting provenance. Numerous unmined sources, notably those owned by the late Robert Lincoln and still closed to researchers per the stipulation in his gift to the Library of Congress, lay unused in archives. Other valuable primary sources had been published only recently. The field was "rich in opportunity." Notably, Randall said nothing about Lincoln the commander in chief; his concerns were thoroughly political.[66] Two years later the "Lincoln Theme" address went into print. By then, Randall's students and fellow Americanists already had taken up his challenge to the degree that, with few exceptions such as Sandburg, the non-academics suddenly felt threatened by the onrushing professors despite Randall's pleas to tread lightly. A decade later the editors of the *American Historical Review* announced a temporary halt to publishing articles about Lincoln. The academics apparently had exhausted the Lincoln Theme after all.[67]

By then, in 1937, with encouragement from author, editor, and historian Allan Nevins, Randall had published a massive, 959-page history of the war simply entitled *The Civil War and Reconstruction.* It became the dominant textbook and history of the war of its time as well as a major pillar of Revisionism. The author thoroughly cited and welcomed "with keenest pleasure" the new revisionism as professional, unbiased, and a great step forward beyond the "superficial, traditionally narrow, and partisan" Civil War histories of past years. Those approaches clearly shaped Randall's evolving views. The shadow of World War I loomed over it as well. Much more than in *Constitutional Problems,* Randall in *Civil War and Reconstruction* depicted the war as an unnecessary tragedy stirred up by extremism, "professional patrioteering, slogan-making, face-saving, political clamoring, and propaganda" and then enacted by a generation of second-rate politicians. Although he defended his work as "a fresh study," in many ways Randall followed the path of Stephenson. The plantation South, admittedly grounded in "white supremacy," also had boasted "romance and aristocratic brilliance" if a "wretched class" of poor whites as well. Citing historian U. B. Phillips's favorable views of slavery, Randall depicted the institution as relatively benign and the enslaved certainly no worse off than the European peasantry. All the South wanted was "to be left alone," but "the Yankee world" would not do that. Admittedly more modern, the North also contained a small but vocal group of reformers and abolitionist "agitators" driven by a thirst for power and status. Their "puritanism in politics" would not let the South go on as it had. The white South understandably responded defensively and coalesced. Sectional conflict grew in the 1850s due to both economic differences and what Randall deemed the false issue of slavery's expansion into the western territories. With weak leadership in Washington other than Stephen Douglas, the drumbeats for division and war North and South grew, with the "bitter zeal of righteous men" lacking "wisdom, toleration, tact, and the sense of human values. . . . Issues were becoming emotionalized, slogans were reducing public sentiment to stereotyped patters. . . . Mass psychology" hatched a needless war.[68]

Into this morass strode Abraham Lincoln. Rough and awkward but a "genius" intellectually, Lincoln also was a Kentucky-born moderate who understood the South better than his fellow Republicans. Yet he foolishly made no effort as president-elect to reassure the South of his intentions or support the various compromise plans that might well have prevented the war. He continued to blunder. Once inaugurated, the inexperienced executive could not unite the polarized country. He came close to giving up Fort Sumter to lessen tensions, changed his mind, and started the war almost accidentally when his own intention was simply to preserve the current status quo. His proclamation of insurrection and call for volunteers alienated southern Unionists and drove out four more slave states. "Four ghastly years of war ensued," Randall lamented. "The South had the advantage of fighting for independence—for something bold, positive, thrilling—while the North was too apt to appear in the role of subjugator." Lincoln had stumbled into a disaster.[69]

Once the war began, Lincoln seized power from Congress and the courts. Following his arguments in *Constitutional Problems* but now with more apprehension, Randall described how Lincoln embraced his second-order warmaking powers. He ignored Congress when he could but could not discount Radicals, "Jacobins. . . . who had never been in the army," who now wanted to control it toward their own extreme antislavery ends. Always more moderate, Lincoln sometimes had to "defer to the coarser influence of the Radicals or Jacobins." While "Congress was nibbling and whacking" away at slavery, however, the president moved deliberately, always preferring state emancipation with Federal compensation to slaveholders. He issued the Emancipation Proclamation as a war measure only when he had no other alternative. Once Lincoln died, the Vindictives moved on to Reconstruction, described in Revisionist terms as an "age of hate."[70]

As in *Constitutional Problems,* Randall maintained that Lincoln's inherent conservativism kept him from becoming a dictator "as the word is understood in the fourth decade of the twentieth century. He did not think of suppressing the legislature and ruling without it. He did not pack his Congress or eject the opposition. . . . No party emblem was adopted as the flag of his country. No rule for the universal saluting of Lincoln was imposed. There was no Lincoln party constituting a super-state and visiting vengeance upon political opponents." Lincoln may have outstripped Wilson and even Franklin Roosevelt in exercising executive power, in other words, but at least he was no Adolf Hitler, the new standard for authoritarianism.[71]

Lincoln was not a masterly commander in chief, either, not when it came to first-order powers and military prowess anyway. The heroic legend appeared nowhere in *Civil War and Reconstruction,* far from it. By and large, Randall described the war's campaigns and battles without any references to Lincoln at all, as if he had not been involved. When the president did appear, it was only to meddle and muck up things. "Pathetically eager that something be done," he erred egregiously in doing the Radicals' bidding and hindering McClellan. Lincoln read his books, but even then, his limited understanding of operational strategy involved little more than keeping an army between Washington and the army. As de facto general in chief, he and Stanton failed to stop Jackson in the Shenandoah Valley while he weakened McClellan on the Peninsula and all but ensured defeat there. "The promotion of Pope to high command in Virginia," Randall went on, "was one of those measures of amateurish experimentation in which the authorities at Washington so often indulged." After Fredericksburg, the citizenry lamented Lincoln's "two years of bungling." At that point, aside from promoting Grant, the president all but disappears entirely from Randall's military narrative. Grant, Sherman, and Thomas won the war without him.[72]

Well into the early years of World War II, Randall hammered away at his main themes with increasing force and deeper personal anguish as he researched and began writing his great opus, a multivolume biography of Lincoln the president. In November 1939, two months after German and Soviet forces invaded Poland, Randall defended both the professionalization of Civil War history and Revisionism in a stirring address to the Southern Historical Society in Kentucky. "No sane historian," he said, "is going to make light of revisionist work competently done." With yet another slap at the Ann Rutledge legend, Randall reiterated some of his main points. He noted the false "triviality" of the issue of slavery's western expansion while defending Buchanan and the compromisers of 1860–61. He also spoke out for McClellan. "The real cleavage of sentiment was not between Lincoln and McClellan," who fundamentally agreed on most social and political issues, but "but between Republican conservatives and Republican radicals." Randall saved his strongest pleadings, however, for peace itself. The Civil War, he said, "was less a matter of yellow sashes and tassels, of swords and roses. It becomes known for the ghastly scourge that it was." There was no glory in soldiers dying from disease or in the squalor of prison camps, much less in "desertion, corruption, and greed." What it did to people's minds was almost worse. "In its mental attitudes the war emerges from restudy as a thing of twisted ideology. Indeed, the war mind is one of the most ghastly features of the struggle; minds that should have kept serene were swept into the excesses of propaganda, intolerance, and hate, . . . an ideological abyss."[73]

Six months later, in May 1940, as German armies swept across western Europe, Randall in his presidential address to the Mississippi Valley Historical Association meeting in Omaha, Nebraska, returned to the false glory of "swords and roses" as he coined the term "blundering generation." With a comparison to the better-known horrors of World War I, Randall noted the Civil War's massive death toll—"about half the Union Army became human waste in one form or another"—as well as the dirt, disease, and horrors. And for what? Even "with all the recent revisionist studies it is difficult to achieve a full realization how Lincoln's generation stumbled into a ghastly war." The president was honest and forgiving, but his generation and party either were greedy and corrupt or else were "misled in [their] unctuous fury." As in most wars, ham-fisted blundering and "at some point a psychopathic case," rather than any great "economic or cultural processes," drove the nation into the bloody abyss. In the Civil War, blundering and a mass psychological breakdown, not slavery or slavery's expansion, paved the road to Lincoln's sad refusal to compromise at Fort Sumter. "The Civil War mind," he lamented, "seems a sorry *melange* of party bile, crisis melodrama, inflated eloquence, unreason, religious fury, self-righteousness, unctuous self-deception, and hate." Always moderate at heart, Lincoln seemed to fear his own people's fury, Randall suggested. The only real heroes other than the common soldiers were the pacifists, ostracized and shouted down then and now.[74]

The Civil War, the Great War, the current war, any war, was—to use Randall's favorite word—"ghastly." War means murder.[75] Never an isolationist, he believed nonetheless that statesmen should strive for compromise and peace at almost any cost.[76] What Randall and his fellow Revisionists could not see in Omaha was that a great shift in the American mood would come along with the nation's entry into the midnight of World War II, an event that would leave him sleepless and despondent. Before Pearl Harbor, a sizable majority of polled American wanted nothing to do with a second world war, even as the Roosevelt administration used Lincoln as a symbol to buttress its expansion and preparations to support the Allies and even join the fighting if need be.[77] After 1945, most Americans would argue that some wars were in fact just after all, and those had to be fought and won. With that turnabout from isolationism and disillusionment to consensus and victorious purpose would come the renunciation of Revisionism and the final canonization of Lincoln's heroic legend. But before that could occur, a separate and different intellectual tradition, which also grew out of the horror of World War I, had to emerge and enter the discussion, too, like one stream feeding into another to form a river. It was in interwar Great Britain, not the United States, where Lincoln again became known as a military genius.

7

BLADES OF GRASS IN THE SHENANDOAH

Great Britain, World War I, and the Heroic Legend Revived, 1916–1939

In August 1914 war began in Europe with the assassination of an Austrian archduke. The conflict spread rapidly through a tangle of international treaties, competing nationalisms, and imperial possessions to engulf most of the planet. An estimated 40 million people died, were maimed, or were declared missing over the following four years of World War I, at the time called the Great War. One in three men of military age living in the major European states died in battle. The sheer scale of death and destruction, the collapse of four empires, the rise of the Soviet Union, economic disaster, and the quick failure of the Versailles peace settlement combined to shake postwar Western society and culture to its knees. Subsequent wars fought over borders and ethnicity, civil wars, and more revolutions left Asia, Europe, and parts of Africa in tumult. A so-called lost generation of survivors abandoned spiritual and secular beliefs that seemed to have failed, including faith in liberal democracy, and turned to the authoritarian extremes of communism or fascism.[1] Fewer democracies existed in 1934 than in 1914. The dehumanization of enemies, new technologies that made killing anonymous, and the erasure of clear lines between combatants and noncombatants pointed to a dark future if another such war ensued.[2] "In scarcely any other period in modern times," historian Jörn Leonhard wrote, "did war, death, and injury mark a postwar period so profoundly."[3]

Out of all the blood and disillusionment came an unexpected, remarkable, and resounding British assertion of Abraham Lincoln's military genius, even as American authors continued to focus on other topics such as his genealogy, religious views, and love affairs. On the Western Front that gouged through Belgium and France, a belt-fed meat grinder killed hundreds of thousands of Tommies in a hellish squalor of muddy trenches, barbed wire, and gore. British soldier-historians had studied America's Civil War for decades, searching for useful models, but now convinced that their teachers had sold them murderous lies before 1914 and led them like lambs to the slaughter, a small coterie of influential British officer-historians rejected those lessons. Some of them turned to Lincoln and his generals for new models. Haunted by the Western Front, they breathed new life into the heroic legend, while adding their own twists.[4]

Despite popular assertions that the British Army of World War I consisted of "lions led by donkeys," a lively intellectual tradition existed within it before 1914. Books and magazines intended for professional soldiers abounded. It is difficult to ascertain how well read the officers were, but attendance at the Royal Military Academy at Sandhurst or the Staff College at nearby Camberley at least provided introductions. The American Civil War figured prominently in instruction at both institutions, but until World War I, the exemplars usually were Confederate. While the British government of the 1860s hewed to neutrality and the public divided between the American sides, officers drawn from the upper class largely embraced the Confederacy and scorned the perceived ineptitude of the Federal military. They especially criticized its much-reported destructiveness and lack of discipline, which they linked to northern democracy and egalitarianism.[5]

As historian Michael Turner explained, Stonewall Jackson especially became a special hero to many Britons in the 1860s. Admirers liked his daring, his piety, and his Anglophilism. To English supporters, Jackson was a quirky modern Cromwell, while Scots saw him as a pseudo-Jacobite. People wrote songs about him and attached his name to everything from ships to prize bulls. Britons mourned his death. After the war, trans-Atlantic Lost Cause hagiography bolstered his celebrity. British officers taught his tactics, lauded his victories, studied his leadership, embraced his stern discipline, and in effect made him one of them. Robert E. Lee never quite achieved the British adoration that his lieutenant received, but he had his fervent disciples, too. He certainly fared much better in the military mind than Lincoln and his generals. Swaths of a previously hostile British society first thought better of Lincoln after the Emancipation Proclamation, and his positive reputation grew after his assassination. He became a symbol of republicanism and democracy to many Britons. In the army, however, Lincoln remained a meddling and bumbling amateur when it came to making war. Grant was his best general, they believed, but even he was an unimaginative plodder whose own presidency further dimmed his military reputation. Nor was Grant a gentleman, any more than Lincoln. Others such as William T. Sherman and Philip Sheridan seemed decidedly second rate and unworthy of much attention at all.[6]

The high priest of the Confederacy within the British Army before World War I was Field Marshal Garnet Joseph Wolseley, 1st Viscount Wolseley. As a young officer, in a biographer's words, Wolseley had "believed that the best possible way to get ahead in the army was to try to get killed every time he had the chance."[7] Wolseley was wounded in Burma, lost an eye in the Crimea, survived a shipwreck, won renown during the Indian Rebellion of 1857 and again in China, led troops against Canadian rebels, fought the Ashanti in Africa, oversaw the end of the Zulu War (1879), secured British control of Egypt, and commanded the relief expedition sent unsuccessfully to save his friend Gen. Charles George Gordon in the Sudan. He was a key player in Britain's imperial expansion, with little to say about the colonized except ugly racial slurs. Wolseley became adjutant general of the army in 1882, which placed him in charge of officer instruction among other duties, and rose to commander in chief from 1895 until retirement in 1900.[8] No single person more shaped the British Army during the era, and no one more epitomized the intellectual officer than the man historian Hugh Dubrulle called "Britain's greatest living general in the late-nineteenth century."[9] Once in power, Wolseley championed controversial parliamentary reforms that modernized the army with new structures and technologies. He also called for better military education, staffed Sandhurst and the Staff College with like-minded officers, and became a prolific author of military history. Such was his fame that he served as the inspiration for Major-General Stanley, Gilbert and Sullivan's comical "modern major general" who was an expert on everything.[10]

No one venerated Lee and Jackson more than Wolseley. When war loomed between the United States and Britain at the end of 1861 due to the Trent Affair, the army sent 11,000 British regulars, including Wolseley, to Canada. An

Anglo-American war never came, but the conflict to the south fascinated him. Wolseley secured a two-month leave to observe the Confederates, slipped across the Potomac, toured the Seven Days battlefields, and found Lee's army after its retreat from Maryland. Lee, Jackson, and their plucky soldiers won him over for life. In January 1863 he breathlessly described his adventures in *Blackwood's Magazine.* Wolseley praised the Confederates for their military prowess and their characters, both allegedly shaped in a proper hierarchical society. "Whilst General Lee is regarded in the light of infallible Jove," he wrote, "a man to be reverenced, Jackson is loved and adored." He begrudgingly praised McClellan, too, but readily dismissed the "dictatorship of an insignificant lawyer" in Washington. Hapless, timid, and dependent upon "mobs of Irish and German mercenaries," Lincoln would never win. Britain should recognize the Confederates and let them end slavery on their own.[11]

The Confederacy did not survive, but Wolseley never repented of his hero-worship of Lee, even as his own growing international reputation as an expert on military science and history increasingly gave his views credence. In 1887, just as the *Century* was publishing Nicolay and Hay's Lincoln excerpts, he wrote a book review for *Macmillan's* that grew into a paean to Lee. The next year brought an essay on "Military Genius" that favorably compared Lee to Julius Caesar, Napoleon, and the Duke of Marlborough. He then authored a seven-part essay evaluating and expanding upon *Battles and Leaders* for Allen Thorndike Rice's *North American Review,* entitled "An English View of the Civil War." Lee biographer Douglas Southall Freeman later called the *Macmillan's* essay "a classic of Confederate literature," but the same could be said of all the officer's efforts. Wolseley defended secession and described Lee as "the greatest of his age, . . . one whom I have always considered to be the most perfect man I ever met, . . . the model Christian gentlemen in thought, word, and of deed, . . . a true hero." Lee's only failing was a "softness of heart" that prevented him from overthrowing an inept Jefferson Davis and establishing a military dictatorship that could have achieved independence. What was new in 1887 was Wolseley's expressed opinion of Lincoln. No longer the "insignificant lawyer," Lincoln now was the other great man of his age, "a far-seeing statesman of iron will, of unflinching determination."[12]

Lincoln's greatness, however, was entirely on the civilian side of the scales. In the *North American Review,* Wolseley praised Lee and Lincoln as the two great men of the war—"a head and shoulders above all others"—but repeatedly gave Lincoln the commander in chief low marks. While his "common-sense" made him at least better than Halleck or Stanton, that was a low bar. Lincoln's regrettable tendency to listen to "that hoary-headed and cruel old rascal, Public Opinion," led him to defeat at First Bull Run and to withdraw support from McClellan on the Peninsula. Had Lincoln really read military history, Wolseley quipped in a jab at Hay and Nicolay, he would have known that Lee had to remain close to his capital. Instead, the president foolishly believed that "the one way to get to Richmond was by making straight there from Washington." Then Jackson thoroughly frightened Lincoln in the Shenandoah Valley. Wolseley continued: "Mr. Lincoln, though doubtless one of the greatest men who have ruled the United States, was entirely ignorant of war. Able and wise as he was in all matters of civil government, he failed here most disastrously. By the course he pursued he wrecked an ably-devised plan for the advance upon Richmond of all the available Federal forces by one single line, whilst the troops intended for the defence of Washington were kept as passive as possible." In promoting Halleck to general in chief and giving an army to Pope, Lincoln and Stanton caused another defeat at Second Bull Run. The administration later wrongly criticized Meade, who "appears to have done all that any one but a man of quite transcendent military genius could have done to organize an effective pursuit" after Gettysburg. Only a joint army-navy attack could have taken Charleston, especially with the alleged genius Gen. P. G. T. Beauregard defending the city.[13]

Like so many other Britons who wrote about Lincoln, Wolseley had an open agenda. As historian James B. Rawley observed, the field marshal wanted his officers to study the Civil War for four practical reasons: observing the model careers of great generals such as Lee and Jackson, studying the many examples of combined operations, learning the importance of having a well-trained standing army in place before war began, and understanding the need for civilian leadership to let the army fight its battles. The last thing party-ridden Britain needed, Wolseley believed, was another Lincoln interfering with its generals.[14] Wolseley thus recommended *Battles and Leaders* to the men under his command. "Educated volunteer officers" would profit from learning what generals did that was right (Lee) or wrong (Grant at Shiloh). Joint army-navy campaigns merited attention "owing to the many wars [the British] have to carry on in wild and distant countries." Wolseley continued: "A German, a French, or a Russian general may frequently, perhaps usually, carry on a campaign without considering what assistance he may expect to derive from the cooperation of his own navy. . . . An English general has almost always to make his calculations in accordance to what the navy can do for him. . . . All European powers, England especially, are deeply interested in this question of naval attack *versus* land defence."[15]

Wolseley was not alone in his opinions. Standing intellectually at his side during his most influential years was another acolyte of Lee and Jackson, Maj. George Francis Robert Henderson. Twenty years Wolseley's junior, Henderson had left Oxford early for Sandhurst. He served conspicuously in Egypt in 1882 under Wolseley at the climax of the Anglo-Egyptian War, gaining a commendation. Like Wolseley, he became a noted military historian. His future commanding officer in the Second Boer War (1899–1902), Field Marshal Frederick Roberts, 1st Earl Roberts, described the young Henderson as a scholar who "read with avidity all military history and carefully studied the plans of the great battles of the world."[16]

In 1885 Henderson took his wife to Virginia, where he examined the battlegrounds of his great hero, Jackson. Four years later he anonymously published *The Campaign of Fredericksburg* as an instruction tool for the volunteer officers that Wolseley had brought to center stage. Such men would profit, Henderson hoped, from studying a battle fought largely by other nonprofessionals to the degree that, with actual war experience, they might "excel even Lee's battalions in mobility and efficiency" in Britain's colonial wars. Largely a top-down depiction of the "master minds" Lee and Jackson's model generalship—Henderson compared Lee to both Alexander the Great and Hannibal—he said little about Lincoln other than noting the president's anxiety to protect Washington and his "loyal determination" to carry on after defeat on the Rappahannock.[17]

The Campaign of Fredericksburg brought Henderson favorable attention throughout the army as well as respectable sales, a new assignment, and powerful new sponsors. Col. Sir John Frederick Maurice, professor of military arts and science at the Staff College, liked the book so much that he recommended it to Wolseley. According to Roberts, "as he found out who the author was, he interested himself in Henderson's future." Within months, Wolseley moved Henderson into the classroom for a decade, first at Sandhurst and then replacing a supportive Maurice at the Staff College. Both Maurice and Wolseley had criticized the college's dependence on German military thinkers—in the ascendancy since Prussian victory over France in 1871—at the expense of the American Civil War. Here was a way to turn the tide. Henderson became the great intellectual force at Camberley, inculcating views marinated in his pro-Confederate leanings. As Carol Reardon noted, British students in uniform in Henderson's era studied the Civil War more than their counterparts in the United States. His assigned paper topics and examination questions often involved the Civil War, especially Jackson in the Shenandoah.[18]

In his public lectures, Henderson increasingly echoed Wolseley in his condemnation of Lincoln, noting the president's alleged meddling, prioritization of political needs, and regrettable deference to public opinion. In 1892 Henderson affirmed that "neither Abraham Lincoln nor his Secretary at War had any previous knowledge of military affairs, but, notwithstanding, they not only attempted to dictate to the generals in the field, but settled for themselves who those generals should be. If their efforts to direct military operations were disastrous, as Lord Wolseley has pointed out, their efforts at selection were little better." He continued, "the Federal generals were much hampered by the President and his advisers, who never ceased, until the coming of Grant, to interfere with the military operations; but the fact that the ideas of these civilian councilors were almost invariably unsound goes to prove the proposition that for judicious strategy something more is needed than mere natural intelligence."[19]

Henderson's negativity about Lincoln derived from his new research. Wolseley had persuaded him to write a biography of Jackson, in part as another instruction manual for British officers. The finished, two-volume work, entitled *Stonewall Jackson and the American Civil War,* came out in 1898, followed by a second edition with an introduction from Wolseley in 1900. It received sterling reviews and reigned as the standard life of Jackson in Britain and the United States for perhaps a century. Henderson conducted extensive research, walked the ground, and corresponded with Jackson's surviving staff and his widow. He mastered nineteenth-century military tactics, operations, and strategy more than most writers since. He was among the first to call the Civil War the first modern war. Maj. Gen. J. F. C. Fuller, no friend to Henderson's overarching thesis, later admitted that Henderson never bowed at the altar of Lee as much as Wolseley. Unfortunately, according to later critics, including Fuller, Henderson also consistently reflected Lost Cause tropes by depicting Jackson as a stainless hero, eliding his mistakes, and minimizing the evils of slavery.[20] "Henderson has painted a vivid portrait of 'Stonewall,'" another critic, Brig. Gen. Colin Ballard, later wrote, "but it would please some of us better if the halo were not so much in evidence."[21]

As for Lincoln, Henderson equivocated. He sympathized with the president's toughness after "insult to the flag" at Fort Sumter and praised his agenda of isolating the Confederacy by sea. "Abraham Lincoln was no ordinary foe," Henderson wrote. "In forcing the Confederates to become the aggressors, and to fire on the national ensign, he had created a united North; in establishing a blockade of their coasts he brought into play a force, which, like the mills of God, 'grinds slowly, but grinds exceeding small.'" Yet the Confederates had valid arguments, too, he added, and the constitutionality of secession was a matter of opinion.[22]

Lincoln as commander in chief was another story. "In these pages Mr. Lincoln has not been spared," Henderson admitted. "He made mistakes, and he himself would have been the last to claim infallibility. He had entered the White House with a rich endowment of common-sense, a high sense of duty, and an extraordinary knowledge of the American character; but his ignorance of statesmanship directing arms was great, and his military errors were numerous."[23] Henderson consistently rejected the heroic legend and routinely depicted Lincoln as an anxious amateur woefully out of his league. The president's "apprehension" about losing Washington, for example, was fair for a variety of reasons, yet he could never grasp that the city already was secure. The "cordon of isolated earthworks" that protected the capital, Henderson quipped, did "not appear as an effective barrier to the civilian mind." When Lincoln withheld troops from McClellan, the "original dissemination of the Federal forces was thus gravely accentuated, and the Confederates had now to deal with four distinct armies . . . dependent for co-operation on the orders of two civilians, President Lincoln and his Secretary of War." As for McClellan, "however inadequately the capital might be defended, it was worse than folly to interfere with the general's plans when he was on the eve of executing them."[24]

Lincoln reached his nadir militarily, according to Henderson, when he took on Jackson in the Shenandoah Valley. He started out already handicapped due to his political generals. "What the President expected," Henderson wrote, "when he gave [Maj. Gen. Nathaniel Banks] an army corps it is difficult to divine; what might have been expected any soldier could have told him. To gratify an individual, or perhaps to conciliate a political faction, the life of many a private soldier was sacrificed." Lincoln himself "knew nothing of war, beyond what he had learned in a border skirmish, and very little of general history. He had not yet got rid of the common Anglo-Saxon idea that a man who has pluck and muscle is already a good soldier, and that the same qualities which serve in a street-brawl are all that is necessary to make a general." Jackson and Lee used Lincoln's inexperience and fears to their advantage. The result was Federal failure. Jackson escaped to join Lee at Richmond because "Lincoln and Stanton had not yet discovered that the best defence is generally a vigorous attack. They had learned nothing from the Valley campaign, and they were infected with the fears of Banks and Frémont."[25]

Henderson concluded his analysis with another damning passage:

> Men who, aware of their ignorance, would probably have shrunk from assuming charge of a squad of infantry in action, had no hesitation whatever in attempting to direct a mighty army, a task which Napoleon has assured us requires profound study, incessant application, and wide experience. They were in fact ignorant—and how many statesmen, and even soldiers, are in like case?—that strategy, the art of manœuvring armies, is an art in itself, an art which none may master by the light of nature, but to which, if he is to attain success, a man must serve a long apprenticeship. The rules of strategy are few and simple. They may be learned in a week. They may be taught by familiar illustrations or a dozen diagrams. But such knowledge will no more teach a man to lead an army like Napoleon than a knowledge of grammar will teach him to write like Gibbon. Lincoln, when the army he had so zealously toiled to organise, reeled back in confusion from Virginia, set himself to learn the art of war. He collected, says his biographer, a great library of military books; and, if it were not pathetic, it would be almost ludicrous, to read of the great President, in the midst of his absorbing labours and his ever-growing anxieties, poring night after night, when his capital was asleep, over the pages of Jomini and Clausewitz.[26]

By the time of Antietam, Henderson conceded, Lincoln had grown a bit as a military thinker. His advice to McClellan after the battle "shows that the lessons of the war had not been altogether lost upon him. Generals Banks and Pope, with some stimulus from Stonewall Jackson, had taught him what an important part is played by lines of supply. He had mastered the strategical truism that an enemy's communications are his weakest point." Yet the president still had much to learn and continued to underestimate Lee, who "had that practical experience which Mr. Lincoln lacked, and without which it is but waste of words to dogmatise on strategy."[27]

Historian Hugh Dubrulle called Henderson's *Stonewall Jackson* "probably the single most influential book in the British army before World War I."[28] Henderson was still at the Staff College in 1899 when the Second Boer War began, hoping eventually to write a biography of Lee but anxious to return to action. Lord Roberts later asserted that his subsequent successful marches into the Orange Free State and the Transvaal derived in part from his reading of *Stonewall Jackson,* and he requested Henderson for his staff. Henderson served for two years under Lord Roberts until bad health forced him home. After a year as editor of the army's official history of the war, Henderson died early in 1903. He was only forty-eight years old.[29]

Yet along with his patron, Henderson left giant footsteps. As Michael Turner observed, the Boer War renewed the appetite for studies of the allegedly comparable American Civil War. In so doing, it kept Wolseley's and Henderson's ideas and writings in the spotlight for decades. Until World War II, British officers regularly toured Jackson's battlefields, while historian Brian Bond maintained that Henderson's views survived in some form in the British Army through the 1960s. In 1958 Winston Churchill followed the Wolseley-Henderson path in his narrative of the American Civil War in the last volume of his monumental *History of the English-Speaking Peoples,* from its veneration of Lee and Jackson to its middling marks for an anxious, inexperienced, and overly political Lincoln's clumsy interference and "vacillations." Lincoln, Churchill concluded, may have saved the Union, but he should have stood by McClellan. The British Army that entered World War I in 1914, in other words, was a military led by a plethora of officers—including Generals Edward Allenby and Douglas Haig—that Wolseley and Henderson had trained to look to the Confederates for tactics and lessons while largely ignoring Federal operations. As historian Jay Luvaas pointed out, Henderson especially used Jackson to argue that mobility and flanking could overcome strong defenses. In contrast, the Staff College largely dismissed German authors and the lessons of the Franco-Prussian War. In 1914 the Confederate-style army that Wolseley and Henderson built encountered the German doctrine of envelopment in the fields of Flanders—with tragic results.[30]

Late-nineteenth-century British authors willing to dispute Wolseley and Henderson were few and far between. The most prominent was the dashing and popular Scottish war correspondent Archibald Forbes, a favorite journalist of authors Arthur Conan Doyle, Rudyard Kipling, and Mark Twain. A poor clergyman's son and formerly a private and acting sergeant in the Royal Dragoons, Forbes turned to writing after an injury earned him an army discharge. In the 1870s he gained fame reporting on the Franco-Prussian War from the German side and then covered a series of other wars in Afghanistan, Burma, South Africa, eastern Europe, and civil war Spain for *The Daily News,* a newspaper originally founded by Charles Dickens. He gave up reporting on war in the 1880s and turned to writing about it and lecturing to international audiences. When it came to the American Civil War, his affections were decidedly with the Federal cause. Forbes met and admired Phil Sheridan in France and later married Montgomery Meigs's youngest daughter Louisa in Washington. Iconoclastically, in British circles anyway, he judged Grant superior to Lee.[31]

In the summer of 1892, just as Henderson began to sour on Lincoln, Forbes published two positive articles entitled "Abraham Lincoln as a Strategist" for the *North American Review,* the same publication in which Wolseley had praised Lee while dismissing Lincoln's strategic vision. To be sure, Forbes lamented many of Lincoln's unsuccessful choices for commanding generals, especially McClellan and Burnside, and he added that Grant, Sheridan, Sherman, and George Thomas were responsible for their own advancement by making themselves indispensable. As a strategist, however, Forbes concluded that Lincoln had been much better than credited. The president indeed was an intuitive general and natural strategist who never needed the great study of warfare that Nicolay and Hay had described. Proof of that, Forbes continued, were Lincoln's post–First Bull Run memoranda, his determination to hold Washington at all costs through the possession of strategic points, and his early insistence of controlling the railroad through East Tennessee. Forbes also praised everything about Lincoln's General War Order No. 1 except its hastiness, and he concluded that the president's 's post-Antietam letters to McClellan proved that he was "a strategist of the first order." Had the generals done what Lincoln asked, Forbes maintained, the war would have ended much earlier. Whether intentional or not—the two men were on good terms otherwise—Forbes had provided a strong rejoinder to Wolseley that nonetheless failed to land a telling blow.[32]

British civilian opinions of Lincoln and his foes continued to shift steadily during the Great War. Actively encouraged by the government, the press sometimes connected their war to Lincoln's. Newspapers editorialized Lincoln's nationalism, military draft, and suppression of dissent to justify the

British war effort and to support unpopular policies such as conscription. David Lloyd George—Liberal prime minister of a Conservative-heavy coalition government beginning in December 1916—had called Lincoln his hero since childhood. "The Great Outsider" grew up with an illustration of Lincoln on a wall of his Welsh cottage, increasingly identified with Lincoln's rise from humble roots to power, centralized the war power in his office, and after the war met Robert Lincoln while touring Lincoln sites in the United States. With an eye toward pleasing Woodrow Wilson, Lloyd George even quoted Lincoln at the beginning of his government to speak out against a negotiated peace and to depict the war as a struggle for democracy. In postwar Paris in 1919, Lloyd George, Wilson, and French Prime Minister Georges Clemenceau—yet another Lincoln buff—frequently talked about the sixteenth president as they redrew the map of the world after victory.[33]

Perhaps most indicative of the new positive attitudes toward Lincoln that emerged in Great Britain during the war was the fact that an English peer wrote the Lincoln biography that Merrill Peterson called "the most readable that had ever been written on the subject" until Benjamin Thomas's book appeared in 1952.[34] Born a commoner in 1864, Godfrey Rathbone Benson attended Oxford, entered the law and Liberal Party politics, and became 1st Baron Charnwood. A lifelong Lincoln admirer, *Abraham Lincoln* was his first book when it appeared in 1916 as part of a series on great statesmen. Charnwood drew heavily upon available published sources, notably Herndon and Weik, Nicolay and Hay, Rhodes, Ropes, Wolseley and Henderson, the published Lincoln papers, and various memoirs. His goals were to depict Lincoln to wartime Britons as a universal hero of democratic government and then to use him to rally support for the war. Charnwood, too, wanted to counter the lingering antipathy between his nation and the United States that Wolseley had embodied in England and that so many Americans still expressed in 1914. The great Radicals and intellectuals of the 1860s supported Lincoln, Charnwood wrote, while it was the president who prevented an Anglo-American war and put the two nations on the road to better relations. Charnwood's *Abraham Lincoln* was a plea for common cause.[35]

In so doing, Charnwood offered a much rosier view of the commander in chief to his British audience that had Wolseley or Henderson. His views were more in line with the American authors of the era that he looked to for ideas. Repeatedly admitting Lincoln's inexperience and lack of preparation, he observed that the president relied upon his generals, "his common-sense and the military books" until time and events developed his military mind. He might have learned more quickly, Charnwood added, had his military advisors endeavored to teach him. Lincoln made mistakes, but none that were fatal to the Union. He learned how to appoint the right men and to be patient until their failures forced him to make changes. The president deliberated too long about Fort Sumter, but he made the right decision in the end. He reacted too strongly to public pressure before First Bull Run but never again, drafting a viable grand strategy for victory. Lincoln tried to work through his top generals, even the lamentable McClellan, whom Charnwood presented with little more sympathy than Nicolay and Hay. The president erred in appointing Burnside and Halleck, but that was understandable given the structure of the army, and he rectified his errors soon enough. He was right to criticize Meade for not destroying Lee's army at the Potomac. Most importantly, Lincoln supported Grant and stayed out of the way after appointing him as general in chief.[36]

Lacking real field experience, Charnwood admitted, Lincoln to be sure never became the tactician that Nicolay and Hay depicted:

> Some Northern military critics, when they came to read his correspondence with his generals, called him, as his chief biographers were tempted to think him, "the ablest strategist of the war." Grant and Sherman did not say this; they said, what is another thing, that his was the greatest intellectual force that they had met with. Strictly speaking, he could not be a strategist. If he were so judged, he would certainly be found guilty of having, till Grant came to Washington, unduly scattered his forces. He could pick out the main objects; but as to how to economise effort, what force and how composed and equipped was necessary for a particular enterprise, whether in given conditions of roads, weather, supplies, and previous fatigue, a movement was practicable, and how long it would take, any clever subaltern with actual experience of campaigning ought to have been a better judge than he.[37]

Nonetheless, Lincoln's overall vision became "the dominant will of his Administration, so too it seems likely that, with his early and sustained grasp of the general problem, he contributed not a little to the clearness and consistency of the strategical plans." Lincoln was a great commander in chief at least at the upper levels of war.[38]

Charnwood wrote about Lincoln as a civilian in a society embracing Lincoln symbolically, but the war and its appalling failures inevitably shook postwar thinking within the British Army as well. After 1918, a few embittered veterans, writing in a time of rising disillusionment, repudiated Wolseley and Henderson while creating a new view of Lincoln and his lieutenants as the men they should have studied. Those new views in turn would shape the canonical historic legend that emerged fully after World War II.

When it came to Lincoln, Capt. B. H. Liddell Hart provided the transition. Young Basil Hart—he dropped the "Liddell" in school only to reclaim it after the war—eagerly left Cambridge for the army in 1914. Expecting a short and romantic war, he obtained a temporary commission and undertook officer-candidate training. He went on to be hospitalized for illness, concussed, wounded, gassed, and briefly listed as missing at the front over the combined space of about seven weeks in action. His heart never fully recovered, but at least he lived. Half of his battalion died at the Somme in the first three days of July 1916, while 27 percent of his first-year college class died in action during the Great War. Reassigned to train recruits, write manuals, and digest the lessons of the war, he bitterly spurned the Wolseley and Henderson legacy as he wondered how armies could avoid another disaster. Eventually forced to retire due to the lingering effects of gas—perhaps for his increasingly avant-garde views of military tactics as well—he became a newspaper correspondent. A well-regarded study of the Roman general Scipio Africanus landed him an interview with new Italian dictator Benito Mussolini. Liddell Hart briefly admired Il Duce for making the trains run on time before firmly rejecting him and fascism.[39]

The Great War was never far from Liddell Hart's mind, however. In a direct slap at Henderson and the brass who revered him, he taunted in 1927 that "to be able to enumerate the blades of grass in the Shenandoah Valley and the yards marched by Stonewall Jackson's men is not an adequate foundation for leadership in a future war where conditions and armaments have radically changed."[40] A year later he seized his moment when he rejected a publisher's overture to write a biography of Lee, whom he regarded as passé. Instead, Liddell Hart suggested Sherman, the general who seemed to offer the real lessons on how to avoid another trench war through swift movement and deception, which the author later enshrined as the "Indirect Approach."[41] Sherman was "the most original genius of the war," he asserted, but the "General Staffs of Europe" had ignored him for the "battledore and shuttlecock tournament in Virginia—which they faithfully imitated with even greater lavishness and ineffectiveness on the battle fields of France from 1914 to 1918."[42] By then, Liddell Hart had come under the wing of an even more jaded and brilliant veteran, J. F. C. Fuller, who looked for battlefield salvation in the mobility of armored vehicles. Fuller—he always preferred Grant to Sherman—later charged that Liddell Hart's Sherman looked too much like the author: restless, nonconformist, pessimistic, and weary of the status quo. Despite that, like Henderson's *Stonewall Jackson and the American Civil War,* Liddell Hart's *Sherman: Soldier, Realist, American* became one of the two standard Sherman biographies in the United States for decades.[43]

Liddell Hart's bitter rejection of Wolseley and Henderson's pro-Confederate bias, however, did not lead him to reject their evaluation of Lincoln. Old Abe was still the same old ham-fisted meddler as far as Lidell Hart was concerned. Acknowledging the president's "moral strength," he observed that by First Bull Run, readers could "perceive the early dawn of that attitude which has made his name a synonym for the wise conduct of war and discerning support of his military executants, and a symbol of the right relation between statesman and general." Yet Lincoln made blunder after blunder when he tried to play general. Liddell Hart criticized him, for example, for obsessively pushing Don Carlos Buell toward East Tennessee and a "'blind alley' advance" into mountains. "Without river or railroad for its communications," he observed, "this movement over country roads, soon impassable in winter, would be in constant peril of a thrust against its rear flank from a foe who had both a railway and a river from which to launch it." Thus, Buell was right to balk. Lincoln also foolishly promoted John McClernand, while his resistance to Sherman's attempts to close railroads to civilians threatened the Atlanta Campaign.[44]

Liddell Hart defended McClellan, too. Acknowledging the general's numerous faults, he criticized the "irritated and uneasy" president's "ignorant midwifery" of the Peninsula plan. "Lincoln and his government interfered repeatedly and harmfully with McClellan" and "repeatedly overstepped the borders of McClellan's sphere," Liddell Hart wrote. Lincoln wanted an advance against the Confederate capital overland, an approach that "was foredoomed as a way to gaining Richmond—because it followed the line of most resistance. McClellan wisely persevered with his plan. . . . [T]he chance was further marred by Lincoln's reluctance to accept a calculated risk, in consequence of which he kept back McDowell's corps for the direct protection of Washington and so deprived McClellan not only of part of his strength but of the element of distraction essential to the success of his expedition." Wolseley or Henderson could have said it no better.[45]

Liddell Hart helped undermine the Wolseley-Henderson legacy—he was well on the way to becoming perhaps the leading military theorist of the twentieth century—but it took three fellow officers writing almost simultaneously between 1926 and 1933 to complete that rejection by elevating Lincoln to the level of genius that Hay and Nicolay, Conger, and Forbes staked out.[46]

The first of them was Maj. Gen. Sir Frederick Barton Maurice. At first glance, Maurice's appearance in the ranks of disillusioned Lincoln champions jars, as he very much had represented the military establishment. He was the son of Maj. Gen. John Frederick Maurice, one of young Liddell Hart's favorite war historians, Henderson's initial sponsor, a central figure in the Wolseley ring, and perhaps Wolseley's best friend and leading interpreter. J. F. Maurice twice served on Wolseley's staff in Africa, taught at Sandhurst, wrote the official history of the Anglo-Egyptian War as well as other books, and championed Henderson's ascent. Like his father, F. B. Maurice became a soldier-scholar in the Wolseley mold. After Sandhurst, he served in India and South Africa, studied at the Staff College after Henderson's departure, wrote a history of the Russo-Turkish War of 1877–78, and taught at Camberley just before World War I, when Maj. Gen. William R. Robertson served as commandant. After a few months at the Western Front, he rejoined Roberston as director of military operations when the latter became Chief of the Imperial General Staff in January 1915. The younger Maurice had reached the pinnacle.[47]

And then it all came crashing down in what came to be known as the Maurice Case. This requires some explanation. Prime Minister Lloyd George and the army's wartime leadership had despised each other since the Second Boer War, which the politician had opposed not only out of sympathy for the Boers but also because of Lord Roberts's scorched-earth policies. As the end of 1917 drew near, Field Marshal Robertson and Lloyd George clashed constantly. The former wanted to continue massing British troops on the Western Front for yet another frontal-assault offensive in 1918. Lloyd George, in contrast, had lost all faith in Robertson and British Expeditionary Force commander Haig, the crony of King George V who had been behind the worst atrocities in South Africa. The prime minister especially blanched at the massive casualty figures from the recent Battle of Passchendaele (July–November 1917). Probably correctly, he suspected that an increasingly hard-pressed, hungry, pessimistic, and angry public would not support another such bloody effort. Moreover, since the war's beginning, the government had sought to gain support from national and ethnic groups submerged in enemy empires. Lloyd George thus despaired of victory in France and advocated a "global strategy" of campaigning in southern Europe, in either Greece or Italy, against Austria-Hungary. He additionally wanted to mount a larger effort in the Middle East, where both London and Paris cast their imperialist eyes, eager to gobble up the collapsing Ottoman Empire. The Allies, Lloyd George maintained, had enough men to hold the western line, while the French—their army was on the verge of mutiny—just wanted to wait for the Americans, who had recently declared war on Germany. In shades of the Lincoln-McClellan struggle, the British brass in turn branded the prime minister as an amateur who needed to listen to his generals.[48]

Over time, the number of British soldiers on the Western Front, as counted officially by Maurice, became a flashpoint. Robertson fumed that Lloyd George was reducing troop strength there for his pet Mediterranean campaigns while forcing him to lengthen a weakened line that increasingly was vulnerable to a growing German threat. In February 1918 Lloyd George finally fired Robertson and took steps to put the army under overall French command, an additional insult to the army. A month later a reinforced German offensive all but wiped out the British Fifth Army; a follow-up campaign nearly seized the Channel ports. Lloyd George's critics charged that Robertson had been right. Either confused by conflicting reports or simply lying, the prime minister told the House of Commons that there had been more men on the front than in the previous year, blaming the generals and the weather for the disaster. Goaded by Robertson, Maurice responded by damning Lloyd George as a liar in a public letter to five London newspapers. The "Maurice Debate" followed in the Commons and divided the Liberal Party forever. Lloyd George denied the charges, attacked Maurice with typical oratorical brutality as both a liar and a coconspirator against the government, survived with Conservative support, and in the end claimed even more control of the military. Maurice soon retired under pressure.[49]

Historians have characterized Maurice's letter as everything from heroic to petty revenge to gross naïveté. Lloyd George charged as late as 1936 that Maurice was mentally ill. Historian John Gooch, however, saw an existential issue. "Underlying Maurice's allegations," he wrote, "was a strong belief that the entire conduct of the war was wrong."[50] To Maurice, Lloyd George was the corrupt and hapless commander in chief of a failed government, too confident in his own nonexistent strategic abilities and too easily frightened and distracted. Casualty lists and favorites swayed the British leader, while he otherwise "had an instinctive distrust of military opinion." He thus dreamed up spurious campaigns against the Austrians and Turks that only cost time and met army disapproval. Maurice alleged that the General Staff wasted "20%" of its efforts responding to the prime minister's "unsound" military fantasies. His criticisms of Lloyd George, in short, mirrored those of Abraham Lincoln's critics.[51]

The next few years further suggested that Maurice remained in the Wolseley-Henderson-Camberley camp. Lauded by some but still persecuted by the prime minister, he took a variety of positions—newspaper correspondent (until Lloyd George's friends bought out the newspaper), cofounder of the British Legion, principal at a school founded by his Christian Socialist grandfather—but increasingly he turned to writing. His first books dealt with the recent war, but then he published a laudatory cowritten biography of Wolseley in 1924 and a well-received life of Robert E. Lee the next year, in part because "the Great War has set before us new standards by which to judge generalship." Referring to the comte de Paris, Henderson, and Ropes among others, he ticked off several Lee mistakes: the First Ride Around McClellan, Malvern Hill, Antietam, his failure to control Longstreet, and most egregiously (and fundamentally), secession. Maurice nevertheless concluded in true Wolseley style that as a general, Lee had been better than the Duke of Wellington—and Stonewall Jackson—while comparable to Alexander the Great and Napoleon.[52]

Maurice's unexpectedly sudden break with tradition came later that year, when he delivered a series of invited lectures at Trinity College, Cambridge on civil-military relations. He focused these on Lincoln and Jefferson Davis. Seemingly out of the blue, he offered Lincoln as a role model for the British, just as an uncited Lord Charnwood had a decade earlier. "I had long been dissatisfied that the judgments of Lord Wolseley and of Colonel F. R. Henderson upon Lincoln's conduct of the war," he explained in the preface to a volume of the lectures published in 1926 as *Statesmen and Soldiers of the Civil War*, "written by the former on incomplete information, and by the latter in a study of one part only of the American Civil War, should stand as the British military criticism of a great statesman." How exactly he came to such an abrupt about-face is murky. The major catalysts seem to have been the recent war and his ongoing feud with Lloyd George, lenses through which he viewed Lincoln. "When I studied again," he explained, "in the light of my own experience in the Great War, the relations between Lincoln and McClellan and between Lincoln and Grant I became more than ever convinced that if, instead of holding up Lincoln's actions in May 1862 as an example of how not to interfere with soldiers, we had made a closer study of the workings of his mind and of the processes by which he evolved a system for the conduct of war, we should have saved ourselves much painful labor in the Great War."[53] *Statesmen and Soldiers*, excerpted in the United States and reviewed favorably there, was as much about the Great War as it was the Civil War.[54]

Maurice's depiction of Lincoln as commander in chief was nonetheless nuanced, a portrait of a man growing into a job. As a statesman, from the first he succeeded in uniting "his people"—the "first task" of any wartime statesman—by allowing Davis to be the aggressor. He weakened the Confederacy by holding the border states. Later in the war, the Emancipation Proclamation served as another rallying point. Maurice was critical of the commander in chief during the early war years, however. Lacking military experience, Lincoln pushed McDowell into battle before his army was properly trained, which led to defeat at Bull Run.[55]

Both Lincoln and McClellan bore the onus for their bad relationship, Maurice concluded. The president lacked enough military knowledge to even write proper orders, but the general did not know how to deal with civilian leadership. Lincoln overreached, just as more recent political leaders had done. McClellan "was quite right to refuse to advance [against Richmond] until he was ready, and prone though he was to be overcautious in preparation and to exaggerate the strength of his enemy, he cannot be said to have asked too much in requiring six months to train and organize the army which had been disrupted by the battle of Bull Run." Maurice compared that to his own experiences, when "the first new divisions created by [Field Marshal the

Earl Kitchener] began to land in France in April 1915, about seven months after the outbreak of war, and they first went into battle at Loos, five months later. The first American divisions were engaged just a year after the United States had entered the war [in 1917]." The "absurdity" of Lincoln's "foolish" general orders to get McClellan moving thus was obvious, Maurice admitted. Yet to be fair, McClellan and Winfield Scott had done nothing to educate the president, the unspoken addition being that his chief did better by the prime minister. "Left without information and means of reply to persistent critics," Maurice continued, "Lincoln was first perplexed and then perturbed, and if in that state of mind he did things which were militarily foolish, the chief cause of this was that his military adviser left him without military advice."[56]

McClellan's Peninsula plan was strong, Maurice judged, and "it was no part of Lincoln's business to have a military plan of his own" when his proper function was only to set "strategic priorities." Maurice added that he had observed that malady firsthand with yet another swipe at Lloyd George. "In 1915," he wrote, "Great Britain was severely hampered by the fact that more than one civilian minister had a plan of his own. . . . The preparation of plans of campaign is a matter which must be left to the experts, who, in their turns, must satisfy their Governments. . . . Statesmen and soldiers must have clear ideas as to their respective functions." Yet McClellan again had failed, too, by dismissing Lincoln's need to protect Washington and providing deceptive troop strengths—a sore spot to Maurice thanks to his own former duties and professional demise.[57]

Lincoln continued for a time to do foolish things that "cannot be defended." Sending a division to John C. Frémont in the Valley was a mistake. Then "Lincoln and Stanton took it upon themselves to devise manoeuvres and combinations of troops which had little relation to the facts of the situation, and to issue military orders which were as bad of their kind as they well could be. The effect of these orders has been well summarized by Henderson as causing 175,000 men to be absolutely paralyzed by 16,000. The best that can be said for Lincoln's bungling in this business is that it was one of the consequences of McClellan's attitude toward him, and that he saw almost at once that he had blundered." As much as he stuck by Grant in 1862 to his great credit, Lincoln meddled in his affairs, too. Indeed, Maurice decided that, with his late nights in the telegraph office and his reading of military science, Lincoln simply was the kind of man with a brain that "finds delight in the intellectual exercise of framing military plans."[58]

But Lincoln was at least no Lloyd George. He learned on the job, stopped making amateurish operational plans, championed Grant, and three years into his war finally developed what Maurice called a "practical and sensible . . . system for the conduct of war," one that was "ahead of any system of which had been devised in Europe until [Prussian Field Marshal Helmuth] von Moltke in 1866 and 1870 displayed the Prussian methods to an astonished military world." In that system, three men ran the war: Lincoln developed grand strategy, communicated it to Halleck, and let Halleck translate it to Grant. Both Lincoln and Halleck then let Grant be "master of his house." Yet Lincoln did not give away "his responsibility for the conduct of the war. The statesman cannot divest himself of such responsibility, and Lincoln made no attempt to do so. He read every line of Grant's reports, and followed all his movements with the closest attention." And he supported his general through dark days. "The situation was indeed not unlike that which in 1916 followed the close of the battle of the Somme," Maurice contended. "It is not surprising in the circumstances that the Allied statesmen wavered in their confidence in their generals, and determined to have 'no more Sommes'; but we, with the recent memory of those days in our minds, may the more admire Lincoln's firmness and constancy." When the eastern armies found themselves in the trenches of Petersburg, Lincoln had Grant's back even though trench warfare was not "the kind of military success which sets the bells ringing and the people cheering. . . . [T]he methods of the bulldog are sure, but they are neither speedy nor showy. . . . Was there ever a finer example of political courage?" Again, Maurice judged Lincoln—and grinding trench warfare—through his own khaki-colored glasses. Lloyd George never gave Robertson and Haig the support that Lincoln granted to Halleck and Grant. The admiring prime minister had been, in fact, the anti-Lincoln.[59]

Much of what happened that was tragic between 1914 and 1918, such as Winston Churchill's operational disaster at Gallipoli, occurred in the end because neither the army nor the politicians had studied Lincoln. Politicians were to make strategy and then trust their generals to carry it out. "More than fifty years after Lincoln," Maurice lamented, "we had, like him, to rough out a system as the result of bitter experience." Robertson finally did so, he contended, but unlike Halleck the field marshal had to deal with a meddling War Cabinet, not Lincoln. That nearly brought Britain to defeat. To avoid that in the future, the army needed to shrug off Henderson, who studied Lincoln at his worst, while Britain needed to realize that "the practice of Rome and the United States should assure us that there is nothing undemocratic in establishing a temporary dictatorship in time of national emergency. We must, in a great war, have a supreme authority to direct all the armed forces of the Empire." Lincoln had been a model dictator. Britain would need one again in a future war.[60]

Maurice, to be sure, was not the first author to refer favorably to Lincoln as a benign dictator. William O. Stoddard and James Ford Rhodes had done so, while Carl Sandburg, Nathaniel Stephenson, and James G. Randall soon would as well. But as Randall also noted, the times were changing the word's power. By the time *Statesmen and Soldiers of the Civil War* was published in 1926, Mussolini ruled Italy, the brutal Communist Joseph Stalin controlled the Soviet Union, and Adolf Hitler's *Mein Kampf* had just appeared in print. Maurice's conservativism left him somewhat sympathetic to such governments. Twelve years later, when Prime Minister Neville Chamberlain handed western Czechoslovakia to Hitler without a fight, a supportive Maurice met with both men and volunteered to take elements of the British Legion to the Sudetenland to ensure a peaceful transfer of power. With democracy in retreat, the concept of dictatorship wore a new patina, one that did not include Lincoln's belief in the people or the legacy of his relatively free American reelection. Indeed, it was in the zeitgeist enough that others—remarkably even that arch-man of the people Sandburg—would make the same perceived connection between Lincoln and positive authoritarianism.[61]

Almost simultaneously with Maurice, Brig. Gen. Colin Robert Ballard offered a defense of Lincoln that was even more enthusiastic. The son of an Indian Army colonel, Ballard was a schoolmate of Rudyard Kipling's. After Sandhurst, he took up Kipling's "white man's burden" in Burma and India. He studied at the Staff College under Henderson and was a classmate of Robertson. After completing his courses, Ballard left for South Africa to fight the Boers. After additional African and Asian service, he became an instructor of military history at Camberley in 1911, during Robertson's tenure as commandant and overlapping the younger Maurice's as an instructor. Ballard took a battalion to the Western Front in 1914, rose to brigade command, and like Liddell Hart fell wounded at the Somme. Once Ballard recovered, Robertson sent him to Romania as a military attaché. He held a postwar appointment in Turkey before retiring in 1923. By then he, too, had become an author. Over the course of a decade, before a stroke stilled his pen, Ballard churned out a history of Russia, four biographies of generals, and in 1926 *The Military Genius of Abraham Lincoln.*[62]

American Civil War scholars positively reviewed and discussed *Military Genius* just as they had Maurice's *Statesmen and Soldiers,* with a few even comparing it to Henderson's *Stonewall Jackson,* Wolseley's articles, and Maurice's *Robert E. Lee.* With reference to his earlier praise of Arthur Conger's similar thesis, reviewer Milo Quaife announced that the "time has arrived for those teachers who are still presenting in the classroom the doctrine that Lincoln was a military blunderer, to overhaul their lectures."[63] One less-positive reviewer chided Ballard for his limited source base. Indeed, Ballard built *Military Genius* on a foundation of fewer than two dozen published sources, including *Battles and Leaders,* Charnwood, Henderson, Maurice's biography of Lee, Rhodes, Ropes, and memoirs—but not Nicolay and Hay or other standard Lincoln books. He characterized his work simply as an extended essay on Lincoln as commander in chief.[64]

Directly criticizing Henderson, Wolseley, and Ropes, Ballard set out to do nothing less than change the entire Lincoln debate. As Maurice had maintained months earlier, the Great War reset the stage. Indeed, Ballard's essential estimation of Lincoln resembled his former Camberley colleague's enough that one cannot help but wonder if they had discussed it or if Ballard had attended Maurice's Trinity College lectures; we do not know. But Ballard was more positive throughout, minimizing the president's learning curve. Lincoln was "an exceptional genius" and "the Strategist of the North—he was the forerunner of that which we now call the Higher Command." Having built and supplied a massive military, which Ballard compared favorably to the work of recent wartime leaders, Lincoln "took upon himself to control the broad lines of strategy, and in some cases he even issued detailed orders for movements of troops. Here the chorus of praise turns to a note of denunciation," he admitted. "The military critics are especially severe, and long sermons have been written about the folly of amateur strategists, the wickedness of politicians who interfere with regular soldiers, the timidity, or to put it more bluntly the cowardice, which reigned in offices at Washington and spread its baneful influence in the Federal Army of the North." The critics, men such as Wolseley and Henderson, were wrong. "My belief," he continued, "is that Lincoln was solely responsible for the strategy of the North and proved himself a very capable strategist."[65]

Lincoln's strategic ideas, moreover, were ahead of their times, according to Ballard. Blinded by Lee's "exploits," historians had failed to see that the president's ideas were "not on the conventional lines of Napoleon and von Moltke, but it is just in its originality that beauty comes out." Lincoln was a "born strategist. . . . [I]nstinctively he grasped the main facts and gave them proper value." He knew that for political reasons, Washington had to be protected and the border states held. He also had to fight an offensive war across a wide front to save the Union. "The true faith is that attack is always the best means of defence," Ballard explained, "and that all force should be concentrated to form a mass for offensive action; this mass should be directed against the main body of the enemy. . . . [A] passive defensive would guard his own States but would never crush the rebellion. He must therefore think out offensive measures of some kind." The blockade could accomplish some of that, but land operations remained necessary.[66]

Ballard focused on the Peninsula Campaign as one example of how his superiors as historians had garbled the story. Like Maurice, he sympathized with McClellan, noting that Lincoln's desire for an overland march would have launched the Army of the Potomac down muddy winter byways against an entrenched enemy. Yet at great length, he also challenged Wolseley's assertion that Lincoln had doomed McClellan at Richmond by holding back troops. The campaign was lost from the first, Ballard asserted. The element of surprise had slipped away through delay, and the Confederates had time to concentrate. Lincoln grasped that even if McClellan did not. "Instinct told him that the plan was unsound," Ballard observed, "but he was quite aware of his own ignorance of military matters, and he felt that he could not override the opinion of the four senior officers whom he himself had appointed." As for holding McDowell, that was McClellan's fault, too, just as Maurice had maintained. "McClellan failed to give the Government an entire feeling of security," Ballard wrote, "his information regarding numbers and geography was hopelessly wrong; and his opponents were brilliant men who seized every opportunity." The general knew that Lincoln had to secure Washington, and he had months to update the president on his plans and explain his questionable numbers. When he did not, Lincoln justifiably held back troops to defend the capital. The president made mistakes in ending recruiting and in dispatching troops to Frémont, but on the whole, McClellan wrecked his own campaign before it started through "thoroughly bad execution. . . . McClellan had only himself to blame. . . . Lincoln would have been warranted in recalling Mc-

Clellan for disobedience of orders." Lincoln knew in his gut that McClellan would never attack, even with more men; holding McDowell back was moot.[67]

So much for Wolseley's arguments. Ballard's rejection of Henderson was more personal, as his jibe about Jackson's "halo" suggests. Seeking to protect Washington—and lacking a crystal ball—Lincoln correctly sent columns into the Valley against "a first-class prig—about as cheerful as Brother Stiggins, as humble as Uriah Heep—and we are prepared to dislike him thoroughly" until Jackson emerged in battle as "a gambler, intoxicated with the red wine of war. His soaring imagination carried him to heights where without exaggeration he can be compared with Alexander, Charles XII of Sweden, [and] Napoleon the Great." Yet Lincoln would have bested even that great general had his commanders only obeyed orders.[68]

Ballard went on to laud Lincoln again and again, with only occasional mild chiding. He defended Pope, supported Lincoln's decision to turn back to McClellan after Second Bull Run, and agreed with Henderson and Ropes that McClellan had to go after Antietam. Appointing Burnside was a mistake but an understandable one, as "it was an error in judging the human factor, which in time of war is of all things the most difficult to judge." Burnside should have moved quickly as Lincoln wanted, just as Hooker should have put in all his men at Chancellorsville. Lincoln correctly replaced Hooker with Meade as the former refused to attack Lee's extended columns. The president was right that Meade should have destroyed Lee at the Potomac; Lincoln's "attitude [after Gettysburg] provides us with the most signal of all the proofs of his genius," Ballard asserted. "It would be too much to say that certain victory was within Meade's reach," he admitted, "for there is no such thing as certainty in war—but it is a fact that he had a better chance than ever presented itself to the Unionists, either before or afterwards. It is easy for us to see this now, in the light of history. Lincoln, the amateur strategist, grasped it at the time, while the professional soldiers were congratulating themselves on 'driving the invader from our soil.'" Lincoln deserved credit for Vicksburg, too, for he had "boldness and perseverance to stick to a man against evil report[s]. There is the charm of absolute simplicity in his summing up of Grant: 'We can't spare this man; he fights.'" That "pair of thorough Anglo-Saxons" became a team in 1864, ending "Lincoln's active part as Strategist of the North," aside from Early's raid. Still, the president was the senior partner.[69]

To fully understand Lincoln's genius, Ballard concluded, readers needed only to consider him in the light of the Great War, just as Liddell Hart and

Maurice argued, while dispensing with the false doctrine that preceded it. "To set a true value in Lincoln as a strategist," he continued, "we must shut our eyes to the glamour which surrounds the statesman and get down to his military work. . . . There is no shame in admitting that in 1914 our ideas on strategy and tactics had to be very much revised." With confidence in himself, Lincoln "was carrying out all the functions of the modern Higher Command. There was no ready-made General Staff to set carefully prepared plans before him, and he had to pick up expert advice as best he could." The president replaced generals, sometimes impatiently, but so did governments during the Great War. He made mistakes, but "on the whole he has a wonderfully clean record." Lincoln understood the value of sea power, unknowingly reflected the German assertion that "every one of the separate units must pull its weight," conscripted men, and weakened the enemy through emancipation. Before his generals, he knew that Lee's army was the true target. Wolseley was wrong to attribute victory to Grant, Ballard observed. Lincoln had set the stage months before.[70]

Ballard closed with a similar argument to Maurice's. Lincoln was a good dictator:

> The position of Dictator was thrust upon [Lincoln] by circumstances; he accepted it, not from personal ambition but because he felt himself to be a bigger man than those around him; having accepted it, he made full use of his power. We see a very masterful Dictator issuing the first call to arms, instituting the blockade, proclaiming emancipation, warding off the intervention of foreign Powers—to say nothing of ruling a nation of free-born Anglo-Saxons. The Anglo-Saxons grumbled at him and disagreed with him, as is their free-born manner, and voted for him and supported him, as is also their manner; and so fought their way to victory.[71]

Chronologically, the final British soldier-scholar to link Lincoln and military genius was the one who most eagerly embraced dictators and fascism in his own times, the brilliant and eccentric Maj. Gen. John Frederick Charles Fuller. Along with Liddell Hart, he was already by then one of the two central military thinkers of his time, with fame exceeding that of Ballard and Maurice. A middle-class clergyman's son who early on rejected Christianity, the isolated youth acquired the nickname "Boney" at Sandhurst, both for his admiration for Napoleon Bonaparte and his small size. Fuller endured a lonely garrison life in Ireland and later South Africa, missing most of the fighting against the Boers due to appendicitis but exceling at scouting. In India, bored by the expected peacetime pursuits of young officers, he read philosophy, studied Eastern religions and yoga, and like Conger dove into mysticism. Back home in England, Fuller immersed himself in the supernatural. For six years, he was a devoted acolyte of Aleister Crowley, the self-proclaimed wizard and a father of the modern occult. Fuller published his first book about Crowley, who saw the young officer in turn as a kindred spirit in their mutual abhorrence of Christianity, democracy, and the lower classes. After an ugly personal break in 1911, however, Fuller applied to the Staff College, substituting professional study for the esoteric. He was there when the Great War began, burning bridges with his instructors for a torrent of ideas and papers that historian Brian Bond called "caustic," "unorthodox," and "heresy." He read what he wanted, which meant deep dives into Clausewitz, Napoleon and his interpreters, and the Social Darwinists.[72]

During the war, Fuller became a solid staff officer, then joined the nascent Tank Corps at the end of 1916. Churchill had championed armored fighting vehicles, but Fuller became the first great theorist and evangelist of armored warfare. He helped plan the attack at Cambrai, the world's first tank battle, and drew up a sweeping if unrealistic plan to win the war in 1919 that resembled what the Germans would do twenty years later with better tanks. After the war, like a human tornado, he championed armored warfare, mobility, new military technologies, and a thorough overhaul of the Ministry of Defence. Becoming chief instructor at Camberley, he eagerly tried to bury the Henderson legacy. Fuller increasingly earned the displeasure of his superiors, however, with his arrogant stridency and unconcealed loathing of the generals who, he charged, had led the army in the Great War as if they were still fighting Napoleon with muskets. Such flippant iconoclasm influenced younger admirers such as Liddell Hart, who embraced both mechanization and Fuller's disgust with the old order. In 1927, however, Fuller haughtily balked at including infantry in an experimental tank brigade that he and Liddell Hart had lobbied into existence and that Fuller would have commanded. His career ground to an ugly halt.[73]

Fuller retired in 1933 to pursue a second career in journalism. By then, he was an internationally known writer on military issues. His prolific early theoretical work on tactics, strategy, and the philosophy of war energetically embraced modernism in technology and in mindset though his advocacy of modern weapons, science, Darwin, Social Darwinism, and psychology. As with Liddell Hart, however, the Great War haunted him. His 1923 book *The Reformation of War* not only advocated aerial bombardment, airships, gas, submarines, and tanks as deterrents to war but also bitterly derided the men who and ideas that created and commanded the Western Front. *The Reformation of War* marked the pinnacle of Fuller's influence at home. His next major book, *The Foundations of the Science of War* (1926), grew out of his Staff College lectures, but it fell flat with officers who had grown weary of his hectoring. Among the most vociferous critics was Sir Frederick Maurice.[74]

Spurned by his peers, Fuller turned tardily to the American Civil War. He steeped himself in the *War of the Rebellion,* Grant's memoirs, *Battles and Leaders,* Nicolay and Hay, Ropes, and a Conger essay on Grant. In 1929 he published *The Generalship of Ulysses S. Grant,* ambitiously hoping that it would supersede Henderson's *Stonewall Jackson.* He followed it up in 1933 with *Grant and Lee.* Both works proved highly controversial. Civil War scholars in the United States preferred Ballard and Maurice when it came to the Civil War. As historian Jay Luvaas has pointed out, Fuller's overall approach differed little from Henderson's in that he, too, wanted to use history to instruct future officers. Brian Holden Reid added that Fuller also was trying to explain what the generals of 1914 had missed, doing so to such a degree that Liddell Hart suggested that his friend saw more genius in Grant than was there. The shadow of the Somme shaped everything else. As Liddell Hart turned to Sherman, Grant became Fuller's tool to pillory the generals of the Great War and shape the future.[75]

Wolseley and Henderson had been right in that the Civil War offered the best lessons to modern officers, Fuller admitted, but they failed to grasp them themselves. They should have studied Grant, for Lee was an especially poor role model. As a tactician, Fuller complained, Lee had "two cardinal defects, . . . his dislike to interfere with his subordinates once battle was engaged, and his reliance on verbal orders." Operationally, he should have fought defensively, especially in 1863, when holding Vicksburg was more vital than launching a quixotic invasion of Pennsylvania later wrecked by poor control of his subordinates and his failure to coordinate his attacks. Lee also hated confrontation, which undermined army discipline. His only idea was to attack.[76]

The previous generation also failed to understand the American Civil War as an extension of the Industrial Revolution, Fuller went on. Both it and World War I utilized modern technologies: rifled projectiles, grenades, mortars, steam-powered blockades, and entrenchments protected by wire. The Civil War was "so wonderfully modern, so close to us and of our day," he believed. Wolseley and Henderson never saw that, however, nor did they realize that the new technologies favored the defense. The Civil War had "foretold the coming of the World War of 1914–18, the tactics of which would have been vastly modified had Moltke studied those of this Civil War." Likewise, "the grand strategical problems which faced President Lincoln and the Union Government at the outbreak of the war were very similar to those which confronted the Allied Governments in 1914." The Allies defeated the Central Powers with "combined economic, moral, and physical pressure," much as Lincoln and Grant had crushed the Confederacy. Clinging to their intellectual bayonets and Confederate battle flags, Henderson and Wolseley had missed the real lessons and inaugurated a bloodbath.[77]

Wolseley and Henderson also had been unfair to Lincoln. While not perfect, Fuller called Lincoln the great statesman of his age. As the war ended, for example, the president crafted a "healthy peace" that put Versailles to shame. But Lincoln was more than a great civil leader; in tandem with Grant, he also became a great commander in chief. "If not to be reckoned with amongst the greatest of grand strategists," Fuller maintained, "there can be no doubt that [Lincoln] is numbered amongst the most successful, because his goodness as a man eclipsed his errors as a strategist." Faced with myriad problems that included building a modern military, Lincoln "had no military experience beyond a few weeks' campaigning against Red Indians in 1832. . . . He had at his disposal a microscopic navy, and a tiny army deprived of many of its best officers. Yet, though he knew nothing about war, he was possessed of a true military instinct." He understood that superior numbers and resources could allow him to win a bloody war of attrition. Lincoln also possessed the moral force and potential manpower of emancipation once the moment was right. When that time came after Antietam, it became "a moral victory" equivalent to "when the Germans most foolishly torpedoed the *Lusitania*."[78]

Despite his real gifts, Lincoln made plenty of mistakes at first, as Fuller admitted in a manner more reminiscent of Maurice than Ballard—without effectively citing either brother officer.[79] But those mistakes usually were the fault of the professional soldiers. The inexperienced president did not trust himself at first. He listened too much to Scott and especially the woeful Halleck, who to Fuller resembled no one as much as the quintessential bad British staff officer of 1914. "Lincoln though he possessed military insight of a kind, such as when he suggested to Hooker 'not to take any risk of being entangled upon the river, like an ox jumped half over a fence,' relied on a military Junta, consisting of himself, the irascible Stanton and the egregious Halleck." First Bull Run was "paralyzing" to them all. It led to the conventional but erroneous emphasis on defending Washington at all costs and taking Richmond from the north, as if the Confederates would have surrendered then and there. McClellan, the best of a poor lot of generals, "behaved like a willful schoolboy. . . . [B]etween Lincoln's ignorance and at times high-handedness, Stanton's infernal temper, and McClellan's secrecy and exaggeration, the first great Federal campaign was utterly ruined" on the Peninsula. Lincoln sapped his generals' initiative, interfered with them too much, and worried much too much about politics, even allowing the rank and file to elect officers. The result was three years of murderous stalemate.[80]

All that changed in 1864, when Lincoln made his greatest military decision and elevated Grant. The general understood that the war had to be won in the West, just as the president himself sensed. "Lincoln," Fuller explained, "who was a strategical visionary, that is to say he could often see what should be done without possessing an idea of how to do it, had long hankered after carrying the war into East Tennessee, not only because this would bring relief to the local population in this area, but because such an advance would threaten Chattanooga, a vital strategic point." Grant had made that a reality, starting at Forts Henry and Donelson in February 1862. But Lincoln still made foolish blunders. He interfered too much at Vicksburg, favored McClernand, and stood by as Halleck scotched Grant's potentially war-winning campaign against Mobile. Fuller compared that error to the younger Helmuth von Moltke, commanding the German Army in 1914, ruining the German's Schlieffen Plan and failing to take Paris. Yet Grant and the president eventually became an effective team. Lincoln could trust him to accomplish what he wanted and took his fingers out of the batter. "Lincoln, who possessed that wonderful gift of looking into the hearts of men," Fuller observed, "[and] said: 'Grant is the first general I have ever had.'" Called to Washington as general in chief, Grant mastered his assignment in eight weeks, a remarkable achievement, "as if in the World War a British general had been called from Mesopotamia to France to take over, not only command of the British armies in the west, but also to direct the strategy of the armies of the entire Empire." What followed was "the first of the modern campaigns; it initiated a tactical epoch, and did not even resemble the wars of ten years before its date." Ultimately, Lincoln became great with Grant at his side. "Grand strategy secures the political object by directing all warlike resources towards the winning of the war," Fuller observed, "whilst grand tactics accomplishes action by converging all means of waging war against the forces of the enemy. In spite of their military ignorance at the outbreak of the war, Lincoln learnt the meaning of the first, and Grant of the second."[81]

Fuller's final conclusions further announced another phase in his restless thought. Increasingly unsatisfied with what he perceived as modern decadence, the messiness of liberal democracy, and a moribund army that rejected him, he joined the British Union of Fascists only months after he completed *Grant and Lee* and retired from the army. Some historians have defended him as naïve, while others have pointed to the attractions of a militarized society or the possibility of forcing reform on the army. Others have argued still that Fuller had always been on the far right. Even his elitist mysticism, as historian Azar Gat noted, leaned that way. Fuller gravitated toward heroes as well. As he had once looked to Napoleon, Crowley, and Grant with schoolboy enthusiasm, he now focused on a fellow Sandhurst graduate and tank enthusiast, British Fascist leader Sir Oswald Mosely, who intended to make Fuller minister of defence if he himself became prime minister. Through Mosely, Fuller in turn came to know Adolf Hitler. While most British and American officers still ignored the former officer—Fuller increasingly loathed Anglo-American society in return—the Nazis welcomed him as a prophet. Future commanders of German tank columns read his works just as they did Liddell Hart, who first tried to save his old friend from his drift toward the far right and then broke with him over his new views. Fuller went on to embrace antisemitism, to attend German military maneuvers, to report as a war correspondent about the Italians in Ethiopia and the Nationalists in Spain, to lament Allied victory in World War I, and to call on Britain either to support the fascists in a coming war of civilizations against the Soviets or get out of the way.[82]

None of this should have been surprising. Fuller had previewed his new beliefs in 1933 in *Grant and Lee*. Of all of Lee's many failings, his worst, according to Fuller, was that he refused to overthrow Davis and his elected civilian government. "It was very clear to many at the time," he contended, "as it will be commonly acknowledged now, that the South could only hope to win under the rule of a Military Dictator." But shackled by his Christan principles, Lee "could not realise that the occasion demanded, if not a military dictator, then the strongest military hold over the Government and the political situation." He refused to act when he had the chance "as a revolutionary general should, because to have ousted Davis would have infringed the prerogative of God." At the end of the war, even with dictatorship thrust upon him, Lee foolishly continued to defer to Davis and the Confederate Congress.[83] Ironically, Wolseley had said the same thing. Fuller the avowed fascist never linked Lincoln directly to dictatorship as his comrades in arms had, but he praised military authoritarianism in theory.

In April 1939 the Nazis staged a massive fiftieth birthday parade for Hitler in Berlin. Fuller stood among the honored guests. For over four hours, warplanes soared across the sky, tanks and other mechanized vehicles rumbled by the grandstand, and 40,000 soldiers or more goose-stepped in time. When it ended, Hitler said to Fuller about the tanks, "I hope you were pleased with your children." Fuller replied, "Your Excellency, they have grown up so quickly that I no longer recognize them."[84] Within months, Fuller's mechanized "children" began rolling through Europe, bringing death and leaving a black mass of destruction in their wake. But they failed to achieve final victory. A new lineup of Allies overcame militarism and fascism. In the long shadow of a Second World War and the Cold War that followed, two American scholars—one of them another veteran of the Western Front—pulled together the threads of so many of the past studies, from Lincoln himself to Maurice, Ballard, Liddell Hart, and Fuller. They not just completed the British reconstruction of the heroic legend, they canonized it.

8

THE STERN STANDARD OF VICTORY

World War II, the Cold War, and the Triumph of the Heroic Legend, 1945–1959

In 1945, as World War II raced to its fiery conclusion, the long-awaited first two volumes of James G. Randall's *Lincoln the President* finally appeared, taking the commander in chief from *Springfield to Gettysburg*. True to his earlier calls to focus on Lincoln's White House years, Randall spent relatively little time on his life before the presidency, except for challenging the popular folklore that he decried before the war. However rough-hewn he may have been, this Lincoln by 1860 was a well-to-do lawyer, a leading Illinois politician, and a renowned speaker and writer who could rise to oratorical heights or spar in the partisan arena. Randall dispensed with the Ann Rutledge legend in an appendix and expressed little faith overall in Herndon's research.[1]

Randall's Revisionist arguments about the early war years largely were familiar as well. His Lincoln remained a conservative who wanted peace, contending like the Revisionists that the crisis was "'artificial.' . . . [T]he fuss was about things that did not count." Lincoln was willing to concede much, if not secession or the expansion of slavery. He did not maneuver Jefferson Davis into ordering the first shot at Fort Sumter. Yet thanks to the abolitionists, President Buchanan's concessions, Secretary of State Seward's ego, confusion in Charleston, and his own inexperience, Lincoln "could not hope to avoid trouble; he could merely choose between alternatives of trouble. . . . packed with psychological dynamite." Fort Sumter brought a war few wanted.

Lincoln defined the conflict as an insurrection, expanded his role through "emergency acts and his wide use of executive power," and ignored Congress when he could. His struggles with the Radicals—Randall also called them "unctuous rebel-haters," "Jacobins," and "Vindictives"—became the "veritable *leitmotif*" of his presidency. "A more unlovely knot of politicians," Randall commented, "would be hard to find."[2]

As for another traditional "leitmotif" of Lincoln historians, however, Randall threw down a fresher gauntlet. "For certain writers," he began, "the military career of George B. McClellan has become a fixed stereotype. It is assumed that if one is pro-Lincoln, he must be anti-McClellan, though the most bitter of McClellan's foes were also opponents of Lincoln." While those writers notably included Nicolay and Hay, they all had blasted McClellan as evasive, political, pompous, slow, rude to Lincoln, whiny, self-deluded when it came to enemy numbers, prone to blame others for his own sins, a poor general, and possibly a traitor as well. Randall rattled off a dozen rebuttal points, noting that "competent military writers" defended McClellan, he built a fine army that needed extensive training, and his men loved him. Lincoln's lack of military experience, impatience, and weak attempts at generalship "ineffectively" hobbled Little Mac. Lincoln was no model commander in chief and indeed was a poor operational general during the Valley Campaign. "Only an amateur," Randall observed, "could suppose that the head of a reorganized and untried army was unwise in demanding full preparation and a heavy force when taking the offensive against Richmond." Lincoln crippled McClellan on the Peninsula with his clumsy interventions just as the general went up against a Confederate army "at its military peak." Despite Lincoln and Lee, McClellan saved Washington, won at Antietam (the real turning point of the war), and never lost to Lee. Compare that, Randall wrote, to the "inadequate, timid, and bungling" failures who followed. Even Grant, he observed, needed over a year to take Richmond while enduring less interference from the White House, "unstable" Secretary of War Stanton, and the Radicals, all the while facing a diminished foe. "Lee's biographer [Douglas Southall Freeman] leaves no doubt on this subject," Randall continued. "He writes: 'Who was the ablest Federal general he had opposed? He [Lee] did not hesitate . . . for the answer. "McClellan, by all odds," he said emphatically.'"[3]

As before Pearl Harbor but now more passionately at the end of a war that had cost perhaps 60 million lives or more, Randall finally announced that he was sick of drums-and-trumpets history altogether:

> One seldom reads of the Civil War in terms of blood and filth, writhing men, spilled brains, and mutilated flesh. Even the terms "sick," "wounded," and "dead" are so generalized as to be almost abstract. Realities are so revolting that writers prefer to tell of flanking movements, of position and assault, of retreat or advance, of batteries opening up handsomely, of divisions doing this or brigades doing that. The very word "war" is a euphemism for "human slaughterhouse." Murder in drama usually occurs offstage. In historical accounts, especially military narratives, the war is offstage in the sense that its hideousness and stench do not appear.[4]

Lincoln the President: Springfield to Gettysburg garnered mixed reviews. Traditionalists balked at Randall's positive treatment of McClellan. Others admitted that it would never unseat Carl Sandburg's lyrical biography in popularity.[5] Paul M. Angle, the secretary of the Abraham Lincoln Association, raised his eyebrows at Randall's contention that "as commander-in-chief . . . [Lincoln's] course left much to be desired."[6]

More significantly, the nation had changed. Revisionism had run its course. During World War II, Lincoln metamorphosed into a symbol of democracy, freedom, just war, and military preparedness, a frequent symbolic adjunct to the expanding Roosevelt administration. In the aftermath of war and the opening days of Cold War, most Americans abandoned isolationism. There was little hand-wringing or soul-searching about "war guilt" resembling the debate that followed the First World War—Pearl Harbor made sure of that. Evil was real in the world, most Americans concluded, while war had become necessary and sometimes even ennobling. Compromise smacked of British Prime Minister Neville Chamberlain's failed "appeasement" of Hitler in Czechoslovakia. Over time, as the "Pax Americana" spread around the globe, World War II eventually became a "good war" fought by "the greatest generation."[7] As historian Wendy Wall explained, much of this new thought was deliberate. Well aware of the "the breakdown of social order" in 1919, still shaken by the turmoil of the 1930s and the rise of fascism, and worried by the nation's ongoing class and racial struggles, American elites from right to center-left—many historians included—called for consensus, pluralism, and unity.[8] In such an environment, Randall's antiwar sentiments and contention that slavery had not been worth the fight found repeated censure. His most significant postwar critics were Carter G. Woodson, Louis M. Hacker, and Arthur M. Schlesinger Jr.[9]

Born ten years after the Civil War to formerly enslaved parents, Woodson by 1945 was the acknowledged "father of black history." Formerly a coal miner and teacher, he became the second African American to earn a doctorate in history at Harvard after W. E. B. Du Bois. Despite his credentials, Woodson largely spent his career teaching in segregated high schools. Facing discrimination from the major professional associations as well as universities, he published prolifically and cofounded the Association for the Study of Negro Life and History in 1915.Woodson then started the *Journal of Negro History* in 1916 and edited it for over three decades. In 1926 he created the forerunner to Black History Month.[10]

As early as 1918, Woodson began criticizing white historians in essays that anticipated Revisionism's postwar critics. Randall actually was one of the last to receive his wrath. In his 1946 review of *Lincoln the President: Springfield to Gettysburg,* Woodson denounced it as a Revisionist polemic laden with questionable interpretations and unfortunate views. While Randall at least was not as bad as the "discredited" Avery Craven—Woodson had accused Craven of "misquoting, misinformation, and misstatement"—he came close. Noting Randall's support for Stephen A. Douglas, Woodson criticized "the author's praise for the temporizing and compromising element in history rather than those who face public evils courageously and deal with them promptly." There was "blundering" and corruption in the Civil War, but that happened in all conflicts. Likewise, Woodson hammered Randall for asserting the war was not "*inevitable* and *necessary.*" Pointing to the contemporary Indonesian War for Independence, Woodson suggested that it would not have been inevitable either if "the natives there did not ardently desire to be free from the exploitation of the Dutch." Likewise, the Civil War would not have been inevitable if the white South had given up slavery. With a slap at McClellan, Woodson asserted that Lincoln and the abolitionists were the heroes of the era.[11] A year later he launched an even more personal broadside. Noting that *Springfield to Gettysburg* was "pleasing pro-southern sympathizers immensely," he accused Randall of using weak evidence to convince modern racists that southern-born Lincoln, married to a southern woman, was a likeminded racial conservative who should be *their* hero as they blocked racial justice. Dismissing such a characterization of the president as nonsense, Woodson defended Lincoln, took another swipe at Craven, and wondered if Randall's marriage to a Virginian had deluded him into a "sectional bent."[12]

Louis Hacker was equally blunt. Born to immigrants, he once had been a Marxist critic of capitalism and disciple of Charles Beard, having also described the Civil War as a clash of competing economic systems. Around 1940, however, Hacker shifted well to the right. He was impressed by how the nation had surmounted the economic disaster of the Depression, and like many American leftists, he expressed dismay at Stalin's temporary alliance with Hitler. Hacker sloughed off his earlier Marxism so radically that he purged new editions of his books and praised capitalism for saving the world. He became a dedicated anticommunist, if also one who defended academic freedom against McCarthyism. To Hacker as to Lincoln, the United States had become the last great hope on earth.[13]

Hacker struck out at Randall and the Revisionists in a withering book review of *Lincoln the President: Springfield to Gettysburg*, tellingly published in 1947 in *Fortune* magazine, an expensive business publication aimed at the wealthy and published by conservative Henry Luce, who long had supported anticommunist movements. Hacker charged the Revisionists with seeking "to undermine the great libertarian tradition of the American Civil War" by claiming that the conflict was "a tragic mistake." Linked to the South if now "teaching in midwestern universities," anti-American intellectuals and "sons of Dixie" like the Indiana-born Randall were "embarked on a dangerous course" in "an increasingly authoritarian world." Revisionism made Hacker seethe, but he particularly castigated Randall for depicting Lincoln as an appeaser who was sympathetic to slave drivers. "This is an unreal and senseless travesty," he complained. Like Woodson, he defended the Radicals for fighting a just war to end slavery. Their capitalist legislation also "laid the broad base for American national greatness" and poured the foundation of what Franklin Roosevelt in 1940 called the nation's "arsenal of democracy."[14]

Two years later, in 1949, Arthur M. Schlesinger Jr. upbraided Randall for "pushing moral issues under the rug" and producing histories that were "pulpy and dangerous."[15] Born in 1917, Schlesinger was a wunderkind. The son of a prominent Harvard historian who had supported Carter Woodson, he was a Harvard man himself. Prominent historian Bernard DeVoto was his mentor. Schlesinger's lectures in Boston in 1941 impressed listeners so much that he published them in revised form in 1945 as *The Age of Jackson*. Depicting Old Hickory as a hero of democracy, it became a seminal work and won Schlesinger a Pulitzer Prize at the age of twenty-seven. He spent World War II first in the Office of War Information, which created pro-American news and propaganda, and then in the Office of Strategic Services, the forerunner to the Central Intelligence Agency. Harvard hired him after the war despite his lack of a doctorate. In 1947 he joined with a group of prominent liberals to create the Americans for Democratic Action, a potential "vital center" of national politics located between conservatism and socialism.[16]

Schlesinger now sought to craft a usable history out of American myth and legend to fight the Cold War. In his 1949 book *The Vital Center,* he imagined in one passage Lincoln's ghost appearing in the Soviet Union "like [Fyodor] Dostoyevsky's Christ" in the novel *The Brothers Karamazov,* reawakening Russian hopes for freedom.[17] To win the Cold War, he believed, the Civil War needed proper interpretation. Like his father, Schlesinger disdained Revisionists. His scathing review of Randall that same year linked him and the others to *Gone with the Wind* (the 1939 movie based on the 1936 novel by Margaret Mitchell), the Old South's modern apologists, and wartime appeasers. Slavery was evil and begged for destruction. Moreover, the antidemocratic methods slaveowners used to defend their cruel institution—"book burning, the censorship of the mails, [and] the gradual illegalization of dissent"—smacked too much of present-day Communist evils. The Civil War was not a repressible conflict, stirred up by fanatics and blundering politicians, but a moral crusade. Randall and the Revisionists had avoided "moral judgment. . . . To say that the Civil War was fought over the 'unreal' issue of slavery," Schlesinger wrote, "is like saying that the Second World War was fought over the 'unreal' issue of the invasion of Poland." Peaceful means would never obliterate all evil either. "The unhappy fact," he added, "is that man occasionally works himself into a log-jam; and the log-jam must be burst by violence. We know that well enough from the experience of the last decade." Dismissing the Civil War as needless, he warned, would lead to "regarding our own struggles against evil as equally needless."[18]

Lincoln had become an anticommunist. In short order, the community of Civil War scholars largely agreed. Revisionism all but evaporated in the 1950s. The wounds of World War II remained opened, the Cold War threatened nuclear destruction, and the broadening movement for African American civil rights blossomed into a new appreciation of abolitionists, Radical Republicans, the rights of the enslaved, and Lincoln the Emancipator. African American scholars rejected the contention that slavery was a minor issue to Lincoln. A "new nationalist tradition" emerged in Civil War historiography, functioning within a broader interpretive movement dubbed the "Consensus School" that minimized internal conflict in the nation's past. This "New

Nationalism" harkened back to James Ford Rhodes, if not William Henry Seward's "irrepressible conflict."[19]

Randall heartily despised the "log-jam thesis," agreeing with his colleague Richard Current that Schlesinger sounded like a fascist himself in glorifying violence. Yet he could not ignore the times entirely. In 1947 he published *Lincoln the Liberal Statesman,* a collection of essays dedicated to Sandburg. The two men's relationship had grown during the war, and the book was the poet's idea. In it, Randall warned against associating the personalities of the Civil War era too closely with modern events. While Lincoln or Thomas Jefferson were role models, they were "best to be considered in their own setting." Randall restated his belief in the blundering generation, adding that "war makers have been too much dignified. . . . The war mind needs to be exposed. The hate, partisan excess, and bombast, and corruption of the time belong to the nation's history"[20]

Five years later Randall published the third volume of his Lincoln biography, *Lincoln the President: Midstream.* More evolution was evident. The bulk of *Midstream* reexamined the war years to 1863, largely covered already in the first volumes, with both a post–World War II sensibility and a decidedly new perspective openly influenced by "Carl Sandburg—that eloquent voice, eminent Lincoln writer, and beloved interpreter of the American spirit." Randall accordingly included chapters on Lincoln's life in the White House, his humor, and his marriage—the last no surprise as Randall's wife Ruth Painter Randall had just completed a biography of Mary Lincoln. In the volume's final chapter, he sought to understand "this strange, quaint, great man." Randall to be sure returned to some of his oldest themes, such as Lincoln's strained relationship with the Radicals as well as his "harsh methods" regarding civil liberties and dissent. But he could not escape the recent war, however much he rejected the Cold War presentism of Hacker or Schlesinger. He again called for understanding Lincoln's actions in their own time and context, as "things regarded as severe in Lincoln's time would have seemed soft and 'decadent' to a Hitler, a [Reinhard] Heydrich, or a [Heinrich] Himmler." Yes, Lincoln had overstretched the Constitution, but he remained "considerate, tolerant, and respectful of civil liberty" as well as lenient to most political opponents. He was no dictator. There was no American "Dachau or Buchenwald," nor were there "witch hunts" for the disloyal.[21]

What Randall still did not do in *Midstream* was reassess Lincoln as commander in chief. Lincoln "carefully pondered eastern and western army problems," Randall observed, but "he studiously avoided interference in military strategy." He was no Davis, nor was he "the military genius or master of strategy which some of his eulogists have made him out to be." Given his "lack of military conceit" and self-awareness, Lincoln "deliberately kept himself in the strategic background." Convinced that George Meade needed to forget about Richmond, draw out Lee, and fight "a decisive battle," the president still refused to order it. Randall went so far as to suggest that Stanton, not Lincoln, deserved credit for Grant's elevation. Comparing Lincoln's generals to squabbling children, he concluded that the president confined himself to "putting in a word of caution, generous compliment, morale-building encouragement, explanation to avoid misunderstanding, and if necessary, rebuke."[22]

But even Randall had second thoughts at the end. He died of cancer in early 1953, leaving eight complete chapters of his final volume and a stack of notes. Richard Current completed this volume as *Lincoln the President: Last Full Measure,* published in 1955. Randall's chapters dealt largely with wartime reconstruction, foreign relations, and Lincoln's renomination. Only in his last chapter did he return to the shooting war. And there for the first time—at the very end of both his life and his career as academe's preeminent Lincoln scholar—Randall finally if briefly praised the commander in chief as a strategist. "Lincoln gave Grant a free hand," he wrote, "but it would be a mistake to suppose that the President had nothing to do with strategy or that he was passively inattentive to military matters. Too much should not be made of Lincoln's statement to Grant, as to other generals, disclaiming military expertness while leaving the field commander to act as the effective military leader." For those new perspectives, Randall cited a recent book that he quietly had fostered, T. Harry Williams's *Lincoln and His Generals.*[23]

While the New Nationalists discredited Revisionism and revived an interpretation of the Civil War that revolved around slavery, irrepressible conflict, and a good war, two unrelated men named Williams finally enshrined the heroic legend in the canon. If postwar America was barren ground for Revisionists, it became remarkably fertile for replanting the heroic legend. Trapped in a Cold War that drew a sharp contrast between democracy and authoritarianism, facing nuclear annihilation, eager for heroic leadership, and not at all incidentally approaching the Civil War centennial, much of the nation was receptive at last to reading about a military genius in the White

House who won a necessary war against evil by being smarter than his own generals. The successful centralization of warmaking in the governments of Winston Churchill and Franklin D. Roosevelt, both charismatic, eloquent, and brilliant leaders working through a small circle of military professionals, seemed to prove that the British soldier-historians had been right about Lincoln as a role model after all. Strategy fascinated Churchill. Both he and Roosevelt established that impatiently micromanaging a military could be positive (despite Churchill's later criticism of Lincoln for exactly that), and the prime minister loved new war technologies just as Lincoln had. It seemed clear to many that Lincoln's centralized warmaking really had pointed the way to victory.[24]

In this new climate, the first of the two new historians to successfully enshrine the heroic legend was Kenneth P. Williams. Like his literary bête noire John Codman Ropes, Williams occupied a transitional place. Born only a generation after the Civil War, he was a contemporary of Liddell Hart and Fuller who did not write Civil War history until after World War II. His unfinished five-volume study, *Lincoln Finds a General,* published between 1949 and 1959, was one of the last written by a soldier-historian of the Great War, yet it also was fully informed by his predecessors and the most recent war.[25]

Williams was a university professor but not a historian. He earned a doctorate in mathematics from Princeton in 1913 and returned to his alma mater, Indiana University. He taught in Bloomington for over forty years, retiring only shortly before his death in 1958. As a mathematician, Williams became a prolific author of everything from basic college mathematics texts to technical and specialized studies such as *The Dynamics of the Airplane* (1921); *The Calculations of Orbits of Asteroids and Comets* (1934); and *The Mathematical Theory of Finance* (1935). His greatest contribution, *The Transits of Mercury* (1939), analyzed observations of that planet from 1723 to 1927. The Smithsonian Institution's Minor Planet Center named a body in the asteroid belt after him.[26]

Unlike Ropes or Randall, however, Williams led a second life in uniform. In 1915, at the relatively advanced age of twenty-eight, he enlisted in the Indiana National Guard. Not long after Arthur Conger left the Mexican border to defend Lincoln in print, Lieutenant Williams spent six months there. Back on campus, he became Indiana University's "Founding Father of ROTC," leading a racially integrated cadre. When the United States entered World War I, Williams was among the first doughboys to arrive in France with the

150th Field Artillery Battalion, the lineal descendant of Capt. Eli Lilly's famed Civil War battery. He fought the Germans as a battery commander himself. Thus, like Conger and the British soldier-historians, Williams was a veteran of the Western Front. But he was not done with military service. He rejoined the National Guard in 1921 and remained in uniform until a month before Pearl Harbor, rising to the rank of colonel and eventually serving as chief of staff of the National Guard's 38th Infantry Division.[27]

While a talented mathematician by vocation, Williams also was a soldier at heart, one with extensive staff experience. And it was Col. "KP" Williams (as the Hoosier cadets called him), the retired officer who just missed a second world war, who decided to rewrite the history of the Civil War with a focus on the two men he most admired, the commander in chief and his best general in chief. *Lincoln Finds a General* was to follow Lincoln's repeated disappointments in the East through 1863 in two volumes, switch to Grant's simultaneous rise in the West, and bring them together at last in Virginia. The first two Lincoln-centric volumes came out in 1949, the same year that also produced Schlesinger's devastating review of Randall and Joseph Campbell's *Hero with a Thousand Faces.*[28]

From the outset, Williams was as fulsome praising Grant as Fuller had been. Grant, he wrote, "remains unique after two world wars; he is still in many ways the most profitable and the most inspiring of all generals to study. He was a soldier's soldier, a general's general . . . always thoughtful of his subordinates," hardworking, uncomplaining, modest, resolutely aggressive at every level, and in sum a modern military genius who remade warmaking.[29] After Williams's death, his publisher admitted that "nothing aroused in him so much as an inaccuracy or falsehood when it involved the character of his hero [Grant]," down to the smallest detail. Small wonder that Williams spent significant ink disputing charges of the general's alleged drunkenness while chiding historians who repeated them.[30]

But Lincoln was no less a military and political genius in Williams's eyes. Like Colin Ballard, whose often cited and glowing analysis best matched his own views, the colonel defended Lincoln's sagacity at every turn. With "tenacious spirit and forthright integrity," the president confronted the Fort Sumter imbroglio. The Confederacy wanted war; "there could not be peace except on the terms of the South." Lincoln "handled" the "pompous governor" of South Carolina "as readily as he had handled a flatboat on the Mississippi" and forced Jefferson Davis to choose war or peace. "The North . . . had a President: a man who then knew almost nothing about war," Williams observed, "but who had toiled hard and was familiar with adversity; a man with an indomitable will, a splendid mind, and a great heart; and over and above, a man who was habitually very honest and truthful." Any mistakes during the initial crisis, such as the confusion over the *Powhatan,* were Seward's fault. Once the war began, Lincoln still "acted with great wisdom." He called for troops and superseded General Scott, who "must often have been near the breaking point." Williams did not know why Lincoln accepted southern officers' resignations, but he had faith that the president "probably did so not only because it seemed the one practicable course, but because he believed it wise and right." Bull Run was lost only because Irvin McDowell was slow and Robert Patterson was afraid.[31]

"And so George B. McClellan came to Washington," Williams continued, "with the idea that he was a savior." Enter the chief villain of *Lincoln Finds a General.* No Confederate came close to edging aside Little Mac, and no author had been more negative since Nicolay and Hay. Vain, cowardly, backbiting, condescending, disrespectful, and politically partisan, Williams's McClellan was a bad engineer to boot. The man "had no military achievement to his credit—except the invention of an uncomfortable saddle," he snorted, and "was not likely to prove fit for high command." Once in Washington, the general did nothing, Williams observing that three months were enough to train soldiers for a more complicated World War II. "The training needed for warfare of the [eighteen] sixties," the mathematician observed, "in comparison with that needed today is like a mathematical education that stops at algebra against one that requires mastery of calculus."[32]

When McClellan went to his sickbed in December 1861, Williams contended, Lincoln had no choice but to step in and act as commander in chief. He learned quickly, as his questions to McClellan and later his general orders proved. "Few military writers have put in a more striking way the points to be kept in mind in forming an 'Estimate of the Situation' than Lincoln did in his letter to McClellan," Williams wrote. "In the pages of history it would be difficult to find an illustration that could more appropriately go into a textbook on strategy." World War II, moreover, should have changed the debate and diffused any criticism of Lincoln's alleged meddling. "Any contention that Lincoln should not have insisted upon very good reasons for adopting a new plan in place of one previously accepted looks foolish at the present time," Williams contended, "when it is taken for granted that it was proper for the

President of the United States and the Prime Minister of Great Britain to sit with the Chiefs of Staff of the two countries and together make the great decisions regarding theaters of operation and the critical 'second front' in World War II. . . . Lincoln was not a trained soldier," Williams concluded, "but he was a political leader of great intelligence, who saw things clearly and was courageous."[33]

As 1862 passed, Williams continued, Lincoln's genius and McClellan's flaws fully emerged. The author sarcastically described McClellan's march to Manassas and the question of numbers left to defend Washington. Lincoln had every reason to demote McClellan and distrust him, he opined. Williams again agreed with Colin Ballard that the president was also right to worry about the security of the capital. Jackson's Valley Campaign was "a real crisis," yet Lincoln never panicked, remaining offensive minded and seeking a way to crush the Confederates. As de facto general in chief, Lincoln fared no worse in the Valley than the professionals had. He "immediately sought to turn the Confederate move to advantage . . . without excitement, and with amazing speed and definiteness." Federal forces would have captured Jackson had McDowell acted more forcefully and Frémont followed orders. There were hiccups, Williams admitted, and excuses as well. The first orders to Frémont were so badly composed for Williams to conjecture that Lincoln had not written them. But even if the president did not know exactly where Jackson was, his confusion caused no delays. Nor was he wrong to redirect McDowell to the Valley.[34]

Williams continued to draw upon the world wars to depict Lincoln as a military genius. Indeed, in many ways *Lincoln Finds a General* became a sort of prequel to the later conflicts as Williams stressed the apparent object lessons of the British soldier-historians. "The spirit of a 'blitz' was in the words 'celerity and vigor' that Lincoln telegraphed to McDowell," Williams contended at one point, pointing to the rapid German campaigns of 1939–40. Moreover, his "scheme of command . . . was at least as good as the Germans used in the opening phases of World War I. . . . Who handled a difficult problem of command best—Moltke and his staff, or Lincoln, McDowell, and [Chief of Staff Lt. Col. Edmund] Schriver?" Lincoln's campaign "to cut off and destroy Jackson was the first case of inspired warfare by the Federals in Virginia since Lew Wallace had made his sudden descent upon Romney and thereby jerked Joe Johnston out of Harpers Ferry."[35]

Down on the Peninsula, McClellan wallowed. Lincoln knew that a breakthrough at Yorktown was possible, but the general refused to try. Even Joe Johnston understood that "'no one but McClellan could have hesitated to attack.' In military history," Williams observed, "it would be difficult to find a more crushing judgment than that." Admittedly ill, Little Mac went on the defensive before Seven Pines and came close enough to a victory there that Williams struggled for several pages to avoid any praise before complaining that the general had held too many men in reserve. Despite good information from Washington—Williams wrote that Stanton would have made a good "G-2" intelligence officer in the mid-twentieth-century U.S. Army—the "complete disintegration of the Commanding General" followed. "For a resolute and able commander the road to Richmond was open," he concluded, "but the real indictment against McClellan is not that he did not have the courage that would allow him to make a vigorous and general counterstroke, but that he did not even act conservatively and maintain a position in front of Richmond." The general's defenders aside, "the retreat to the James is found to be incomprehensibly bad when it is carefully examined." The Harrison's Landing Letter proved that "McClellan's lack of balance was growing worse instead of better. . . . Perhaps no soldier ever presumed to write a document more out of order. . . . McClellan's offense was not in what he said, but in the fact that he should say anything."[36]

Williams continued to hammer away at McClellan in describing the Second Bull Run and Antietam Campaigns while consistently defending John Pope's aggressiveness and shift to hard war. Unlike so many chroniclers, he admired Pope as a "good soldier." Almost every bad thing that happened to him was McClellan's fault, with General in Chief Halleck responsible for the rest. Old Brains should have combined the two armies in Virginia into a modern "little army group," perhaps commanded by seventy-eight-year-old Maj. Gen. John Wool, another Williams favorite. Still, "it was a tonic for generals to know that the President was at the side of a telegraph operator at seven o'clock in the morning." Unfortunately for Pope, however, Jackson slipped north in yet another precursor to modern war. "What had taken place," Williams explained, "was the prototype of an airborne operation of World War II. Between Pope and Washington was Stonewall Jackson with some 23,000 infantry and artillery and [Maj. Gen. Jeb] Stuart's cavalry. Not by gliders and parachutes had they arrived there, but by their legs and feet, after one of the famous marches of history." Yet "no blow by Jackson could be quite as paralyzing as an order by McClellan," who did everything he could do to ruin

Pope. Lincoln was perhaps "too patient," but Stanton demonstrated "a touch of the spirit of [French Commander in Chief Joseph] Joffre's great order of September 4, 1914, a touch of the boldness that would have brought victory on the banks of Bull Run as surely as it did a half-century later along the Marne." Instead, disaster occurred. Lincoln asked McClellan to protect Washington but never intended to keep him for long. After Antietam, he dawdled until Lincoln fired him. "Surely the verdict must be: McClellan was not a real general," Williams concluded. He "was not even a disciplined, truthful soldier. McClellan was merely [an] attractive but vain and unstable man, with considerable military knowledge, who sat a horse well and wanted to be President."[37]

Williams despised no one in the Civil War more than McClellan, but at this point Lincoln was yet to find his general. Ambrose Burnside at least had the good sense not to endorse McClellan's plans and "was soldier enough to realize that the Confederate capital was a less important objective than the main Confederate army which Lincoln was eager to have destroyed." It was Halleck's failure to get Burnside's pontoons to the Rappahannock River that doomed the Fredericksburg advance. Burnside was rational as well: "Although Lincoln had not found the general he needed, he at least had one to whom he could speak as man to man without offending or being misunderstood." Yet Burnside became too enmeshed in Army of the Potomac politics and his own self-doubts. Lincoln accepted his resignation after the Mud March and turned to Joseph Hooker. He, too, started out well, but the fighting at Chancellorsville shook him. When Lee went north across the Potomac River, Lincoln expressed superior operational ideas to his general and encouraged him to follow. When Hooker continued to fuss with Halleck, the president gave the army to George Meade. Although he won at Gettysburg, Meade's "feeble" McClellan-like pursuit troubled Lincoln, especially when he contrasted it to Grant at Vicksburg. Stalemate followed. Williams praised the decision to send troops to Chattanooga without mentioning Lincoln's bitter opposition to the operation. He decried Meade's weakness, citing "a complete surrender by Meade of all initiative, although he had much the larger army. . . . [H]e was in awe of Lee and believed that he could do almost anything. Lincoln saw the truth to which his general was blind."[38]

In three subsequent volumes—the author died in 1958 before he could write the final books, leaving his story unfinished at Chickamauga—Williams turned to his hero Grant in the West. Lincoln took center stage less often, but when he did, it was always as the wise military genius and father of modern war. His September 1861 "paper" on Tennessee, Williams observed, was by that early date in his presidency "not that of the ordinary amateur or armchair strategist; it savors strongly of the professional." Constantly reading reports, Lincoln was an active commander in chief. He developed a strong grasp of the far-flung western theater, made cogent suggestions, and attempted to encourage coordinated campaigns. Williams defended the president in his confrontation with the frustrating Frémonts, championed his deliberate shift toward emancipation, and explained how Lincoln consistently tried to liberate East Tennessee. With vigor, he repeatedly derided the claims of Maryland author, political reformer, and Federal spy Anna Ella Carroll, a "pretentious woman" who allegedly gave Lincoln the ideas for both the Tennessee River and Mississippi campaigns. General War Order No. 1 dealt with the West as well as the East; Williams linked those orders to the fall of Fort Donelson. Giving Halleck western overall command was a stab at achieving success there while reigning in McClellan. Despite his impatience in the winter of 1862–63, Lincoln defended Grant. Williams's deep regard for both men led him to deal gingerly with the devious John McClernand before concluding that Lincoln made a rare mistake in being too lenient with that general while allowing him to ignore the chain of command. Williams likewise explained away the president's decision to disagree with Grant and prioritize Texas over Mobile in a way that did credit to both men.[39]

Wanting to do more than exalt Lincoln and Grant, Williams's aim was to silence once and for all the generations of critics who had disputed their military genius and thus reinvigorate the heroic legend. He vowed to do so by grounding his analysis in "the most reliable of documents," the *Official Records*, promising to refer to later works only to augment the documents or to weigh into controversies against "fashionable" interpretations. As it turned out, those exceptions proved to be legion. Williams in fact frequently entered the literary lists, corrected what he perceived as errors to the smallest detail, and sometimes brutally addressed the shortcomings of other authors. He could be scathing when dealing with writers who suggested that Lincoln's handling of the war was less than masterful, to the point of adding lengthy, multipart appendices to damn a handful of recent works that he found especially egregious. He devoted several pages, for example, to Confederate apologist John Shipley Tilley's obscure *Lincoln Takes Command,* which in Williams's view was blatantly prosecession and unfairly "censorious of President Lincoln" for deceitfully manipulating events at Fort Sumter. He found it "difficult to write either briefly or with restraint" about Fred A. Shannon, who had replaced Randall in the Civil War classroom at the University of Illinois. Williams feared that Shannon's Pulitzer Prize–winning *The Organization and Administration of the Union Army* (1928) had "done much harm" to the nation's college students by convincing their professors that Lincoln had mishandled raising troops and acquiring weapons, issues that garnered appendices of their own. Shannon lacked military experience and allegedly ignored key documents, leaving Williams to huff that he was unqualified to write about army administration. Equally unqualified in his eyes was pioneering military historian Maj. R. M. Johnston, later chief of the U.S. Army's Historical Section. Williams complained that he botched his discussion of raising troops before Bull Run, misunderstood terminology, garbled the death of Elmer Ellsworth, and exhibited "something of a bias against Lincoln" by misquoting James Ford Rhodes and calling Lincoln a "demagogue."[40]

Williams was equally defensive about the president's relationship with Secretary of War Stanton. He disliked Revisionist George Fort Milton Jr.'s history of the war for depicting Lincoln as "a weak man" who allowed Stanton to control him. He likewise attacked young T. Harry Williams for suggesting, in his first book, that Stanton had set up Fitz John Porter in an unfair court-martial. Here was another so-called scholar who clearly had never worn a uniform, Colonel Williams complained. Otto Eisenschiml's accusation that Stanton played a role in the Lincoln assassination was blasphemous, but the main complaint about *Why Was Lincoln Murdered?* was that the author depicted Lincoln as ignorant of tactics and strategy, unable to grasp topography, and wed tactically to wasteful frontal assaults.[41]

Kenneth Williams's favorite targets, however, were McClellan defenders who spouted "nonsense" and criticized the commander in chief or the eventual general in chief. Randall drew shockingly little criticism—he seemed to write for another world—as did Sandburg. Williams expressed mixed opinions about Conger's biography of Grant, Rhodes's histories, and Lee biographer Douglas Southall Freeman. But G. F. R. Henderson and John Codman Ropes attracted his frequent sarcasm and bitter disdain. He accused both of sloppy research and personal bias, which led them to questionable narratives and unfair interpretations. To counter if not ridicule their assertions, he often turned to J. F. C. Fuller, Frederick Maurice, and especially Colin Ballard. Williams once countered Ropes's "distorted and false" contention that Lincoln and Stanton were unfit to direct troops in the Valley by citing all three British authors. Williams did criticize Fuller's and Liddell Hart's views of Grant in the later volumes, but Ballard still could do no wrong. As for Americans, Williams praised soldier-historian Francis Greene's history of the Mississippi campaigns while treating Nicolay and Hay as beyond reproach.[42]

Lincoln Finds a General came out over the course of a decade to mixed reviews. Many readers loved it. Bernard DeVoto, Schlesinger's mentor at Harvard, praised the first two volumes in the *New York Herald Review* "as close to being final as we are ever likely to get." Williams was a finalist for the National Book Award in nonfiction in 1950.[43] Other academic reviewers were appreciative. Frank Vandiver compared Williams to Freeman. Despite the author's tendency "to talk down to the reader from the heights of professional military analysts," he found the first two volumes "for the most part, an excellent exposition of the Federal side of military operations in Virginia. . . . Williams has at last given the Army of the Potomac its rightful place in the literature of the Civil War."[44] Military historian Theodore Ropp likewise praised Williams for writing "the standard Union military history of the war" despite a pro-Grant bias.[45] After Williams's death, Allan Nevins lauded his final entry for "the same mastery of fine detail, the same strong opinions based on thorough research, the same readiness to combat fashionable views, and the same virile if somewhat awkward style, as the volumes written in full health." The entire work would "stand as one of the enduring monuments in the field of military history."[46]

Not everyone agreed, however. The old guard of Revisionists and other pro-southern writers fought back tenaciously. Randall claimed to find much to like in the first volumes, including the author's ready facility with army terminology. But he took exception to Williams's constant denigration of McClellan, with extended reference to his own more positive arguments in *Lincoln the President: Springfield to Gettysburg,* as well as his positive view of Stanton. Williams was just as guilty of misunderstanding documents and ignoring contradictory evidence as those he criticized, Randall charged.[47]

E. Merton Coulter of the University of Georgia, representing the pro-Confederate rear guard within academia, praised Williams's interest in the still-neglected western theater and suggested that in some ways he had indeed written the companion piece to Freeman's *R. E. Lee* and *Lee's Lieutenants.* "Probably no one unless Freeman," he observed, "has ever combed through the 128 volumes of the Official Records of the Union and Confederate Armies as thoroughly as Professor Williams did." Yet he disdained the author's "provocative" approach and especially his "ever-sharpening and sarcastic pen. . . . If McClellan was utterly bad," the reviewer wondered, "not even given credit for a victory he won . . . , the reader is made to wonder why Lincoln, whom Professor Williams considers no mean strategist, kept him so long." As for Lee and Jackson, the author did "not to seem to think it possible for a commander in a later report, when he had fuller information, to change a statement without being guilty of dishonesty." Williams further seemed to believe that his army experience made him an expert, Coulter observed. He complained that "the author does not stop with passing judgment on the actors in the great drama; he lines up for execution in his notes and appendices various writers of the present day and generation. . . . Perhaps this style of writing by the author comes from the fact that he is a scientist, a mathematician, who deals with exactitudes. If formulas work in mathematics, they should be devised and made to work in historical narrative. When once the true formula has been found, then all deviators, of course, must be wrong."[48]

Yet another notable Revisionist, William B. Hesseltine, found in the volumes "a tone of distinct bias." Just as McClellan "could do no right," he observed, Grant "could do no wrong." It was a wonder, he added, that Lincoln took so long to find his general.[49] Hesseltine's former doctoral student, T. Harry Williams—Kenneth Williams had pilloried him in volume 2—weighed in as well. He was generous to a point. In 1957 he described the ongoing series as a "tremendous venture" that boasted "a painstaking, fact-laden narrative." Once completed, it would "undoubtedly rank as one of the most impressive achievements in Civil War historiography." He liked the author's treatments of Don Carlos Buell, William Rosecrans, and Grant, he admitted; no one would ever dismiss Grant as "a blundering butcher" again. Yet with understandable reasons, he also lamented the author's tendency to take "issue with other writers for their opinions, generalizations, and errors, all of which he essays to correct in his narrative and notes." And he had no idea what the author wanted to do. Was *Lincoln Finds a General* "a record of the command system of the North, an analysis of Northern generalship . . . a story of campaigns and battles . . . an over-all military history of the war," or all of those things?[50]

Three years later T. Harry Williams reviewed Kenneth Williams's final volume on the precipice of the Civil War Centennial and answered his own questions. *Lincoln Finds a General* was in the end, he concluded, "a military history of the Northern armies. The shift in emphasis," he added, "was fortunate both for his own and for Civil War scholarship." Each volume had been better, something "often observed in writers who are not professional historians." Kenneth Williams had expanded his research in the final installment beyond the orders and reports he revered. That had made him less "impatient with the errors of others," as he had been "far too testy and patronizing in calling attention to such errors." Grant remained his "pet. . . . [H]is greatest service was in fixing the greatness of Grant beyond question"—and McClellan his "pet dislike." Yet "the merits . . . outweigh its defects. The most detailed and the most careful study of the Union military organization yet written, it will remain a treasury of information and reference for years to come. . . . [as] one of the essays in grand writing of the history of the Civil War."[51]

T. Harry Williams was right. *Lincoln Finds a General* has endured. As historian Gary Gallagher observed, Bruce Catton followed Kenneth Williams's lead as he wrote the grand histories of the Civil War Centennial, books that in turn shaped how Americans still consider the war. *Lincoln Finds a General* itself may not be read as widely as before, and some of the volumes are currently out of print, but its ideas about Lincoln and McClellan still dominate popular Civil War discussions. Kenneth Williams did nothing less than revive the heroic legend for new generations of Americans. Yet when he wrote his review, T. Harry Williams was modest. His competing narrative, *Lincoln and His Generals,* already had superseded *Lincoln Finds a General* as the standard work on the subject. In many ways, it still is.[52]

In December 1947 Editor Robert H. Glauber of Alfred A. Knopf's publishing house wrote a letter to T. Harry Williams. Glauber was back from Chicago, where he had met Ralph Newman, owner of the Abraham Lincoln Book Shop. "It occurred to me," he explained, "that there exists no book on the subject [of] Lincoln and the War Generals. Surely this is a worthwhile field. . . . [A] full and comprehensive evaluation of Lincoln as the first executive Commander-in-Chief of the army had yet to be done." The time seemed ripe, with the end of World War II and the opening of the Lincoln Papers at the Library of Congress. Glauber had approached Randall, but deep in his own biography of Lincoln, he suggested Williams.[53]

T. Harry Williams was not an obvious choice to many others. Born "two axe handles and a twist of tobacco" from Grant's Galena, Illinois, he grew up north of the state border as an admirer of Lincoln from boyhood and a child of Progressive Wisconsin. He graduated from Plattsburg State Teachers College in 1931 at the depths of the Depression and could find no job. Instead, he took his father's advice, went on to graduate school at the University of Wisconsin, and began to study Civil War history, eventually under Hesseltine.[54] In 1936 the University of Wisconsin Extension Service hired him to teach around the state. It fired him two months later after an incident in Wausau, where he drew the ire of the local American Legion and Veterans of Foreign Wars for comments made in a speech entitled "The Technic of War Propaganda." According to a supporter, Williams was "bitterly denounced for an Armistice Day speech in the Senior High School for some remarks which were interpreted as an attack on the Civil War President. One local patriot sought to round up a group for the purpose of 'throwing Williams into the drink.'" A local newspaper "denounced him as a 'Communist at heart who takes delight in assailing the great men of this and former generations who have made this country what it is.'"[55] Williams insisted that he had been misquoted and his words about Lincoln taken out of context. He really had not blamed Lincoln and the Republicans for starting the Civil War, he said, and viewed the Gettysburg Address favorably as "sincere propaganda" designed to "bring others to your way of thinking." Revisionism apparently was already out of favor in Wausau. Thanks to the intercession of the American Federation of Teachers as well as letters of support from scholars across the country, he regained his job.[56]

Two years later Williams completed his dissertation about Lincoln's relationship with the Joint Committee on the Conduct of the War. In 1941 it grew into *Lincoln and the Radicals,* the successful work of late Revisionism that Kenneth Williams took to task and whose author himself later thought too far afield. By then, T. Harry Williams had left Wisconsin for a teaching job in Omaha, Nebraska, but he soon moved on again to Louisiana State University. In Baton Rouge he edited a compilation of Lincoln speeches and writings, yet he also began to move on as a scholar. With a congenial new home and increasingly appreciative southern students, he turned his scholarly interests to the Confederates, while studiously avoiding any military or government service in World War II. When Glauber wrote him after the war, Williams was hard at work on a biography of P. G. T. Beauregard.[57]

Glauber's offer intrigued the scholar nonetheless. Williams outlined what he thought such a book should contain, with a telling clue. It would need, he suggested, "a brief discussion of the role of the president in military affairs in a democracy at war (something like Maurice does in his *Statesmen and Soldiers of the Civil War*)." The author also would need to narrate chronologically Lincoln's relationships with his generals, examine his "developing ideas of strategy (there was undoubtedly improvement here)," consider how much Lincoln imposed his views and how much politics informed those views, look at his relationship with the Radicals, and include "some discussion of the battles."[58]

Over the next months, the two men discussed the project, renamed by Glauber to its eventual published title, *Lincoln and His Generals*. The editor, not Williams, shaped its broad outlines as well. He wanted either a military or political study, "lest the book fall between two stools." He preferred the latter, he added, although much could be said, too, for a northern version of Freeman's *Lee's Lieutenants*. Also, the scholar absolutely needed to conduct original archival research in Washington, as both Paul Angle and Randall had suggested and agreed to succor. Williams wrote both men almost immediately, telling Glauber that he still had his dissertation notes but agreed on the necessity for returning to the archives.[59] "I am *dee*-lighted that you are going to do Lincoln and the War Generals," Randall responded, adding some research advice, and concluding, "we will watch your future career with a good deal of interest."[60]

In March 1948 Williams agreed to deliver his manuscript in two years, a fast turnaround for a book that required time and travel. The timetable proved too ambitious. In September 1949 he asked for a year's extension. Glauber left the press that same month, replaced by the prolific Civil War historian Earl Schenck Miers, who promptly discovered that unknown Kenneth Williams was about to publish the first two volumes of *Lincoln Finds a General*. The prospect did not worry Miers too much given that he expected a projected four-volume history of military operations to attract a different audience. In Baton Rouge, meanwhile, T. Harry Williams toiled. He completed his research in the summer of 1950, set up a card table under some trees in the summer heat, and began writing in longhand.[61] Roughly a year later, in May 1951, he submitted the completed manuscript, now retitled to the press's displeasure "Lincoln and the Generals;" there was a recent book with their original title, he explained. His haste was obvious. Alfred A. Knopf himself expressed "very great pleasure" with the manuscript yet chided Williams for its "many, many typographical errors which you could and should have caught and virtually no corrections whatsoever." Knopf added that Miers thought the manuscript was weaker when it came to Grant and the West. The publisher promised to consult an anonymous subject specialist to review the manuscript.[62]

Based on the reader's comments, Williams submitted a new draft just three months later. Editor in Chief Harold Strauss expressed delight with his willingness to make changes, yet he stressed the need for even greater speed. The book needed illustrations, and Strauss distrusted the ability of anyone in Baton Rouge to render proper maps. He also insisted upon the original title as specified in the contract, observing that "they were *his* generals, after all, and not just any generals." Then in November 1951, Knopf signed a deal with the popular subscriber-based Book-of-the-Month Club, a major achievement and a sure path to sales with the American middle class, yet one that piled on more pressure to finish in a timely fashion. Book designer Sidney Jacobs became nearly apoplectic when Williams suggested that he would deliver the index in a month—send it next week, Jacobs pleaded.[63]

Written hurriedly and rushed to the shelves, *Lincoln and His Generals* appeared early in 1952. The scramble to publication was evident. Williams cited the manuscript material that he had amassed as Randall advised and Knopf required, notably including documents from the papers of Simon Cameron, Zachariah Chandler, John Dahlgren, Charles Dana, William B. Franklin, Samuel Heintzelman, Andrew Johnson, George McClellan, Montgomery Meigs, Carl Schurz, Edwin Stanton, Ben Wade, Elihu Washburne, and above all the recently opened Robert Todd Lincoln manuscripts at the Library of Congress. Much of this was familiar to him thanks to *Lincoln and the Radicals.* Yet the primary-source base as revealed in the footnotes largely was published and familiar: the *Official Records, Battles and Leaders,* the published Lincoln papers, Nicolay and Hay, and the then-standard memoirs and diaries. As for secondary sources, the bibliography included a who's who of writers who had debated the heroic legend since 1865: the pathbreakers Isaac Arnold and Henry Raymond, soldiers Arthur Conger and Francis Greene, William Kelley, Alexander McClure, Donn Piatt, Allen Thorndike Rice, John Codman Ropes, Carl Sandburg, the brand-new first volumes of Kenneth Williams, and especially the British soldier-historians, with preeminence given to Sir Frederick Maurice instead of Colin Ballard. As Williams's student Roger Spiller later pointed out, serious students of American military history still read the British soldier-historians at the time, if only because there was little else available on Civil War military history. *Lincoln and His Generals,* if nothing else, was the culmination of nearly a century of transatlantic debating and writing about Lincoln as commander in chief. Yet there were notable omissions, too, mostly Lincoln skeptics. Gideon Welles's papers and diaries were nowhere to be found. Nor did Williams cite Herndon and Weik, William O. Stoddard, the comte de Paris, Ida Tarbell, G. F. R. Henderson, Viscount Wolseley, or curiously enough, Randall.[64]

The major influence, however, as it had been on Kenneth Williams, was more recent. World War II provided the retrospective lenses T. Harry Williams used to reevaluate Lincoln the war president through "the perspective of modern war." The Civil War itself, he argued, was "the first of the modern total wars." Influenced especially by Fuller and Maurice—but not interested in discussing the recent world war with actual participants—Williams declared in his first paragraphs that he would explain Lincoln's "influence in developing a modern command system for this nation . . . from the perspective of military developments since 1865 and to measure the correctness of his decisions by the standards of modern war." He continued: "Judged by modern standards, Lincoln stands out as a great war president, probably the greatest in our history, and a great natural strategist, a better one than any of his generals. He was in actuality as well as in title the commander in chief who, by his larger strategy, did more than Grant or any general to win the war for the Union." Using Ballard's and Maurice's earlier assertions, in other words, Williams maintained that Lincoln created the foundation of "the modern command system," one that achieved victory over the Nazis and Japanese militarism. Such a presentist perspective was a strong selling point to the publisher.[65]

Given how *Lincoln and His Generals* became a foundational and indeed canonical Civil War text for the centennial and succeeding generations, much of what followed in the narrative was familiar. Williams's Lincoln—like Nicolay and Hay's, Ballard's, Maurice's, and indeed Kenneth Williams's commander in chief—was once again the "better natural strategist than were most of the trained soldiers." Despite his limited military background, Lincoln "saw the big picture of the war from the start. . . . He grasped immediately the advantage that numbers gave the North and urged his generals to keep up a constant pressure on the whole strategic line of the Confederacy until a weak spot was found—and a break-through could be made." The "proper objective" was "the destruction of the Confederate armies and not the occupation of Southern territory." To ensure success, the president functioned not only politically, as Franklin Roosevelt had done, but also had been his own George Marshall and Joint Chiefs of Staff, too. "He formulated policy, drew up strategic plans, and even devised and directed tactical movements," Williams continued. "Judged by modern standards, he did some things that a civilian director of war should not do. Modern critics say that he 'interfered' too much with military operations," he added. Because of his inexperience and his flawed generals, he "made bad mistakes" early on, yet his developing skills in planning, establishing policies, and choosing the right generals ensured that by 1864, he had created the nation's first "modern command system" and ensured victory.[66]

Lincoln did not do that by being perfect, however, as Ballard and Kenneth Williams had implied. T. Harry Williams's professional analysis was much more nuanced, again more resembling Fuller's and Maurice's assessments than Ballard's, with Maurice the guiding star. The president had to learn and grow before he became a master of war. One of his first successes in creating that "system" was establishing his preeminence over Winfield Scott. Rejecting the Anaconda Plan, Lincoln began formulating his own blueprints for victory, schemes that admittedly bore the marks of military ignorance early on. He overemphasized East Tennessee; Buell was right to balk at marching into the region. Yet Lincoln was right to "initiate" and plan the First Bull Run Campaign, and "for reasons he considered militarily sound" rather than to please the press or politicians. His reactions to the disastrous battle showed growing judgment. As for McClellan and his relationship with the White House, Williams again reflected the British soldier-historians as well as what one of his own students later identified as his own lifelong aversion to West Pointers. Elevating McClellan was defensible, Williams believed, as "Lincoln could not have picked a better man" to rebuild the eastern army. McClellan deserved credit for building what became the Army of the Potomac, as others—but not Kenneth Williams—had admitted. Yet the general was also a poor strategic planner due to his flights of fancy, proved to be condescending, pursued limited war aims, and was unable to accept the straitjacket of available resources. Given no choice when McClellan took ill, Lincoln "took over the function of general in chief." The relationship grew worse thereafter. General Order No. 1 was silly, but Lincoln wrote it to get McClellan moving, Williams believed, not to be taken seriously.[67]

Lincoln's greatest error was allowing the Peninsula operation to proceed despite his doubts. He "undoubtedly made a mistake in grudgingly approving a plan which he distrusted," Williams concluded. "If he did not like the Urbana scheme, he should have said so." Instead, Lincoln wavered, first approving it, then expressing second thoughts, and finally letting it go forward because only McClellan would reap the blame if he failed. Williams observed that "there was something bizarre in the spectacle of the President refusing to adopt the plan of his chief general until it had been approved by a majority vote of subordinates." Lincoln was not wrong to remove McClellan as commander in chief, he judged, but the White House bungled the demotion and sent troops to Frémont that Little Mac really needed. Looking back, Lincoln should have just axed him rather than put the general in the bind where he found himself. "McClellan was about to embark on a campaign to which the government was opposed but one which would largely depend for success upon the support and cooperation it got from several agencies of government. . . . [Yet] McClellan was leaving behind him in Washington a President who believed the plan of operation of his commanding general was dangerous and a Secretary of War who thought the commander ought to be removed." The question of numbers in Washington made a bad situation worse. McClellan had not obeyed orders and had not helped Lincoln realize that the capital was safe. Once the general landed at Fort Monroe, the president pushed him to advance quickly, a reasonable assessment proven during the "vacation jaunt" at Norfolk.[68]

While McClellan dawdled, Jackson struck, giving Lincoln the opportunity to be commander in chief in fact as well as in title, Williams observed. The final grades were mixed. Ever aggressive, the president "was designing both strategy and tactics. His plan to capture Jackson was strategic in nature." It might have worked had Frémont held up his end, but the chances were "slim from the beginning," given the "poor positions" of Federal columns. However much Lincoln had grown as a strategist, he remained a novice at tactics. "In particular," Williams wrote, "he showed an unawareness with the problem of logistics and of the effects of hard marching on troops. He seemed to think that McDowell could go to the Valley, defeat Jackson, and immediately return and be ready for the Peninsula." Indeed, "as his misgivings about the abilities of the generals increased, Lincoln tended to exercise more control over tactical movements and arrangements." He "took direct charge of the defence system of the Valley. . . . down to fine details."[69]

On the Peninsula Lincoln and Stanton did their best to meet McClellan's requests for men and supplies, yet their insistence that McDowell travel overland rather than by sea, as McClellan wanted, put him in a poor position when Lee struck to begin the Seven Days. Listening to Pope at this time did not help matters. Unlike Kenneth Williams, T. Harry Williams was not enamored by the western general. During the Seven Days' Battles, McClellan became "unhinged by events." In contrast, "Lincoln kept his head better during the Peninsula crisis than did many of the military men." At Harrison's Landing McClellan gave Lincoln his letter, which Williams found no worse than anything Pope was saying in Washington. It "was nothing more than a well-meant piece of advice from an egotistical young general who thought he was much greater than he was." Still, it led to the unfortunate ascent of Halleck to general in chief. Lincoln "wanted a military man," Williams explained, "to make the decisions he found so difficult to make." He was ready to fire McClellan, except Burnside declined command, leaving Lincoln no alternative. Instead, he withdrew McClellan from the Peninsula and turned to Pope's new Army of Virginia. Williams thought that was a bad decision, too. Lincoln should have replaced McClellan but left the Army of the Potomac where it stood, keeping Lee's back to the wall covering Richmond. Instead, the Confederates wriggled free and pounced at Second Bull Run. Lincoln blamed McClellan, somewhat unfairly given the logistical difficulties Little Mac had faced, and only reluctantly turned to him to protect Washington after Pope's defeat. "Lincoln was now judging generals by a single standard—the stern standard of victory." After Antietam, Lincoln grew frustrated with McClellan's "timidity" and "kept poking sharp sticks under McClellan's ribs" until he fired him at last.[70]

Victories still proved hard to come by. Burnside was not a bad general, and Halleck again was partially responsible for Fredericksburg, having delayed the pontoons, according to Williams, because the general in chief misunderstood Burnside's plans. But Lincoln had appointed Halleck. "The whole episode showed that there was something badly wrong with the command system," Williams opined, "or with the humans running it." Burnside and Halleck, on the other hand, should have taken Lincoln's alternate operational plan seriously. It was "a bold one, and it would have employed sea power." The defeat at Fredericksburg was Burnside's, and so was the failure of the Mud March. Reluctantly but correctly, Lincoln removed a general he liked, ignored Halleck, and chose Hooker as the next obvious man. Williams understood the choice but regretted it; Hooker was no strategist, he concluded. Lincoln stuck by him after Chancellorsville but came to rue his decision as Hooker floundered, grew unhinged, and became obsessed over Halleck's role in the campaign into Pennsylvania. A recurrent theme in *Lincoln and His Generals* is the mental breakdown of Federal generals. Increasingly, Lincoln looked at Hooker and saw McClellan. And so came Meade, a general Williams found lacking as well. He fought Gettysburg "with great tactical skill" but "no aggressive spirit" and was happy just to let Lee go. Williams defended Lincoln's frustrations with Meade's pursuit of Lee and his unsent letter of reprimand as well, "an excellent essay in military art . . . it demonstrated . . . that Meade and many generals seemed never to have heard of: that the destruction of the enemy armies was the primary objective of Union armies."[71]

A general more to Lincoln's thinking was in the West. Yet the president did not recognize it immediately, although he supported Grant during the general's nadir. Lincoln put too much faith in incompetent Nathaniel Banks—a "case of Lincoln misreading his man"—and the pompous McClernand. Williams struggled to explain the president's thinking before shrugging his shoulders. Yet his plans to coordinate Grant's and Banks's advances against Vicksburg demonstrated "increasing stature as a strategist." He offered increasing support to Grant while becoming less besotted by McClernand after more handwringing about Grant's drinking. Vicksburg cemented Grant's ascendance; here was the general Lincoln wanted. In Tennessee Lincoln had despaired of Rosecrans for months even before the general's defeat at Chickamauga. With input from Stanton, the president "made a complete and intelligent change in the command system in the West." When Grant arrived in Tennessee as western commander and broke the entrapped Army of the Cumberland out of Chattanooga, "the second of Lincoln's great strategic objectives had been achieved and like the first—the opening of the Mississippi—achieved by Grant." Yet "even in his great joy, Lincoln was still the strategist. He wanted to complete Grant's work by running down and destroying [James] Longstreet [in East Tennessee], and he thought that the job [of winning the war] could be done if only he had good generals in the East."[72]

Williams contended, as Maurice and Fuller had argued previously, that Lincoln's military genius came to fruition through his association with Grant, the war's best military commander. The general was a modern thinker, unlike Lee, just as Fuller wrote. In the winter of 1863–64, when Lincoln and Congress elevated Grant to lieutenant general and command of all Union armies, they became the "principal architects" of "a modern command system." They "put into institutional form the result of the nation's experience after three years of modern war. In a fundamental sense," he continued, "the new arrangement represented the total military thought of the country." Grant developed a modern staff and made good use of Halleck, now U.S. Army chief of staff, as an intermediary. Yet Lincoln remained the senior partner. Despite Grant's assertions in his *Memoirs*—Williams found that source untrustworthy—the president never gave the general a "free hand." Indeed, he overrode Grant's early strategic and operational ideas. Together, they developed the plan for winning the war in 1864 through coordinated campaigns, which Williams named "Operation Crusher" in imitation of the "modern terms" used by the mid-twentieth-century U.S. Army. The president was not always happy with the results, especially the siege at Petersburg, Grant's slow reaction to Jubal Early's raid on Washington, and later the general's intention to fire George Thomas at Nashville. Lincoln could do little about Petersburg, but he pulled rank in Virginia, and he saved Thomas. "Again the President had been more right than Grant," Williams concluded. Lincoln's last "important" order—"let the *thing* be pressed"—was, according to Williams, "like most of his orders a good one."[73]

The man, the book, and the hour finally met. Seven decades later, in a digital world marked by a plethora of voices and public opinions, it is difficult to grasp how much *Lincoln and His Generals* gripped a portion of the American mind in 1952. It was a tremendous success, the main selection of the Book-of-the-Month Club for February, in a year that the club also featured Ernest Hemingway's *The Old Man and The Sea.* It spent weeks on the *New York Times* Best Sellers list. Williams made enough money to replace his card table under the trees with a sizable, detached office he called "Lincolnand." Early in March 1952, President Harry Truman wrote Williams about how much he liked the book. A year earlier, just as Williams was completing it, Truman had fired his own McClellan, Gen. Douglas MacArthur. That created a public brouhaha that not only besieged the president but also, according to historian Ethan Rafuse, increased the audience of *Lincoln and His Generals.* Truman the Missourian now commented that he hoped that Williams would write about the western theater, which he thought still neglected. Williams mentioned the letter to a friend, who was happy to make it public. An Associated Press wire story subsequently quoted the president. Lesser-known readers wrote Williams as well. One in New Hampshire complained that there were too many footnotes. Another in Delaware wrote directly to LSU's president complaining that Williams had written "Northern propaganda" if not "Russian propaganda" by saying that Grant was a better general than Lee. Her children, she snorted, would never attend LSU. But they were rare exceptions.[74]

Book reviews, almost always glowing except for a strong demurral from Randall's student David Donald in the *New York Herald Tribune*, simultaneously appeared in daily newspapers and the era's popular magazines. Williams and Lincoln appeared together on the cover of *Saturday Review*, accompanied by a glowing review from Allan Nevins that favorably placed the book openly and firmly in the Maurice tradition. Henderson's and Ropes's earlier volumes had reached their expiration date, Nevins added, and here was their replacement. An Ohio publisher, meanwhile hastily reissued Ballard's *Abraham Lincoln as a Military Genius* in hopes of cashing in. Reviewers occasionally reviewed both books together, with Williams garnering the better comments. He preserved all the reviews in a scrapbook without comment, except for one letter to the editor extoling the book in the *Wausau Record Herald*, published in the Wisconsin town where he once lost a job for allegedly criticizing Lincoln.[75] Across that clipping, Williams wrote, "Revenge is Sweet!"[76]

Academic book reviews were favorable as well, if sometimes less fulsome.[77] Williams even almost won over the arch-Revisionist Avery Craven, who again noted the author's debt to Ballard and Fuller as well as the book's overall fairness and grasp of military affairs. As good a scholar as he was, however, Craven complained that Williams also was "favored by the growing disposition to glorify Lincoln and transform him into an Olympian figure. The public is willing to accept as sound fact almost any assertion or claim made in his favor. To discover that he was a military genius is, therefore, only a logical step in the growth of the Lincoln myth."[78]

But it was an obscure retired cavalryman, Lt. Col. Henry S. Merrick, who provided the most fitting last word. A former Iowa National Guardsman who had risen from the ranks, he was a fixture in Washington's new Civil War Round Table, cofounded by Bruce Catton and soon to be the cradle of the Civil War Centennial. Writing in *Military Affairs*, he joked that Williams should have entitled the book "Lincoln and His Prima Donnas." He added, "nowhere is a volume so replete with evidence of Lincoln's Christ-like humility, patience, and forbearance with the weak vessels who headed his forces, especially during the early years of the war." The pious early Lincoln biographers Isaac Arnold and Josiah Holland, not to mention John Hay and John Nicolay, surely would have smiled and nodded at that comment. Merrick had closed the Lincoln circle where it began in 1865, with the heroic legend vibrant and ascendant.[79]

CONCLUSION

FOR WELL OVER A decade beginning in 2005, the pioneering Civil War blogger Dimitri Rotov took aim on what he called the "Centennial School" of Civil War history. Rotov worked in a new and wide-open digital world that John Hay or Colin Ballard could never have imagined. A self-perceived cybervoice crying in the wilderness of the internet, he drew a large readership while criticizing many aspects of Civil War historiography and historians who recycled the same sources and stories, privileged dramatic commercial narratives over analysis, and reasserted the irrepressible conflict and the modernity of the war. But he especially disliked the liturgy of Abraham Lincoln's genius as compared to George McClellan's alleged perfidy. Such "Centennialism," he maintained, began with Kenneth P. Williams and T. Harry Williams, then wormed its way into the American mind in the 1960s. Rotov regularly criticized more recent writers for keeping Centennialism alive. "The story elements that defined Centennial ideology," he complained, "are now embedded in pop culture; in that sense, the ideology's work is done. For most readers, Lincoln found a general, [Ulysses S.] Grant saved the Union, and the Republican newspapers of 1861–1865 had it exactly right . . . there is very little perceived need for historical analysis."[1] Historian Brooks Simpson once summed up Rotov's definition of Centennialism nicely as "the 'Lincoln Finds a General/Lincoln and His Generals' school of interpretation."[2]

Rotov's personal attacks on certain historians were unfortunate. Yet he was not that far off the mark when it came to *Lincoln and His Generals* and the heroic legend. Six decades after publication, it remained the central work for understanding Lincoln as commander in chief. T. Harry Williams's specific analysis and Kenneth Williams's wider conclusions really have not been superseded. Both men placed Lincoln at the heart of the strategy that won the Civil War, while cementing in place the heroic legend of Lincoln as a brilliant modern strategist who rose above his generals as a military thinker. He remains in scholarship and in the popular mind the nation's greatest wartime president. T. Harry Williams's reach was especially long. A cowritten college textbook published initially by Knopf in 1959, once the most assigned general survey in the nation, extended his ideas about Lincoln, McClellan, and the modernity of the war. So did a popular Civil War history published during the Civil War Centennial in 1963 by Time-Life Books. His classic essay, "Military Leadership North and South," in David Donald's equally beloved edited work, *Why the North Won the Civil War* (1960)—yet another signal product of the centennial—became a standard text for decades. Well into the twenty-first century, the U.S. Army chief of staff recommended *Lincoln and His Generals* as professional reading for officers, one of only four Civil War books remaining on that list.[3]

Williams and Williams did not create the heroic legend, of course. Rotov was wrong about that. Historians once recognized their progenitors—Colin Ballard, J. F. C. Fuller, and Sir Frederick Maurice especially—but only Fuller has escaped modern obscurity. Sometimes people conflate the two men named Williams as well, to the detriment of T. Harry Williams's greater nuance and willingness to criticize the president in *Lincoln and His Generals.* It is not unusual to hear his name attached loosely and incorrectly to the essential ideas of Kenneth Williams's essential hagiography. To be fair, in later years T. Harry Williams himself contributed to such confusion. He increasingly became more favorable to Lincoln and more negative about McClellan in other writings, the classroom, and public lectures. "Military Leadership North and South" reflected Kenneth Williams's more black-and-white thinking on Lincoln and Grant almost more than it did T. Harry Williams's own *Lincoln and His Generals,* to the degree that it even borrows the "Lincoln finds a general" trope in its conclusion.[4]

In essence if not in exact details, "the 'Lincoln Finds a General/Lincoln and His Generals' school of interpretation" survives. Indeed, as Ethan Rafuse maintained, it shaped most later writing on Lincoln as commander in chief.[5] At the end of the twentieth century, for example, Stephen Sears's powerful, deeply researched, and ultimately negative depiction of McClellan carried the heroic legend's assertion of that general's foibles into new generations.[6] The continuing power of the heroic legend conversely meant that only four prominent and mainstream dissidents have challenged it openly in the last six decades, setting aside the cottage industry of "neo-Confederates" who attack Lincoln reflexively from every possible angle and a small redoubt of doughty McClellan defenders. For various reasons, all four dissenters failed to land a telling blow.[7]

Brooks Simpson's *Abraham Lincoln and the Gettysburg Campaign* (1998), a sixty-four-page pamphlet published by a small Pennsylvania press, came first. Still the best recent analysis of Lincoln as commander in chief despite its brevity and eastern focus, Simpson directly challenged T. Harry Williams. He warned that Williams's "glowing accolades . . . blind readers to qualifications, reservations, and dissents: they are testimony to the pervasiveness as well as the persuasiveness of Williams' account. . . . [I]f Abraham Lincoln was all that his advocates claim him to have been as commander-in-chief, one must wonder why Union fortunes prospered in the West and not in the East, where the president was far more involved in military planning." The president was no "bumbler," Simpson readily admitted, adding, "it is remarkable that he did as well as he did," given his lack of military experience. But his inexperience, impatience for a decisive battle against Lee, interference, backbiting criticism, and open door to carpers and critics all undermined his gifts. As historian Ethan Rafuse later observed, the booklet unfortunately drew little attention. Simpson enunciated some of its criticisms in better-known later works, notably those about Grant, but there the focus shifted enough to lighten its effect.[8]

Geoffrey Perret's *Lincoln's War: The Untold Story of America's Greatest President as Commander in Chief* (2004) failed to dent the heroic legend for quite different reasons. It boasted a successful author, a major trade-publisher's imprint, and a whirl of popular interest in presidential war powers during the era of Commander in Chief George W. Bush's war on terrorism. If *Lincoln and His Generals* was about World War II, *Lincoln's War* was very much about the Iraq War and especially Bush's suspension of habeas corpus for suspected terrorists and their ongoing imprisonment. His administration sometimes defended such actions using Lincoln administration precedents. While Perret's treatment of Lincoln himself thus included the familiar—his quick study of warfare, fascination with military technology, and indomitable will to preserve the Union whatever the cost in blood—he was quite critical as well, easily outdistancing Simpson. Perret's Lincoln was a distant dreamer, a military dilettante, an impatient and incompetent micromanager, a self-pitying worrier, sometimes the pawn of unscrupulous men, occasionally a liar, and ultimately a hypocrite "eager enough to get other men's sons into uniform, but not his own." Lincoln's rejection of Winfield Scott's military advice prolonged the war by as much as three years, Perret opined, while his first suspension of the writ of habeas corpus was "on its face, a rejection of more than six hundred years of legal development" going back to the Magna Carta. "As he shaped the role of commander in chief," he continued, "Lincoln was altering the cosmology of American wars by making the president the sun around which all else—and all others—revolved. . . . It is unlikely that any president before Lincoln would have asserted that he possessed the power to jail people without evidence, to free slaves in rebellious territories, to impose conscription, to create his own currency and, all in all, to exercise what amounted to dictatorial powers, even during a national emergency." Ongoing expansion of the executive powers since 1861, Perret believed, became an existential threat to the nation under George W. Bush.[9]

Such a provocative, political, and indeed neo-Revisionist thesis was always going to jar readers. Yet *Lincoln's War* quickly sank out of sight due to a stormy sea of details. Reviewers correctly pointed to the author's weak grasp of basics. James McPherson counted well over a hundred errors. Some of the Lincoln "quotations" were spurious. The president was not obsessed with taking Richmond, nor did he embrace African American enlistment after reading an obscure pamphlet. Accounts of conscription and the creation of a national currency, as well as descriptions of battles, were muddled. Neither Corinth, Mississippi, nor Paducah, Kentucky, lay on the Mississippi River, for example, while Perret had the Tennessee and Shenandoah Rivers flowing in the wrong direction. The listed errors piled up until the overall conclusion was that *Lincoln's War* was so flawed regarding basic facts that it must be untrustworthy interpretively as well. It became easy to dismiss.[10]

Unlike Perret, the prolific William Marvel already had spent two decades writing about various aspects of the Civil War. Marvel had earned a reputation not only for his mastery of details and primary sources but also for challenging conventional wisdom and some of the war's cherished legends. He favorably revived the reputation of Ambrose Burnside and rewrote the history of Andersonville prison. No one would be able to challenge a Lincoln Prize winner with botching basic facts about the war. Starting in 2006, Marvel wrote a four-volume history of the Union's war: *Mr. Lincoln Goes to War* (2006), *Lincoln's Darkest Year* (2008), *The Great Task Remaining* (2010), and *Tarnished Victory* (2011). He followed up in 2015 with an unfavorable biography of Edwin Stanton and in 2021 added a sympathetic defense of Fitz John Porter.[11]

Marvel, in these six works combined, came closer than any other modern historian to resurrecting pre–World War II Revisionism's portrait of Lincoln and the war. The president, he asserted at the outset, had been much too much "revered" by historians as one possessing "commendable genius" ever since "sympathetic" T. Harry Williams had obscured his many failures. As a result, Lincoln had "escaped substantial revision by mainstream scholars." Those historians had propagated instead "a single nationalistic legend," a "gospel of Lincoln," and a "New Testament of American history" that declared the Civil War's "orgy of violence" and "irretrievable flood of misery" were well worth the cost in lives for ending slavery. Lincoln was the man primarily responsible for provoking that unnecessary war, Marvel maintained, with emancipation its only redeeming if collateral feature. Slavery aside, peaceful secession and the breakup of the nation into two or more nation-states might well have been preferable to the terrible war that followed, Marvel suggested, as it "might not have produced unmitigated misfortune" and resulted in a "loose confederation" of likeminded states resembling the modern European Union. Slavery might have lasted decades longer in such an event, he admitted, but Lincoln went into war unconcerned about the institution anyway. Instead, the ardent nationalist took "a singularly destructive and unimaginative course" at Fort Sumter and "committed the nation to a bloodbath" well beyond his imagination. Once the war began, the administration illegally and steadily veered toward autocracy. Lincoln unconstitutionally began to suspend the writ of habeas corpus, "the fundamental element in the tapestry of law that had always protected American citizens against tyrannical government." He and his party equated disagreement with treason, jailed political opponents, destroyed honest men's careers, shut down opposition newspapers, unleashed mobs of soldiers and civilians, and otherwise declared a second war on "the most fundamental elements of democracy. . . . [T]he war to preserve the Union quickly eviscerated the First Amendment." When unable to win elections fairly, Republicans turned to military intimidation and mob violence. Increasingly, Radical Republican abolitionists—once again styled "Jacobins"—pulled Lincoln's strings, with help from duplicitous Edwin Stanton. Meanwhile, the war widened into an unmitigated disaster, "growing completely out of hand and overwhelming the people who started it." Corruption, "military ineptitude and political perfidy" cheapened the sacrifices of heroic boys in blue. Nor was the war that popular at home. A sizable minority of northerners opposed Lincoln's war, Marvel reminded readers, which only led to more repression and coerced conscription. Copperheads and other opponents of the war had been the villains of most histories, but instead they numbered among the real heroes of the era, just as James G. Randall had argued decades earlier.[12]

Yet despite his overall indictment of Lincoln as well as disdain for T. Harry Williams, Marvel was somewhat more conventional when it came to the heroic legend. Like many who had come before, he depicted an exhausted and initially mistake-prone tyro commander in chief who grew into the job in the second half of the war. Lincoln militantly dispatched the Fort Sumter expedition and started the war, but he seemingly played little role in its planning. He indirectly helped cause defeat at Bull Run by forcing Virginia's hand, but not through ignoring Scott's advice, consulting his maps, and ordering Irvin McDowell to advance. He "pestered McClellan with plans and ideas for campaigns" but to little effect. It was only in 1862, according to Marvel's broader narrative, that a more active Lincoln proved that he was possessed of no superior knowledge or talent as commander in chief despite "the accolades reaped upon him." Just as G. F. R. Henderson once argued, the "primary responsibility" for defeat in the blades of grass of the Shenandoah Valley lay at Lincoln's feet for "depleting his Valley divisions and appointing incompetent politicians to command them." After Stonewall Jackson's initial victories, Lincoln's "obsessive fear for the safety of Washington" took hold. The president "fell into a panic, scattering his Fredericksburg troops into the Valley in a needless effort to repel Jackson—and in a vain attempt to capture him." By weakening McClellan, whom Marvel depicted traditionally as inept, Lincoln threw away "an unprecedented opportunity to overwhelm Richmond." The president "emasculated the overpowering dual movement against Richmond" and "may have cost the country another three years of war and several hundred thousand lives," dooming "his war to either failure or catastrophic escalation. . . . [T]he greatest chance for an early, meaningful victory was lost through one impulsive decision" to stop McDowell's march to Richmond. Seemingly aloof from the subsequent Second Bull Run and Kentucky Campaigns, Lincoln tried to prod McClellan after Antietam. His decision to remove Little Mac to please the Radicals "spawned a debilitating mistrust and antagonism between generals," elevated lesser men, undermined enlistments, and led directly to conscription and civil repression.[13]

But after Antietam, Lincoln began to grow to an extent as an operational thinker as well, just as T. Harry Williams had suggested. Marvel described the president's attempt to provide an alternate course for Burnside at the Rappahannock, for example, as an "entirely sensible option." He was perhaps too obsessed with Charleston in 1863, unfairly suspected George Meade of "'bad faith'" after Gettysburg, and he opposed reinforcing William Rosecrans after Chickamauga. Yet he largely avoided repeat performances of his earlier bungling. Indeed, Marvel's Lincoln largely stayed out of his generals' way after Antietam, confining himself to raising troops and securing their votes while (meticulously described) battles and campaigns swept by without his intervention.[14]

Marvel's Lincoln tetralogy won praise from many Civil War lay readers, but it failed to sway the scholarly community. Some academic reviewers to be sure welcomed his deep primary research, iconoclasm, deft prose, and provocative assertions as a useful counterbalance to rosier prevailing interpretations. Others, however, recoiled at his dark portrait of the president and his era, his treatment of the Radicals, the author's refusal to cite and confront modern secondary sources, and especially Marvel's expressed antiwar preference for peaceful secession, the breakup of the Union, and delayed emancipation instead of an orgy of bloodshed.[15]

Elizabeth Brown Pryor's *Six Encounters with Lincoln: A President Confronts Democracy and Its Demons* (2017) became the final challenger to the heroic legend. Formerly a National Park Service historian, Pryor had become an accomplished State Department diplomat who specialized in arms control, advised Congress, served in Sarajevo during the Bosnian War (1992–95), acted as a spokesperson for NATO, helped write the constitution of Moldova, and eventually penned a biography of Clara Barton. Her biggest splash as a historian, however, came in 2007 with *Reading the Man,* a biography of Robert E. Lee. Pryor depicted a complex and often unlikeable Lee who was haunted by a shameful father, prone to anger and depression, authoritarian as a leader, unhappy as a husband, flirtatious with other women, and smothering as a father. He supported both slavery and secession, and he was cruel to the enslaved on his wife's Arlington plantation. Even as a general, Pryor found him disappointing. *Reading the Man*'s iconoclasm won an enthusiastic audience and took home four major book awards. Its heterodoxy matched a developing national rejection of reconciliationism and Confederate iconography as emancipationism came to the fore.[16]

Over the next decade, Pryor immersed herself in Lincoln. Her negative conclusions shocked even herself. In *Six Encounters* Lincoln is well meaning and hard working enough, but he is also clumsy, coarse, conflicted, egotistical, thin-skinned, sometimes unprincipled, often inarticulate, and altogether a disappointment, "something less than the mythologizers have told us." As president, she concluded, he stumbled into war and repressed dissent and civil liberties. Worse still, according to Pryor, Lincoln was a misogynist who disliked strong women and a reluctant emancipator who feared racial amalgamation and routinely used racist slurs. He treated Native Americans condescendingly and crudely while encouraging assimilation and the surrender of their lands, staffing the Indian Bureau with greedy party hacks and cronies.[17]

Lincoln's greatest sin in Pryor's eyes, however, was that he was a pitiful excuse for a commander in chief. Her diplomatic service in the wartime Balkans, ties to NATO, and deep admiration for the modern U.S. military shaped her views of Lincoln. She cited a laundry list of his failings as commander in chief. Opposed to a standing army as a congressman and prone to making jokes at the army's expense, he needed to win over the military in 1861. Instead, he made the situation worse. As a manager he was undisciplined. He never bothered to learn military protocol or grasp the importance of rank and pomp, made corrupt Simon Cameron secretary of war over the army's justifiable dismay, and doubted the loyalty of good officers. Lincoln appointed bad generals from civilian life while shying away from better men he distrusted for their place of birth or army connections. He repeatedly ignored the chain of command and floundered trying to direct operations himself. His susceptibility to flattery and his favoritism for its practitioners in uniform left a bad taste with officers who suspected that they lost out thanks to the "chaotic disobedience" in the White House. He looked the other way at his army's far western atrocities. "Many have credited him with improving his skills and, finally, learning to entrust more to the professionals and stay out of their way," she concluded in a stinging rebuke, specifically citing T. Harry Williams among others. "But however laudable his self-education, it also meant that he was forever catching up. Terrible tragedies occurred and thousands lost their lives in the time it took Lincoln to comprehend strategy and tactics, discipline and military protocol, staffing and morale; and to back away from his unfortunate experiments with hands-on direction of the war."[18]

Given the absolute triumph of her Lee book, expectations for *Six Encounters* were high. Tragically, Pryor died in a car crash in April 2015, leaving a manuscript that still lacked a preface and final editing. Both the final text and the public rollout suffered from her absence.[19] Even the most laudatory reviewers noted that her heretical treatment of a beloved president would not please modern admirers. They were right. Lincoln was not ripe for deconsecrating as Lee had been. Some reviewers openly defended Lincoln while criticizing Pryor as one sided, neo-Revisionist, and too presentist in her concerns with race, gender, and modern notions of democracy. Lincoln was no worse to Native Americans than other president, they argued, nor were his racial views unusual for the times.[20] The weight of the heroic legend rested heavily upon such reviews. One reviewer cited as irrefutable fact that "the North *won* the war, largely due to Lincoln's military shrewdness. He was a tyro at the start, but he endorsed attacking the enemy's armies simultaneously in different arenas while occupying Southern locales when possible, a strategy that worked brilliantly when it was adopted by Grant and [William Tecumseh] Sherman."[21]

The heroic legend had withstood all four challenges without flinching.

The heroic legend has a long and tangled history. Its origins can be found in the words and actions of Lincoln himself. From the beginnings of his presidency, with or without any additional reading and instruction, he concluded that he had a better grasp than his generals on how the war could be won: forcefully, directly from point A to point B, and quickly. He developed strategic and operational ideas dialectically to the professionals, and he came to favor the straight-ahead Euclidian "chord" over the tactical "arc" of what he derided as "strategy." He favored those officers who agreed, and he disposed of those who did not. In the immediate aftermath of the president's assassination, his pious first biographers were inclined to agree with his positive self-assessment, assigning him military talents that literally were God given. William Herndon, however, launched a countertradition that ignored Lincoln as commander in chief and the heroic legend. Despite the strenuous efforts of devoted White House insiders John Nicolay and John Hay to combat Herndon and enshrine the heroic legend as canon, most contemporary writers of their generation and the one that followed chose not to follow their path when it came to exalting Lincoln as commander in chief, except for denigrating McClellan almost universally. Most authors depicted the president as exemplary in seemingly every category *except* military genius, especially when it came to tactics. In the United States, with the notable exceptions of the soldiers Francis Greene and Arthur Conger, otherwise admiring historians in the first half of the twentieth century continued to play down the heroic legend if not dismissing it entirely. As late as Pearl Harbor, the dominant Revisionists all but sank Lincoln's reputation as a strategist, even as Carl Sandburg cemented the counterimage of the folksy prairie Lincoln of another legend.

It was in Great Britain, amid the bloody shambles of World War I, that agenda-driven officers-turned-historians first turned the tide, looking to Lincoln and his chief generals as antidotes to pro-Confederate influences and doctrines in the British Army that they believed had failed them miserably on the Western Front. Judging Lincoln as a modern war thinker and benevolent dictator in an era of rising authoritarianism, they called for their own powerful Lincolns and Grants in the next expected cataclysm. The subsequent successes of Winston Churchill and Franklin Roosevelt in winning World War II seemed to bear out their ideas. Victory encouraged postwar American scholars to reassess Lincoln through British eyes, as did the ongoing struggle with the Soviet Union, which in the American mind pitted Lincolnian democracy against totalitarianism. Kenneth Williams and T. Harry Williams did not create the heroic legend—they had numerous shoulders to stand upon going back to 1865—but at the depth of the Cold War, they resurrected, borrowed, and restated the essential ideas of Nicolay and Hay, Conger, Forbes, Charnwood, and the British soldier-historians for a modern audience that was coming to accept powerful presidents and ongoing world conflicts as facts of life. That Lincoln resonated with postwar Americans. The Civil War Centennial, similarly steeped in the Cold War and grounded in the revitalized heroic legend, drew deeply upon Williams and Williams while stoking a renewed interest in Lincoln and the Civil War that occasionally ebbed but more often flowed with the times, right up through Ken Burns's *The Civil War* television series in 1990 and the sharp uptick in interest in the war that followed.[22]

More recently, the ongoing national discussion of the relevance of the Civil War in modern America has kept the war in mind but increasingly raised newer questions about Lincoln's racial views. To many Americans, as Barry Schwartz argued, Lincoln emerged chiefly as the Great Emancipator, with his role as Savior of the Union relegated to lesser importance. Others were disappointed.[23] Like his Confederate counterparts, Lincoln statues and schools named in his honor have not escaped recent opposition, defacement, and removal due to what protesters condemn as his settler colonialism and racism toward African Americans and Indigenous peoples. Lincoln came to seem less central and less relevant to many Americans, as his relatively tame sesquicentennial revealed. But even programs and protests only challenged the heroic legend itself with at best an occasional glancing blow.[24]

The complicated, politicized, and often presentist history of the heroic legend does not by itself make it untrue. Hay and Nicolay, Conger, Forbes, Charnwood, Ballard, Maurice, Kenneth Williams, T. Harry Williams, and all those who follow on their path may very well be right after all. T. Harry Williams's *Lincoln and His Generals* holds up well enough under modern scrutiny, except for the overarching presentist theme of the "modern command system" in war. Yet the heroic legend remains too shrouded in reverence for an American icon and too steeped in the various agendas of its creators to accept it uncritically, not while we dissect every other aspect of Lincoln's life and career. It deserves similar reconsideration.

What would that look like? A "more balanced assessment of Lincoln," Brooks Simpson concluded, would need to "first question prevailing orthodoxy, verging on uncritical praise, of his performance in the role."[25] It also remains an interpretation often based upon the same familiar reminiscences, secondary sources, and comfortable "great stories." We must go back to the beginning to reassess Lincoln as commander in chief, just as scholars have with every other facet of his life and career. Accomplishing that will not be easy for future historians, however. The early chapters of this book suggest a more complicated, exhausted, edgy, impatient, self-confident, and thoroughly human commander in chief and would-be tactician who may well have prolonged the war in his zeal to shorten it. But those chapters also remain grounded in a century-and-a half of scholarship that still swamps deep reconsideration of the heroic legend. Kenneth Williams promised to go back to basics by delving deeply into the *Official Records,* but not only did he end up deviating from that course to wade gleefully into historiographical debates with a metaphorical meataxe, but the *Official Records* themselves also turned out to be problematic. As historian Yael Sternhell pointed out, the editors of the compilation started out with their own agendas and biases as they selected what to include and what to ignore. Many of the documents that would further illuminate the commander in chief and the Union armies in their routine day-to-day operations are not found in the *Official Records* at all. They remain in folders and boxes in the National Archives and other repositories throughout the United States. Truly reconsidering Lincoln and the heroic legend, in short, means having to start with trying to forget what we think we know, working in archives that themselves are selective and incomplete, moving on to the other primary sources produced during the war while accepting the existence of their inherent biases, and then treading even more carefully through sources produced in the terrible afterglow of Ford's Theatre.[26]

As if that was not enough, historians will need to broaden their vistas as well. Abraham Lincoln was commander in chief of all U.S. forces, not just those battling the insurgent Confederates. As he was the superior officer of Generals U. S. Grant, George McClellan, and William Tecumseh Sherman, he also was the chief commander of Maj. Gen. James H. Carleton during the Long Walk, Col. John Chivington at Sand Creek, and Col. Patrick Edward Connor at Bear River. Civil War historians continue to debate with spirit whether the Indian Wars of 1861–65 should be considered as part of the Civil War or something separate. Both sides make good points. Yet here is an opportunity. If we are to understand Lincoln fully as commander in chief, we cannot exclude part of his charge and then make judgments because it does not involve a particular delineation of that war. The man who stayed up all night in the telegraph office awaiting battle reports was the same Lincoln who used the Dakota War as an excuse to send away John Pope and who avoided commenting on his military's western atrocities. To truly understand Lincoln as commander in chief, we must integrate these two Lincolns.[27]

All this promises to be a herculean task for scholars of the future, but only after its accomplishment will we be able to understand truly Lincoln as a commander in chief, free of past agendas, heroes' journeys, the American Monomyth, and the heroic legend.

An afterword.

In the end, the heroic legend matters for a more fundamental reason. A decade after his service in President John F. Kennedy's administration, Arthur Schlesinger Jr., who once belittled James G. Randall and held up Lincoln as a symbol of popular democracy and freedom, warned Americans about the development of an "Imperial Presidency." His idea was based exactly on the same Lincoln policies that worried Randall before World War II. Schlesinger saw recent presidents constantly carving out increasing executive power from Congress and the courts, leading to more foreign wars, domestic scandals, and centralization of power in the White House. He did not soft-pedal his new concerns, even confessing that, for a time, he had played a role in their expansion during the Kennedy years. Now like Randall, he described Lincoln's expansion of power in 1861 at the expense of Congress. He cited Congressman Lincoln's opposition to any president having such wide authority during the war with Mexico before outdoing Polk in his own administration. Schlesinger admitted that Lincoln had acted unconstitutionally at times. He especially drew attention to Lincoln's claim to "the war power," along with his expansion of the constitutionally limited role of commander in chief, as the beginning of a slippery slope. Yet Schlesinger still defended the president, much as Randall had. The gravity of the secession crisis and the real threat to American nationhood itself, he wrote, as well as Lincoln's transparency, his expectations that Congress would support him, and finally his determination that his powers would be temporary all mitigated what he had done. Lincoln had acted, Schlesinger believed, in the defensible tradition of John Locke and Thomas Jefferson as well as in "the spirit" of the Constitution, at least, "if not the letter" of the law. Lincoln had said that he never meant to set precedent. The real problem in Schlesinger's view was that too many of Lincoln's modern successors, beginning with Harry Truman—the same Truman who once wrote a fan letter praising T. Harry Williams—and up through Richard Nixon and George W. Bush (in later editions), had used and abused Lincoln's legacy to claim that he had created for them exactly such precedents. They also insisted that, thanks to Lincoln, they possessed "inherent" and "routine" powers to do what Lincoln always thought to be extraordinary, temporary, and potentially dangerous, especially when it came to making war or squelching political opposition. Sometimes they had exercised those doubtful powers behind multiplying layers of secrecy, denial, and criminality.[28]

Geoffrey Perret, less sympathetic to Lincoln than Schlesinger, nonetheless agreed with his overall argument. In a subsequent book to his Lincoln biography, written on more familiar twentieth-century ground, he too pointed to Truman as starting the post-World War II United States down the road to ever-more powerful commanders-in-chief while citing Lincoln for his authority. Truman, followed eventually by Lyndon Johnson and George W. Bush, Perret wrote, looked to Lincoln as they waged wars around the globe without the express consent of Congress, sometimes ignoring their generals' advice and curtailing freedoms at home. William Marvel expressed frustration with Schlesinger's admiration of Lincoln and his willingness to excuse what he saw as Lincoln's egregious record on civil liberties, but he agreed as well that Lincoln had supplied precedents for modern presidents to threaten American liberty.[29]

If Schlesinger was right, then the heroic legend is more than a didactic historiographical interpretation fit for discussion in a graduate-school seminar or at a Civil War Round Table meeting. It then would be an unintentional foundation of modern imperial presidencies and ever more powerful commanders in chief who look back to Lincoln to curtail and control legislative power, ignore or threaten the courts, justify limitations of civil liberties such as habeas corpus, round up dissenters, tolerate presidential lawbreaking as a justifiable norm, and blissfully accept ever more presidential bending of the Constitution to somehow save the Constitution. More than ever the heroic legend would empower both the rogue protagonists of the American Monomyth and their ever-compliant followers. In the wake of unilateral executive actions—including recent commanders in chief Barack Obama's, Donald Trump's, and Joseph Biden's sporadic executive orders to authorize armed drone attacks and missile strikes in the Middle East, as well as Trump's second-term rhetoric about deploying the military abroad while sending troops into American streets—perhaps it behooves us all to reconsider as much of the reality behind the heroic legend as we can and to amend the record if it indeed requires correction.[30] As Lincoln himself said, "we—even we *here*—hold the power and bear the responsibility."[31]

NOTES

INTRODUCTION

1. *Life, Speeches, and Public Services of Abram Lincoln.* See also Burlingame, *Abraham Lincoln,* 1:648–49; Donald, *Lincoln,* 252–53; Guelzo, "Lincoln and His Biographers," 239–41; Holzer, *Lincoln as I Knew Him,* 1; Oates, *With Malice Toward None,* 3–5; Reynolds, *Abe,* xiv. In lieu of a massive endnote listing numerous works, see the best recent overview of Lincoln historiography, Pinsker, "Lincoln Theme 2.0," 417–40. See also these responses to Pinsker in the same *Journal of American History* issue: Ayers, "Lincoln's America 2.0," 441–46; Clinton, "Turning and Turning," 447–50; Holt, "Lincoln Reconsidered," 451–55; Neely, "Lincoln, Slavery, and the Nation," 456–58; and Wilson, "Prospects for Lincoln 2.5," 459–61. Two older essays are still useful as well: Neely, "Lincoln Theme," 10–70 (which Pinsker partially updates); and Zarefsky, "Continuing Fascination," 337–70.

2. Grossman, "Lincoln Compulsion." For a popular exploration of these issues, see Ferguson, *Land of Lincoln.*

3. Peterson, *Lincoln in American Memory,* esp. 26–35. Frank J. Wetta and Martin A. Novelli added a sixth category, the "Man of Sorrows." *Abraham Lincoln & Women in Film,* 3–4, 20, 36, 37, 54, 90, 99, 104, 105, 109, 112, 141, 177.

4. Barr, *Loathing Lincoln,* 17–62, 72–95, 100–102, 105–35, 137–41; Peterson, *Lincoln in American Memory,* 38–50, 243, 251–55.

5. Barr, *Loathing Lincoln,* 10–16, 201–41, 257–77, 290–324; Guelzo, *Our Ancient Faith,* 74–75; Schwartz, *Abraham Lincoln and the Forge,* 79–86. There is a sizable literature along these lines, as discussed in Pinsker, "Lincoln Theme 2.0," 434; and Monroe, "Lincoln the Dwarf," 32–42.

6. Donald, "Getting Right with Lincoln," 3–18; Zarefsky, "Continuing Fascination," 368.

7. Schwartz, *Abraham Lincoln and the Forge,* 251–55 (quotations, 251, 255). For Lincoln's fictional struggle with the undead, see Grahame-Smith, *Abraham Lincoln: Vampire Hunter.* On Lincoln as a comic character and "benign ridicule," see Schwartz, *Abraham Lincoln in the Post-Heroic Era,* 158–66.

8. For solid historiographical introductions to a massive literature, see Gallagher, "Blueprint for Victory," 8–35 (esp. 10–15); Neely, "Abraham Lincoln vs. Jefferson Davis," 96–111 (esp. 103–8); Holt, "Elusive Synthesis," 112–34 (esp. 121); and Benedict, "Constitutional Crisis," 154–73 (esp.

159). See also *Emancipation at 150;* Fields, "Historiographical Trends, Part I," 150–67, and Fields, "Historiographical Trends, Part II," 11–30; Guelzo, *Our Ancient Faith,* 114–22; Neely, "Lincoln Theme," 60–62; Pinsker, "Lincoln Theme 2.0," 430–34; and Zarefsky, "Continuing Fascination," 338–41, 343–44, 353–55, 357–63. Several new works that also touch on these issues appeared after the Pinsker essay and its responses: see especially Burlingame, *Abraham Lincoln;* Foner, *Fiery Trial;* Reynolds, *Abe;* and White, *A. Lincoln.*

9. Thomas, *Portrait for Posterity,* x. David Donald was concerned about dividing authors of books about Lincoln into "idealists" and "realists," however, as "each was legendary in character." Donald, *Lincoln's Herndon,* 372.

10. Randall, *Lincoln the President: Springfield to Gettysburg,* 2:321–42; Niven, *Carl Sandburg,* 492, 583, 628; Wetta and Novelli, *Abraham Lincoln & Women in Film,* 2, 28–57. For the opening of papers and their content, see Mearns, "Lincoln Papers," 369–85.

11. Donald, *Lincoln,* 608–9n55; Simon, "Abraham Lincoln and Ann Rutledge," 13–33; Wilson, "Abraham Lincoln, Ann Rutledge, and the Evidence," 301–24; Wilson, "Herndon's Dilemma," 2–9; Wilson, "Herndon and His Lincoln Informants," 15–34.

12. For introductions to these themes, see Holt, "Lincoln Reconsidered," 451; Neely, "Lincoln Theme," 10–15, 45–49, 66–67; Peterson, *Lincoln in American Memory,* 256–57, 298–310; Pinsker, "Lincoln Theme 2.0," 418–19, 421–33; Randall, "Has the Lincoln Theme Been Exhausted?," 270–94; Wilson, "Prospects for Lincoln 2.5," 459; Zarefsky, "Continuing Fascination," 339–44, 346–49. Several new works that also touch on these issues appeared after the Pinsker essay and its responses: see especially Burlingame, *Abraham Lincoln;* Reynolds, *Abe* (which deals directly with the questions of Lincoln's cultural context); Shenk, *Lincoln's Melancholy;* and White, *A. Lincoln.*

13. Bell and Smallwood, "Pragmatic Lincoln," 134–42; Clinton, "Turning and Turning," 447–50; Holt, "Elusive Synthesis," 112–25; Holt, "Lincoln Reconsidered," 452–55; Neely, "Lincoln Theme," 13–23, 30–40; Pinsker, "Lincoln Theme 2.0," 420–21, 430–32.

14. Heather Cox Richardson, with *West from Appomattox,* and Elliott West, with *The Last Indian War,* initiated the scholarly project of integrating the American West and Civil War history while looking at the latter as an episode of a wider period of nation building. West does not mention Lincoln, however, and Richardson mentions him in passing only a few times. Later books and essays on the West and the Civil War that deal with the president at times include Arenson and Graybill, *Civil War Wests,* 6–7, 228–29; Nelson, *Three-Cornered War,* xiv, xviii, 92–98, 132–33, 201–3; Schulten, "Civil War and the Origins of the Colorado Territory," 21–46; and Warde, *When the Wolf Came,* esp. 38–39, 42–43, 64–67, 225–26, 242–43. More tightly focused on Lincoln are Mason, "Indian Policy of Abraham Lincoln"; Etulain, *Lincoln and the Oregon Country;* Green, *Lincoln and Native Americans;* Nichols, *Lincoln and the Indians;* and Vorenberg, *Lincoln's Peace,* xxiii–xxiv, 154–74, 345, 346–52. As for Lincoln biographers, see Burlingame, *Abraham Lincoln,* 2:480–83; Donald, *Lincoln,* 392–64; Foner, *Fiery Trial,* 204, 261–62; Guelzo, *Our Ancient Faith,* 121; Neely, *Last Best Hope,* 150–51; and Reynolds, *Abe,* 665–70, 673. A notable exception is Pryor, *Six Encounters,* 154–210.

15. Green, *Lincoln and Native Americans,* 106.

16. Ballard, *Military Genius;* Boritt, *Lincoln the War President;* Davis, "Creating a Military Image," 19–23; Dirck, "Lincoln as Commander-in-Chief," 20–27; Fuller, *Generalship of U. S. Grant;* Glatthaar, *Partners in Command,* chaps. 3, 7; LaFantasie, "Lincoln and the American

Military Tradition," 8–34; Liddell Hart, *Sherman;* Hearn, *Lincoln and McClellan;* Houghton, "Lincoln and Gettysburg," 243–46; Marszalek, *Lincoln and the Military;* Maurice, *Statesmen and Soldiers;* McDonough, "Commander in Chief and Military Operations in Tennessee," 93–105; McPherson, "Lincoln as Commander in Chief," 32–35; McPherson, *Tried by War;* Nicolay and Hay, *Abraham Lincoln;* Rable, *Conflict of Command;* Simpson, *Lincoln and the Gettysburg Campaign;* Stoker, *Grand Design;* Symonds, *Lincoln and His Admirals;* Waugh, *Lincoln and McClellan;* Weigley, *Great Civil War;* Williams, "Abraham Lincoln"; Williams, *Lincoln Finds a General,* vols. 1–2; Williams, *Lincoln and His Generals.* The major biographies and near-biographies also deal with this aspect of Lincoln's presidency in varying degrees. For crucial examples, see Burlingame, *Abraham Lincoln;* Donald, *Lincoln;* Foner, *Fiery Trial;* Gienapp, *Abraham Lincoln;* Goodwin, *Team of Rivals;* Neely, *Last Best Hope;* Oates, *With Malice Toward None;* Perret, *Lincoln's War;* Reynolds, *Abe;* Thomas, *Abraham Lincoln;* and White, *A. Lincoln.*

17. See Williams, *Lincoln and His Generals;* Williams, *Lincoln Finds a General;* LaFantasie, "Lincoln and the American Military Tradition," 18; and Marvel, *Mr. Lincoln Goes to War,* xiii. Notable dissenters are Grimsley, "Lincoln as Commander-in-Chief," 62–87; Grimsley, "Lincoln-McClellan Relationship," 63–81; Perret, *Lincoln's War;* Pryor, "Conflict, Chaos, and Confidence," 2–79; Pryor, *Six Encounters;* Simpson, *Lincoln and the Gettysburg Campaign;* Simpson, *Ulysses S. Grant;* and four notable books by William Marvel: *Great Task Remaining; Lincoln's Darkest Year; Mr. Lincoln Goes to War;* and *Tarnished Victory.*

18. LaFantasie, "Lincoln and the American Military Tradition," 19.

19. Pryor, *Six Encounters,* 5.

20. Venville, *Abraham Lincoln,* eps. 1–3; Goodwin, *Team of Rivals;* Goodwin, *Leadership in Turbulent Times.* Ironically, in 2010 Obama had removed McCrystal as the commander of American troops in Afghanistan in a moment that reminded some at the time of Lincoln relieving McClellan. See Greenblatt, "Generals Gone Rogue"; and Grimsley, "Lincoln-McClellan Relationship," 65–66.

21. Levin, "Rethinking the Role of Talking Heads in Documentaries."

22. Venville, *Abraham Lincoln,* eps. 1–3. For important books that deal in similar ways with this aspect of Lincoln's presidency, see Ballard, *Military Genius,* 5–6, 17–23; Boritt, *Lincoln the War President,* 184–87, 200–205; Burlingame, *Abraham Lincoln,* 1:49, 67–71, 2:248, 285–87, 492–93; Davis, "Creating a Military Image," 19–21; Dirck, "Lincoln as Commander-in-Chief," 20–26; Donald, *Lincoln,* 44–46; "Eisenhower on Lincoln as Commander-in-Chief," 8–9; Liddell Hart, *Sherman,* 92; Marszalek, *Lincoln and the Military,* x, 1, 3–4, 7, 109–13; Maurice, *Statesmen and Soldiers,* vii, 118–21; McPherson, *Tried by War,* xv–xvii, 2–8; Neely, *Last Best Hope,* 7–11, 83–84, 95–96, 123, 142–44; Oates, *With Malice Toward None,* 24–25; Perret, *Lincoln's War,* 8–11, 75, 144–49, 156–61, 233, 260, 270; Reardon, *With a Sword in One Hand,* 28; Reynolds, *Abe,* 123–24, 687–716; Stoker, *Grand Design,* 14–15, 18; Symonds, *Lincoln and His Admirals,* ix, x–xiv; Thomas, *Abraham Lincoln,* 30–34, 465, 469–70; White, *A. Lincoln,* 50–52, 438, 540; Williams, "Abraham Lincoln"; Williams, *Lincoln and his Generals,* vii, 7–12; Weigley, *Great Civil War,* 90, 177–78; Wolseley, *American Civil War,* 55, 120–21, and Zander, *Army Under Fire,* 14-16.

23. Boritt, *Lincoln the War President,* 186–87; Burlingame, *Abraham Lincoln,* 1:67–71; Donald, *Lincoln,* 44–46; Gienapp, *Abraham Lincoln,* 17; Hearn, *Lincoln and McClellan,* 8–9; LaFantasie, "Lincoln and the American Military Tradition," 29; Marszalek, *Lincoln and the Military,* 3–4, 110; Oates, *With Malice Toward None,* 24–25; Perret, *Lincoln's War,* 8–11; Pryor, "Conflict,

Chaos, and Confidence," 7–8; Pryor, *Six Encounters,* 176–81; Rable, *Conflict of Command,* 13–14; Thomas, *Abraham Lincoln,* 30–34; White, *A. Lincoln,* 50–52; Williams, "Abraham Lincoln."

24. Nicolay and Hay, *Abraham Lincoln,* 5:155–56.

25. Rable, *Conflict of Command,* 7.

26. See Noe, *Howling Storm,* 122–43, 276–97.

27. Simpson, *Ulysses S. Grant,* 136, 155–59, 178–84, 197–98, 214–15, 251–53, 257–63, 271–77, 289–90, 393–99, 400–401.

28. Bray, "'Power to Hurt,'" 43–51; Guelzo, *Our Ancient Faith,* 47 (quotation). See also Burlingame, *Abraham Lincoln,* 1:155–57, 190–94, 357–62; Gienapp, *Abraham Lincoln,* 32–33; Pryor, *Six Encounters,* 79–81; Reynolds, *Abe,* 163–67; Thomas, *Abraham Lincoln,* 84; White, *A. Lincoln,* 94, 114–16; and Wilson, *Honor's Voice,* 266–72, 300–304.

29. Luke 2:46–47 (King James Version).

30. Dundes, *Sacred Narrative,* 1–3. Chapters in *Sacred Narrative* by William Bascom (5–29), Jan DeVries (30–40), Lauri Honko (41–52), G. S. Kirk (53–61), J. W. Rogerson (62–71) illustrate some of those differences.

31. Bascom, "Forms of Folklore," 5–29 (quotations, 8, 9).

32. Kirk, "On Defining Myths," 55–58 (quotation, 56).

33. Shaara, *Gods and Generals.* See also Grimsley, "Lincoln-McClellan Relationship," 63.

34. Blight, *Race and Reunion,* 191, 189. For my earlier use of the word "myth," see Noe, "'Deadened Color'"; and Noe, "Toward the Myth of Unionist Appalachia."

35. Consider, for example, Thomas Carlyle, "The American Iliad in a Nutshell," *New York Times,* Aug. 14, 1863; Eisenschiml and Newman, *American Iliad;* Roland, *American Iliad;* and Mark Grimsley's regular column American Iliad, which ran in *Civil War Monitor* from Fall 2015 through Winter 2020. See also Blight, *Race and Reunion,* 181–98; and Grimsley, "Lincoln-McClellan Relationship,"63–64.

36. Rowland, *George B. McClellan,* 43.

37. Grant, *Personal Memoirs,* 2:488. Wallace Hettle discusses this quotation in *Inventing Stonewall Jackson,* 12.

38. David Powell, comment to Dan Masters, "Just read this in Sam Hood's book," July 28, 2022, Facebook, https://www.facebook.com/dan.masters.94/posts/pfbid031ro2r7Qgu1A9ZhXAp1GTfoEU5NJiXqwHE6Gt1RD8cAc7C1c6RtjqjPeEM4zT4hSDl.

39. I compiled much of this list by posting a query to Civil War historians and other friends on my Facebook page. See Kenneth Noe, "Civil War peeps: here's a list of cliches we hear all the time," July 28, 2022, Facebook, https://www.facebook.com/kenneth.noe.10/posts/pfbid0cZYBSVLHmjQcWzvK9tiGPVhY5xucp7La9R278Ay3MSraEna69mhznks73GxVt7. I am very grateful to Terry Beckenbaugh, Robert Bradley, Bryan Cheeseboro, Jake Clawson, Daniel Cone, Barbara Gannon, Andy Hall, Will Haynes, Richard Heisler, Jordan Henderson, Bob Huddleston, Martin Husk, Bob Hutton, Chuck Kays, Ari Kelman, Kelly Kennington, Chris Kolakowski, Kevin Levin, Dan Masters, Jennifer Murray, Dan Modes, Steve Nash, Bruce Nave, Al Nofi, Mike Peters, David Powell, Logan Shaddix, Donald Shaffer, Darryl Smith, Cara Stoddard, Bruce Tap, Lee White, and David Woodbury. I also will add one personal anecdote. A student once complained to our department chair that one of my colleagues had referred to "Lee" in a lecture. "His name is Robert E. Lee," the student complained, "never just Lee." See also Blight, *Race and Reunion,*

189; Grimsley, "Lincoln-McClellan Relationship," 63; and Harsh, "On the McClellan-Go-Round," 101–18. For an extension of Harsh's argument, see Rowland, *George B. McClellan,* vii, 25–33, 43–53, 70–71, 74–75.

40. Shaara, *Killer Angels;* Maxwell, *Gettysburg;* Murray, *On a Great Battlefield,* 143, 150, 166; Rable, *Conflict of Command,* 7; Harris, "Searching for Buster Kilrain"; "Little Round Top Rehabilitation Project," *National Park Service, Gettysburg National Military Park,* last updated Oct. 22, 2024.

41. Harsh, "On the McClellan-Go-Round," 106, 110, 117. See also Grimsley, "Lincoln-McClellan Relationship," 64–70; and Rowland, *George B. McClellan,* 4–8, 11, 14, 16–20.

42. Moody, *Seven Myths of the Civil War;* Varon, *Appomattox,* esp. 1–4, 208–58 (quotation, 1); Vorenberg, *Lincoln's Peace,* esp. xv–xxix, 343–57.

43. Nolan, "Anatomy of the Myth," 11-29; Wilson, *Baptized in Blood.*

44. Pollard, *Lost Cause;* Nolan, "Anatomy of the Myth," 12–19 (quotation, 12).

45. Wilson, *Baptized in Blood,* 38–40; Campbell, *Hero with a Thousand Faces.*

46. Larsen and Larsen, *Fire in the Mind,* esp. 334–49. See also "About Joseph Campbell"; and Campbell, *Hero with a Thousand Faces.*

47. Campbell, *Hero with a Thousand Faces,* 1, 28–29.

48. Campbell, *Hero with a Thousand Faces,* 211.

49. Larsen and Larsen, *Fire in the Mind,* xvii, xix, 540–43, 548–51; Batty, "Are You Monomythic?"; Bridgman, "Richard Adams at Eighty"; Clarke, *Lost Worlds of 2001,* 34; Vogler, "Memo That Started It All"; Vogler, *Writer's Journey,* ix–x, xxvii–xxxi, 3–8. Campbell also influenced artists as varied as musicians Bob Dylan and The Grateful Dead, director Stanley Kubrick, and novelists Richard Adams, Dan Brown, and Arthur C. Clarke.

50. Quoted in Larsen and Larsen, *Fire in the Mind,* 347–48.

51. See, for example, Christensen and Bond, "Man Behind the Myth"; Crespi, film review of *People of the Klamath,* 1103–5; Dundes, "Folklorists in the Twenty-First Century," 391–402; Ellwood, *Politics of Myth,* vii–xiii, 6–7, 126–69; Lefkowitz, "Myth of Joseph Campbell," 429–34; Northrup, "Myth-Placed Priorities," 5–10; Segal, "Campbell's Theory of Myth," in Dundes, *Sacred Narratives,* 256–69; Segal, "Romantic Appeal of Joseph Campbell," 332–35; and Toelken, *Dynamics of Folklore,* 257, 413. For a concise abstract of Dundes's negative opinion of Campbell's work, see Dundes, *Sacred Narratives,* 256–57.

52. Frankel, *From Girl to Goddess,* 1, 2–3, 4, 6, 18–19, 51, 146, 150, 164, 174, 251; Murdock, *Heroine's Journey,* 2, 3, 7, 13–14; Morgan, *Demon Lover,* 58–60, 67–70.

53. Christensen and Bond, "Man Behind the Myth."

54. For a discussion of these issues, see, for example, Ellwood, *Politics of Myth,* vii–xviii, 131–33, 138–40, 145–46, 149–51, 153, 162–67; Friendman, "Why Joseph Campbell's Psychologizing of Myth Precludes the Holocaust," 385–401; Gill, "Faces of Joseph Campbell," 16–19; Grede, "Bashing Joseph Campbell," 50–52; Konner et al., "Joseph Campbell," 57–61; Larsen and Larsen, *Fire in the Mind,* 9, 510–11; Lefkowitz, "Myth of Joseph Campbell," 430, 432–33, 434; Segal, "Campbell on Jews and Judaism," 151–70; and Segal, "Romantic Appeal of Joseph Campbell," 332–35. The weight of the evidence unfortunately suggests that the charges of Campbell's casual antisemitism carry real weight. In addition, see Brin, "'Star Wars' Despots vs. 'Star Trek' Populists"; and Lawrence and Jewett, *Myth of the American Superhero,* 265–82. Lawrence and Jewett

reference in particular the last scene of the original *Star Wars* film, which they link convincingly to Leni Riefenstahl's *Triumph of the Will* (1935), as well as Lucas's depiction of a "stabbed in the back" ideology among the Jedi Knights and the subservience of the individual to the Force.

55. Jewett and Lawrence, *American Monomyth,* xx, 170, 210, 215, 216, 219, 224. The authors updated and expanded their argument past the events of September 11, 2001, in Lawrence and Jewett, *Myth of the American Superhero.* Campbell himself articulated the difficulty of transporting his hero's journey to a pluralistic United States. See Ellwood, *Politics of Myth,* 165.

56. Thomas, *Portrait for Posterity,* 3–7 (quotations, 3, 7).

57. Donald, *Lincoln's Herndon,* 371.

58. Rossiter quoted in Schwartz, *Abraham Lincoln in the Post-Heroic Era,* 9.

59. Grimsley, "Lincoln as Commander-in-Chief," 82–84; Grimsley, "Lincoln-McClellan Relationship," 77, 78–80.

60. Lawrence and Jewett, *Myth of the American Superhero,* 131–32, 138–42 (quotations, 131, 132, 142). From *Young Mr. Lincoln,* they add, it was then only a few short hops to the alien-fighting superpresident of the 1996 blockbuster *Independence Day.* See also Schwartz, *Abraham Lincoln in the Post-Heroic Era,* 30.

61. See, for example, Bishop, "Teaching Lincoln at the Abraham Lincoln Presidential Library and Museum," 39–41; Decker, review of the Abraham Lincoln Presidential Library and Museum, 934–38; Erekson, "Engulfed by the Past," 93–100; Ferguson, *Land of Lincoln,* 91–116; Pine and Gilmore, "Museums and Authenticity," 76–80, 92–93; and Pryor, *Six Encounters,* 1–2, 5–9. For the record, I like the tours at the Lincoln Presidential Library and Museum, but the debt to Campbell through the former Disney employees who helped design them is obvious.

62. Rable, *Conflict of Command,* 5.

63. Harsh, "McClellan-Go-Round," esp. 105, 112–13 (quotation, 112). See also Grimsley, "Lincoln-McClellan Relationship," 64–67; and Rable, *Conflict of Command,* 1–7.

64. Grimsley, "Lincoln-McClellan Relationship," 70, 76. On this point see also Rowland, *George B. McClellan,* 45–53.

65. Williams, *Lincoln Finds a General,* 1:ix–x.

66. Schlesinger, *Imperial Presidency.*

1. THE WAR POWER

1. Basler et al., *Collected Works of Abraham Lincoln,* 4:518–37 (quotation, 537). There is a vast literature on Lincoln and his colonization proposal. See, for example, Burlingame, *Abraham Lincoln,* 2:235–36, 333–63, 383–96, 439–43; Foner, *Fiery Trial,* 168–71, 184–87, 195–202, 222–26, 233–49, 269; Donald, *Lincoln,* 343–46, 363–68, 396–98; McPherson, *Tried by War,* 128–29, 212–13, 226–30; and Symonds, *Lincoln and His Admirals,* 167–68, 177–81.

2. Holzer, *Lincoln President-Elect,* 421.

3. Weigley, *Great Civil War,* 177–78. Weigley sees this expansion as unfortunate, suggesting that whether any president has these powers is "constitutionally debatable" and "a most vital question" for today. The Supreme Court eventually did uphold Lincoln's views in the 1863 Prize Cases decision, but only by a slim majority. For other views, see Boritt, *Lincoln the War President,* 201; Degler, "One Among Many," 108–9; Dirck, "Lincoln as Commander-in-Chief," 20–21;

Gienapp, *Abraham Lincoln,* 122; Marszalek, *Lincoln and the Military,* 1–2; Neely, *Last Best Hope,* 81, 95–97; Stoker, *Grand Design,* 6; and Williams, "Abraham Lincoln."

4. Dirck, "Lincoln as Commander-in-Chief," 23–26 (quotations, 23, 26). See also Gienapp, *Abraham Lincoln,* 141.

5. Nicolay and Hay, *Abraham Lincoln,* 4:76.

6. Geoffrey Perret maintained, "Lincoln defined the war powers of the president in a way that no member of his Cabinet understood or agreed with, including [Attorney General] Edward Bates." In "a struggle for its very survival," Lincoln countered, "the United States could claim all the war powers allowed under international law, and none of those powers could be circumscribed by any of the guarantees and prohibitions of the Constitution. The only limitation Lincoln faced was his reliance on Congress to provide the Army and Navy and the money needed to support them." Perret, *Lincoln's War,* 38–40, 382 (quotation). See also Dirck, "Lincoln as Commander-in-Chief," 20–22; Foner, *Fiery Trial,* 162; Paludan, "'Dictator Lincoln,'" 8–12; and Pryor, *Six Encounters,* 17–18. For the ramifications, see the conclusion as well as Schlesinger, *Imperial Presidency,* esp. xiii–xiv, xxv–xxviii, 42–43, 58–69, 109, 113–14, 142, 157, 165, 187–88, 192–83, 285–86, 321–22, 335, 460.

7. Dirck, "Lincoln as Commander-in-Chief," 22–26 (quotations, 23, 24).

8. Grimsley, "Lincoln as Commander-in-Chief," 62.

9. For specific examples, see Ballard, *Military Genius,* 233, 315; Burlingame, *Abraham Lincoln,* 2:319; Donald, *Lincoln,* 489, 500; Hearn, *Lincoln and McClellan,* 48; Liddell Hart, *Sherman,* 137; Marszalek, *Lincoln and the Military,* 15, 23–25; McDonough, "Commander in Chief and Military Operations in Tennessee," 102, 103; McPherson, *Tried by War,* 63, 181; Neely, *Last Best Hope,* 72; Perret, *Lincoln's War,* 91, 338; Pryor, *Six Encounters,* 222–23; Simpson, *Ulysses S. Grant,* 181; Simpson, *Lincoln and the Gettysburg Campaign,* v, 29, 45, 58; Stoker, *Grand Design,* 72; Waugh, *Lincoln and McClellan,* 129; Weigley, *Great Civil War,* 82; Williams, *Lincoln Finds a General,* 1:472; and Wolseley, *American Civil War,* 80, 112–13.

10. Pryor, *Six Encounters,* 5.

11. See, for example, Wolseley, *American Civil War,* 80, 98, 99, 100, 112–13. On Lincoln's "logical and analytical" mind, see Rable, *Conflict of Command,* 62. On his indecisiveness, see LaFantasie, "Lincoln and the American Military Tradition," 24–26.

12. See, for example, Donald, *Lincoln,* 437–38; Hearn, *Lincoln and McClellan,* 80; Neely, *Last Best Hope,* 123; and Pryor, *Six Encounters,* 60.

13. Basler et al., *Collected Works of Abraham Lincoln,* 4:438.

14. Gienapp, *Abraham Lincoln,* 99–100; Meacham, *And There Was Light,* 154.

15. This paragraph is based largely on Robins and Dorn, "Stress and Political Leadership," 3–17; Gienapp, *Abraham Lincoln,* 126–27, 151–52, 164–65, 184–86, 190–91; Stanley, "War Duration," 178–200; and Stanley and Larsen, "Stressed Out," 793–808. But see also Carucci, "Stress Leads to Bad Decisions"; Harms, "Stress and Exploitative Decision-Making," 10035–37; Porcelli and Delgado, "Stress and Decision Making," 33–39; and Yaribeygi et al., "Impact of Stress on Body Function," 1057–72. I am grateful to Darin Rock and Daniel Svyantek for pointing me to these articles. Harold Holzer, who described Lincoln himself as "a man of inexhaustible energy and robust health," also fairly noted John Speed's and Henry Villard's contrary opinions of Lincoln's health. See Holzer, *Lincoln as I Knew Him,* 6 (quotation), 45, 92–93. George Rable has

emphasized Lincoln's melancholy, while William Marvel has drawn attention to Lincoln's "debilitating physical and mental strain" caused in part by his attention to political appointments and other "trivia." Rable, *Conflict of Command;* Marvel, *Mr. Lincoln Goes to War,* 22 (quotation).

16. Robins and Dorn, "Stress and Political Leadership," 3–17.

17. Donald, *Lincoln,* 14, 15.

18. Robins and Dorn, "Stress and Political Leadership," 3–17; Basler et al., *Collected Works of Abraham Lincoln,* 7:281–83 (quotation, 282). See also Gienapp, *Abraham Lincoln,* 127.

19. See the analysis in Pryor, "Conflict, Chaos, and Confidence," 24–56.

20. Boritt, *Lincoln and the Economics of the American Dream,* 267–67; Boritt, *Lincoln the War President,* 184–204; Bruce, "Shadow of Coming War," 26; Burlingame, *Abraham Lincoln,* 1:70–71, 421–35; Dirck, "Lincoln as Commander-in-Chief," 21–22; Gienapp, *Abraham Lincoln,* 39; LaFantasie, "Lincoln and the American Military Tradition," 21–24; Marszalek, *Lincoln and the Military,* 2–4, 7, 109; Meacham, *And There Was Light,* 98–101; Neely, *Last Best Hope,* 61; Pryor, "Conflict, Chaos, and Confidence," 5–6, 7–8; Pryor, *Six Encounters,* 15–17; Reynolds, *Abe,* 306–7; Zander, *Army Under Fire,* 1–11, 17–68.

21. Basler et al., *Collected Works of Abraham Lincoln,* 4:157–60, 162 (quotation, 159). See also Rable, *Conflict of Command,* 29.

22. Basler et al., *Collected Works of Abraham Lincoln,* 4:157–60, 162, 164, 176, 183, 191–246; Burlingame, *Abraham Lincoln,* 2:2, 4–5, 8, 18, 30–31, 36, 40, 45–49, 65–66; Burton, *Age of Lincoln,* 116–18; Donald, *Lincoln,* 283–84; Foner, *Fiery Trial,* 157, 159; Gienapp, *Abraham Lincoln,* 72–74; Goodwin, *Team of Rivals,* 323–24, 326, 330; Guelzo, *Our Ancient Faith,* 162–63; McPherson, *Tried by War,* 10; Meacham, *And There Was Light,* 199–203, 218, 225–27; Neely, *Last Best Hope,* 63; Oates, *With Malice Toward None,* 234; Pryor, *Six Encounters,* 13, 287–93; Reynolds, *Abe,* 521; Stoker, *Grand Design,* 14–15; Thomas, *Abraham Lincoln,* 247–48; White, *A. Lincoln,* 383–84. Harold Holzer offers the most detailed examination of this period, as well as a spirited refutation of the stereotype of President-elect Lincoln as weak and wrongheaded in his silence, in *Lincoln President-Elect,* 1–5, 77, 155–396.

23. Basler et al., *Collected Works of Abraham Lincoln,* 4:249–71 (quotations, 266, 271). See also Nicolay and Hay, *Abraham Lincoln,* 3:321–23; Holzer, *Lincoln President-Elect,* 242–43, 254–59 262–71, 312, 337, 341–43, 345–46, 417, 439–40, 444, 457–75; and Pryor, *Six Encounters,* 14.

24. Basler et al., *Collected Works of Abraham Lincoln,* 4:279–80, 284–85; Beale, *Diary of Edward Bates,* 177–78; Burlingame, *With Lincoln in the White House,* 46–47; Burlingame and Ettlinger, *Inside Lincoln's White House,* 5; Pease and Randall, *Diary of Orville Hickman Browning,* 476, 563; Welles, *Diary of Gideon Welles,* 1:47–48; Burlingame, *Abraham Lincoln,* 2:99–103; Donald, *Lincoln,* 285–87; Gienapp, *Abraham Lincoln,* 79–81; Goodwin, *Team of Rivals,* 334–39; Marvel, *Mr. Lincoln Goes to War,* xvi, 14–16, 27; McPherson, *Tried by War,* 10–11, 13–17; Oates, *With Malice Toward None,* 238, 240; Pryor, "Conflict, Chaos, and Confidence," 23; Pryor, *Six Encounters,* 12–15, 34–36; Thomas, *Abraham Lincoln,* 250–51; White, *A. Lincoln,* 397–401; Williams, *Lincoln Finds a General,* 1:37–41, 42, 44, 47.

As discussed in a later chapter, readers should note that Gideon Welles's actual diary did not begin until August 1862. The earliest published version cited here included much revisionist editing as well as a long narrative leading up to the diary, all prepared by an increasingly bitter Welles, as well as further editing and censoring from his editor-son Edgar. Sadly, it is all we have for the first seventeen months of the war from Lincoln's secretary of the navy. For the cleanest edition of his actual diary, see Gienapp and Gienapp, *Civil War Diary of Gideon Welles,* esp. xii–xxii for details.

25. Beale, *Diary of Edward Bates,* 178–80; Nicolay and Hay, *Abraham Lincoln,* 3:375–95; Welles, *Diary of Gideon Welles,* 1:6–16; Burlingame, *Abraham Lincoln,* 2:105–9; Donald, *Lincoln,* 287–91; Gienapp, *Abraham Lincoln,* xi, 80–81, 92; Goodwin, *Team of Rivals,* 339–40; Marvel, *Mr. Lincoln Goes to War,* 17, 20; McPherson, *Tried by War,* 17–20; Oates, *With Malice Toward None,* 240–42; Pryor, *Six Encounters,* 8, 15, 34, 37–39; Symonds, *Lincoln and His Admirals,* 8–14; Weigley, *Great Civil War,* 1–6, 19; White, *A. Lincoln,* 400–401; Williams, *Lincoln and His Generals,* 15.

26. Welles, *Diary of Gideon Welles,* 1:13; Niven, *Gideon Welles,* 326–29.

27. Gordon, *Dread Danger,* 18; Gordon, "'Novices in Warfare,'" 194–208; Gordon, "Zouave," 48–53; Groeling, *First Fallen,* 1–150: Reynolds, *Abe,* 528–32.

28. Basler et al., *Collected Works of Abraham Lincoln,* 4:177–78, 273; Herndon and Weik, *Abraham Lincoln,* 2:319; Burlingame, *Abraham Lincoln,* 2:177; Gordon, *Dread Danger,* 34–38, 49, 58; Gordon, "'Novices in Warfare,'" 194–97, 208–15; Gordon, "Zouave," 50, 52, 57, 68; Groeling, *First Fallen,* 151–212; Reynolds, *Abe,* 531–44.

29. Basler et al., *Collected Works of Abraham Lincoln,* 4:313–16; Beale, *Diary of Edward Bates,* 180; "General M. C. Meigs on the Conduct of the War," 287–88, 299–302; Nicolay and Hay, *Abraham Lincoln,* 3:434–41; Porter, *Incidents and Anecdotes,* 13–23; Current, *Lincoln and the First Shot,* 194–99; Niven, *Gideon Welles,* 328–39; Gienapp, *Abraham Lincoln,* 75, 80–81, 90; Holzer, *Lincoln President-Elect,* 121–24, 153–55, 171; Meacham, *And There Was Light,* 236–38; Pryor, "Conflict, Chaos, and Confidence," 8, 14–16; Pryor, *Six Encounters,* 37–39, 51–54, 56–57; Welles, *Diary of Gideon Welles,* 1:16–18, 136–37. Howard Holzer explained why rewarding loyal Republicans with patronage positions was vital to party unity and why Lincoln embraced it despite his other cares. Holzer, *Lincoln President-Elect,* 121–24.

30. Basler et al., *Collected Works of Abraham Lincoln,* 4:316–18, 323–24, 329–31; Beale, *Diary of Edward Bates,* 180–83; Burlingame, *With Lincoln in the White House,* 33; Nicolay and Hay, *Abraham Lincoln,* 3:445–49, 4:5–7, 33–34; Pease and Randall, *Diary of Orville Hickman Browning,* 563; Welles, *Diary of Gideon Welles,* 1:6–8, 16–32, 36–40, 136–37; Burlingame, *Abraham Lincoln,* 2:111–16, 125; Current, *Lincoln and the First Shot,* 190–94; Degler, "One Among Many," 108; Donald, *Lincoln,* 291–93; Goodwin, *Team of Rivals,* 342–46; Holzer, *Lincoln as I Knew Him,* 91–92; Marszalek, *Lincoln and the Military,* 12; McPherson, *Tried by War,* 14; Oates, *With Malice Toward None,* 242–44; Stampp, "One Alone?," 135; Symonds, *Lincoln and His Admirals,* 15–27; Thomas, *Abraham Lincoln,* 254–55; White, *A. Lincoln,* 402–4, 408; Williams, *Lincoln Finds a General,* 1:54–55. On Fort Sumter itself, see Klein, *Days of Defiance;* Goodheart, *1861;* and Swanberg, *First Blood.*

31. The classic examination is Current, *Lincoln and the First Shot.* For a history of the discussion, see ibid., 182–208. Current concluded that Lincoln did not want a war but was willing to accept one if the Confederates fired first. For other interpretations, see Ballard, *Military Genius,* 54; Burlingame, *Abraham Lincoln,* 2:125–29; Donald, *Lincoln,* 293; Goodwin, *Team of Rivals,* 345; Marszalek, *Lincoln and the Military,* 12; Marvel, *Mr. Lincoln Goes to War,* xvii–xviii, 20–27, 153; McPherson, *Tried by War,* 20; Stampp, *And the War Came,* 280–86; Stampp, *Imperiled Union,* 163–88; Stampp, "One Alone?," 135; White, *A. Lincoln,* 408; and Williams, *Lincoln Finds*

a General, 1:57–58, 789–93. Donald Stoker blamed Davis, adding that militarily, the decision to fire on Sumter was a rash idea that hurt Confederate procurement abroad and crippled the southern economy. Stoker, *Grand Design,* 23–23.

32. Pease and Randall, *Diary of Orville Hickman Browning,* 476.

33. Nicolay and Hay, *Abraham Lincoln,* 4:44–45.

34. Johnson, "Fort Sumter and Confederate Diplomacy," 441–77; Potter, *Lincoln and His Party,* 371–75; Stampp, *And the War Came,* 280–86; Stampp, *Imperiled Union,* 163–88; Symonds, *Lincoln and His Admirals,* 30–36. See also Sherman, *Memoirs,* 1:167–68; Stoddard, *Inside the White House,* 15–16; and Pryor, *Six Encounters,* 7–8, 52–56, 293–96.

35. Welles, *Diary of Gideon Welles,* 1:40, 38.

36. Richard Current shifted the blame to Davis, who could have chosen not to contest the resupply mission. Current, *Lincoln and the First Shot,* 199–201.

37. Foner, *Fiery Trial,* 162. See also Rable, *Conflict of Command,* 33.

38. Burlingame, *With Lincoln in the White House,* 40; Burlingame and Ettlinger, *Inside Lincoln's White House,* 5; Welles, *Diary of Gideon Welles,* 1:16–21, 36–37; Burlingame, *Abraham Lincoln,* 2:166, 362; Donald, *Lincoln,* 298; Gienapp, *Abraham Lincoln,* xi, 91–92; Marszalek, *Lincoln and the Military,* 3; Marvel, *Mr. Lincoln Goes to War,* 15, 22; McPherson, *Tried by War,* 30; Oates, *With Malice Toward None,* 251–57; Paludan, "'Dictator Lincoln,'" 10; Perret, *Lincoln's War,* 40; Pryor, "Conflict, Chaos, and Confidence," 5–7, 8–9; Pryor, *Six Encounters,* 15, 7–23, 24–31, 34, 41–49, 50–51; White, *A. Lincoln,* 415.

39. Basler et al., *Collected Works of Abraham Lincoln,* 4:331–33, 338–39, 340–41, 343, 344, 346–47, 356, 385–86; Burlingame, *With Lincoln in the White House,* 35, 39; Burlingame and Ettlinger, *Inside Lincoln's White House,* 13; Nicolay and Hay, *Abraham Lincoln,* 4:72–75, 77, 125–27, 152–53; Paludan, "'Dictator Lincoln,'" 10. See also Burlingame, *Abraham Lincoln,* 2:131–49; Donald, *Lincoln,* 298–99; Foner, *Fiery Trial,* 162–63; Gienapp, *Abraham Lincoln,* 82–83, 85; Goodwin, *Team of Rivals,* 348–54, 355–56; Guelzo, *Our Ancient Faith,* 94–106; Holzer, *Lincoln President-Elect,* 156–59, 211–13, 221, 223; Marszalek, *Lincoln and the Military,* 13–15; Marvel, *Mr. Lincoln Goes to War,* 42–44, 70–72, 185, 197–99; McPherson, *Tried by War,* 22–24; Niven, *Gideon Welles,* 347–48, 356–58; Oates, *With Malice Toward None,* 251–57; Pryor, "Conflict, Chaos, and Confidence," 6–7; Pryor, *Six Encounters,* 65–66, 102–3; Symonds, *Lincoln and His Admirals,* 38–39, 41; Perret, *Lincoln's War,* 31–32; Thomas, *Abraham Lincoln,* 266–68; Weigley, *Great Civil War,* 30, 56, 180, 183; White, *A. Lincoln,* 415–17; and Williams, *Lincoln Finds a General,* 1:60, 65–66, 72–73, 115, 121, 796–800. Chief Justice Roger Taney later ruled against Lincoln, claiming that only Congress had such powers. The president ignored him.

40. Basler et al., *Collected Works of Abraham Lincoln,* 4:351–52, 353–54, 364–65, 372, 394–95, 409–10, 419; Boritt, *Lincoln the War President,* 201; Burlingame, *Abraham Lincoln,* 2:149–53, 163–65; Dirck, "Lincoln as Commander-in-Chief," 20–21; Donald, *Lincoln,* 299, 301–5; Gienapp, *Abraham Lincoln,* 82–83; Goodwin, *Team of Rivals,* 365–69; Marszalek, *Lincoln and the Military,* 1–2, 15; McPherson, *Tried by War,* 23–24; Neely, *Last Best Hope,* 61, 81; Perret, *Lincoln's War,* 105–6; Pryor, "Conflict, Chaos, and Confidence," 6–7; Pryor, *Six Encounters,* 58–60; Reynolds, *Abe,* 675–81; Simpson, *Ulysses S. Grant,* 89; Symonds, *Lincoln and His Admirals,* 57–59; Thomas, *Abraham Lincoln,* 266–68; White, *A. Lincoln,* 444–45; Zander, *Army Under Fire,* 74–76.

41. Basler et al., *Collected Works of Abraham Lincoln,* 4:421–41 (quotations, 426, 440, 429). See also Burlingame, *Abraham Lincoln,* 2:169–74; Donald, *Lincoln,* 305; Gienapp, *Abraham*

Lincoln, 83; Guelzo, *Our Ancient Faith,* 95–96; and Marszalek, *Lincoln and the Military,* 3, 17. On the "Lincoln as dictator" argument, see Paludan, "'Dictator Lincoln.'"

42. Koistinen, *Beating Ploughshares into Swords,* 188.

43. Burlingame and Ettlinger, *Inside Lincoln's White House,* 11.

44. "General M. C. Meigs on the Conduct of the Civil War," 289–90; Nicolay and Hay, *Abraham Lincoln,* 4:298–303; Sears, *Civil War Papers of George B. McClellan,* 12–13; Burlingame, *Abraham Lincoln,* 2:176; Donald, *Lincoln,* 306–7; Harsh, "McClellan-Go-Round," 117–18; Hearn, *Lincoln and McClellan,* 25–26; Rable, *Conflict of Command,* 4, 12, 36–37; Rafuse, *McClellan's War,* 2–7, 96–98; Rowland, *George B. McClellan,* 53–54, 81–85; Stoker, *Grand Design,* 36–37; Williams, *Lincoln and His Generals,* 19–22; Williams, *Lincoln Finds a General,* 1:75. In regards to McClellan's boastful letters to his wife and their effect of later scholarship, one can cite almost any letter to Mary Ellen Marcy McClellan in Sears, *Civil War Papers of George B. McClellan.* But see also Grimsley, "Lincoln-McClellan Relationship," 76–77; Harsh, "McClellan-Go-Round," 108–9, 112; and Rowland, *George B. McClellan,* 22–33, 57–58.

45. Pease and Randall, *Diary of Orville Hickman Browning,* 481; "General M. C. Meigs on the Conduct of the Civil War," 289–90; Nicolay and Hay, *Abraham Lincoln,* 4:303, 321–23; Burlingame, *Abraham Lincoln,* 2:176–81; Donald, *Lincoln,* 306–7; Gienapp, *Abraham Lincoln,* 86–87; Goodwin, *Team of Rivals,* 371–73; Marszalek, *Lincoln and the Military,* 15–16; McPherson, *Tried by War,* 34–39; Oates, *With Malice Toward None,* 270, 271, 275; Pryor, *Six Encounters,* 65–66; Rafuse, *McClellan's War,* 102–3; Rowland, *George B. McClellan,* 137–39; Simpson, *Lincoln and the Gettysburg Campaign,* 44; Stoker, *Grand Design,* 39–40; Thomas, *Abraham Lincoln,* 270; Weigley, *Great Civil War,* 58–60; White, *A. Lincoln,* 430–31; Williams, "Abraham Lincoln"; Williams, *Lincoln Finds a General,* 1:75.

46. Williams, *Lincoln and His Generals,* 20. See also Gienapp, *Abraham Lincoln,* 87.

47. Nicolay and Hay, *Abraham Lincoln,* 4:352–56, 358–59; Bates, *Lincoln in the Telegraph Office,* 91–92; Burlingame, *With Lincoln in the White House,* 51–52; Burlingame, *Abraham Lincoln,* 2:181–85; Davis, "Creating a Military Image," 21; Donald, *Lincoln,* 307–8, 313–14; Gienapp, *Abraham Lincoln,* 86–87; Goodwin, *Team of Rivals,* 371–73; Hearn, *Lincoln and McClellan,* 32; Marszalek, *Lincoln and the Military,* 21–22; McPherson, *Battle Cry of Freedom,* 339–48; Oates, *With Malice Toward None,* 275–77; Thomas, *Abraham Lincoln,* 270–74; White, *A. Lincoln,* 437–38; Williams, *Lincoln and His Generals,* 20–22; Williams, *Lincoln Finds a General,* 1:84, 90, 99. For the battle itself, see Davis, *Battle at Bull Run;* Hennessy, *First Battle of Manassas;* and Rafuse, *Single Grand Victory.*

48. Nicolay and Hay, *Abraham Lincoln,* 4:354.

49. Basler et al., *Collected Works of Abraham Lincoln,* 4:457–58, 460, 463, 468–69 (quotation, 458). See also Nicolay and Hay, *Abraham Lincoln,* 4:358–59, 367, 368–69; Pease and Randall, *Diary of Orville Hickman Browning,* 488; Burlingame, *Abraham Lincoln,* 2:187–88; Burton, *Age of Lincoln,* 146–49; Goodwin, *Team of Rivals,* 373–74; McPherson, *Tried by War,* 41–43; Oates, *With Malice Toward None,* 277–80; Rable, *Conflict of Command,* 45; Stoker, *Grand Design,* 42–43; White, *A. Lincoln,* 433–45; and Williams, *Lincoln and His Generals,* 32–33. "Here was Lincoln the maturing strategist," historian Donald Stoker wrote of the period immediately after First Bull Run. "He was beginning to see the broad sweep of war, not just defaulting to a single campaign against Richmond or down the Mississippi. He established strategic goals . . . as well as operational objectives, and envisioned campaigns in the East and West." The president

"was [not only] establishing separate spheres of responsibility for civilian and military leaders" but also "blurring them as he began partially assuming the de facto mantle of general in chief." Stoker, *Grand Design*, 43. William Marvel, meanwhile, blames Lincoln for the Bull Run defeat because he helped start the war and then drove Virginia out of the Union but says little about Lincoln's role in instigating and planning the campaign. Marvel, *Mr. Lincoln Goes to War*, 153.

50. Greene, "Lincoln as Commander-in-Chief," 106.

51. Nicolay and Hay, *Abraham Lincoln*, 4:338–40 (quotation, 340); Sears, *Civil War Papers of George B. McClellan*, 67, 70; Glatthaar, *Partners in Command*, 58–61; Harsh, "McClellan-Go-Round," 104; Hearn, *Lincoln and McClellan*, 37–40; Rable, *Conflict of Command*, 26–27, 51; Rafuse, *McClellan's War*, 118–24; Rowland, *George B. McClellan*, 140–42; Zeitz, *Lincoln's Boys*, 279, 296–98.

52. Stoker, *Grand Design*, 52–53.

53. U.S. War Department, *War of the Rebellion*, ser. 1, 5:6–8 (hereafter cited as *OR*, all citations to ser. 1); Sears, *Civil War Papers of George B. McClellan*, 28–30, 71–75; Hearn, *Lincoln and McClellan*, 40–42; Pryor, *Six Encounters*, 53–55; Rable, *Conflict of Command*, 56–7; Rafuse, *McClellan's War*, 120–23; Reardon, *With a Sword in One Hand*, 25–27; Rowland, *George B. McClellan*, 86–88; Stoker, *Grand Design*, 55–59; Waugh, *Lincoln and McClellan*, 43; Williams, *Lincoln and His Generals*, 29–33.

54. Stoker, *Grand Design*, 63.

55. Reardon, *With a Sword in One Hand*, 27–28, 29–32.

56. Nicolay and Hay, *Abraham Lincoln*, 8:158–60; Maurice, *Statesmen and Soldiers*, 236; Liddell Hart, *Sherman*, 102; McDonough, "Commander in Chief and Military Operations in Tennessee," 94–95; Pryor, "Conflict, Chaos, and Confidence," 53; Williams, *Lincoln and His Generals*, 48.

57. Russell, *My Diary North and South*, 317–18 (quotations, 317). A "navvy" was an unskilled laborer on an engineering project, such as a canal or railroad. The condescending Russell essentially was describing Lincoln as someone of the lower classes. Note that William Gienapp dates this event to the period immediately after First Bull Run. Gienapp, *Abraham Lincoln*, 87.

58. Basler et al., *Collected Works of Abraham Lincoln*, 4:497, 544–45; Nicolay and Hay, *Abraham Lincoln*, 5:60–64 (quotations, 61, 63). See also Gienapp, *Abraham Lincoln*, 85; Marszalek, *Lincoln and the Military*, 24; Niven, *Gideon Welles*, 355–56; Stoker, *Grand Design*, 62, 68, 95; Symonds, *Lincoln and His Admirals*, 61–69; Williams, *Lincoln and His Generals*, 48. The Port Royal operation eventually succeeded under Du Pont's command in early November.

59. Nicolay and Hay, *Abraham Lincoln*, 8:158–60; Sherman, *Memoirs*, 1:102, 190, 192–93, 199; Hess, *Civil War Supply and Strategy*, 25–26; McDonough, "Commander in Chief and Military Operations in Tennessee," 95–96; McPherson, *Tried by War*, 61–62; Noe, *Howling Storm*, 98–99; Rable, *Conflict of Command*, 134; Williams, *Lincoln and His Generals*, 48–49.

60. Burlingame and Ettlinger, *Inside Lincoln's White House*, 29.

61. Nicolay and Hay, *Abraham Lincoln*, 5:65–67; Hess, *Civil War Supply*, 26–27; McDonough, "Commander in Chief and Military Operations in Tennessee," 96.

62. Beale, *Diary of Edward Bates*, 194, 196–97, 199–200; Burlingame and Ettlinger, *Inside Lincoln's White House*, 30, 35; Nicolay and Hay, *Abraham Lincoln*, 4:465-66; Sears, *Civil War Papers of George B. McClellan*, 81–84, 85–86, 89, 103–4, 106–7, 109, 114–19, 122–24, 127, 128; Grimsley, "Overthrown," 20–29; Glatthaar, *Partners in Command*, 52, 55–62; Goodwin, *Team of Rivals*, 383–88; McPherson, *Tried by War*, 51–53; Oates, *With Malice Toward None*, 286–88;

Rable, *Conflict of Command,* 63, 66; Rafuse, *McClellan's War,* 142–47; Weigley, *Great Civil War,* 82–83; Williams, *Lincoln and His Generals,* 43–45. Scott became increasing exasperated with McClellan's "disrespect." Welles, *Diary of Gideon Welles,* 1:240–43. William Gienapp suggests that Lincoln's willingness to defend McClellan went to Little Mac's head and ultimately worsened the situation. Gienapp, *Abraham Lincoln,* 97.

63. Sears, *Civil War Papers of George B. McClellan,* 127 (quotation), 128.

64. Rable, *Conflict of Command,* 40, 61.

65. Rowland, *George B. McClellan,* 47–48. See also Stoddard, *Inside the White House,* 112–19; Marvel, *Mr. Lincoln Goes to War,* 263–64; Rable, *Conflict of Command,* 15, 67–68, 70–72, 77–78, 82–83, 88–90; and Rafuse, *McClellan's War,* 157–58. Rowland offers a strong critique of the often-told story.

66. Nicolay and Hay, *Abraham Lincoln,* 4:466–70, 5:99–100, 149–52; Burlingame, *Abraham Lincoln,* 2:191–200, 213–19; Donald, *Lincoln,* 318–19, 326–28; Glatthaar, *Partners in Command,* 65–66; Goodwin, *Team of Rivals,* 378–83; Harsh, "McClellan-Go-Round," 115; Hearn, *Lincoln and McClellan,* 36–64; McPherson, *Tried by War,* 53–54, 137; Rable, *Conflict of Command,* 12, 86, 90–92; Rafuse, *From the Mountains to the Bay,* 5, 31; Stoker, *Grand Design,* 55–64, 71–72; Waugh, *Lincoln and McClellan,* 43, 48–50, 53–60; Weigley, *Great Civil War,* 82–83; White, *A. Lincoln,* 483; Williams, *Lincoln and His Generals,* 29–53. The Virginia focus may have been a mistake. Brooks Simpson opined, "That one of the principles of military operations is to force the enemy to fight on terms of one's own choosing seemed to elude both him [McClellan] and the president." Simpson, *Lincoln and the Gettysburg Campaign,* 8.

67. Beale, *Diary of Edward Bates,* 219; Rable, *Conflict of Command,* 100 (quotation); Taaffe, *Commanding the Army of the Potomac,* 9.

68. OR, Series I, vol. 7, 530–35, 537–38, 545–46; Nicolay and Hay, *Abraham Lincoln,* 5:69–74, 91–92, 98–100, 103–4, 155; Niven, *Salmon P. Chase Papers,* 321–22; Sears, *Civil War Papers of George B. McClellan,* 147–50; Burlingame, *Abraham Lincoln,* 2:290; Donald, *Lincoln,* 326–29; Gienapp, *Abraham Lincoln,* 98; Goodwin, *Team of Rivals,* 380–82; Hearn, *Lincoln and McClellan,* 64; Holzer, *Lincoln as I Knew Him,* 91–92; Marvel, *Burnside,* 40–61; Marvel, *Mr. Lincoln Goes to War,* 261–65, 267, 268; McPherson, *Tried by War,* 63, 65–67; Niven, *Gideon Welles,* 370–73; Oates, *With Malice Toward None,* 307–8; Paludan, *"A People's Contest,"* 64–67; Rable, *Conflict of Command,* 93–94, 98–100; Rafuse, *McClellan's War,* 166–72; Stoker, *Grand Design,* 72–74, 77; Thomas, *Abraham Lincoln,* 287–89, 291–92; Weigley, *Great Civil War,* 96–99; Williams, *Lincoln and His Generals,* 53–55.

69. *OR,* 7:535.

70. Nicolay and Hay, *Abraham Lincoln,* 5:155–56; Reardon, *With a Sword in One Hand,* 28.

71. Nicolay and Hay, *Abraham Lincoln,* 5:155–56.

72. Stoddard, *Abraham Lincoln,* 245. See also Holzer, *Lincoln's White House Secretary,* 1, 4–9.

73. Stoddard, *Inside the White House,* 151–52 (quotation, 151).

74. Brooks, *Abraham Lincoln and the Downfall of American Slavery,* 326–27.

75. Gienapp, *Abraham Lincoln,* 87; Henderson, *Stonewall Jackson,* 1:407; McPherson, *Tried by War,* 137, 142; Rable, *Conflict of Command,* 96; Reynolds, *Abe,* 708; White, *A. Lincoln,* 442. David S. Reynolds also sees Clausewitz's and Cromwell's influence as filtered through Lieber. Reynolds, *Abe,* 571. For Jomini and his debatable influence on the entire generation, see Reardon, *With a Sword in One Hand.*

76. The authority is Bray, *Reading with Lincoln,* esp. ix–x, 4, 10–13, 16–20, 28–29, 35, 41–42, 46–49, 69–80, 82–84, 87–118, 140–50, 168–70, 189–90, 194, 200–15. See also Bates, *Lincoln in the Telegraph Office,* 184–90; Carpenter, *Inner Life of Abraham Lincoln,* 153–54; Holzer, *Lincoln as I Knew Him,* 14–23, 57–58, 67–68, 72–75, 96–101; Stoddard, *Abraham Lincoln,* 282; Boritt, *Lincoln the War President,* 189; Burlingame, *Abraham Lincoln,* 1:36, 62–64, 79, 87–90, 185–86, 333–34, 2:188–89; Davis, "Creating a Military Image," 19–20; Donald, *Lincoln,* 30–31, 47–49, 51, 53–55, 99, 102; Gienapp, *Abraham Lincoln,* 6–7, 19, 28, 41, 42, 44, 90–91; Guelzo, *Our Ancient Faith,* 64–73; Meacham, *And There Was Light,* 28–31, 39–41, 125–27; Oates, *With Malice Toward None,* 12, 22, 30–32, 269–70; Pryor, *Six Encounters,* 84–85, 91–100, 329–33; Reynolds, *Abe,* 51–52, 219, 242–44, 847; Thomas, *Abraham Lincoln,* 54–55, 135, 476; and White, *A. Lincoln,* 32–34, 53–55, 65–67, 168–71, 490.

77. Carpenter, *Six Months at the White House,* 114–15 (quotation, 115). Carpenter reissued this book in 1868 as *Inner Life.* See also Gabbard, "Lincoln Through the Eyes of History"; and Holzer, *Lincoln President-Elect,* 256.

78. Herndon, "Analysis of the Character of Abraham Lincoln," 431. Herndon originally delivered this lecture in Springfield on December 26, 1865. Ibid., 403. See also Donald, *Lincoln's Herndon,* 202–4; Gienapp, *Abraham Lincoln,* 42; and John H. Littlefield as excerpted in Holzer, *Lincoln as I Knew Him,* 72–75.

79. Donald, *Lincoln's Herndon,* 36–38.

80. Reardon, *With a Sword in One Hand,* 28 (quotation); Bray, "What Abraham Lincoln Read," 28–81; Stoddard, *Inside the White House,* 152.

81. Halleck, *Elements of Military Art and Science,* 3, 5 (quotations); Marszalek, *Commander of All Lincoln's Armies,* 36–47, 98, 114, 125, 167.

82. Marszalek, *Commander of All Lincoln's Armies,* 44, 46.

83. Bray, "What Abraham Lincoln Read"; Busk, *Rifle;* Callan, *Military Laws of the United States.* I am grateful to Terry Beckenbaugh, Barbara Gannon, and Tim Talbott for identifying Busk as the author.

84. Reardon, *With a Sword in One Hand,* 32–40 (quotation, 38).

85. Bray, "What Abraham Lincoln Read"; Donald, *Lincoln,* 355; Maurice, *Statesmen and Soldiers,* 152; Oates, *With Malice Toward None,* 340; White, *A. Lincoln,* 500; Williams, *Lincoln and His Generals,* 257. Elizabeth Brown Pryor maintained that, despite his eloquence in major speeches and writings, Lincoln's everyday communications skills could be lacking. Pryor, *Six Encounters,* 4–5.

86. *OR,* 7:524–33 (quotations, 533). See also Nicolay and Hay, *Abraham Lincoln,* 5:107; Burlingame, *Abraham Lincoln,* 2:188–89; and Rable, *Conflict of Command,* 99.

87. Here I rely on Bruce, *Lincoln and the Tools of War,* 156–65; and Symonds, *Lincoln and His Admirals,* 106–25. But see also Bates, *Lincoln in the Telegraph Office,* 4–5, 415–16; Porter, *Incidents and Anecdotes,* 63–66; Stoddard, *Inside the White House,* 39–44; Boritt, *Lincoln and the Economics of the American Dream,* 269; Burlingame, *Abraham Lincoln,* 2:291–92; Donald, *Lincoln,* 330–31; and Niven, *Gideon Welles,* 381–82. On Lincoln and technology, see Donald, *Lincoln,* 431–32; Marszalek, *Lincoln and the Military,* x–xiii; Neely, *Last Best Hope,* 142–44; and Perret, *Lincoln's War,* 144–49, 156–86.

88. "General M. C. Meigs on the Conduct of the Civil War," 292. See also Burlingame, *Abraham Lincoln,* 2:112, 163, 178–81, 207; Donald, *Lincoln,* 291, 329–30; Gienapp, *Abraham Lin-*

coln, 98; Goodwin, *Team of Rivals,* 426; Hearn, *Lincoln and McClellan,* 66; Oates, *With Malice Toward None,* 307–8; Pryor, "Conflict, Chaos, and Confidence," 32; Pryor, *Six Encounters,* 56–57; Rafuse, *McClellan's War,* 170–72; Reynolds, *Abe,* 675; Symonds, *Lincoln and His Admirals,* 15–16, 20–21, 102–3; Waugh, *Lincoln and McClellan,* 61; Williams, *Lincoln and His Generals,* 53–55.

89. Beale, *Diary of Edward Bates,* 218–19, 220, 223–26 (quotation, 220). See also McPherson, *Tried by War,* 65; Oates, *With Malice Toward None,* 307, 320; Rable, *Conflict of Command,* 99; White, *A. Lincoln,* 463.

90. Pease and Randall, *Diary of Orville Hickman Browning,* 523. See also McPherson, *Tried by War,* 70–71, 213, 268–69; Rable, *Conflict of Command,* 105–6; Rowland, *George B. McClellan,* 85; Symonds, *Lincoln and His Admirals,* 102–3; and White, *A. Lincoln,* 471. I am grateful to Kevin Brock for explaining what Browning meant by "Pensacola."

91. *OR,* 5:9–11; Basler et al., *Collected Works of Abraham Lincoln,* 4:457–58, 544–45; Glatthaar, *Partners in Command,* 53–55, 59–62; Goodwin, *Team of Rivals,* 371–73; Marszalek, *Lincoln and the Military,* 19–21, 24; Oates, *With Malice Toward None,* 277–78; Stoker, *Grand Design,* 36–43, 55–59; Williams, *Lincoln and His Generals,* 19–23, 27–33, 48; Williams, "Abraham Lincoln."

92. "Memorandum of General McDowell," in Raymond, *Life and Public Services of Abraham Lincoln,* 772–74; Hettle, *Inventing Stonewall Jackson,* 56–57; Oates, *With Malice Toward None,* 307–8; Paludan, *"A People's Contest,"* 61–63; Rafuse, *From the Mountains to the Bay,* 27; Reardon, *With a Sword in One Hand,* 55–88; Thomas, *Abraham Lincoln,* 291–92; Williams, *Lincoln Finds a General,* 1:136–37; Work, *Lincoln's Political Generals,* 2–3; Zander, *Army Under Fire,* 74-83. Brooks Simpson observed, "Lincoln's behavior promised to open up a conduit for dissatisfied subordinates to air their grievances, circumventing the chain of command; in turn, army commanders began to chafe at the thought that politicians might wreak havoc with their careful plans." Simpson, *Lincoln and the Gettysburg Campaign,* 9.

93. "Memorandum of General McDowell," 773.

94. Nicolay and Hay, *Abraham Lincoln,* 5:156–69 (quotation, 158); Niven, *Salmon P. Chase Papers,* 324–26; Burlingame, *Abraham Lincoln,* 2:237–45; Hearn, *Lincoln and McClellan,* 73–74; Neely, *Last Best Hope,* 77; Rable, *Conflict of Command,* 101–2; and Stoker, *Grand Design,* 79–80. William Gienapp suspected that Lincoln only appointed Cameron because he did not expect a war. See Gienapp, *Abraham Lincoln,* 76.

95. Basler et al., *Collected Works of Abraham Lincoln,* 5:98–99. See also Nicolay and Hay, *Abraham Lincoln,* 5:155–56; Hearn, *Lincoln and McClellan,* 73–74; Neely, *Last Best Hope,* 77; and Stoker, *Grand Design,* 79–80.

96. Nicolay and Hay, *Abraham Lincoln,* 5:157–58; "General M. C. Meigs on the Conduct of the War," 292–93; Burlingame, *Abraham Lincoln,* 2:163, 174, 220–21; Donald, *Lincoln,* 330; Foner, *Fiery Trial,* 187–88; Glatthaar, *Partners in Command,* 65–68; Goodwin, *Team of Rivals,* 366; Hearn, *Lincoln and McClellan,* 66–68; Marszalek, *Lincoln and the Military,* 26–27; Marvel, *Lincoln's Autocrat,* 151–52, 153–55; McPherson, *Tried by War,* 65–67; Oates, *With Malice Toward None,* 309–10; Rable, *Conflict of Command,* 103–4, 117; Rafuse, *McClellan's War,* 162, 170–71; Reynolds, *Abe,* 651, 676; Stoker, *Grand Design,* 54, 77–78; Symonds, *Lincoln and His Admirals,* 59, 102, 104; Waugh, *Lincoln and McClellan,* 61–65; Weigley, *Great Civil War,* 65; Williams, *Lincoln Finds a General,* 1:136–37; White, *A. Lincoln,* 461; Williams, *Lincoln and His Generals,* 55–58.

97. Basler et al., *Collected Works of Abraham Lincoln,* 6:327–29. John Hoffmann made a strong case for the veracity of the younger Lincoln's recollections. See Hoffmann, "Robert Todd Lincoln's 'Gettysburg Story,'" 1-13. See also Burlingame, *Abraham Lincoln,* 2:295; Rable, *Conflict of Command,* 100.

2. THE ARC AND THE CHORD

1. Basler et al., *Collected Works of Abraham Lincoln,* 5:111–12 (quotation, 111). See also Bates, *Lincoln in the Telegraph Office,* 7–10, 113, 389–99; Burlingame, *With Lincoln in the White House,* 68; Burlingame and Ettlinger, *Inside Lincoln's White House,* 35; Burlingame, *Abraham Lincoln,* 2:237–45; Gienapp, *Abraham Lincoln,* 128; Goodwin, *Team of Rivals,* 410–41; Koistinen, *Beating Ploughshares into Swords,* 136–38, 168–69; Marvel, *Lincoln's Autocrat,* xi–xvi, 148–60; Pryor, "Conflict, Chaos, and Confidence," 17–19; Rafuse, *McClellan's War,* 177–78; Rable, *Conflict of Command,* 107, 113–14; Rowland, *George B. McClellan,* 50–53; Thomas, *Abraham Lincoln,* 295–97; and Williams, *Lincoln and His Generals,* 62.

2. Williams, *Lincoln and His Generals,* 62. For scholars in more or less agreement with this, see Burlingame, *Abraham Lincoln,* 2:294; Donald, *Lincoln,* 334–35; Glatthaar, *Partners in Command,* 69; Hearn, *Lincoln and McClellan,* 74–75; Marszalek, *Lincoln and the Military,* 26; Neely, *Last Best Hope,* 65–66; Oates, *With Malice Toward None,* 310; Pryor, "Conflict, Chaos, and Confidence," 48; Rable, *Conflict of Command,* 104; and White, *A. Lincoln,* 471.

3. Hearn, *Lincoln and McClellan,* 74–75.

4. Basler et al., *Collected Works of Abraham Lincoln,* 5:115; Nicolay and Hay, *Abraham Lincoln,* 5:159–60; Burlingame, *Abraham Lincoln,* 2:294–95; Neely, *Last Best Hope,* 65–66; Oates, *With Malice Toward None,* 310–11. James McPherson states that Lincoln really did want concerted campaigns at least, while Craig Symonds defends General Order No. 1 as a good idea that would have given the Confederates a hard time. McPherson, *Tried by War,* 68–69; Symonds, *Lincoln and His Admirals,* 105. I agree with George Rable's assessment that Lincoln "showed a limited understanding of military affairs, plotting strategy on a map without paying much attention to geographical barriers . . . or logistical considerations." Rable, *Conflict of Command,* 134.

5. Sears, *Civil War Papers of George B. McClellan,* 162–71; Marvel, *Lincoln's Autocrat,* 169–70; Noe, *Howling Storm,* 75–77; Rable, *Conflict of Command,* 114, 122; Rafuse, *McClellan's War,* 178–82; Weigley, *Great Civil War,* 93.

6. Basler et al., *Collected Works of Abraham Lincoln,* 5:119–20. See also Nicolay and Hay, *Abraham Lincoln,* 5:160–61 (they silently corrected Lincoln's misspelling of "enemy's"). Mark Neely observed: "Nothing in Lincoln's foolish and unrealistic orders, which ignored the intentions of the enemy, the weather, and myriad factors any conscientious general would have to consider before advancing, was calculated to increase McClellan's confidence in the commander in chief." Neely, *Last Best Hope,* 66.

7. Nicolay and Hay, *Abraham Lincoln,* 5:161–63. See also Williams, *Lincoln and His Generals,* 62–65.

8. Nicolay and Hay, *Abraham Lincoln,* 5:168–69; Burlingame, *With Lincoln in the White House,* 69; Burlingame, *Abraham Lincoln,* 2:291, 297; Donald, *Lincoln,* 335, 338; LaFantasie, "Lincoln and the American Military Tradition," 24–26; McPherson, *Tried by War,* 72; Oates, *With Malice Toward None,* 310–11; Rable, *Conflict of Command,* 119–20; Rafuse, *McClellan's*

War, 186–88; Stoker, *Grand Design,* 112–15; White, *A. Lincoln,* 480–82. Elizabeth Brown Pryor blamed Willie's death for his father's "series of poor military decisions." Pryor, *Six Encounters,* 242–43. Ethan Rafuse, meanwhile, doubted that Urbanna and its limited capacity could have supported the army. Rafuse, *From the Mountains to the Bay,* 52.

9. Nicolay and Hay, *Abraham Lincoln,* 5:167–68; Sears, *Civil War Papers of George B. McClellan,* 193–95; Burlingame, *Abraham Lincoln,* 2:295–96; Donald, *Lincoln,* 339; Glatthaar, *Partners in Command,* 70; Noe, *Howling Storm,* 125–26; Oates, *With Malice Toward None,* 319; Rable, *Conflict of Command,* 119–21; Rafuse, *McClellan's War,* 189–90; Williams, *Lincoln Finds a General,* 1:141.

10. Rowland, *George B. McClellan,* 65.

11. Burlingame, *With Lincoln in the White House,* 72–73. See also Marvel, *Lincoln's Darkest Year,* 18; and McPherson, *Tried by War,* 75.

12. Nicolay and Hay, *Abraham Lincoln,* 5:169; Marvel, *Lincoln's Autocrat,* 172–73, 175–76; Marvel, *Lincoln's Darkest Year,* 25; McPherson, *Tried by War,* 75–77; Rable, *Conflict of Command,* 133; Rafuse, *From the Mountains to the Bay,* 75.

13. Nicolay and Hay, *Abraham Lincoln,* 5:221–22 (quotation, 221).

14. Beale, *Diary of Edward Bates,* 239–40; Burlingame and Ettlinger, *Inside Lincoln's White House,* 35; Nicolay and Hay, *Abraham Lincoln,* 5:167, 221–22, 226–28, 231; Sears, *Civil War Papers of George B. McClellan,* 199; Stoddard, *Inside the White House,* 124–27; Welles, *Diary of Gideon Welles,* 1:54–68; Burlingame, *Abraham Lincoln,* 2:306–7; Marvel, *Lincoln's Autocrat,* 171–72; Marvel, *Lincoln's Darkest Year,* 21; Niven, *Gideon Welles,* 404–8; Rable, *Conflict of Command,* 128–29; Symonds, *Lincoln and His Admirals,* 131–32, 134, 138. Much has been written about the Battle of Hampton Roads, but a good place to start is Davis, *Duel Between the First Ironclads.*

15. Nicolay and Hay, *Abraham Lincoln,* 5:167, 171–73; Pease and Randall, *Diary of Orville Hickman Browning,* 532–33; Burlingame, *Abraham Lincoln,* 2:302–4; Donald, *Lincoln,* 341, 348; Glatthaar, *Partners in Command,* 71; Goodwin, *Team of Rivals,* 427–30; Grimsley, "Lincoln-McClellan Relationship," 71; Hearn, *Lincoln and McClellan,* 81–97; Marvel, *Lincoln's Autocrat,* 169–70; Marvel, *Lincoln's Darkest Year,* 24; McPherson, *Tried by War,* 77–80; Neely, *Last Best Hope,* 66; Oates, *With Malice Toward None,* 319–21; Rable, *Conflict of Command,* 122–25; Rafuse, *McClellan's War,* 190–93; Simpson, *Lincoln and the Gettysburg Campaign,* 11–12; Thomas, *Abraham Lincoln,* 309–10; Waugh, *Lincoln and McClellan,* 73–77; Williams, *Lincoln and His Generals,* 46, 70–72; Williams, *Lincoln Finds a General,* 1:153–59.

16. Williams, *Lincoln and His Generals,* 67. Note that Williams's source for the quotation—Flower, *Edwin McMasters Stanton,* 139—provides no citation for his quotation.

17. Burlingame and Ettlinger, *Inside Lincoln's White House,* 35 (quotation); Sears, *Civil War Papers of George B. McClellan,* 200. Mark Grimsley found it "astounding" that Lincoln would not let an army commander "choose his own senior subordinates." "Lincoln-McClellan Relationship," 71–72. Ethan Rafuse observed that Lincoln's decision and appointments were much like what President Polk had done in the Mexican-American War, while George Rable has noted how much both McClellan and Scott had abhorred Polk's interference. Rafuse, *From the Mountains to the Bay,* 54; Rable, *Conflict of Command,* 16. See also ibid., 125; and Taaffe, *Commanding the Army of the Potomac,* 10–13.

18. Basler et al., *Collected Works of Abraham Lincoln,* 5:149–51, 155. See also Bates, *Lincoln in the Telegraph Office,* 115–17; Nicolay and Hay, *Abraham Lincoln,* 5:169–72, 173, 178–81; Sears,

Civil War Papers of George B. McClellan, 207; Burlingame, *Abraham Lincoln,* 2:302–4; Donald, *Lincoln,* 341, 348; Glatthaar, *Partners in Command,* 71; Goodwin, *Team of Rivals,* 427–30; Hearn, *Lincoln and McClellan,* 81–97; Marvel, *Lincoln's Autocrat,* 173–74; McPherson, *Tried by War,* 77–80; Neely, *Last Best Hope,* 66; Oates, *With Malice Toward None,* 319–21; Pryor, "Conflict, Chaos, and Confidence," 48; Rable, *Conflict of Command,* 130–31; Rafuse, *McClellan's War,* 195–96; Reardon, *With a Sword in One Hand,* 29; Rowland, *George B. McClellan,* 49; Simpson, *Lincoln and the Gettysburg Campaign,* 11–12; Stoker, *Grand Design,* 144; Thomas, *Abraham Lincoln,* 309–10; Waugh, *Lincoln and McClellan,* 73–77; Williams, *Lincoln and His Generals,* 46, 70–72; and Williams, *Lincoln Finds a General,* 1:153–59. McClellan had wanted to wait and appoint the corps commanders himself after judging his division commander's performance in the field. But he made no objection to his removal as general in chief. "*The President is all right,*" he wrote an ally, "he is my strongest friend." Sears, *Civil War Papers of George B. McClellan,* 213.

19. Sears, *Civil War Papers of George B. McClellan,* 215–16; Hearn, *Lincoln and McClellan,* 97; Rafuse, *McClellan's War,* 198–200; Rowland, *George B. McClellan,* 106–7; Stoker, *Grand Design,* 144; Waugh, *Lincoln and McClellan,* 80–82.

20. Nicolay and Hay, *Abraham Lincoln,* 5:170, 180–81 (quotation, 181); Basler et al., *Collected Works of Abraham Lincoln,* 5:159; Williams, *Lincoln and His Generals,* 73.

21. Williams, *Lincoln and His Generals,* 73–74. See also Hearn, *Lincoln and McClellan,* 99–103; Rable, *Conflict of Command,* 134; and Williams, *Lincoln Finds a General,* 1:159–60. Mark Grimsley criticized T. Harry Williams's habit of writing these sorts of things but then asserting that McClellan should have paid attention to the president anyway. "This is just plain crazy," he has chided. Grimsley, "Lincoln-McClellan Relationship," 71.

22. Rowland, *George B. McClellan,* 128.

23. Basler et al., *Collected Works of Abraham Lincoln,* 5:175–76, 179, 184; Nicolay and Hay, *Abraham Lincoln,* 5:182–84; Sears, *Civil War Papers of George B. McClellan,* 222–23; Donald, *Lincoln,* 349–50; Goodwin, *Team of Rivals,* 431; Grimsley, "Lincoln as Commander-in-Chief," 65; Hearn, *Lincoln and McClellan,* 105–10; Marvel, *Lincoln's Darkest Year,* 25; Oates, *With Malice Toward None,* 321–22; Rafuse, *From the Mountains to the Bay,* 72, 99, 112–13; Rable, *Conflict of Command,* 137–38; Rafuse, *McClellan's War,* 204–7; Rowland, *George B. McClellan,* 52, 104–5, 108–12; Stoker, *Grand Design,* 143; Thomas, *Abraham Lincoln,* 316; Williams, *Lincoln and His Generals,* 73–82; Williams, *Lincoln Finds a General,* 1:144–45, 159–60. James McPherson has maintained: "McClellan may have been correct in asserting that his offensive on the Peninsula would force Johnston to hasten south to defend his own capital instead of attacking Washington. But Lincoln was right in saying that he could not risk it." McPherson, *Tried by War,* 81. Meanwhile, Mark Grimsley has noted: "Lincoln plainly expected the required troops to be in the immediate vicinity of Washington: what military men would call a 'point defense' posture. McClellan's dispositions instead reflect a 'defense in depth.' . . . [O]n the whole, most military historians concur that McClellan's dispositions were adequate." Grimsley, "Lincoln as Commander-in-Chief," 62.

24. Pease and Randall, *Diary of Orville Hickman Browning,* 537–39 (quotations, 539, 537). See also Marvel, *Lincoln's Autocrat,* 175–77; Rable, *Conflict of Command,* 143–44; and Rafuse, *McClellan's War,* 201.

25. Basler et al., *Collected Works of Abraham Lincoln,* 5:182; Nicolay and Hay, *Abraham Lincoln,* 5:358–61; Sears, *Civil War Papers of George B. McClellan,* 228, 232–34; Harsh, "McClellan-Go-Round," 114; Rable, *Conflict of Command,* 137–41; Rafuse, *From the Mountains to the Bay,*

115–18, 139; Rowland, *George B. McClellan,* 107–8, 129; Stoker, *Grand Design,* 146; Waugh, *Lincoln and McClellan,* 86–87; White, *A. Lincoln,* 483–84; Williams, *Lincoln and His Generals,* 82–83; Williams, *Lincoln Finds a General,* 1:163–66. The standard history of the Peninsula Campaign remains Sears, *To the Gates of Richmond,* but note its strong bias against McClellan. Also useful is Gallagher, *Richmond Campaign of 1862.*

26. Koistinen, *Beating Ploughshares into Swords,* 171; Marvel, *Lincoln's Autocrat,* 178–81; Marvel, *Lincoln's Darkest Year,* 30–35, 39–40, 46; McPherson, *Battle Cry of Freedom,* 437; Rable, *Conflict of Command,* 363n30; Sword, *Shiloh,* 432, 460.

27. Basler et al., *Collected Works of Abraham Lincoln,* 5:182. See also Rafuse, *From the Mountains to the Bay,* 138–39.

28. Sears, *Civil War Papers of George B. McClellan,* 234. See also Hearn, *Lincoln and McClellan,* 104, 112–15.

29. Pease and Randall, *Diary of Orville Hickman Browning,* 540. See also Marvel, *Lincoln's Darkest Year,* 26.

30. Nicolay and Hay, *Abraham Lincoln,* 5:362; Hearn, *Lincoln and McClellan,* 112–13; McPherson, *Tried by War,* 82; Rable, *Conflict of Command,* 146; Waugh, *Lincoln and McClellan,* 89–91 (quotation, 89). Nicolay and Hay wrote specifically that Lincoln answered McClellan "with as much consideration and kindness as a father would use toward a querulous and petulant child." On the "power to hurt," see the introduction.

31. Basler et al., *Collected Works of Abraham Lincoln,* 5:184–85.

32. Basler et al., *Collected Works of Abraham Lincoln,* 5:203. See also Nicolay and Hay, *Abraham Lincoln,* 5:366, 371, 376; Sears, *Civil War Papers of George B. McClellan,* 236–37, 239, 241–42, 246–49, 252–58; Burlingame, *Abraham Lincoln,* 2:308–11; Goodwin, *Team of Rivals,* 431–32; Hearn, *Lincoln and McClellan,* 115–25; Marvel, *Lincoln's Autocrat,* 196–97; Noe, *Howling Storm,* 130–33; Simpson, *Lincoln and the Gettysburg Campaign,* 13; Stoker, *Grand Design,* 146–48; Thomas, *Abraham Lincoln,* 318–19; Waugh, *Lincoln and McClellan,* 91–92; Williams, *Lincoln and His Generals,* 87–91; Williams, *Lincoln Finds a General,* 1:167, 169.

33. Nicolay and Hay, *Abraham Lincoln,* 5:366.

34. Nicolay and Hay, *Abraham Lincoln,* 5:234 (quotation); Beale, *Diary of Edward Bates,* 256, 257–58.

35. Basler et al., *Collected Works of Abraham Lincoln,* 5:209; Nicolay and Hay, *Abraham Lincoln,* 5:234–38; Niven, *Salmon P. Chase Papers,* 336–48; Pease and Randall, *Diary of Orville Hickman Browning,* 545; Burlingame, *Abraham Lincoln,* 2:311–14; Goodwin, *Team of Rivals,* 436–39; Hearn, *Lincoln and McClellan,* 120–22; Marszalek, *Lincoln and the Military,* 32; McPherson, *Tried by War,* 89–90; Noe, *Howling Storm,* 137; Rable, *Conflict of Command,* 153; Stoker, *Grand Design,* 148; Symonds, *Lincoln and His Admirals,* 145–57; White, *A. Lincoln,* 484–85; Williams, *Lincoln and His Generals,* 81–82. Chase wrote: "I think it quite certain that if he had not come down Norfolk would still have been in possession of the enemy, and the Merrimac [*Virginia*] grim and defiant and as much a terror as ever. The whole coast is now virtually ours." See Nicolay and Hay, *Abraham Lincoln,* 5:238; and Niven, *Salmon P. Chase Papers,* 344.

36. Basler et al., *Collected Works of Abraham Lincoln,* 5:208–9 (quotations). See also Nicolay and Hay, *Abraham Lincoln,* 5:380–81; Sears, *Civil War Papers of George B. McClellan,* 258–59, 264–65, 270–73; Holzer, *Lincoln President-Elect,* 280–82, 354–55, 391–93; and Rafuse, *McClellan's War,* 211–12.

37. Basler et al., *Collected Works of Abraham Lincoln,* 5:209; Burlingame, *Abraham Lincoln,* 2:314–15; Taaffe, *Commanding the Army of the Potomac,* 17–20.

38. Basler et al., *Collected Works of Abraham Lincoln,* 5:219–20, 226–27; Grimsley, "Lincoln as Commander-in-Chief," 69; Marvel, *Lincoln's Darkest Year,* 51, 53; Stoker, *Grand Design,* 150; Rafuse, *From the Mountains to the Bay,* 99, 182; Rafuse, *McClellan's War,* 213–14; Thomas, *Abraham Lincoln,* 325–27; Waugh, *Lincoln and McClellan,* 93–97; Williams, *Lincoln and His Generals,* 92–95; Williams, *Lincoln Finds a General,* 1:169–71.

39. Basler et al., *Collected Works of Abraham Lincoln,* 5:230–40, 243, 246–52, 254, 258, 264, 267, 269–70 (quotations, 236, 240, 246); Nicolay and Hay, *Abraham Lincoln,* 5:392–412; Sears, *Civil War Papers of George B. McClellan,* 275–76; Burlingame, *Abraham Lincoln,* 2:314–19; Donald, *Lincoln,* 355–56; Glatthaar, *Partners in Command,* 75; Goodwin, *Team of Rivals,* 442; Grimsley, "Lincoln as Commander-in-Chief," 68–69, 70–82; Grimsley, "Lincoln-McClellan Relationship," 73–74; Hearn, *Lincoln and McClellan,* 128–31; Marvel, *Lincoln's Autocrat,* 183, 195–96, 202; Marvel, *Lincoln's Darkest Year,* xii, 54–55, 57–59; McPherson, *Tried by War,* 91–95; Noe, *Howling Storm,* 144–53; Oates, *With Malice Toward None,* 327–28; Pryor, "Conflict, Chaos, and Confidence," 48–49; Rable, *Conflict of Command,* 161–62; Rafuse, *McClellan's War,* 215–17; Rowland, *George B. McClellan,* 110–12, 113–15, 129; Simpson, *Lincoln and the Gettysburg Campaign,* 13–14; Stoker, *Grand Design,* 150–51; Symonds, *Lincoln and His Admirals,* 157; Thomas, *Abraham Lincoln,* 321–24; Weigley, *Great Civil War,* 129; Williams, "Abraham Lincoln"; Williams, *Lincoln and His Generals,* 97–104; Williams, *Lincoln Finds a General,* 1:181–213. The Valley Campaign continues to receive great attention. For starters, see Cozzens, *Shenandoah 1862;* Gallagher, *Shenandoah Valley Campaign of 1862;* and Tanner's classic *Stonewall in the Valley.*

40. Burlingame, *Abraham Lincoln,* 2:319–20; Sears, *Civil War Papers of George B. McClellan,* 280, 285, 290–92, 295, 297–98, 299, 304; Glatthaar, *Partners in Command,* 75; Hearn, *Lincoln and McClellan,* 132–39; Noe, *Howling Storm,* 138–39; Rable, *Conflict of Command,* 165–66; Stoker, *Grand Design,* 151–59; Waugh, *Lincoln and McClellan,* 97–106; Weigley, *Great Civil War,* 131–32; Williams, *Lincoln and His Generals,* 105–9; Williams, *Lincoln Finds a General,* 1:182–86, 214–21.

41. Basler et al., *Collected Works of Abraham Lincoln,* 5:287; Burlingame, *With Lincoln in the White House,* 82; "General M. C. Meigs on the Conduct of the War," 298; Nicolay and Hay, *Abraham Lincoln,* 6:1–2; Burlingame, *Abraham Lincoln,* 2:320; Czarnecki, "Lincoln's Secret Visit to West Point," 6–7, 8–9, 11, 16, 25, 40–41; Donald, *Lincoln,* 361; Hearn, *Lincoln and McClellan,* 154–55; Marvel, *Lincoln's Autocrat,* 205–6; Marvel, *Lincoln's Darkest Year,* 66–69; Oates, *With Malice Toward None,* 319; Pryor, "Conflict, Chaos, and Confidence," 28; Rafuse, *McClellan's War,* 218; Rowland, *George B. McClellan,* 91–92, 117; Stoker, *Grand Design,* 159; Sutherland, "Lincoln, John Pope, and the Origins of Total War," 569, 570–71; Waugh, *Lincoln and McClellan,* 106; Williams, *Lincoln Finds a General,* 1:252–53, 329; Williams, *Lincoln and His Generals,* 113–14.

42. Pease and Randall, *Diary of Orville Hickman Browning,* 552.

43. Basler et al., *Collected Works of Abraham Lincoln,* 5:286–87. See also Sears, *Civil War Papers of George B. McClellan,* 309–10, 312–22; Rafuse, *McClellan's War,* 219.

44. Nicolay and Hay, *Abraham Lincoln,* 6:114. See also Rafuse, *McClellan's War,* 220–21; Sutherland, "Lincoln, John Pope, and the Origins of Total War," 570–71.

45. Freeman, *Lee's Dispatches,* 7. See also Grimsley, "Lincoln as Commander-in-Chief," 80–81; Grimsley, "Lincoln-McClellan Relationship," 74–75; and Rowland, *George B. McClellan,* 116–18.

46. Glatthaar, *Partners in Command,* 76–79; Grimsley, "Lincoln-McClellan Relationship," 75; Hearn, *Lincoln and McClellan,* 140–43; Marvel, *Lincoln's Darkest Year,* 70–79; Rable, *Conflict of Command,* 174–86; Rafuse, *McClellan's War,* 227–29; Waugh, *Lincoln and McClellan,* 109–11; Williams, *Lincoln Finds a General,* 1:224–43.

47. Basler et al., *Collected Works of Abraham Lincoln,* 5:290; *OR,* 11(1):60–61; Sears, *Civil War Papers of George B. McClellan,* 322–23; Marvel, *Lincoln's Autocrat,* 208–9. See also Bates, *Lincoln in the Telegraph Office,* 413–14; and Williams, *Lincoln and His Generals,* 126–27.

48. Basler et al., *Collected Works of Abraham Lincoln,* 5:289–90. See also Hearn, *Lincoln and McClellan,* 148–50; and Rable, *Conflict of Command,* 184.

49. Basler et al., *Collected Works of Abraham Lincoln,* 5:288–89, 292–97; Nicolay and Hay, *Abraham Lincoln,* 5:443, 6:5; Sears, *Civil War Papers of George B. McClellan,* 329–30, 333, 336–39; Burlingame, *Abraham Lincoln,* 2:322–26, 333; Donald, *Lincoln,* 357–59, 369; Goodwin, *Team of Rivals,* 445–49; Hearn, *Lincoln and McClellan,* 155–56; McPherson, *Tried by War,* 113; Pryor, "Conflict, Chaos, and Confidence," 32–33; Rafuse, *McClellan's War,* 240; Sutherland, "Lincoln, John Pope, and the Origins of Total War," 569; Williams, *Lincoln and His Generals,* 119–30; Williams, *Lincoln Finds a General,* 1:242–49. Lincoln wrote the governor of New York: "I should not want the half of 300,000 new troops if I could have them now. If I had 50,000 additional troops here now, I believe I could substantially close the war in two weeks. But time is everything; and if I get 50,000 new men in a month I shall have lost 20,000 old ones during the same month, having gained only 30,000, with the difference between old and new troops still against me. The quicker you send, the fewer you will have to send." Nicolay and Hay, *Abraham Lincoln,* 6:118-9. This call for new recruits was poorly received. See Burlingame, *Abraham Lincoln,* 2:326.

50. Basler et al., *Collected Works of Abraham Lincoln,* 5:298 (quotation), 301; Oates, *With Malice Toward None,* 331.

51. Basler et al., *Collected Works of Abraham Lincoln,* 5:309–12; Burlingame, *With Lincoln in the White House,* 85; Nicolay and Hay, *Abraham Lincoln,* 6:119, 202; Burlingame, *Abraham Lincoln,* 2:327–31, 365–66; Donald, *Lincoln,* 359–61; Gienapp, *Abraham Lincoln,* 105–6; Glatthaar, *Partners in Command,* 80–82; Goodwin, *Team of Rivals,* 449–51; Hearn, *Lincoln and McClellan,* 154, 157–61; McPherson, *Tried by War,* 97; Noe, *Howling Storm,* 162; Rable, *Conflict of Command,* 187–89; Rafuse, *McClellan's War,* 232–33; Rowland, *George B. McClellan,* 91–95; Simpson, *Lincoln and the Gettysburg Campaign,* 15; Sutherland, "Lincoln, John Pope, and the Origins of Total War," 572, 576–80; Waugh, *Lincoln and McClellan,* 113–15; Williams, *Lincoln and His Generals,* 130–39. Mark Grimsley discussed the shift from "soft war" in *Hard Hand of War,* esp. 1–6, 31–35, 85–92. William Marvel suggests that Stanton may have written most of the orders, citing Pope himself. Marvel, *Lincoln's Autocrat,* 218, 510n27.

52. Sears, *Civil War Papers of George B. McClellan,* 348. See also Basler et al., *Collected Works of Abraham Lincoln,* 5:309–12.

53. Sears, *Civil War Papers of George B. McClellan,* 344–45 (quotations); Nicolay and Hay, *Abraham Lincoln,* 5:446–53; Noe, *Howling Storm,* 158–59; Oakes, *Freedom National,* 211–13; Rable, *Conflict of Command,* 74–75.

54. Donald, *Lincoln,* 359–61; Grimsley, *Hard Hand of War,* 74–75; Rable, *Conflict of Command,* 190–91; Williams, *Lincoln and His Generals,* 132–34; Williams, *Lincoln Finds a General,* 1:249–51.

55. Grimsley, *Hard Hand of War,* 75.

56. Burlingame, *Abraham Lincoln,* 2:235–36, 366, 370–75, 386–93, 398–410, 414, 417–23, 434, 520–21, 530, 534–37. See also Basler et al., *Collected Works of Abraham Lincoln,* 5:2–3, 48, 126–27, 317–19, 324–25; 336–38, 341–42, 370–75, 388–89, 414, 418–19, 433–36; Nicolay and Hay, *Abraham Lincoln,* 6:41–42, 90–91, 94–98, 108–11, 120, 123–27, 153–54, 158–60, 178–79, 354, 357–60, 8:33–34; and Rowland, *George B. McClellan,* 91, 97–99, 101. On the movement toward an emancipation proclamation, see Pease and Randall, *Diary of Orville Hickman Browning,* 541, 549–50, 555, 558; Welles, *Diary of Gideon Welles,* 1:70–71, 142–45, 150–53; Brasher, *Peninsula Campaign and the Necessity of Emancipation,* 188–224; Burlingame, *Abraham Lincoln,* 2:333–64; Burton, *Age of Lincoln,* 162–67; Donald, *Lincoln,* 343–46, 363–68; Foner, *Fiery Trial,* 184–87, 195–202, 206–38; Gienapp, *Abraham Lincoln,* 109–13; Goodwin, *Team of Rivals,* 459–71, 481–83; Guelzo, *Our Ancient Faith,* 130–34; Guyatt, ""Future Empire of Our Freedmen,'" 95–105; Marvel, *Lincoln's Darkest Year,* 109–33; McPherson, *Tried by War,* 107–9, 128–33, 157–58; Meacham, *And There Was Light,* 159–65,270–76; Neely, *Last Best Hope,* 101–16, 125; Oates, *With Malice Toward None,* 337, 340; Pryor, *Six Encounters,* 124–25, 132–37; Rafuse, *McClellan's War,* 233–36; Reynolds, *Abe,* 568–72, 584–91, 651; Sutherland, "Lincoln, John Pope, and the Origins of Total War," 567–68, 573–74, 580–82; Symonds, *Lincoln and His Admirals,* 167–68, 177–81; Weigley, *Great Civil War,* 167–68, 174, 187; and White, *A. Lincoln,* 511–12. On the origins of a draft, see Neely, *Last Best Hope,* 125–28.

57. Niven, *Salmon P. Chase Papers,* 349–52; Pease and Randall, *Diary of Orville Hickman Browning,* 557–60, 563 (quotation, 559–60). See also Basler et al., *Collected Works of Abraham Lincoln,* 5:301, 305–6; Rable, *Conflict of Command,* 197–99; Rafuse, *McClellan's War,* 245; and Rowland, *George B. McClellan,* 118. On Turchin and the "Sack of Athens," see Bradley and Dahlen, *From Conciliation to Conquest,* 18–30, 109–234.

58. Nicolay and Hay, *Abraham Lincoln,* 5:454–55; Burlingame, *Abraham Lincoln,* 2:370–71; Marszalek, *Commander of All Lincoln's Armies,* 129–37; Marsalek, *Lincoln and the Military,* 34; Marvel, *Lincoln's Darkest Year,* 107; Rable, *Conflict of Command,* 200–202; Reardon, *With a Sword in One Hand,* 71–73; Sutherland, "Lincoln, John Pope, and the Origins of Total War," 574; White, *A. Lincoln,* 500. Oregon already had elected its lone congressman, a Republican, on June 2.

59. Donald, *Lincoln,* 361 (quotation), 369–70.

60. "General M. C. Meigs on the Conduct of the War," 296–97; Nicolay and Hay, *Abraham Lincoln,* 6:3; Pease and Randall, *Diary of Orville Hickman Browning,* 563; Sears, *Civil War Papers of George B. McClellan,* 380–82, 383–85; Welles, *Diary of Gideon Welles,* 1:1–92; Burlingame, *Abraham Lincoln,* 2:370–72; Donald, *Lincoln,* 369–70; Goodwin, *Team of Rivals,* 451–54; Hearn, *Lincoln and McClellan,* 161–67; Marszalek, *Commander of All Lincoln's Armies,* 135–41; Marvel, *Burnside,* 99–100; Marvel, *Lincoln's Autocrat,* 217–19; McPherson, *Tried by War,* 101, 112–13; Pryor, "Conflict, Chaos, and Confidence," 50; Rable, *Conflict of Command,* 205, 209–10; Rafuse, *McClellan's War,* 246–52; Sears, *To the Gates of Richmond,* 351; Taaffe, *Commanding the Army of the Potomac,* 26, 27–28; Waugh, *Lincoln and McClellan,* 120–30; Weigley, *Great Civil War,* 135–36; Williams, *Lincoln and His Generals,* 135–39, 142–48. William Marvel and George Rable have made similar points. Lincoln's influence on the 1862 Virginia campaigns, Marvel observed, "may have cost the country another three years of war and several hundred thousand lives." Marvel, *Lincoln's Darkest Year,* xiv (quotation), 107; Rable, *Conflict of Command,* 205. The casualty estimate is based upon figures given in Marvel, "Battles," *A Concise History of the Civil War,* National Park Service, https://npshistory.com/publications/civil_war_series/1/sec2.htm.

61. Nicolay and Hay, *Abraham Lincoln,* 6:18–20; Sears, *Civil War Papers of George B. McClellan,* 389–93, 394, 397, 404–7, 411–12, 416 (quotation), 423–24; Burlingame, *Abraham Lincoln,* 2:371–75; Glatthaar, *Partners in Command,* 83–84; Goodwin, *Team of Rivals,* 474; Hartwig, *To Antietam Creek,* 36–40; Hearn, *Lincoln and McClellan,* 168–77; Marszalek, *Commander of All Lincoln's Armies,* 141–46; Marsalek, *Lincoln and the Military,* 35–37; Marvel, *Lincoln's Darkest Year,* 140–66; McDonough, "Commander in Chief and Military Operations in Tennessee," 98; McPherson, *Tried by War,* 114–16, 118–19; Oates, *With Malice Toward None,* 340, 342; Rable, *Conflict of Command,* 212–16; Rafuse, *McClellan's War,* 250, 257–67; Rowland, *George B. McClellan,* 203–4; Stoker, *Grand Design,* 166, 169–83; Waugh, *Lincoln and McClellan,* 129–30; Weigley, *Great Civil War,* 142–43; Williams, *Lincoln and His Generals,* 148–59, 163; Williams, *Lincoln Finds a General,* 1:255–352. For Cedar Mountain, see Krick, *Stonewall Jackson at Cedar Mountain.* For Second Manassas, begin with Hennessy, *Return to Bull Run.*

62. Burlingame and Ettlinger, *Inside Lincoln's White House,* 37–38. See also Basler et al., *Collected Works of Abraham Lincoln,* 5:395, 397, 399, 400–402, 404; Bates, *Lincoln in the Telegraph Office,* 118–22; Pryor, *Six Encounters,* 129.

63. Bates, *Lincoln in the Telegraph Office,* 118–22; Gienapp and Gienapp, *Civil War Diary of Gideon Welles,* 17–29, 31–36, 38–47; Nicolay and Hay, *Abraham Lincoln,* 6:21–24 (quotation, 23); Niven, *Salmon P. Chase Papers,* 366–71; Pease and Randall, *Diary of Orville Hickman Browning,* 590–91; Sears, *Civil War Papers of George B. McClellan,* 428, 430–31; Welles, *Diary of Gideon Welles,* 1:62, 93–99, 100–109, 112–18, 122, 124, 130–32; Burlingame, *Abraham Lincoln,* 2:371–80; Donald, *Lincoln,* 371–74; Gienapp, *Abraham Lincoln,* 114; Glatthaar, *Partners in Command,* 84; Goodwin, *Team of Rivals,* 474–79; Hartwig, *To Antietam Creek,* 43–47; Hearn, *Lincoln and McClellan,* 176–84; Marszalek, *Commander of All Lincoln's Armies,* 144–51; Marsalek, *Lincoln and the Military,* 37; Marvel, *Burnside,* 111; Marvel, *Lincoln's Autocrat,* 229–33, 512n72; Marvel, *Lincoln's Darkest Year,* 167–71, 186–87; McPherson, *Tried by War,* 119–21; Neely, *Last Best Hope,* 81; Niven, *Gideon Welles,* 411–16; Noe, *Howling Storm,* 174–75; Oates, *With Malice Toward None,* 343; Rable, *Conflict of Command,* 216–19; Simpson, *Lincoln and the Gettysburg Campaign,* 16; Stoker, *Grand Design,* 166, 185; Taaffe, *Commanding the Army of the Potomac,* 20, 28, 37–39; Thomas, *Abraham Lincoln,* 335–36; Waugh, *Lincoln and McClellan,* 133–34; Williams, *Lincoln and His Generals,* 159–65; Williams, *Lincoln Finds a General,* 1:356–61.

64. Basler et al., *Collected Works of Abraham Lincoln,* 5:410, 412, 415, 418, 426; Gienapp and Gienapp, *Civil War Diary of Gideon Welles,* 64; Nicolay and Hay, *Abraham Lincoln,* 6:145–46, 179–801; Niven, *Salmon P. Chase Papers,* 393–96; Sears, *Civil War Papers of George B. McClellan,* 435–70; Welles, *Diary of Gideon Welles,* 1:156; Burlingame, *Abraham Lincoln,* 2:407–10, 417–20; Donald, *Lincoln,* 385–86; Foner, *Fiery Trial,* 231, 235; Gienapp, *Abraham Lincoln,* 114; Glatthaar, *Partners in Command,* 89; Goodwin, *Team of Rivals,* 481–83; Harsh, "McClellan-Go-Round," 114–15; Hearn, *Lincoln and McClellan,* 196; McPherson, *Tried by War,* 123–26, 132–33, 135–37; Neely, *Last Best Hope,* 69; Oates, *With Malice Toward None,* 345–46; Rable, *Conflict of Command,* 222–41; Rafuse, *McClellan's War,* 273–343; Stoker, *Grand Design,* 189–92; Thomas, *Abraham Lincoln,* 345–47; Waugh, *Lincoln and McClellan,* 139–44, 157–67; Weigley, *Great Civil War,* 177; White, *A. Lincoln,* 518; Williams, *Lincoln and His Generals,* 163–69; Williams, *Lincoln Finds a General,* 1:363–71. Much has been written on the Maryland Campaign itself, but for an introduction, see McPherson, *Crossroads of Freedom;* and Sears, *Landscape Turned Red.* For events between McClellan's appointment and the eve of battle, see Hartwig, *To Antietam*

Creek, 50–652. For the battle itself, see Hartwig, *I Dread the Thought of the Place,* 20–669; for the Emancipation Proclamation and its ramifications within the Army of the Potomac, 729–40; and for McClellan in the days following the battle, 754–60.

65. Gienapp and Gienapp, *Civil War Diary of Gideon Welles,* 22–23; Niven, *Salmon P. Chase Papers,* 411, 415, 417; Welles, *Diary of Gideon Welles,* 1:99; Sears, *Civil War Papers of George B. McClellan,* 488–90; Burlingame, *Abraham Lincoln,* 2:424–27; Donald, *Lincoln,* 387–88; Glatthaar, *Partners in Command,* 86–88; Hartwig, *I Dread the Thought of the Place,* 760–63; Hearn, *Lincoln and McClellan,* 197; Marvel, *Lincoln's Darkest Year,* 267–74; Rable, *Conflict of Command,* 242–45, 247–50; Waugh, *Lincoln and McClellan,* 167; Williams, *Lincoln and His Generals,* 173–78; Williams, *Lincoln Finds a General,* 2:465–68.

66. Nicolay and Hay, *Abraham Lincoln,* 6:175. See also Rafuse, *McClellan's War,* 344–46.

67. Burlingame, *Abraham Lincoln,* 2:427–28; Glatthaar, *Partners in Command,* 88–89; Hartwig, *I Dread the Thought of the Place,* 763–67; Hearn, *Lincoln and McClellan,* 197–200; Marszalek, *Lincoln and the Military,* 41; Neely, *Last Best Hope,* 70–71 (quotation, 71); Rable, *Conflict of Command,* 250–51; Rafuse, *McClellan's War,* 346–52; Simpson, *Lincoln and the Gettysburg Campaign,* 16–19; Stoker, *Grand Design,* 192–93; Waugh, *Lincoln and McClellan,* 167–71; Williams, *Lincoln Finds a General,* 2:468–70. On October 5 Hay published an unsigned letter in a Missouri newspaper attacking McClellan for his constant excuses, which historian James McPherson thinks Lincoln must have seen and approved. See McPherson, *Tried by War,* 139.

68. Basler et al., *Collected Works of Abraham Lincoln,* 5:460–61. See also Neely, *Last Best Hope,* 71; and Hartwig, *I Dread the Thought of the Place,* 767–70.

69. *OR,* 19(1):13–14; Basler et al., *Collected Works of Abraham Lincoln,* 5:460–62; Nicolay and Hay, *Abraham Lincoln,* 6:181–84. See also Neely, *Last Best Hope,* 71; Pryor, "Conflict, Chaos, and Confidence," 50; Rable, *Conflict of Command,* 245–46; and Rafuse, *McClellan's War,* 362–64.

70. Hartwig, *I Dread the Thought of the Place,* 768–69.

71. Neely, *Last Best Hope,* 71. See also Pryor, "Conflict, Chaos, and Confidence," 27; and Rable, *Conflict of Command,* 254–55.

72. Basler et al., *Collected Works of Abraham Lincoln,* 5:474–75 (quotation, 474); Hartwig, *I Dread the Thought of the Place,* 769–70.

73. Burlingame, *With Lincoln in the White House,* 89, 90–91; Gienapp and Gienapp, *Civil War Diary of Gideon Welles,* 84–87; Nicolay and Hay, *Abraham Lincoln,* 6:186–90, 279–81; Pease and Randall, *Diary of Orville Hickman Browning,* 590–91; Sears, *Civil War Papers of George B. McClellan,* 520–22; Welles, *Diary of Gideon Welles,* 1:179–80; Goodwin, *Team of Rivals,* 485; Hartwig, *I Dread the Thought of the Place,* 763, 770–80; Hearn, *Lincoln and McClellan,* 200–205; Marszalek, *Commander of All Lincoln's Armies,* 152–54; Marvel, *Burnside,* 159–61; Neely, *Last Best Hope,* 71–73; McPherson, *Tried by War,* 140–42; Noe, *Howling Storm,* 201–2; Oates, *With Malice Toward None,* 352–53; Rable, *Conflict of Command,* 256–63, 268; Rafuse, *McClellan's War,* 364–79; Taaffe, *Commanding the Army of the Potomac,* 54–55; Waugh, *Lincoln and McClellan,* 178–84; Williams, *Lincoln Finds a General,* 2:472–77. On the Kentucky Campaign and the Battle of Perryville, see Noe, *Perryville.*

74. Burlingame and Ettlinger, *Inside Lincoln's White House,* 232. See also Goodwin, *Team of Rivals,* 485.

75. Brooks, *Washington in Lincoln's Time,* 16.

76. Livermore, *My Story of the War,* 554–61 (quotations, 554, 555, 556, 557). Don Fehrenbacher and Virginia Fehrenbacher warn that Livermore's account contains "a good deal of literary invention" and was doubtful as a true account, yet they admitted that similar accounts existed, notably from Hay. Fehrenbacher and Fehrenbacher, *Recollected Words of Lincoln,* 210, 300–302 (quotation, 302). James McPherson describes the statement as "Clausewitzian." McPherson, *Tried by War,* 142. For Lincoln's obsession with absent men, see his October 20, 1862, memorandum on the army's numbers in Basler et al., *Collected Works of Abraham Lincoln,* 5:469–70. See also Pease and Randall, *Diary of Orville Hickman Browning,* 594; and Marvel, *Lincoln's Darkest Year,* 180. For Lincoln's "impatience" with women like Livermore who visited the White House, see Pryor, *Six Encounters,* 213–23 (quotation, 222).

77. Halleck, *Elements of Military Art and Science,* 35–60 (quotations, 37, 38, 44); Fehrenbacher and Fehrenbacher, *Recollected Words,* 210, 300–302. Lincoln did not refer to the modern practice that separates overlapping "levels of warfare" into "strategy" (political and military leaders setting key military and logistical policies designed to achieve the political goals of the war), "operations" (generals' military campaigns within a given theater as part of the larger strategy), and specific "tactics" in the presence of the enemy that shape a specific battle within a wider campaign. The concept of operations as separate from strategy is an idea that emerged in the Soviet Union only during the 1920s. See, for example, Bateman, "Understanding Military Strategy"; Hagerman, *American Civil War and the Origins of Modern Warfare,* 6–27; Harvey, "Levels of War," 75–81; Rafuse, *From the Mountains to the Bay,* 12; Stoker, *Grand Design,* 7–11; and Weigley, *Great Civil War,* xx–xxi.

78. Hattaway and Jones, *How the North Won,* 11–17; Stoker, *Grand Design,* 7–11; Weigley, *Great Civil War,* xx–xxiv.

79. Reardon, *With a Sword in One Hand,* 19–20, 24, 31, 32–33, 43, 49–50 (quotation, 19).

80. Simpson, *Lincoln and the Gettysburg Campaign,* 19, 24. See also Burlingame, *Abraham Lincoln,* 2:420; Burton, *Age of Lincoln,* 170; Gienapp, *Abraham Lincoln,* 109, 120–21, 159, and Zander, *Army Under Fire,* 94.

3. I COULD HAVE WHIPPED THEM MYSELF

1. Burlingame, *Abraham Lincoln,* 2:432–33; Donald, *Lincoln,* 388–90; Long, *Civil War Day by Day,* 284, 288; Gienapp, *Abraham Lincoln,* 118, 126; McPherson, *Tried by War,* 141–42; Neely, *Last Best Hope,* 82–87; Stoker, *Grand Design,* 197, 201–3. Edwards, "Saving the Republic," attributes Republican losses to the fact that so many Republican voters were away from home in uniform.

2. For transcripts of Porter's trial, see *OR,* vol. 12, pt. 2 supplement. For transcripts of the Buell Commission hearings, see *OR,* 16(1):66–726. See also Basler et al., *Collected Works of Abraham Lincoln,* 5:485, 6:67; Burlingame, *With Lincoln in the White House,* 89, 90–91, 103; Nicolay and Hay, *Abraham Lincoln,* 6:279–81; Burlingame, *Abraham Lincoln,* 2:420, 423, 431–33; Donald, *Lincoln,* 388–90; Engle, *Don Carlos Buell,* 311–42; Goodwin, *Team of Rivals,* 485; Marvel, *Radical Sacrifice,* xi–xviii, 269–91; Marvel, *Lincoln's Autocrat,* 258–61, 270–72, 316; McPherson, *Battle Cry of Freedom,* 560–63; McPherson, *Tried by War,* 141–42; Meacham, *And There Was Light,* 284–85; Rable, *Conflict of Command,* 272–73; and Williams, *Lincoln Finds a General,* 1:477. Earlier in September, Lincoln had summarily dismissed from the U.S. Army staff officer Maj. John J. Key for answering a colleague's question, "Why was not the rebel army

bagged immediately after the battle near Sharpsburg?" by allegedly replying: "That is not the game. . . . [T]he object is that neither army shall get much advantage of the other; that both shall be kept in the field till they are exhausted, when we will make a compromise and save slavery." See Basler et al., *Collected Works of Abraham Lincoln,* 5:442–43, 508–9, 6:20; Gienapp and Gienapp, *Civil War Diary of Gideon Welles,* 64; and Welles, *Diary of Gideon Welles,* 1:156. I am grateful to Jennifer Murray, the author of a forthcoming biography of George G. Meade, for her thoughts on the political nature of the Porter trial.

3. Hartwig, *I Dread the Thought of the Place,* 773; Sears, *To the Gates of Richmond,* 351; Sears, *Civil War Papers of George B. McClellan,* 376–78.

4. Pease and Randall, *Diary of Orville Hickman Browning,* 590.

5. Nicolay and Hay, *Abraham Lincoln,* 6:196–98; Burlingame, *Abraham Lincoln,* 2:443–44; Marvel, *Burnside,* 159–63; Simpson, *Lincoln and the Gettysburg Campaign,* 20; Taaffe, *Commanding the Army of the Potomac,* 60–63; Williams, *Lincoln and His Generals,* 179–80, 182, 194.

6. Nicolay and Hay, *Abraham Lincoln,* 6:198–200; Burlingame, *Abraham Lincoln,* 2:443–45; Marszalek, *Commander of All Lincoln's Armies,* 156–57; Marvel, *Burnside,* 163–65; Marvel, *Lincoln's Darkest Year,* 274–78 (quotation, 278); McPherson, *Tried by War,* 142–43; Neely, *Last Best Hope,* 73–74; Perret, *Lincoln's War,* 225–27; Stoker, *Grand Design,* 211–12; Williams, *Lincoln and His Generals,* 194–98; Williams, *Lincoln Finds a General,* 2:482–83, 497–505.

7. Basler et al., *Collected Works of Abraham Lincoln,* 5:485, 514–15; Nicolay and Hay, *Abraham Lincoln,* 6:200–209; Pease and Randall, *Diary of Orville Hickman Browning,* 590; Burlingame, *Abraham Lincoln,* 2:445–48; Gienapp, *Abraham Lincoln,* 121; Marszalek, *Commander of All Lincoln's Armies,* 156–59; Marszalek, *Lincoln and the Military,* 42–43, 45; Marvel, *Burnside,* 165–206; Marvel, *Lincoln's Darkest Year,* 279–96, 308; McPherson, *Tried by War,* 144; Meacham, *And There Was Light,* 284–85; Perret, *Lincoln's War,* 227; Simpson, *Lincoln and the Gettysburg Campaign,* 20–21; Stoker, *Grand Design,* 216–20; Williams, *Lincoln and His Generals,* 197–201; Williams, *Lincoln Finds a General,* 2:507–8, 516–17. For more on the battle, see O'Reilly, *Fredericksburg Campaign;* and Rable, *Fredericksburg! Fredericksburg!*

8. Basler et al., *Collected Works of Abraham Lincoln,* 6:13–14; Nicolay and Hay, *Abraham Lincoln,* 6:210-11; Burlingame, *Abraham Lincoln,* 2:448; McPherson, *Tried by War,* 144; Oates, *With Malice Toward None,* 355; White, *A. Lincoln,* 525.

9. Quoted in Burlingame, *Abraham Lincoln,* 2:446.

10. Pease and Randall, *Diary of Orville Hickman Browning,* 600. See also Marvel, *Lincoln's Darkest Year,* 308.

11. Burton, *Age of Lincoln,* 177.

12. Stoddard, *Inside the White House,* 179. See also Burlingame and Ettlinger, *Inside Lincoln's White House,* 268n14; Zeitz, *Lincoln's Boys,* 2–3, 92.

13. Boritt, *Lincoln the War President,* 204, 205.

14. Casualty figures and total strengths are interpolated from Livermore, *Numbers and Losses,* 96–97; and McPherson, *Battle Cry of Freedom,* 570, 572. Gabor Boritt noted the problems with Lincoln's addition and subtraction. See Boritt, *Lincoln and the Economics of the American Dream,* 357n10.

15. Brooks, *Washington in Lincoln's Time,* 41.

16. Basler et al., *Collected Works of Abraham Lincoln,* 6:15–16, 22; Brooks, *Washington in Lincoln's Time,* 41; Burlingame, *Lincoln Observed,* 15–17; Nicolay and Hay, *Abraham Lincoln,*

6:213–16; Burlingame, *Abraham Lincoln,* 2:474–75, 479, 485; Donald, *Lincoln,* 409–10; Goodwin, *Team of Rivals,* 498; Hartwig, *I Dread the Thought of the Place,* 773, 778–80; Marszalek, *Lincoln and the Military,* 45; Marvel, *Burnside,* 206–11; McPherson, *Tried by War,* 147–48; Oates, *With Malice Toward None,* 365; Pryor, *Six Encounters,* 139–42; Rafuse, "'Spirit Which You Have Aided to Infuse'"; Thomas, *Abraham Lincoln,* 364; Taaffe, *Commanding the Army of the Potomac,* 68, 73–75; Williams, *Lincoln and His Generals,* 201–4; Williams, *Lincoln Finds a General,* 2:540–41, 543.

17. Basler et al., *Collected Works of Abraham Lincoln,* 6:23–26, 48–49, 56, 73, 178–80; Burlingame, *With Lincoln in the White House,* 98–102; Nicolay and Hay, *Abraham Lincoln,* 5:126–27, 148–49, 153, 6:90–91, 94–98, 108–11, 120, 123–27, 129–30, 153–54, 158–60, 360–63, 420, 8:208–9; Pease and Randall, *Diary of Orville Hickman Browning,* 591, 611–12, Burlingame, *Abraham Lincoln,* 2:393–96, 442, 463–66; Donald, *Lincoln,* 396–98, 429–31; Foner, *Fiery Trial,* 232–40, 244–51, 257–59, 269; Goodwin, *Team of Rivals,* 497, 500–501; Guelzo, *Our Ancient Faith,* 132–34; McPherson, *Tried by War,* 157–59; Meacham, *And There Was Light,* 276–77, 356–57; Neely, *Last Best Hope,* 118; Oates, *With Malice Toward None,* 359, 369; Page, *Black Resettlement,* 131–39, 143, 165–67; Page, "Time and Place," 147–54; Stampp, "One Alone?," 140.

18. Foner, *Fiery Trial,* 245.

19. Basler et al., *Collected Works of Abraham Lincoln,* 6:31, 46–48; Nicolay and Hay, *Abraham Lincoln,* 6:215–16 (quotation, 215).

20. Marszalek, *Lincoln and the Military,* 46.

21. Basler et al., *Collected Works of Abraham Lincoln,* 6:46–48 (quotation, 46); Nicolay and Hay, *Abraham Lincoln,* 6:217.

22. Basler et al., *Collected Works of Abraham Lincoln,* 6:78–79; Gienapp and Gienapp, *Civil War Diary of Gideon Welles,* 130–31; Nicolay and Hay, *Abraham Lincoln,* 6:217–21; Pease and Randall, *Diary of Orville Hickman Browning,* 619–20; Welles, *Diary of Gideon Welles,* 1:229–30; Burlingame, *Abraham Lincoln,* 2:485–86; Donald, *Lincoln,* 409–10; Hartwig, *I Dread the Thought of the Place,* 779–81; Marvel, *Burnside,* 211–17; Marvel, *Lincoln's Darkest Year,* 310–14; McPherson, *Tried by War,* 161–62; Noe, *Howling Storm,* 218–26; Oates, *With Malice Toward None,* 365–66; Simpson, *Lincoln and the Gettysburg Campaign,* 21; Taaffe, *Commanding the Army of the Potomac,* 77–79; Thomas, *Abraham Lincoln,* 365; Williams, *Lincoln and His Generals,* 204–5; Williams, *Lincoln Finds a General,* 2:540–46; White, *A. Lincoln,* 535.

23. Basler et al., *Collected Works of Abraham Lincoln,* 6:78–79. See also Niven, *Salmon P. Chase Papers,* 400–401; Gienapp, *Abraham Lincoln,* 130–31; Marszalek, *Commander of All Lincoln's Armies,* 166–67, 170; Marszalek, *Lincoln and the Military,* 48–49; McPherson, *Tried by War,* 163–64; Neely, *Last Best Hope,* 82–87; Stoker, *Grand Design,* 252–53; Taaffe, *Commanding the Army of the Potomac,* 20, 28, 54, 55, 62–63, 79–84; Williams, *Lincoln and His Generals,* 210–14; and Williams, *Lincoln Finds a General,* 2:548–51.

24. *OR,* 13:590–91, 595, 597, 599–600, 613, 616–18, 620–21, 631–32, 637–38, 642, 644, 648–53, 658–69, 662–64, 666–67, 669–70, 679–80, 685–88, 694–95, 705–6, 707–12, 716–18, 722–24 (quotations, 599, 686); Basler et al., *Collected Works of Abraham Lincoln,* 5:493, 537–38, 542–43, 6:6–7; Burlingame, *With Lincoln in the White House,* 88; Gienapp and Gienapp, *Civil War Diary of Gideon Welles,* 77, 91–92; Welles, *Diary of Gideon Welles,* 1:171, 186; Burlingame, *Abraham Lincoln,* 2:480–83; Donald, *Lincoln,* 392–95; Foner, *Fiery Trial,* 261; Pryor, *Six Encounters,* 182–90, 200–202; Reynolds, *Abe,* 668–69; Zeitz, *Lincoln's Boys,* 127–29. Much has been written

on the Dakota Uprising—albeit not by Civil War historians—but good places to start include Berg, *38 Nooses;* Cox, *Lincoln and the Sioux Uprising;* and Schultz, *Over the Earth I Come.*

25. Basler et al., *Collected Works of Abraham Lincoln,* 6:78–79; 39, 101, 108–9, 138–40, 148; Burlingame, *With Lincoln in the White House,* 102, 105; Burlingame, *Abraham Lincoln,* 2:484; Donald, *Lincoln,* 408; Goodwin, *Team of Rivals,* 527–28; Marszalek, *Commander of All Lincoln's Armies,* 159–60; Marszalek, *Lincoln and the Military,* 49; McDonough, "Commander in Chief and Military Operations in Tennessee," 99–100; McPherson, *Tried by War,* 137, 155, 189–90; Noe, *Howling Storm,* 248–49, 256–58, 31; Pryor, *Six Encounters,* 56; Stoker, *Grand Design,* 221–22, 240–42; Williams, *Lincoln and His Generals,* 206–8, 248–49. On the Battle of Stones River, see Cozzens, *No Better Place to Die.* As historian James McPherson pointed out, Napoleon had traveled on half the rations and with only one-third of the wagons that Federal regulations recommended. He suggests that Lincoln "may have" read about Napoleon's rations and wagon allotments "in his crash course of reading military history," something I question earlier. McPherson, *Tried by War,* 137. Moreover, Napoleonic armies were more likely to live off the land. For the high command's growing disdain of long trains and deliberate movement in general, see ibid., 136–38; Hess, *Civil War Logistics,* 142–43; and Hess, *Civil War Supply,* 46–47.

26. Basler et al., *Collected Works of Abraham Lincoln,* 5:505. Banks blamed the request on a staff officer. See ibid., 5:506.

27. Basler et al., *Collected Works of Abraham Lincoln,* 6:101, 108–9, 138–40, 148 (quotation, 108); Nicolay and Hay, *Abraham Lincoln,* 8:43–50; Goodwin, *Team of Rivals,* 527–28; Marszalek, *Commander of All Lincoln's Armies,* 159–60; Oates, *With Malice Toward None,* 378; Stoker, *Grand Design,* 240–42; Williams, *Lincoln and His Generals,* 250–51. Nicolay and Hay later wrote that Rosecrans "was, like McClellan, always demanding impossibilities from the Government in the way of troops and supplies; but the great difference between them was, that, while in McClellan's case delay was an instinct, in the case of Rosecrans delay seemed to spring from a certain controversial insubordination." Nicolay and Hay, *Abraham Lincoln,* 8:45.

28. Nicolay and Hay, *Abraham Lincoln,* 6:440–41; Pease and Randall, *Diary of Orville Hickman Browning,* 553, 562; Porter, *Incidents and Anecdotes,* 95–98, 120; Welles, *Diary of Gideon Welles,* 1:71–72; Glatthaar, *Partners in Command,* 192; Stoker, *Grand Design,* 135–37; Symonds, *Lincoln and His Admirals,* 127–29, 188–90; White, *A. Lincoln,* 548.

29. Porter, *Incidents and Anecdotes,* 95–96.

30. Basler et al., *Collected Works of Abraham Lincoln,* 5:453; Nicolay and Hay, *Abraham Lincoln,* 6:440–41; Donald, *Lincoln,* 429–30; Stoker, *Grand Design,* 207–8, 225, 227. The navy had enlisted African American sailors for many years and reintroduced Black enlistment in the spring of 1862, albeit with the rating of "boys." In late August, as permitted by recent legislation, Lincoln did authorize the first African American regiments, which would be raised in South Carolina. See Nicolay and Hay, *Abraham Lincoln,* 6:441–42; and Symonds, *Lincoln and His Admirals,* 160–62, 165.

31. Pryor, *Six Encounters,* 54.

32. Gienapp and Gienapp, *Civil War Diary of Gideon Welles,* 70–71; Porter, *Incidents and Anecdotes,* 121–22; Welles, *Diary of Gideon Welles,* 1:163–65; Symonds, *Lincoln and His Admirals,* 188–91.

33. Basler et al., *Collected Works of Abraham Lincoln,* 5:468–69; Gienapp and Gienapp, *Civil War Diary of Gideon Welles,* 119–20; Nicolay and Hay, *Abraham Lincoln,* 7:135–36; Niven,

Salmon P. Chase Papers, 404, 406; Porter, *Incidents and Anecdotes,* 122–24; Welles, *Diary of Gideon Welles,* 1:217; Burlingame, *Abraham Lincoln,* 2:433–38; Gienapp, *Abraham Lincoln,* 138–39; McPherson, *Tried by War,* 149–52; Noe, *Howling Storm,* 238–39; Pryor, *Six Encounters,* 58–59; Stoker, *Grand Design,* 209–10; Williams, *Lincoln and His Generals,* 187–90; Zander, *Army Under Fire,* 75–76.

34. Williams, *Lincoln and His Generals,* 187–94 (quotation, 193–94). See also Burlingame, *Abraham Lincoln,* 2:433, 438; and Noe, *Howling Storm,* 238–39.

35. Porter, *Incidents and Anecdotes,* 122–23 (quotation, 123).

36. Simpson, *Ulysses S. Grant,* 157–59 (quotation, 159).

37. Sherman, *Memoirs,* 1:296–303; Marszalek, *Commander of All Lincoln's Armies,* 139–40, 161–62; McPherson, *Tried by War,* 152–54; Simpson, *Ulysses S. Grant,* 167–72, 182–84; Williams, *Lincoln and His Generals,* 215–24.

38. Basler et al., *Collected Works of Abraham Lincoln,* 6:70. See also Gienapp and Gienapp, *Civil War Diary of Gideon Welles,* 119–20; Nicolay and Hay, *Abraham Lincoln,* 7:143; and Welles, *Diary of Gideon Welles,* 1:217.

39. Grant, *Personal Memoirs,* 1:446; Porter, *Incidents and Anecdotes,* 181–83; Brady, *War upon the Land,* 42–42; Burlingame, *Abraham Lincoln,* 2:516; Donald, *Lincoln,* 445; Fiege, *Republic of Nature,* 156–98, 222–23; Glatthaar, *Partners in Command,* 192–94; Goodwin, *Team of Rivals,* 528–29; Marszalek, *Lincoln and the Military,* 50–51; McPherson, *Tried by War,* 166–69; Noe, *Howling Storm,* 243–45, 494–95; Simpson, *Ulysses S. Grant,* 119–24, 167–72, 182–84, 214–15; Williams, *Lincoln and His Generals,* 224–28.

40. Burlingame, *With Lincoln in the White House,* 108.

41. Simpson, *Ulysses S. Grant,* 157–59.

42. Donald, *Lincoln,* 432.

43. Gienapp and Gienapp, *Civil War Diary of Gideon Welles,* 70–71, 140–41, 168–69; Welles, *Diary of Gideon Welles,* 1:2–66, 239–40, 277; Burlingame, *Abraham Lincoln,* 2:306–7; Niven, *Gideon Welles,* 383–87; Symonds, *Lincoln and His Admirals,* 109–10, 137–40, 191–94; Thomas, *Abraham Lincoln,* 310.

44. Gienapp and Gienapp, *Civil War Diary of Gideon Welles,* 70–71, 140–41, 168–69, 222–23 (quotations, 70, 141, 222); Welles, *Diary of Gideon Welles,* 1:163–65, 239–40, 341 (quotations, 240, 341). Here I follow the original diary entry instead of Welles's later effort, which included an addition of condemning "the army practice of favoritism and political partyism." See Gienapp and Gienapp, *Civil War Diary of Gideon Welles,* 70; and Welles, *Diary of Gideon Welles,* 1:164.

45. Basler et al., *Collected Works of Abraham Lincoln,* 6:111–12; Gienapp and Gienapp, *Civil War Diary of Gideon Welles,* 137–40, 146–47, 154, 157–61; Nicolay and Hay, *Abraham Lincoln,* 7:58–67; Welles, *Diary of Gideon Welles,* 1:236–39, 247, 259, 262–64 (quotation 237); Symonds, *Lincoln and His Admirals,* 62–70, 192–94, 200–11. See also Burlingame, *Abraham Lincoln,* 2:488–90; Marvel, *Great Task Remaining,* 38; McPherson, *Tried by War,* 165–66; and Niven, *Gideon Welles,* 424–39. Welles initially tried to replace Du Pont with Rear Admiral Andrew H. Foote, but the latter's poor health made that impossible.

46. Symonds, *Lincoln and His Admirals,* 206–7 (Dahlgren Diary, Feb. 14, 1863, quoted, 206).

47. Burlingame and Ettlinger, *Inside Lincoln's White House,* 43–45, 53 (quotations, 43, 53). See also Basler et al., *Collected Works of Abraham Lincoln,* 6:165–67, 170, 173–74; Brooks, *Washington in Lincoln's Time,* 35–37, 45; Burlingame, *With Lincoln in the White House,* 108–9;

Gienapp and Gienapp, *Civil War Diary of Gideon Welles,* 156–60, 161, 163, 165, 168–69, 175, 195–97, 199–200, 200–201, 219–20, 222–23, 258–59; Welles, *Diary of Gideon Welles,* 1:262–64, 266, 268–69, 273, 276–77, 288, 309–13, 315, 317–18, 337, 341, 382–84, 2:128–29; Nicolay and Hay, *Abraham Lincoln,* 7:68–75; Burlingame, *Abraham Lincoln,* 2:490–91; Marvel, *Great Task Remaining,* 41; Pryor, *Six Encounters,* 58; and Symonds, *Lincoln and His Admirals,* 214–18, 236–49.

48. Burlingame and Ettlinger, *Inside Lincoln's White House,* 96 (quotation), 101–2.

49. Gienapp and Gienapp, *Civil War Diary of Gideon Welles,* 48–49; Welles, *Diary of Gideon Welles,* 1:128–29; Symonds, *Lincoln and His Admirals,* 236–49, 292. For the wider campaign, see Wise, *Gate of Hell.*

50. Basler et al., *Collected Works of Abraham Lincoln,* 5:338–39, 359, 436–37, 6:215–16, 237; Nicolay and Hay, *Abraham Lincoln,* 7:3, 6–7; Burlingame, *Abraham Lincoln,* 2:503–7, 530; Burton, *Age of Lincoln,* 225–28; Goodwin, *Team of Rivals,* 522–24; Marvel, *Great Task Remaining,* 116–19; McPherson, *Tried by War,* 171–75; Meacham, *And There Was Light,* 291–96; Neely, *Fate of Liberty,* 65–68; Oates, *With Malice Toward None,* 371–73; Pryor, *Six Encounters,* 96–104; Thomas, *Abraham Lincoln,* 376–81. The definitive work on Lincoln and civil liberties remains Neely, *Fate of Liberty.*

51. Foner, *Fiery Trial,* 264–65; Goodwin, *Team of Rivals,* 502–3; Noe, *Howling Storm,* 261–67; Stoker, *Grand Design,* 197, 254; Williams, *Lincoln Finds a General,* 2:560.

52. Brooks, *Washington in Lincoln's Time,* 45–56; Burlingame, *Abraham Lincoln,* 2:491–97; Donald, *Lincoln,* 434; Goodwin, *Team of Rivals,* 513–14; Marvel, *Great Task Remaining,* 29–30; McPherson, *Tried by War,* 175–76; Noe, *Howling Storm,* 268–69; Oates, *With Malice Toward None,* 374; Simpson, *Lincoln and the Gettysburg Campaign,* 20–23, 29; Stoker, *Grand Design,* 253–58; Williams, *Lincoln and His Generals,* 233–38; Williams, *Lincoln Finds a General,* 2:564.

53. Gienapp and Gienapp, *Civil War Diary of Gideon Welles,* 180 (quotation); Welles, *Diary of Gideon Welles,* 1:293. See also Basler et al., *Collected Works of Abraham Lincoln,* 6:196–99, 198; and Burlingame, *With Lincoln in the White House,* 110–12. Chancellorsville has amassed a lengthy bibliography, but good overviews can be found in Furgerson, *Chancellorsville 1863;* and Sears, *Chancellorsville.*

54. Marvel, *Great Task Remaining,* 60; Meacham, *And There Was Light,* 299.

55. Brooks, *Washington in Lincoln's Time,* 57–60 (quotation, 57–58). See also Burlingame, *With Lincoln in the White House,* 113–14; Nicolay and Hay, *Abraham Lincoln,* 7:90–111; Stoddard, *Inside the White House,* 198–205; Burlingame, *Abraham Lincoln,* 2:498; Goodwin, *Team of Rivals,* 520; Marszalek, *Lincoln and the Military,* 53; McPherson, *Tried by War,* 176–77; Williams, *Lincoln and His Generals,* 238–42; Williams, *Lincoln Finds a General,* 2:606–9.

56. Basler et al., *Collected Works of Abraham Lincoln,* 6:201 (quotation), 215, 217; Brooks, *Washington in Lincoln's Time,* 58–60; Gienapp and Gienapp, *Civil War Diary of Gideon Welles,* 178–79; Nicolay and Hay, *Abraham Lincoln,* 7:197–200; Welles, *Diary of Gideon Welles,* 1:291–93; Burlingame, *Abraham Lincoln,* 2:499–500; Donald, *Lincoln,* 435–36; Goodwin, *Team of Rivals,* 521; Marszalek, *Commander of All Lincoln's Armies,* 171–72; Marszalek, *Lincoln and the Military,* 53–55; Simpson, *Lincoln and the Gettysburg Campaign,* 29–32; Williams, *Lincoln Finds a General,* 2:609; Williams, *Lincoln and His Generals,* 233–47.

57. Gienapp and Gienapp, *Civil War Diary of Gideon Welles,* 218. See also Welles, *Diary of Gideon Welles,* 1:336.

58. Donald, *Lincoln,* 437.

59. Reynolds, *Abe,* 636.

60. Basler et al., *Collected Works of Abraham Lincoln,* 6:235, 237, 248, 260–69; Nicolay and Hay, *Abraham Lincoln,* 7:343–49, 352–54; Gienapp, *Abraham Lincoln,* 132–34; Guelzo, *Our Ancient Faith,* 102–6; Marvel, *Burnside,* 230–37; McPherson, *Tried by War,* 173–74; Neely, *Fate of Liberty,* 66–67; White, *A. Lincoln,* 564–67.

61. Basler et al., *Collected Works of Abraham Lincoln,* 6:235, 237, 260–69 (quotations, 266, 265, 269). See also Gienapp, *Abraham Lincoln,* 133–34; Marvel, *Great Task Remaining,* 74–87, 103–5; and Pryor, *Six Encounters,* 60, 102–6, 111–15. Published in pamphlet form, the "Corning Letter" became remarkably popular with Republicans but only made steps toward healing the northern political divide. Lincoln sent a similar letter to Ohio Democrats in late June. See Basler et al., *Collected Works of Abraham Lincoln,* 6:300–306.

62. Basler et al., *Collected Works of Abraham Lincoln,* 6:236; Nicolay and Hay, *Abraham Lincoln,* 8:61–65; McPherson, *Tried by War,* 189–92; Noe, *Howling Storm,* 320–23; Williams, *Lincoln and His Generals,* 273–77. The definitive study of this campaign is Powell and Wittenberg, *Tullahoma.*

63. Basler et al., *Collected Works of Abraham Lincoln,* 6:244; Burlingame, *With Lincoln in the White House,* 113–15; Gienapp and Gienapp, *Civil War Diary of Gideon Welles,* 154, 181–82, 192–93, 203–4; Nicolay and Hay, *Abraham Lincoln,* 7:153–54; Welles, *Diary of Gideon Welles,* 1:259, 295, 308, 320; Burlingame, *Abraham Lincoln,* 2:517; McPherson, *Tried by War,* 169–70; Simpson, *Ulysses S. Grant,* 182–83, 190–209; Symonds, *Lincoln and His Admirals,* 195–99; Williams, *Lincoln and His Generals,* 229–30. Grant's relationship with alcohol remains disputed and controversial, but see, for example, Marvel. *Lincoln's Autocrat,* 305, 518n5; and Simpson, *Ulysses S. Grant,* 223. Vicksburg boasts an impressive bibliography. Among the most useful one-volume introductions are Ballard, *Vicksburg;* Grabau, *Ninety-Eighty Days;* and Shea and Winschel, *Vicksburg Is the Key.*

64. Burlingame, *With Lincoln in the White House,* 115.

65. Nicolay and Hay, *Abraham Lincoln,* 7:154.

66. Historian James McPherson wonders if Lincoln kept Hooker only to squelch a developing movement to bring back McClellan, who remained out of action. See McPherson, *Tried by War,* 177–79. See also Taaffe, *Commanding the Army of the Potomac,* 98, 101–3, 105–6.

67. No Civil War campaign has amassed more books about it than Gettysburg. The classic one-volume study still preferred by many serious students of the battle is Coddington, *Gettysburg.* A modern one-volume treatment is Guelzo, *Gettysburg.* On the march north, see also McPherson, *Battle Cry of Freedom,* 646–55.

68. Basler et al., *Collected Works of Abraham Lincoln,* 6:249–51 (quotation, 250). See also Nicolay and Hay, *Abraham Lincoln,* 7:203–5; Noe, *Howling Storm,* 276–78; Stoker, *Grand Design,* 285–86; and Williams, *Lincoln Finds a General,* 2:618–21.

69. Basler et al., *Collected Works of Abraham Lincoln,* 6:249. See also Nicolay and Hay, *Abraham Lincoln,* 7:204–5.

70. Basler et al., *Collected Works of Abraham Lincoln,* 6:257–58 (quotation, 257). See also Nicolay and Hay, *Abraham Lincoln,* 7:208 (they silently corrected Lincoln's spelling of "opportunity"); Noe, *Howling Storm,* 277–78; White, *A. Lincoln,* 572–73; and Williams, *Lincoln Finds a General,* 2:622–26. "Halleck gave no orders," Donald Stoker has observed. "He thought it wasn't

his place to do so. Lincoln also dispatched none, believing he should bow to Halleck's superior military wisdom. Hooker lacked the confidence to act on his own. He sat, and the opportunity to wrest control of the summer campaign by striking Lee's rear passed untaken. The Union command system was broken." Stoker, *Grand Design,* 287.

71. Simpson, *Lincoln and the Gettysburg Campaign,* 32–34; Stoker, *Grand Design,* 287–90. See also Burlingame, *Abraham Lincoln,* 2:501; Donald, *Lincoln,* 438–40; Houghton, "Lincoln and Gettysburg," 243–44; Marszalek, *Lincoln and the Military,* 56–57; McPherson, *Tried by War,* 179–80; Williams, *Lincoln and His Generals,* 251–53; and Williams, *Lincoln Finds a General,* 2:609; 622–27.

72. Gienapp and Gienapp, *Civil War Diary of Gideon Welles,* 212. For an edited version of the quotation, see Welles, *Diary of Gideon Welles,* 1:328.

73. Basler et al., *Collected Works of Abraham Lincoln,* 6:271, 273 (quotation), 276–77. See also Gienapp and Gienapp, *Civil War Diary of Gideon Welles,* 311–22; Nicolay and Hay, *Abraham Lincoln,* 7:210; Welles, *Diary of Gideon Welles,* 1:328; and Simpson, *Lincoln and the Gettysburg Campaign,* 34–35.

74. Basler et al., *Collected Works of Abraham Lincoln,* 6:277–78. See also Burlingame, *With Lincoln in the White House,* 117; Gienapp and Gienapp, *Civil War Diary of Gideon Welles,* 211–12, 214; Welles, *Diary of Gideon Welles,* 1:328, 331; Simpson, *Lincoln and the Gettysburg Campaign,* 35; and Williams, *Lincoln and His Generals,* 254.

75. Marszalek, *Commander of All Lincoln's Armies,* 172–73.

76. Gienapp and Gienapp, *Civil War Diary of Gideon Welles,* 214. See also Welles, *Diary of Gideon Welles,* 1:331.

77. Basler et al., *Collected Works of Abraham Lincoln,* 6:281–82 (quotation, 282). Basler added, "Throughout the day the exchange of telegrams between Hooker and Halleck up to this time had indicated beyond question that Hooker and Halleck did not understand either the military situation or their respective relations to each other." Ibid., 282. See also Nicolay and Hay, *Abraham Lincoln,* 7:210–13.

78. Gienapp and Gienapp, *Civil War Diary of Gideon Welles,* 228–29; Nicolay and Hay, *Abraham Lincoln,* 7:226; Welles, *Diary of Gideon Welles,* 1:348–49; Burlingame, *Abraham Lincoln,* 2:501–3, 509–10; Donald, *Lincoln,* 444–45; Goodwin, *Team of Rivals,* 530–31; Marszalek, *Commander of All Lincoln's Armies,* 173–75; McPherson, *Tried by War,* 180; Simpson, *Lincoln and the Gettysburg Campaign,* 35–37; Stoker, *Grand Design,* 290–92; Williams, *Lincoln and His Generals,* 254–59; Williams, *Lincoln Finds a General,* 2:627–55.

79. Gienapp and Gienapp, *Civil War Diary of Gideon Welles,* 229. See also Welles, *Diary of Gideon Welles,* 1:349.

80. Gienapp and Gienapp, *Civil War Diary of Gideon Welles,* 228–29. See also Welles, *Diary of Gideon Welles,* 1:348; Carpenter, *Inner Life of Abraham Lincoln,* 142–43; and Taaffe, *Commanding the Army of the Potomac,* 105–6.

81. Brooks, *Washington in Lincoln's Time,* 59–60. Welles was harsher still, writing that Hooker was worse than McClellan: "There was confidence in McClellan's ability to organize, to defend, and to repel, though he was worthless in attack, but there is no such feeling towards Hooker. He has not grown in public estimation since placed in command. If he drinks, as is reported, God help us." Gienapp and Gienapp, *Civil War Diary of Gideon Welles,* 64, 212–13.

82. Burlingame, *Abraham Lincoln,* 2:510; Donald, *Lincoln,* 445; Marszalek, *Commander of All Lincoln's Armies,* 175–77; Noe, *Howling Storm,* 218–26; 282–83; Oates, *With Malice Toward None,* 379–80; Taaffe, *Commanding the Army of the Potomac,* 103, 108–9; White, *A. Lincoln,* 574–75; Williams, *Lincoln and His Generals,* 230, 260–64, 271. On supplies, see Brown, *Retreat from Gettysburg.*

83. Bates, *Lincoln in the Telegraph Office,* 155–56; Meacham, *And There Was Light,* 303–4.

84. Rusling, *Men and Things I Saw,* 16, 17.

85. Burlingame, *Abraham Lincoln,* 2:517–18; Donald, *Lincoln,* 445–46; Goodwin, *Team of Rivals,* 532–35; Marszalek, *Lincoln and the Military,* 58.

86. Basler et al., *Collected Works of Abraham Lincoln,* 6:326. See also Meacham, *And There Was Light,* xxv–xxvii.

87. *OR,* 27(3):519. See also Simpson, *Lincoln and the Gettysburg Campaign,* 40–41.

88. James B. Fry in Rice, *Reminiscences of Abraham Lincoln,* 402. See also McPherson, *Tried by War,* 181.

89. Burlingame and Ettlinger, *Inside Lincoln's White House,* 62. See also Nicolay and Hay, *Abraham Lincoln,* 7:278; Taliaferro, *All the Great Prizes,* 72.

90. Basler et al., *Collected Works of Abraham Lincoln,* 6:318. See also Bates, *Lincoln in the Telegraph Office,* 156–57; Burlingame, *Abraham Lincoln,* 2:510–12; Marszalek, *Lincoln and the Military,* 58; McPherson, *Tried by War,* 182; Neely, *Last Best Hope,* 79–80, 163; Simpson, *Lincoln and the Gettysburg Campaign,* 40–41; Williams, *Lincoln and His Generals,* 265–66; Williams, *Lincoln Finds a General,* 2:739–41. Mark Neely observed that "such suspicions gained the upper hand only when Lincoln was under great stress and especially aggravated, but he was under stress a great deal of the time." Neely, *Last Best Hope,* 163.

91. Weigley, *Great Civil War,* 254, 272.

92. McPherson, *Tried by War,* 183; Noe, *Howling Storm,* 286–98; Weigley, *Great Civil War,* 254, 272. On the retreat and pursuit, see Brown, *Retreat from Gettysburg;* Murray, "'Your Golden Opportunity Is Gone,'" 71–72, 76–83; and Wittenberg, Petruzzi, and Nugent, *One Continuous Fight.* Federal casualty figures can be found in Livermore, *Numbers and Losses,* 100, 102–3; McPherson, *Battle Cry of Freedom,* 664; and "Battle Detail: Vicksburg," accessed May 7, 2025.

93. *OR,* 27(1):83–84 (quotations, 83, 84).

94. *OR,* 27(1):83–95 (quotations, 84, 92, 93). See also Basler et al., *Collected Works of Abraham Lincoln,* 6:319; Burlingame and Ettlinger, *Inside Lincoln's White House,* 61–63; Gienapp and Gienapp, *Civil War Diary of Gideon Welles,* 241–42; Nicolay and Hay, *Abraham Lincoln,* 7:274–75; Welles, *Diary of Gideon Welles,* 1:363–64; Burlingame, *Abraham Lincoln,* 2:512–13; Marszalek, *Lincoln and the Military,* 59; Marvel, *Great Task Remaining,* 155–56; Murray, "'Your Golden Opportunity Is Gone,'" 83–86; Simpson, *Lincoln and the Gettysburg Campaign,* 42–49; Stoker, *Grand Design,* 300–303; Williams, *Lincoln Finds a General,* 2:741–45.

95. Burlingame and Ettlinger, *Inside Lincoln's White House,* 62.

96. Burlingame and Ettlinger, *Inside Lincoln's White House,* 62, 63. See also Burlingame, *Abraham Lincoln,* 2:513; Hoffmann, "Robert Todd Lincoln's 'Gettysburg Story,'" 1–13; McPherson, *Tried by War,* 184. John Nicolay and John Hay wrote that Lincoln "regretted that he had not himself gone to the army and personally issued the order for an attack." Nicolay and Hay, *Abraham Lincoln,* 7:278.

97. Gienapp and Gienapp, *Civil War Diary of Gideon Welles,* 247. See also Welles, *Diary of Gideon Welles,* 1:370–71; and Marvel, *Great Task Remaining,* 155.

98. Basler et al., *Collected Works of Abraham Lincoln,* 6:327–28. In addition to Meade, Lincoln specifically blasted Generals Couch and "Baldy" Smith, who had arrived with reserves too late to see action at Gettysburg. See also Nicolay and Hay, *Abraham Lincoln,* 7:279–81; Burlingame, *Abraham Lincoln,* 2:513–14; McPherson, *Tried by War,* 184–85; and Simpson, *Lincoln and the Gettysburg Campaign,* 49–51.

99. Basler et al., *Collected Works of Abraham Lincoln,* 6:328; Donald, *Lincoln,* 446–47; Goodwin, *Team of Rivals,* 535–38; Marszalek, *Lincoln and the Military,* 59–60; McPherson, *Tried by War,* 183–87; Stoker, *Grand Design,* 303–5; White, *A. Lincoln,* 574–81; Williams, *Lincoln and His Generals,* 267–71.

100. Nicolay and Hay, *Abraham Lincoln,* 7:278–79 (quotation, 278).

101. Gienapp and Gienapp, *Civil War Diary of Gideon Welles,* 251, 259. See also Welles, *Diary of Gideon Welles,* 1:374, 383.

102. Basler et al., *Collected Works of Abraham Lincoln,* 6:350, 354, 381; Burlingame and Ettlinger, *Inside Lincoln's White House,* 68, 73–74; Nicolay and Hay, *Abraham Lincoln,* 8:234–36; McPherson, *Tried by War,* 198–200; Noe, *Howling Storm,* 295–98, 359–64; Simpson, *Lincoln and the Gettysburg Campaign,* 52–55; Stoker, *Grand Design,* 309–12; Symonds, *Lincoln and His Admirals,* 252–54; Taaffe, *Commanding the Army of the Potomac,* 130; Williams, *Lincoln Finds a General,* 2:767–69.

103. *OR,* 29(2):207–8. See also Williams, *Lincoln Finds a General,* 2:769.

104. *OR,* 29(2):208. Jennifer Murray suggested that Lincoln held on to Meade only because he worried about the upcoming October 1863 elections in Pennsylvania. Jennifer Murray, email message to the author, June 15, 2024.

105. Basler et al., *Collected Works of Abraham Lincoln,* 6:519 (quotation), 7:7; Burlingame and Ettlinger, *Inside Lincoln's White House,* 92–93, 109; Gienapp and Gienapp, *Civil War Diary of Gideon Welles,* 308; Nicolay and Hay, *Abraham Lincoln,* 8:234–36; Welles, *Diary of Gideon Welles,* 1:469, 471–72; McPherson, *Tried by War,* 200–201; Noe, *Howling Storm,* 364–70; Oates, *With Malice Toward None,* 391; Simpson, *Lincoln and the Gettysburg Campaign,* 53–56; Stoker, *Grand Design,* 312–15; Taaffe, *Commanding the Army of the Potomac,* 134–35; Williams, *Lincoln and His Generals,* 285–88; Williams, *Lincoln Finds a General,* 2:769–73.

106. Simpson, *Lincoln and the Gettysburg Campaign,* 56.

4. MARTYR VICTORIOUS

1. Marszalek, *Commander of All Lincoln's Armies,* 185–86; McPherson, *Tried by War,* 192–93; Noe, *Howling Storm,* 325–32; Oates, *With Malice Toward None,* 390; Stoker, *Grand Design,* 319; Williams, *Lincoln and His Generals,* 278–79. On the Battle of Chickamauga, see Cozzens, *This Terrible Sound;* Woodworth, *Six Armies in Tennessee;* and three books by David A. Powell: *Chickamauga Campaign: A Mad Irregular Battle; Chickamauga Campaign: Glory or the Grave;* and *Chickamauga Campaign: Barren Victory.*

2. Burlingame and Ettlinger, *Inside Lincoln's White House,* 85. See also Bates, *Lincoln in the Telegraph Office,* 158–59; and Burlingame, *Abraham Lincoln,* 2:555.

3. Gienapp and Gienapp, *Civil War Diary of Gideon Welles,* 295. See also Welles, *Diary of Gideon Welles,* 1:439–40; Marszalek, *Lincoln and the Military,* 63–64; Oates, *With Malice Toward None,* 390–91; White, *A. Lincoln,* 593–97; and Williams, *Lincoln and His Generals,* 278–79.

4. Basler et al., *Collected Works of Abraham Lincoln,* 6:534–35 (quotation, 534).

5. *Washington (DC) Sunday Herald,* Dec. 5, 1886, quoted in Burlingame, *Abraham Lincoln,* 2:555. See also Basler et al., *Collected Works of Abraham Lincoln,* 6:478; and Nicolay and Hay, *Abraham Lincoln,* 8:108–9.

6. Basler et al., *Collected Works of Abraham Lincoln,* 6:498.

7. Bates, *Lincoln in the Telegraph Office,* 202. See also Nicolay and Hay, *Abraham Lincoln,* 8:164–66; Burlingame, *Abraham Lincoln,* 2:556; Marvel, *Burnside,* 284–89; McDonough, "Commander in Chief and Military Operations in Tennessee," 100; White, *A. Lincoln,* 595–96; and Williams, *Lincoln and His Generals,* 281.

8. Basler et al., *Collected Works of Abraham Lincoln,* 6:469–70, 480–81 (quotation), 483, 484, 485; Nicolay and Hay, *Abraham Lincoln,* 8:164–67; Williams, *Lincoln and His Generals,* 282; McPherson, *Tried by War,* 194.

9. Niven, *Salmon P. Chase Papers,* 450–54 (quotation, 454); Basler et al., *Collected Works of Abraham Lincoln,* 6:486; Bates, *Lincoln in the Telegraph Office,* 172–79; Burlingame and Ettlinger, *Inside Lincoln's White House,* 78–79, 86, 87; Gienapp and Gienapp, *Civil War Diary of Gideon Welles,* 299–300; Nicolay and Hay, *Abraham Lincoln,* 8:112–13; Welles, *Diary of Gideon Welles,* 1:444; Burlingame, *Abraham Lincoln,* 2:556–57; Donald, *Lincoln,* 458; Goodwin, *Team of Rivals,* 557; Marszalek, *Commander of All Lincoln's Armies,* 186; Marvel, *Lincoln's Autocrat,* 301–3; Marvel, *Great Task Remaining,* 198; McPherson, *Tried by War,* 195; White, *A. Lincoln,* 596; Williams, *Lincoln and His Generals,* 283–84. Kenneth Williams examined the situation but said nothing about Lincoln's opposition to sending Hooker to Tennessee. Williams, *Lincoln Finds a General,* 2:763–64. Lincoln may have been mistaken to oppose the transfer effort, but he was not totally wrong about the Army of the Potomac. Maj. Gen. Henry Slocum, who commanded one of the shifting corps, threatened to resign rather than serve under Hooker again. Lincoln asked Rosecrans to swap Slocum's units from Hooker's command for some of his own when the relief force arrived, which he refused to do. See Basler et al., *Collected Works of Abraham Lincoln,* 486.

10. Bates, *Lincoln in the Telegraph Office,* 162–64, 204–5; Burlingame and Ettlinger, *Inside Lincoln's White House,* 86, 94, 98–99, 107–8 (quotation, 99). See also Basler et al., *Collected Works of Abraham Lincoln,* 6:472, 474, 480, 486. 492–93, 498, 499–504, 510–11, 523–24, 543–45, 7:78–79, 84–85; Gienapp and Gienapp, *Civil War Diary of Gideon Welles,* 299–300; Nicolay and Hay, *Abraham Lincoln,* 8:224–29, 471–74; Welles, *Diary of Gideon Welles,* 1:444–45; Burlingame, *Abraham Lincoln,* 2:534–42, 555, 557; Donald, *Lincoln,* 458; Foner, *Fiery Trial,* 278; Goodwin, *Team of Rivals,* 527, 557; Marvel, *Lincoln's Autocrat,* 305–6; McPherson, *Tried by War,* 196–97; Stoker, *Grand Design,* 325–57; White, *A. Lincoln,* 597–98; and Williams, *Lincoln and His Generals,* 284–85.

11. Noe, *Howling Storm,* 336–50; Oates, *With Malice Toward None,* 397–98; Thomas, *Abraham Lincoln,* 403–5; Williams, *Lincoln and His Generals,* 290. On the battles at Chattanooga, see Cozzens, *Shipwreck of Their Hopes;* and Woodworth, *Six Armies.*

12. Basler et al., *Collected Works of Abraham Lincoln,* 6:496–97, 7:17-23, 30–31 (first two quotations, 7:23); Burlingame and Ettlinger, *Inside Lincoln's White House,* 117–18, 327–28n299 (third and fourth quotations, 117). See also Grant, *Memoirs,* 2:98; Stoddard, *Inside the White House,* 189–92; Burlingame, *Abraham Lincoln,* 2:579; Meacham, *And There Was Light,* 317–18; and Stoker, *Grand Design,* 327. Armond S. Goldman and Frank C. Schmalstieg Jr. believe that Lincoln's symptoms suggest a dangerously full-blown case of smallpox, not its milder presentation. Goldman and Schmalstieg, "Abraham Lincoln's Gettysburg Illness."

13. Basler et al., *Collected Works of Abraham Lincoln,* 7:35, 53. See also Simpson, *Ulysses S. Grant,* 243.

14. Burlingame, *With Lincoln in the White House,* 121

15. Donald, *Lincoln,* 489. See also Nicolay and Hay, *Abraham Lincoln,* 6:473–75, 481; Goodwin, *Team of Rivals,* 549–51; McPherson, *Tried by War,* 204–5; and Reynolds, *Abe,* 806–9.

16. Neely, *Last Best Hope,* 75.

17. Basler et al., *Collected Works of Abraham Lincoln,* 7:53–56, 126, 178, 222, 226; Burlingame, *With Lincoln in the White House,* 129; Gienapp and Gienapp, *Civil War Diary of Gideon Welles,* 288–90; Nicolay and Hay, *Abraham Lincoln,* 8:34–35; Welles, *Diary of Gideon Welles,* 1:431–44; Burlingame, *Abraham Lincoln,* 2:532–34; Donald, *Lincoln,* 489–90; Marvel, *Lincoln's Autocrat,* 327–29; Marvel, *Great Task Remaining,* 274–76, 285, 289–93; Marvel, *Tarnished Victory,* 5; Nulty, *Confederate Florida,* 71–218; Sears, *Controversies and Commanders,* 232–48; Symonds, *Lincoln and His Admirals,* 290–92. William Marvel, Stephen Sears, and Eric J. Wittenberg have argued that the Dahlgren papers were real, believing that Stanton—but not Lincoln—was in on the plot. See Marvel, *Great Task Remaining,* 291–93; Sears, *Controversies and Commanders,* 232–48; and Wittenberg, *Like a Meteor Blazing Brightly,* 3–4, 161–247. Marvel's *Confederate Resurgence of 1864* deals specifically with this period of thwarted Federal efforts.

18. Donald, *Lincoln,* 489–90 (quotation, 490).

19. *OR,* 31(2):72–73, 31(3):349–50, 457–58, 32(2):40–42, 99–101, 126–27; Gienapp and Gienapp, *Civil War Diary of Gideon Welles,* 396–97, 404–5; Welles, *Diary of Gideon Welles,* 2:18, 26–27; Glatthaar, *Partners in Command,* 200–201; Johnson, *Red River Campaign,* 42–49; LaFantasie, "Lincoln and the American Military Tradition," 31–32; McPherson, *Tried by War,* 209–11; Noe, *Howling Storm,* 350–58, 375–79; Williams, *Lincoln and His Generals,* 291–94.

20. *OR,* 32(2):40–42, 99–101, 126–27, 411–43, 33:394–95; Burlingame, *Abraham Lincoln,* 2:646; Glatthaar, *Partners in Command,* 201–5; Marszalek, *Commander of All Lincoln's Armies,* 192–94; McPherson, *Tried by War,* 211; Noe, *Howling Storm,* 350–58, 379–96; Simpson, *Ulysses S. Grant,* 249, 251–53; Williams, *Lincoln and His Generals,* 294–96.

21. Glatthaar, *Partners in Command,* 202–3. Supporting this, see Gienapp, *Abraham Lincoln,* 160.

22. Simpson, *Ulysses S. Grant,* 252.

23. Basler et al., *Collected Works of Abraham Lincoln,* 7:234–36, 239–40; Brooks, *Washington in Lincoln's Time,* 139–41, 144–47; Gienapp and Gienapp, *Civil War Diary of Gideon Welles,* 372–73; Grant, *Memoirs,* 2:114–21; Nicolay and Hay, *Abraham Lincoln,* 8:334–36, 340–42; Welles, *Diary of Gideon Welles,* 1:538–39; Burlingame, *Abraham Lincoln,* 2:627–30; Donald, *Lincoln,* 490–97; Glatthaar, *Partners in Command,* 206; Goodwin, *Team of Rivals,* 614–15; Marszalek, *Commander of All Lincoln's Armies,* 197–99; Marszalek, *Lincoln and the Military,* 73; McPherson, *Tried by War,* 211–12; Simpson, *Ulysses S. Grant,* 246–47, 253–72, 275–82;

Stoker, *Grand Design*, 349–51; Taaffe, *Commanding the Army of the Potomac*, 145–46; Williams, *Lincoln and His Generals*, 297–302.

24. Williams, *Lincoln Finds a General*, 2:776.

25. Stoddard, *Inside the White House*, 221.

26. Grant, *Memoirs*, 2:122. See also Stoddard, *Inside the White House*, 221.

27. Grant, *Memoirs*, 2:123. See also McPherson, *Tried by War*, 213; and Simpson, *Ulysses S. Grant*, 272–73.

28. Grant, *Memoirs*, 2:124–40; Nicolay and Hay, *Abraham Lincoln*, 8:347–49; Burlingame, *Abraham Lincoln*, 2:646–47 (quotation, 646); Donald, *Lincoln*, 498; Glatthaar, *Partners in Command*, 206–10; LaFantasie, "Lincoln and the American Military Tradition," 31–32; Oates, *With Malice Toward None*, 417–18; Thomas, *Abraham Lincoln*, 419–20; Williams, *Lincoln and His Generals*, 303–8.

29. Burlingame and Ettlinger, *Inside Lincoln's White House*, 193–94. For Grant's version of Lincoln's response, see Grant, *Memoirs*, 2:142–43. See also Goodwin, *Team of Rivals*, 617–18; McPherson, *Tried by War*, 214; and Stoker, *Grand Design*, 353.

30. Simpson, *Ulysses S. Grant*, 273–91 (quotation, 282). See also Basler et al., *Collected Works of Abraham Lincoln*, 7:248, 272, 324–25; Pease and Randall, *Diary of Orville Hickman Browning*, 668; Nicolay and Hay, *Abraham Lincoln*, 8:335–36, 354–57; Burlingame, *Abraham Lincoln*, 2:647; Donald, *Lincoln*, 498–99; Gienapp, *Abraham Lincoln*, 160–61; Goodwin, *Team of Rivals*, 617–18; and Williams, *Lincoln and His Generals*, 309.

31. Burlingame and Ettlinger, *Inside Lincoln's White House*, 188, 191; McPherson, *Battle Cry of Freedom*, 724–43. On the Overland Campaign, see Gordon C. Rhea's several now-standard works: *Battle of the Wilderness; Battles for Spotsylvania Court House and the Road to Yellow Tavern; To the North Anna River; Cold Harbor; In the Footsteps of Grant and Lee;* and *On to Petersburg*. An excellent recent one-volume survey is Grimsley, *And Keep Moving On*. For Banks' ill-fated Red River Campaign, see Johnson, *Red River Campaign*, 79–276. For the Atlanta Campaign, see Castel, *Decision in the West*.

32. Arnold, *Life of Abraham Lincoln*, 375; Brooks, *Washington in Lincoln's Time*, 148–49; Gienapp and Gienapp, *Civil War Diary of Gideon Welles*, 402–3, 405–6; Keckley, *Behind the Scenes*, 133 (quotation); Sherman, *Memoirs*, 2:109–10; Welles, *Diary of Gideon Welles*, 2:25, 28; Burlingame, *Abraham Lincoln*, 2:648–53; Donald, *Lincoln*, 500–516; Gienapp, *Abraham Lincoln*, 158, 161; Goodwin, *Team of Rivals*, 619–20; Marvel, *Tarnished Victory*, 155; McPherson, *Tried by War*, 218–21; Meacham, *And There Was Light*, 318–19; Oates, *With Malice Toward None*, 418–20; Reynolds, *Abe*, 746–47; Simpson, *Ulysses S. Grant*, 322; Thomas, *Abraham Lincoln*, 420–24; Williams, *Lincoln and His Generals*, 313–18, 334–35.

33. Arnold, *Life of Abraham Lincoln*, 375 (quotation); Rawley, "Isaac Newton Arnold," 39–53; Thomas, *Abraham Lincoln*, 423.

34. Donald, *Lincoln*, 513–15 (quotation, 514). See also Bates, *Lincoln in the Telegraph Office*, 284–86; Gienapp, *Abraham Lincoln*, 164–65; Guelzo, *Abraham Lincoln: Redeemer President;* esp. 311–463; Marvel, *Great Task Remaining*, 198; Marvel, *Lincoln's Darkest Year*, 181–82; and Meacham, *And There Was Light*, 317–18.

35. *OR*, 36(2):627 (quotation); Basler et al., *Collected Works of Abraham Lincoln*, 7:374, 384; Burlingame, *With Lincoln in the White House*, 139, 141; Burlingame and Ettlinger, *Inside Lincoln's White House*, 195, 196, 197, 198; Gienapp and Gienapp, *Civil War Diary of Gideon Welles*,

428, 431; Welles, *Diary of Gideon Welles,* 2:55, 58; Donald, *Lincoln,* 501; Simpson, *Ulysses S. Grant,* 341, 353; Thomas, *Abraham Lincoln,* 432.

36. Brooks, *Washington in Lincoln's Time,* 149.

37. Basler et al., *Collected Works of Abraham Lincoln,* 7:393, 394–95; Donald, *Lincoln,* 513; Marszalek, *Commander of All Lincoln's Armies,* 205–7; Neely, *Last Best Hope,* 84–85; Noe, *Howling Storm,* 414–21; Williams, *Lincoln and His Generals,* 319–20. On the opening weeks of the Petersburg Campaign, see Greene, *Campaign of Giants;* and Sommers, *Richmond Redeemed.*

38. Porter, *Incidents and Anecdotes,* 218. See also Burlingame and Ettlinger, *Inside Lincoln's White House,* 210.

39. Basler et al., *Collected Works of Abraham Lincoln,* 7:448–49, 452; Gienapp and Gienapp, *Civil War Diary of Gideon Welles,* 458–59; Welles, *Diary of Gideon Welles,* 2:90, Noe, *Howling Storm,* 423–26; Simpson, *Ulysses S. Grant,* 351.

40. Basler et al., *Collected Works of Abraham Lincoln,* 7:437–39, 444–45 (quotation, 437); Bates, *Lincoln in the Telegraph Office,* 251–54; Brooks, *Washington in Lincoln's Time,* 177–78; Burlingame and Ettlinger, *Inside Lincoln's White House,* 221–23; Gienapp and Gienapp, *Civil War Diary of Gideon Welles,* 445–46, 448–49, 458, 465–66; Nicolay and Hay, *Abraham Lincoln,* 9:163––75, 179–80; Pease and Randall, *Diary of Orville Hickman Browning,* 676; Welles, *Diary of Gideon Welles,* 2:74, 77–78, 88, 96–97; Burlingame, *Abraham Lincoln,* 2:655–58; Donald, *Lincoln,* 517–21; Glatthaar, *Partners in Command,* 210–16; Goodwin, *Team of Rivals,* 641–44; Marszalek, *Commander of All Lincoln's Armies,* 205–8; Marszalek, *Lincoln and the Military,* 87; Marvel, *Lincoln's Autocrat,* 338–41; McPherson, *Tried by War,* 224–29; Noe, *Howling Storm,* 421–26; Oates, *With Malice Toward None,* 427; Simpson, *Ulysses S. Grant,* 367–69; Taaffe, *Commanding the Army of the Potomac,* 185–86; Thomas, *Abraham Lincoln,* 434, 436; Williams, *Lincoln and His Generals,* 324–33. Sheridan initially would only command the troops in the field, while Hunter retained overall departmental command, but that arrangement soon ended.

41. *OR,* 43(1):917.

42. Nicolay and Hay, *Abraham Lincoln,* 9:180. See also Gienapp and Gienapp, *Civil War Diary of Gideon Welles,* 458; and Welles, *Diary of Gideon Welles,* 2:88.

43. Basler et al., *Collected Works of Abraham Lincoln,* 7:476 (quotation); Grant, *Memoirs,* 2:318; Nicolay and Hay, *Abraham Lincoln,* 9:179.

44. Basler et al., *Collected Works of Abraham Lincoln,* 7:499. See also Marszalek, *Lincoln and the Military,* 88; and Simpson, *Ulysses S. Grant,* 372.

45. Burlingame, *With Lincoln in the White House,* 150.

46. Gienapp, *Abraham Lincoln,* 151–52, 168–71; McPherson, *Tried by War,* 234–36, 238–40; Neely, *Last Best Hope,* 121.

47. Basler et al., *Collected Works of Abraham Lincoln,* 7:514; Burlingame and Ettlinger, *Inside Lincoln's White House,* 247. On Lincoln's mood, see Rable, *Conflict of Command,* 315.

48. McPherson, *Battle Cry of Freedom,* 760–62, 772–76.

49. Carpenter, *Inner Life of Abraham Lincoln,* 143.

50. Burlingame, *With Lincoln in the White House,* 157, 158; Gienapp, *Abraham Lincoln,* 171–72; Goodwin, *Team of Rivals,* 656; McPherson, *Tried by War,* 238, 243–44; Meacham, *And There Was Light,* 339; Sears, *George B. McClellan,* 371–81.

51. Burlingame, *With Lincoln in the White House,* 157, 158.

52. Burlingame, *With Lincoln in the White House,* 161; Nicolay and Hay, *Abraham Lincoln,* 9:298–304; McPherson, *Tried by War,* 244–46; Rable, *Conflict of Command,* 321; Simpson, *Ulysses S. Grant,* 378–81.

53. Basler et al., *Collected Works of Abraham Lincoln,* 7:504–5, 512, 528–29, 8:11, 24, 45, 46, 48–49, 128–30, 153; Bates, *Lincoln in the Telegraph Office,* 276–81; Burlingame and Ettlinger, *Inside Lincoln's White House,* 247; Gienapp and Gienapp, *Civil War Diary of Gideon Welles,* 527–28; Nicolay and Hay, *Abraham Lincoln,* 9:365–66; Welles, *Diary of Gideon Welles,* 2:175; Burlingame, *Abraham Lincoln,* 2:713, 717–18; Gienapp, *Abraham Lincoln,* 172–75; Goodwin, *Team of Rivals,* 663; Marszalek, *Lincoln and the Military,* 88–89; Marvel, *Lincoln's Autocrat,* 353–54; McPherson, *Battle Cry of Freedom,* 803–6; McPherson, *Tried by War,* 249–50; Meacham, *And There Was Light,* 340–43; Noe, *Howling Storm,* 433; Rable, *Conflict of Command,* 330–32; Simpson, *Ulysses S. Grant,* 383, 388–90; Symonds, *Lincoln and His Admirals,* 338; Weigley, *Great Civil War,* 380–81; Williams, "Abraham Lincoln." Delaware, Illinois, Indiana, Massachusetts, New Jersey, and Oregon required soldiers to vote at home. Jonathan W. White maintained that Republican-Union and/or army coercion and fraud before and during 1864 either silenced large numbers of Democrats or forced them to vote instead for Lincoln and his party, in so doing skewing the soldier vote unfairly. See White, "How Lincoln Won the Soldier Vote"; and White, *Emancipation,* esp. 98–128. This argument is also made in Marvel, *Tarnished Victory,* 220–27. Zachary A. Fry has disputed this analysis and downplayed such intimidation. He countered that the Republican vote was a sincere reflection of at least veteran soldiers' ideology in late 1864, as previously molded by politically committed junior officers and, especially, as stimulated more recently by their hatred of Copperheads and the Democratic Party's peace platform. As for intimidation tactics, Fry added that partisans on both sides utilized them. *Fry, Republic in the Ranks,* 8–9, 14, 155, 160–84, 186, 210–25.

54. Brooks, *Washington in Lincoln's Time,* 298–99; Burlingame, *With Lincoln in the White House,* 260, Marszalek, *Lincoln and the Military,* 92–98; Grant, *Memoirs,* 2:366–67; McPherson, *Tried by War,* 250–53; Simpson, *Ulysses S. Grant,* 382–83, 390. On the March to the Sea, see Glatthaar, *March to the Sea and Beyond;* Kennett, *Marching through Georgia;* and Rubin, *Through the Heart of Dixie.*

55. Basler et al., *Collected Works of Abraham Lincoln,* 8:181–82; Nicolay and Hay, *Abraham Lincoln,* 9:494–95; Sherman, *Memoirs,* 2:166–67. See also Gienapp, *Abraham Lincoln,* 178.

56. Sherman, *Memoirs,* 2:166. See also Noe, *Howling Storm,* 474–78.

57. Basler et al., *Collected Works of Abraham Lincoln,* 8:181.

58. *OR,* 45(1):15–16; Basler et al., *Collected Works of Abraham Lincoln,* 8:169; Bates, *Lincoln in the Telegraph Office,* 310–20; Brooks, *Washington in Lincoln's Time,* 293; Marszalek, *Lincoln and the Military,* 95; McDonough, "Commander in Chief and Military Operations in Tennessee," 102–3; McDonough, *Western Confederacy's Final Gamble;* McPherson, *Tried by War,* 250–53; Simpson, *Ulysses S. Grant,* 394; Williams, *Lincoln and His Generals,* 342–47; Sword, *Confederacy's Last Hurrah.*

59. Brooks, *Washington in Lincoln's Time,* 293.

60. Basler et al., *Collected Works of Abraham Lincoln,* 8:187, 207–8, 215; Gienapp and Gienapp, *Civil War Diary of Gideon Welles,* 489–90, 560–61, 562–63; Nicolay and Hay, *Abraham Lincoln,* 10:55–65; Welles, *Diary of Gideon Welles,* 2:127, 210, 213–14; Noe, *Howling Storm,* 473–74;

Simpson, *Ulysses S. Grant,* 400–401; Symonds, *Lincoln and His Admirals,* 188–91; Taaffe, *Commanding the Army of the Potomac,* 168–71, 197–98; Williams, *Lincoln and His Generals,* 349–50.

61. Basler et al., *Collected Works of Abraham Lincoln,* 8:171, 316–17, 320–21; Noe, *Howling Storm,* 426–35, 479–81, 485. See also Greene, *Final Battles of the Petersburg Campaign.*

62. Barnes, "With Lincoln from Washington to Richmond," pt. 1, 515–22; Basler et al., *Collected Works of Abraham Lincoln,* 8:332–33, 367, 369, 372, 373–74, 377; Bates, *Lincoln in the Telegraph Office,* 343–44; marquis de Chambrun, "Personal Recollections of Mr. Lincoln," 27–28; Nicolay and Hay, *Abraham Lincoln,* 10:213–16; Porter, *Incidents and Anecdotes,* 282–88; Burlingame, *Abraham Lincoln,* 2:777–80; Donald, *Lincoln,* 568, 573; Gienapp, *Abraham Lincoln,* 162, 187, 193; Marvel, *Tarnished Victory,* 297–98, 308–10; Meacham, *And There Was Light,* 376–78; Oates, *With Malice Toward None,* 445; Simpson, *Ulysses S. Grant,* 413–16; Vorenberg, *Lincoln's Peace,* 3–9; Williams, *Lincoln and His Generals,* 348–51. Lincoln was never a hearty eater. See Gienapp, *Abraham Lincoln,* 126.

63. Barnes, "With Lincoln from Washington to Richmond," pt. 1, 521–22.

64. Basler et al., *Collected Works of Abraham Lincoln,* 8:250–51, 256, 258, 269, 274–85, 330–31; Gienapp and Gienapp, *Civil War Diary of Gideon Welles,* 583–85; Porter, *Incidents and Anecdotes,* 282–90, 314–17; Sherman, *Memoirs,* 2:324–30, 352–53; Welles, *Diary of Gideon Welles,* 2:235–36; Burlingame, *Abraham Lincoln,* 2:780–88; Donald, *Lincoln,* 559; Marszalek, *Lincoln and the Military,* 101–5; Meacham, *And There Was Light,* 376–81; Neely, *Last Best Hope,* 92; Vorenberg, *Lincoln's Peace,* 9–12; Weigley, *Great Civil War,* 401.

65. Sherman, *Memoirs,* 2:326.

66. Porter, *Incidents and Anecdotes,* 294.

67. Basler et al., *Collected Works of Abraham Lincoln,* 8:378–86, 390; Barnes, "With Lincoln from Washington to Richmond," pt. 2, 745–51; Porter, *Incidents and Anecdotes,* 286–87, 293–304; Burlingame, *Abraham Lincoln,* 2:787–97; Noe, *Howling Storm,* 486–88; Vorenberg, *Lincoln's Peace,* 14–20, 24–29.

68. Basler et al., *Collected Works of Abraham Lincoln,* 8:392.

69. Burlingame, *Abraham Lincoln,* 2:799–806; Donald, *Lincoln,* 580–85, 589–92; Goodwin, *Team of Rivals,* 724–31; Oates, *With Malice Toward None,* 458–63; Thomas, *Abraham Lincoln,* 513–15; Vorenberg, *Lincoln's Peace,* 50–63; White, *A. Lincoln,* 670–72.

70. Gienapp and Gienapp, *Civil War Diary of Gideon Welles,* 623–25; Welles, *Diary of Gideon Welles,* 2:282–83.

71. Burlingame, *Abraham Lincoln,* 2:806–19; Donald, *Lincoln,* 592–96; Goodwin, *Team of Rivals,* 731–45; William Herndon, excerpted interview with Mary Lincoln, in Holzer, *Lincoln as I Knew Him,* 30–33; Oates, *With Malice Toward None,* 463–71; Reynolds, *Abe,* 885–95, 907–15; Thomas, *Abraham Lincoln,* 515–21; White, *A. Lincoln,* 672–75.

72. Much has been written about the assassination and its aftermath, but here I rely on Hodes, *Mourning Lincoln.* See also Peterson, *Lincoln in American Memory,* 3–46, 50–66; Schwartz, *Abraham Lincoln and the Forge,* 23, 26–65; and Zeitz, *Lincoln's God,* 240–48. For context, see also Faust, *This Republic of Suffering,* esp. 156–61. For Lincoln's parallels to Jesus as the son of a carpenter, see Thomas, *Portrait for Posterity,* 3.

73. Hettle, *Inventing Stonewall Jackson,* 4 (quotation), 33, 38–40.

74. Donald, *Lincoln's Herndon,* 167–70, 212–16; Holzer, *Lincoln as I Knew Him,* 2–3 (quotation); Peterson, *Lincoln in American Memory,* 3–34, 66–70; Thomas, *Portrait for Posterity,* 3–7.

75. Thomas, *Portrait for Posterity,* x, 28; Schwartz, *Abraham Lincoln and the Forge,* 71, 147, 256–90.

5. LINCOLN MEN

1. Matthew 13:3–9 (King James Version).

2. Raymond, *Administration of President Lincoln;* Raymond, *Life and Public Services of Abraham Lincoln;* Maverick, *Henry J. Raymond and the New York Press;* Burlingame, *Abraham Lincoln,* 2:144, 288, 340, 342, 674, 668; Donald, *Lincoln,* 347, 504–5, 529, 532; LaFantasie, "Lincoln and the American Military Tradition," 18–19; Gabbard, "Lincoln Through the Eyes of History"; Peterson, *Lincoln in American Memory,* 66–68, 84–85.

3. Carpenter, *Inner Life of Abraham Lincoln;* Carpenter, *Six Months;* Peterson, *Lincoln in American Memory,* 66–68, 84–85 (quotation, 85). Another early biographer, L. P. Brockett, not only drew on Raymond's work for his own military discussion but also included material from Carpenter. See Brockett, *Life and Times of Abraham Lincoln,* esp. 345.

4. Holland, *Life of Abraham Lincoln,* 456, 542. See also Barr, *Loathing Lincoln,* 62–64; Donald, *Lincoln's Herndon,* 167–70, 212–16; Guelzo, "Lincoln and His Biographers," 242–43; Peterson, *Lincoln in American Memory,* 3–34, 66–70; Thomas, *Portrait for Posterity,* 3–7; Zeitz, *Lincoln's Boys,* 234–35; Zeitz, *Lincoln's God,* ix–x.

5. Schwartz, *Abraham Lincoln and the Forge,* 71.

6. Holland, *Life of Abraham Lincoln,* 277–544 (quotations, 383–84, 390, 406, 411); Dirck, "Lincoln as Commander-in-Chief," 22–26.

7. Arnold, *History of Abraham Lincoln,* esp. 173–725 (quotation, 361); Donald, *Lincoln's Herndon,* 239–40; Guelzo, "Lincoln and His Biographers," 242n6; Holzer, *Lincoln President-Elect,* 109; Rawley, "Isaac Newton Arnold," 39–54; Thomas, *Portrait for Posterity,* 91–93.

8. Arnold, *History of Abraham Lincoln,* esp.173–725 (quotations, 326, 685).

9. Donald, "Getting Right with Lincoln," 3–4; Peterson, *Lincoln in American Memory,* 40–47.

10. There is a vast literature on this topic, but for significant examples, see Barr, *Loathing Lincoln,* 8–9, 59–61, 107, 110, 115–17, 131–41, 153–86, 240; Blight, *Race and Reunion,* esp. 64–210, 255–99, 338–80; Gannon, *Won Cause;* Janney, *Remembering the Civil War;* Nolan and Gallagher, *Myth of the Lost Cause;* Peterson, *Lincoln in American Memory,* 46–49; Rubin, *Shattered Nation,* 126–30; Rubin, *Through the Heart of Dixie;* and Schwartz, *Abraham Lincoln and the Forge,* 79–82. For the Lost Cause and deliberate falsehood, see Domby, *False Cause.* For the "battle of the books," see Noe, "'Damned North Carolinians,'" 1089–1115. While weaker today, the Lost Cause's continuing power can be seen in fights over Confederate flag displays and monuments and the Confederate battle flags waved outside and even inside the U.S. Capitol during the insurrection of January 6, 2021.

11. Blight, *Race and Reunion,* 2 (quotation).

12. Blight, *Race and Reunion;* Wilson, *Baptized in Blood.* Gannon, *Won Cause;* and Janney, *Remembering the Civil War.* These authors have essentially argued for acknowledging four postwar interpretations of the era instead of Blight's three while questioning the extent of the reconciliationist vision, an argument I follow here.

13. Adams, *Address of Charles Francis Adams,* 28–33 (quotations, 29, 32, 33); Peterson, *Lincoln in American Memory,* 82–83; Zeitz, *Lincoln's Boys,* 250.

14. Burlingame, *Abraham Lincoln,* 1:229–30, 757–58 (quotation, 230); Donald, "Herndon and Mrs. Lincoln," 37–42; Donald, *Lincoln's Herndon,* esp. 12–14, 18–38, 50–63, 102, 126–57, 153–66, 167–96, 201–3, 212; Donald, *Lincoln,* 100–104, 160; Guelzo, "Lincoln and His Biographers," 243–44; Mearns, "Lincoln Papers," 370; Oates, *With Malice Toward None,* 78–81, 105–7, 111–12, 224; Peterson, *Lincoln in American Memory,* 66–72; Pryor, *Six Encounters,* 239; Reynolds, *Abe,* 161, 202–3, 206, 212, 215–18, 282–83, 508; Thomas, *Abraham Lincoln,* 96–100, 238–39; Thomas, *Portrait for Posterity,* 7–17; Zeitz, *Lincoln's Boys,* 231–38.

15. Carpenter, *Inner Life of Abraham Lincoln,* 323–50; Townsend, *Real Life of Abraham Lincoln;* Barr, *Loathing Lincoln,* 63–72, 71–72; Donald, "Herndon and Mrs. Lincoln," 42–44; Donald, *Lincoln's Herndon,* 184–88, 197–250; Donald, *Lincoln,* 160, 608–9n55; Guelzo, "Lincoln and His Biographers," 244–45; Gabbard, "Lincoln Through the Eyes of History"; Peterson, *Lincoln in American Memory,* 72–77; Pryor, *Six Encounters,* 229–30, 232, 234; Reynolds, *Abe,* 150–51, 156–59, 202–3, 212, 282–83; Schwartz, *Abraham Lincoln and the Forge,* 146–47, 157–58; Simon, "Abraham Lincoln and Ann Rutledge," 13–33; Thomas, *Abraham Lincoln,* 49–51; Thomas, *Portrait for Posterity,* 18–21; Wilson, "Abraham Lincoln, Ann Rutledge, and the Evidence," 301–24; Wilson, "Herndon's Dilemma," 2–9; Wilson, "Herndon and His Lincoln Informants," 15–34.

16. Lamon, *Life of Abraham Lincoln;* Robert T. Lincoln to John G. Nicolay, Jan. 10, 1874, Chicago, John G. Nicolay Papers, Library of Congress (hereafter cited as JGN-LC); Barr, *Loathing Lincoln,* 63–64, 68–71; Donald, *Lincoln's Herndon,* 250–84; Guelzo, "Lincoln and His Biographers," 245–47; Peterson, *Lincoln in American Memory,* 77–81; Thomas, *Portrait for Posterity,* 18–94; Zeitz, *Lincoln's Boys,* 238–50.

17. Thomas, *Portrait for Posterity,* x, 28.

18. John G. Nicolay to Richard Gilder, Dec. 26, 1887, Washington; John G. Nicolay to Robert Lincoln, Jan. 1, 1888, Washington; and clipping, *Philadelphia Public Ledger and Daily Transcript,* Dec.16, 1872, both JGN-LC; Taliaferro, *All the Great Prizes,* 3, 4–7, 86, 89–91, 99, 101–2, 106–263; Peterson, *Lincoln in American Memory,* 118; Temple, *Lincoln's Confidant,* 158–61; Zeitz, *Lincoln's Boys,* 174–227.

19. John G. Nicolay to Robert Lincoln, May 31, 1873, Springfield, IL, JGN-LC. See also Isaac Arnold to John G. Nicolay, Sept. 11, 1874, Chicago, JGN-LC; Taliaferro, *All the Great Prizes,* 105–6, 115, 160, 180–83; Thomas, *Portrait for Posterity,* 94, 98–101; and Zeitz, *Lincoln's Boys,* 247–52, 281.

20. M. Hay to John G. Nicolay, Dec. 24, 1872, Springfield, IL, JGN-LC. See also John G. Nicolay to J. A. Reed, Dec. 24, 1872, Washington, DC, JGN-LC; Holzer, *Lincoln President-Elect,* 116, and Peterson, *Lincoln in American Memory,* 118,

21. John G. Nicolay to Robert T. Lincoln, [Jan. 1874?], n.p., JGN-LC. Lincoln was not convinced at first. See Robert T. Lincoln to John G. Nicolay, July 10, 1874, Chicago; and Nicolay to Lincoln, July 17, 1874, Bethlehem, NH, JGN-LC. See also Peterson, *Lincoln in American Memory,* 82–83, 122–23; Taliaferro, *All the Great Prizes,* 3, 39–40.

22. John G. Nicolay to Robert T. Lincoln, Mar. 3, 1874, Washington, DC, JGN-LC.

23. John G. Nicolay to Robert T. Lincoln, July 17, 1874, Bethlehem, NH, JGN-LC.

24. M. Hay to John G. Nicolay, Dec. 24, 1872, Springfield, IL; and John G. Nicolay to Robert Lincoln, July 17, 1874, Bethlehem, NH, both JGN-LC; Mearns, "Lincoln Papers," 373; Thomas, *Portrait for Posterity,* 98–101; Zeitz, *Lincoln's Boys,* 247–52.

25. Isaac Arnold to John G. Nicolay, Sept. 11, 1874, Chicago; John G. Nicolay to Isaac Arnold, Sept. 17, 1874, Bethlehem, NH; Isaac Arnold to John G. Nicolay, Nov. 16, 1874, Chicago; John G. Nicolay to John Hay, Nov. 16, 1875, Washington; Isaac Arnold to John G. Nicolay, Nov. 16, 1874, Chicago; Isaac Arnold to Robert Lincoln, Oct. 13, 1882, Chicago; Robert Lincoln to John G. Nicolay, Oct. 16, 1882, Chicago; John G. Nicolay to John Hay, Aug. 7, 1885, Bethel, VT; Roswell Smith to John Hay and John G. Nicolay, Jan. 19, 1889, New York; and John G. Nicolay to Roswell Smith, Jan. 22, 1889, Washington (quotation), all JGN-LC; Burlingame, "Nicolay and Hay," 18–20; Taliaferro, *All the Great Prizes,* 36, 235; Thomas, *Portrait for Posterity,* 98–103; Zeitz, *Lincoln's Boys,* 252–62, 266–67.

26. Nicolay, *Outbreak of the Rebellion,* 206; John G. Nicolay to John Hay, Nov. 11, 1876, Washington; E. L. Burlingame to John G. Nicolay, July 17, 1880, New York; John Nicolay to E. L. Burlingame, Aug. 2, 1880, Greenland, NH; E. L. Burlingame to John Nicolay, Aug. 13, 1880, New York; John G. Nicolay to E. L. Burlingame, Mar. 1, 1864, Washington; Edward L. Burlingame to John G. Nicolay, Mar. 4, 1881, New York; John G. Nicolay to Charles Scribner's Sons, Mar. 15, 1881, Washington; John G. Nicolay to E. L. Burlingame, Nov. 4, 1881, Washington; and E. L. Burlingame to John G. Nicolay, Nov. 9, 1881, New York, all JGN-LC; Taliaferro, *All the Great Prizes,* 213–22, 224–32; Zeitz, *Lincoln's Boys,* 286–87. After Therena Nicolay's sudden death in November 1885—she was only forty-nine years old—her widower wrote Hay that her contributions were to be found all through the manuscript. See John G. Nicolay to John Hay, Nov. 25, 1885, Washington, JGN-LC.

27. G. V. Fox to John G. Nicolay, n.d., Washington [?]; and D. Hunter to John G. Nicolay, Oct. 31, 1881, Washington, both JGN-LC (quotation).

28. W. T. Sherman to John G. Nicolay, Feb. 4, Mar. 24, 1882, Washington; and W. T. Sherman to John G. Nicolay, Apr. 2, 1882, Fort Grant, AZ, all JGN-LC. Several additional letters in the collection over the next few months contained nothing but praise.

29. "American Literature," 838. For more on Beresford Hope, see Turner, *Stonewall Jackson.*

30. John Hay to John G. Nicolay, Aug. 10, 1885, Cleveland, OH, Box 4, John Hay Collection, John Hay Library, Brown University Library (hereafter cited as JH-BU, all items from Box 4). "Lincoln men" is also quoted without attribution in Thomas, *Portrait for Posterity,* 104. See also Zeitz, *Lincoln's Boys,* 257–60.

31. Mearns, "Lincoln Papers," 374–76 (quotation, 374). Mearns, who supervised the collection's opening in 1947, argued that it was possible but unlikely that Robert Lincoln purged any material before sending the boxes to Nicolay, aside from a few items he gave away as keepsakes.

32. John G. Nicolay to Robert Lincoln, July 17, 1874, Bethlehem, NH, JGN-LC. See also Zeitz, *Lincoln's Boys,* 254–57.

33. John G. Nicolay to Robert Lincoln, July 17, 1874, Bethlehem, NH; John G. Nicolay to Robert Lincoln, Feb. 17, 1875, Washington; Robert Lincoln to John G. Nicolay, Feb. 20, 1875, Chicago; Robert Lincoln to John G. Nicolay, June 14, 1878, Chicago; John G. Nicolay to Robert Lincoln, June 25, 1878, Burlington, KS; and John G. Nicolay to Robert Lincoln, Sept. 5, 1881, Colorado Springs, CO, all JGN-LC; Burlingame, "Nicolay and Hay," 6–11; Taliaferro, *All the Great Prizes,* 18–19, 207–8, 245–46; Thomas, *Portrait for Posterity,* 98, 110–19; Zeitz, *Lincoln's Boys,* 252–60.

34. John Hay to John G. Nicolay, Aug. 10, 1885, Cleveland, OH, JH-BU; Taliaferro, *All the Great Prizes,* 162–63, 169, 178–80, 183, 232–33, 243–45; Thomas, *Portrait for Posterity,* 98–103;

Zeitz, *Lincoln's Boys,* 252–62, 266–67. Taliaferro maintained that Hay also returned to Washington to live next door to friend Adams while they both pursued their clandestine infatuations with neighbor Lizzie Sherman Cameron, General Sherman's niece and former Secretary of War Simon Cameron's daughter-in-law.

35. Arnold, *Life of Abraham Lincoln.* For Arnold on the military situation, see esp. 4, 203–4, 232–30, 237–305, 313, 369–84. See also Rawley, "Isaac Newton Arnold," 54–56.

36. Burlingame, *Abraham Lincoln,* 2:70–71, 73; Holzer, *Lincoln's White House Secretary,* 2–9, 11–13; Taliaferro, *All the Great Prizes,* 46, 52. 53, 61, 94, 237, 336.

37. Stoddard, *Abraham Lincoln,* esp. 3–4, 216, 223–226, 232, 237, 245–46, 257, 268, 271–74, 284, 285 (quotations, 4, 225–26, 232, 245). "Dictator" as a full word or root word appears on 9, 222, 225, 226, 238, 257, 276, 289, 290, 294, 308, 329, 330, 331, 386, 418, as well as in the title of chapter 37. Fords, Howard, and Hulbert reissued the book in 1888 as *Abraham Lincoln: The Man and the War President* as part of the series Red Letter Life of the Republic. See also Holzer, *Lincoln's White House Secretary,* 12–13; and Schwartz, *Abraham Lincoln and the Forge,* 71.

38. Stoddard, *Abraham Lincoln,* esp. 291, 294, 315, 325–26, 356–57, 408 (quotations, 291–92, 356).

39. Brooks, *Washington in Lincoln's Time,* 2; Burlingame, *Lincoln Observed,* 1–11; Taliaferro, *All the Great Prizes,* 99; Temple, *Lincoln's Confidant,* esp. xiii–xiv, 7–9, 46–49, 56–69, 74–79, 119–22, 136–38; Zeitz, *Lincoln's Boys,* 2, 90, 161–64, 194, 255, 305 (quotation, 161).

40. Noah Brooks, *Abraham Lincoln: A History for Young People* (New York: G. T. Putnam's Sons, 1888), republished as Brooks, *Abraham Lincoln and the Downfall of American Slavery,* esp. vii–viii, 255–58, 270–71, 285, 290, 293–321, 325–27, 331–32, 337, 347–48, 365–66 (quotations, 320, 321, 326–27). Page numbers refer to the republished edition. G. T. Putnam's Sons reissued and retitled Brooks's work yet again in 1909 as *Abraham Lincoln: The Nation's Leader in the Great Struggle Through Which Was Maintained the Existence of the United States* (New York: G. T. Putnam's Sons, [1909]). See also Temple, *Lincoln's Confidant,* 141–82, 199–200, 203–5.

41. John G. Hay to John Nicolay, July 14, 1888, Colorado Springs, CO, JH-BU. See also Burlingame, *Lincoln Observed,* 12.

42. John Hay to John G. Nicolay, Mar. 2, 1885, Cleveland, OH, JH-BU. See also Zeitz, *Lincoln's Boys,* 271; and Taliaferro, *All the Great Prizes,* 237.

43. John G. Nicolay to Robert Underwood Johnson, Mar. 21, 1882, Washington; R.U.J. [Robert Underwood Johnson] to John G. Nicolay, Mar. 22, 1882, New York; John G. Nicolay to Robert Underwood Johnson, Mar. 25, 1882, Washington; and R.U.J. to John G. Nicolay, June 30, July 6, 22, 1882, New York, all JGN-LC; Blight, *Race and Reunion,* 164, 173–84, 216–17, 242–43, 294–95, 431n10; Janney, *Remembering the Civil War,* 165–66, 203, 204–5; Johnson and Buel, *Battles and Leaders;* Schwartz, *Abraham Lincoln and the Forge,* 136; Taliaferro, *All the Great Prizes,* 232–33, 235–39, 243–45, 249–51; Zeitz, *Lincoln's Boys,* 267–70. Another divisive topic that *Century* ignored until after 1890 was Civil War prison camps. See Blight, *Race and Reunion,* 183–84.

44. Roswell Smith to John Hay, Mar. 19, 1885, New York, JGN-LC. See also Roswell Smith to John Hay, Mar. 19 (second letter of that date), Mar. 20, 1885, New York, JGN-LC; and Thomas, *Portrait for Posterity,* 103.

45. John G. Nicolay to John Hay, Mar. 26, 1885, Washington; Roswell Smith to John Hay, Mar. 27, 30, 1885, New York; Richard Gilder to John G. Nicolay, June 12, 1885, New York; Ros-

well Smith to John Hay, June 13, 1885, New York; John G. Nicolay to Roswell Smith, June 20, 1885, Washington; Richard Gilder to John G. Nicolay, July 8, 1885, Marion, MA; John G. Nicolay to Richard Gilder, July 4, 1885, Bethel, VT (two letters); Richard Gilder to John G. Nicolay, July 29, 1885, Marion, MA; John G. Nicolay to John Hay, July 19, 1885, Washington; John G. Nicolay to Richard Gilder, Aug. 5, 1885, Bethel, VT; Roswell Smith to John G. Nicolay, Oct. 1, 1885, New York; John G. Nicolay to Roswell Smith, Oct. 14, 1885, Washington; Frank H. Scott to John G. Nicolay, Oct. 15, 1885, Boston; Frank Scott to John G. Nicolay, Oct. 20, 1885, New York; Roswell Smith to John G. Nicolay, Oct. 22, 1885, New York; Roswell Smith to John Hay, Oct. 22, 1885, New York; John G. Nicolay to Roswell Smith, Oct. 24, 1885, Washington; Roswell Smith to John G. Nicolay, Oct. 26, 1885, New York; Roswell Smith to John G. Nicolay, Mar. 26, 1888, New York; and Roswell Smith to John Hay, Dec. 30, 1885, New York, all JGN-LC; Peterson, *Lincoln in American Memory,* 118–20; Zeitz, *Lincoln's Boys,* 270–72.

46. Richard Gilder to John G. Nicolay, Aug. 1, 1885, Marion, MA (quotation); John G. Nicolay to Richard Gilder, Aug. 5, 1885, Bethel, VT; John G. Nicolay, Bethel, VT, to John Hay, Aug. 7, 1885, Bethel, VT; Richard Gilder to John G. Nicolay, Aug.11, 1885, n.p.; John G. Nicolay to Richard Gilder, Aug. 13, 1885, Bethel, VT; Richard Gilder to John G. Nicolay, Nov. 2, 1885, New York; John G. Nicolay to Richard Gilder, Nov. 13, 1885, Washington; Roswell Smith to John G. Nicolay, Dec. 3, 1885, New York; Richard Gilder to John G. Nicolay, Dec. 11, 1885, New York; Richard Gilder to John G. Nicolay, Dec. 29, 1885, New York; Richard Gilder to John G. Nicolay, May 26, 1887, New York; John G. Nicolay to Robert Underwood Johnson, May 30, 1887, Washington; and Richard Gilder to John G. Nicolay, July 12, 1888, New York, all JGN-LC; John Hay to John G. Nicolay, Aug. 10, 1885, Cleveland, OH, JH-BU; Peterson, *Lincoln in American Memory,* 1118–20; Taliaferro, *All the Great Prizes,* 37–38, 192–94, 249–51, 257–58, 261–63; Thomas, *Portrait for Posterity,* 106–10; Zeitz, *Lincoln's Boys,* 272–77, 286–94.

47. Richard Gilder to John G. Nicolay, July 12, 1888, New York, JGN-LC. See also Richard Gilder to John G. Nicolay, Aug. 28, 1889, New York, JGN-LC; and Thomas, *Portrait for Posterity,* 107–10.

48. John G. Nicolay to Robert Underwood Johnson, May 30, 1887, Washington, JGN-LC. See also John G. Nicolay to Richard Gilder, June 7, 1887, Washington; and John G. Nicolay to Richard Gilder, Oct. 9, 1887, Washington, both JGN-LC.

49. Taliaferro, *All the Great Prizes,* 249–51; Thomas, *Portrait for Posterity,* 107–10.

50. Roswell Smith to John G. Nicolay, Mar. 27, 1886, New York; W. H. Herndon to John G. Nicolay, Oct. 8, 1886, Springfield, IL; Richard Gilder to John G. Nicolay, Jan. 15, 1887; Richard Gilder to John G. Nicolay, Jan. 18, 1887, New York; J. A. Mitchell to Richard Gilder, Mar. 28, 1888, [New York?]; Richard Gilder to J. A. Mitchell, Mar. 30, 1887, New York; Richard Gilder to John G. Nicolay, Mar. 30, 1887, New York; John G. Nicolay to Richard Gilder, Apr. 24, 1887, Washington; John G. Nicolay to Richard Gilder, Nov. 6, 1887, Washington; Richard Gilder to John G. Nicolay, June 16, 1888, New York; Fitz John Porter to John G. Nicolay and John G. Hay, Nov. 14, 1889, New York; and Richard Gilder to My Dear Authors, Jan. 2, 1890, New York, all JGN-LC; Burlingame, "Nicolay and Hay," 1–2; Taliaferro, *All the Great Prizes,* 249–51; Thomas, *Portrait for Posterity,* 103, 120–31; Zeitz, *Lincoln's Boys,* 278–80, 301–3, 307–8. The *Century* editors generally advised the offended to write letters to the editor, as it was too late to amend published articles. See, for example, Richard Gilder to John G. Nicolay, June 3, 1887, New York; and Richard Gilder to Samuel D. Lecompte, June 7, 1887, New York, both JGN-LC.

51. Richard Gilder to John G. Nicolay, Jan. 18, 1887, New York, JGN-LC. See also A. N. Drake to John G. Nicolay, Apr. 11, 1887, New York; and John G. Nicolay to Richard Gilder, Mar. 30, 1888, n.p., both JGN-LC.

52. Unsent letter, John G. Nicolay to Richard Gilder, Jan. 8, 1890, Washington, JGN-LC. See also Richard Gilder to My Dear Authors, Jan. 2, 1890, New York; and John G. Nicolay to Richard Gilder, Jan. 24, 1890, Washington, both JGN-LC. Nicolay repeated the first paragraph of his unsent letter in his letter of January 24, but he omitted the rest. See also Burlingame, "Nicolay and Hay," 3–4; and Peterson, *Lincoln in American Memory,* 120–21.

53. Robert Lincoln to John G. Nicolay, Dec. 6, 1890, Chicago, JGN-LC. See also John G. Nicolay to Richard Gilder, Apr.12, 1888, Washington; Frank Scott to John G. Nicolay, May 7, 1888, New York; John G. Nicolay to Richard Gilder, July 18, 1890, Washington; John G. Nicolay to William Dean Howells, Jan. 25, 1891, Washington; John Work to John G. Nicolay, July 10, 1891, Chicago; Parker Mann to John G. Nicolay, July 11, 1891, East Gloucester, MA; Bye and Co., Philadelphia, to John G. Nicolay, July 10, 1891; John Hay to John G. Nicolay, July 1891, Cleveland; and O. M. Hatch to John G. Nicolay, Aug. 13, 1891, Springfield, IL, all JGN-LC. The two July 1891 files in the Nicolay Papers contains many clippings about the affair that Nicolay amassed. See, for example, clipping, *Bangor (ME) Weekly Courier,* July 10, 1891; clipping, *The Independent,* July 16, 1891; clipping, *New York Herald,* July 10, 19, 1891; clipping, *Northwest News* (Grand Forks, ND), July 11, 1891; clippings, *Evening Star* (Washington, DC), July 7, 9, 17, 1891; and clippings, *Washington Post,* July 9, 11, 12, 13, 14, 16, 1891, all JGN-LC. Many of the letters in the collection from July 1891 also deal with the McClure controversy. As for prominent reviews, see the *Athanaeum* 97 (Apr. 11, 1891): 468–70; Bancroft, "Lincoln and Seward," 711–24; "Editor's Study," 481–82; "Nicolay and Hay's Lincoln—1," 13–14; and Schurz, "Abraham Lincoln," 721–50. See also Burlingame, "Nicolay and Hay," 1–4, 14–15; Peterson, *Lincoln in American Memory,* 86, 95–96, 126–27; Thomas, *Portrait for Posterity,* 125–31; and Zeitz, *Lincoln's Boys,* 301–4.

54. John Hay to John G. Nicolay, July 25, 1891, Cleveland, OH, JGN-LC.

55. Zeitz, *Lincoln's Boys,* 279. See also Peterson, *Lincoln in American Memory,* 125–26; and Thomas, *Portrait for Posterity,* 128–30.

56. Nicolay and Hay, *Abraham Lincoln,* 1:ix–x; Schwartz, *Abraham Lincoln and the Forge,* 71.

57. Nicolay and Hay, *Abraham Lincoln,* 3:321–23, 375–95, 434–41, 445–49, 4:5–7, 33–34, 44–45, 64, 72–77, 321–23, 352–56, 358–59, 367–68, 5:149–77, 403–5, 6:113–14 (quotations, 4:321, 367, 5:148, 174, 403, 6:114).

58. Nicolay and Hay, *Abraham Lincoln,* 5:99–103, 107 (quotation).

59. Nicolay and Hay, *Abraham Lincoln,* 4:412–38, 5:65–70, 99–108, 403–9, 6:279–81 (quotation, 4:412); Thomas, *Portrait for Posterity,* 101–6.

60. Nicolay and Hay, *Abraham Lincoln,* 8:335. See also ibid., 5:339–41, 352, 6:1–4, 19–27, 197–200, 215–17, 8:63–67, 164–65, 234–36.

61. Nicolay and Hay, *Abraham Lincoln,* 6:197–220, 7:74–76, 90–92, 197–281, 8:43–50, 63–67, 108, 112–15 (quotations, 6:220, 7:210).

62. Roswell Smith to John G. Nicolay, Mar. 26, 1888, New York, JGN-LC; Blight, *Race and Reunion,* 212–16 (quotation, 212); Waugh, *U. S. Grant,* 168–82.

63. Grant, *Personal Memoirs,* 2:489–90 (quotation, 489).

64. Grant, *Personal Memoirs,* 1:215, 430–33, 446–47, 459–60, 2:121–23, 132, 142–43, 332–33, 375, 423, 459, 508–10 (quotations, 1:430, 2:143, 509).

65. Nicolay and Hay, *Abraham Lincoln,* 7:135–44, 153–54, 8:334–42, 347–56, 9:163–79, 298, 10:196.

66. Comte de Paris, *Histoire de la Guerre Civile en Amérique;* comte de Paris, *History of the Civil War in America,* 1:164, 214–15, 259–64, 270, 396, 405, 417, 431–33, 572–75, 611–13, 615–17, 626–28, 2:7–9, 11–12, 33–35, 44–45, 73, 68–81, 83, 105–7, 112, 241–43, 251, 263, 294, 305, 353, 445, 540–41, 549, 558, 601 (quotations, 1:573, 616, 2:105). See also (unattributed) review of *History of the Civil War in America,* 41–54; "Reviews: Military Literature of the Civil War," 290–91; "Scenes from the Peninsula Campaign," 38–43; Sears, *George B. McClellan,* 115–16; and Thomas, *Portrait for Posterity,* 104–5.

67. Peterson, *Lincoln in American Memory,* 123–24; Thomas, *Portrait for Posterity,* 101–2, 104.

68. Ropes, *Army Under Pope,* esp. 1–18, 88–101, 122–28, 154–71 (quotation, 163–64). For Ropes, see Fiske, "John Codman Ropes," 629–34; May, *Memoir of the Life of John Codman Ropes;* and Reardon, *Soldiers and Scholars,* 27–28.

69. McClellan, *McClellan's Own Story.* See also Burlingame and Ettlinger, *Inside Lincoln's White House,* 32–33, 35–39, 40–41, 59, 62, 214, 230–32; Rable, *Conflict of Command,* 1–2; Sears, "Curious Case," 101–14; Sears, *George B. McClellan,* 393–94, 398–401; Taliaferro, *All the Great Prizes,* 49–50, 56, 90–91, 238; and Thomas, *Portrait for Posterity,* 104–5.

70. Kelley, *Lincoln and Stanton* (quotations, 1, 2, 28); Brockett, *Men of Our Day,* 466–74. Yael Sternhell has discussed the complicated history of the *War of the Rebellion*—the familiar *Official Records* or "*OR.*" See *War on Record,* esp. 8–9, 120–21, 152–55, 178–84, 214–17.

71. [Ropes], "General McClellan," 546–59 (quotation, 554); Sears, "Curious Case," 102–3.

72. Piatt, *Memories,* esp. v–vi, xviii, 28–32, 43–46; Bridges, *Donn Piatt;* Burlingame, *Abraham Lincoln,* 2:566–67; Miller, *Donn Piatt,* esp. 93, 131, 135–41, 162–67, 306–13; Thomas *Portrait for Posterity,* 45–46.

73. Piatt, *Memories,* 280–81.

74. John Hay to John G. Nicolay, Aug. 10, 1885, Cleveland, OH, JH-BU. With small differences, this letter is quoted as well in Taliaferro, *All the Great Prizes,* 238; Thomas, *Portrait for Posterity,* 104; and Zeitz, *Lincoln's Boys,* 296. See also Taliaferro, *All the Great Prizes,* 50. "Mugwumps" were anticorruption Republicans who supported Democratic presidential candidate Grover Cleveland in 1884 rather than GOP nominee James G. Blaine.

75. Nicolay and Hay, *Abraham Lincoln,* 4:281–98, 327–40, 440–70, 5:99, 148–84, 358–460, 6:1–29, 131–47, 173–94 (quotations, 4:445, 446, 5:164, 171, 174, 177, 443, 6:188).

76. Zeitz, *Lincoln's Boys,* 277, 280, 316. The Burns quotation is found on the cover of the paperback edition of Zeitz.

77. Herndon and Weik, *Herndon's Lincoln,* 3:498–520, 539–81; Herndon and Weik, *Abraham Lincoln,* 2:249–91; Donald, *Lincoln's Herndon,* 296–363; Hill, "Henry Clay Whitney," 177–84; Peterson, *Lincoln in American Memory,* 127–35; Thomas, *Portrait for Posterity,* 131–77; Zeitz, *Lincoln's Boys,* 303. Whitney went on to produce two published works about Lincoln: a rambling reminiscence entitled *Life on the Circuit with Lincoln, with Reminiscences of Generals Grant, Sherman, and McClellan, Judge Davis, Leonard Swett, and Other Contemporaries* (Boston: Estes and Lauriat, 1892), which includes a harsh depiction of McClellan (see 296–316), and a posthumous two-volume *Life of Lincoln,* edited by Marion Mills Miller (New York: Baker & Taylor, 1908).

78. Piatt, *Memories,* v–vii.

79. Piatt, *Memories,* v–vi, xviii–xviii, xx–xxiv, 28–41, 50–94, 172–279 (quotations, xviii, xxii, xxiii, 30, 33, 37, 39, 41, 75, 93).

80. Peterson, *Lincoln in American Memory,* 86–97.

81. Oldroyd, *Lincoln Memorial* (quotation, 239). See also Peterson, *Lincoln in American Memory,* 86, 144–45. For more on the "gentle legend," see Peterson, *Lincoln in American Memory,* 103–9; and Schwartz, *Abraham Lincoln and the Forge,* 176–80.

82. Rice, *Reminiscences of Abraham Lincoln,* esp. 52–56, 327–29, 396–400, 579–80 (quotations, xvii, xli); Peterson, *Lincoln in American Memory,* 86–87.

83. Rice, *Reminiscences of Abraham Lincoln,* esp. 1–4, 52, 56, 73–75, 128–29, 139–54, 187, 242–44, 276–78, 337–39, 342–45, 352–61, 391–400, 450, 477–500, 501–9. Merrill Peterson describes Butler's entry as "patently self-serving." Peterson, *Lincoln in American Memory,* 92.

84. Stoddard, *Inside the White House,* esp. 15–19, 25, 26, 39–47, 105 (quotation), 111–19, 151, 124–27, 159–63, 178–79, 220–22. Four years later Stoddard followed up with *The Table Talk of Abraham Lincoln,* a collection of excerpts from letters and speeches. He asserted that Lincoln was the first true "general in chief" since George Washington, "supervising, if need should be, his subordinate generals," but otherwise steered clear of warmaking. *Table Talk of Abraham Lincoln,* 89. Henry Clay Whitney dismissed the book as a "most vapid thing . . . a cancer among letters." Quoted without attribution in Thomas, *Portrait for Posterity,* 174. John Hoffman has identified the quote's source in his yet-to-be published annotated edition of *Portrait to Posterity* as a postcard from Whitney to Jesse Weik dated November 5, 1895. Hoffman, email message to author, Feb. 20, 2025. Stoddard eventually rounded out his Lincolniana in 1905 with *The Boy Lincoln.*

85. Chittenden, *Recollections of President Lincoln,* esp. 72–78, 10–14, 153–57, 212–14, 265–83, 316, 366–69, 415–19, 442, 446–51, 453 (quotation, 155).

86. Marquis de Chambrun, "Personal Recollections of Mr. Lincoln," 26–31, 34–38 (quotation, 28).

87. McClure, *Abraham Lincoln and Men of War-Times,* 3, 180. A. C. Lambdin, who wrote the introduction to McClure's book, made his views of Nicolay and Hay clear as well: "With the exception of Mr. Blaine's delightful narrative of *Twenty Years in Congress* . . . we have nothing relating to this period that approaches to the dignity of history. The *Life of Lincoln* by Nicolay and Hay is an admirable compilation of the political records of the time, and its narrative of public events is invaluable. But as an actual biography of Lincoln it is unsatisfactory, and as a comprehensive view of the great forces for which Lincoln stood it is lacking in proportion as in insight." Ibid., 10. See also Peterson, *Lincoln in American Memory,* 95–97.

88. Brooks, *Washington in Lincoln's Time,* esp. 15–16, 32, 36–37, 45–59, 94–96, 134–41, 144–47, 177–78, 425. See also "Minor Notices," 372–77; Peterson, *Lincoln in American Memory,* 86, 94–95; and Temple, *Lincoln's Confidant,* 204–8.

89. Brooks, *Washington in Lincoln's Time,* 36–37, 177.

90. Bates, *Lincoln in the Telegraph Office,* 6–10, 40–44, 91–123, 138–53, 156–71, 175–76, 183–216, 218–24, 248–49, 252, 56, 277–82.

91. Dodge, *Personal Recollections,* 1–31 (quotation, 30).

92. Doster, *Lincoln and Episodes of the Civil War,* 1–45 (quotations, 2, 12–13).

93. Welles, *Lincoln and Seward,* iii, iv, 55, 214. See also John G. Nicolay to Robert T. Lincoln, [Jan. 1874?], n.p.; John G. Nicolay to Robert T. Lincoln, Mar. 3, 1874, Washington; and

Robert T. Lincoln to John G. Nicolay, July 10, 1874, Chicago, all JGN-LC; and Niven, *Gideon Welles,* 570–77.

94. Welles, *Diary of Gideon Welles,* 1:i–liii, 1–71, 83–84, 126, 134–37 (quotations, vi, 3). See also Bancroft, "Gideon Welles and His Diary," 598; Beale, "Is the Printer Diary of Gideon Welles Reliable?," 547–52; Dunning, "Diary of Gideon Welles," 109–24; Gallagher, "Father Neptune's War," 18–20; Gienapp and Gienapp, *Civil War Diary of Gideon Welles,* xvii–xxii; Henry Barrett Learned, letter to the editor, *The Nation,* May 12, 1910, 480; Niven, *Gideon Welles,* 396–402; Thomas, *Portrait for Posterity,* 110.

95. Welles, *Diary of Gideon Welles,* esp. 1:112, 121–26, 131–36, 150–51, 163–65, 179–80, 217, 229, 236–40, 265, 273–87, 312–20, 341, 363, 373, 383, 439–40, 2:9–10, 55, 69–70, 91–93, 127, 130, 160–61, 167, 269 (quotations, 1:131, 135, 265, 364); Niven, *Gideon Welles,* 577–80.

96. Bancroft, "Gideon Welles and His Diary," 598–601 (quotations, 599, 600).

6. ABRAHAM LINCOLN WALKS AT MIDNIGHT

1. Ropes, *Story of the Civil War,* pt. 1; Ropes, *Story of the Civil War,* pt. 2, esp. 384–85.

2. Ropes, *Story of the Civil War,* pt. 1, esp. 11, 74, 80, 91, 107, 111, 163–68, 180, 193–94, 219–20, 234–56, 262–65n4, 265–72n5 (quotations, 91, 226, 235, 236); Ropes, *Story of the Civil War,* pt. 2, 6, 116 (quotation), 420–21.

3. Ropes, *Story of the Civil War,* pt. 2, 103, 132–33.

4. Ropes, *Story of the Civil War,* pt. 2, 116, 127–28, 220–21, 227, 234, 420–21, 442.

5. Livermore, *Story of the Civil War,* pt. 3, esp. 1:iii–iv, 70–71, 110–12, 200, 2:352–59; Reardon, *Soldiers and Scholars,* 43, 160.

6. Greene, "Lincoln as Commander-in-Chief," 104–15 (quotations, 107, 111, 115). See also Greene, *The Mississippi.* On the wider trends, see Reardon, *Soldiers and Scholars.* Reardon praised Greene's work on the Russo-Turkish War of 1877–78 and added that War College students often "criticized governmental policies in their proper historical contexts." Ibid., 94, 131 (quotation).

7. "Contributors of Historical Papers," 104; Conant, *Colonel Arthur L. Conger;* Reardon, *Soldiers and Scholars,* 14–15, 34–35, 66, 68–78, 82–83, 126–27, 145, 168, 172, 175–81, 186–87, 196–97, 206; Vestal, "First Wartime Water Torture by Americans," 36–37, 46–47. Drawing from Buddhism and Hinduism as well as the ancient Western past, theosophy is a philosophical and religious movement that emerged in 1875 through the Russian émigré Helena Blavatsky; see "Theosophy."

8. Reardon, *Soldiers and Scholars,* 69.

9. "Contributors of Historical Papers," 104. Carol Reardon pointed out that Conger spoke frequently at meetings of civilian historical associations, including the American Historical Association, and taught a summer seminar on military history at Harvard University. Reardon, *Soldiers and Scholars,* 168, 172, 186–87, 196–97.

10. Conger, "President Lincoln as War Statesman," 106–40 (quotation, 106–7).

11. Conger, "President Lincoln as War Statesman," 106–40 (quotations, 111, 114).

12. Conger, "President Lincoln as War Statesman," 106–40 (quotation, 128).

13. Quaife, review of *The Military Genius of Abraham Lincoln,* 412. Conger retired as a colonel the next year, 1928, and devoted the rest of his life to the American Theosophical Society.

14. Brady, *Ida Tarbell,* 22–24, 95–106, 120–33, 135–49, 152–53, 235–36, 241–42; Gorton, *Citizen Reporters,* 3–4, 7, 17–32, 76, 79–89, 113–18, 177–86, 210; Guelzo, "Lincoln and His Biographers," 252–54; Rice, "Ida M. Tarbell," 57–72; Schwartz, *Abraham Lincoln and the Forge,* 158–60; Thomas, *Portrait for Posterity,* 178–85; Zeitz, *Lincoln's Boys,* 305–6.

15. Rice, "Ida M. Tarbell," 61–64, 68–72; Schwartz, *Abraham Lincoln in the Post-Heroic Era,* 21; Thomas, *Portrait for Posterity,* 178–202 (quotation, 178).

16. Tarbell, *Life of Abraham Lincoln,* 1:396–97, 2:16–17, 39–58, 69–72, 83–87, 90–110, 127–29, 131–32, 135, 142–69 (quotations, 2:50, 83, 105). An appendix of documents makes up the second half of Tarbell's volume 2.

17. Dana, *Recollections of the Civil War,* 181; Holzer, *Lincoln as I Knew Him,* 149. Writing for Dana, Tarbell said in full:

> Another interesting fact about Abraham Lincoln is that he developed into a great military man; that is to say, a man of supreme military judgment. I do not risk anything in saying that if one will study the records of the war and study the writings relating to it, he will agree with me that the greatest general we had, greater than Grant or Thomas, was Abraham Lincoln. It was not so at the beginning; but after three or four years of constant practice in the science and art of war, he arrived at this extraordinary knowledge of it, so that Von Moltke was not a better general, or an abler planner or expounder of a campaign, than was President Lincoln.

18. McPherson, "Long-Legged Yankee Lies," 103.

19. Rhodes, *History of the Civil War, 1861–1865;* Rhodes, *History of the United States,* vols. 3–5; Blight, *Race and Reunion,* 357–59; Cruden, *James Ford Rhodes;* Janney, *Remembering the Civil War,* 276; McPherson, "Long-Legged Yankee Lies," 103; Peterson, *Lincoln in American Memory,* 164; Pressly, *Americans Interpret Their Civil War,* 166–81. Harper and Brothers published the first four volumes of Rhodes's *History of the United States* before they surrendered their rights in 1899. Macmillan took over the series from that point.

20. Rhodes, *History of the Civil War;* Rhodes, *History of the United States,* esp. 3:114–49, 164–67, 439–42, 459–63, 554–58, 607, 4:1, 20–56, 171, 271, 5:2, 45, 56, 83 (quotations, 3:347, 442, 4:171, 271, 5:56); Pressly, *Americans Interpret Their Civil War,* 172–78; Sternhell, *War on Record,* 215–17; Zeitz, *Lincoln's Boys,* 302, 307.

21. Rhodes, *History of the United States,* esp. 3:325, 343–47, 459–60, 604, 615–16, 4:105–7, 209, 271, 280, 293–99 (quotations, 3:604, 4:209, 271); Rhodes, *History of the Civil War,* esp. 1–6, 11, 27, 31, 37, 291–92, 302, 438.

22. Rhodes, *History of the United States,* esp. 4:12, 20–22, 47–50, 105–7, 188, 199, 203 (quotations, 12, 20–21); Rhodes, *History of the Civil War,* esp. 142, 157–63, 179, 182–87, 246–47.

23. Rhodes, *History of the Civil War,* 438.

24. For the Civil War, see Wilson, *History of the American People,* 4:145–264. See also Cooper, *Woodrow Wilson,* 16, 74, 76, 110, 155, 168, 425; and Peterson, *Lincoln in American Memory,* 164–67.

25. Elson, *History of the United States,* esp. 584–603, 626–27, 648, 662, 687, 693–703, 716, 726, 735, 756, 767–70, 774–76, 783 (quotations, 603, 626, 667, 703, 774, 776).

26. Peterson, *Lincoln in American Memory,* 175–94 (quotation, 182); Schwartz, *Abraham Lincoln and the Forge,* 109–34.

27. Lindsay, *The Congo and Other Poems,* 83–84; Peterson, *Lincoln in American Memory,* 158, 163–64, 198.

28. Lindsay, *The Congo and Other Poems,* 84 (quotation); Barr, *Loathing Lincoln,* 135–37; Cooper, *Woodrow Wilson,* 11, 16, 74, 79, 110, 114, 153, 155, 168, 178, 225, 349, 387, 394, 397–401, 405, 410, 425, 432–33, 499, 512, 535, 574, 599; Hochschild, *American Midnight,* esp. 43, 47–48, 69–70, 155, 325; Peterson, *Lincoln in American Memory,* 195, 198–99, 204–5; Schwartz, *Abraham Lincoln and the Forge,* 225–40; Schwartz, *Abraham Lincoln in the Post-Heroic Era,* xii. For Wilson's speech, see Wilson, "July 4, 1913, Address at Gettysburg."

29. Peterson, *Lincoln in American Memory,* 166, 196, 241–42, 257, 298, 299, 335, 339, 340; Thomas, *Portrait for Posterity,* 214–66 (quotations, 214).

30. Barton, *Autobiography,* 25–35 (quotation, 25).

31. Barton, *Autobiography,* 272–84; Peterson, *Lincoln in American Memory,* 196, 221–26, 235–41, 244–46, 260, 262, 288; Thomas, *Portrait for Posterity,* 214–42, 312.

32. Barton, *Life of Abraham Lincoln,* vol. 1, 2:76 (quotation); Thomas, *Portrait for Posterity,* 223–32.

33. Barton, *Life of Abraham Lincoln,* 1:454–56, 460–61, 468–69, 474–75, 2:3–10, 63–64, 71, 75–76, 88–106, 123–27, 167–238, 248–70, 296 (quotations, 2:231, 237, 238); Barton, *Autobiography,* 277–78.

34. Sandburg, *Abraham Lincoln: The Prairie Years,* esp. 1:34–37, 54, 112; Sandburg, *Abraham Lincoln: The Prairie Years and the War Years;* Hurt, "Sandburg's *Lincoln,*" 55–65; Johannsen, "Sandburg and Lincoln," 267–73; Niven, *Carl Sandburg,* esp. 408–9, 414–19, 424–38, 461–62; Peterson, *Lincoln in American Memory,* 273–77; Thomas, *Portrait for Posterity,* 187–88, 285–301.

35. Hurt, "Sandburg's *Lincoln,*" 55, 58–65 (quotations, 55, 64); Johannsen, "Sandburg and Lincoln," 273–74; Niven, *Carl Sandburg,* 44; Schwartz, *Abraham Lincoln in the Post-Heroic Era,* 21.

36. Johannsen, "Sandburg and Lincoln," 273–78; Niven, *Carl Sandburg,* 436–38, 470–71; Peterson, *Lincoln in American Memory,* 257, 294–99; Wetta and Novelli, *Abraham Lincoln & Women in Film,* 31–50, 81–90.

37. Niven, *Carl Sandburg,* 470–71 (quotation, 470); Schwartz, *Abraham Lincoln in the Post-Heroic Era,* 220–58.

38. Hurt, "Sandburg's *Lincoln,*" 55, 56, 62–65 (quotations, 55, 56). See also Hoffmann, "How the Sandburg Collection Came to Illinois"; Niven, *Carl Sandburg,* 419–20, 461–62, 470–71, 475, 477–78, 481–82, 492–93, 517, 519, 522–23, 525–37, 562, 623–25, 627–28, 635–36; Peterson, *Lincoln in American Memory,* 277–78, 304–8, 321–23; and Schwartz, *Abraham Lincoln in the Post-Heroic Era,* 25, 87, 88–89, 112–13, 183.

39. Johannsen, "Sandburg and Lincoln," 278–81; Niven, *Carl Sandburg,* 423; Hurt, "Sandburg's *Lincoln,*" 58.

40. Peterson, *Lincoln in American Memory,* 306–7 (quotation, 307); Niven, *Carl Sandburg,* 525–31.

41. Sandburg, *Abraham Lincoln: The War Years,* esp. 1:35–84, 95–97, 125, 188–237, 301–33, 413–22, 479–510, 527–51, 591–604 (quotations, 231, 301, 319, 321, 417, 508–9, 510).

42. Sandburg, *Abraham Lincoln: The War Years,* 1:462–68, 550–52, 623–35, 2:6, 78–102, 106–20, 224–46, 293–96, 339–75, 420–48, 477–87, 533–47, 3:13–16, 43–63, 153–55, 191–93, 229–38, 481–512, 615–35, 4:24–26, 80–86 (quotations, 2:430, 444).

43. Sandburg, *Abraham Lincoln: The War Years,* 3:138–52, 4:135–64 (quotation, 3:142).

44. Johannsen, "Sandburg and Lincoln," 274. Dying in 2011, Johannsen did not live to see the publication of a popular wave of new Lincoln biographies written by nonacademics.

45. Thomas, *Portrait for Posterity,* 274–76.

46. "Nathaniel Wright Stephenson," 13–14. Stephenson remained in Charleston two decades before leaving to edit a series for Yale University Press, then decamped again for California's new Scripps College.

47. Stephenson, *Abraham Lincoln and the Union;* Stephenson, *Autobiography of Abraham Lincoln;* Stephenson, *Lincoln.*

48. Stephenson, *Abraham Lincoln and the Union,* x, 19.

49. Stephenson, *Abraham Lincoln and the Union,* 99, 136, 137. See also Schwartz, *Abraham Lincoln in the Post-Heroic Era,* 21.

50. Stephenson, *Abraham Lincoln and the Union,* 137–38.

51. Stephenson, *Lincoln and the Union,* 151.

52. Stephenson, *Lincoln.*

53. Peterson, *Lincoln in American Memory,* 271.

54. Stephenson, *Lincoln,* 1–108 (quotations, 16, 27, 29).

55. Stephenson, *Lincoln,* 109–244 (quotations, 5, 9, 119, 129, 171, 193, 219).

56. Stephenson, *Lincoln,* 244–69 (quotation, 242).

57. Stephenson, *Lincoln,* 269–422 (quotations, 269, 271).

58. Bonner, "Civil War Historians," 193–216; Barr, *Loathing Lincoln,* 156–60; Greenberg, "Civil War Revisionism," 202–8 (quotation, 202); Neely, "Lincoln Theme," 13, 15–16; Stanley and Phillips, "New Civil War Revisionism," 372–73, 376–77; Peterson, *Lincoln in American Memory,* 300, 302–4, 308–10, 334 (quotations, 302, 334); Pressly, *Americans Interpret Their Civil War,* 182–95, 221–26, 229–48, 291–320 (quotation, 183); Sternhell, "Revisionism Reinvented?," 239–42, 252n3–4. Bonner counted Stephenson among the Revisionists. See "Civil War Historians," 194. For the secretary of state's famous speech, see Seward, *Irrepressible Conflict.* For "repressible conflict," see Craven, *Repressible Conflict.* For "needless war," see Milton, *Eve of Conflict.* For "blundering generation," see Randall, "Blundering Generation," 3–28. For "tragic era," see Bowers, *Tragic Era.* For "age of hate," see Milton, *Age of Hate.* The original editions of both Bowers and Milton include a frontispiece photograph of their hero, Andrew Johnson. Describing the rough period between the end of Reconstruction and roughly the era of Woodrow Wilson as the "nadir" of American race relations began with Logan, *The Negro in American Life and Thoughts,* but has become a commonplace term in histories of the era.

59. Craven, *Coming of the Civil War,* v, 1–3, 312, 314, 318, 319, 386, 391–92, 417, 423, 430, 435–38 (quotations, 386, 392, 423, 438). See also Craven, "Coming of the Civil War," 303–22; Craven, *Edmund Ruffin,* 211–12; Pressly, *Americans Interpret Their Civil War,* 307–20; Thomas, review of *The Repressible Conflict,* 345–48; and Bonner, "Civil War Historians," 197–202.

60. Randall, "Blundering Generation," 3–28; Guelzo, "Lincoln and His Biographers," 254; Peterson, *Lincoln in American Memory,* 299–300; Pratt, "James Garfield Randall," 119–20, 122; Pressly, *Americans Interpret Their Civil War,* 307–20; Randall, *I, Ruth,* 43–124; Young, "Randall's Lincoln," 1–4.

61. Randall, *Constitutional Problems,* 35, 147, 477, 513 (quotations); Randall, *I, Ruth,* 121–24.

62. Randall, *Constitutional Problems,* 45, 47, 59.

63. J. G. Randall, "Has the Lincoln Theme Been Exhausted?," 270–94; Neely, "Lincoln Theme," Randall, *I, Ruth,* 124–26; Peterson, *Lincoln in American Memory,* 300–301; Thomas, *Portrait for Posterity,* 275–76; Young, "Randall's Lincoln," 3–4. The Mississippi Valley Historical Association is now the Organization of American Historians.

64. Thomas, *Portrait for Posterity,* 275. See also Guelzo, "Lincoln and His Biographers," 255; and Peterson, *Lincoln in American Memory,* 256–57.

65. Current, introduction to Randall and Current, *Lincoln the President: Last Full Measure,* ix.

66. Randall, "Has the Lincoln Theme been Exhausted?," 270–94 (quotation, 272); Guelzo, "Lincoln and His Biographers," 255; Neely, "Lincoln Theme," 10–11, 13–23.

67. Neely, "Lincoln Theme," 10–13, 45–46; Peterson, *Lincoln in American Memory,* 256–57, 298–302; Thomas, *Portrait for Posterity,* 275–78; Young, "Randall's Lincoln," 5.

68. Randall, *Civil War and Reconstruction,* v–221 (quotations, v, vi, vii, viii, 5, 25, 27, 73, 74, 145, 146, 147, 170); Randall, *I, Ruth,* 126–30; Peterson, *Lincoln in American Memory,* 299–300, 300–301; Young, "Randall's Lincoln," 4. For U. B. Phillips's conservatism and importance, see Pressly, *Americans Interpret Their Civil War,* 265–72.

69. Randall, *Civil War and Reconstruction,* 161–64, 178–81, 202–3, 222–61 (quotations, 161, 259, 261).

70. Randall, *Civil War and Reconstruction,* 259–81, 317–404, 477–505, 689–879 (quotations, 368, 373, 480, 689, 722); Young, "Randall's Lincoln," 6–8.

71. Randall, *Civil War and Reconstruction,* 388–404 (quotation, 402).

72. Randall, *Civil War and Reconstruction,* 274–316, 405–36, 512–93, 665–88 (quotations, 289, 303, 315, 435).

73. Randall, "Civil War Restudied," 439–57 (quotations, 443, 447, 452, 456); Pressly, *Americans Interpret Their Civil War,* 3–7-9.

74. Randall, "Blundering Generation," 3–28 (quotations, 3, 5, 7, 8, 10, 18, 27).

75. Randall, *I, Ruth,* 159–60; Pressly, *Americans Interpret Their Civil War,* 307–9.

76. Current, introduction to Randall and Current, *Lincoln the President: Last Full Measure,* x.

77. Schwartz, *Abraham Lincoln in the Post-Heroic Era,* 59, 61, 64–72.

7. BLADES OF GRASS IN THE SHENANDOAH

1. The literature on World War I is vast—a full citation would result in an endnote longer than the rest of this book—but in this paragraph and chapter, I draw particular inspiration from Fussell, *Great War and Modern Memory;* Gat, *Fascist and Liberal Visions of War,* 130–38; Gerwarth, *Vanquished;* Gilbert, *First World War;* Gregory, *Last Great War;* Gregory, *War of Peoples;* Keegan, *First World War*; Leonhard, *Pandora's Box;* and my ragged schoolboy copy of Taylor, *First World War.* See also Guelzo, *Our Ancient Faith,* 14–15. For the calculation of one in three deaths of men of military age, see Keegan, *First World War,* 423.

2. Gat, *Fascist and Liberal Visions of War,* 134–36; Gerwarth, *Vanquished,* 1–13, 250–63; Leonhard, *Pandora's Box,* 837–45, 864, 871–95, 900.

3. Leonhard, *Pandora's Box,* 886.

4. Bond, *Liddell Hart,* 20–28, 37–49; Gat, *Fascist and Liberal Visions of War,* 130–38; Higham, *Military Intellectuals in Britain,* 3–5, 242; Luvaas, *Education of an Army,* 331–33; Tal, "American Civil War in British Thought," 411.

5. Beckett, *Victorians at War,* 179–80, 188–90, 203; Dubrulle, "Military Legacy of the Civil War," 156–75; Foreman, *World on Fire,* 458–59; McPherson, *Battle Cry of Freedom,* 546–57; Wolseley, *American Civil War,* ix, xviii–xxxviii; Tal, "American Civil War in British Thought," 414–15; Turner, *Stonewall Jackson,* 137–38, 145–69, 184–86, 200–230 (quotations, 99, 147). For "lions led by donkeys," see, for example, Clark, *Donkeys.* Clark attributed the phrase to German General Erich Ludendorff.

6. Dubrulle, "Military Legacy of the Civil War," 170; Hettle, *Inventing Stonewall Jackson,* 19, 62; Tal, "American Civil War in British Thought," 415–20, 422; Turner, *Stonewall Jackson,* 237–38, 145–69, 184–87, 200–230; Wolseley, *American Civil War,* xxx.

7. Lehmann, *All Sir Garnet,* 13.

8. Bond, *Victorian Army and the Staff College,* 17, 117–22, 127–48; Lehmann, *All Sir Garnet,* 13–379.

9. Dubrulle, "Military Legacy of the Civil War," 176.

10. Wolseley's life is described in detail in Lehmann, *All Sir Garnet* (quotation, 14). See also Bond, *Victorian Army and the Staff College,* 17, 20, 24–45, 82, 112, 117–22, 127–31; Wolseley, *American Civil War,* x–xvi; and Dubrulle, "Military Legacy of the Civil War," 176.

11. An English Officer [Wolseley], "Month's Visit to the Confederate Headquarters," 5–48 (quotations, 36, 38, 48). See also Dubrulle, "Military Legacy of the Civil War," 176–77; Foreman, *World on Fire,* 180–85; Lehmann, *All Sir Garnet,* 114–23; and Wolseley, *American Civil War,* ix, xii–xiv.

12. Wolseley, "General Lee," 51–70 (quotations, 51, 53, 55, 57, 67, 69). See also Wolseley, "Military Genius," 297–312; Beckett, *Victorians at War,* 3–4, 5–6; and Tal, "American Civil War in British Thought," 417–18, 421. Wolseley's essay, originally appearing in *Macmillan's Magazine* in 1887, later was published as a limited-run book.

13. Wolseley, "English View of the American Civil War," esp. xix–xxii, xxiii–xxv, 80, 101, 112–21, 129, 173, 191–93, 221 (quotations, 101, 115, 121, 173, 221). Wolseley's controversial remarks did not go unanswered in the United States. William Tecumseh Sherman defended Grant and condemned secession. See "Grant, Thomas, Lee," 437–50. For Jefferson Davis's self-defense, see "Lord Wolseley's Mistakes," 472–83. And for James B. Fry's angry attack on Wolseley and defense of Lincoln, see "Lord Wolseley Answered," 728–40.

14. Wolseley, *American Civil War,* xix–xxxviii. See also Bond, *Victorian Army and the Staff College,* 111, 143; and Turner, *Stonewall Jackson,* 226–27.

15. Wolseley, *American Civil War,* 179–81, 191–203 (quotations, 80, 94, 108, 191).

16. Roberts, "Memoir," xviii–xxiv (quotation, xix); Henderson [A Line Officer], *Campaign of Fredericksburg;* Bond, *Victorian Army and the Staff College,* 155–56; Fastabend, "G. F. R. Henderson," 6–67; Luvaas, *Education of an Army,* 216–18; Luvaas, "G. F. R. Henderson," 139.

17. Henderson [A Line Officer], *Campaign of Fredericksburg,* 25, 141, 144. See also Luvaas, *Education of an Army,* 216–20; and Luvaas, "G. F. R. Henderson," 139, 141–42.

18. Roberts, "Memoir," xxiv–xxxiv (quotation, xxv); Beckett, *Victorians at War,* 188–89; Bond, *Victorian Army and the Staff College,* 128, 131, 155–5,9 166–70; Dubrulle, "Military Legacy of the Civil War," 176; Fastabend, "G. F. R. Henderson," 66–67; Luvaas, *Education of an Army,* 220–25, 242–43; Luvaas, "G. F. R. Henderson," 139–42, 149–52; Reardon, *Soldiers and Scholars,* 98, 118.

19. Henderson, "American Civil War," 230–79 (quotations, 240, 258–59). For two additional Henderson lectures on the war, see "The Battle of Gettysburg," in Malcolm, *Science of War,*

280–306; and "The Campaigns in the Wilderness of Virginia, 1864," ibid., 307–37. See also Luvaas, "G. F. R. Henderson," 143.

20. Henderson, *Stonewall Jackson;* Fuller, *Generalship of U. S. Grant,* 23; Fuller, *Grant and Lee,* 106–18, 126; Hettle, *Inventing Stonewall Jackson,* 42, 67–68, 81–82, 84, 112–13, 130–312; Luvaas, *Education of an Army,* 242; Maurice, *Statesmen and Soldiers,* vi; Luvaas, *Education of an Army,* 225–29, 235–36; Luvaas, "G. F. R. Henderson," 142–44; Peterson, *Lincoln in American Memory,* 204–5; Turner, *Stonewall Jackson,* 225–28, 319n181.

21. Ballard, *Military Genius,* 77.

22. Henderson, *Stonewall Jackson,* 1:101, 112–13 (quotations, 101, 113). See also Tal, "American Civil War in British Thought," 417, 421–22.

23. Henderson, *Stonewall Jackson,* 2:334.

24. Henderson, *Stonewall Jackson,* 1:233–36, 250 (quotations, 233, 250). See also Ballard, *Military Genius,* 20–21; Fuller, *Grant and Lee,* 126; and Maurice, *Statesmen and Soldiers,* vi. Wolseley absolutely agreed with Henderson:

> McClellan, who was selected to command the army which was to capture Richmond and end the war, was a soldier of known ability, and, in my opinion, if he had not been interfered with by the Cabinet in Washington, he would probably have succeeded. . . . What Lincoln did not see was that to divide the Federal army into three portions, working on three separate lines, was to run a far greater risk than would be incurred by leaving Washington weakly garrisoned. I cannot bring myself to believe that he in the least realised all that was involved in changing a plan of operations so vast as McClellan's.

Wolseley, introduction to Henderson, *Stonewall Jackson,* 1:xiii–xiv.

25. Henderson, *Stonewall Jackson,* 1:226–27, 289, 306, 351, 358, 401, 405 (quotations, 226, 401).

26. Henderson, *Stonewall Jackson,* 1:406–7.

27. Henderson, *Stonewall Jackson,* 2:295–97, 300 (quotations, 295, 296).

28. Dubrulle, "Military Legacy of the Civil War," 178.

29. Roberts, "Memoir," xxviii–xxx, xxxiv–xxxviii; Wolseley, *American Civil War,* x; Beckett, *Victorians at War,* 4–5, 88–91; Bond, *Victorian Army and the Staff College,* 155–67; Dubrulle, "Military Legacy of the Civil War," 152–53, 175–80; Luvaas, *Education of an Army,* 216–17, 237–45; Luvaas, "G. F. R. Henderson," 148–53; Holden Reid, *America's Civil War,* 14, 21; Turner, *Stonewall Jackson,* 226–28.

30. Bond, *Victorian Army and the Staff College,* 155–67, 304–6; Churchill, *History of the English-Speaking Peoples,* 99–158 (quotation, 118); Luvaas, *Education of an Army,* 226–27, 243–47; Luvaas, "G. F. R. Henderson," 147–48, 153; Turner, *Stonewall Jackson,* 226–28. Bond added that the easily distracted Allenby and especially the dullish Haig were by no means Henderson's best students at the Staff College, although the instructor suspected correctly that Haig's friendship with the Prince of Wales, coupled with his work ethic and keen ambition, would someday place him at the top of the army. See Bond, *Victorian Army and the Staff College,* 163–67. Generations of World War I historians have since questioned whether that was a positive or negative result.

31. Forbes, *Memories and Studies; New York Times,* June 20, 1886; Forbes, "Archibald Forbes"; Bullard, *Famous War Correspondents,* 69–114; Weigley, *Quartermaster-General of the Army,* 361.

32. Forbes, "Lincoln as a Strategist," pt. 1, 55–65; Forbes, "Lincoln as a Strategist," pt. 2, 160–69 (quotation, 164).

33. Doyle, *Cause of All Nations,* 46–49, 76–82, 145–50, 235, 245–49; Fleche, *Revolution of 1861,* 86, 114–16, 199, 133–34, 148–49; Foreman, *World on Fire,* 139–41, 184–86, 189–92, 199–203; 281–84, 395–97, 773–77; Gregory, *Last Great War,* 6–7, 39–62; Hattersley, *Lloyd George,* 1, 65, 426–39, 578; Jones, *Blue & Gray Diplomacy,* 94–111; Leonhard, *Pandora's Box,* 48, 120, 136–37, 315–16, 322–25, 389, 404–6, 439–40, 524–25, 633, 650–54, 682–83, 831; Luvaas, "G. F. R. Henderson," 149; McPherson, *Battle Cry of Freedom,* 544–57; Peterson, *Lincoln in American Memory,* 198–200, 208–17; Schwartz, *Abraham Lincoln and the Forge,* 238–40; Tal, "American Civil War in British Thought," 411–13, 415–17, 422–23; Turner, *Stonewall Jackson,* 46, 68, 86, 99–101, 129, 146, 149, 177; Wolseley, *American Civil War,* xxx.

34. Peterson, *Lincoln in American Memory,* 201.

35. Charnwood, *Abraham Lincoln,* esp. 216–17, 220, 233–35, 255–64, 284–85, 361–84, 423–24, 451–53. Henry Holt published an American edition the following year. See also Guelzo, "Lincoln and His Biographers," 251; Morel, "Charnwood's Lincoln," 24–41; Peterson, *Lincoln in American Memory,* 200–201; and Thomas, *Portrait for Posterity,* 208–10, 213. On internal divisions over the war, see Gregory, *Last Great War,* 10–25, 113–31, 118–21.

36. Charnwood, *Abraham Lincoln,* 202–8, 216–17, 244–49, 272–93, 307–8, 336–37, 342–46, 355–61 (quotation, 277).

37. Charnwood, *Abraham Lincoln,* 277.

38. Charnwood, *Abraham Lincoln,* 359.

39. Bond, *Liddell Hart,* 12–34, 35n21; Danchev, *Alchemist of War,* esp. 1, 6–7, 20, 24, 34–86, 97–123, 196–98; Gat, *Fascist and Liberal Visions of War,* 136, 139–43, 147–49, 164–65, 167–68; Luvaas, *Education of an Army,* 46–49, 82–95, 113–16; Luvaas, *Education of an Army,* 376–81, 416–17. Liddell Hart's liberal rejection of J. F. C. Fuller's fascism is a major theme of Gat's study.

40. Liddell Hart, *Remaking of Modern Armies,* 170–71. See also Beckett, *Victorians at War,* 4–5; Bond, *Liddell Hart,* 19–22, 26–30; Danchev, *Alchemist of War,* 135; Gat, *Fascist and Liberal Visions of War,* 178–81; and Holden Reid, *America's Civil War,* 14.

41. Bond, *Liddell Hart,* 37–61; Cook, "From Liddell Hart to Keegan," 23–24, 30; Danchev, *Alchemist of War,* 113–23, 137–46, 155–64, 176, 257–58; Gat, *Fascist and Liberal Visions of War,* 147–49, 164–66, 244; Luvaas, *Education of an Army,* 91–95; Luvaas, "*Sherman* and the 'Indirect Approach,'" vii–x; Tal, "American Civil War in British Thought," 430–32. Liddell Hart already had listed Lee among the "great captains" and then dismissed him briefly in *Great Captains Unveiled,* 77. He later lamented that he could have made twice the money writing about Lee and briefly considered Nathan Bedford Forrest as the topic for another book. See Danchev, *Alchemist of War,* 158.

42. Liddell Hart, *Sherman,* xiii–xiv. See also Bond, *Liddell Hart,* 47.

43. Danchev, *Alchemist of War,* 151–53; Gat, *Fascist and Liberal Visions of War,* 138–39, 143–50, 163–64; Luvaas, *Education of an Army,* 46–49, 83–86; Luvaas, *Education of an Army,* 381–83, 398–400, 422. The close relationship between Fuller and Liddell Hart ended in part over a spat about Sherman and Grant, although the larger issue was that the student was becoming the master. Through *Sherman,* however, Liddell Hart also won devoted readers in uniform, such as the American officer George S. Patton and the German father of the blitzkrieg, Heinz Guderian. His exact influence on the latter, however, is much disputed, with Liddell Hart sometimes accused of exaggerating his importance (and through him, Sherman's) to the development of the

blitzkrieg. See Danchev, *Alchemist of War,* 224–26, 233–37; Gat, *Fascist and Liberal Visions of War,* 127–29; and Higham, *Military Intellectuals in Britain,* 12–14, 92–93. Nimrod Tal asserted that Liddell Hart used Sherman to dissect a modern American culture he disliked. See Tal, "American Civil War in British Thought," 423–27.

44. Liddell Hart, *Sherman,* 67, 92, 102–13, 171, 175, 234–35, 386 (quotations, 92, 113).

45. Liddell Hart, *Sherman,* 137–38.

46. Liddell Hart's centrality to modern military theory and his genius are continuing themes in Bond, *Liddell Hart.* But see also other takes in Danchev, *Alchemist of War,* 1, 6–7; Gat, *Fascist and Liberal Visions of War,* 127–29, 306–10; and Luvaas, *Education of an Army,* 376–77, 419, 421–24. Gat in particular viewed Liddell Hart as both a forward thinker on strategic theory who deserves reconsideration and a tireless self-promoter with a healthy ego who exaggerated his own importance.

47. *Times* (London), Jan. 13, 1912; Maurice, *Maurice Case,* 91, 237–39; Beckett, *Victorians at War,* 8, 11, 85, 88–92, 148, 179, 188–89, 220, 228, 231–32, 234; Bond, *Victorian Army and the Staff College,* 128, 131, 134, 136–38, 155–56, 278, 303–17; Gooch, "Maurice Debate," 211–12; Luvaas, *Education of an Army,* 170–215.

48. Gooch, "Maurice Debate," 211–28 (quotation, 212); Gat, *Fascist and Liberal Visions of War,* 168–71; Gregory, *Last Great War,* 213–48; Gregory, *War of Peoples,* 98–99, 113–14, 120–21, 126, 186–89; Hattersley, *Lloyd George,* 119–44, 186, 357, 363–66, 373, 391–99, 421–25, 442–62; Leonhard, *Pandora's Box,* 206–10, 406–11, 428, 439–44, 650–57, 679, 682–84, 715, 723, 742, 812–15. *The Maurice Case 1918,* edited and published by Nancy Maurice, the general's daughter, is a defensive compendium of reports, speeches, statements, magazine and newspaper articles, and diary entries that the general wrote or compiled in his defense.

49. Gooch, "Maurice Debate," 211–28; Hattersley, *Lloyd George,* 39, 53, 55, 82, 177, 462–68; Leonhard, *Pandora's Box,* 773–74, 832; Maurice, *Maurice Case,* esp. 3–54, 91–137 (quotation, 96). Major General Maurice mailed five letters, but only four newspapers printed them. Nancy Maurice and Maj. Gen. Edward Spears depict him as a hero for his stand. In contrast, Lloyd George castigated Maurice as a mentally ill liar and catspaw of Robertson. See Lloyd George, *War Memoirs,* 5:295, 309, 367, 374, 6:31, 52–72. For the text of Maurice's letter, see ibid., 6:61–62. In it he also attacked Conservative leader and Lloyd George ally Andrew Bonar Law.

50. Gooch, "Maurice Debate," 211 (quotation), 228. See also Sir Frederick Maurice, "Intrigues of the War," in Maurice, *Maurice Case,* 176–77, 181–207; Hattersley, *Lloyd George,* 466; Leonhard, *Pandora's Box,* 773–74; Lloyd George, *War Memoirs,* 5:295, 309, 6:52–72. In 1936 the former prime minister bitterly attacked Maurice as more politician than soldier, "the architect" of Robertson's "downfall"; "subservient and rather unbalanced, . . . one of those foolish devotees who bring their idols they worship down with them"; and "the tool of astuter men." Lloyd George, *War Memoirs,* 5:295, 309, 6:63.

51. Maurice, "Intrigues of the War," 181–220 (quotations, 183, 207). See also Edward Spears, "Appreciation," in Maurice, *Maurice Case,* 9, 34–36, 52–56.

52. Maurice, *Robert E. Lee,* v (quotation), 274–94. See also Maurice and Arthur, *Life of Lord Wolseley,* esp. 6, 33–38, 234–36; Maurice, "Intrigues of the War," 181–20; Lloyd George, *War Memoirs,* 5:295, 309, 6:52–72; Maurice, *Maurice Case,* 237–39; Hattersley, *Lloyd George,* 532; and Hettle, *Inventing Stonewall Jackson,* 130–31. Before the smoke had settled on the Western Front, Maurice dashed out two books about the beginning and end of the Great War: *Forty Days*

in 1914 and *The Last Four Months: The End of the War in the West,* both published in 1919. In the latter book, he repeated his criticism of Lloyd George but with less anger than he expressed privately. See Maurice, *Last Four Months,* 2–7, 11, 23–24, 62, 69–70, 96, 134, 149–50, 242. Proto-Nazis in Germany mistakenly embraced *The Last Four Months* as reinforcing the "stabbed in the back myth" that blamed socialists and Jews for Germany's defeat. William L. Shirer pointed out that the Germans based their opinions on bad German-language reviews of the book and that Maurice vigorously denied their allegations. See Shirer, *Rise and Fall of the Third Reich,* 31.

53. Maurice, *Statesmen and Soldiers,* vi–vii (quotations), 165–66.

54. Excerpts from the book appeared in the United States as Maurice, "Lincoln as a Strategist," 161–69; Maurice, "Soldiers and Statesmen of the Civil War: I," 52–61; and Maurice, "Soldiers and Statesmen of the Civil War: II," 224–36. For reviews, see, for example, (unattributed) review of *Statesmen and Soldiers of the Great War,* in *Military Engineer,* 536; Spaulding, review of *Statesmen and Soldiers of the Great War,* 111–13; and Ware, review of *Statesmen and Soldiers of the Great War,* 242–43.

55. Maurice, *Statesmen and Soldiers,* 59–65, 87 (quotation, 59).

56. Maurice, *Statesmen and Soldiers,* 68–75 (quotations, 68, 71, 72–73, 74).

57. Maurice, *Statesmen and Soldiers,* 75–80 (quotations, 76–77).

58. Maurice, *Statesmen and Soldiers,* 82–83, 88–95 (quotations, 82, 83, 95).

59. Maurice, *Statesmen and Soldiers,* 95–114, 121, 152–54 (quotations, 97, 98, 99, 100, 101, 111, 112).

60. Maurice, *Statesmen and Soldiers,* 120–22, 143–45 (quotations, 121, 144).

61. Gerwarth, *Vanquished,* esp. 11–13, 19–68, 153–76, 250–65; *New York Times,* Dec. 8, 1938; *Times* (London), Sept. 13, 1938.

62. For a brief biography of Ballard by his son-in-law, a former British officer and military historian, see Cook, "Ballard Letters," 145–47. See also Robertson, *From Private to Field Marshal,* 173–74; Robertson, foreword to *Russia in Rule and Misrule,* v–vi; and Bond, *Victorian Army and the Staff College,* 158–59, 162, 196. Although Ballard was a classmate of Robertson's, Bond did not include him among the "future stars" of the college during that era.

63. Quaife, review of *The Military Genius of Abraham Lincoln,* 412–13 (quotation, 413). For other American reviews, see, for example, Millard, review of *Soldiers and Statesmen of the Great War,* ii, iv; Pennypacker, "Military History and Historians," 141–61; and (unattributed) review of *Abraham Lincoln as Military Genius,* in *Military Engineer,* 357.

64. Ballard, *Military Genius,* 6, 8, 56, 66–67, 72, 77, 97–98, 108–9, 136, 237. Merrill Peterson mentioned Ballard's book in a few sentences in connection with Arthur Conger and Sir Frederick Maurice. See Peterson, *Lincoln in American Memory,* 205.

65. Ballard, *Military Genius,* 1–4 (quotations, 2, 4). For Ballard's mention of Maurice, see ibid., 97. See also Gallagher, "Blueprint for Victory," 22.

66. Ballard, *Military Genius,* 8, 41–43 (quotations, 8, 42–43).

67. Ballard, *Military Genius,* 66–76, 91–113 (quotations, 72–73, 75).

68. Ballard, *Military Genius,* 77–90 (quotation, 78). Brother Stiggins and Uriah Heep were two unsavory characters in the Charles Dickens novels *The Pickwick Papers* and *David Copperfield,* respectively.

69. Ballard, *Military Genius,* 114–37, 143–71, 192–93, 201–28 (quotations, 151, 171, 192–93, 203, 204).

70. Ballard, *Military Genius,* 229–42 (quotations, 229, 230, 231, 235, 236).

71. Ballard, *Military Genius,* 240–41. Sir Frederick Maurice also discussed Anglo-Saxons, noting in *Soldiers and Statesmen* (91–92):

> even the more phlegmatic Anglo-Saxon races tend in such times to become neurotic, and are apt to be aroused to enthusiasm or indignation on very slight grounds. This is one of the difficulties with which the statesmen of modern democracies must reckon. The experienced soldier knows how manifold are the chances and the uncertainties of war; how incomplete in normal circumstances is the information on which he has to make decisions; he is only too aware that with the highest skill and the best judgment he cannot hope to guess right all the time. It is the duty of the statesman to know this too, for the public does not read the maxims of Napoleon, and is not aware that the victory falls to the general who makes fewest mistakes; it judges by results and readily become intolerant of any error which has caused loss of life. The statesman who understands his business will stand between his soldiers and hasty popular judgment. Both Lincoln and Davis have it to their eternal credit that they did this, and prevented the outstanding military figures of the war from being swept by blasts of popular criticism into oblivion in the early days of the conflict.

72. Beckett, *Victorians at War,* 180, 220, 234; Bond, *Liddell Hart,* 21, 25, 27–29; Bond, *Victorian Army and the Staff College,* 278, 290–93, 303 (quotations, 290, 291, 292); Boot, *War Made New,* 216; Danchev, *Alchemist of War,* 114–15; Gat, *Fascist and Liberal Visions of War,* 14–26; Higham, *Military Intellectuals in Britain,* 67; Luvaas, *Education of an Army,* 336–39; Holden Reid, *J. F. C. Fuller,* 1–3, 7–26; Trythall, *"Boney" Fuller,* 1–40. Crowley attributed the break to Fuller's embarrassed mortification that Crowley's involvement in a legal case, one that touched on the magician's bisexuality, might harm the young officer's career. Crowley in turn dismissed Fuller as a "swelled head" with no more talent than a "'clerk.'" See Crowley, *Confessions,* 335–37, 521, 530–33, 539–43, 561–65, 594, 634–35, 638, 642.

73. Bond, *Liddell Hart,* 22, 29; Bond, *Victorian Army and the Staff College,* 303; Boot, *War Made New,* 216–17; Danchev, *Alchemist of War,* 98, 113–22, 125–30, 132–33, 137–45; Gat, *Fascist and Liberal Visions of War,* 27–31, 138; Higham, *Military Intellectuals in Britain,* 67–68, 84–86; Luvaas, *Education of an Army,* 339–46, 356–58; Holden Reid, *J. F. C. Fuller,* 30–106, 128–51; Trythall, *"Boney" Fuller,* 40–80, 91–92, 97–105, 117–22, 125–32, 133–45, 153–63, 170–79. Trythall pointed out correctly that Fuller was not the first to think about tanks in action and also noted the relationship between "Plan 1919—which drew on the ideas of others as well—and actions in the later Arab-Israeli wars." See ibid., 32–48, 60, 71–74.

74. Beckett, *Victorians at War,* 4; Danchev, *Alchemist of War,* 118–19, 128–29; Higham, *Military Intellectuals in Britain,* 68–70, 80–81; Luvaas, *Education of an Army,* 336–65, 367–68, 370–72; Holden Reid, *J. F. C. Fuller,* 56–99; Trythall, *"Boney" Fuller,* 82–91, 105–7, 122–27, 132–33, 145–55, 163–72, 180–81. Brian Holden Reid maintained that Maurice failed to understand Fuller, as they were not so diametrically opposite in their views of strategy. See Holden Reid, *J. F. C. Fuller,* 90–99.

75. Danchev, *Alchemist of War,* 73, 151–52; Luvaas, *Education of an Army,* 336–65, 367–69; Gallagher, "Blueprint for Victory," 21–22; Higham, *Military Intellectuals in Britain,* 74; Holden

Reid, *J. F. C. Fuller*, 107–10, 115–21, 127; Tal, "American Civil War in British Thought," 431–34; Trythall, *"Boney" Fuller*, 159–60, 177–78. Brian Holden Reid noted that Fuller's *Generalship of Ulysses S. Grant* failed to replace Henderson, but it at least found its way to the required reading list for promotions within the British Army, along with Liddell Hart's *Sherman*. See Holden Reid, *J. F. C. Fuller*, 127. Liddell Hart himself found *Generalship of Ulysses S. Grant* too polemic, charging that Fuller started with his own views and looked for evidence to support them. He was not alone. The American author Thomas Robson Hay agreed that the book was much too positive about the general. See Hay, review of *Generalship of Ulysses S. Grant*, 891–92. William B. Hesseltine, meanwhile, slammed *Grant and Lee* for Fuller's slight research and conclusions. See Hesseltine, review of *Grant and Lee*, 404–5.

76. Fuller, *Generalship of Ulysses S. Grant*, 118–26; Fuller, *Grant and Lee*, 162 (quotation), 194–98; Holden Reid, *J. F. C. Fuller*, 109–10.

77. Fuller, *Generalship of Ulysses S. Grant*, vii, 19, 20, 23, 26–28, 35, 46, 65 (quotations, vii, 20, 35, 46); Fuller, *Grant and Lee*, 43–49, 133, 185; Holden Reid, *J. F. C. Fuller*, 111–12.

78. Fuller, *Generalship of Ulysses S. Grant*, 30–33, 38–39, 46, 126 (quotations, 31, 39, 46).

79. Fuller mentioned Maurice only once—*Grant and Lee*, 168—and then only to dismiss his argument about Lee before Antietam.

80. Fuller, *Generalship of Ulysses S. Grant*, 6–7, 38–43, 96, 183, 184 (quotations, 43, 184); Fuller, *Grant and Lee*, 30, 151, 251–52 (quotation, 30); Holden Reid, *J. F. C. Fuller*, 110.

81. Fuller, *Generalship of Ulysses S. Grant*, 6–7, 126, 132, 136, 159–60, 183, 184, 197, 209–10, 212, 357–59, 379 (quotations, 7, 210, 357); Fuller, *Grant and Lee*, 30, 38–42, 89, 93, 140, 144, 177 (quotations, 89, 140, 197, 249).

82. Fuller, *Generalship of Ulysses S. Grant*, 389; Bond, *Liddell Hart*, 78, 215, 219–23, 235, 273; Boot, *War Made New*, 217; Danchev, *Alchemist of War*, 115, 197–98, 234–38; Gat, *Fascist and Liberal Visions of War*, 3–6, 14–19, 27–96, 233–34; Higham, *Military Intellectuals in Britain*, 71–73, 78–81, 111–12, 115; Luvaas, *Education of an Army*, 364–67, 374–75; Holden Reid, *J. F. C. Fuller*, 175–200; Tal, "American Civil War in British Thought," 427–30; Trythall, *"Boney" Fuller*, 170–71, 180–218. As much as Fuller disliked what he perceived as American crudity and materialism, he saw the United States as "the great hope of Western civilization." Tal, "American Civil War in British Thought," 427. Luvaas noted ironic interest in Fuller's ideas about mechanization in the Soviet Union, while with a few exceptions Americans mostly knew him for *The Generalship of Ulysses S. Grant*. A larger question here concerns the subsequent war. Were Grant, Sherman, and Lincoln, as interpreted by Fuller and Liddell Hart anyway, the actual godfathers of blitzkrieg?

83. Fuller, *Grant and Lee*, 37, 116, 122–26 (quotations, 122, 123); Wolseley, "General Lee," 67.

84. Fuller, quoted in Trythall, *"Boney" Fuller*, 205; and Boot, *War Made New*, 224. When war finally came in 1939, only Churchill's intervention saved Fuller from prison, although the prime minister also denied him a uniform or active role in the military. He reacted ungratefully. For the rest of his life, Fuller denied the worst of Nazi atrocities while maintaining that Britain should have made peace with Berlin so that the Germans could have destroyed the Soviet Union. Nonetheless, he renewed his relationship with Liddell Hart and quickly rebuilt much of his reputation as a postwar military theorist and popular author, especially in the United States. See Trythall, *"Boney" Fuller*, 213–75.

8. THE STERN STANDARD OF VICTORY

1. Randall, *Lincoln the President: Springfield to Gettysburg,* 1:1–272, 2:321–42; Guelzo, "Lincoln and His Biographers," 254–55; Peterson, *Lincoln in American Memory,* 308; Pratt, "James Garfield Randall," 123; Pressly, *American Interpret their Civil War,* 316–17; Thomas, *Portrait for Posterity,* 277–82, 283–84. Only the first two volumes of *Lincoln the President* had appeared at the time of Thomas's publication.

2. Randall, *Lincoln the President: Springfield to Gettysburg,* 1:272–395, 2:1–64, 126–238 (quotations, 1:282, 315, 316, 373, 2:1, 63, 173, 204–5, 210); Neely, "Lincoln Theme," 13–14; Peterson, *Lincoln in American Memory,* 308–9; Thomas, *Portrait for Posterity,* 280–83.

3. Randall, *Lincoln the President: Springfield to Gettysburg,* 2:65–125, 239–302 (quotations, 68, 69, 77, 83, 125, 251); Peterson, *Linooln in American Memory,* 308–9.

4. Randall, *Lincoln the President: Springfield to Gettysburg,* 2:277. Some modern historians have compared the Revisionists to the "New Revisionists" and the "dark turn" school of early twenty-first-century Civil War historians, which also emphasizes the ugly side of the war. See Sternhell, "Revisionism Reinvented?" For World War II's disputed death toll, see Roberts, *Storm of War,* 579.

5. Peterson, *Lincoln in American Memory,* 308–9; Thomas, *Portrait for Posterity,* 282–83.

6. Angle, review of *Lincoln the President: Springfield to Gettysburg,* 157.

7. The literature on World War II and its immediate aftermath is as vast as that of its predecessor. Here I have relied especially upon Mawdsley, *World War II,* esp. 442–50 (quotation, 442); Overy, *Blood and Ruins,* esp. 618–32, 647–49, 870–76; Overy, *Why the Allies Won,* esp. 261, 327; Roberts, *Storm of War;* and Weinberg, *World at Arms,* esp. 913–14. On the end of Revisionism, see Current, introduction to Randall and Current, *Lincoln the President: Last Full Measure,* vii–viii; Peterson, *Lincoln in American Memory,* 334–37; Neely, "Lincoln Theme," 14–18, 59–60; and Sternhell, "Revisionism Reinvented?," 241. For "the good war," see Terkel, *"Good War."* For "the greatest generation," see Brokaw, *Greatest Generation.* For Lincoln as symbol, see Schwartz, *Abraham Lincoln in the Post-Heroic Era,* 64–84.

8. Wall, *Inventing the "American Way,"* esp. 3–12, 163–84, 280–86 (quotation, 168).

9. Wall, *Inventing the "American Way,"* 4–5, 114, 117, 167.

10. Dagbovie, *Carter G. Woodson;* Goggin, "Countering White Racist Scholarship," 355–75; Hine, "Carter G. Woodson," 405–25; Winston, "Carter Godwin Woodson," 459–63.

11. Woodson, review of Randall, *Lincoln the President,* 107–11 (quotations, 108, 110).

12. Woodson, "Lincoln as a Southern Man," 105–6.

13. Current, introduction to Randall and Current, *Lincoln the President: Last Full Measure,* vii–viii; Gerstung, "Louis M. Hacker's Reappraisal," 140–66; Olch, "Louis M. Hacker Civil Libertarian"; Pressly, *Americans Interpret their Civil War,* 256–62; Zeman, "Louis M. Hacker's 'Coincidental Conversion,'" 85–99.

14. Hacker, "Professor Hacker v. Some Sons of Dixie," 6, 9; Current, introduction to Randall and Current, *Lincoln the President: Last Full Measure,* vii–viii; Pressly, *Americans Interpret Their Civil War,* 262; "About Us," *Fortune,* https://fortune.com/about-us/ (accessed May 9, 2025). The acerbic William B. Hesseltine responded for the Revisionists by referring to Hacker as "the most recent example of historical obscurantism" and citing his "weird Republican–Neo Marxist Faith."

Hesseltine, "Lincoln Parade," 35. For the "arsenal of democracy" and the American war economy's role in arming the Allies, see Mawdsley, *World War II,* 444; Overy, *Blood and Ruins,* 397–419, 526–77, 606–9; Overy, *Why the Allies Won,* 109–10, 193–98, 223–25, 331–32; Roberts, *Storm of War,* 87, 109, 129–31, 214–15, 604; and Weinberg, *World at Arms,* 154–59, 241–45, 307–8, 469.

15. "Tragedy of History," *Time* (Oct. 24, 1949): 51–52.

16. Schlesinger, *Age of Jackson;* Schlesinger, *Vital Center.* For Schlesinger's biography, see Aldous, *Schlesinger;* Diggins, *Liberal Persuasion,* 3–83; and Cole, "Age of Jackson," 149–59. See also Hine, "Carter G. Woodson," 417–18.

17. Schlesinger, *Vital Center,* 88–91 (quotation, 88).

18. Schlesinger, "Cause of the Civil War," 969–81 (quotations, 976–77, 978, 980, 981). See also Aldous, *Schlesinger,* 135–37; Peterson, *Lincoln in American Memory,* 334–35; and Pressly, *American Interpret Their Civil War,* 341–42. As Peterson noted, Pressly also disliked Revisionism.

19. Guelzo, "Lincoln and His Biographers," 258; Lilly, *Set My People Free;* Pressly, *American Interpret Their Civil War,* 340–60; Schwartz, *Abraham Lincoln in the Post-Heroic Era,* 84–87, 92–102, 105–14. Writing in 1954 before the full emergence of the new approach, Pressly emphasized Allan Nevins's multivolume history of the war, *Ordeal of the Union,* but admitted that it reflected some Revisionist concerns, notably the "blundering generation." See also Higham, "Beyond Consensus," 615–16; and Peterson, *Lincoln in American Memory,* 334–35. Amid the struggle with communism, consensus historians minimized class and racial divisions in American history, celebrated the continuity of American values, and proclaimed the nation's essential unity. Consensus School history dominated American historical scholarship until the rise of the "New Left" in the 1960s. For an introduction, see three essays by John Higham: "Cult of the American Consensus," 93–100; "Beyond Consensus," 609–25; and "Changing Paradigms," 460–66.

20. Randall, *Lincoln the Liberal Statesman,* xi, xii, xiii (quotations); Randall, *I, Ruth,* 162–64, 177–78, 185, 196–98, 203, 209, 220, 222–23, 225.

21. Randall, *Lincoln the President: Midstream,* xi, 149, 152, 178, 210, 393. Heydrich and Himmler were closely associated with the Nazi death camps such as those at Dachau and Buchenwald. See also Pratt, "James Garfield Randall," 123–24.

22. Randall, *Lincoln the President: Midstream,* 363–92, 410–11 (quotations, 375, 376, 410–11).

23. Randall and Current, *Lincoln the President: Last Full Measure,* vii–xiv, 138–67 (quotation, 143); Randall, *I, Ruth,* 226–36. Harry E. Pratt wrote that Randall had completed nine chapters and dictated a tenth. See Pratt, "James Garfield Randall," 126.

24. Churchill, *History of the English-Speaking Peoples,* 106, 112–13, 116, 118, 120, 126–27, 130, 131, 132, 158; Mawdsley, *World War II,* 116–17, 200–201, 216–17, 236–36, 291, 298–99, 304–19, 350, 377–80, 394–94, 436, 443; Overy, *Blood and Ruins,* 73–74, 104–7, 114, 129–31, 170–76, 244–47, 266–69, 274, 288–91, 298, 303, 338–39, 342–45, 472–75, 526–27, 538, 547, 549, 647–49, 674, 870–76; Overy, *Why the Allies Won,* 4, 25–27, 32–34, 97–98, 116–17, 137–38, 141–45, 156–57, 178, 245–47, 248–55, 261–68, 272, 293–94, 317–19, 323, 326–28; Rafuse, "Two Harrys," 58–65; Roberts, *Storm of War,* 45–47, 58, 68, 126–31, 142–43, 193, 198–200, 205–7, 302–3, 309–10, 369, 382–84, 403, 437–40, 545, 564, 568, 594, 603; Weinberg, *World at Arms,* 327–32, 349, 351, 354–59, 388–89, 418–20, 436, 611–16, 625–31, 656–64, 682–83, 724–26, 777, 829–36; Williams, *Lincoln Finds a General,* 1:139, 147–48.

25. Williams, *Lincoln Finds a General,* vols. 1–5.

26. Finding aid, Kenneth P. Williams Papers C193, Indiana University Archives, https://archives.iu.edu/catalog/InU-Ar-VAA2736 (accessed May 9, 2025); K. P. Williams to C. H. Gingrich, Feb. 27, 1935, n.p.; and C. H. Gingrich to K. P. Williams, Feb. 12, 1835, Northfield, MN, all Kenneth P. William Papers C193, Indiana University Archives, Bloomington (hereafter cited as Williams Papers, IU); Schmadel, *Dictionary of Minor Planet Names,* 140–41. See also Williams, *Calculation of the Orbits of Asteroids and Comets;* Williams, *College Algebra;* Williams, *Dynamics of the Airplane;* Williams, *Mathematical Theory of Finance;* Williams, *Transits of Mercury;* Williams, "Transits of Mercury (Supplement)," 1–5; and Williams and Williams, *Plane Geometry.*

27. For Williams military biography, see State of Indiana, Adjutant General's Officer, General Orders No. 42, Sept. 18, 1958, Williams Papers, IU. See also finding aid, ibid.; "Our Proud History," *Indiana University ROTC,* https://iu.go-rotc.com/history/ (accessed May 9, 2025); and *In Memory of the 150th Field Artillery, August 5, 1917, to May 9, 1919* (n.p., 1927), Indiana State Library Digital Collections, https://indianamemory.contentdm.oclc.org/digital/collection/p16066coll47/id/2755/, Indiana State Library, Indianapolis. *In Memory* is a photocopy of a unit history that General of the Armies John J. Pershing placed in the cornerstone of the Indiana World War Memorial on July 4, 1927.

28. Williams, *Lincoln Finds a General,* 1:ix–x, 5:vii–xiii.

29. Williams, *Lincoln Finds a General,* 1:ix–x (quotations, ix).

30. Williams, *Lincoln Finds a General,* 3:452–56, 4:439–51, 551–53n73, 580–81n49–50, 582n53–54, 5:xi–xii (quotation, 5:xi). See also Gallagher, "Blueprint for Victory," 22–23.

31. Williams, *Lincoln Finds a General,* 1:37–121 (quotations, 37, 44, 59, 73, 115, 121).

32. Williams, *Lincoln Finds a General,* 1:104–31, 141, 147–48 (quotations, 104, 108, 147); Peterson, *Lincoln in American Memory,* 337.

33. Williams, *Lincoln Finds a General,* 1:136–48, 171 (quotations, 139, 147). For example, American leadership in Europe, Williams argued, knew as early as 1942 that they needed to stage a cross-channel campaign into France rather than fight around the edges of the Axis powers.

34. Williams, *Lincoln Finds a General,* 1:152–61, 172–82, 188–213 (quotations, 173, 174, 213).

35. Williams, *Lincoln Finds a General,* 1:210–13, 252–53 (quotations, 210–11, 212, 213, 253).

36. Williams, *Lincoln Finds a General,* 1:160–67, 188–251 (quotations, 166, 221, 228, 231, 232, 249–50).

37. Williams, *Lincoln Finds a General,* 1:251–383, 2:445–79 (quotations, 1:280, 291, 301, 302, 324, 331, 2:479).

38. Williams, *Lincoln Finds a General,* 2:482–757, 763–69 (quotations, 483, 543, 730, 768).

39. Williams, *Lincoln Finds a General,* 3:30, 37, 59–67, 76–77, 92, 109–12, 114, 118–19, 132, 145, 153–65, 187, 229, 253, 261, 277, 283, 308, 342, 432, 448–52, 4:21–22, 26, 38, 53–59, 117–20, 135–37, 146–48, 305, 333–38, 421–23, 431–39, 455–57, 5:20, 27, 48, 81–91, 99, 118–20, 126–29, 140–42, 160, 210–11, 241 (quotations, 3:76, 109). For Carroll, see also Coryell, "Anna Ella Carroll," 120–37; and Coryell, *Neither Heroine nor Fool.*

40. Williams, *Lincoln Finds a General,* 1:ix–xi, 2:777–85, 789–803 (quotations, 1:x, xi, 2:789, 796, 795, 804). The books in question were Johnston, *Bull Run;* Shannon, *Organization and Administration of the Union Armies;* and Tilley, *Lincoln Takes Command.* See also *Montgomery (AL) Advertiser,* Mar. 1, 1968.

41. Williams, *Lincoln Finds a General,* 2:803–10 (quotation, 804). The books in question are Eisenschiml, *Why Was Lincoln Murdered?;* Milton, *Conflict;* and Williams, *Lincoln and the*

Radicals. Mark Neely has compared T. Harry Williams's views of the Radicals to Randall's. See Neely, "Abraham Lincoln vs. Jefferson Davis," 103.

42. Williams, *Lincoln Finds a General,* 1:75, 101, 131, 137–40, 155, 157, 159–60, 166, 173, 195, 197, 198, 200, 205, 207, 208, 212–13, 217, 232, 238, 257, 264, 300, 302, 312, 318, 337, 357, 376, 387n55, 390n117, 397n118, 399n28, 400n30, 402n16, 404n48, 407n30, 424n111, 425n12, 426n17, 430n106, 2:450, 452, 454, 505, 508, 514, 520, 548, 549, 556, 614–15, 628, 650, 689–91, 725–27, 784, 795, 803, 808, 830n16, 852n38, 854n72, 3:74, 78, 87, 94, 245, 247, 313, 331, 352, 414, 441, 456, 529n92, 4:335, 357, 358, 367, 371, 424–25, 436, 455, 527n17, 532, 555n73, 572, 575n17, 577, 5:89, 133 (quotation, 1:140); Conger, *Rise of U. S. Grant;* Greene, *The Mississippi.*

43. *New York Times,* Mar. 17, 1950. DeVoto's praise, and that of others, is found on the dust jacket of Williams, *Lincoln Finds a General,* vol. 3.

44. Vandiver, review of *Lincoln Finds a General,* 125–28 (quotations, 127, 128).

45. Ropp, review of *Lincoln Finds a General,* 3:321–22 (quotation, 321).

46. Nevins, review of *Lincoln Finds a General,* 5:154–55.

47. Randall, review of *Lincoln Finds a General,* 627–29.

48. Coulter, review of *Lincoln Finds a General,* 83–86 (quotations, 83–84, 84–85, 86); Pressly, *Americans Interpret Their Civil War,* 311,

49. Hesseltine, review of *Lincoln Finds a General,* 651–52 (quotations, 652).

50. Williams, review of *Lincoln Finds a General,* vol. 4, 243–45 (quotations, 243, 244).

51. Williams, review of *Lincoln Finds a General,* vol. 5, 119–22 (quotations, 120, 121, 122).

52. Gallagher, "Blueprint for Victory," 18–23; Madden, "Rediscovering Civil War Classics."

53. Robert H. Glauber to T. Harry Williams, Dec. 17, 1946, New York, T. Harry Williams Papers, Mss 2489, 2510, Louisiana and Lower Mississippi Collections, Special Collections, Hill Library, Louisiana State Universities Libraries, Baton Rouge (hereafter cited as Williams Papers, LSU).

54. Williams, biographical introduction to *Selected Essays of T. Harry Williams,* 1–3; "The Author," 11 (quotation); Dawson, "T. Harry Williams," 432–33; Spiller, "Williams Among the Rebels," 275–76, 276–77; Wetta, "T. Harry Williams," 1–3; "Williams, T(homas) Harry," 601–2.

55. Clipping of George Johnson, Letter to the Editor, *Wausau (WI) Record Herald,* [1952], Scrapbook, Williams Papers, LSU. See also *Hartford (CT) Courant,* Nov. 14, 1936; *Rhinelander (WI) Daily News,* Nov. 13, 1936; and Wetta, "T. Harry Williams," 1–2.

56. *Rhinelander (WI) Daily News,* Nov. 13, 1936. See also *Hartford (CT) Courant,* Nov. 14, 1936; and Wetta, "T. Harry Williams," 1–2.

57. T. Harry Williams to Robert H. Glauber, Feb. 2, 1948, Baton Rouge, LA, Williams Papers, LSU; Williams, biographical introduction, 5–6; Dawson, "T. Harry Williams," 434–35; Hewitt and Schott, *Lee and His Generals,* xi–xii; Launius, "Bibliography of the Works of T. Harry Williams," 5–10, 13; Spiller, "Williams Among the Rebels," 273, 275–78; Wetta, "T. Harry Williams," 2–3, 4, 10–13; "Williams, T(homas) Harry," 601–2. Williams also taught a single summer at West Virginia University before finishing his dissertation and moving to Nebraska.

58. T. Harry Williams to Robert H. Glauber, Jan. 13, 1948, Baton Rouge, LA, Williams Papers, LSU.

59. Robert H. Glauber to T. Harry Williams, Jan. 27, Mar. 2 (quotation), 11, 1948, New York; J. G. Randall to T. Harry Williams, Feb. 24, 1948, Urbana, IL; Paul W. Angle to T. Harry Williams, Jan. 27, Mar. 2, 11, 1948, Chicago; E. G. Campbell to T. Harry Williams, Apr. 9, 1948, Washington, DC; and Robert H. Glauber, Mar. 11, 1948, all Williams Papers, LSU.

60. J. G. Randall to T. Harry Williams, Feb. 24, 1948, Urbana, IL, Williams Papers, LSU.

61. Robert H. Glauber to T. Harry Williams, Mar. 2, 1948, New York; and Earl Schenck Miers to T. Harry Williams, Sept. 14, 23, 1949, New York, all Williams Papers, LSU; Williams, biographical introduction, 6.

62. Alfred A. Knopf to T. Harry Williams, May 31, 1951, New York (quotation); and Harold Strauss to T. Harry Williams, Sept. 4, 13, 1951, New York, all Williams Papers, LSU.

63. Harold Strauss to T. Harry Williams, Sept. 4 (quotation), 13, 1951, New York; and Sidney R. Jacobs to T. Harry Williams, Nov. 15, 1951, all Williams Papers, LSU; Lee, *Hidden Public;* Radway, *Feeling for Books,* esp. 1–14, 105–14.

64. Williams, *Lincoln and His Generals,* esp. 355–63. By standard diaries, I mean the writings of Grant, Sherman, Noah Brooks, Orville Browning, Francis Carpenter, Ward Lamon (but not Herndon, still out of favor in the profession), McClellan, and Horace Porter. See also Spiller, "Williams Among the Rebels," 274–75.

65. Williams, *Lincoln and His Generals,* vii–viii, 3 (quotations); Spiller, "Williams Among the Rebels," 277–79.

66. Williams, *Lincoln and His Generals,* 7–14 (quotations, 7, 8, 14). One of his doctoral students, George Rable, remembered that in the classroom, Williams commented, "Lincoln was so self-confident he could appear to be humble but did not have a humble bone in his body." George Rable, email message to author, June 6, 2024.

67. Williams, *Lincoln and His Generals,* 15–24, 29–64 (quotations, 20, 29, 53); Spiller, "Williams Among the Rebels," 279–81; Wetta, "T. Harry Williams" 10. Williams grew more pro-Lincoln and anti-McClellan in later years, especially in his classroom, where he compared Lincoln to Gen. Dwight Eisenhower and commented negatively on McClellan's character. George Rable, email message to author, June 3, 2024; Frank Wetta (another Williams student), email messages to author, June 6, 23, 2024.

68. Williams, *Lincoln and His Generals,* 64–91 (quotations, 66, 67–68, 74, 91).

69. Williams, *Lincoln and His Generals,* 97–104 (quotations, 98, 101, 102, 104).

70. Williams, *Lincoln and His Generals,* 92–178 (quotations, 126, 130, 133, 134, 151, 168, 176).

71. Williams, *Lincoln and His Generals,* 179–206, 215–47, 251–71 (quotations, 197, 198, 264, 269).

72. Williams, *Lincoln and His Generals,* 84–86, 187–94, 215–32, 247–51, 271–90 (quotations, 188, 189, 275, 283, 284, 290).

73. Williams, *Lincoln and His Generals,* 291–335, 342–54 (quotations, 291, 305, 306, 336, 345, 354). On Williams's high opinion of Grant, see Hewitt and Schott, *Lee and His Generals,* xii–xiii.

74. For the Book-of-the-Month Club, see Lee, *Hidden Public,* 186; "The Author," 11; and Wetta, "T. Harry Williams," 12. Williams told the *Saturday Review* that having his book selected for the club was "going to bring me a lot of money. . . . That sure is a nasty thought, isn't it?" "The Author," 11. For correspondence, see Sam Ross to Harry, Feb. 23, 1956, Sacramento, CA; Philip R. Sherman to T. Harry Williams, Apr. 16, 1952, Hanover, NH; and M. McDonald Wilson to President of Louisiana State University, Feb. 12, 1952, Newark, DE (quotation), all Williams Papers, LSU. The Associated Press picked up the Truman story on March 10, 1952, and it quickly appeared in other newspapers. See, among others, *Lafayette (LA) Advertiser,* Mar. 11, 1952; *New Orleans States,* Mar. 11, 1952; *New Orleans Times Picayune,* Mar. 11, 1952; and *Shreveport Times,* Mar. 12, 1952. See also Scrapbooks, Williams Papers, LSU; Rafuse, "Two Harrys," 58–65; and Schwartz, *Abraham Lincoln in the Post-Heroic Era,* 102. For the book as best seller, see "*New*

York Times Best Seller List," Mar. 23, 1952, Scrapbooks, Williams Papers, LSU. On a happier note, Williams received a letter from undergraduate James I. Robertson Jr., whom the book had helped inspire to become a Civil War historian. See Robertson to T. Harry Williams, Sept. 13, 1954, Ashland, VA, ibid.

75. For popular reviews, see Nevins, "Able Strategist & President," 10–11; *Cleveland (OH) News,* Feb. 27, 1952; *Columbia (SC) Record,* Feb. 28. 1952; *Dayton (OH) News,* Mar. 9, 1952; *Durham (NC) Herald,* Mar. 9, 1952; *Library Journal,* Mar. 15, 1952; Hesseltine, *Milwaukee Journal,* Mar. 23, 1952; Johnson, Letter to the Editor, *Wausau (WI) Record Herald,* [1952]; *Newsweek,* n.d.; *The New Yorker,* Mar. 8, 1952; Rubin, *Richmond (VA) News Leader,* Feb. 26, 1952; *Time,* Mar. 10, 1952; and Wiley, *Jackson (MS) Sun,* May 30, 1952; all clippings in Scrapbooks, Williams Papers, LSU. David Donald called the book "on the whole disappointing," "curiously inconsistent," and "more provocative than convincing. . . . [H]is conclusions are obiter dicta." Clipping, *New York Herald Tribune,* Feb. 24, 1952, ibid,

76. George Johnson, Letter to the Editor, *Wausau (WI) Record Herald,* [1952], Scrapbooks, Williams Papers, LSU.

77. See, for example, H.E.P., review of *Lincoln Finds a General,* 176; Henry, review of *Lincoln Finds a General,* 991–92; and Perkins, review of *Lincoln and His Generals,* 368–69.

78. Craven, review of *Lincoln Finds a General,* 337–39 (quotation, 338). David M. Potter likewise commented on Williams's debt to Ballard as a springboard as well as his contentions that Lincoln was a better strategist than his generals—Potter found these convincing—and the more dubious notion that he had created a modern system of warmaking. See Potter, review of *Lincoln and His Generals,* 508–9.

79. Merrick, review of *Lincoln and His Generals,* 38; Clark, "Report of the Chronicler," 377; *Official National Guard Register for 1930,* 322; Cook, *Troubled Commemoration,* 22–25; Civil War Round Table of the District of Columbia.

CONCLUSION

1. Dimitri Rotov, *Civil War Bookshelf* (blog), https://cwbn.blogspot.com/; Rotov, "Book Sales and New Thinking: In Summary," ibid., Dec. 24, 2004, https://cwbn.blogspot.com/2004/12/book-sales-and-new-thinking-in-summary_24.html (quotation). See also Rotov's posts of Dec. 10, 13, 15, 20, and 21, 2004; Nov. 7, 23, 29, Dec. 2, 7, 2005; Dec. 27, 2006; Dec. 13, 18, 19, 2007; Nov. 7, Dec. 23, 2008; Dec. 10, 14, 2009; Sept. 24, 2010; May 8, 28, June 2, 2011; Nov. 4, 2012; Sept. 9, 2015; and May 7, June 20, 2017. Rotov's blog has not been updated since 2019 at this writing. On Rotov as an internet pioneer, see Schulte, "Guide to Civil War Books for Beginners." On the Civil War Centennial itself, see Cook, *Troubled Commemoration.*

2. Brooks Simpson, June 12, 2009, comment on Kevin Levin, "Dimitri Rotov Historiography," *Civil War Memory* (blog), June 10, 2009.

3. Williams, Current, and Freidel, *History of the United States;* Williams, *Union Restored,* 6–107; Williams, "Military Leadership of North and South," 33–54. I am grateful to Frank Wetta for suggesting that I look at these volumes. See also Gallagher, "Blueprint for Victory," 18–22; Marszalek, *Lincoln and the Military,* ix–x; McDonough, "Commander in Chief and Military Operations in Tennessee," 93; Peterson, *Lincoln in American Memory,* 336; Prokopowicz, "Five Best Books on Lincoln and His Commanders"; Rafuse, review of *Lincoln and the Civil War,*

53–55; Rafuse, "Two Harrys," 58; George Rable, email message to author, June 3, 2024; Frank Wetta, email messages to author, June 6, 23, 2024. For the U.S. Army reading list, see "The Chief of Staff's Professional Reading List," *Army* (Mar. 2012): 22–23. The other three Civil War books included in that list are Grant, *Personal Memoirs;* McPherson, *Battle Cry of Freedom;* and Shaara, *Killer Angels.*

4. Williams, "Military Leadership of North and South"; George Rable, email message to author, June 3, 2024; Wetta, email messages to author, June 6, 23, 2024. On T. Harry Williams as the creator of the heroic legend, see also Craig Symonds's comments in *The Civil War: Lincoln and His Generals,* Gettysburg College Civil War Institute, C-SPAN, June 10, 2023.

5. Rafuse, review of *Lincoln and the Civil War,* 53–55.

6. Sears, *George B. McClellan;* Sears, *Landscape Turned Red;* Sears, *To the Gates of Richmond.*

7. For modern "neo-Confederate" views of Lincoln, the trendsetter has been the Austrian School economist Thomas J. DiLorenzo: see his *Real Lincoln;* and *Lincoln Unmasked.* For notable examples of defending McClellan, see Grimsley, "Lincoln as Commander-in-Chief"; Grimsley, "Lincoln-McClellan Relationship"; Harsh, "On the McClellan-Go-Round"; and Rowland, *George B. McClellan.*

8. Simpson, *Lincoln and the Gettysburg Campaign,* iv–v, 7–14, 16–19, 24–26, 58–59 (quotations, iv, v, 59); Rafuse, "'Spirit Which You Have Aided to Infuse,'" 4n6; Brooks Simpson, email message to author, May 13, 2024.

9. Perret, *Lincoln's War,* esp. 40–45, 53–60, 75, 105–6, 112, 144–49, 156–68, 250–60, 270, 291–305, 334–58, 382 (quotations, 291, 300, 342, 358). Perret would continue his analysis of the growing powers of the commander in chief more directly with *Commander in Chief.*

10. McPherson, "Top Gun"; Baker, review of *Lincoln's War,* 698–99; Furgurson, review of *Lincoln's War,* 73–74; Tap, review of *Lincoln's War,* 89–94.

11. For Stanton, see Marvel, *Lincoln's Autocrat.* For Porter, see Marvel, *Radical Sacrifice.*

12. Marvel, *Great Task Remaining,* xi, xiii; Marvel, *Lincoln's Darkest Year,* xi; Marvel, *Mr. Lincoln Goes to War,* xiii, xiv, xvii, xviii, 42, 71, 186, 264, 282, 284.; Marvel, *Tarnished Victory.*

13. Marvel, *Mr. Lincoln Goes to War,* esp. xviii, 14–24, 26–27, 106–48, 151–54; Marvel, *Lincoln's Darkest Year,* esp. xii–xv, 14–30, 51–78, 107–8, 140–44, 151–65, 187, 248–55 (quotations, xii, xiv, xv, 58, 107).

14. Marvel, *Lincoln's Darkest Year,* 267–74, 278 (quotation); Marvel, *Great Task Remaining,* esp. 38–41, 85–87, 116–19, 155–56, 198, 334 (quotation, 155); Marvel, *Tarnished Victory,* esp. 5–9, 175–85, 220–27.

15. See, for example, Cimprich, review of *Lincoln's Darkest Year,* 228; Davis, review of *Mr. Lincoln Goes to War,* 299–300; Marszalek, review of *Tarnished Victory;* McClintock, review of *Lincoln's Darkest Year,* 88–89; McColley, review of *Mr. Lincoln Goes to War,* 419–20; Norman, review of *The Great Task Remaining,* 204–5; Rafuse, "Jaundiced View of Yanks," 68; Ramold, review of *Mr. Lincoln Goes to War,* 510–11; and Simpson, review of *The Great Task Remaining.*

16. Pryor, *Reading the Man;* Pryor, *Six Encounters,* viii–xi; *New York Times,* Apr. 28, 2015; *Washington Post,* Apr. 16, 2015.

17. Pryor, *Six Encounters,* 7.

18. Pryor, *Six Encounters,* 11–62, 353n99 (quotations, 54, 61).

19. Pryor, *Six Encounters,* vii–viii, x–xi; *New York Times,* Apr. 28, 2015; *Richmond (VA) Times Dispatch,* Apr. 14, 2015; *Washington Post,* Apr. 16, 2015. For anticipation of the book,

see, for example, Levin, "My Brief Encounter with Elizabeth Brown Pryor," and John Hennessy comment, Jan. 31, 2017, on Levin's post.

20. Bundy, "Honest, Narcissistic, Ambitious Abe"; Chaput, "Two Tales of Lincoln," 65–71; Crofts, review of *Six Encounters with Lincoln,* 69–73; Alice Kessler-Harris, "Lincoln Served Six Ways: Reframing a President," *New York Times,* Feb. 6, 2017; Norman, review of *Six Encounters with Lincoln;* Reynolds, "Taking Old Abe to Task"; Stevenson, review of *Six Encounters with Lincoln,* 141–44. Allen C. Guelzo especially lacerated Pryor as "prickly, condescending, and schoolmarmish, contemptuous not only of Lincoln but of everyone who sees him as more than an oafish political hack." With its "querulous, fault-finding tone" and errors, he continued, "*Six Encounters* is, unquestionably, a book for the snobbish end of the anti-Lincoln sofa." Guelzo, "Lincoln's Forgotten Middle Years."

21. Reynolds, "Taking Old Abe to Task."

22. Cook, *Troubled Commemoration,* esp. 22, 46, 59, 86, 113, 123, 128–29, 269.

23. For recent examples, see Faust, "'We Should Grow to Fond of It,'" 368–83; and its subsequent companion piece, Downs et al., "'Does the Civil War Matter?,'" 50–73.

24. Faust, "'We Should Grow to Fond of It,'" 368–83; Downs et al., "'Does the Civil War Matter?,'" 50–73. For debate over Lincoln and race, see, for example, Maria Cramer, "Chicago Lists Lincoln Statues," *New York Times,* Feb. 18, 2021; Marie Fazio, "Boston Removes Statue of Formerly Enslaved Man Kneeling Before Lincoln," *New York Times,* Dec. 29, 2020; Elbaum, "Portland Protesters Tear Down Statues"; "San Francisco to Remove Washington, Lincoln, and Feinstein from School Names"; and Chappell, "Statue of Lincoln with Formerly Enslaved Man at His Feet Is Removed." See also Cook, *Troubled Commemoration,* esp. 22, 46, 59, 86, 113, 123, 128–29, 269; Guelzo, *Our Ancient Faith,* 112–13; and Schwartz, *Abraham Lincoln in the Post-Heroic Era,* 2, 6, 13, 15–16, 112, 115–278.

25. Simpson, *Lincoln and the Gettysburg Campaign,* 59.

26. Sternhell, *War on Record.*

27. See, for example, Arenson and Graybill, *Civil War Wests;* Nelson, *Three-Cornered War;* and West, *Last Indian War.*

28. Schlesinger, *Imperial Presidency,* esp. xiii–xiv, xxv–xxviii, 42–43, 58–69, 109, 113–14, 142, 157, 165, 187–88, 192–93, 285–86, 321–22, 335, 460 (quotations, xiv, 193, 460). The 2004 edition took the narrative up to President George W. Bush. See also Aldous, *Schlesinger,* 353–57, 363, 373, 384.

29. Perret, *Commander in Chief;* Marvel, *Mr. Lincoln Goes to War,* xiv, 71, 281–82; Marvel, *Great Task Remaining,* xiii–xv.

30. Beaumont, "Trump's Expansionism Threatens the Rules-Based Order"; Wargaski, "U.S. Drone Warfare and Civilian Casualties." One might also refer to the *Trump v. United States* Supreme Court decision of July 2024, which seemingly granted a president broad immunity from criminal prosecution for all "official acts." See *Trump v. United States,* Certiorari to the United States, Court of Appeals for the District of Columbia Circuit, 603 U.S. ____ (2024). Although it does not deal specifically with the role of commander in chief, one might as well note the expansion of executive power more generally through the Supreme Court decision in *Donald J. Trump v. Norma Anderson et al.,* 601 U.S. ____ (2024).

31. Basler et al., *Collected Works of Abraham Lincoln,* 4:537.

BIBLIOGRAPHY

PRIMARY SOURCES

Manuscripts

Indiana University Archives, Bloomington
Kenneth P. Williams Papers C193

John Hay Library, Brown University Library, Providence, RI
John Hay Collection, Box 4

Library of Congress, Washington, DC
John G. Nicolay Papers: General Correspondence, 1811–1943, Manuscript/Mixed Material, https://www.loc.gov/collections/john-g-nicolay-papers/about-this-collection

Louisiana State Universities Libraries, Hill Memorial Library, Special Collections, Louisiana and Lower Mississippi Collections, Baton Rouge
T. Harry Williams Papers, Mss 2489, 2510

Books and Articles

Adams, Charles Francis. *The Address of Charles Francis Adams, of Massachusetts, on the Life, Character, and Services of William H. Seward. Delivered by Invitation of the Legislature of the States of New York, in Albany, April 18, 1873.* New York: D. Appleton, 1873.

"American Literature." *Saturday Review of Politics, Literature, Science, and Arts* 52 (December 31, 1881): 837–39.

Arnold, Isaac N. *The History of Abraham Lincoln and the Overthrow of Slavery.* Chicago: Clarke, 1866.

——. *The Life of Abraham Lincoln.* Introduction by E. B. Washburne. Chicago: Jackson, McClurg, 1884.

Bancroft, Frederic. "Gideon Welles and His Diary." *The Nation* 93 (December 21, 1911): 598–601.

——. "Lincoln and Seward and Their Latest Biographers." *Political Science Quarterly* 6 (December 1891): 711–24.

Barnes, John S. "With Lincoln from Washington to Richmond in 1865." Pts. 1 and 2. *Appleton's Magazine* 9 (May 1907): 515–24; 9 (June 1907): 742–51.

Basler, Roy P., Lloyd A. Dunlap, and Marion Dolores Pratts, eds. *The Collected Works of Abraham Lincoln.* 8 vols. New Brunswick, NJ: Rutgers University Press, 1953–55.

Bates, David Homer. *Lincoln in the Telegraph Office: Recollections of the United States Military Telegraph Corps During the Civil War.* New York: Century, 1907.

Beale, Howard K. ed. *The Diary of Edward Bates, 1859–1866.* Washington, DC: Government Printing Office, 1933.

Brockett, L. P. *The Life and Times of Abraham Lincoln, Sixteenth President of the United States. Including His Speeches, Messages, Inaugurals, Presentations, Etc. Etc.* Philadelphia: Jones Brothers, 1865.

——. *Men of Our Day; or, Biographical Sketches of Patriots, Orators, Statesmen, Generals, Reformers, Financiers and Merchants, Now on the Stage of Action: Including Those Who in Military, Political, Business and Social Life, Are the Prominent Leaders of the Time in This Country.* St. Louis: Zeigler, McCurdy, 1868.

Brooks, Noah. *Abraham Lincoln and the Downfall of American Slavery.* New York: G. T. Putnam's Sons, 1888; new ed., 1894.

——. *Washington in Lincoln's Time.* New York: Century, 1895.

Burlingame, Michael, ed. *Lincoln Observed: Civil War Dispatches of Noah Brooks.* Baltimore: Johns Hopkins University Press, 1998.

——, ed. *With Lincoln in the White House: Letters, Memoranda, and Other Writings of John G. Nicolay, 1860–1865.* Carbondale: Southern Illinois University Press, 2000.

Burlingame, Michael, and John R. Turner Ettlinger, eds. *Inside Lincoln's White House: The Complete Civil War Diary of John Hay.* Carbondale: Southern Illinois University Press, 1997.

Busk, Hans. *The Rifle, and How to Use It. Comprising a Description of That Valuable Weapon in All Its Variants.* 8th ed. London: Routledge, Warne, and Routledge, 1861.

Callan, John F. *The Military Laws of the United States, Relating to the Army, Volunteers, Militia, and to Bounty Lands and Pensions, from the Foundation of the Government to the Year 1863. To Which Are Prefixed the Constitution of the United*

States (with an Index Thereto), and a Synopsis of the Military Legislation of Congress During the Revolutionary War. Philadelphia: George W. Childs, 1863.

Carpenter, F. B. *The Inner Life of Abraham Lincoln: Six Months at the White House.* New York: Hurd and Houghton, 1868.

———. *Six Months at the White House with Abraham Lincoln: The Story of a Picture.* New York: Hurd and Houghton, 1866.

Chittenden, L. E. *Recollections of President Lincoln and His Administration.* New York: Harper and Bros., 1891.

Comte de Paris. *Histoire de la Guerre Civile en Amérique.* Paris: Michel Lévy Fréres, 1874–90.

———. *History of the Civil War in America.* 4 vols. Philadelphia: Porter & Coates, 1875–88.

Cook, Hugh. "The Ballard Letters: The Boer War Writings of C. R. Bond, Part 1." *Quarterly Bulletin of the South African Library* 45 (1991): 145–58.

Coryell, Janet L. *Neither Heroine nor Fool: Anna Ella Carroll of Maryland.* Kent, OH: Kent State University Press, 1990.

Crowley, Aleister. *The Confessions of Aleister Crowley: An Autohagiography.* Edited by John Symonds and Kenneth Grant. London: Arkana, 1979.

Dana, Charles A. *Recollections of the Civil War: With the Leaders at Washington and in the Field in the Sixties.* New York: D. Appleton, 1898.

Davis, Jefferson Davis. "Lord Wolseley's Mistakes." *North American Review* 149 (October 1889): 472–83.

Dodge, Grenville. *Personal Recollections of President Abraham Lincoln, General Ulysses S. Grant, and General William T. Sherman.* Council Bluffs, IA: Monarch, 1914.

Doster, William E. *Lincoln and Episodes of the Civil War.* New York: G. P. Putnam's Sons, 1915.

Douglass, Frederick. "Oration in Memory of Abraham Lincoln." *Teaching American History.* https://teachingamericanhistory.org/document/oration-in-memory-of-abraham-lincoln/.

"Editor's Study." *Harper's New Monthly Magazine* 82 (February 1891): 481–83.

An English Officer [Garnet Wolseley]. "A Month's Visit to the Confederate Headquarters." In Wolseley, *American Civil War,* 51–70. Previously published in *Blackwood's Edinburgh Magazine* 93 (January 1863): 1–29.

Forbes, Archibald. *Memories and Studies of War and Peace.* 2nd ed. London: Cassell, 1895.

Freeman, Douglas Southall, ed. *Lee's Dispatches: Unpublished Letters of General Robert E. Lee, C.S.A., to Jefferson Davis and the War Department of the Confederate States of America, 1862–1865.* Baton Rouge: Louisiana State University Press, 1994.

Fry, James B. "Lord Wolseley Answered." *North American Review* 149 (December 1889): 728–40.

"General M. C. Meigs on the Conduct of the Civil War." *American Historical Review* 26 (1921): 285–303.

Gienapp, William E., and Erica L. Gienapp, eds. *The Civil War Diary of Gideon Welles, Lincoln's Secretary of the Navy. The Original Manuscript Edition.* Urbana: Knox College Lincoln Studies Center and University of Illinois Press, 2014.

Grant, U. S. *Personal Memoirs of U. S. Grant.* 2 vols. New York: Charles L. Webster, 1885–86.

Greene, Francis V. "Lincoln as Commander-in-Chief." *Scribner's Magazine* 46 (July 1909): 104–15.

Halleck, H. Wager. *Elements of Military Art and Science; or, Course of Instruction in Strategy, Fortification, Tactics of Battles, &c., Embracing the Duties of Staff, Infantry, Cavalry, Artillery, and Engineers. Adapted to the Use of Volunteers and Militia.* Boston, D. Appleton, 1846.

Herndon, William H. "Analysis of the Character of Abraham Lincoln: A Lecture by William H. Herndon." *Abraham Lincoln Quarterly* 1 (December 1941): 403–41.

Herndon, William H., and Jesse W. Weik. *Abraham Lincoln: The True Story of a Great Life.* Introduction by Horace White. 2 vols. New York: D. Appleton, 1892.

——. *Herndon's Lincoln: The True Story of a Great Life.* 2 vols. Chicago: Belford, Clarke, 1889.

Holland, J.G. *The Life of Abraham Lincoln.* Springfield, MA: Gurdon Bill, 1866.

Holzer, Harold, ed. *Lincoln as I Knew Him: Gossip, Tributes & Revelations from His Best Friends and Worst Enemies. A Collected Biography.* Chapel Hill, NC: Algonquin Books, 2009.

Johnson, Richard Underwood, and Clarence Buel, eds. *Battles and Leaders of the Civil War Era.* 4 vols. New York: Century, 1884.

Keckley, Elizabeth. *Behind the Scenes; or, Thirty Years a Slave, and Four Years in the White House.* New York: G. W. Carleton, 1868.

Kelley, William D. *Lincoln and Stanton: A Study of the War Administration of 1861 and 1862, with Special Consideration of Some Recent Statements of General Geo. B. McClellan.* New York: G. Putnam's Sons, 1885.

Lamon, Ward H. *The Life of Abraham Lincoln, from His Birth to His Inauguration as President.* Boston: James R. Osgood, 1872.

Life, Speeches, and Public Services of Abram Lincoln, Together with a Sketch of the Life of Hannibal Hamlin, Wigwam ed. New York: Rudd and Carlton, 1860.

Lindsay, Vachel. *The Congo and Other Poems.* New York: Macmillan, 1915. Reprint, New York: Dover, 1992.

Livermore, Mary. *My Story of the War: A Woman's Narrative of Four Years Personal Experience as Nurse in the Union Army, and in Relief Work at Home, in Hospitals, Camps, and at the Front during the War of the Rebellion, with Anecdotes, Pathetic Incidents, and Thrilling Reminiscences Portraying the Lights and Shadows of*

Hospital Life and the Sanitary Service of the War. Hartford, CT: A. D. Worthington, 1889.

Lloyd George, David. *War Memoirs of David Lloyd George.* 6 vols. Boston: Little, Brown, 1936.

Marquis de Chambrun [Adolphe Pineton]. "Personal Recollections of Mr. Lincoln." *Scribner's Magazine* 13 (January 1893): 26–38.

Maurice, Nancy, ed. *The Maurice Case: From the Papers of Major-General Sir Frederick Maurice K.C.M.G., C.B.* With an appreciation by Major-General Sir Edward Spears, Bart. K.B.E., C.B., M.C. Hamden, CT: Archon, 1972.

McClellan, George B. *McClellan's Own Story: The War for the Union, the Soldiers Who Fought It, the Civilians Who Directed It, and His Relations to It and Them.* New York: Charles L. Webster, 1887.

McClure, A. K. *Abraham Lincoln and Men of War-Times: Some Personal Recollections of War and Politics During the Lincoln Administration.* Introduction by A. C. Lambdin. Philadelphia: Times Publishing, 1892.

"Minor Notices." *American Historical Review* 1 (January 1896): 372–77.

Nicolay, John G. *The Outbreak of the Rebellion.* Campaigns of the Civil War 1. New York: Charles Scribner's Sons, 1881.

Nicolay, John G., and John Hay. *Abraham Lincoln: A History.* 10 vols. New York: Century, 1890.

"Nicolay and Hay's Lincoln—1." *The Nation* (January 1, 1891): 13–14.

Niven, John, ed. *The Salmon P. Chase Papers.* Vol. 1, *Journals, 1829–1872.* Kent, OH: Kent State University Press, 1994.

Official National Guard Register for 1930. Washington, DC: Militia Bureau, 1930.

Oldroyd, Osborn H., ed. *The Lincoln Memorial: Album-Immortelles. Original Life Pictures, with Autographs, from the Hands and Hearts of Eminent Americans and Europeans, Contemporaries to the Great Martyr to Liberty Abraham Lincoln, Together with Extracts from His Speeches, Letters and Sayings.* Introduction by Matthew Simpson. "Sketch of the Patriot's Life," by Isaac N. Arnold. New York: G. W. Carleton, 1882.

Pease, Theodore Calvin, and James G. Randall, eds. *The Diary of Orville Hickman Browning.* Vol. 1, *1850–1864.* Springfield: Illinois State Historical Library, 1925.

Piatt, Donn. *Memories of the Men Who Saved the Union.* New York: Belford, Clarke, 1887.

Pollard, Edward A. *The Lost Cause; A New Southern History of the War of the Confederates, Comprising a Full and Authentic Account of the Rise and Progress of the Late Southern Confederacy—the Campaigns, Battles, Incidents, and Adventures of the Most Gigantic Struggle of the World's History, Drawn from Official Sources, and Approved by the Most Distinguished Confederate Leaders.* New York: E. B. Treat, 1867.

Porter, Admiral [David Dixon]. *Incidents and Anecdotes of the Civil War.* New York: D. Appleton, 1885.

Randall, Ruth Painter. *I, Ruth: Autobiography of a Marriage, the Self-Told Story of the Woman Who Married the Great Lincoln Scholar, James G. Randall, and Through Her Interest in His Work Became a Lincoln Author Herself.* Boston: Little, Brown, 1968.

Raymond, Henry J. *History of the Administration of President Lincoln: Including His Speeches, Letters, Addresses, Proclamations, and Messages, with a Preliminary Sketch of His Life.* New York: J. C. Derby and N. C. Miller, 1864.

———. *The Life and Public Services of Abraham Lincoln, Sixteenth President of the United States, Together with His State Papers, Including His Speeches, Addresses, Messages, Letters, and Proclamations, and the Closing Scenes Connected with his Life and Death, to Which Are Added Anecdotes and Personal Reminiscences of President Lincoln, by Frank B. Carpenter.* New York: Derby and Miller, 1865.

Rice, Allen Thorndike, ed. *Reminiscences of Abraham Lincoln, by Distinguished Men of His Time.* New York: North American Publishing, 1888.

Robertson, Sir William. Foreword to *Russia in Rule and Misrule: A Short History,* by C. R. Ballard. London: John Murray, 1920.

———. *From Private to Field Marshal.* Boston: Houghton Mifflin, 1926.

Russell, William Howard. *My Diary North and South.* Edited by Eugene H. Berwanger. New York: Alfred A. Knopf, 1988.

Rusling, James Fowler. *Men and Things I Saw in Civil War Days.* New York: Methodist Book Concern, 1914.

Schurz, Carl. "Abraham Lincoln." *Atlantic Monthly* 67 (June 1891): 721–50.

Sears, Stephen W., ed. *The Civil War Papers of George B. McClellan: Selected Correspondence, 1860–1865.* New York: Ticknor & Fields, 1989.

Seward, William Henry. *The Irrepressible Conflict. A Speech by William H. Seward, Delivered at Rochester, Monday Oct. 25, 1858.* New York: *New York Tribune,* 1858.

Sherman, William T. "Grant, Thomas, Lee." *North American Review* 144 (May 1887): 437–50.

———. *Memoirs of William T. Sherman, by Himself.* Foreword by B. H. Liddell Hart. 2 vols. complete in 1. Bloomington: Indiana University Press, 1957.

Stoddard, William O. *Abraham Lincoln: The True Story of a Great Life, Showing the Inner Growth, Special Training, and Peculiar Fitness of the Man for His Work.* New York: Fords, Howard, and Hulbert, 1885.

———. *The Boy Lincoln.* New York: D. Appleton, 1905.

———. *Inside the White House in War Times.* New York: Charles C. Webster, 1890.

———. *The Table Talk of Abraham Lincoln.* Centenary ed. New York: Frederick A. Stokes, 1894.

Townsend, George Alfred. *The Real Life of Abraham Lincoln: A Talk with Mr. Herndon, His Late Law Partner.* New York: Bible House, 1867.

U.S. War Department. *The War of the Rebellion: A Compilation of the Official Records of the Union and Confederate Armies.* 129 vols. Washington, DC: Government Printing Office, 1880–1901.

"*Washington in Lincoln's Time.*" *The Critic* (December 21, 1895), 425.

Welles, Edgar T., ed. *Diary of Gideon Welles, Secretary of the Navy Under Lincoln and Johnson.* 3 vols. Introduction by John T. Morse Jr. Boston: Houghton Mifflin, 1911.

Welles, Gideon. *Lincoln and Seward: Remarks upon the Memorial Address of Chas. Francis Adams, on the Late Wm. Henry Seward, with Incidents and Comments Illustrative of the Measures and Policies of the Administration of Abraham Lincoln, and Views as to the Relative Positions of the Late President and Secretary of State.* New York: Sheldon, 1874.

Wolseley, Garnet. "An English View of the American Civil War." In Wolseley, *American Civil War,* 71–223. Previously published in *North American Review* 148 (May 1889): 538–63; 149 (July): 30–43; (August): 164–81; (September): 278–92; (October): 446–59; (November): 564–606; (December): 713–27.

——. "General Lee." In Wolseley, *American Civil War,* 51–70. Previously published in *Macmillan's Magazine* 55 (March 1887): 321–31.

Newspapers

Hartford (CT) Courant

Montgomery (AL) Advertiser

New York Times

Rhinelander (WI) Daily News

Richmond Times Dispatch

Times (London)

SECONDARY SOURCES

Books

Aldous, Richard. *Schlesinger: The Imperial Historian.* New York: W. W. Norton, 2017.

Arenson, Adam, and Andrew R. Graybill, eds. *Civil War Wests: Testing the Limits of the United States.* Berkeley: University of California Press, 2015.

Ballard, Colin Robert. *The Military Genius of Abraham Lincoln.* London: Oxford University Press, 1926.

——. *Russian in Rule and Misrule: A Short History.* London: John Murray, 1920.

Ballard, Michael B. *Vicksburg: The Campaign That Opened the Mississippi.* Chapel Hill: University of North Carolina Press, 2004.

Barr, John McKee. *Loathing Lincoln: An American Tradition from the Civil War to the Present.* Baton Rouge: Louisiana State University Press, 2014.

Barton, William E. *The Autobiography of William E. Barton.* Introduction by Bruce Barton. Indianapolis: Bobbs-Merrill, 1932.

——. *The Life of Abraham Lincoln.* 2 vols. Indianapolis: Bobbs-Merrill, 1925.
Bearss, Edwin C. *The Campaign for Vicksburg.* 3 vols. Dayton, OH: Morningside House, 1985.
Beckett, Ian F. W. *The Victorians at War.* London: Hambledon and London, 2003.
Berg, Scott W. *38 Nooses: Lincoln, Little Crow, and the Beginning of the Frontier's End.* New York: Pantheon, 2012.
Blight, David. *Race and Reunion: The Civil War in American Memory.* Cambridge, MA: Belknap Press, 2002.
Bond, Brian. *Liddell Hart: A Study of His Military Thought.* New Brunswick, NJ: Rutgers University Press, 1977.
——. *The Victorian Army and the Staff College, 1854–1914.* London: Eyre Methuen, 1972.
Boot, Max. *War Made New: Technology, Warfare, and the Course of History, 1500 to Today.* New York: Gotham Books, 2006.
Boritt, Gabor S. *Lincoln and the Economics of the American Dream.* Urbana: University of Illinois Press, 1978.
——, ed. *Lincoln the War President: The Gettysburg Lectures.* New York: Oxford University Press, [1992].
Bowers, Claude G. *The Tragic Era: The Revolution After Lincoln.* New York: Houghton Mifflin, 1929.
Bradley, George C., and Richard L. Dahlen. *From Conciliation to Conquest: The Sack of Athens and the Court-Martial of Colonel John B. Turchin.* Tuscaloosa: University of Alabama Press, 2006.
Brady, Kathleen. *Ida Tarbell: Portrait of a Muckraker.* Pittsburgh: University of Pittsburg Press, 1989.
Brady, Lisa M. *War upon the Land: Military Strategy and the Transformation of Southern Landscapes during the Civil War.* Athens: University of Georgia Press, 2012.
Brasher, Glenn David. *The Peninsula Campaign and the Necessity of Emancipation: African Americans and the Fight for Freedom.* Chapel Hill: University of North Carolina Press, 2012.
Bray, Robert. *Reading with Lincoln.* Carbondale: Southern Illinois University Press, 2010.
Bridges, Peter. *Donn Piatt: Gadfly of the Gilded Age.* Kent, OH: Kent State University Press, 2012.
Brokaw, Tom. *The Greatest Generation.* New York: Random House, 1998.
Brown, Kent Masterson. *Retreat from Gettysburg: Lee, Logistics, and the Pennsylvania Campaign.* Chapel Hill: University of North Carolina Press, 2011.
Bruce, Robert V. *Lincoln and the Tools of War.* Indianapolis: Bobbs-Merrill, 1956.
Bullard, F. Lauriston. *Famous War Correspondents.* Boston: Little, Brown, 1914.
Burlingame, Michael. *Abraham Lincoln: A Life.* 2 vols. Baltimore: Johns Hopkins University Press, 2008.
Burton, Orville Vernon. *The Age of Lincoln.* New York: Hill and Wang, 2007.

Campbell, Joseph. *The Hero with a Thousand Faces.* 3rd ed. Bollingen Series 17. Novato CA: Joseph Campbell Foundation and New World Library, 2008.

Castel, Albert. *Decision in the West: The Atlanta Campaign of 1864.* Lawrence: University Press of Kansas, 1992.

Charnwood, Lord. *Abraham Lincoln.* London: Constable, 1916.

Churchill, Winston S. *A History of the English-Speaking Peoples.* Vol. 4, *The Great Democracies.* London: Castle, 1958. Reprint, London: Bloomsbury Academic, 2015.

Clark, Alan. *The Donkeys.* New York: William Morrow, 1962.

Clarke, Arthur C. *The Lost Worlds of 2001.* New York: New American Library/Signet, 1972.

Coddington, Edwin B. *The Gettysburg Campaign: A Study in Command.* New York: Charles Scribner's Sons, 1968.

Conant, Alan E. *Colonel Arthur L. Conger.* Pasadena, CA: Theosophical University Press, 1999.

Conger, Arthur. *The Rise of U. S. Grant.* New York: Century, 1931.

Cook, Robert J. *Troubled Commemoration: The American Civil War Centennial, 1961–1965.* Baton Rouge: Louisiana State University Press, 2007.

Cooper, John Milton, Jr. *Woodrow Wilson: A Biography.* New York: Vintage, 2011.

Cox, Hank. *Lincoln and the Sioux Uprising of 1862.* Nashville: Cumberland House, 2005.

Cox, Karen L. *No Common Ground: Confederate Monuments and the Ongoing Fight for Racial Justice.* Chapel Hill: University of North Carolina Press, 2021.

Cozzens, Peter. *No Better Place to Die: The Battle of Stones River.* Urbana: University of Illinois Press, 1990.

———. *Shenandoah 1862: Stonewall Jackson's Valley Campaign.* Chapel Hill: University of North Carolina Press, 2008.

———. *The Shipwreck of Their Hopes: The Battles for Chattanooga.* Urbana: University of Illinois Press, 1994.

———. *This Terrible Sound: The Battle of Chickamauga.* Urbana: University of Illinois Press, 1992.

Craven, Avery. *The Coming of the Civil War.* 1942. 2nd ed., Chicago: University of Chicago Press, 1957.

———. *Edmund Ruffin, Southerner.* New York: D. Appleton, 1932. Reprint, Baton Rouge: Louisiana State University Press, 1972.

———. *The Repressible Conflict, 1830–1861.* Baton Rouge: Louisiana State University Press, 1939.

Cruden, Robert. *James Ford Rhodes: The Man, the Historian, and His Work, with a Complete Bibliography of the Writings of James Ford Rhodes.* Cleveland, OH: Press of Western Reserve University, 1961.

Current, Richard N. *Lincoln and the First Shot.* Critical Periods of History. Philadelphia: J. B. Lippincott, 1963.

Dagbovie, Pero Gaglo. *Carter G. Woodson in Washington, D.C.: The Father of Black History*. Charleston, SC: History Press, 2014.

Danchev, Alex. *Alchemist of War: The Life of Basil Liddell Hart*. London: Weidenfeld & Nicolson, 1998.

Davis, William C. *Battle at Bull Run: A History of the First Major Campaign of the Civil War*. Baton Rouge: Louisiana State University Press, 1977.

——. *Duel Between the First Ironclads*. New York: Doubleday, 1975.

Diggins, John Patrick, ed. *The Liberal Persuasion: Arthur Schlesinger, Jr., and the Challenge of the American Past*. Princeton, NJ: Princeton University Press, 1997.

DiLorenzo, Thomas J. *Lincoln Unmasked: What You're Not Supposed to Know About Dishonest Abe*. New York: Crown Forum, 2006.

——. *The Real Lincoln: A New Look at Abraham Lincoln, His Agenda, and an Unnecessary War*. Foreword by Walter E. Williams. Roseville, CA: Prima, 2002.

Domby, Adam H. *The False Cause: Fraud, Fabrication, and White Supremacy in Confederate Memory*. Charlottesville: University of Virginia Press, 2020.

Donald, David Herbert. *Lincoln*. New York: Simon and Schuster, 1995.

——. *Lincoln Reconsidered: Essays on the Civil War Era*. New York: Vintage, 1947.

——. *Lincoln's Herndon*. Introduction by Carl Sandburg. New York: Alfred A. Knopf, 1948.

Doyle, Don H. *The Cause of All Nations: An International History of the American Civil War*. New York: Basic Books, 2015.

Dundes, Alan, ed. *Sacred Narrative: Readings in the Theory of Myth*. Berkeley: University of California Press, 1984.

Eisenschiml, Otto. *Why Was Lincoln Murdered?* Boston: Little, Brown, 1937.

Eisenschiml, Otto, and Ralph Newman. *The American Iliad: The Epic Story of the Civil War as Told by Eyewitnesses and Contemporaries*. Indianapolis: Bobbs Merrill, 1948.

Ellwood, Robert. *The Politics of Myth: A Study of C. G. Jung, Mircea Eliade, and Joseph Campbell*. Albany: State University of New York Press, 1999.

Elson, Henry W. *History of the United States of America*. New York: Macmillan, 1904.

Emancipation at 150: The Impact of the Emancipation Proclamation. N.p: National Trust for Historic Preservation, 2013.

Engle, Stephen D. *Don Carlos Buell: Most Promising of All*. Chapel Hill: University of North Carolina Press. 1999.

Etulain, Richard W. *Lincoln and the Oregon Country: Politics in the Civil War Era*. Corvallis: Oregon State University Press, 2013.

Fehrenbacher, Don E., and Virginia Fehrenbacher, comps. and eds. *Recollected Words of Abraham Lincoln*. Stanford, CA: Stanford University Press, 1996.

Ferguson, Andrew. *Land of Lincoln: Adventures in Abe's America*. New York: Grove, 2007.

Fiege, Mark. *The Republic of Nature: An Environmental History of the United States.* Seattle: University of Washington Press, 2012.

Fleche, Andre M. *The Revolution of 1861: The American Civil War in the Age of Nationalist Conflict.* Chapel Hill: University of North Carolina Press, 2012.

Flower, Frank A. *Edwin McMasters Stanton: The Autocrat of Rebellion, Emancipation, and Reconstruction.* New York: W. W. Wilson, 1905.

Foner, Eric. *The Fiery Trial: Abraham Lincoln and American Slavery.* New York: W. W. Norton, 2010.

Foreman, Amanda. *A World on Fire: Britain's Crucial Role in the American Civil War.* New York: Random House, 2010.

Foster, Gaines M. *Ghosts of the Confederacy: Defeat, the Lost Cause, and the Emergence of the New South.* New York: Oxford University Press, 1987.

Frankel, Valerie Estelle. *From Girl to Goddess: The Heroine's Journey Through Myth and Legend.* Jefferson, NC: McFarland, 2010.

Fry, Zachery A. *A Republic in the Ranks: Loyalty and Dissent in the Army of the Potomac.* Chapel Hill: University of North Carolina Press, 2020.

Fuller, J. F. C. *The Generalship of Ulysses S. Grant.* London: J. Murray, 1929. Reprint, Boston: Da Capo, [1956].

——. *Grant and Lee: A Study in Personality and Generalship.* Bloomington: Indiana University Press, 1982.

Furgerson, Ernest B. *Chancellorsville 1863: The Souls of the Brave.* New York: Knopf, 1992.

Fussell, Paul. *The Great War and Modern Memory.* New York: Oxford University Press, 1975.

Gallagher, Gary W., ed. *The Richmond Campaign of 1862: The Peninsula & the Seven Days.* Chapel Hill: University of North Carolina Press, 2000.

——. *The Shenandoah Valley Campaign of 1862.* Chapel Hill: University of North Carolina Press, 2003.

Gannon, Barbara. *The Won Cause: Black and White Comradeship in the Grand Army of the Republic.* Chapel Hill: University of North Carolina Press, 2011.

Gat, Azar. *Fascist and Liberal Visions of War: Fuller, Liddel Hart, Douhet, and Other Modernists.* Oxford: Clarendon, 1998.

Gerwarth, Robert. *The Vanquished: Why the First World War Failed to End.* New York: Farrar, Straus, and Giroux, 2016.

Gienapp, William E. *Abraham Lincoln and Civil War America.* Oxford: Oxford University Press, 2002.

Gilbert, Martin. *The First World War: A Complete History.* New York: Henry Holt, 1994.

Glatthaar, Joseph T. *The March to the Sea and Beyond: Sherman's Troops in the Savannah and Carolinas Campaigns.* Baton Rouge: Louisiana State University Press, 1985.

———. *Partners in Command: The Relationships Between Leaders in the Civil War.* New York: Free Press, 1994.

Goodheart, Adam. *1861: The Civil War Awakening.* New York: Vintage, 2011.

Goodwin, Doris Kearns. *Leadership in Turbulent Times.* New York: Simon & Schuster, 2018.

———. *Team of Rivals: The Political Genius of Abraham Lincoln.* New York: Simon & Schuster, 2005.

Gordon, Lesley J. *Dread Danger: Cowardice and Combat in the American Civil War.* Cambridge: Cambridge University Press, 2025.

Gorton, Stephanie. *Citizen Reporters: S. S. McClure, Ida Tarbell, and the Magazine That Rewrote America.* New York: Ecco/Harper Collins, 2020.

Grabau, Warren E. *Ninety-Eighty Days: A Geographer's View of the Vicksburg Campaign.* Knoxville: University of Tennessee Press, 2000.

Grahame-Smith, Seth. *Abraham Lincoln: Vampire Hunter.* New York: Grand Central, 2010.

Green, Michael S. *Lincoln and Native Americans.* Carbondale: Southern Illinois University Press, 2021.

Greene, A. Wilson. *A Campaign of Giants: The Battle for Petersburg.* Vol. 1, *From the Crossing of the James to the Crater.* Chapel Hill: University of North Carolina Press, 2018.

———. *The Final Battles of the Petersburg Campaign: Breaking the Backbone of the Rebellion.* Knoxville: University of Tennessee Press, 2008.

Greene, Francis Vinson. *The Mississippi.* Campaigns of the Civil War 8. New York: Charles Scribner's Sons, 1882.

Gregory, Adrian. *The Last Great War: British Society and the First World War.* Cambridge: Cambridge University Press, 2008.

———. *A War of Peoples, 1914–1919.* Oxford: Oxford University Press, 2014.

Grimsley, Mark. *And Keep Moving On: The Virginia Campaign, May–June 1864.* Lincoln: University of Nebraska Press, 2002.

———. *The Hard Hand of War: Union Military Policy Toward Southern Civilians, 1861-1865.* Cambridge: Cambridge University Press, 1995.

Groeling, Meg. *First Fallen: The Life of Elmer Ellsworth, the North's First Civil War Hero.* El Dorado, CA: Savas Beatie, 2021.

Guelzo, Allen C. *Abraham Lincoln: Redeemer President.* Grand Rapids, MI: Wm. B. Eerdmans, 1999.

———. *Gettysburg: The Last Invasion.* New York: Alfred A. Knopf, 2013.

———. *Our Ancient Faith: Lincoln, Democracy, and the American Experiment.* New York: Alfred A. Knopf, 2024.

Hagerman, Edward. *The American Civil War and the Origins of Modern Warfare: Ideas, Organization, and Field Command.* Bloomington: Indiana University Press, 1988.

Hartwig, D. Scott. *I Dread the Thought of the Place: The Battle of Antietam and the End of the Maryland Campaign.* Baltimore: Johns Hopkins University Press, 2023.

———. *To Antietam Creek: The Maryland Campaign of September 1862.* Baltimore: Johns Hopkins University Press, 2019.

Hattaway, Herman, and Archer Jones. *How the North Won: A Military History of the Civil War.* 1983. Reprint, with a new introduction, Urbana: University of Illinois Press, 1991.

Hattersley, Roy. *David Lloyd George: The Great Outsider.* London: Little, Brown, 2010.

Hearn, Chester G. *Lincoln and McClellan at War.* Baton Rouge: Louisiana State University Press, 2010.

Henderson, G. F. R. [A Line Officer, pseud.]. *The Campaign of Fredericksburg, Nov.–Dec. 1862: A Study for Officers of Volunteers.* London: Kegan Paul, Trench, 1886.

———. *Stonewall Jackson and the American Civil War.* 2 vols. 2nd ed. Introduction by Viscount Wolseley. London: Longmans, Green, 1900.

Hennessy, John J. *The First Battle of Manassas: An End to Innocence, July 18–21, 1861.* Rev. and updated ed. Mechanicsburg, PA: Stackpole Books, 2015.

———. *Return to Bull Run: The Campaign and Battle of Second Manassas.* New York: Simon & Schuster, 1993.

Hess, Earl J. *Civil War Logistics: A Study of Military Transportation.* Baton Rouge: Louisiana State University Press, 2017.

———. *Civil War Supply and Strategy: Feeding Men and Moving Armies.* Baton Rouge: Louisiana State University Press, 2020.

Hettle, Wallace. *Inventing Stonewall Jackson: A Civil War Hero in Memory and History.* Baton Rouge: Louisiana State University, 2011.

Hewitt, Lawrence Lee, and Thomas E. Schott, eds. *Lee and His Generals: Essays in Honor of T. Harry Williams.* Knoxville: University of Tennessee Press, 2012.

Higham, Robin. *The Military Intellectuals in Britain: 1918–1939.* New Brunswick, NJ: Rutgers University Press, 1966.

Hochschild, Adam. *American Midnight: The Great War, a Violent Peace, and Democracy's Forgotten Crisis.* New York: Mariner, 2022.

Hodes, Martha. *Mourning Lincoln.* New Haven, CT: Yale University Press, 2015.

Holden Reid, Brian. *America's Civil War: The Operational Battlefield, 1861–1863.* New York: Prometheus, 2008.

———. *J. F. C. Fuller: Military Thinker.* New York: St. Martin's, 1987.

Holzer, Harold. *Lincoln President-Elect: Abraham Lincoln and the Great Secession Winter, 1860–1861.* New York: Simon & Schuster, 2008.

———, ed. *Lincoln's White House Secretary: The Adventurous Life of William O. Stoddard.* Carbondale: Southern Illinois University Press, 2007.

Janney, Caroline E. *Remembering the Civil War: Reunion and the Limits of Reconciliation.* Chapel Hill: University of North Carolina Press, 2013.

Jewett, Robert, and John Shelton Lawrence. *The American Monomyth.* Foreword by Isaac Asimov. Garden City, NY: Anchor Press, Doubleday, 1977.

Johannsen, Robert W. *The Frontier, the Union, and Stephen A. Douglas.* Urbana: University of Illinois Press, 1989.

Johnson, Ludwell H. *Red River Campaign: Politics and Cotton in the Civil War.* Kent, OH: Kent State University Press, 1993.

Johnston, R. M. *Bull Run: Its Strategy and Tactics.* Boston: Houghton Mifflin, 1913.

Jones, Howard. *Blue & Gray Diplomacy: A History of Union and Confederate Foreign Relations.* Chapel Hill: University of North Carolina Press, 2010.

Keegan, John. *The First World War.* New York: Alfred A. Knopf, 1999.

Kennett, Lee. *Marching Through Georgia: The Story of Soldiers and Civilians During Sherman's Campaign.* New York: HarperCollins, 1995.

Klein, Maury. *Days of Defiance: Sumter, Secession, and the Coming of the Civil War.* New York: Alfred A. Knopf, 1997.

Koistinen, Paul A. C. *Beating Ploughshares into Swords: The Political Economy of American Warfare, 1606–1865.* Lawrence: University Press of Kansas, 1996.

Krick, Robert K. *Stonewall Jackson at Cedar Mountain.* Chapel Hill: University of North Carolina Press. 1990.

Larsen, Stephen, and Robin Larsen. *A Fire in the Mind: The Life of Joseph Campbell.* New York: Doubleday, 1991.

Lawrence, John Shelton, and Robert Jewett. *The Myth of the American Superhero.* Grand Rapids, MI: William B. Eerdman's, 2002.

Lee, Charles. *The Hidden Public: The Story of the Book-of-the-Month Club.* Garden City, NY: Doubleday, 1958.

Lehmann, Joseph H. *All Sir Garnet: A Life of Field Marshal Lord Wolseley.* London: Jonathan Cape, 1964.

Leonhard, Jörn. *Pandora's Box: A History of the First World War.* Cambridge, MA: Belknap Press of Harvard University Press, 2018.

Levin, Kevin M. *Searching for Black Confederates: The Civil War's Most Persistent Myth.* Chapel Hill: University of North Carolina Press, 2019.

Liddell Hart, B. H. *Great Captains Unveiled.* Edinburgh: William Blackwood and Sons, 1927.

———. *The Remaking of Modern Armies.* London: John Murray, 1927.

———. *Sherman: Soldier, Realist, American.* Boston: Dodd, Mead, 1929. Reprint, with new introduction by Jay Luvaas, [Boston]: Da Capo, [1993].

Lilly, William E. *Set My People Free: A Negro's Life of Lincoln.* New York: Farrar and Rinehart, 1932.

Livermore, Thomas M. *Numbers and Losses in the Civil War in America, 1861–1865.* Boston: Houghton, Mifflin, 1900.

Livermore, William Roscoe. *The Story of the Civil War: A Concise Account of the War in the United States Between 1861 and 1865, in Continuation of the Story by John Codman Ropes.* Pt. 3, *The Campaigns of 1863 to July 10.* 2 vols. New York: G. P. Putnam's Sons, 1913.

Logan, Rayford W. *The Negro in American Life and Thoughts: The Nadir, 1877–1901.* New York: Dial, 1954.

Long, E. B., with Barbara Long. *The Civil War Day by Day: An Almanac, 1861–1865.* Foreword by Bruce Catton. Garden City, NJ: Doubleday, 1971.

Luvaas, Jay. *The Education of an Army: British Military Thought, 1815–1940.* Chicago: University of Chicago Press, 1964.

Malcolm, Capt. Neill, ed. *The Science of War: A Collection of Essays and Lectures, 1891–1903, of the Late Colonel G. F. R. Henderson, CB.* London: Longmans, Green, 1912.

Marszalek, John F. *Commander of All Lincoln's Armies: A Life of Henry W. Halleck.* Cambridge, MA: Harvard University Press, 2004.

———. *Lincoln and the Military.* Carbondale: Southern Illinois University Press, [2014].

Marvel, William. *Burnside.* Chapel Hill: University of North Carolina Press, 1991.

———. *The Confederate Resurgence of 1864.* Baton Rouge: Louisiana State University Press, 2024.

———. *The Great Task Remaining: The Third Year of Lincoln's War.* Boston: Houghton Mifflin, 2010.

———. *Lincoln's Autocrat: The Life of Edwin Stanton.* Chapel Hill: University of North Carolina Press, 2015.

———. *Lincoln's Darkest Year: The War in 1862.* Boston: Houghton Mifflin, 2008.

———. *Mr. Lincoln Goes to War.* Boston: Houghton Mifflin, 2006.

———. *Radical Sacrifice: The Rise and Ruin of Fitz John Porter.* Chapel Hill: University of North Carolina Press, 2021.

———. *Tarnished Victory: Finishing Lincoln's War.* Boston: Houghton Mifflin, 2011.

Maurice, F. [Sir Frederick]. *British Strategy: A Study of the Application of the Principles of War.* Introduction by Field Marshal Sir G. Milne. London: Constable, 1929.

———. *Forty Days in 1914.* London: Constable, 1919.

———. *The Last Four Months: The End of the War in the West.* London: Cassell, 1919.

———. *Robert E. Lee the Soldier.* London: Constable, 1925.

———. *Statesmen and Soldiers of the Civil War: A Study of the Conduct of War.* Boston: Little, Brown, 1926.

Maurice, F. [Sir Frederick], and George Arthur. *The Life of Lord Wolseley.* Foreword by R. Wingate. Garden City, NJ: Doubleday, Page, 1924.

Maverick, Augustus. *Henry J. Raymond and the New York Press for Thirty Years: Progress of American Journalism from 1840 to 1870.* Hartford, CT: A. S. Hale, 1870.

Mawdsley, Evan. *World War II: A New History*. Cambridge: Cambridge University Press, 2009.

May, Joseph, ed. *A Memoir of the Life of John Codman Ropes, with the Proceedings of Various Societies Addresses, Papers, and Resolutions in Commemoration of Him*. Boston: Privately printed, 1891.

McDonough, James Lee. *The Western Confederacy's Final Gamble: From Atlanta to Franklin to Nashville*. Knoxville: University of Tennessee Press, 2013.

McPherson, James M. *Battle Cry of Freedom: The Civil War Era*. New York: Oxford University Press, 1988.

———. *Crossroads of Freedom: Antietam, the Battle That Changed the Civil War*. New York: Oxford University Press, 2002.

———. *Tried by War: Abraham Lincoln as Commander in Chief*. New York: Penguin Books, 2008.

McPherson, James M., and William J. Cooper Jr. *Writing the Civil War: The Quest to Understand*. Columbia: University of South Carolina Press, 1998.

Meacham, Jon. *And There Was Light: Abraham Lincoln and the American Struggle*. New York: Random House, 2022.

Miller, Charles Grant. *Donn Piatt: His Work and His Ways*. Cincinnati: Robert Clarke, 1893.

Milton, George Fort. *The Age of Hate: Andrew Johnson and the Radicals*. New York: Coward-McCann, 1930.

———. *Conflict: The American Civil War*. New York: Coward-McCann, 1941.

———. *The Eve of Conflict: Stephen A. Douglas and the Needless War*. Boston: Houghton Mifflin, 1934.

Moody, Wesley, ed. *Seven Myths of the Civil War*. Indianapolis: Hackett, 2017.

Morgan, Robin. *The Demon Lover: The Roots of Terrorism*. New York: Washington Square Books, 2001.

Murdock, Maureen. *The Heroine's Journey*. Boston: Shambhala, 1990.

Murray, Jennifer M. *On a Great Battlefield: The Making, Management, and Memory of Gettysburg National Military Park, 1933–2013*. Knoxville: University of Tennessee Press, 2014.

Neely, Mark E., Jr. *The Fate of Liberty: Abraham Lincoln and Civil Liberties*. New York: Oxford University Press, 1991.

———. *The Last Best Hope: Abraham Lincoln and the Promise of America*. Cambridge, MA: Harvard University Press, 1993.

Nelson, Megan Kate. *The Three-Cornered War: The Union, the Confederacy, and Native Peoples in the Fight for the West*. New York: Scribner, 2020.

Nichols, David A. *Lincoln and the Indians: Civil War Policies and Politics*. Columbia: University of Missouri Press, 1978.

Niven, John. *Gideon Welles: Lincoln's Secretary of the Navy*. New York: Oxford University Press, 1973. Reprint, Baton Rouge: Louisiana State University Press, 1994.

Niven, Penelope. *Carl Sandburg: A Biography.* New York: Charles Scribner's Sons, 1991.

Noe, Kenneth W. *The Howling Storm: Weather, Climate, and the American Civil War.* Baton Rouge: Louisiana State University Press, 2020.

——. *Perryville: This Grand Havoc of Battle.* Lexington: University Press of Kentucky, 2001.

Nolan, Alan T., and Gary W. Gallagher, eds. *The Myth of the Lost Cause and Civil War History.* Bloomington: Indiana University Press, 2000.

Nulty, William H. *Confederate Florida: The Road to Olustee.* Tuscaloosa: University of Alabama Press, 1990.

Oakes, James. *Freedom National: The Destruction of Slavery in the United States, 1861–1865.* New York: Norton, 2013.

Oates, Stephen B. *With Malice Toward None: The Life of Abraham Lincoln.* New York: Harper & Row, 1977.

O'Reilly, Francis Augustín. *The Fredericksburg Campaign: Winter War on the Rappahannock.* Baton Rouge: Louisiana State University Press, 2003.

Overy, Richard. *Blood and Ruins: The Last Imperial War, 1931–1945.* New York: Viking, 2022.

——. *Why the Allies Won.* London: Jonathan Cape, 1995.

Page, Sebastian N. *Black Resettlement and the American Civil War.* Cambridge: Cambridge University Press, 2002.

Paludan, Phillip Shaw. *"A People's Contest": The Union and the Civil War, 1861–1865.* New York: Harper & Row, 1988.

Perret, Geoffrey. *Commander in Chief: How Truman, Johnson, and Bush Turned a Presidential Power into a Threat to America's Future.* New York: Macmillan, 2007.

——. *Lincoln's War: The Untold Story of America's Greatest President as Commander in Chief.* New York: Random House, 2004.

Peterson, Merrill D. *Lincoln in American Memory.* New York: Oxford University Press, 1994.

Potter, David M. *Lincoln and His Party in the Secession Crisis.* New Haven, CT: Yale University Press, 1942.

Powell, David A. *The Chickamauga Campaign: A Mad Irregular Battle: From the Crossing of Tennessee River Through the Second Day, August 22–September 19, 1863.* El Dorado Hills, CA: Savas Beatie, 2014.

——. *The Chickamauga Campaign: Barren Victory: The Retreat into Chattanooga, the Confederate Pursuit, and the Aftermath of the Battle, September 21 to October 20, 1863.* El Dorado Hills, CA: Savas Beatie, 2016.

——. *The Chickamauga Campaign: Glory or the Grave: The Breakthrough, the Union Collapse, and the Defense of Horseshoe Ridge, September 20, 1863.* El Dorado Hills, CA: Savas Beatie, 2015.

Powell, David A., and Eric J. Wittenberg. *Tullahoma: The Forgotten Campaign That Changed the Course of the Civil War, June 23–July 4, 1863*. El Dorado Hills, CA: Savas Beatie, 2020.

Pressly, Thomas J. *Americans Interpret Their Civil War*. 1954. Reprint, with a new introduction, New York: Free Press, 1962.

Pryor, Elizabeth Brown. *Reading the Man: A Portrait of Robert E. Lee Through His Private Letters*. New York: Viking, 2007.

———. *Six Encounters with Lincoln: A President Confronts Democracy and Its Demons*. New York: Penguin, 2017.

Rable, George C. *Conflict of Command: George McClellan, Abraham Lincoln, and the Politics of War*. Baton Rouge: Louisiana State University Press, 2023.

———. *Fredericksburg! Fredericksburg!* Chapel Hill: University of North Carolina Press, 2002.

Radway, Janice A. *A Feeling for Books: The Book-of-the-Month Club, Literary Taste, and Middle-Class Desire*. Chapel Hill: University of North Carolina Press, 1997.

Rafuse, Ethan S. *From the Mountains to the Bay: The War in Virginia, January–May 1862*. Lawrence: University Press of Kansas, 2023.

———. *McClellan's War: The Failure of Moderation in the Struggle for the Union*. Bloomington: Indiana University Press, 2005.

———. *A Single Grand Victory: The First Campaign and Battle of Manassas*. Wilmington, DE: SR Books, 2002.

Randall, James G. *The Civil War and Reconstruction*. Boston: D. C. Heath, 1937.

———. *Constitutional Problems under Lincoln*. New York: D. Appleton, 1926.

———. *Lincoln the Liberal Statesman*. New York: Dodd, Mead, 1947.

———. *Lincoln the President: Springfield to Gettysburg*. 2 vols. New York: Dodd, Mead, 1945.

———. *Lincoln the President: Midstream*. New York: Dodd, Mead, 1952.

Randall, James G., and Richard N. Current. *Lincoln the President: Last Full Measure*. New York: Dodd, Mead, 1953. Reprint, with a new introduction by Richard N. Current, New York: Dodd, Mead, 1991.

Reardon, Carol. *Soldiers and Scholars: The U.S. Army and the Uses of Military History, 1865–1920*. Lawrence: University Press of Kansas, 1990.

———. *With a Sword in One Hand & Jomini in the Other: The Problem of Military Thought in the Civil War North*. Chapel Hill: University of North Carolina Press, 2012.

Reynolds, David S. *Abe: Abraham Lincoln in His Times*. New York: Penguin, 2020.

Rhea, Gordon C. *The Battle of the Wilderness May 5–6, 1864*. Baton Rouge: Louisiana State University Press, 1994.

———. *The Battles for Spotsylvania Court House and the Road to Yellow Tavern May 7–12, 1864*. Baton Rouge: Louisiana State University Press, 1997.

——. *Cold Harbor: Grant and Lee, May 26—June 3, 1864*. Baton Rouge: Louisiana State University Press, 2002.

——. *In the Footsteps of Grant and Lee: The Wilderness Through Cold Harbor.* Baton Rouge: Louisiana State University Press, 2007.

——. *On to Petersburg: Grant and Lee, June 4–15, 1864.* Baton Rouge: Louisiana State Press, 2017.

——. *To the North Anna River: Grant and Lee, May 13–25, 1864.* Baton Rouge: Louisiana State University Press, 2000.

Rhodes, James Ford. *History of the Civil War, 1861-1865.* New York: Macmillan, 1917.

——. *History of the United States from the Compromise of 1850.* Vols. 1–4. New York: Harper and Brothers, 1893–99. Vols. 5–8. New York: Macmillan, 1904–6.

Richardson, Heather Cox. *West from Appomattox: The Reconstruction of America after the Civil War.* New Haven, CT: Yale University Press, 2007.

Roberts, Andrew. *The Storm of War: A New History of the Second World War.* London: Penguin, 2010.

Roland, Charles Pierce. *An American Iliad: The Story of the Civil War.* Lexington: University Press of Kentucky, 2004.

Ropes, John Codman. *The Army Under Pope.* Campaigns of the Civil War 4. New York: Charles Scribner's Sons, 1881.

——. *The Story of the Civil War: A Concise Account of the War in the United States Between 1861 and 1865.* Pt. 1, *To the Opening of the Campaigns of 1862.* New York: G. P. Putnam's Sons, 1895.

——. *The Story of the Civil War: A Concise Account of the War in the United States Between 1861 and 1865.* Pt. 2, *The Campaigns of 1862.* New York: G. P. Putnam's Sons, 1898.

Rowland, Thomas J. *George B. McClellan and Civil War History: In the Shadow of Grant and Sherman.* Kent, OH: Kent State University Press, 1998.

Rubin, Anne Sarah. *A Shattered Nation: The Rise and Fall of the Confederacy, 1861–1868.* Chapel Hill: University of North Carolina Press, 2005.

——. *Through the Heart of Dixie: Sherman's March and American Memory.* Chapel Hill: University of North Carolina Press, 2014.

Sandburg, Carl. *Abraham Lincoln: The Prairie Years.* 2 vols. New York, Harcourt, Brace, 1926.

——. *Abraham Lincoln: The Prairie Years and the War Years.* New York, Harcourt, Brace, 1954.

——. *Abraham Lincoln: The War Years.* 4 vols. New York, Harcourt, Brace, 1939.

Schlesinger, Arthur M., Jr. *The Age of Jackson.* Boston: Little, Brown, 1945.

——. *The Imperial Presidency.* Boston: Houghton Mifflin, 1973. Reprint, Boston: Mariner Books, 2004.

——. *The Vital Center: The Politics of Freedom.* Boston: Houghton Mifflin, 1949.

Schmadel, Lutz D. *Dictionary of Minor Planet Names*. Berlin: Springer, 2007.

Schultz, Duane. *Over the Earth I Come: The Great Sioux Uprising of 1862*. New York: St. Martin's Griffin, 1993.

Schwartz, Barry. *Abraham Lincoln and the Forge of National Memory*. Chicago: University of Chicago Press, 2000.

———. *Abraham Lincoln in the Post-Heroic Era*. Chicago: University of Chicago Press, 2008.

Sears, Stephen W. *Chancellorsville*. Boston: Houghton Mifflin, 1996.

———. *Controversies and Commanders: Dispatches from the Army of the Potomac*. Boston: Houghton Mifflin, 1999.

———. *George B. McClellan: The Young Napoleon*. New York: Ticknor & Fields, 1988.

———. *Landscape Turned Red: The Battle of Antietam*. Boston: Houghton Mifflin, 1983.

———. *To the Gates of Richmond: The Peninsula Campaign*. New York: Ticknor & Fields, 1992.

Shaara, Jeff. *Gods and Generals*. New York: Ballantine Books, 1996.

Shaara, Michael. *The Killer Angels*. New York: David McKay, 1974.

Shea, William L., and Terrence J. Winschel. *Vicksburg Is the Key: The Struggle for the Mississippi River*. Lincoln: University of Nebraska Press, 2003.

Shenk, Joshua Wolf. *Lincoln's Melancholy: How Depression Challenged a President and Fueled His Greatness*. New York: Houghton Mifflin Harcourt, 2005.

Shirer, William L. *The Rise and Fall of the Third Reich: A History of Nazi Germany*. New York: Simon & Schuster, 1960.

Simpson, Brooks D. *Abraham Lincoln and the Gettysburg Campaign*. Gettysburg, PA: Farnsworth Military Impressions, 1998.

———. *Ulysses S. Grant: Triumph over Adversity, 1822–1865*. New York: Houghton Mifflin, 2000.

Sommers, Richard J. *Richmond Redeemed: The Siege at Petersburg*. Garden City, NY: Doubleday, 1981.

Stampp, Kenneth M. *And the War Came: The North and the Secession Crisis, 1860–61*. 1950. Reprint, Baton Rouge: Louisiana State University Press, 1967.

———. *The Imperiled Union*. New York: Oxford University Press, 1980.

Stephenson, Nathaniel Wright. *Abraham Lincoln and the Union: A Chronicle of the Embattled North*. New Haven, CT: Yale University Press, 1918.

———. *An Autobiography of Abraham Lincoln: Consisting of the Personal Portions of His Letters Speeches and Conversations*. Indianapolis: Bobbs-Merrill, 1926.

———. *Lincoln: An Account of His Personal Life, Especially of Its Springs of Action as Revealed and Deepened by the Ordeal of War*. Indianapolis: Bobbs-Merrill, 1922.

Sternhell, Yael A. *War on Record: The Archive and Afterlife of the Civil War*. New Haven, CT: Yale University Press, 2023.

Stoker, Donald. *The Grand Design: Strategy and the U.S. Civil War.* New York: Oxford University Press, 2010.

Swanberg, W. A. *First Blood: The Story of Fort Sumter.* New York: Charles Scribner's Sons, 1957.

Sword, Wiley. *The Confederacy's Last Hurrah: Spring Hill, Franklin, and Nashville.* Lawrence: University Press of Kansas, 1993.

———. *Shiloh: Bloody April.* Foreword by S. L. A. Marshall. Dayton, OH: Morningside Bookshop, 1988.

Symonds, Craig L. *Lincoln and His Admirals: Abraham Lincoln, the U.S. Navy, and the Civil War.* New York: Oxford University Press, 2008.

Taaffe, Stephen R. *Commanding the Army of the Potomac.* Lawrence: University Press of Kansas, 2006.

Taliaferro, John. *All the Great Prizes: The Life of John Hay, from Lincoln to Roosevelt.* New York: Simon & Schuster, 2013.

Tanner, Robert G. *Stonewall in the Valley: Thomas J. "Stonewall" Jackson's Shenandoah Valley Campaign, Spring 1862.* Garden City, NY: Doubleday, 1976.

Tarbell, Ida M. *The Life of Abraham Lincoln: Drawn from Original Sources and Containing Many Speeches, Letters, and Telegrams Heretofore Unpublished.* 2 vols. New York: Doubleday and McClure, 1900.

Taylor, A. J. P. *The First World War: An Illustrated History.* New York: Capricorn Books, G. P. Putnam's Sons, 1972.

Temple, Wayne C. *Lincoln's Confidant: The Life of Noah Brooks.* Edited by Douglas L. Wilson and Rodney O. Davis. Introduction by Michael Burlingame. Urbana: Knox College Lincoln Studies Center and University of Illinois Press, 2019.

Terkel, Studs. *"The Good War": An Oral History of World War II.* New York: Pantheon, 1984.

Thomas, Benjamin P. *Abraham Lincoln: A Biography.* New York: Alfred A. Knopf, 1952.

———. *Portrait for Posterity: Lincoln and His Biographers.* New Brunswick, NJ: Rutgers University Press, 1947.

Toelken, Barre. *The Dynamics of Folklore.* Logan: Utah State University Press 1996.

Trythall, Anthony John. *"Boney" Fuller: The Intellectual General, 1878–1966.* London: Cassell, 1977.

Turner, Michael J. *Stonewall Jackson, Beresford Hope, and the Meaning of the American Civil War in Britain.* Baton Rouge: Louisiana State University Press, 2020.

Varon, Elizabeth R. *Appomattox: Victory, Defeat, and Freedom at the End of the Civil War.* New York: Oxford University Press, 2014.

Vogler, Christopher. *The Writer's Journey: Mythic Structure for Writers.* 3rd ed. Studio City, CA: Michael Wiese Productions, 2007.

Vorenberg, Michael. *Lincoln's Peace: The Struggle to End the American Civil War.* New York: Alfred A. Knopf, 2025.

Wall, Wendy L. *Inventing the "American Way": The Politics of Consensus from the New Deal to the Civil Rights Movement.* Oxford: Oxford University Press, 2008.

Warde, Mary Jane. *When the Wolf Came: The Civil War and Indian Territory.* Fayetteville: University of Arkansas Press, 2013.

Waugh, Joan. *U.S. Grant: American Hero, American Myth.* Chapel Hill: University of North Carolina Press, 2009.

Waugh, John C. *Lincoln and McClellan: The Troubled Partnership Between a President and His General.* New York: Palgrave Macmillan, 2010.

Weigley, Russell F. *A Great Civil War: A Military and Political History, 1861–1865.* Bloomington: Indiana University Press, [2000].

——. *Quartermaster-General of the Army: A Biography of M. C. Meigs.* New York: Columbia University Press, 1959.

Weinberg, Gerhard L. *A World at Arms: A Global History of World War II.* 2nd ed. Cambridge: Cambridge University Press, 2005.

West, Elliott. *The Last Indian War: The Nez Perce Story.* New York: Oxford University Press, 2009.

Wetta, Frank J., and Martin A. Novelli. *Abraham Lincoln & Women in Film: One Hundred Years of Hollywood Mythmaking.* Baton Rouge: Louisiana State University Press, 2024.

White, Jonathan W. *Emancipation, the Union Army, and the Reelection of Abraham Lincoln.* Baton Rouge: Louisiana State University Press, 2014.

White, Ronald C. *A. Lincoln: A Biography.* New York: Random House, 2009.

Williams, John H., and Kenneth P. Williams. *Plane Geometry.* Chicago: Lyons and Carnahan, 1915.

Williams, Kenneth P. *The Calculation of the Orbits of Asteroids and Comets.* Bloomington, IN: Principia, 1934.

——. *College Algebra.* Boston: Ginn, 1928.

——. *The Dynamics of the Airplane. Mathematical Monographs.* New York: John Wiley, 1921.

——. *Lincoln Finds a General: A Military Study of the Civil War.* 5 vols. New York: Macmillan, 1949–59.

——. *The Mathematical Theory of Finance.* New York: Macmillan, 1935.

——. *The Transits of Mercury: Determination of Corrections to the Elements of Mercury's Orbit, the Semi-Diameters of the Sun and Mercury, the Mass of Venus, and the Secular Retardation of the Earth's Rotation.* Bloomington: Indiana University, 1939.

Williams, T. Harry. *Lincoln and His Generals.* New York: Alfred A. Knopf, 1952. Reprint, New York: Gramercy Books, 2000.

——. *Lincoln and the Radicals.* Madison: University of Wisconsin Press, 1941.

——. *The Union Restored.* Vol. 6 of *The Life History of the United States.* 1963. Reprint, New York: Time-Life Books, 1975.

Williams, T. Harry, Richard Current, and Frank Freidel. *A History of the United States [to 1876]*. New York: Alfred A. Knopf, 1959.

Wilson, Charles Reagan. *Baptized in Blood: The Religion of the Lost Cause, 1865–1920*. Athens: University of Georgia Press, 1980.

Wilson, Douglas L. *Honor's Voice: The Transformation of Abraham Lincoln*. New York: Alfred A. Knopf, 1998.

Wilson, Woodrow. *A History of the American People*. 5 vols. New York: Harper & Brothers, 1901–2.

Wise, Stephen R. *Gate of Hell: Campaign for Charleston Harbor, 1863*. Columbia: University of South Carolina Press, 1994.

Wittenberg, Eric J. *Like a Meteor Blazing Brightly: The Short but Controversial Life of Colonel Ulric Dahlgren*. Roseville, MN: Edinborough, 2009.

Wittenberg, Eric J., David Petruzzi, and Michael F. Nugent. *One Continuous Fight: The Retreat from Gettysburg and the Pursuit of Lee's Army of Northern Virginia, July 4–14, 1863*. El Dorado Hills, CA: Savas Beatie, 2008.

Wolseley, Garnet. *The American Civil War: An English View: The Writings of Field Marshal Viscount Wolseley*. Edited with an introduction by James A. Rawley. Mechanicsburg, PA: Stackpole, 2002.

———. *General Lee*. Rochester, NY: George P. Humphrey, 1906.

Woodworth, Steven E. *Six Armies in Tennessee: The Chickamauga and Chattanooga Campaigns*. Lincoln: University of Nebraska Press, 1998.

Work, David. *Lincoln's Political Generals*. Urbana: University of Illinois Press, [2009].

Zander, Cecily N. *The Army Under Fire: The Politics of Antimilitarism in the Civil War Era*. Baton Rouge: Louisiana State University Press, 2024.

Zeitz, Joshua. *Lincoln's Boys: John Hay, John Nicolay, and the War for Lincoln's Image*. New York: Penguin, 2014.

———. *Lincoln's God: How Faith Transformed a President and a Nation*. New York: Viking, 2023.

Articles and Chapters

Angle, Paul M. Review of *Lincoln the President: Springfield to Gettysburg*, by James G. Randall. *The Atlantic* (November 1945), 157.

Ayers, Edward L. "Lincoln's America 2.0." *Journal of American History* (September 2009): 441–46.

Baker, Jean. Review of *Lincoln's War*, by Geoffrey Perret. *Journal of Southern History* 71 (August 2005): 698–99.

Bascom, William. "The Forms of Folklore: Prose Narratives." In Dundes, *Sacred Narrative*, 5–29.

Beale, Howard K. "Is the Printer Diary of Gideon Welles Reliable?" *American Historical Review* 30 (1925): 547–52.

Bell, Samuel E., and James M. Smallwood. "The Pragmatic Lincoln: A Historiographical Assessment of His Western Policy." *Lincoln Herald* 86 (Fall 1984): 134–42.

Benedict, Michael Les. "A Constitutional Crisis." In McPherson and Cooper, *Writing the Civil War,* 154–73.

Bishop, Erin I. "Teaching Lincoln at the Abraham Lincoln Presidential Library and Museum." *OAH Magazine of History* (January 2007): 39–41.

Bonner, Thomas N. "Civil War Historians and the 'Needless War' Doctrine." *Journal of the History of Ideas* 17 (April 1956): 193–216.

Bray, Robert. "'The Power to Hurt': Lincoln's Early Use of Satire and Invective." *Journal of the Abraham Lincoln Association* 16 (Winter 1995): 43–51.

———. "What Abraham Lincoln Read—An Evaluative and Annotated List." *Journal of the Abraham Lincoln Association* 28 (Summer 2007): 28–81.

Bruce, Robert V. "The Shadow of Coming War." In Boritt, *Lincoln the War President,* 1–28.

Bundy, Carol. "Honest, Narcissistic, Ambitious Abe." *Wall Street Journal,* February 13, 2017.

Burlingame, Michael. "Nicolay and Hay: Court Historians." *Journal of the Abraham Lincoln Association* 19 (Winter 1998): 1–20.

Chaput, Eric J. "Two Tales of Lincoln and the Meaning of Democracy." *Reviews in American History* 46 (March 2018): 65–71.

Cimprich, John. Review of *Lincoln's Darkest Year,* by William Marvel. *Journal of American History* 96 (June 2009): 228.

Clark, Elizabeth G. "Report of the Chronicler, 1960." *Records of the Columbia Historical Society, Washington, D.C.* 60/62 (1960/1962): 330–93.

Clinton, Catherine. "Turning and Turning in the Widening Gyre." *Journal of American History* (September 2009): 447–50.

Cole, Donald B. "The Age of Jackson: After Forty Years." *Reviews in American History* 14 (March 1986): 149–59.

Conger, Arthur Latham. "President Lincoln as War Statesman." In *Publications of the State Historical Society of Wisconsin: Proceedings of the Society at its Sixty-Fourth Annual Meeting, held October 19, 1919,* 106–40. Madison: State Historical Society of Wisconsin, 1916.

"Contributors of Historical Papers." In *Publications of the State Historical Society of Wisconsin: Proceedings of the Society at its Sixty-Fourth Annual Meeting, held October 19, 1919,* 104. Madison: State Historical Society of Wisconsin, 1916.

Cook, Joseph J. "From Liddell Hart to Keegan: Examining the Twentieth Century Shift in Military History Embodied by Two British Giants in the Field." *Saber and Scroll* 4 (2015): 23–35.

Coryell, Janet L. "Anna Ella Carroll and the Historians." *Civil War History* 35 (June 1989): 120–37.

Coulter, E. Merton. Review of *Lincoln Finds a General,* vols. 1–2, by Kenneth P. Williams. *Indiana Magazine of History* 46 (March 1950): 83–86.

Craven, Avery. "The Coming of the Civil War: An Interpretation." *Journal of Southern History* 2 (August 1936): 303–22.

———. Review of *Lincoln Finds a General.,* vols. 1–2, by Kenneth P. Williams. *Indiana Magazine of History* 49 (December 1950): 423–24.

Crespi, Muriel. Film review of *People of the Klamath: Of Land and Life* and *The Hero's Journey: The World of Joseph Campbell. American Anthropologist* 92 (December 1990): 1103–5.

Crofts, Daniel W. Review of *Six Encounters with Lincoln,* by Elizabeth Brown Pryor. *Journal of the Abraham Lincoln Association* 41 (Summer 2020): 69–73.

Czarnecki, Anthony J. "Mr. Lincoln's Secret Visit to West Point: The Sesquicentennial of a Military Mission." *New York History* 93 (Winter 2012): 4–51.

Davis, Rodney O. Review of *Mr. Lincoln Goes to War,* by William Marvel. *Civil War History* 53 (September 2007): 299–300.

Davis, William C. "Creating a Military Image: Lincoln as Commander in Chief." *OAH Magazine of History* (January 2009): 19–23.

Dawson, Joseph G., III. "T. Harry Williams." *Dictionary of Literary Biography* 17: *Twentieth-Century American Historians.* Detroit: Gale, 1983.

Decker, John R. Review of the Abraham Lincoln Presidential Library and Museum. *Journal of American History* 92 (December 2005): 934–38.

Degler, Carl N. "One Among Many: The United States and National Unification." In Boritt, *Lincoln the War President,* 89–119.

Dirck, Brian. "Lincoln as Commander-in-Chief." *Perspectives on Political Science* 39 (2010): 20–27.

Donald, David Herbert. "Getting Right with Lincoln." In Donald, *Lincoln Reconsidered,* 3–18. Previously published in *Harper's Magazine* 102 (April 1951): 74–80.

———. "Herndon and Mrs. Lincoln." In Donald, *Lincoln Reconsidered,* 37–56.

Downs, Jim, et al. "'Does the Civil War Matter?': A Roundtable Discussion." *Civil War History* 70 (March 2024): 50–73.

Dubrulle, Hugh. "A Military Legacy of the Civil War: The British Inheritance." *Civil War History* 49 (June 2003): 153–80.

Dundes, Alan. "Folklorists in the Twenty-First Century." *Journal of American Folklore* 118 (Fall 2005): 385–408.

Dunning, William A. "The Diary of Gideon Welles." *Political Science Quarterly* 27 (March 1912): 109–24.

Edwards, Richard. "Saving the Republic, Sinking the Republicans: Unraveling the Anomalous 1862 Midterms and Their Consequences," *Civil War History* 71 (Sept. 2025): 48–82.

"Eisenhower on Lincoln as Commander-in-Chief." *Lincoln Herald* 65 (June 1963): 55–57.

Erekson, Keith A. "Engulfed by the Past: History and Experience at the Abraham Lincoln Presidential Library and Museum." *Indiana Magazine of History* 103 (March 2007): 93–100.

Fastabend, David A. "G. F. R. Henderson and the Challenge of Change." *Military Review* 69 (October 1989): 66–74.

Faust, Drew Gilpin. "'We Should Grow Too Fond of It': Why We Love the Civil War." *Civil War History* 50 (December 2004): 368–83.

Fields, Kevin. "Historiographical Trends and Interpretations of President Abraham Lincoln's Reputation and the Morality on the Slavery Question: Part I." *Lincoln Herald* 106 (2004): 150–67.

———. "Historiographical Trends and Interpretations of President Abraham Lincoln's Reputation and the Morality on the Slavery Question: Part II." *Lincoln Herald* 107 (2005): 11–30.

Fiske, John. "John Codman Ropes." *Proceedings of the American Academy of Arts and Sciences* 35 (1900): 629–34.

Forbes, Archibald. "Abraham Lincoln as a Strategist." Pts. 1 and 2. *North American Review* 155 (July 1892): 53–68; 155 (August 1892): 160–70.

Friendman, Maurice. "Why Joseph Campbell's Psychologizing of Myth Precludes the Holocaust as a Touchstone of Reality." *Journal of the American Academy of Religion* 66 (Summer 1998): 385–401.

Furgurson, Ernest B. Review of *Lincoln's War*, by Geoffrey Perret. *Virginia Magazine of History and Biography* 112 (2004): 73–74.

Gallagher, Gary W. "Blueprint for Victory: Northern Strategy and Military Policy," in McPherson and Cooper, *Writing the Civil War*, 8–35.

———. "Father Neptune's War." *Civil War Times* 54 (August 2015): 18–20.

Gerstung, John F. "Louis M. Hacker's Reappraisal of Recent American History." *Historian* 12 (Spring 1950): 140–66.

Gill, Brendan. "The Faces of Joseph Campbell." *New York Review of Books* 36 (September 28, 1989): 16–19.

Goggin, Jacqueline. "Countering White Racist Scholarship: Carter G. Woodson and the *Journal of Negro History*." *Journal of Negro History* 68 (Autumn 1983): 355–75.

Goldman, Armond S., and Frank C. Schmalstieg. "Abraham Lincoln's Gettysburg Illness." *Journal of Medical Biography* 15, no. 2 (May 2007): 104–10. https://doi.org/10.1258/j.jmb.2007.06-14.

Gooch, John. "The Maurice Debate 1918." *Journal of Contemporary History* 3 (October 1968): 211–28.

Gordon, Lesley J. "'Novices in Warfare': Elmer E. Ellsworth and Militia Reform on the Eve of the Civil War." *Journal of the Civil War Era* 11 (June 2021): 194–223.

———. "The Zouave." *Civil War Monitor* 14 (Fall 2024): 48–57, 68, 70–71.

Grede, Coralee. "Bashing Joseph Campbell: Is He Now the Hero of a Thousand Spaces?" *Mythlore* 18 (August 1991): 50–52.

Greenberg, Kenneth S. "Civil War Revisionism." *Reviews in American History* 7 (June 1979): 202–8.

Grimsley, Mark. "Lincoln as Commander-in-Chief: Forays into Generalship." In *The War Worth Fighting: Abraham Lincoln's Presidency and Civil War America,* edited by Stephen D. Engle, 62–87. Gainesville: University Press of Florida, 2015.

———. "The Lincoln-McClellan Relationship in Myth and Memory." *Journal of the Abraham Lincoln Association* 38 (Summer 2017): 63–81.

———. "Overthrown: The Truth about the McClellan-Scott Feud." *Civil War Times Illustrated* 19 (November 1980): 20–29.

Guelzo, Allen Carl. "Lincoln and His Biographers." *Civil War History* 64 (September 2018): 239–71.

Guyatt, Nicholas. "'The Future Empire of Our Freedmen': Republican Colonization Schemes in Texas and Mexico, 1861–1865." In Arenson and Graybill, *Civil War Wests*, 95–117.

Hacker, Louis M. "Professor Hacker v. Some Sons of Dixie." Books and Ideas. *Fortune* (July 1947): 6, 9.

Harms, Madeline B. "Stress and Exploitative Decision-Making." *Journal of Neuroscience* 37 (October 18, 2017): 10035–37.

Harsh, Joseph L. "On the McClellan-Go-Round." *Civil War History* 19 (June 1973): 101–18.

Harvey, Andrew S. "The Levels of War as Levels of Analysis." *Military Review* (November–December 2021): 75–81.

Hay, Thomas Robson. Review of *The Generalship of U. S. Grant,* by J. F. C. Fuller. *American Historical Review* 35 (July 1930): 891–92.

Henderson, G. F. R. "The American Civil War." Pts. 1 and 2. In Malcolm, *Science of War,* 230–79.

Henry, Robert S. Review of *Lincoln Finds a General,* by Kenneth P. Williams. *American Historical Review* 57 (July 1952): 991–92.

H.E.P. Review of *Lincoln Finds a General,* by Kenneth P. Williams. *Journal of the Illinois State Historical Society* 45 (Summer 1952): 176.

Hesseltine, William B. "The Lincoln Parade." *Progressive* 12 (February 1948): 35.

———. Review of *Grant and Lee,* by J. F. C. Fuller. *Journal of Southern History* 1 (August 1935): 404–5.

———. Review of *Lincoln Finds a General,* by Kenneth P. Williams. *American Historical Review* 58 (April 1953): 651–52.

Higham, John. "Beyond Consensus: The Historian as Moral Critic." *American Historical Review* 67 (April 1962): 609–25.

———. "Changing Paradigms: The Collapse of Consensus History." *Journal of American History* 76 (September 1989): 460–66.

———. "The Cult of the American Consensus: Homogenizing Our History." *Commentary* 27 (February 1959): 93–100.

Hill, Douglas W. "Henry Clay Whitney: A Reliable Source for Lincoln Research?" *Lincoln Herald* 102 (Winter 2000): 177–84.

Hine, Darlene Clark. "Carter G. Woodson, White Philanthropy, and Negro Historiography." *History Teacher* 19 (May 1986): 405–25.

Hoffmann, John. "How the Sandburg Collection Came to Illinois: Historical Notes in Anticipation of the Library's New Project to Enhance a Major Collection, Part 1: 1950–1967." *Non Solus* 8 (1981): 25–35.

———. "Robert Todd Lincoln's 'Gettysburg Story.'" *Journal of the Abraham Lincoln Association* 38 (Winter 2017): 1–13.

Holt, Michael F. "An Elusive Synthesis: Northern Politics During the Civil War." In McPherson and Cooper, *Writing the Civil War,* 112–34.

———. "Lincoln Reconsidered." *Journal of American History* (September 2009): 451–55.

Houghton, Rick. "Lincoln and Gettysburg: A Study of America's Most Forceful Commander-in-Chief." *Military Collector & Historian* 61 (Winter 2009): 243–46.

Hurt, James. "Sandburg's *Lincoln* Within History." *Journal of the Abraham Lincoln Association* 20 (Winter 1999): 55–65.

Johannsen, Robert W. "Sandburg and Lincoln: The Prairie Years." In Johannsen, *Frontier, the Union, and Stephen A. Douglas,* 267–84.

Johnson, Ludwell H. "Fort Sumter and Confederate Diplomacy." *Journal of Southern History* 26 (November 1960): 441–77.

Kirk, G. S. "On Defining Myths," In Dundes, *Sacred Narrative,* 53–61.

Konner, Joan, et al. "Joseph Campbell: An Exchange." *New York Review of Books* 36 (November 9, 1989): 57–61.

LaFantasie, Glenn W. "Abraham Lincoln and the American Military Tradition." *Journal of the American Lincoln Association* 44 (2023): 18–34.

Launius, Roger A. "A Bibliography of the Works of T. Harry Williams." *Louisiana History* 25 (Winter 1984): 5–28.

Lefkowitz, Mary R. "The Myth of Joseph Campbell." *American Scholar* 59 (Summer 1990): 429–34.

Luvaas, Jay. "G. F. R. Henderson and the American Civil War." *Military Affairs* 20 (Autumn 1956): 139–53.

———. "*Sherman* and the 'Indirect Approach.'" Introduction to Liddell Hart, *Sherman,* vi–xi.

Maurice, Frederick. "Lincoln as a Strategist." *The Forum* 75 (February 1926): 161–69.

———. "Soldiers and Statesmen of the Civil War: I. President Davis and General Joseph Johnston." *Atlantic Monthly* 138 (July 1926): 52–61.

———. "Soldiers and Statesmen of the Civil War: II. Lincoln and Grant." *Atlantic Monthly* 138 (August 1926): 224–36.

McClintock, Russell. Review of *Lincoln's Darkest Year,* by William Marvel. *Virginia Magazine of History and Biography* 118 (2010): 88–89.

McColley, Robert. Review of *Mr. Lincoln Goes to War,* by William Marvel. *Journal of the Illinois State Historical Society* 101 (Fall-Spring 2008): 419–20.

McDonough, James Lee. "The Commander in Chief and Military Operations in Tennessee." *Lincoln Herald* 84 (June 1982): 93–105.

McPherson, James M. "Lincoln as Commander in Chief." *American Heritage* 58 (Winter 2009): 32–35.

———. "Long-Legged Yankee Lies: The Lost Cause Textbook Crusade." In *This Mighty Scourge: Perspectives on the Civil War,* by James M. McPherson, 93–106. New York: Oxford University Press, 2007.

Mearns, David C. "The Lincoln Papers." *Abraham Lincoln Quarterly* 4 (December 1947): 369–85.

Merrick, Henry S. Review of *Lincoln and His Generals,* by T. Harry Williams. *Military Affairs* 16 (Spring 1952): 38.

Millard, C. I. Review of *Statesmen and Soldiers of the Great War. Current History* 26 (September 1927): ii, iv.

Mitchell, Reid. "'Not the General but the Soldier': The Study of Civil War Soldiers." In McPherson and Cooper, *Writing the Civil War,* 81–95.

Monroe, Dan. "Lincoln the Dwarf: Lyon Gardiner Tyler's War on the Mythical Lincoln." *Journal of the Abraham Lincoln Association* 24 (Winter 2003): 32–42.

Morel, Lucas E. "Charnwood's Lincoln: Biography as Civic Lesson." *Journal of the Abraham Lincoln Association* 27 (Summer 2006): 24–41.

Murray, Jennifer M. "'Your Golden Opportunity Is Gone': George Gordon Meade, the Expectations of Decisive Battle, and the Road to Williamsport." In *Upon the Fields of Battle: Essays on the Military History of America's Civil War,* edited by Andrew S. Bledsoe and Andrew F. Lang, 71–91. Baton: Rouge: Louisiana State University Press, 2018.

"Nathaniel Wright Stephenson." *Proceedings of the American Antiquarian Society* 47 (April 1937): 13–14.

Neely, Mark E., Jr. "Abraham Lincoln vs. Jefferson Davis: Comparing Presidential Leadership in the Civil War." In McPherson and Cooper, *Writing the Civil War,* 96–111.

———. "Lincoln, Slavery, and the Nation." *Journal of American History* (September 2009): 456–58.

——. "The Lincoln Theme Since Randall's Call: The Promises and Perils of Professionalism." *Papers of the Abraham Lincoln Association* 1 (1979) 10–70.

Nevins, Allan. "Able Strategist & President." *Saturday Review* 35 (February 23, 1952): 10–11.

——. Review of *Lincoln Finds a General,* vol. 5, by Kenneth P. Williams. *American Historical Review* 67 (October 1961): 154–55.

Noe, Kenneth W. "'Damned North Carolinians' and 'Brave Virginians': The Lane-Mahone Controversy, Honor, and Civil War Memory." *Journal of Military History* 72 (October 2008): 1089–1115.

——. "'Deadened Color and Colder Horror': Rebecca Harding Davis and the Myth of Unionist Appalachia." In *Confronting Appalachian Stereotypes: Back Talk from an American Region,* ed. Dwight B. Billings, Gurney Norman, and Katherine Ledford, 67–84. Lexington: University Press of Kentucky, 1999.

——. "Toward the Myth of Unionist Appalachia, 1865–1883." *Journal of the Appalachian Studies Association* 6 (1994): 73–80.

Nolan, Alan T. "The Anatomy of the Myth." In Nolan and Gallagher, *Myth of the Lost Cause,* 11–34.

Norman, Matthew. Review of *The Great Task Remaining,* by William Marvel. *Journal of American History* (June 2011): 204–5.

Northrup, Lesley A. "Myth-Placed Priorities: Religion and the Study of Myth." *Religious Study Review* 32 (January 2006): 5–10.

Olch, Norman A. "Louis M. Hacker Civil Libertarian." *Columbia Spectator* (New York City), January 15, 1962, 2.

Page, Sebastian N. "Time and Place, Time and Chance." *Journal of the Civil War Era* 13 (June 2023): 147–54.

Paludan, Philip Shaw. "'Dictator Lincoln': Surveying Lincoln and the Constitution." *OAH Magazine of History* (January 2007): 8–13.

Pennypacker, Isaac R. "Military History and Historians, Second Paper." *Pennsylvania Magazine of History and Biography* 52 (1928): 141–61.

Perkins, Howard C. Review of *Lincoln and His Generals,* by T. Harry Williams. *Pennsylvania Magazine of History and Biography* 76 (July 1952): 368–69.

Pine, B. Joseph, II, and James H. Gilmor. "Museums and Authenticity." *Museum News* (May-June 2007): 76–80, 92–93.

Pinsker, Matthew. "Lincoln Theme 2.0." *Journal of American History* (September 2009): 417–40.

Porcelli, Anthony J., and Mauricio R. Delgado. "Stress and Decision Making: Effects on Valuation, Learning, and Risk-Taking." *Current Opinion in Behavioral Science* 14 (April 2017): 33–39.

Potter, David M. Review of *Lincoln and His Generals,* by T. Harry Williams. *Journal of Southern History* 18 (November 1952): 508–9.

Pratt, Harry E. "James Garfield Randall, 1881–1953." *Journal of the Illinois State Historical Society* 46 (Summer 1953): 119–31.

Pryor, Elizabeth Brown. "Conflict, Chaos, and Confidence: Abraham Lincoln's Struggle as Commander in Chief." *Virginia Magazine of History and Biography* 129 (2021): 2–79.

Quaife, M. M. Review of *The Military Genius of Abraham Lincoln,* by Colin Ballard. *Mississippi Valley Historical Review* 14 (December 1927): 412–13.

Rafuse, Ethan S. "A Jaundiced View of Yanks." *Civil War Times* (August 2012): 68.

———. Review of *Lincoln and the Civil War,* by Michael Burlingame. *Journal of the Abraham Lincoln Association* 33 (2012): 53–55.

———. "'The Spirit Which You Have Aided to Infuse': A. Lincoln, Little Mac, Fighting Joe, and the Question of Accountability in Union Command Relations." *Journal of the Abraham Lincoln Association* 38 (Summer 2017): 1–39.

———. "Two Harrys and 'A Most Interesting Story': A Document of Note." *Civil War History* 60 (March 2014): 58–65.

Ramold, Steven J. Review of *Mr. Lincoln Goes to War,* by William Marvel. *Virginia Magazine of History and Biography* 114 (2006): 510–11.

Randall, J. G. "The Blundering Generation." *Mississippi Valley Historical Review* 27 (June 1940): 3–28.

———. "The Civil War Restudied." *Journal of Southern History* 6 (November 1940): 439–57.

———. "Has the Lincoln Theme Been Exhausted?" *American Historical Review* 41 (January 1936): 270–94.

———. Review of *Lincoln Finds a General,* vols. 1–2, by Kenneth P. Williams. *American Historical Review* 55 (April 1950): 627–29.

Rawley, James A. Introduction to Wolseley, *American Civil War.*

———. "Isaac Newton Arnold, Lincoln's Friend and Biographer." *Journal of the Abraham Lincoln Association* 19 (Winter 1998): 39–56.

Review of *Abraham Lincoln as Military Genius. Military Engineer* 19 (July–August 1927): 357.

Review of *History of the Civil War in America,* by the comte de Paris. *Edinburgh Review* 145 (July 1876): 41–54.

Review of *Statesmen and Soldiers of the Great War. Military Engineer* 19 (November–December 1927): 536.

"Reviews: Military Literature of the Civil War." *The Critic* (June 16, 1888): 290–91.

Rice, Judith A. "Ida M. Tarbell: A Progressive Look at Lincoln." *Journal of the Abraham Lincoln Association* 19 (Winter 1998): 57–72.

Roberts, Field Marshal Earl Roberts. "Memoir." In Malcolm, *Science of War,* xviii–xxiv.

Robins, Robert S., and Robert M. Dorn. "Stress and Political Leadership." *Politics and the Life Sciences* 12 (February 1993): 3–17.

[Ropes, John Codman]. "General McClellan." *Atlantic Monthly* 59 (April 1887): 546–59.

Ropp, Theodore. Review of *Lincoln Finds a General*, vol. 3, by Kenneth P. Williams. *South Atlantic Quarterly* 52 (April 1953): 321–22.

"Scenes from the Peninsula Campaign." *America's Civil War* (January 1, 2012): 38–43.

Schlesinger, Arthur M., Jr. "The Cause of the Civil War: A Note on Historical Sentiments." *Partisan Review* (November 10, 1949), 969–81.

Schulten, Susan. "The Civil War and the Origins of the Colorado Territory. *Western Historical Quarterly* 44 (Spring 2013): 21–46.

Sears, Stephen W. "The Curious Case of General McClellan's Memoirs." *Civil War History* 34 (June 1988): 101–14.

Segal, Robert A. "Joseph Campbell on Jews and Judaism." *Religion* 22 (1992): 151–70.

———. "Joseph Campbell's Theory of Myth." In Dundes, *Sacred Narrative*, 256–79.

———. "The Romantic Appeal of Joseph Campbell." *Christian Century* (April 4, 1990): 332–35.

Shannon, Fred A. *The Organization and Administration of the Union Army, 1861–1865*. 2 vols. Cleveland, OH: Arthur H. Clark, 1928.

Simon, John Y. "Abraham Lincoln and Ann Rutledge." *Journal of the Abraham Lincoln Association* 11 (1990): 13–33.

Spaulding, Oliver L., Jr. Review of *Statesmen and Soldiers of the Great War*. *Mississippi Valley Historical Review* 14 (June 1927): 111–13.

Spiller, Roger. "Williams Among the Rebels: Southern Generalship in the Civil War." In Hewitt and Schott, *Lee and His Generals*, 274–93.

Stampp, Kenneth M. "One Alone?: The United States and National Self-Determination." In Boritt, *Lincoln the War President*, 121–44.

Stanley, Elizabeth A. "War Duration and the Micro-Dynamics of Decision Making Under Stress." *Polity* 50 (April 2018): 178–200.

Stanley, Elizabeth A., and Kelsey L. Larsen. "Stressed Out: The Missing Influence of Stress Arousal in Emotion's Role in Political Decision-Making." *Political Psychology* 43 (2022): 793–808.

Stanley, Matthew E., and Christopher Phillips, eds. "The New Civil War Revisionism: Twenty Years Later: A Roundtable in Honor of Edward L. Ayers." *Civil War History* 65 (December 2019): 372–404.

Sternhell, Yael A. "Revisionism Reinvented?: The Antiwar Turn in Civil War Scholarship." *Journal of the Civil War Era* 3 (June 2013): 239–56.

Stevenson, Louise L. Review of *Six Encounters with Lincoln*, by Elizabeth Brown Pryor. *Journal of the Civil War Era* 8 (March 2018): 141–44.

Sutherland, Daniel E. "Abraham Lincoln, John Pope, and the Origins of Total War." *Journal of Military History* 56 (October 1992): 567–86.

Tal, Nimrod. "The American Civil War in British Thought from the 1880s to the 1930s." *Civil War History* 60 (December 2014): 409–35.

Tap, Bruce. Review of *Lincoln's War,* by Geoffrey Perret. *Journal of the Abraham Lincoln Association* 26 (Summer 2005): 89–94.

Thomas, E. R. Review of *The Repressible Conflict,* by Avery Craven. *Journal of Negro History* 24 (July 1939): 345–48.

Tilley, John Shipley. *Lincoln Takes Command.* Chapel Hill: University of North Carolina Press, 1941.

"Tragedy of History." *Time,* October 24, 1949, 51–52.

Vandiver, Frank. Review of *Lincoln Finds a General,* vols. 1–2, by Kenneth P. Williams. *Southwestern Historical Quarterly* 54 (July 1950): 125–28.

Vestal, Allen W. "The First Wartime Water Torture by Americans." *Maine Law Review* 69 (January 2017): 2–66.

Ware, S. L. Review of *Statesmen and Soldiers of the Great War. Sewanee Review* 36 (April 1928): 242–43.

Wetta, Frank J. "T. Harry Williams: Pragmatic Historian." In Hewitt and Schott, *Lee and His Generals,* 1–14.

Williams, Estelle. Biographical introduction to *The Selected Essays of T. Harry Williams.* Baton Rouge: Louisiana State University Press, 1983.

Williams, Kenneth P. "The Transits of Mercury (Supplement)." *Publications of the Kirkwood Observatory of Indiana University* 1 (1940): 1–5.

Williams, T. Harry. "The Military Leadership of North and South." In *Why the North Won the Civil War,* edited by David Donald, 33–54. New York: Macmillan, 1960. Reprint, New York: Collier, 1962.

———. Review of *Lincoln Finds a General,* vol. 4, by Kenneth P. Williams. *Journal of Southern History* 23 (May 1957): 243–45.

———. Review of *Lincoln Finds a General,* vol. 5, by Kenneth P. Williams. *Journal of Southern History* 26 (February 1960): 119–22.

"Williams, T(homas) Harry." In *Contemporary Authors: A Bio-Bibliographical Guide to Current Writers in Fiction, General Nonfiction, Poetry, Journalism, Drama, Motion Pictures, Television, and Other Fields,* 3:601–2. New Revision Series. Detroit: Gale, 1981.

Wilson, Douglas L. "Abraham Lincoln, Ann Rutledge, and the Evidence of Herndon's Informants." *Civil War History* 36 (December 1990): 301–24.

———. "Herndon's Dilemma: Abraham Lincoln and the Privacy Issue." *Lincoln Lore* (Summer 2004): 2–9.

———. "Prospects for Lincoln 2.5." *Journal of American History* (September 2009): 459–61.

———. "William H. Herndon and His Lincoln Informants." *Journal of the Abraham Lincoln Association* 14 (Winter 1993): 15–34.

Winston, Michael R. "Carter Godwin Woodson: Prophet of a Black Tradition." *Journal of Negro History* 60 (October 1975): 459–63.

Wolseley, Garnet, ed. "Military Genius." *Fortnightly Review* 44 (September 1888): 297–312.

Woodson, Carter G. "Lincoln as a Southern Man." *Negro History Bulletin* 10 (February 1947): 105–6.

———. Review of *Lincoln the President,* by James G. Randall. *Journal of Negro History* 31 (January 1946): 107–11.

Yaribeygi, Habib, et al. "The Impact of Stress on Body Function: A Review." *ECCLI Journal* 16 (2017): 1057–72.

Young, James Harvey. "Randall's Lincoln: An Academic Scholar's Biography." *Journal of the Abraham Lincoln Association* 19 (Summer 1998): 1–13.

Zarefsky, David. "The Continuing Fascination with Lincoln." *Rhetoric & Public Affairs* 6 (2003): 337–70.

Zeman, Scott C. "Louis M. Hacker's 'Coincidental Conversion' to the Truth." *Historian* 61 (Fall 1998): 85–99.

Video and Online Sources

"About Joseph Campbell." Joseph Campbell Foundation. https://www.jcf.org/learn/joseph-campbell-biography.

Abraham Lincoln Presidential Library and Museum. https://presidentlincoln.illinois.gov/.

Bateman, Robert. "Understanding Military Strategy and the Four Levels of War." *Esquire,* November 25, 2015. https://www.esquire.com/news-politics/politics/news/a39985/four-levels-of-war.

"Battle Detail: Vicksburg." National Park Service. https://www.nps.gov/civilwar/search-battles-detail.htm?battleCode=ms011.

Batty, Craig. "Are You Monomythic?: Joseph Campbell and the Hero's Journey." *The Conversation,* June 25, 2014. https://theconversation.com/are-you-monomythic-joseph-campbell-and-the-heros-journey-27074.

Beaumont, Peter. "Trump's Expansionism Threatens the Rules-Based Order in Place Since Second World War." *The Guardian,* March 23, 2025. https://www.theguardian.com/us-news/2025/mar/23/trump-expansionism-threatens-the-rules-based-order-in-place-since-second-world-war.

Bridgman, Joan. "Richard Adams at Eighty." *Contemporary Review,* August 1, 2000. https://www.thefreelibrary.com/richard+adams+at+eighty.-a064752236.

Brin, David. "'Star Wars' Despots vs. 'Star Trek' Populists." *Salon,* June 15, 1999. https://www.salon.com/1999/06/15/brin_main/.

Carucci, Dan. "Stress Leads to Bad Decisions. Here's How to Avoid Them." *Harvard Business Review,* August 29, 2017. https://hbr.org/2017/08/stress-leads-to-bad-decisions-heres-how-to-avoid-them.

Chappell, Bill. "Statue of Lincoln with Formerly Enslaved Man at His Feet Is Removed in Boston. *NPR,* December 29, 2020. https://www.npr.org/2020/12/29/951206414/statue-of-lincoln-with-freed-slave-at-his-feet-is-removed-in-boston.

Christensen, Joel, and Sarah E. Bond. "The Man Behind the Myth: Should We Question the Hero's Journey?" *Los Angeles Review of Books,* August 12, 2021. https://www.lareviewofbooks.org/article/the-man-behind-the-myth-should-we-question-the-heros-journey/.

The Civil War: Lincoln and His Generals. Gettysburg College Civil War Institute. C-SPAN, June 10, 2023. https://www.c-span.org/video/?528650-4/lincoln-generals.

Elbaum, Rachel. "Portland Protesters Tear Down Statues of Abraham Lincoln, Theodore Roosevelt." *NBC News,* October 12, 2020. https://www.nbcnews.com/news/us-news/portland-protesters-tear-down-statues-abraham-lincoln-theodore-roosevelt-n1242913.

Forbes, Bart. "Archibald Forbes, War Correspondent and Author." Clan Forbes Society, June 27, 2023. https://www.clan-forbes.org/post/archibald-forbes.

"Fredericksburg." American Battlefield Trust. https://www.battlefields.org/learn/civil-war/battles/fredericksburg.

The Civil War Round Table of the District of Columbia. https://www.cwrtdc.org/.

Gabbard, Sara. "Lincoln Through the Eyes of History: Harold Holzer on Francis Carpenter." *Lincoln Lore* 1932 (Winter 2021): 3–7. Friends of the Lincoln Collection. https://www.friendsofthelincolncollection.org/lincoln-lore/lincoln-through-the-eyes-of-history/.

Greenblatt, Alan. "General Gone Rogue: A History of Friction." NPR, June 23, 2010. https://www.npr.org/2010/06/23/128008712/generals-gone-rogue-a-history-of-friction.

Grossman, Lev. "The Lincoln Compulsion." *Time,* January 31, 2008. https://content.time.com/time/subscriber/article/0,33009,1708828,00.html.

Guelzo, Allen C. "Lincoln's Forgotten Middle Years." *Washington Monthly,* June 11, 2017. https://washingtonmonthly.com/2017/06/11/lincolns-forgotten-middle-years/.

Harris, Keith. "Searching for Buster Kilrain. . . ." *Keith Harris History* (blog), June 18, 2014. https://keithharrishistory.com/keith-harris-history/searching-for-buster-kilrain.

In Memory of the 150th Field Artillery United States Army, August 5, 1917, to May 9, 1919 (n.p., 1927). Indiana State Library Digital Collections. https://indianamemory.contentdm.oclc.org/digital/collection/p16066coll47/id/2755/.

Levin, Kevin. "Dimitri Rotov Historiography." *Civil War Memory* (blog), June 10, 2009, https://cwmemory.com/2009/06/10/dimitri-rotov-historiography/.

———. "My Brief Encounter with Elizabeth Brown Pryor." *Civil War History* (blog), Jan. 31, 2017, https://cwmemory.com/2017/01/31/my-brief-encounter-with-elizabeth-brown-pryor/.

———. "Rethinking the Role of Talking Heads in Documentaries." *Civil War Memory* (blog), February 23, 2022. https://cwmemory.com/2022/02/23/another-lincoln-documentary/.

"Little Round Top Rehabilitation Project." *National Park Service, Gettysburg National Military Park,* last updated October 22, 2024. https://www.nps.gov/gett/learn/historyculture/little-round-top.htm.

Madden, David. "Rediscovering Civil War Classics: Lincoln Books That Should Get Reprinted." *Civil War Book Review* 10, no. 1 (Winter 2008). https://repository.lsu.edu/cwbr/vol10/iss1/4.

Marszalek, John. Review of *Tarnished Victory,* by William Marvel. *Civil War Book Review* 14, no. 4 (Fall 2012). https://repository.lsu.edu/cwbr/vol14/iss4/8/.

Mason, W. Dale. "The Indian Policy of Abraham Lincoln." *Indigenous Policy Journal* (Fall 2009). https://ipjournal.wordpress.com/2009/12/16/the-indian-policy-of-abraham-lincoln/.

Maxwell, Ron, dir. *Gettysburg.* Turner Pictures, 1993.

McPherson, James M. "Top Gun: Of the Making of Many Books About Abraham Lincoln There Is No End." *The Nation,* May 27, 2004. https://www.thenation.com/article/archive/top-gun/.

Norman, Matthew. Review of *Six Encounters with Lincoln,* by Elizabeth Brown Pryor. *Civil War Monitor,* February 15, 2017. https://www.civilwarmonitor.com/pryor-six-encounters-with-lincoln-2017/.

"Our Proud History." Indiana University ROTC. https://iu.go-rotc.com/history/.

Prokopowicz, Gerald J. "The Five Best Books on Lincoln and His Commanders." *Civil War Monitor,* June 21, 2022. https://www.civilwarmonitor.com/the-five-best-books-on-lincoln-and-his-commanders/.

Reynolds, David S. "Taking Old Abe to Task." *American Scholar,* March 6, 2017. https://theamericanscholar.org/taking-old-abe-to-task/.

"San Francisco to Remove Washington, Lincoln, and Feinstein from School Names." *CBS News,* January 27, 2021. https://www.cbsnews.com/news/san-francisco-renaming-schools/.

Schulte, Brett. "A Guide to Civil War Books for Beginners, Part 1: Civil War Overviews." *TOCWOC—A Civil War Blog,* July 21, 2008. https://www.brettschulte.net/CWBlog/2008/07/21/a-guide-to-civil-war-books-overviews/.

Simpson, Brooks. Review of *The Great Task Remaining,* by William Marvel. *Civil War Book Review* 12, no. 3 (Summer 2010). https://repository.lsu.edu/cwbr/vol12/iss3/9/.

"Theosophy." https://www.theosophical.org/about/theosophy.

Venville, Malcolm, dir. *Abraham Lincoln.* Episodes 1–3. Aired February 20–22, 2022, on History.

Vogler, Christopher. "The Memo That Started It All." https://livingspirit.typepad.com/files/chris-vogler-memo-1.pdf.

Wargaski, Robert. "U.S. Drone Warfare and Civilian Casualties." *Eagleton Political Journal,* Rutgers University, May 9, 2022. https://eagletonpoliticaljournal.rutgers.edu/us-the-world/u-s-drone-warfare-and-civilian-casualties/.

White, Jonathan W. "How Lincoln Won the Soldier Vote." Disunion, *New York Times,* November 7, 2014. https://archive.nytimes.com/opinionator.blogs.nytimes.com/2014/11/07/how-lincoln-won-the-soldier-vote/.

Williams, Frank J. "Abraham Lincoln: The President Who Changed the Role of Commander-in-Chief." *White House Studies* 2, no. 1 (Winter 2002): 3–15. Gale Academic OneFile. link.gale.com/apps/doc/A86851219/AONE?u=anon~ee96cd65&sid=googleScholar&xid=c55aded5. Subscription required.

Wilson, Woodrow. "July 4, 1913, Address at Gettysburg." University of Virginia Miller Center. https://millercenter.org/the-presidency/presidential-speeches/july-4-1913-address-gettysburg.

INDEX